THE WILL TO SURVIVE

BRYAN CARTLEDGE

The Will to Survive

A History of Hungary

Columbia University Press
New York

Columbia University Press
Publishers Since 1893
New York   Chichester, West Sussex
Copyright © Bryan Cartledge, 2011
All rights reserved

Library of Congress Cataloging-in-Publication Data

Cartledge, Bryan, Sir.
  The will to survive : a history of Hungary / Bryan Cartledge.
      p. cm.
  Includes bibliographical references and index.
  ISBN 978-0-231-70224-9 (cloth: alk. paper)
  ISBN 978-0-231-70225-6 (pb: alk. paper)
  ISBN 978-0-231-80021-1 (eBook)
  1. Hungary—History. I. Title.

  DB925.C374 2010
  943.9—dc22

2010047008

Columbia University Press books are printed on permanent and durable acid-free paper.
This book is printed on paper with recycled content.
Printed in India

c 10 9 8 7 6 5 4 3 2 1
p 10 9 8 7 6 5 4 3 2 1

References to Internet Web sites (URLs) were accurate at the time of writing. Neither the author nor Columbia University Press is responsible for URLs that may have expired or changed since the manuscript was prepared.

To Freda
In Memoriam

CONTENTS

Part One

THE MEDIEVAL KINGDOM

Part Two

THE HABSBURG KINGDOM

CONTENTS

CONTENTS

Part Three

TRIPLE TRAGEDY AND REBIRTH

CONTENTS

LIST OF ILLUSTRATIONS

The author and publisher are grateful to the Director of the Hungarian National Museum for his kind permission to reproduce the following paintings and engravings from the Museum's Historical Picture Gallery:

LIST OF ILLUSTRATIONS

The author and publisher are grateful to the Director of the Hungarian National Museum for his kind permission to reproduce the following photographs from the Museum's Photographic Archive:

LIST OF ILLUSTRATIONS

The following photographs are reproduced with the kind permission of Getty Images, London:

LIST OF MAPS

(Computer aided map design by Mátyás Márton and Judit Paksi, Department of Cartography & Geoinformatics (Head of Department László Zentai), Eötvös Loránd University, Budapest; and M & P Térképműhely Bt.)

PREFACE

I began this book in order to satisfy my own curiosity about Hungary's past. While serving as British Ambassador to Hungary in the early 1980s, I was frequently struck by how little British visitors to Budapest, both official and private, knew of the country's history; and also by the small margin by which their ignorance exceeded my own. I resolved to do what I could to remedy both deficits when I had the time to do so, a circumstance that did not arise until fifteen years later. Once begun, the project developed a momentum of its own and took over much of my life for seven years. Computer crashes apart, I have enjoyed every minute of it.

I am particularly glad that *The Will to Survive* is being published in 2006, the fiftieth anniversary of one of Hungary's finest but most tragic moments, the 1956 Revolution. For many people, '1956' encapsulates all that they know about Hungary. The anniversary, and the many commemorations which will mark it both in print and in other media, may spark a wider curiosity—a desire to know more about the long and eventful history of this small country and about its survival against heavy odds.

One historian has written a little cynically of the spell Hungary cast over many British visitors during the nineteenth and early twentieth centuries. 'Ever since 1848–49', wrote Harry Hanak, 'when they had so valiantly upheld the cause of Magyar liberty they [the Magyars] had been the darlings of England, a fact of which they made the greatest possible use. They successfully pretended to the English that their constitutional development was similar [to Great Britain's]'. Englishmen, 'captivated by the charm of the Magyars became their vociferous advocates. Nearly all travellers to Hungary were struck by Magyar hospitality and this tradition of hospitality became a legend in Europe'.[1] I did develop, during the three and a half years I spent there, great respect and affection for Hungary but not merely for her hospitality. When I left Budapest in 1983, I fully shared—and still share—the sentiments expressed by an English visitor to Hungary who left the country nearly two centuries earlier, in 1793: 'I could not leave [Hungary] behind without regret', wrote Robert Townson; 'and I frequently looked back to thank its generous inhabitants for the friendly reception they had given me, and to wish them every kind of public prosperity. The Hungarians are a noble race of men; and, of the variety of nations amongst which I have travelled, the one I esteem the most. This small tribute of praise I owe them, and I say it with pleasure'.[2] This book is my own small tribute. It is not uncritical and some of its judgements may be unpalatable to Hungarians; but anything less than the objectivity I have tried to achieve would be inconsistent with my respect for the Hungarian people.

This book does not pretend to be a work of original scholarship. My first debt, therefore, is to the scholars, mostly British and Hungarian, whose findings from primary sources I have attempted to synthesize in this narrative; unless otherwise stated, the interpretation of their findings is mine. I am immensely grateful to Professor Robert Evans, Regius Professor of Modern History at Oxford University and one of the leading Western experts on Central and Eastern Europe, who read the entire manuscript as it progressed and made innumerable constructive comments, as well as saving me from many errors. István Pálffy (to whom I am also indebted for the genealogical trees) and Mark Odescalchi both read the manuscript, made useful suggestions and gave me invaluable assistance in preparing the book for publication. Dr Tibor Frank of the Eötvös Loránd University (ELTE) in Budapest was generous with his time and knowledge in helping me to find and select the book's illustrations and commission its maps. In this context, the Press, Cultural and Scientific Co-operation Department of the Hungarian Ministry of Foreign Affairs provided invaluable support. I am also most grateful to Professor István Petrovics of the University of Szeged in Hungary, for his comments on and corrections to the chapters dealing with the medieval period; to Professor László Kontler of the Central European University, Budapest, for his wise comments on the Habsburg period; to Dr Andrea Velich, of ELTE; to Sir John Birch, who served with me in the British Embassy in Budapest and subsequently returned as Ambassador, for his comments on the closing chapters; to George Gömöri, who as a student played an active part in the early days of the 1956 revolution, for his advice on the chapter dealing with those events; to Dr John Clarke and Dr Marianne Fillenz, of Oxford University, for reading most of the manuscript and identifying a number of infelicities and opacities; to Richard Thorpe, László Mathé, Dr Kinga Deák, and Mrs Nori Paterson (née Vattay) for valuable information and advice; to Stanley and Judy Price for their practical advice and support; to Carolyn Murphy for her computing skills; to my agent, Andrew Lownie, for introducing me to and guiding me through the complex world of publishing; to Andreas Campomar, for his faith in the book and his help in making it publishable; to the Librarian and staff of the Cambridge University Library, surely the most user-friendly academic library in Britain; to the Hungarian Cultural Centre in London and to its energetic Director, Katalin Bogyay. I am especially grateful to the Gyula Andrássy Foundation for providing invaluable support. Finally, I must record my gratitude to my late wife, Freda Newcombe, who sadly did not live to see this book completed; the half of it which she read benefited enormously from her eagle eye for faulty grammar or unclear expression. The responsibility for any errors or flaws which have remained impervious to the generous advice and assistance I have received is, of course, mine alone.

Bryan Cartledge
Oxford, January 2006

PREFACE TO THE SECOND EDITION

Several readers have taken the trouble to point out misspellings and other inaccuracies in the first edition of The Will to Survive. This corrected second edition gives me the opportunity to thank them. I am especially grateful to Andrew Alchin and to George Gomori for their suggestions.

Bryan Cartledge
February 2007

PREFACE TO THE THIRD EDITION

In 2008 *The Will to Survive* was published in Budapest in a Hungarian translation, under the title *Megmaradni: A magyar történélem egy angol szemével* ('To Survive: Hungarian history through English eyes'). Hungarians, to their credit, take their history very seriously; and I was not surprised when the process of translation and editing exposed a number of flaws in the English text. The publication of this Third Edition has given me the opportunity to correct them and also to take account of the many helpful comments which I have received from Hungarian readers.

I am especially grateful to my heroic Hungarian translator, Veronika Bánki and to her friends in Hungary's academia; to Katalin Balogh of the Officina publishing house in Budapest and her editorial staff; and to all those, from many countries, who have taken the trouble to write to me about the book, particularly Professor Thomas Széll and Mrs. Erzsébet Courage (née Studinka). I owe a special debt to Professor Géza Jeszenszky, a founder member of the Hungarian Democratic Forum (MDF) and Foreign Minister in the first democratically elected Hungarian government, for his comments on the final chapter of this book, which now better reflects the course of events in that dramatic year, 1989. Finally, I am very grateful to my new publisher, Michael Dwyer of C. Hurst & Co., for his decision to publish a new edition of *The Will to Survive*; and to Daisy Leitch and Jonathan de Peyer for their invaluable help in putting it into shape.

Like several countries in Europe, east and west, Hungary is currently experiencing a period of intense economic and political difficulty; this book will, I hope, help to explain why she is certain to survive it.

Bryan Cartledge
London, 2010

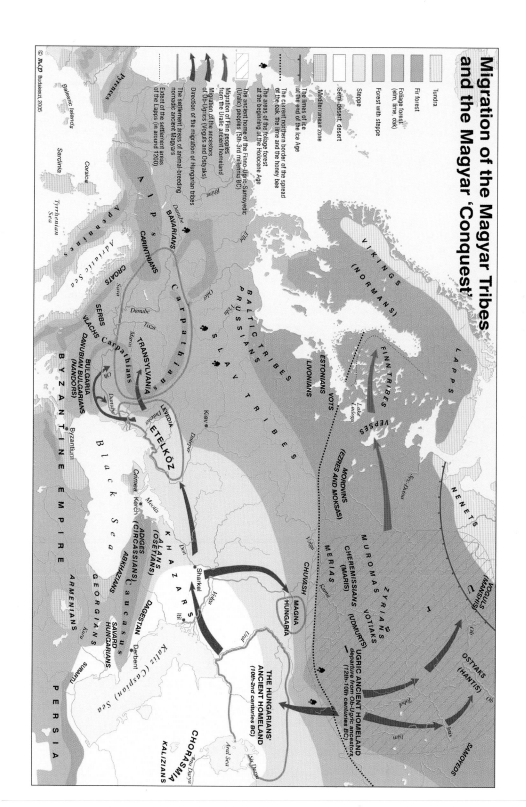

Migration of the Magyar Tribes and the Magyar 'Conquest'

Tundra

Fir forest

Foliage forest
(elm, lime, oak)

Forest with steppe

Steppe

Semi-desert, desert

Mediterranean zone

The lines of ice
at the end of the Ice Age

The current northern border of the spread
of the oak, the lime and the honey bee

The areas of the foliage forest
at the beginning of the Holocene Age

The ancient home of the Finno-Ugric-Samoyedic
(Uralic) peoples (5th-3rd millennia BC)

Migration of Finn peoples
from the Uralic ancient homeland

Migration of the ancestors
of Ob-Ugrics (Voguls and Ostyaks)

Direction of the migration of Hungarian tribes

The settlement areas of animal-breeding
nomadic ancient Magyars

Extent of the settlement areas
of the Lapps (in around 1200)

© mcp Budakeszi, 2005

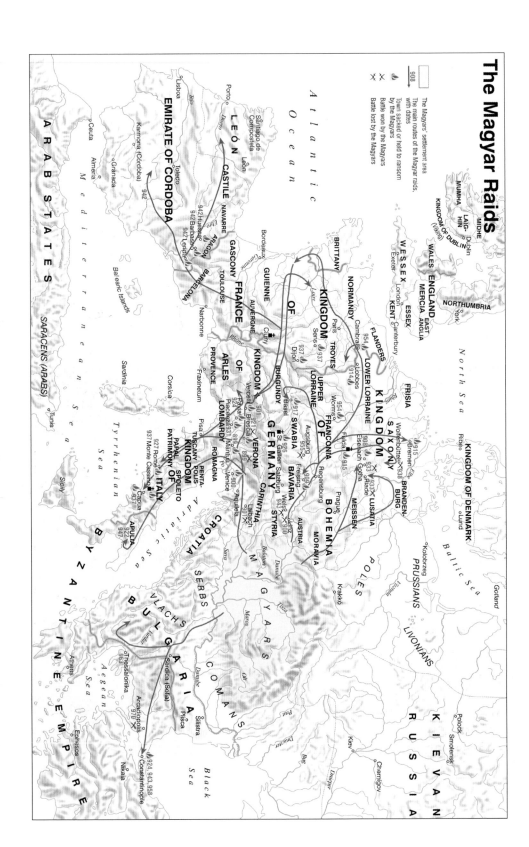

The Magyar Raids

908 | The Magyars' settlement area

The main routes of the Magyar raids, with dates.

Town sacked or held to ransom by the Magyars

✕✕ | Battle won by the Magyars
✕✕ | Battle lost by the Magyars

KINGDOM OF DUBLIN (Viking)
MIDHE
LAIG- Dublin
HIN
MUMHA

WALES
ENGLAND
WESSEX
MERCIA EAST
ANGLIA
ESSEX
London Canterbury
Exeter KENT
York
NORTHUMBRIA

Atlantic Ocean

Santiago de Compostela
Lisboa
Porto
León
Toledo
EMIRATE OF CORDOBA
Karmona (Córdoba)
Almería
Granada
Ceuta
LEÓN
CASTILE **NAVARRE**
942 Huesca
942 Barbastro
942 Barbastro
942 Lleida
942
ARAGON
BARCELONA
GASCONY
Bordeaux
GUIENNE
Toulouse
Narbonne
TOULOUSE
FRANCE
AUVERGNE
Cluny

North Sea

FLANDERS
954
NORMANDY
Paris
BRITTANY
KINGDOM OF FRANCE
Sens 937
Dijon 937
937
914
Cambrai
Lobbes 914
TROYES
LOWER LORRAINE
UPPER LORRAINE
954
Worms
Basel 926
917
BURGUNDY
KINGDOM OF ARLES
PROVENCE
Fraxinetum

FRISIA
KINGDOM OF SAXONY
Bremen 915
938
933 ✕ LUSATIA
Wolfenbüttel 938
906 933
Eisenach Gotha
Fulda 915
FRANCONIA
Worms
Augsburg 955
Freising 945
SWABIA 917
St. Gallen 926
GERMANY
Regensburg
Weißenburg 913
BAVARIA
Salzburg 943
Wels.
AUSTRIA 901
900
CARINTHIA
Laibach
STYRIA
Aquileia
Venice 900
Pisa o
TUSCANY
LOMBARDY
Pavia 921
Piacenza 931
Vercelli ✕ 899
Brescia
VERONA 899
ROMAGNA
PENTA-POLIS
927 Rome
937 Monte Cassino
PAPAL PATRIMONY OF
KINGDOM OF ITALY
SPOLETO
Capua 937
APULIA
922
947

BRANDEN-BURG
MEISSEN
BOHEMIA
Prague
MORAVIA
Krakkó

KINGDOM OF DENMARK
Ribe o
Lund

Baltic Sea
Gotland
Kołobrzeg
PRUSSIANS
POLES
LIVONIANS
Polock
Smolensk

KIEVAN RUSSIA
Charnigov
Kiev

COMANS
MAGYARS

CROATIA
SERBS
VLACHS
BULGARIA
Serdica (Sofia)
Pliska
Silistra

BYZANTINE EMPIRE
Thessalonika 904
Athens
Ephesos
Nikaia
Arcadiopolis 970 ✕
924, 943, 958
Constantinople

Black Sea

Mediterranean Sea
ARAB STATES
SARACENS (ARABS)
Tunis
Sardinia
Corsica
Balearic Islands
Sicily
Tyrrhenian Sea
Adriatic Sea
Aegean Sea

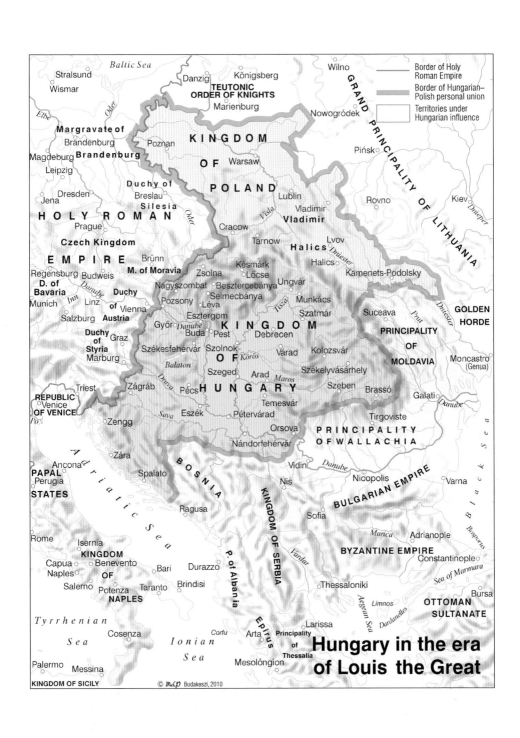

Hungary in the era of Louis the Great

Legend:
- Border of Holy Roman Empire
- Border of Hungarian–Polish personal union
- Territories under Hungarian influence

Baltic Sea
Stralsund
Wismar
Danzig
Königsberg
TEUTONIC ORDER OF KNIGHTS
Marienburg
Wilno
GRAND PRINCIPALITY OF LITHUANIA
Nowogródek
Pińsk
Elbe
Oder
Margravate of Brandenburg
Poznan
KINGDOM OF POLAND
Warsaw
Magdeburg Brandenburg
Leipzig
Dresden
Jena
Duchy of Silesia
Breslau
Lublin
Vladimir
Vladimir
Rovno
Kiev
Dnieper
HOLY ROMAN
Prague
Oder
Cracow
Tarnow
Lvov
Halics
Dniester
EMPIRE
Czech Kingdom
Brünn
M. of Moravia
Zsolna
Késmárk
Lőcse
Halics
Kamenets-Podolsky
Regensburg
Budweis
D. of Bavaria
Duchy
Danube
Inn
Nagyszombat
Besztercebánya
Ungvár
Munkács
Munich
Linz
of
Vienna
Pozsony
Léva
Selmecbánya
Tisza
Szatmár
Suceava
GOLDEN HORDE
Salzburg
Austria
Esztergom
Duchy of Graz
Győr
Danube
Buda Pest
KINGDOM
Debrecen
Várad
Kolozsvár
PRINCIPALITY OF MOLDAVIA
Prut
Dniester
Styria
Marburg
Székesfehérvár
Szolnok
OF
Körös
Várad
Székelyvásárhely
Moncastro (Genua)
Balaton
Szeged
Arad
Maros
Triest
Zágráb
Drava
Pécs
HUNGARY
Szeben
Brassó
Galati
Danube
REPUBLIC
Venice
OF VENICE
Po
Zengg
Sava
Eszék
Temesvár
Pétervárad
Tirgoviste
Orsova
PRINCIPALITY OF WALLACHIA
Zára
Nándorfehérvár
Ancona
PAPAL
Perugia
STATES
Spalato
BOSNIA
Vidin
Danube
Nis
Nicopolis
Varna
Black Sea
Ragusa
KINGDOM OF SERBIA
Sofia
BULGARIAN EMPIRE
Rome
Isernia
KINGDOM
Capua
Benevento
OF
Bari
Durazzo
P. of Albania
Vardar
Marica
Adrianople
BYZANTINE EMPIRE
Constantinople
Bosporus
Naples
Salerno
Potenza
Taranto
Brindisi
Thessaloniki
Sea of Marmara
NAPLES
Bursa
OTTOMAN SULTANATE
Tyrrhenian Sea
Cosenza
Corfu
Arta
Epirus
Principality of Thessalia
Larissa
Aegean Sea
Limnos
Durdanelles
Ionian Sea
Mesolóngion

Hungary in the era of Louis the Great

Palermo
Messina
KINGDOM OF SICILY
© map Budakeszi, 2010

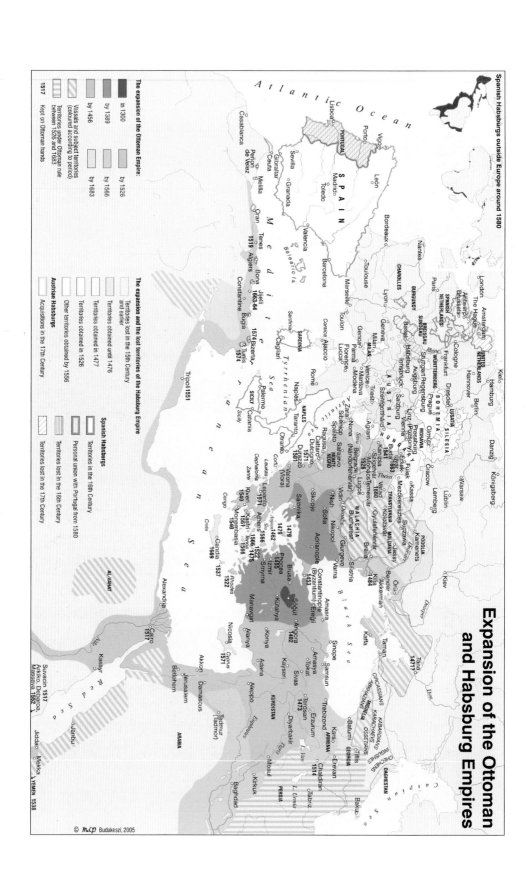

Expansion of the Ottoman and Habsburg Empires

Spanish Habsburgs outside Europe around 1580

The expansion of the Ottoman Empire:

- in 1300
- by 1389
- by 1683
- by 1526
- by 1566
- by 1683
- Vassals and subject territories (coloured according to period)
- Territories under the Ottoman rule between 1526 and 1683
- 1517 Kept on Ottoman hands

The expansion and the lost territories of the Habsburg Empire:

- Territories lost in the 15th century and earlier
- Territories obtained until 1476
- Territories obtained in 1477
- Territories obtained in 1526
- Other territories obtained by 1556

Austrian Habsburgs

- Acquisitions in the 17th Century

Spanish Habsburgs

- Territories in the 16th Century
- Personal union with Portugal from 1580
- Territories lost in the 16th century
- Territories lost in the 17th century

© map Budakeszi, 2005

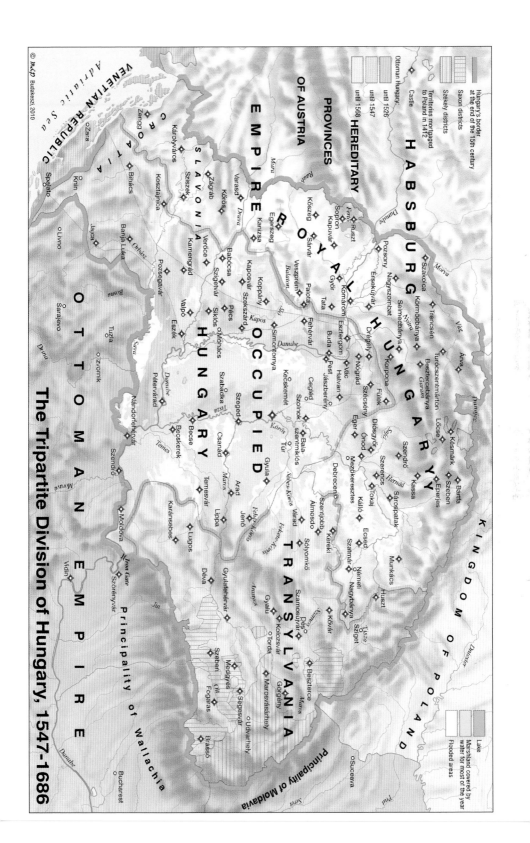

The Tripartite Division of Hungary, 1547-1686

Hungary's border at the end of the 15th century
Saxon districts
Székely districts
Territories mortgaged to Poland in 1472
Castle

Ottoman Hungary:
until 1526
until 1547
until 1568

HEREDITARY
PROVINCES
OF AUSTRIA

Lake
Marshland covered by water for most of the year
Flooded areas

© MÁP Budakeszi 2010

HABSBURG

ROYAL HUNGARY

EMPIRE

OCCUPIED HUNGARY

OTTOMAN EMPIRE

TRANSYLVANIA

CROATIA

SLAVONIA

KINGDOM OF POLAND

VENETIAN REPUBLIC

Adriatic Sea

Principality of Wallachia

Principality of Moldavia

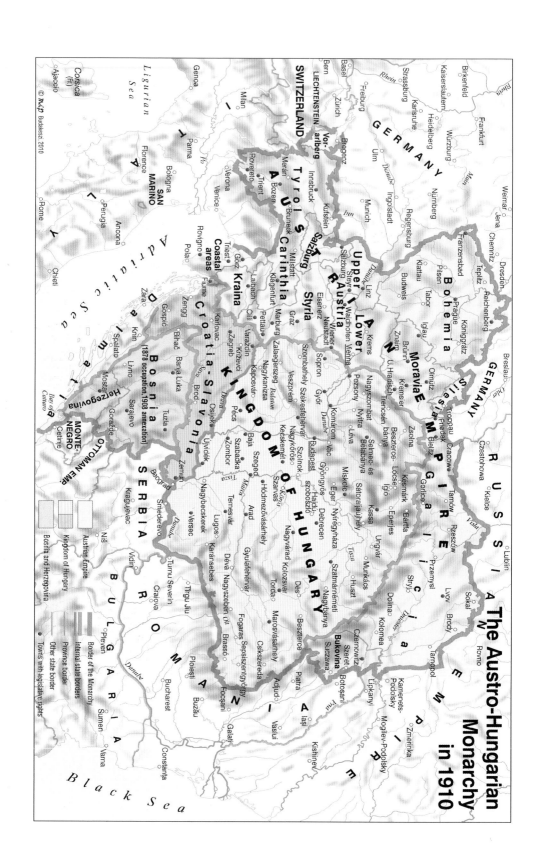

The Austro-Hungarian Monarchy in 1910

© M.Cp Budakeszi 2010

Legend:
- Border of the Monarchy
- Internal state borders
- Province border
- Other state border
- Towns with legislative rights

- Austrian Empire
- Kingdom of Hungary
- Bosnia and Herzegovina

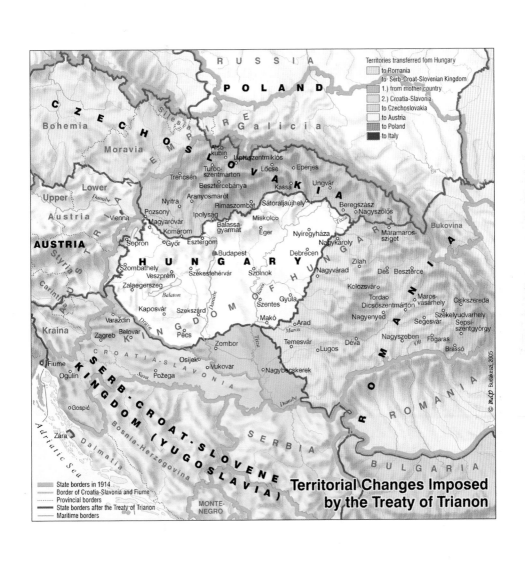

Territorial Changes Imposed by the Treaty of Trianon

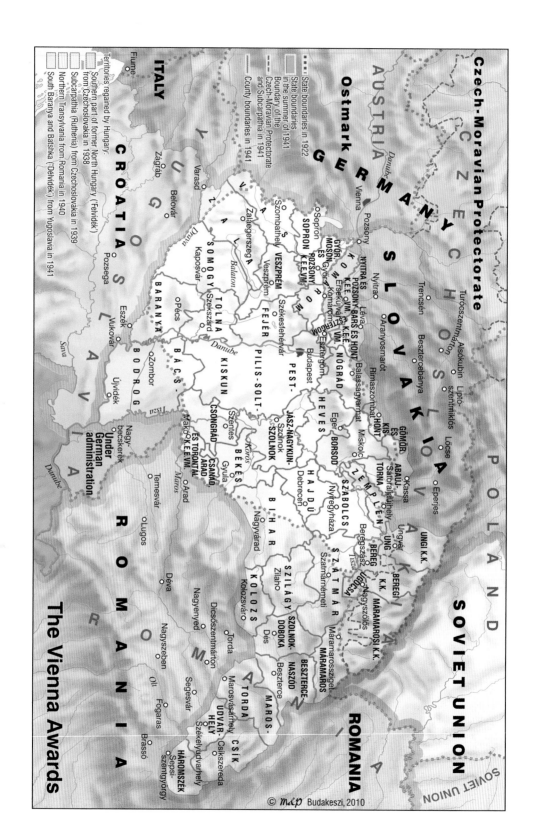

Part One

THE MEDIEVAL KINGDOM

1

THE MAGYARS

(400 BC–AD 1000)

The Migrations

Nations need myths. Hungary, a country that became conscious of nationhood rather late in its history, has its fair share. Hungarian myths are more concerned with origins than with gods or heroes. Finding themselves on a cultural island in the centre of Europe, speaking a language incomprehensible to their Slav or German neighbours, Hungarians are fascinated by the question of how they came to be there in the first place. There are no certain answers, despite the immense amount of scholarly research devoted to the question: but it seems unlikely that the grandmother of Árpád, who led the Magyar tribal confederacy into the Carpathian Basin, was made pregnant by a giant eagle (*turul*) or that the Hun and Magyar peoples were the descendants of two princely brothers, Hunor and Magor. In a less scientific era, Hungarian scholars were inclined to search hopefully for evidence of ancestral links with Attila's Huns, the conquering scourge of Europe in the fourth and fifth centuries AD, and to appropriate by association their military renown—Attila remains a popular Hungarian personal name to this day. The probable truth—and the account which follows is an amalgam of probabilities—is less dramatic but far from prosaic.

Documentary sources for the very early history of the tribes that eventually became the Hungarian people are naturally sparse, although near-contemporary accounts such as 'The Governing of Empire' (*De Administrando Imperio*) by the Byzantine Emperor Constantine VII (913–959) contain valuable clues. Hungarian historians have been obliged to rely largely on the scientific tools of linguistics, archaeology and anthropology to throw even a dim light on the train of events which began over fifteen hundred years ago in western Siberia: the images that emerge are blurred and contradictory, the theories arising from them numerous and hotly disputed.[1] It seems probable that the Ugrian group of peoples, inhabiting a region in the central Urals between the River Kama in the west and the River Ob in the east, began to break up into smaller groups in the third millennium BC. One of these groups, the Finno-Ugrians, moved gradually westwards, beyond the Urals; and from it emerged a linguistic offshoot, a group of tribes that eventually called themselves Magyars.* By the sixth century BC, the Magyars had settled in the area between the Urals and the River Volga, later known as Bashkiria, and embarked on their long history as an identifiably distinct ethnic and linguistic group. There were, however, as yet no formal links between the individual tribes or central control over them. Although their lifestyle became more nomadic than it had been in their ancient home, they engaged in primitive arable farming and livestock rearing, supplementing the meagre returns from this by equestrian raids on their neighbours for loot. The Magyar tradition of equestrian skills, often put to predatory use, was born at this time.

Between AD 700 and about AD 830, the Magyars resumed their westward drift, occupying a region of the north Caucasus, between the Rivers Donets and Dniester, which the Onogur-Bulgars, a powerful group of tribes who were also moving westwards, had recently vacated. Some Magyars elected to remain in Bashkiria, where their descendants were to be discovered four centuries later by a Hungarian friar seeking the origins of his people. The location and designation of the region in which the majority group of Magyars now made their home, for about a hundred years, has given rise to lively controversy among historians. It was known to the Greeks of Byzantium as Levedia, probably in honour of the first identified leader of the Magyar tribes at that time, Levedi; the Magyars and others called their new home Etelköz, a name that probably meant 'the space between the rivers'. But it is not clear whether Levedia was an eastern region of the Etelköz or a separate area in which the Magyars lived before moving into the Etelköz. It is certain, however, that both areas lay to the northwest of the Crimea; and that the eastern part of the region formed part of the Khanate of the Khazars, whose empire stretched from the southern Ukraine down through the northern Caucasus to the Caspian Sea and who had been converted to Judaism. The Magyars' most important neighbours in Levedia/Etelköz were the Onogur-Bulgars to the north and the Aláns to the south; from both groups, but especially from the Onogur-Bulgars, the hitherto mainly nomadic Magyars learned a great deal. Tools and pots recovered from graves in the region testify to a much more developed agriculture than the Magyars had known in Bashkiria: iron-tipped ploughs were used to cultivate wheat, barley and millet, for which there were storage facilities, and the Onogurs also grew—and introduced the Magyars to—vines, melons and cucumbers. Winter shelter was provided for cattle and pigs, increasing their survival rate. Onogur influence on the Magyars at this time is demonstrated not only by archaeological finds but also by the modern Hungarian language, in which many of the most important words in agriculture and horticulture are of Onogur-Bulgar origin. The influence of the Aláns was evident in less peaceful pursuits; the Magyars copied much of their military hardware including, importantly, their harnesses and stirrups.

---

* A note on nomenclature is needed. 'Magyar' was the name of the dominant tribe in the group to which it belonged; and the seven tribes in the Magyar-led tribal confederacy used it to describe themselves. But outsiders used a variety of names for the Magyars: the Byzantine Greeks called them 'Turks', the Bulgars 'Bashkirs', the Khazars 'Majgars' and the Slavs 'Onoghurs'. The word 'Onoghur' gradually became transformed by West European (Latin) usage into 'Hungary' and 'Hungarian'. The Hungarians still call themselves 'Magyars' and their country 'Magyarország'.

The relationship between the Magyars and the Khazars was uncertain in both its duration and its substance. It lasted for, at most, a century and a half or, at least, twenty years of the early ninth century. The Magyars apparently fought alongside the Khazars against the Bulgars, possibly as early as AD 670, and served the Khazars as guardians of the eastern and northern frontiers of their empire. Early in the ninth century, the Khazars attempted to bind the Magyars into a closer alliance by giving a Khazar princess in marriage to the Magyar leader, Levedi, although—probably to the embarrassment of the Magyars—the union failed to produce an heir. Relations subsequently deteriorated when the Magyars gave at least tacit support to a rebellion against the Khazar Khan, possibly triggered by a campaign of forcible conversion to Judaism; and they offered refuge in the Etelköz, and eventually alliance, to three tribes of Khavars (or Qabars) who fled Khazar retribution when the rebellion had been crushed.

The sojourn of the Magyars in Levedia/Etelköz was marked by two important political developments: Levedi began, and his successors continued, the process of welding the seven Magyar tribes into a tribal confederacy, pledged to mutual support; and the Magyars adopted the Khazar system of dual kingship, under which the supreme leader, the *kende*, delegated much of his executive authority to a deputy, the *gyula*. Levedi, the first Magyar *kende*, in the mid-ninth century, ceded his position to the leader of a clan dominant in the western Etelköz, Álmos; according to a Hungarian chronicle written three centuries later, the election of Álmos to the supreme leadership was marked by a blood-oath, by which the leaders of the seven tribes mingled and drank their blood as an affirmation of their loyalty to Álmos and his descendants. This established the dynasty that was to rule the Magyars and Hungary for over four hundred years. It was in Etelköz, too, that the Magyars were first exposed to Christianity. The Greek monk Kyrill—inventor of the Glagolitic alphabet—came across them in the Crimea in about 860 and his brother Methodius had an apparently fruitful encounter with them in the lower Danube region twenty years later; the Christian cross features in the decoration of saddlebags found in graves of the Etelköz period. Finally, during their sojourn in Etelköz, the Magyars asserted their dominance over the indigenous Slavs, on whom they imposed heavy taxes and many of whom they sold to Byzantium as slaves in return for brocade and woollen cloth. This early relegation of the Slavs to inferior status contained the seeds of racial attitudes, by no means unique to Hungary, that were to prove troublesome in the country's later history.

Álmos's son, Árpád, in his capacity as *gyula*, established an early reputation as a formidable military commander. Greek merchants from Byzantium, visiting the Etelköz to trade, reported back to their Emperor that Árpád was wise and valiant. Similar reports must have reached Arnulf, King of the Eastern Franks, who needed military help against the rising tribal confederation of Great Moravia; he sought and received the assistance of Árpád's horsemen in defeating the Moravian leader Svyatopluk in 892. This brief campaign was significant for two reasons. It opened Magyar eyes to the relative wealth of central Europe by comparison with the steppe that had been their home, whetting their appetite for plunder and booty; and it gave the Magyars their first proper glimpse of the well-watered and sparsely populated Carpathian Basin. The Magyars soon had another client. The Byzantine Emperor, Leo VI, was already worried about the growing strength of the Bulgars under King Simeon; the appearance on the scene of the Magyars, and the possibility of an alliance between them and the Bulgars, increased his concern. In 895, therefore, Leo encouraged the Magyars to attack the Bulgars and provided barges to transport the Magyar horsemen, led by Árpád's son Levente, across the lower Danube. Initial Magyar successes impelled Simeon to arrange an armistice with Byzantium so that he could concentrate his forces against the new enemy; he did so to such good effect that the Magyars were soon in full retreat back to the Etelköz after sustaining heavy losses. Simeon then clinched matters by informing the formidable Pechenegs, a nomadic warrior people who dominated the region to the east of the Etelköz, of the Magyar plight.

It so happened that in the meantime, in a classic instance of the domino effect that determined the rhythm of the Asian migrations, the Pechenegs were themselves under heavy pressure from a Khazar-Arab alliance and needed no urging to displace the Magyars from the well-watered pastures of the Etelköz. With the bulk of their warrior force still straggling back from the lower Danube, the Etelköz Magyars were in no position to stand and fight. Árpád, whose father Álmos died at about this time—possibly the victim of a ritual killing—led his people north, towards Kiev, and then west towards the Carpathians; he had doubtless already determined in his own mind that the Carpathian Basin should be the Magyars' future home and sent word to the retreating warriors that they, too, should change course and cross the Carpathians from the south. The Magyars thus converged on the Carpathian Basin by the most direct routes open to them: the main contingent, under Árpád, through the Verecke Pass and the warrior force through the mountains of Transylvania or up the Danube valley. There is some evidence that the tribes now closely associated with the Magyars, the Khavars and perhaps the Székely, were already ensconced in Transylvania, having remained there after taking a prominent part in the campaigns against the Moravians. By the summer of 895, the main body of the Magyar tribal confederacy, including the women and children who had survived the devastation of the Etelköz by the Pechenegs, had moved into the eastern half of the Carpathian Basin. The final migration was over. The Magyars were poised to enter the history of Europe.

The 'Conquest'

Hungarian chroniclers and historians have been wont to refer to the arrival of the Magyars in the Carpathian Basin as the 'conquest' (honfoglalás). This is a little too dramatic. What actually happened was more akin to an occupation, against little opposition. A leading Hungarian archaeologist and historian, Gyula László, has advanced the theory that the 'conquest' of 895 was not the first but the second wave of settlement by Magyar-speakers in the Carpathian Basin, the first having taken place in the mid-seventh century, by the Avar-Onoghurs.[2] For the time being, the combined weight of other archaeological and linguistic evidence, together with the testimony (admittedly, not always reliable) of the early medieval chroniclers, favours the more traditional view that, brief military raids apart, the Magyar tribal confederacy made its first appearance west of the Carpathians in 895. The region in which the Magyars and their subordinate tribes now—and finally—settled was divided into two by the River Danube. West of the Danube—

the area that came to be known as Transdanubia (*Dunántúl*)—lay the former Roman province of Pannonia. The Romans had held the line of the Danube from, roughly, the site of present-day Vienna in the north to what is now Belgrade in the south. Apart from the hazards of campaigns against the barbarian tribes east of the river, Pannonia must have been quite a popular posting for the Roman military and their families: the climate was pleasant, vines grew well and both gold and salt were mined with profit. Evidence of a pleasant and cultivated expatriate lifestyle can be seen today in the excavated settlement of Aquincum, within the city limits of Budapest. After three hundred years of mounting pressure from Germanic tribes, however, the Romans finally ceded Pannonia to Attila, leader of the Huns, in 434 as the price of his aid (which proved short-lived) against the Visigoths.

East of the Danube lay the Great Plain (Alföld), flat as a pancake and watered by the River Tisza with its tributaries; and, to the south-east, the mountainous region of Transylvania with its valuable salt and gold mines. After Attila's death and the disintegration of the Hunnish Empire, the plain was home to, successively, Gepids, Lombards and Avars. The short-lived Avar Empire, of which the Carpathian Basin formed the core, had been crushed by Charlemagne in 796 and the region fell under the loose control of the rapidly strengthening Kingdom of Bulgaria. The Bulgars, however, were preoccupied with their running contest against Byzantium to the south and never attempted seriously to incorporate Transdanubia or the Great Plain into their empire.

When the Magyars arrived in the Carpathian Basin, therefore, it was populated—rather sparsely—by a mixture of Avars, Bulgars and other Slavs, occupying what had temporarily become a power vacuum in the heart of Europe, over whom the Magyars had little difficulty in imposing their authority. A further component of this ethnic mix, and one that was to play a significant part in the subsequent history of Hungary, were the Székely. The provenance of the Székely has been hotly debated and hard evidence is even sparser than in the case of the Magyars themselves. According to medieval accounts, the Székely were already living in the Carpathian Basin when the Magyars occupied it; others maintain that they must have joined up with the Magyars at an earlier stage since their descendants speak a particularly pure form of the Magyar language. The most persuasive theory is that the Székely were among those who, like the Khavars, sought Magyar protection after the failed rebellion against the Khazars; whatever their origins, however, the Székely undoubtedly excelled in military skills and came to fulfil a similar role in Hungary to that of the Cossacks in Russia—as guardians of the frontier lands, in which they were given privileged land tenure. All these peoples enjoyed a more developed culture than that of the semi–nomadic Magyars: they engaged in both animal and arable husbandry, and in handicrafts. Together, they numbered about 200,000 as against the Magyar strength of about 400,000.

The Magyars adapted to their new, more settled lifestyle without apparent difficulty. The majority pushed west to Transdanubia, while others remained on the Great Plain. Initially, each tribe settled in a separate territory, usually close to rivers, the prime consideration being adequate pasture for horses and cattle. As time passed, tribal identity became less important; with migration and its attendant disciplines a distant memory, mixing between tribes became more common, although the three Khavar tribes and the Székely remained distinct. Although the tribe for some time remained the dominant social unit, the clan (extended family), of which there were about fifty, became increasingly important. The indigenous Avar and Slav population in each region was quickly subjected to the local Magyar chief; but the Magyars adapted to the seasonal rhythm of the natives: fishing by the rivers in winter, ploughing and sowing in the spring, moving livestock to new pastures in the hills during summer while the crops ripened, returning to harvest them in the autumn. The typical dwelling was a thatched hut partially sunk below ground level. An open hearth occupied the centre of the earthen floor and some dwellings boasted a clay oven; but there were no windows or chimneys and during the summer months most Magyars escaped the resulting discomfort by moving into tents. The Magyar leaders settled in Transdanubia: Árpád (*kende*) near Pécs in the south but wintering on Csepel Island in the Danube, downstream from today's Budapest, and Kurszán (*gyula*) near the Roman town of Aquincum.

The Magyars differed in one vital respect from all the preceding migrants into Central and Western Europe: they did not allow their language to be absorbed by those of the indigenous population. On the contrary, the Avars, Bulgars and others who had settled in the Carpathian Basin before the Magyars arrived were eventually expected to speak some Magyar. A linguistic island was thus created in the Germanic and Slavic sea. As one historian has put it: 'Magyar served as a linguistic wedge driven into the heart of Slavonic Europe'.[3] This single fact can be said largely to have determined the subsequent history of what was to become the Hungarian nation.

The Raids

Nominally, the sovereign of Transdanubia was the Frankish king, Arnulf, whom the Hungarians had helped to defeat Svyatopluk of Moravia and who had not, therefore, resisted their occupation. When Arnulf died in 899, the Magyars asked his successor, Louis IV (the Child) of Bavaria, formally to acknowledge the status quo. Louis refused, thus triggering an astonishing series of Magyar incursions into central, western and southern Europe that continued for half a century. These predatory raids proceeded in parallel with the process of settlement into the Carpathian Basin; there was no pause for breath after the arduous trek from the Etelköz. Shortly before his death, Arnulf of Bavaria asked the Magyars to help him dispose of his rival for influence in northern Italy, Berengar I. The Magyars obliged by defeating Berengar, sacking every Italian town as far south as Bologna and attempting, but failing, to attack Venice in 900. Meanwhile, the Moravians had taken advantage of Arnulf's death to move into Transdanubia; the returning Magyars, having been bribed by Berengar to end their Italian campaign, expelled the Moravians, pursued them northwards and occupied their homeland. The Magyars now controlled the entire Carpathian Basin: the 'conquest' was complete.

The military prowess of the Magyars, which had commended them to Arnulf and Emperor Leo VI, was based on their horsemanship. Their horses were small, fast and tough. Both horse and rider were unencumbered by the heavy armour favoured by west European cavalry. During their long migration across the steppes, the Magyars had adopted from other tribes the use of the iron stirrup, which allowed a rider to turn through more than ninety degrees at full gallop. Their strategy was to launch a surprise attack against their opponents, made possible by the speed of their mounts, then to turn about as if in retreat; when the enemy had thus been tempted into headlong and undisciplined pursuit, the Hungarians turned in the saddle and launched a hail of arrows on the pursuers. This inflicted carnage on the enemy cavalry and caused a threshing pile-up of wounded horses and riders; the Magyars were then able to administer the *coup de grace* in hand-to-hand combat. Although the initial motive for attacks on Louis of Bavaria was to punish his refusal to cede sovereignty over Transdanubia, subsequent raids were motivated primarily by the quest for loot. The Magyar leadership needed a warrior class to enforce its authority; this class had to be paid. Regular opportunities for lucrative pillage were the best means of ensuring the warriors' loyalty; the disintegration of the Carolingian Empire ensured that these opportunities would be frequent.*

In 904, Louis of Bavaria tempted fate. Feigning a desire for peace with the Hungarians, he invited *gyula* Kurszán to a reconciliatory feast and had him murdered there. Retribution quickly followed: an extraordinary succession of Hungarian military successes terrorised Europe and gave rise to contemporary, and subsequent, confusion between the Hungarians and the perpetrators of the previous scourge of Europe, the Huns. Hungarian raiding parties reached, sacked and looted towns as far afield as Basle, Bremen, Pavia and Cambrai; they reconnoitred the Pyrenees and threatened Spain. They defeated the Bavarians twice, in 907 and 910, and pillaged Saxony and Thuringia. A new prayer was inserted into the Christian liturgy: 'O save and deliver us, Thine unworthy servants, from the arrows of the Hungarians'. In 924 the German King, Henry the Fowler, bought the Hungarians off by agreeing to pay an annual tribute in return for a seven-year armistice. He then set about improving his defences and re-equipping his military force, the better to counter Hungarian tactics in future: after nine years, his preparations completed, he defied the Hungarians by refusing to pay his tribute. As he expected, the Hungarians—led by Árpád's son, Zoltán, since the death of his father in 907—launched a strong punitive expedition against him; and, as he had hoped, Henry inflicted a comprehensive defeat on the Hungarian force at Merseburg (933).

This sobered the Hungarians, at least so far as Germany was concerned, but by no means extinguished their appetite for other people's treasure. Under their new military commander, Bulcsu, they waged a series of campaigns which took them to Lorraine, the south of France, Burgundy, present-day Switzerland, Lombardy, Italy and Constantinople. As in the pre-Merseburg period, these operations were frequently conducted at the request of a Western ruler who wished to get even with a rival or to punish a rebel; and they were greatly facilitated by the continuing disarray of the former Carolingian Empire. This favourable situation began to change in 936, however, with the election of Otto I to the German crown; Otto

---

* This is a convenient point at which to begin to use the word 'Hungarians' to describe the inhabitants of the geographical area known to their contemporaries as Hungary; and to reserve the word 'Magyar' for what became the dominant language spoken by Hungarians.

methodically set about uniting the German dukedoms, subduing the Slavs to the east and occupying northern Italy, which had so often been a happy hunting ground for the Hungarians. Impressed, the Hungarians suggested to Otto that an alliance would be appropriate; when Otto snubbed them, they unwisely supported a rebellion against him. In 955 Otto brought the Hungarians to battle on the Lechfeld, near Augsburg. The Hungarians were annihilated. The two Hungarian leaders, Bulcsu and Lél, were hanged. According to legend, only seven survivors completed the journey back to Hungary, there to be reviled by their compatriots for saving their own skins rather than giving their lives in battle.

The Lechfeld put an end, for the time being, to Hungary's military adventurism in the west; but it was by no means a knock-out blow. The warrior caste at this time probably numbered no more than 40,000 out of a total population of about 400,000; and the warriors who fought on the Lechfeld came predominantly from those clans that had settled in Transdanubia; the clans of the Great Plain and Transylvania were not significantly affected. Moreover, Hungary was still a pagan society. Polygamy was common and by custom a man was obliged to marry his brother's widow; the losses sustained on the Lechfeld were therefore made good relatively quickly, within two decades. But the glory days were over. Raids on Hungary's southern neighbours continued sporadically for some years, but these, too, were brought to an end by a decisive Hungarian defeat at Arcadiopolis, in Turkey, in 970. A sobered Hungary was obliged to reassess her long-term interests.

Hungary and Christendom

The fact that 'ifs' are meant to be taboo to the historian does not diminish their fascination.* One of the great 'ifs' of Hungary's history is the question of how different that history would have been had Byzantium, rather than Rome, presided over the Hungarian conversion to Christendom; if Hungary, like Serbia, Bulgaria and Kievan Russia, had embraced Greek Orthodox rather than Roman Christianity. The odds against the survival of Magyar as the national language would have been even greater than they were already. With Brother Kirill's Church Slavonic as its liturgical language, Hungary would have found it hard to resist absorption into Slavdom.[4] The question gains in interest from the fact that, initially, Byzantium and Orthodoxy seemed to be having it all their own way. We have already seen that the first contacts between Hungarians and Christianity were with the Orthodox monks Kirill and Methodius. In 948 the third-ranking Hungarian leader (harka) and brilliant military commander, Bulcsu, travelled to Constantinople in order to negotiate a peace treaty that would give him a free hand to continue raiding Hungary's northern neighbours: as part of the bargain he accepted conversion to Orthodox Christianity. Five years later, the ruling chieftain of Transylvania, Zombor, did the same and for good measure took an Orthodox bishop back to Hungary with him to start work on converting his people.

---

* The current vogue for 'counter-factual' historiography and the study of 'contingency' has in any case partly lifted the taboo.

In 961, however, the tide began to turn against Byzantium when Taksony, the new paramount chief* and a grandson of Árpád, asked Pope John XII to send a missionary bishop to Hungary. Although this came to nothing, Taksony's successor Géza made another overture, this time to the newly crowned Emperor Otto I. Otto gladly seized the opportunity of installing an agent of influence in Hungary and despatched Bishop Bruno, who began by baptising Géza himself and then went to work on the nobility, apparently with scant success. Bruno nevertheless established a bridgehead which the Bishop of Prague, Adalbert, was subsequently able to widen; in particular, Adalbert played a key role in the education of Géza's son and heir. Géza's motives in promoting Christianity in Hungary were first and foremost political: pagan shamanism strengthened tribal loyalties and weakened central authority. He also needed a powerful ally on his north-west border and sensibly declined to be drawn into the continuing struggle between successive Holy Roman Emperors and the kings of Bavaria. But although Géza married a Christian (albeit Orthodox) lady from Transylvania, he seems to have maintained his own pagan worship as an insurance policy; and as soon as Otto I died in 973, Géza sent a goodwill mission to Constantinople.

Prudence was clearly Géza's watchword and it served Hungary well during its period of vulnerability after the Lechfeld disaster. When Henry II of Bavaria succeeded in asserting his autonomy within the Holy Roman Empire, Géza hastened to conclude an alliance with him; and in 996, one year before his death, Géza crowned his quarter-century of skilful leadership by persuading Henry II to offer his daughter Gisella in marriage to Géza's son, who took the name István (Stephen).** At the same time Géza concluded an agreement with Henry on the Bavarian Hungarian frontier: it was to follow the line of the Rivers Leitha and Morava—and did so, as Hungary's frontier with Austria, until 1919.

When Stephen, still in his twenties, succeeded his father in 997, he immediately faced a challenge from his older cousin, Koppány. Koppány represented the old Magyar traditions: the pagan religion and the custom that a leader was succeeded by the senior member of his family rather than by his eldest son. With the help of Bavarian knights, Stephen defeated the rebel force. Koppány himself was killed in the battle; his body was quartered and displayed at four fortresses as a warning to malcontents. With that local difficulty behind him, and doubtless encouraged by Adalbert, Stephen created a defining moment in the history of Hungary: he sought from Pope Sylvester II recognition as a Christian king. The Pope, after consulting the Holy Roman Emperor Otto III, acceded to his petition. Stephen's emissaries returned to Esztergom—on the Danube Bend north of present-day Budapest—where his father had established the ruling family's permanent seat, bearing symbolic gifts of a crown and an apostolic cross. On Christmas Day in the year 1000,*** Stephen was crowned King of Hungary. Hungary thus joined the family of Christian kingdoms, formally embraced the

---

* The traditional hierarchy of *kende, gyula* and *harka* had by now died out.
** To make life easier for the reader, this account will use the anglicised versions (where they exist) of the names of Hungarian Kings. All other Hungarian names retain their original form and spelling.
*** Or, according to some authorities, on 1 January 1001.

Western tradition of Christianity and, in theory, won immunity from attack by any other Christian prince. Only a hundred years after their arrival in the Carpathian Basin and fewer than fifty years after ending their marauding raids, the Hungarians had become Europeans.

2

THE YOUNG HUNGARIAN STATE

(1000–1301)

Stephen I, King and Saint (1000–38)

It is to the credit of the Hungarians that they have chosen to make King Stephen I, rather than any of his more martial and flamboyant successors, the prime symbol of Hungarian statehood. Although he established his credentials as a military leader early in his reign by his comprehensive defeat of three powerful malcontents, Stephen was above all a man of peace and order. He gave Hungary its Western orientation, its church, and its state organisation, of which the central feature—the county (*megye*)— has survived to the present day. For a man who was to be canonised fifty years after his death, he does not seem to have been outstandingly pious until, in his declining years, grief over the death of his son drove him to religious contemplation; but he possessed remarkable political talents which justify the reverence that Hungarians still, nearly a thousand years later, accord to his memory.

Having disposed of cousin Koppány, Stephen was confronted by further serious threats to his authority. The first came from one of his uncles, Gyula of Transylvania; Stephen defeated and captured him after a short campaign, establishing his authority over this strategically and economically vital region. He subsequently encouraged the Székely to settle on the southern and eastern frontiers of Transylvania, rewarding them with grants of land and the status of freemen. Stephen next had to deal with the defiant hostility of Ajtony, ruler of the Maros region in the south east of the country. Ajtony had accepted baptism from the Byzantine Emperor, who was using him to subvert Stephen's authority; Ajtony, for example, with encouragement from Constantinople, had taken it upon himself to impose a tax on the salt which was conveyed westwards along the Maros river from the Transylvanian salt mines, thus infringing the crown's monopoly. Stephen sent one of his nephews at the head of an army to bring Ajtony to heel. In the resulting battle Ajtony was defeated and killed: his extensive estates were confiscated, further to swell the royal demesne.

Whatever the physical attractions of the lands on which the young Hungarian state was established, and they were many, its position was bound to prove politically uncomfortable. Interposed between two empires—the Holy Roman and the Byzantine, later to be replaced by the Habsburg and the Ottoman—Hungary was doomed to excite the acquisitive ambitions of her neighbours to the north west and south east. Stephen managed this situation, which was to dominate Hungary's history for nine centuries, with greater skill than most of his successors. When, first, the Polish King and then the German Emperor challenged Hungarian independence by seizing territory along its northern borders, Stephen repelled their incursions but then concluded sensible treaties of peace. In the south, Stephen helped the Byzantine Emperor Basil II to vanquish Bulgaria and then arranged the marriage of his son Imre to a Byzantine princess. Despite his strong commitment to Western Catholicism, he endowed an Orthodox church in Byzantium and welcomed Byzantine subjects to his court. Another marriage, between Stephen's sister and the Doge of Venice, gave Hungary an alliance with the other leading power in the region. The relative security provided by these arrangements enabled Stephen to concentrate on his first priorities, the consolidation of royal authority and the conversion of Hungary to the Christian faith.

Stephen inherited from his father, Géza, the rudiments of a system of government, based on the county (megye); Géza had confiscated a number of forts and their adjacent lands from clan leaders, converting them into local outposts of royal authority. Stephen developed and expanded this structure. By the end of his reign, Hungary was divided into over forty counties, each administered by a count (ispán) from a fortress (vár); the counts were royal appointees, selected either from the king's entourage—which included a number of Bavarian knights who had come to Hungary with Queen Gisella—or from the leadership of the local clan or kindred.* The count's responsibilities included the collection of taxes, of which he was allowed to retain a third for local purposes; the administration of justice, in which he was assisted by a county magistrate; and the maintenance of order with the help of a small personal militia (the 'castle warriors' or várjobbágy). The count, his officers and the militia, together with their families, lived within the fortress perimeter, typically defined by a thick circular wall of compacted earth about 400 metres in diameter, in wooden thatched buildings that also comprised storehouses, stabling and, usually, a prison. Outside the fortress walls were the church and, surrounding a marketplace, the dwellings of the many families who depended on the count and his entourage for their livelihood: butchers, blacksmiths, carpenters, potters, weavers, goldsmiths, fowlers and the rest. A typical fortress commanded the labour of one-third of its county's population. Although the day-to-day administration of the counties was conducted by the counts and their officers, Stephen (and his successors) exercised close supervision by travelling round the country with the senior members of the royal court, assessing the performance and honesty of the counts, hearing appeals against their jurisdiction and reminding the populace of where power and final authority resided.

As well as bringing order to the Hungarian lands, Stephen was determined to transform it into a Christian kingdom. This was the more difficult task of the two.

---

* The term 'kindred' (Latin genus) was applied to an extended family, or network of families, sharing a common ancestor real or imagined. During most of the Middle Ages, it was an important social unit in Hungary, with its own recognised legal personality.

Shortly after his coronation, Stephen had sought and obtained papal authority for a campaign to convert the Hungarian people. He conducted it with energy and commitment; but it was uphill work, made no easier by lingering memories of the German Bishop of Passau's heavy-handed efforts at conversion under Géza, which had given Christianity a bad reputation and an uncomfortable association with foreign interference. The French and Italian monks whom Stephen now put into the front line were more skilful and put to good use the fact that the pagan Hungarians were already accustomed to the concept of a single supreme power, *Isten. Isten* now became the Hungarian word for God.

With the help of the newly consecrated primate of Hungary, Archbishop Aschrik of Esztergom, Stephen established two archbishoprics and eight bishoprics, covering the entire realm between them. He required every ten villages in each diocese to build and maintain a church, for which the king supplied the furnishings and the bishop religious texts. Church attendance on Sundays was compulsory for everybody except the village fire-watcher; the counts and priests were responsible for enforcing this. The penalties for non-attendance, and even for talking during the service, were severe. Since Sunday was also market day, the villagers were usually herded into church straight from the marketplace. Against this background, it is perhaps not surprising that Christianity gained in popularity very slowly indeed. At the end of Stephen's reign, the majority of the Hungarian population was still hostile to the Christian Church or at least reluctant to co-operate with it. Shamanism remained strong; it was left to Andrew I (1046–60) to inflict its final defeat. Stephen nevertheless gave the Church a leading role in Hungarian governance and society. He endowed a number of monasteries from the royal estates, including the great Benedictine abbey of Pannonhalma, and senior members of the Church hierarchy were prominent in the royal court. As in Western Christendom, the Church in Hungary was sustained by the tithe, the tenth part of the produce of a family or estate which was paid to the Church in kind or, later, in cash.

The status of the Church and the rules—very strict rules[1]—of religious observance took pride of place in the first of the two Books of Laws attributed to Stephen I. The two books, which were probably compendia of oral judgments made by the king or his court judge and recorded by the court chaplain, gave Hungary the rudiments of a penal code and constituted an important first step towards the establishment of a law-governed state. The laws were not concerned with sin, which was left to the Church to deal with; and they placed greater emphasis on the protection of property than on the protection of life. In many respects, however, Stephen's laws were both more comprehensive and more humane than those of the neighbouring states—France, Germany and Bavaria—from which they probably drew their initial inspiration. The monks and scribes who fell out of favour in the court of Henry of Bavaria and found employment in the royal court of Hungary may well have brought some legal texts with them. They also introduced to Hungary the skill of writing in Latin (it was to be two centuries before Magyar became a written language). The existence of the Laws, and their enforcement through the judgments of the ruler and his representatives had an important consequence for Hungary: the country became a popular destination for immigrants who, for whatever reason, were seeking land and a new life. Stephen encouraged them. In the *Admonitions*, summarising for his son Imre the lessons of his experience as a ruler, Stephen enjoined him to honour guests who, 'from however many diverse countries they arrive, so many languages, precepts and arms do they bring with them, all of which adorn the Royal Court and frighten the enemies ...For a state which owns but one language and one habit is feeble and fragile'.[2]

Hungary's reputation for being a well-ordered society, by medieval standards, attracted not only would-be settlers but also a growing number of transients, both pilgrims and merchants, travelling to the territories controlled by Byzantium, to Constantinople itself or to the Holy Land. Hungary became the recognised bridge between the two Empires, a status that proved to be a very mixed blessing when the Crusades began towards the end of the century. In the meantime, however, it brought significant economic advantages. In order to maximise them, Stephen moved the royal court south west from Esztergom to Székesfehérvár, a place through which the majority of travellers passed. Here he built a basilica in which pilgrims could worship. It was also the royal chapel and burial place; and members of the court could purchase their luxuries from foreign merchants with the newly minted Hungarian silver dinars, coinage that quickly acquired a good reputation in Europe.

The death of his son and heir, Imre, in a hunting accident in 1031 cast a heavy cloud over the closing years of Stephen's reign, not only of paternal grief but also of bitterness over the disputed succession. In the absence of a male heir, the crown should have passed to the eldest Arpád, Stephen's cousin Vazul. As Stephen had a poor opinion of Vazul, he nominated his nephew Peter, son of the Doge of Venice, to succeed him; when Vazul conspired to overturn this decision, Stephen ordered him to be blinded and, according to one account, to have his ears filled with molten lead. Vazul's three sons fled into exile. Stephen himself retreated into prayer and died a few years later, in 1038.

Every year on 20 August, the date of Stephen's canonisation and a national holiday, a casket containing what is believed to be the mummified right hand of King St Stephen I is carried in solemn procession round the outside of the basilica which bears his name in Budapest; and in 1996 the purported remains of Queen Gisella were brought from Passau to be ceremoniously re-interred in the Church of St. Michael in Veszprém. The crown of St. Stephen, and its replacement, quickly became the central symbol of royal legitimacy: the validity of a coronation depended upon the use of this crown, and no other, in the ceremony. The original crown given to Stephen by Pope Sylvester was lost or stolen shortly after the king's death—there are many theories as to its ultimate fate. It is certain, however, that the lower half of the crown as it exists today was a gift from the Byzantine Emperor Michael VII to the Hungarian King, Géza I;* and that the upper half was made in Hungary, probably in the twelfth century, to replace the lost original. The two halves were welded together in order to make an appropriate support for the cross that surmounts the crown. The original cross may have contained a purported fragment of the True Cross, hence 'Holy Crown'. After an extraordinary series of adventures over eight centuries, the crown fell into the hands of the

* See page 26.

United States army, in Austria, in 1945. The US government held it in Fort Knox, for safe keeping, until its ceremonial return to Hungary in 1978. The crown, and other royal regalia thought to have belonged to Stephen I, were then installed, by a Communist regime striving for national respectability, in a large shrine in the National Museum in Budapest, under armed guard. To mark the millennium of the Hungarian state in the year 2000, the liberal/conservative government of Viktor Orbán transferred it with great ceremony to the Parliament Building, where it now resides.

Nine and a half centuries later, the reverence still accorded in Hungary to Stephen's memory may seem disproportionate to his achievement, which was to give Hungary forty years of relative peace and sound but unspectacular rule. His canonisation, and that of his son Imre, in 1083, owed more to the political acumen of the then reigning Árpád, Ladislas I, who was keen to consolidate the prestige of the dynasty, than to saintly qualities in their characters or lifestyle, as the punishment meted out to the unfortunate Vazul showed. There is also a tendency to attribute to Stephen an anachronistic concept of 'nationhood'. Like all monarchs in medieval Europe, Stephen acted first and foremost in the interests of his family and dynasty; those of his subjects, to whose descendants the term 'nation' could not in any case be properly applied for several hundred years, were subordinate. During Stephen's reign, however, the interests of dynasty and people coincided to a greater extent than during those of most of his successors. Hungary's entry into Western Christendom not only conferred respectability on the Árpáds and gave them their entry ticket into the European royal marriage market;[3] it also gave their subjects a degree of security and the beginnings of access to Western culture (in the mid-twelfth century, for example, Thomas à Becket of Canterbury engaged in a long correspondence with the Archbishop of Esztergom).[4] It should also be borne in mind that Hungary experienced two catastrophic interruptions to the course of its history: the Mongol invasions of 1241–42 and the Ottoman occupation, which lasted for 160 years in the sixteenth and seventeenth centuries, not to mention subsequent occupations by the Austrians, Germans and Russians. It is understandable that Hungarians should find reassurance and a sense of identity in reaching over these traumatic events to their roots and to the foundation of their state; innumerable Hungarian institutions and commodities therefore bear the name of St Stephen and keep his memory alive.

Histories of medieval Europe sometimes fail adequately to stress the impact on political events of the low level of life expectancy then prevailing: in Hungary, for example, only a small minority survived what would now be regarded as early middle age. This meant that the heir in direct line of succession to the throne was frequently a minor—often a very young child—or that there was no direct heir at all. This situation encouraged rival claimants and pretenders to chance their arms in bidding for power and created a frequent requirement for regencies, usually destabilising in themselves. Between the death of Stephen I in 1038 and the end of the Árpád dynasty in 1301, there were twenty occupants of the Hungarian throne.* Most of them were too preoccupied with fending off rival claimants and with securing the throne for their preferred successors to make any significant

* See Appendix I.

contribution to the history of the Hungarian kingdom; to list them all in this chapter would simply be a distraction from those developments in twelfth and thirteenth-century Hungary that were of greater importance. The few Hungarian kings who left a significant imprint on the development of their kingdom were those who beat the odds and reigned for twenty years or more; most of the events and developments summarised in the remainder of this chapter occurred during their reigns.

With the exceptions of Kálmán the Learned (1095–1116) and Béla III (1172–96) in the twelfth century, and Béla IV (1235–70) in the thirteenth, Hungary was not well served by its Árpád rulers during this period; but even an intelligent and determined ruler, such as Béla IV, had relatively few resources from which to impose his authority. The first royal standing army still lay in the future; in the meantime, the king raised an army for a specific purpose or campaign, at the end of which the army dispersed. To advise and assist him in the business of government, the king could look only to the Royal Council;[5] but since this body consisted largely of barons and prelates, its co-operation could by no means be taken for granted. A more reliable ally, since he held office at the king's pleasure, was the chief officer of the royal court, the Palatine (*Nádor*), to whom the king usually delegated many of his judicial duties. It became customary for the Palatine to tour the counties in order to dispense justice in cases that could not be dealt with locally, either because the offence was too serious—murder or robbery, for example—or because the defendant was a member of the nobility; the Palatine also led the army when the king was absent or sick and generally acted as his deputy. Andrew II's (1205–35) 'Golden Bull', of which more below, further enhanced the Palatine's status, making him in effect the chief intermediary between crown and people and custodian of the people's rights. Among the officers of the court, the Master of the Treasury was next in importance; as well as administering the royal treasure chest, he supervised the collection of taxes and of revenues from the royal estates. These revenues, supplemented by income from the tax on salt, from tolls and duties paid by merchants and traders, and from the royal monopoly of minting coins, were very considerable: when Béla III had to produce evidence of his financial worth when seeking the hand of Princess Margaret of France, the French were surprised to find that Béla's annual income was equal to that of their own king. After Béla's death, the royal finances deteriorated, particularly under Andrew II, who was profligate and incompetent; he began the practice of debasing the coinage, for the sake of a quick profit, which his successors continued until the fourteenth century. The wealth of the richest barons rivalled the over-stretched resources of the crown.

The royal chancellery, headed by a senior member of the Church hierarchy as Chancellor, drafted the king's correspondence and decrees (the Chancellor was also keeper of the royal seal); during the late twelfth century, partly as a result of Béla III's marriage, French clerics and scribes replaced the predominantly Bavarian staff of the chancellery, writing, of course, in Latin. The royal court, when not on tour, was based first in Székesfehérvár and Esztergom, then in Óbuda (Old Buda, now the northern part of Budapest) and finally, under Béla IV, in Buda itself; a fortress was built on Buda's Castle Hill (*Várhegy*) in 1247. The general assembly of tribal chiefs in pre-conquest times survived in the shape of the Diet (*gyűlés*), which met to elect a sovereign's successor but otherwise only at the king's pleasure. Stephen I, doubtless apprehensive of convening a largely pagan assembly, never summoned it at all; his successors summoned the Diet for specific purposes, usually related to money or a national emergency. The Diet became an integral part of the government of the realm only under the last Árpád, Andrew III (1290–1301), who called upon every baron and noble to attend a Diet annually in order to deliberate on affairs of state and oversee the conduct of the counts in their counties. In 1298, the Diet came of age as a legislative assembly and as an equal partner with the king in the governance of the realm: laws were to be discussed and approved by the Diet and only then submitted to the sovereign for confirmation. Moreover, the nobility and the clergy were each to send two representatives to the Royal Council, hitherto composed only of barons and bishops, in order to monitor royal appointments. These innovations, in European terms considerably in advance of their time, did not long survive the death of their progenitor; but they provided a precedent which the nobility, in particular, was to find valuable many years later.

Hungarian Society in the Twelfth and Thirteenth Centuries

The summit of the Hungarian social pyramid consisted of the king, his family, and the personal entourage that made up the royal court: originally, under Stephen I, this had included the leaders of the clans that had arrived in the Carpathian Basin with Árpád, the Bavarian knights loyal to Queen Gisella, the newly installed archbishops and those whom Stephen had honoured for an outstanding service, usually in battle. Of equivalent status, although not often physically present in the royal household, were the counts, among whom two were *primus inter pares*: the governors in charge of two crucial but distant regions of the kingdom, Transylvania in the east and Slavonia in the south, bearing the titles of '*voivod*' and '*bán*' respectively. This group comprised the original nobility, about one hundred kindreds all claiming descent from leaders of the tribes and clans of Hungary's preChristian era. Below this elite stratum, society consisted of the free and the unfree: freemen and serfs. The former, the minority, enjoyed freedom of movement, at least in theory, and the right to seek redress in the courts; among their number were foreign immigrants (*hospites* or 'guests'). But free status was by no means incompatible with duties of service, typically military in character, to a lord; and most freemen entered into or inherited such obligations, which meant that their freedom of movement was constrained in practice. A serf, on the other hand, was the property of his lord, a chattel like the livestock he tended; he had no rights, no legal personality and usually no property. Marriage, and sexual intercourse, between the nominally free and the unfree were forbidden.

Already in the eleventh century, and continuing into the twelfth, the class of freemen was becoming differentiated by the accident of birth, by the granting of favours or by misfortune. Within a community which lived in and around the same castle or abbey and acknowledged the authority of the same lord, the military element—the 'castle warriors'—came to enjoy a significantly higher standing than those who, though nominally free, fulfilled a less glamorous (and less hazardous) role by working their lord's estate and raising his livestock. During the course of the thirteenth century, these social distinctions became more clearly defined. The original, 'true', nobility began to call themselves, and to be called, 'barons', a title usually associated with tenure of an important office under the crown. The military class, whose members had usually been rewarded by king or lord for their service in battle with grants of land, gradually acquired 'noble' status; while the 'agrarian' freemen, cultivating land they did not own, came to form Hungary's largest social stratum, the peasantry.

This process of social differentiation received a strong impetus from the decision of Andrew II, in 1217, to 'alter the conditions of our realm that has been conserved by the ancients, and distribute castles, counties, lands and other revenues of our abundant Hungary to our barons and knights as inheritable possession given in perpetuity'.[6] Andrew evidently hoped by this means to cement the loyalty of his leading subjects and to enable them to increase their military contribution to the royal army in time of war. The scale of the ensuing alienation of the royal estates, however, had social and political consequences that were not, in the long term, by any means to the advantage of the crown. It resulted in a dangerous increase in baronial wealth and power. At the beginning of the thirteenth century there were twenty-six baronial families in Hungary, of which nine were foreign. They posed a constant threat to the crown. Ever mindful of the elective nature of the Hungarian monarchy and of the power this placed in their hands as the dominant presence in the Diet, the barons invariably regarded their loyalty as conditional; they always kept half an eye on rivals for the succession, and even on foreign rulers, such as Frederick II of Austria who coveted the Hungarian crown, in case the potential rewards, in terms of both office and wealth, might be greater from those patrons than from the reigning king. Moreover, the distribution of royal estates to buy or reward baronial loyalty caused real hardship, and widespread discontent, among those who suddenly found themselves subject to a new and possibly more exacting lord, in the person of the baron, bishop or abbot to whose ownership their castle community and its villages had been transferred. This had two consequences. The first, Andrew II's promulgation of the Golden Bull, is described below. The second consisted of a process, which continued during much of the thirteenth century, by which members of the emerging class of nobles applied to the king to be granted the status of 'royal servants' (*servientes*). Andrew, and his son Béla IV who succeeded him, almost invariably acceded to these petitions, thereby freeing the petitioner from his obligations to his former lord and, usually, granting him the ownership of the land he occupied on his former lord's estate. In return, a royal servant was required to join the king's armed retinue whenever the need arose. This was a bad bargain for the crown. The royal servants acquired enhanced prestige, the land to go with it, the right to sue for justice before the king and the right to take part in an annual deliberation, in the royal presence, on the state of the realm; but they frequently lacked the means to equip themselves for military service. Weapons, armour, sturdy mounts and squires were expensive. The king's hopes of bringing large numbers of well-equipped retainers to fight beneath the royal standard therefore remained largely unfulfilled.

Andrew II returned from the disastrous Fifth Crusade—which he abandoned when it failed to enhance his chances of claiming the vacant Byzantine throne—to find Hungary in a state of turmoil and imminent rebellion. Andrew acceded to the demand of the malcontents—freemen supported by some barons and, importantly, by Andrew's own son and heir, Béla—that he should sign a charter confirming, among other things, the rights and privileges of the emerging class of nobles. The charter should also remove another cause of popular discontent, the appointment of foreigners (including Jews and Muslims) to offices in the gift of the crown. The result was the Golden Bull, so called because its seal was encased in gold, which Andrew II signed in 1222. The preamble proclaimed the king's wish to satisfy the petitions of the nobles 'in all respects, as we are obliged to do-especially because between them and us this circumstance has often led to no inconsiderable bitterness, which ought rightly to be avoided for the better preservation of the royal dignity....We grant both to them and to other men of our kingdom the liberty given by the holy king [Stephen]...'.[7] The Bull went on to affirm the nobility's freedom from taxation by crown or Church; their release from the obligation to serve in the king's army outside the kingdom, while confirming their duty to help him repel an invasion; and their right, in the absence of a male heir, to bequeath their estates and possessions as they wished,* subject to the allocation of one-quarter of their possessions to a daughter if they had one. The Bull also decreed that foreign immigrants could not be raised to high office without the approval of the Royal Council; and barred 'Ishmaelites' (Muslims) and Jews from employment in the royal treasury or mint, or in the collection of taxes or management of the royal salt monopoly. In a rash concession, the Bull gave nobles the right of armed resistance to the crown if a ruler failed to respect its provisions.

The Church was far from pleased with the Golden Bull, complaining both to the King and to Pope Honorius III that its interests had been ignored; the nobles, for their part, protested after a few years that the barons continued to flout its provisions. Andrew was therefore compelled in 1231 to issue a supplementary Bull, which confirmed the extension to churchmen of the nobles' privileges and added a few useful liberties to those already granted: nobles and ecclesiastics were exempted from contributing to the cost of royal fortifications and buildings; and court officials were obliged to compensate households in which they lodged while on tour for the cost of their stay.[8] The Archbishop of Esztergom now received authority to apply the sanction of excommunication against a ruler who flouted the Bull, a sanction to which the Archbishop gave almost immediate effect against Andrew II himself, shortly before the latter's death in 1235.

Despite this, the two Bulls were honoured more in their breach than in their observance, not only by Andrew II but also by his successors and, of course, by the barons. In 1267 Béla IV, whose preoccupation with defending the realm in the wake of the Mongol invasion had led him further to enlarge the noble class by wholesale ennoblements in return for military service, was obliged to force through the Diet a set of laws that provided for the return to nobles of land usurped by the barons, reaffirmed the nobility's freedom from taxation and confirmed the right of nobles to refuse to accompany their king on military campaigns outside Hungary. The barons gave their consent to these laws, secure in the

---

* Under existing law, the estate of a landowner who died without a male heir had automatically reverted to the crown.

belief—subsequently justified—that they could flout them as they had flouted the Golden Bull. The Bulls did, however, become useful later on, in the sixteenth century, when the Hungarian nobility succeeded in convincing the Habsburg King of Hungary, Ferdinand I (1526–64), that the Golden Bull and its supplement were the true and revered cornerstones of noble liberties, which it was incumbent on every monarch to respect. Thenceforth, the Bull's provisions were reaffirmed in the coronation oath of every Habsburg ruler for the next century and a half.

The Golden Bull has naturally been compared with Magna Carta, which preceded it by seven years; and it is a fact that one of the Bull's witnesses, a bishop, was of English descent while another had fought alongside English barons in the Fifth Crusade. There was, however, a crucial difference between the two documents: whereas Magna Carta was designed to protect baronial rights and privileges against the King of England, the Golden Bull was intended to protect the lesser nobility against the barons. It can also be argued that whereas the long-term influence of Magna Carta was benign, the eventual effect of the Golden Bull was to entrench the privileges, in particular immunity from taxation, of a significant segment of the Hungarian population and thus increase the burdens borne by the lower strata—an ugly flaw in Hungarian society, which was to persist into the nineteenth century. In the thirteenth century, however, that society was still in a state of flux: nobles impoverished by baronial oppression or by simple misfortune merged into the peasantry, while free peasants could acquire noble status in return for services rendered to the king.

Despite the limited impact in practice of the Golden Bull and its successor decrees, the emergence of a self-conscious noble class was the most important social development in thirteenth century Hungary. Consisting largely of 'royal servants', who from about 1250 onwards were referred to as *nobiles* rather than *servientes*, together with warriors in the castles and ecclesiastical estates who had remained with their lords rather than transferring their direct loyalty to the king, the common and distinguishing characteristic of the nobility was the ownership of land, whether inherited or donated by the ruler. The nobility, and the Church, constituted the crown's potential allies against the growing might of the supernobles, the barons. Hungarian kings needed the military power of the barons for the defence of the realm; but they also needed the nobility, whose loyalty they were very ready to purchase with grants of liberties and land, as a counterweight to baronial might. The nobility was not, however, by any means a royal instrument. On the contrary, the last years of the thirteenth century saw the beginnings of a process by which the counties were transformed from units of royal administration into semi–autonomous units of noble self-government.

Meanwhile, baronial power had continued to increase. After the Mongol invasion,* Béla IV (1235–70) was obliged to make further substantial grants of royal land to the barons in order to encourage them to build stone castles, which experience had shown to be the only sound defence against invaders. Stone castles could also be used to defy the ruler: the royal army consisted mainly of light cavalry, unsuitable for siege warfare. A leading baronial kindred, the Kőszegis, successfully resisted a siege by Ladislas IV (1272–90) in 1283. Castle building in the late

---

* See page 29.

thirteenth century proceeded at a phenomenal pace. In 1270 there were thirty-two royal castles and forty-four owned by baronial kindreds: by 1300 these figures had increased to forty-two and 124 respectively, a massive shift in military and thence political strength in favour of the barons. One clan, the Csáks, owned forty-one castles in north-west Hungary, ruling the region as a family fiefdom; the Kőszegis (fourteen castles) had similar power over the western part of the country. These developments imposed strains on the 'county' system of administration which, in some parts of the country, it could not withstand; the framework of local government established by Stephen I was replaced in those regions by oligarchic anarchy. By no means untypical of baronial behaviour was the destruction of Veszprém Cathedral by Péter Csák in 1276, simply in order to steal its treasures as an act of spite against the bishop, who belonged to the rival Kőszegi clan.

Stephen I's successors took his admonition concerning the value of 'guests', or immigrants, seriously. Foreigners were encouraged to settle in Hungary and found much to attract them, including the low density of population in a well-watered and fertile land. By early medieval standards and despite the activities of the barons, the rule of law was firmly rooted. Ladislas I (1077–95) reacted to the period of anarchy that followed Stephen's death by introducing a penal code of great severity, giving priority to the protection of property: the theft of anything more valuable than a chicken was punishable by hanging and the reduction of the thief's children to slavery. Kálmán the Learned promulgated an improved and less draconian version (it contained no provision for the punishment of witches, on the enlightened grounds that they did not exist) and clarified the laws on land tenure, an important consideration for potential immigrants. Hungary's reputation as a law-governed state was spread abroad by the Crusades, which passed through the country—initially to its misfortune but eventually to its benefit—on their way to the Near East. In the 1090s, the pillage and devastation wrought by the early 'people's crusades' obliged Kálmán to confront and disperse them by force; but in 1096 he allowed the First Crusade to transit Hungary in return for strict promises of good behaviour, guaranteed by hostages. Subsequent Crusades brought Hungary little trouble, some useful trade and much renown; the Second, led by Louis VII of France, resulted in a surge of French (Walloon) immigration. The Walloons introduced the heavy plough and the open-field system to Hungary, and helped to improve its viticulture, especially in the Tokaj region; they established permanent settlements on the outskirts of both Esztergom and Székesfehérvár, introducing the Hungarians to new skills in craftsmanship, and developed the growing trade in imported luxuries. Under Géza II (1141–62), peasants from the Rhineland (all Germans were known to the Hungarians, without distinction, as 'Saxons') were encouraged to settle in Transylvania as freemen owning their own land and brought with them useful advances in agricultural practice (the asymmetric plough, the three-field system and the horse-collar) while German miners virtually monopolised the working of the rich seams of gold, silver and copper in the mountains of Transylvania and in the northern Carpathians.

During the thirteenth century the development of towns in Hungary introduced a new element in Hungarian society: the burghers and merchants, of whom the great majority were foreign immigrants. Many of them had been persuaded to settle in Hungary by the public relations efforts of the so-called 'locators', who toured the towns of western Europe extolling the virtues of one or another country of central eastern Europe and the great opportunities that beckoned the enterprising townsman. These agents were able to promise prospective immigrants that in Hungary's eight already existing towns, protected by royal charter, and in the new towns which the 'locators' hoped to establish, they would live under 'German law', which guaranteed municipal self-government, judicial autonomy for all except capital offences and, usually, freedom from taxation for a given number of years. Béla IV, in his efforts to improve Hungary's defences following the Mongol invasion, promised charters embodying these privileges to new settlements which undertook to build fortifications. These incentives proved effective in attracting to Hungary the merchants and craftsmen from France, Italy and Germany who made up the country's first urban class. When Béla IV granted a royal charter to the embryo settlement of Buda in 1247, large numbers of townsfolk, predominantly of German origin, moved across from Pest on the opposite bank of the Danube and the town grew rapidly. By 1300 there were two large churches, two priories and a synagogue within Buda's walls. A stone that stood at one of the town gates at this time bore the inscription:

> Gaudeat hic hospes
> Veniens huc cives et ospes
> Ac veniam lapsi
> Capiant et premia iusti.

('May citizens and guests arriving here rejoice in safety; may sinners find pardon and good men reward'.)

This sketch of early medieval Hungarian society would be incomplete without a note on the position of the Jews, whose fortunes and misfortunes were to be a factor of constant and ultimately tragic significance in the history of Hungary. The Khavar tribes that accompanied the Magyars into the Carpathian Basin in 895 were largely Jewish by faith, as the Khazar empire from which they came had been converted to Judaism many years before; there was also a small Jewish minority in the indigenous population of the Carpathian Basin. From the very outset, therefore, Jewry was a phenomenon of which Hungary's rulers had to take account; Esztergom, the first seat of the royal court, already had a well-organised Jewish community in the eleventh century. Kálmán the Learned's dispersal of the early 'peoples' Crusades' spared the Jews of Hungary the massacres to which they had been and would be subjected in other countries on the Crusaders' route; Hungary gained the reputation of being a country in which Jews could live without fear and Jewish immigration increased accordingly. Already in Kálmán's time, however, Jews were disadvantaged in important respects: they were forbidden to marry Christian women and to own or hire Christian slaves, a prohibition that virtually excluded them from farming and channelled their talents into money-lending and pawnbroking. Their gifts for financial management nevertheless made them indispensable to successive Hungarian rulers, whose forte this was not. Despite repeated protests from popes, barons and nobles alike, Jews were usually to be found in key positions in the royal treasury, and those who held such offices were often allowed to own or manage landed estates. The Golden Bull and its 1231 supplement specifically excluded both Jews and Muslims from holding office under the crown; but they continued to do so and the Hebrew characters on thirteenth-century Hungarian coins show that Jews remained in charge of the royal mint. As part of his effort to rebuild the Hungarian kingdom after the Mongol invasion, Béla IV took measures to encourage Jewish immigration; a law of 1251 safeguarded the personal rights of all Jews in Hungary, laid down that crimes against them were to be punished as if they were Christian and stipulated that Christian testimony against a Jew had to be supported by Jewish testimony. Thus protected, Jews continued to play a key role in the royal administration as treasurers, tax–farmers and rent-collectors. This goaded the Papacy and the Hungarian Church to further protest and the ecclesiastical Council of Buda in 1279—a body which Ladislas IV (1272–90) subsequently forced to dissolve itself by forbidding the townsfolk of Buda to sell food to its participants—passed a number of anti–Jewish resolutions, including a renewed prohibition from holding public office and the obligation for Jews to wear a distinctive badge, a circle of red cloth, on their outer clothing (Muslims, who shared all these disabilities, were to wear yellow badges). Although these measures, like their predecessors, had little immediate effect they remained on the table to be revived, with grave consequences, in the fourteenth century.

The Seeds of Ambition

Hungary's geographical situation, sandwiched between two empires, held obvious threats to the security of the young state but also tempting opportunities for Árpád kings ambitious for their dynasty. To the north west, successive German kings and emperors coveted Hungary; while to the north east the ebb and flow of rivalries between Bohemia, Poland and Russia appeared to offer, from time to time, opportunities for gain by Hungarian arms. To the south east, Byzantium was concerned to prevent the southward expansion of the Holy Roman Empire through the absorption of Hungary but also to curb such ambitions as Hungarian rulers, with papal encouragement, might harbour towards Byzantium's Balkan backyard.

The relatively modest armed force a Hungarian king, in the twelfth and thirteenth centuries, could summon to his standard proved considerably more effective in defence against an invader than in campaigning beyond Hungary's borders. Already in the eleventh century successive invasions by two German Emperors, Henry III and Henry IV, had been successfully repulsed before imperial preoccupation with the long struggle with the papacy over investiture spared Hungary further unwelcome attentions for nearly half a century. Henry V of Germany tried again in 1108, in alliance with Bohemia; fortunately for Kálmán the Learned of Hungary, Bohemia's involvement alarmed Boleslaw III in neighbouring Poland and the Polish king helped Kálmán drive the Czechs and Germans from Hungarian soil. Although Frederick, Duke of Austria, took advantage of King Béla IV's defeat by the Mongols to grab a significant slice of north-west Hungary when Hungarian fortunes were at their nadir, Béla exacted just retribution in 1246 by inflicting a defeat on the Austrians in which Frederick was killed. Béla's next adversary, Otokar II of Bohemia, hoped to absorb Hungary into a Slav empire stretching southwards to the Adriatic: Béla fended him off in 1250, Stephen V

(1270–72) drove him out of Hungary in 1271 and in 1276 Ladislas IV, in a rare Hungarian-German alliance, again forced him to withdraw, abandoning the four northern Hungarian towns he had occupied. The same alliance between Ladislas IV and the German King, Rudolf Habsburg, inflicted a final, comprehensive defeat on Otokar on Marchfeld Plain in 1278, a success that, as it laid the foundation for the subsequent rise of the Habsburg dynasty, proved in the long term a mixed blessing for Hungary.

The forays of Árpád kings beyond Hungary's northern borders provided a sharp contrast to this string of successes in defending the young state's territorial integrity. When Kálmán the Learned (whose sound judgement in domestic matters deserted him in issues further afield) sought to fish in troubled Russian waters by coming to the aid of the Prince of Kiev in 1099, he sustained a bruising defeat at Przemysl. His successor, Stephen II, for no good reason, launched a campaign *against* Kiev but with the same outcome, a humiliating reverse in 1123. Béla III seized an opportunity to add Galicia to the Árpád domain but found it beyond his capacities to hold it; and Andrew II launched no fewer than fourteen campaigns against Galicia between 1205 and 1233. Otokar II's only success against the Árpáds came when he drove Béla IV out of Styria, territory Béla had tried to hold on to after Frederick of Austria's death. The lesson to be drawn from these events was that the ruler of a kingdom of only moderate extent, thinly populated, could expect to carry his unruly, occasionally treacherous, barons and a far from subservient nobility with him only when the security of the kingdom and of their own estates was at stake; and that in the absence of a royal standing army he could do nothing without them.

Hungary's involvement beyond her southern borders, in the Balkan lands, began virtually by accident. It was to last for nearly five hundred years and then resulted in Hungary's loss of independence for a further four hundred. Towards the end of the ill-starred reign of Solomon (1063–74),* Emperor Michael VII of Byzantium encouraged Hungary's old enemies to the east, the Pechenegs, to invade Transylvania and southern Hungary; in 1071 they were defeated by the Prince Royal, Géza (later Géza I, 1074–77), who besieged, captured and occupied the strategic fort of Belgrade in the process. Concluding that a direct confrontation with Géza would be unproductive, the Emperor opted for reconciliation, symbolised by the crown Géza accepted from him in 1074 after succeeding Solomon, which became the lower half of the Holy Crown. Fifteen years later, in 1089, King Zvonimir of Croatia died without leaving an heir; his widow, Helen, was the sister of Ladislas I of Hungary, who had succeeded his brother Géza in 1077. Because of this dynastic link, and probably also because Géza's capture of Belgrade had established Hungary as a power in the region, a delegation of nobles from Spalato (Split) invited Ladislas to accept the Croatian crown, an offer of dynastic aggrandisement which no Árpád could refuse. Ladislas thereupon annexed northern Croatia in 1091 and installed his nephew Álmos as ruler; a by-product of this campaign was the incorporation into the Hungarian kingdom of Slavonia, the region to the north east of Croatia lying between the Drava and Sava rivers.

---

* Solomon's reign was dominated by friction with his first cousin, Géza, who eventually drove him out of Hungary and succeeded him as Géza I.

By establishing a dynastic interest in the Balkans, Hungary acquired a new and powerful enemy: Venice. The Venetians needed the Dalmatian ports as components of the maritime trading pattern on which they depended; and they needed Dalmatian oak for their shipbuilding. During the next three hundred years, Hungary was sometimes able to neutralise Venetian hostility through alliance with the other great regional power, Byzantium, and occasionally *vice versa;* but if Venice and Byzantium were to combine against Hungary, the latter's chances of maintaining a Balkan presence would be questionable. Of equal and ominous importance was the birth in Hungarian—or at least in royal Hungarian—minds of the 'what we have, we hold' syndrome in relation to the Balkans. There was no compelling Hungarian national interest in a Balkan presence. Unlike Byzantium, Hungary was not concerned to maintain the Eastern Orthodox faith in the region; unlike Venice, Hungary was not a naval nor a maritime trading power. But once Balkan territory and the fealty of Balkan communities had been acquired, however adventitiously, no Hungarian ruler could afford to turn his back on them or have them wrested from him without sustaining a politically damaging blow to his prestige and domestic standing. Hungary's Balkan commitments and ambitions which, in the absence of a viable buffer state, brought her into dangerous contiguity with the Byzantine, and subsequently Ottoman, Empires were to have fateful consequences.

Venice lost no time in recapturing the Dalmatian coastal towns from Ladislas I and they changed hands frequently thereafter, shuttling between the Venetian Doge and the Hungarian crown. Kálmán the Learned pursued a notably active Balkan policy, reoccupying Dalmatia—apart from the coastal towns—in 1097; and having himself crowned King of Croatia in 1102 and of Dalmatia in 1105. Three years later, he succeeded in winning the allegiance of Spalato, Zara and Trogir; in order to retain it, he imposed only the lightest of taxes on their population, thus removing even a financial rationale for Hungarian suzerainty. *Báns* (viceroys) were appointed to rule Slavonia, Croatia and Dalmatia; thanks to his good relations with Pope Paschal II, Kálmán—himself a former bishop—was able to win papal recognition of their titles and of Hungarian rule. Kálmán's son, Stephen II (1116–31), quickly lost most of Dalmatia and three city-ports to Venice and Belgrade to Byzantium; but Béla II (1131–41) the Blind[9] recovered these losses and added Ráma, the northern half of Bosnia, to the incipient Hungarian empire.

These successes inevitably provoked a reaction. In 1150 the Byzantine Emperor Manuel I Comnenus, in alliance with Venice, began a series of onslaughts on the Hungarian position in the Balkans, which continued sporadically until his death thirty years later. As a weapon against Géza II (1141–62), who had succeeded his father Béla the Blind, Manuel used Géza's two disloyal brothers, Stephen and Ladislas, to whom he gave refuge in Constantinople and who formed their own court-in-exile of Hungarian émigrés. When Géza II died, both the brothers in turn, supported by Manuel, challenged Géza's son Stephen III (1162–72) for the succession. The sudden death of Ladislas and the defeat of the pretender Stephen by barons loyal to Stephen III foiled this strategy but Manuel did not give up: in 1164 he offered the hand of his daughter Maria and eventual succession to the imperial throne to Stephen III's younger brother Béla, Duke of Croatia and Dalmatia, hoping by this means eventually to secure the incorporation of those territories into the Byzantine Empire. For his part, Stephen III could not resist the prospect of seeing an Árpád mount the imperial throne; he signed a peace treaty with Manuel, which ceded Croatia and Dalmatia to Byzantium. Shortly afterwards Manuel seized by force all Hungarian territory in the Balkans not covered by the treaty, including the coastal cities, and held on to it until he died in 1180. Late in life, Manuel had unexpectedly fathered a son; this deprived young Béla of the imperial succession and in 1172 he had become Béla III of Hungary instead.

After Manuel's death, Béla acted quickly to restore Hungarian fortunes in the Adriatic. Hungarian rule was re-established over Croatia and the Dalmatian ports; Bosnia and Serbia were retaken, Belgrade and Sofia occupied. Béla then used his Byzantine background to good effect by marrying his daughter Margit to the new Emperor, Isaac II, and concluding a peace treaty with him. Venice now replaced Byzantium as Hungary's principal opponent in the south. During the next half-century, the Dalmatian ports changed hands several times as truces between Venice and Hungary were proclaimed and broken. For the time being, however, Hungary's southward expansion seemed secure. By the middle of the fourteenth century, the original area of the Hungarian state had been doubled and its population increased to 2 million. At this, the zenith of the Árpád dynasty, Hungary had become the dominant power in south-east Europe.

Béla IV and the Mongol Invasion

Like his contemporary, King John of England, Andrew II of Hungary was 'a bad king'. Fortunately for Hungary his son and successor, Béla IV (1235–70), was cast in a different mould. Béla spent the first years of his reign clearing up after his father: repossessing the royal estates, which had been alienated to pay for Andrew's pointless military adventures, reasserting the authority of the crown and repudiating his father's promise of tribute to Emperor Frederick II. When Pope Gregory IX rebuked him for repossessing lands Andrew had given to the ecclesiastical hierarchy, Béla negotiated a deal by which the Church kept its newly acquired estates and the collection of taxes was once again entrusted to Jews and Muslims, with papal approval. Within two years of his accession, Béla IV had put the Hungarian monarchy back in business; but a storm was rising in the east which threatened to destroy all that the Árpád dynasty had achieved.

In 1237 a Dominican friar, Julian, returned from the second of two remarkable journeys into Muscovy and beyond. He had first set out from Hungary in 1235, with the intention of finding those elements of the Magyar tribes that had not joined the westward drift between 400 BC and AD 700 but had remained—or so legend had it—in Bashkiria. Friar Julian did in fact claim to have discovered a Magyar-speaking community somewhere east of Suzdal, on the banks of the Volga, although it is barely credible that he could have travelled as far east as Bashkiria; it is sufficiently extraordinary that he should have got as far as Suzdal, and back—a round trip of well over two thousand miles—within the space of little more than a year. Julian returned with news of more immediate importance than the results of his quest for Magyar roots: he brought with him an eye-witness account of the Mongol tide that had swept across the southern Russian steppe fifteen years before and had now returned with redoubled strength and fury, devastating everything in its path and still driving westwards. Béla responded to the news by sending a force under the Voivod of Transylvania south east into Wallachia, where the Cuman tribe, whom Hungarian missionaries had largely converted to Christianity and whose king Kötöny acknowledged Béla's suzerainty, was under Mongol attack. After an initial success, the Cumans and their ally were overwhelmed and fled towards Hungary, where Béla agreed to give them refuge and settled them along the River Tisza, doubtless hoping that they would constitute a useful second line of defence against the Mongols. In fact, the irruption of over 200,000 nomads into what was now a well-cultivated region proved to be a social and economic disaster, which Béla soon had reason to regret.

By 1240 the Mongols had sacked Kiev and, infuriated by Béla's provision of sanctuary to the Cumans, demanded his submission to their Great Khan Ogotai, Genghiz Khan's son and successor. Early in the following year, Béla declared a state of emergency and began to look to Hungary's defences. During the preceding two hundred years, successive Hungarian kings had worked to perfect a system of border defence which consisted of a belt of scorched earth several miles deep guarded by settlements whose inhabitants were awarded land and free status in return for military service; in addition, natural obstacles to invasion were enhanced where possible and in 1241 Béla's first move was to order the barricading of mountain passes. Béla then convened a Diet, in Buda, at which he hoped to convince the barons that the situation was serious and that a national effort was called for to defend the realm. True to form, the barons were interested only in extracting further privileges from the crown and offered Béla no practical support. By this time, four columns of Mongols were debouching on to the Great Plain; the strongest, 50,000 horsemen under Batu Khan, forced the Verecke Pass through which Árpád had led the Magyar tribes three and a half centuries earlier. Hungary's traditional defence system, and Béla's barricades, were shown to be totally ineffective and barely gave the Mongols pause. By the time Béla had concentrated such troops as the barons were willing to make available on Pest, the Mongols had reached Vác, only 25 miles to the north, and sacked it. Frederick, Duke of Austria, chose this moment for some characteristic self-promotion by bringing a force of his own to Pest to show the Hungarians how to fight. Unfortunately for Béla, Frederick succeeded in surprising and defeating a Mongol detachment just as the Archbishop of Kalocsa, attacking the Mongols prematurely, was going down to defeat. This double humiliation provoked a violent popular reaction. Inevitably, the unpopular Cumans were cast as scapegoat and accused of conniving in the Mongol invasion, a charge reinforced when Cumans were discovered among the prisoners taken by Frederick of Austria (having been forced earlier to fight alongside their Mongol conquerors). Scores of Cumans were massacred by the mob in Pest and their king, Kötöny, was either murdered or committed suicide; the surviving Cumans abandoned their erstwhile hosts and made for the southern frontier, looting and burning along the way. Béla thus lost a potentially valuable light cavalry force; meanwhile, his uninvited ally Frederick, his point made, had retired to Austria leaving Béla to face the Mongols alone.

The Mongols now employed a favourite stratagem of the early Magyars, the feigned withdrawal, and disappeared eastwards into the Great Plain. The Hungarians followed, eventually pitching camp near the village of Muhi at the junction of the Sajó and Hernád Rivers. Béla surrounded his encampment with a wagon stockade, leaving no gaps through which the Mongols might infiltrate and thus effectively sealing his force of 50,000 men in a trap of their own making. Having forded the River Sajó north and south of the Hungarian camp, the Mongols launched an exploratory attack at dawn on 11 April 1241 and then withdrew. Batu Khan's main assault followed a few hours later: a shower of flaming arrows ignited the wagon stockade and encircled the Hungarians with fire. Apart from Béla and his immediate entourage, who somehow managed to escape through the stockade and flee northwards to the Bükk hills, the entire Hungarian force was massacred. Within three days the Mongols had returned to Pest and sacked it. All of central Hungary, and Transylvania, lay at their feet.

Béla IV made his way to Austria, where Duke Frederick exploited his humiliation by extracting two Hungarian counties, Moson and Sopron, as the price for granting him temporary refuge. Béla fled to Slavonia and from Zagreb launched a salvo of pleas to the monarchs of Western Christendom, and to Pope Innocent IV, for their help in rescuing Hungary from Mongol oppression. Not for the last time, Western Christendom ignored the Hungarian ruler's appeal for aid. Béla, pursued by a Mongol column, sought refuge in the Dalmatian islands. Meanwhile, on 1 February 1242, Batu Khan led his forces across the frozen Danube, captured Óbuda and laid siege to Esztergom, Székesfehérvár and Pannonhalma. Frederick of Austria seized the opportunity to invade Hungary from the north, laying the country waste as far south as Győr.

A rare stroke of good fortune now saved Hungary from irreparable devastation. News reached Batu Khan that his brother, the Great Khan Ogotai, had died in December. A struggle for the succession and a redivision of the Mongol Empire was inevitable. Batu Khan, determined to protect his own interests, decided to head for home; almost overnight, the Mongol horde melted away. Batu Khan may have intended to return to Hungary and to complete unfinished business at Esztergom and Székesfehérvár where the besieged Hungarian garrisons were still holding out; but in the event no further Mongol onslaught materialised—despite Béla IV's subsequent defiance of two Mongol ultimata, in 1259 and 1264, demanding alliance and tribute—until 1285.

Meanwhile, Hungary had survived; but it was a different country. In less than two years, the Hungarian population had been reduced by between 20 and 50 per cent. On the plains, well over half the towns and villages had been destroyed; of the settlements in the hills and forests, at least a quarter had vanished. Wolves and other scavengers roamed freely. The surviving population, as well as enduring starvation and disease, lived in fear of the robber bands that scoured the ruins. Cannibalism was unconcealed. This was the land to which Béla IV returned in May 1242, to begin the work of reconstruction that won him the posthumous accolade 'second founder of the state'. He quickly demonstrated that he had learned the main strategic lesson of the Mongol invasion, namely that only stone castles built on high ground—such as that at Esztergom, which the Mongols failed to capture—offered adequate protection against invaders; Béla therefore decreed that 'in the entire territory subject to the crown castles be built on suitable sites where the people may find refuge if they have to retreat from threatening dangers'. We have already seen how this decree was put into effect; we have seen, too, how—because of the pressing need to repopulate the country through immigration—one significant legacy of the Mongol invasion was Hungary's ethnic heterogeneity. An aspect of Béla's resettlement policy that was to have troublesome consequences for his successors was the recall of the Cumans who, once again, were granted land on the Great Plain; in the hope of making their return permanent, Béla arranged the marriage of his son Stephen to a Cuman princess. Béla also lost no time in punishing the perfidy of Frederick of Austria, who was killed in Béla's successful campaign, in 1246, to regain the territory in northwestern Hungary that had been extorted or grabbed by the Austrian.

In 1270, the year of his death, Béla IV could look back on over thirty years of remarkable achievement. Despite continuous and sometimes armed conflict with his own son Stephen (later Stephen V) and inevitable obstruction from the barons, Béla rebuilt the Hungarian kingdom. He reorganised the structure of government, re-established the rule of law, repopulated a devastated countryside, encouraged the growth of towns, created the new royal town of Buda and revived the commercial life of the country. Hungarian rule in Croatia and authority in the Balkans generally was as strong as ever. To Hungary's misfortune, Béla's successors did not measure up to the legacy he bequeathed to them.

Twilight of the Árpáds

Stephen V (1270–72), for so many years a thorn in his father's flesh, quickly succumbed to a nervous collapse apparently induced by the intrigues of his Cuman Queen, Elisabeth, who organised the abduction of their son, Ladislas, in order to keep him away from the influence of the Anjou court into which he had been married (at the age of eight). The ten-year-old boy now succeeded his father as Ladislas IV (1272–90), his mother Elisabeth acting as Regent during his minority. Elisabeth presided over a chaotic court, riven by intrigue and steeped in debauchery. Ladislas's Cuman genes turned out to be dominant: he adopted Cuman customs, Cuman dress and several Cuman mistresses. During the eighteen years of his reign, Hungary fell apart; the country became little more than a battleground for rival barons, united only by their detestation of the Cuman ascendancy. Following his excommunication for consorting with pagans, Ladislas went to the extreme, in 1285, of inviting the Mongols to make common cause with him and the Cumans against the Hungarian Church and nobility. After pillaging settlements in the eastern Alföld and northern Transylvania the Mongols departed, this time for good. Ladislas deserted his Anjou Queen, Isabella; and when he was murdered in 1290—ironically by Cumans, in the course of some internecine feud—he left no heir. The only Árpád claimant to the throne was a grandson of Andrew II, also named Andrew, who had been brought up in Venice as a protégé of the Habsburgs: the Archbishop of Esztergom, in a notable coup, succeeded in exfiltrating the young man to Hungary and crowning him Andrew III. The most notable events in a reign dominated by the competition between foreign claimants to the Hungarian throne were the Diets of 1290 and 1298, which showed that in calmer times Andrew would have made a politically astute and effective ruler; but three years later he was dead, possibly murdered by poison. The House of Árpád died with him.

Over a period of four centuries, the Árpáds had built—from nothing—a Christian state, socially top-heavy and therefore unstable, but rich by the standards of the time, dominant in central southern Europe and a prize coveted by most of its neighbours. Although prevented from realising its potential by periods of misrule, by the anarchic behaviour of the barons and, above all, by devastation at the hands of the Mongols, Hungary at the dawn of the fourteenth century possessed the basis for a healthy agrarian economy, the rudiments of urban and commercial activity and proven mineral wealth. Hungary's structure of government, when effectively managed by a competent ruler, was if anything a little ahead of its time. Laws were in place which offered protection to person and property in times of peace and stability. The Church was firmly established as a partner in government. The monastic orders were a stimulus to literacy and tended the first shoots of an indigenous culture: although Latin dominated as the language of discourse and record, the first unbroken original texts in Magyar appeared during the late twelfth century, along with translations into Magyar of parts of the Gospels and of sermons. The achievement of King St Stephen I in bringing the Hungarian people into the community of Western Christendom survived the follies of some of his successors and was further consolidated by the wiser of them. The question that remained as the Árpád era ended was whether the Hungarian state was strong enough, actually or even potentially, to withstand pressures from the north and to justify its ambitions in the south. The internal anarchy in which Hungary began the new century, with baronial factions jostling for advantage in their support for two rival claimants to the throne, was an unpromising augury.

3

HUNGARY ASCENDANT

(1301–1444)

The First Angevin: Charles I Robert

The nine years following the death of Andrew III were marked by an almost far-
cical sequence of coronations. The Hungarian state had temporarily ceased to
exist, having disintegrated into virtually autonomous regions ruled by the locally
dominant baronial family. In the absence of a direct heir to the throne, foreign
claimants jostled for the succession (it was perhaps a measure of the Árpáds' success in establishing the concept of royal legitimacy that no Hungarian baron
attempted to grab the crown for himself). The leading contender, because he
enjoyed the backing of Pope Boniface VIII, was Charles I (Charles Robert or
Caroberto) of Naples, great-grandson of Charles I of Anjou and grandson of
Stephen V's daughter Maria. He was crowned in Esztergom in May, 1301, but not
with the 'genuine' Holy Crown; this had been purloined by the barons, of whom
the majority supported the claim of Vencel (Wenceslas) III of Bohemia, a descendant of Béla IV through the female line. The Archbishop of Kalocsa crowned Vencel in Székesfehérvár, in August, with the Holy Crown, thus giving Vencel the
edge over Charles in terms of legitimacy; but Charles's determination to pursue
his claim by force—he attacked Buda in 1302—finally unnerved Vencel, who fled
back to Prague in 1304, taking the Holy Crown and coronation regalia with him.
Vencel then resigned his claim in favour of Otto Wittelsbach of Bavaria, who was
duly crowned (with the Holy Crown) in Székesfehérvár in 1306. Only eighteen
months later, however, Otto fell victim to baronial anarchy when he was kidnapped by the Voivod (Governor-General) of Transylvania, László Kán, who eventually released Otto but hung on to the Holy Crown and regalia.

Meanwhile, Charles—now in alliance with Rudolf Habsburg against the leading barons—had steadily strengthened his position and attracted the support of a
number of lesser baronial families who had scores to settle with the Csáks and
Kőszegis. In 1307 the town of Buda declared for Charles and two years later he
was given his second coronation there, in the church which later became the
Matthias Church (*Mátyás Templom*), but with a crown made for the occasion rather
than with the Holy Crown, which remained in the hands of László Kán of Tran-

sylvania. László was eventually persuaded by the Papal Legate to disgorge the Crown and regalia, which enabled Charles to have his third coronation, in Székesfehérvár and with the Holy Crown, in 1310, thus establishing the Angevin dynasty in Hungary. He was now able to set about rebuilding royal authority and the Hungarian state.

Charles I tackled this formidable task with energy and determination. Having established his base at Temesvár (Timişoara) in the south he began a series of military campaigns which reduced the baronial strongholds one by one; his key victories were over the Aba clan (1312), Máté Csák (1315) and the Kőszegis (1316). Máté Csák's death in 1321 marked the end of two decades of anarchy in Hungary and enabled Charles to transfer his court to Visegrád, on the Danube Bend north of Buda. He used his triumph over the barons to reclaim a high proportion of the alienated royal estates and to appropriate castles with which to defend them: by 1323, when his capture of Pozsony (Pressburg, later Bratislava) completed the reunification of the country, Charles I held a hundred of Hungary's 210 castles, a major shift in the balance of power between crown and barons.[1] He formed the first royal standing army, of a few thousand men, which supplied small garrisons for the royal castles and supplemented the private armies of the nobility and the ecclesiastical hierarchy. In an astute exercise in public relations, Charles used the distribution among the nobility of coats of arms and the other trappings of west European chivalry as an incentive to the conscientious fulfilment of their military obligations. In 1326 he founded the elite Order of St. George, membership of which was limited to fifty deserving barons and nobles. These distractions offered the nobility some compensation for Charles's disappointing (to them) eschewal of foreign adventures. Charles also used to good effect the system of 'honours', which he grafted on to the existing mechanisms of royal governance. An 'honour' consisted of a high office under the crown, such as Palatine, count (ispán), royal judge or castellan of a royal castle, in which the incumbent, usually a baron, was entitled to retain all the revenues which accrued from it, for his own enrichment and to cover his expenses. A baron holding an honour was not even required to carry out in person the duties associated with it; he could use part of its revenue to pay subordinates to do this for him while he remained at court or in his own castle. Honours were held at the king's pleasure, although in practice a baron deprived of one could usually expect to be compensated with another, subject to good conduct.

Charles I made intelligent and effective use of Hungary's main economic asset: the relative wealth of its mineral resources. Significant deposits of gold-bearing ore had recently been discovered to complement the silver deposits mined since the Roman occupation. Happily for Hungary, this discovery coincided with a critical shortage of gold in Europe. Charles I stimulated prospecting by promising landowners a share of the profits from mining operations on their property; all profits had hitherto gone to the royal exchequer, a disincentive to the opening up of new mines. By 1330, Hungary was refining 3,000 pounds of gold a year, one-third of the known world's production; Hungarian and Bohemian mines together accounted for half of Europe's silver and nearly all its gold. The main alternative sources of precious metals were in the Muslim world but papal Bulls forbade Christians to use them. As well as swelling the crown's revenue—the royal treasury typically appropriated one-eighth of precious metal production—Hungary's newly discovered wealth enabled Charles I to reform the country's currency. At the time of his accession, there were thirty-four different currencies in circulation. He replaced them with one gold-based currency, the *gulden* or golden florin, with a gold content equal to that of the Florentine florin; it quickly acquired a high international reputation. Although Hungary's wealth in precious metals enhanced the country's prestige and that of its ruler, in the longer term it proved to be economically debilitating. Imports of luxury goods for the nobility were financed by the export of currency; consequently, incentives for the development of native crafts and industries were almost completely lacking.

The royal share of gold and silver production was not the only increment to crown revenue under Charles I. He encouraged the exploitation of the salt mines at Máramaros in Transylvania, to the extent that by 1400 the salt monopoly was to become the most important component of royal income. He also improved the system of taxation and took the politically courageous step of extracting more money from the Church, including one-third of the tithes levied to finance the Crusades; he levied payments from bishops at their installation, retained for the crown the income from vacant benefices and required the hierarchy to make gifts to the crown at the start of each new year. As well as introducing new taxes, Charles made tax collection more efficient, for example by levying customs duties on imported goods at the point of sale in the markets rather than at the frontier. Immigrants and 'guests' (*hospites*), including Jews, were subject to a special tax as the price of their free status and exemption from military service.

An essential condition for the success of Charles I's domestic reforms and consolidation was a period of peace with Hungary's northern neighbours. He worked hard to secure it, beginning with his marriage in 1320 (his fourth) to Elizabeth, daughter of Wladislaw IV of Poland; this inaugurated a lasting alliance with Poland, which served Hungary well after the accession to the Polish throne of Elizabeth's brother Casimir (Casimir III the Great) in 1333.[2] In establishing good relations with Poland, however, Charles I had an objective that went beyond the preservation of peace on Hungary's northern frontier. He was not blind to the fact that after ten years of marriage Casimir and his Queen had failed to produce an heir; giving priority, like most medieval monarchs, to the interests of his dynasty as distinct from those of his kingdom, Charles perceived an eventual possibility of winning the Polish, in addition to the Hungarian, crown for the House of Anjou. In the meantime, he invited the Kings of Poland and Bohemia (John I of Luxembourg) in 1335 to meet him at Visegrád with the aim of forging a more formal alliance; the immediate impetus for the meeting came from Casimir of Poland, who hoped to secure Hungarian support for his efforts to fend off German and Bohemian claims to his kingdom. Charles, acting as mediator, persuaded John Luxembourg of Bohemia to renounce his claim to the Polish crown in return for the cession by Poland of Silesia. An equally important result of the Visegrád meeting was the agreement of the three participants to co-operate in developing new trade routes between their countries and southern Germany that would bypass Vienna. Vienna's staple rights had hitherto exerted a stranglehold on central European trade.[3] The new trade routes, their use encouraged by customs concessions, would link Brno (Brünn) with Buda and Buda with Cracow; they soon came to be dominated by the merchants of southern Germany, especially Nuremburgers, who used them to establish the dominant position in east central European trade which they have never lost.[4]

At a time when intra-European trade was already beginning to eclipse the traditional Mediterranean trading patterns in importance, the decisions taken at Visegrád made Hungarian ambitions to retain an empire on the Adriatic all the more pointless and, in economic terms, irrelevant. Charles I nevertheless succumbed to the itch that had beset his predecessors, fighting a succession of campaigns against the kings of Serbia in an attempt to regain control of the Serbian marches. Such success as he enjoyed was short-lived: Stephen Dušan of Serbia inflicted a major defeat on Hungarian forces in 1340 and recaptured Belgrade. Charles also failed to strengthen his grip on Croatia and Dalmatia; and an attempt to conquer Wallachia ended in disaster in 1330.

Charles I bequeathed to his son Louis two legacies that inevitably encouraged dreams of further expansion. The first was a bulging exchequer and an effective system of taxation which ensured a healthy revenue. The second consisted of an agreement with Casimir III of Poland that if (as turned out to be the case) he were to die childless he would be succeeded by Charles I's son, Louis, or by the son of his sister, Queen Elizabeth of Hungary. In return, Charles I undertook that Hungary would recover and restore to Poland all territories alienated from the Polish crown without imposing any additional tax on the Polish people. Three years after entering into this uncharacteristically rash commitment, Charles I was dead.

Louis I, the Great, of Hungary and Poland (1342–82)

Louis I is the only Hungarian ruler to have been accorded the title 'the Great'. During the period of Communist rule in Hungary (1949–89) political correctness required Hungarian historians to belittle Louis's achievements and to deny him his sobriquet; he was referred to simply as 'Louis I' and condemned for pursuing policies of acquisitive imperialism and for oppressing the peasantry. Anachronistic value judgements of this kind are inseparable from historiography in an ideological straitjacket. Louis began to be called 'Great' by chroniclers after his death, because by the standards of his time the title was well merited. Dynastic aggrandisement won for a monarch the respect of his peers and the admiration of the nobility; and if he also preserved peace and order within the borders of his kingdom, peasant farmer and serf had no complaint. On both counts, as well as for his evidently chivalrous and knightly personal qualities, Louis I deserved his title. The long-term consequences of his policies, unforeseeable at the time, were nonetheless deeply injurious to Hungary's fortunes.

Louis was crowned, five days after his father's death, at the age of sixteen. His education had been enlightened for his day, in that it included a solid grounding in French and German as well as in Latin and the Latin classics. His particular heroes, apparently, were Alexander the Great and Ladislas I of Hungary (who had initiated Hungary's southward expansion into Croatia) and he lost no time in emulating them. Only two years after his accession, Louis led his army against Alexander of Wallachia, whose father had thrown off Hungarian vassalage, and won his fealty; and in 1345 he launched his first Balkan campaign, which won for Hungary the as yet unconquered regions of southern Croatia and, temporarily, the allegiance of the Dalmatian port of Zadar. Towards the end of that year, however, disturbing news reached Louis from Naples, which compelled him to adjust his military priorities.

Charles I had betrothed his younger son, András, to Joanna, granddaughter of his uncle Roberto, King of Naples. It had been agreed between the two kings that since Roberto had no male heir, the Neapolitan crown should pass to András and Joanna when Roberto died; faced with opposition within his court to the prospect of a Hungarian king, Roberto subsequently reneged on this understanding and bequeathed his crown to Joanna alone. When Roberto died in 1343, Joanna was duly crowned. Queen Elizabeth, Charles I's widow and mother of András, at once set off for Naples to defend her son's interests and to secure his coronation: to this end she took with her a substantial proportion of the gold in the well-stocked Hungarian royal treasury. The influx onto the gold-starved Italian, and thence European, market of a quantity of gold equivalent to the world supply for two years did nothing to help young András, but it did put an end to the European gold crisis: the price of gold quickly returned to its pre-crisis level of about ten times the value of silver, an outcome far from helpful to Hungarian economic interests. Urgent representations on András's behalf by emissaries from Louis to Pope Clement VI in Avignon produced no result: the Pope had no interest in helping the Hungarian Angevins to establish themselves on the borders of the Papal States. Meanwhile Joanna, a lady of considerable strength of character, relegated her husband to a subordinate role in the Neapolitan court and eventually, in 1345, connived in his murder by the anti–Hungarian faction.

As soon as he could disengage from his Balkan campaign, Louis invaded Italy to avenge his brother, attacking from the north and reaching Naples by way of Verona, Bologna and Rimini; he arrived in Aversa, where András had been murdered and buried, early in 1348. Thanks in part to the German mercenaries with whom Louis had reinforced his army of nobles and their retainers, the campaign was victorious: Joanna fled to Marseilles and thence to Avignon to seek the protection of the Pope. Having awarded himself the title of 'King of Jerusalem and Sicily', Louis returned to Hungary, leaving small garrisons to defend his southern Italian conquests. The garrisons, whose morale cannot have been improved by the arrival of the Black Death in Naples, quickly succumbed to attacks by the local nobility and Joanna returned from Avignon to reclaim her kingdom. As soon as Louis learned of this he returned to Italy, this time by sea, to wage a second punitive campaign; he besieged and captured Bari in the spring of 1350. As before, Louis carried all before him on the approach march to Naples, although he was wounded while scaling the walls of Canosa di Puglia and again, more seriously, during the siege of Aversa; he nevertheless entered Naples for the second time, at the head of his army, on 1 August. Once again, however, Hungarian rule in southern Italy survived Louis's departure for only a few months: in March 1351 Joanna returned to Naples, this time for good.[5]

Louis was compelled to accept that without the support and sanction of the Pope, which Clement VI had consistently withheld, he could not maintain Hungarian rule over the Neapolitan kingdom. He consequently had very little to show for two expensive campaigns apart from an enhanced reputation for military leadership and personal bravery. It has been argued that the Italian campaigns produced, by osmosis, a beneficial cultural influence on Hungary and heightened Hungarian awareness of Italian humanism. This seems unlikely. The barons who fought alongside their King doubtless took back with them to Hungary a quantity of loot, but they are more likely to have been attracted by precious metal, silks and jewellery than by books, sculptures or paintings; humanism was indeed gaining a foothold in Hungary but through the influence of the scholars and clerks in Charles I's reconstituted Chancellery rather than through soldiers' campaigns abroad.

Louis the Great spent most of his reign at war. His campaigns, particularly in the Balkans and on the Adriatic coast, were too numerous to describe in detail and since few of them achieved more than ephemeral results, it is unnecessary to do so. His objective was to compel as many Balkan rulers as possible to accept vassalage to the Hungarian House of Anjou; and, as a deeply committed Catholic, to assist the conversion to Roman Catholicism of populations loyal to Eastern Orthodoxy. He succeeded in forcing the submission, as vassals, of the rulers of Bosnia, Serbia, Bulgaria and Wallachia; religious conversion, however, was a tougher proposition and continued, with varying degrees of success, throughout his reign. As the Italian campaigns had shown, Hungary lacked the resources and the manpower to garrison conquered territory effectively and Louis's southern 'empire' was more symbolic than real. In alliance with the Genoese, who supplied the sea-power, Louis waged three wars against Venice for the Dalmatian city-ports: under the Treaty of Zára (Zadar), 1358, Venice ceded to Hungary not only all the coastal towns that had already fallen in and out of Hungarian control during the previous two hundred years but also the important city-port of Ragusa (Dubrovnik). Hungary now exercised nominal suzerainty over the entire Dalmatian coast; but there was irony in the provision of the treaty that Venice would hand over to Hungary twenty-four galleys with which to defend it, since Hungary had none of her own. Venice proved reluctant to accept the situation and renewed hostilities from time to time, notably in 1378 when three towns were recovered from Hungary; but Genoa's naval strength proved decisive and the Treaty of Turin (1381) not only confirmed Hungarian sovereignty over the Dalmatian coast but guaranteed freedom of trade for the city-ports in the Venetian sphere of influence.

Louis had inherited from his father an obligation to support Polish interests in return for the right of succession to the Polish throne; but he also had a genuinely close relationship with the Polish King, his uncle Casimir III, to whom he gave frequent assistance in wars against the Lithuanians and with whom he allied on various occasions against the German Empire, Bohemia and Austria. When Casimir died in 1370, therefore, the Polish nobility had few qualms in electing Louis to the Polish throne; they were also quick to exploit his inexperience of Polish affairs by extracting from him, at Kassa (Košice, Slovakia) in 1374, significant privileges for themselves and limitations on royal authority. The arrangement did not, however, work well. Louis rarely visited his Polish kingdom and entrusted its governance mainly to his mother, Queen Elizabeth, who established a largely Hungarian court in Cracow and made herself deeply unpopular with the Poles, who became determined to frustrate Louis's ambition to bequeath both the Hungarian and the Polish crowns to one of his three daughters.

Meanwhile, events had been taking place in Asia Minor and Byzantium which were to change the destinies of the Balkan states and eventually those of Hungary. The Ottoman Turks, one of the successor principalities to the Seljuk Empire, had been invited in 1345 by the self-proclaimed Byzantine Emperor, John Cantacuzene, to cross the Bosporus into Europe in order to aid him in his struggle against the supporters of the legitimate Emperor, John Paleologue (the two Johns were eventually recognised as co-Emperors). The Turks established themselves in Gallipoli and their formidable army quickly became the arbiter of events in south-eastern Europe. The Ottoman Turkish occupation rapidly spread north and west, assisted by the political and social fragmentation of the region; by 1366 the Turks controlled Thrace, Macedonia and most of southern Bulgaria. In that year, John Paleologue, now sole Emperor following the enforced abdication of Cantacuzene but in effect the Ottoman Sultan Murad I's vassal, travelled to Buda to seek the aid of Louis I in restoring imperial fortunes; he hinted at the possibility of a reunion of the two Christian communions, Catholic and Orthodox. Louis received the Emperor courteously and at the conclusion of his visit escorted him personally to Vidin, on the northern Bulgarian border; but no Hungarian assistance was promised. It had been at Vidin, in 1365, that the first skirmish involving Hungarian and Turkish troops had taken place: the chroniclers of both sides subsequently claimed victory. Whatever the true outcome of this encounter, now that the Ottomans were pressing against Hungarian-controlled territory it was bound to be the first of many; but such was the measured rhythm of the Turkish advance—lightning campaigns punctuated by long periods of consolidation—that there was no serious engagement until the century was nearly over.[6]

Until its closing decade, a reign that consisted mainly of almost continuous military campaigns had little room for attention to domestic issues or for internal reform. In general, the country enjoyed a period of internal peace and stability, largely because foreign campaigning kept the barons and, to a lesser extent, the nobles occupied and happy with the opportunities for looting that Louis gave them. The arrival of the Black Death in 1349, however, caused a change of mood among the nobility. Although the plague was less devastating in Hungary than in western Europe, probably owing to the country's lower population density, the death toll was sufficiently severe to diminish the appetite of the nobles for prolonged and costly absences from their estates at a time when the number of peasants and serfs available to sow, harvest and tend livestock had been drastically reduced. In 1351, Louis convened the only Diet of his reign to approve an Edict, the *Decretum Unicum*, the text of which indicates fairly clearly that it represented an attempt by Louis to assuage noble discontents; but at the same time to establish a more solid financial base for his military activities. It is an interesting and subtle document. With further campaigns in mind, Louis had to ensure the continuing loyalty of the noble class which provided the bulk of his army. The main purpose of the Edict, therefore, was to reproduce and reaffirm Andrew II's Golden Bull, in its original 1222 version; and to supplement it with a number of additional privileges for the nobility. 'At the request of the nobles', the Edict proclaimed that all 'true' nobles were entitled to the same liberties, whether they lived in Hungary or in the Banates (dukedoms) of Transylvania, Croatia, Dalmatia or Slavonia; they were all exempt from taxation and enjoyed all the other privileges set out in the Golden Bull. This provision finally ended the distinction between the hereditary nobility (the kindreds which claimed descent from the original Magyars of the 'conquest'), the castle warriors and the ennobled royal servants (servientes).

The Edict also contained two innovations that were of benefit to the crown as well as to the nobility. It confirmed the institution of entail which, although commonly practised, had been negated, at least on paper, by the Golden Bull, which had authorised nobles without a male heir to dispose of their estates as they wished, including by sale. Now, such nobles were no longer to have this right: in the absence of a direct heir, an estate 'should descend to their brothers, cousins and kinsmen'.[7] This provision had two important consequences. First, entail made the nobility an exclusive caste, tied to the land and prevented from raising credit (because they could not offer their estates as security) for any economic activity, agrarian or industrial: in the long term, this imposed a crippling straitjacket on Hungary's economic development and guaranteed foreign domination of such industrial and commercial activity as might be generated. Second, the estates of extinct kindreds—and given the low level of life expectancy families died out much more frequently than in modern times—automatically reverted to the crown: this gave a useful boost to royal revenues. The crown in any case restricted collateral inheritance to relationships up to the third degree, unleashing the royal lawyers to fight, and invariably win, disputed cases. As a result, Louis acquired twenty-one castles and several other large estates by escheat during his reign. The second important innovation in the Edict of 1351 lay in obliging, rather than simply entitling, all nobles to collect from their peasants the existing tax of 'the ninth' of all farm produce and wine produced on their land, in fact a tenth of what remained after the first tenth, the 'tithe', had been paid to the Church. This prevented the richer barons and nobles from enticing peasants away from their landlords by promising them exemption from 'the ninth'. Like the accompanying provision banning the abduction of serfs and permitting their migration only with the authority of their landlord, the clause was designed to prevent barons from using their muscle to entice or steal serfs from lesser nobles during the period of acute labour shortage caused by the Black Death. More importantly from the crown's viewpoint, it helped to ensure that nobles could not credibly plead poverty as an excuse for not maintaining and equipping their private armies (banderia) on which Louis depended for the conduct of his military campaigns.

During the closing years of his reign Louis, in constant ill-health, largely withdrew from the business of government; his Queen, Elizabeth, became the dominant influence at court and, mindful of the vulnerability of her young daughter to whom the crown would pass on Louis's death, used her position to loosen the grip of the barons on the royal council and royal offices. Under her protection, a new class of experienced administrators, some of them newly ennobled, replaced the barons whose families had monopolised the leading positions at court for generations. The royal chancellery, the royal courts of justice and the royal treasury were now headed by men—such as Miklós Garai, Archbishop Demetrius and Miklós Zámbó—whose interest lay in service to the crown rather than self-enrichment and the enlargement of their estates. Under their auspices, governance of the realm and the administration of justice benefited from the employment of educated clerks and notaries with a good knowledge of Latin and of common law.

A major social event of Louis's reign was his expulsion of the Jews from Hungary in 1360. Hungary had hitherto been immune from the spasm of anti–Semitism that swept through Europe during the first half of the fourteenth century; the Jews had been subjected in many countries to particularly savage persecution in the aftermath of the Black Death, which they were accused of causing. In Hungary, however, the Jews flourished, even in the urban communities that elsewhere had been the first to turn against them. Louis's zeal for the Catholic cause, however, drove him to attempt the conversion to Christianity of the Jews in his kingdom; in return for their abandonment of Judaism, he promised them not only full equality of rights but also exemption from taxation. When his campaign achieved no result, Louis released all Jews from their fealty to the crown and expelled them *en masse*, while allowing them to take with them all their moveable goods. The expellees settled quickly, and for the most part successfully, in Austria, Moravia and Poland; but the Hungarian court and nobility soon began to suffer from the loss of their financial skills and services and in 1364 they were invited to return. Most of them did so. Louis not only desisted from any further attempt to convert them but also elevated to national level the existing institution of the 'Jew judges', Christian noblemen whose duty it was to adjudicate in legal disputes between Jews and Christians in order to ensure fair treatment for the former; in 1371 Louis appointed the first 'Jew judge of the whole kingdom', with status equivalent to that of the royal judges. In this important instance, Louis's attachment to social justice prevailed over his religious fervour.

Louis I died in 1382, respected and admired by contemporaries who knew him and revered by his subjects. Johannes de Cardailhac, Papal Envoy to Hungary, paid Louis this tribute in 1372: 'I call God to witness that I never saw a monarch more majestic and more powerful … or one who desires peace and calm as much as he'.[8] Given Louis's obsessive campaigning, Johannes's eulogy was perhaps a little over the top; but there can be no doubt that in his personal qualities Louis came very close to the medieval ideal of the 'perfect knight'. Another contemporary, the Archpriest of Küküllő, wrote of Louis that 'he ruled neither with passion, nor with arbitrariness, but rather as the guardian of righteousness'.[9] The true value of the legacy of forty years of campaigns and conquest is more open to question. The Hungarian 'Empire of the Three Seas' (Adriatic, Black and Baltic) extolled nostalgically by nationalist Hungarian historians of the nineteenth and early twentieth centuries was both an inaccurate and a misleading construct. Conquest of the Dalmatian coast certainly gave Hungary access to the Adriatic and the subjection of Moldavia in theory brought Hungarian rule to the shores of the Black Sea; but the Polish crown did not extend Louis's 'empire' to the Baltic coast, which the Teutonic Knights were to control for several decades yet. More seriously, Louis did not establish an 'empire' but a conglomeration of regions the rulers of which, for the time being, acknowledged Hungarian suzerainty; since that allegiance was not enforced by a military presence, it could be (and soon was) revoked whenever the threat of retribution lost credibility. In Poland, Louis reigned but did not rule. In the Balkans, Louis's campaigns brought little political and no economic advantage—no attempt was made to exploit Hungarian access to the Adriatic by developing a Hungarian navy or merchant fleet—and frittered away much of the wealth he had inherited from his father. Louis I gave Hungary the appearance of a great European power but, operating as he did from an under-populated and economically undeveloped heartland, not the substance. It would be hard to improve on the judgement of an Austrian historian, sympathetic to Hungary: 'The limitation of Hungary to its natural frontier, its reduction to a ter-ritory corresponding to its inner capacity, would have promised durability; while the audacious encroachments to north and south already brought a foreboding of an imminent disintegration'.[10]

Sigismund I, King and Emperor

The death of Louis the Great, without a male heir, plunged Hungary into a debili-tating repetition of the factional strife and civil conflict that had preceded the accession of Charles I eighty years before. Although Louis's eldest daughter Mária, already betrothed at the age of eleven to Sigismund of Luxembourg, was duly crowned 'king' of Hungary a few days after her father's death, a significant faction of barons opposed her accession; this opposition grew stronger when it became clear that Louis's unpopular widow Elizabeth would be acting as regent. The Poles, for their part, leapt at the chance to end the personal union of the Polish and Hun-garian kingdoms under which they had chafed since 1370 and refused to accept Mária as their ruler unless she promised to live in Poland. The Polish nobles even-tually agreed instead to elect Mária's youngest sister Hedvig to the Polish throne; her subsequent marriage to Vladislav Jagiello of Lithuania led to the union of those countries and established the Jagiellonian dynasty in Poland. Meanwhile the barons of southern Hungary including János Horváti, Ban of Mačva in Serbia, found a rival claimant to the Hungarian crown in Charles Durazzo, the Angevin King of Naples, who in 1385 landed on the Dalmatian coast, rode with his supporters to Buda, scared Mária into abdication and was crowned Charles II of Hungary on the last day of the year. Two months later Charles was dead, assassinated on the orders of Queen Elizabeth's Palatine, Miklós Garai. The Neapolitan party thereupon declared for Charles's young son László and agreed to discuss terms with the two Queens, Elizabeth and Mária, who travelled south for the purpose with their Pala-tine, Garai. János Horváti kidnapped the whole party *en route*, killed Garai and locked up the Queens; Elizabeth was strangled in prison shortly afterwards. Mária, now married to Sigismund of Luxembourg, survived. The southern barons, now united in a formal alliance, the self-styled 'league', faced with a choice between another minor (László) and the adult, apparently capable Sigismund, opted to elect the latter, subject to his acceptance of their terms. When Sigismund was crowned in Székesfehérvár in 1387, therefore, he made a formal promise to uphold the tra-ditional freedoms and privileges of the barons and bishops, to rule only with their advice, to appoint no foreigners to royal or ecclesiastical office, to pardon his oppo-nents in the recent succession struggle and to recognise the right of armed resist-ance to the crown if he were ever to renege on these undertakings. Within a year Sigismund had broken one of these promises by torturing and executing Stephen Hédervári, a leader of the Angevin party, together with thirty-two of his noble supporters, an act of revenge he subsequently had cause to regret.

Partly because of the Hédervári executions and partly because of his German provenance (whereas the Angevins were by now regarded as honorary Hungarians), Sigismund faced an uphill task in establishing his authority over the barons, many of whom continued to oppose him for most of his fifty-year reign. The death of Queen Mária in 1395, in a riding accident, was held to cast further doubt on the legitimacy of Sigismund's rule. In 1401 he rashly accepted an invitation to attend a meeting with a number of barons in Buda, only to be abducted and imprisoned in the castle of Visegrád for two months while the barons argued over who should replace him; Sigismund's principal supporters, the Garai family, eventually rescued him but the act of *lèse majesté* went unpunished. Sigismund eventually found a solution of sorts in the creation of the Order of Knights of the Dragon, an elite group of twenty-four barons (including the Garais) whose loyalty to the crown was purchased with lavish grants of land and castles, a group in which the king claimed no greater status than that of first among equals. During Sigismund's frequent absences from Hungary, particularly after his election and coronation as King of the Romans in 1414, the order operated virtually as a collective regency and this did something to satisfy the baronial thirst for power. The shift in the balance of forces in the kingdom was none the less real. Already by 1407 the number of royal castles and estates had shrunk from a hundred to forty-seven; and during the half-century of Sigismund's reign the proportion of Hungary's 22,000 towns and villages owned by the crown was reduced from 15 to 5 per cent. The barons, meanwhile, doubled their share and in the process usurped the royal pre-eminence in local administration, which Charles I and Louis I had painstakingly restored.

Sigismund did succeed, however, in asserting royal authority over the Church. When Pope Boniface IX, in 1403, reaffirmed the right of the papacy to appoint bishops and other members of the ecclesiastical hierarchy in the Hungarian Church, Sigismund defied him and claimed the right of investiture first granted to St Stephen I. In the following year, he won the approval of the Diet for a decree that forbade papal appointments in Hungary, affirmed the crown's sole right of investiture and made the pronouncement of Papal Bulls and Encyclicals in Hungary dependent on royal assent. The Pope eventually conceded defeat on these issues, perhaps in recognition of Sigismund's zealous opposition to the Hussite movement in Bohemia, opposition that until 1436, a year before his death, barred him from election to the Bohemian throne although it was his by inheritance.

During the early years of the fifteenth century Jan Hus's campaign in Bohemia for reform of the church had gathered strength and his attacks on abuses such as the sale of indulgences commanded widespread support. Excommunicated by the Pope in 1411, Hus established his base in southern Bohemia, where he enjoyed powerful protection. When he was summoned to appear before the Church's Council in Constance in 1414, Sigismund granted Hus safe conduct for his journey and for his stay there. When, in the following year, the Council accused Hus of heresy and condemned him to death, Sigismund declined to honour his guarantee of personal safety. This outraged the Hussite movement in Bohemia, now strengthened further by Hus's martyrdom, and inaugurated a running conflict between Sigismund and Bohemia that lasted for twenty years: during that time,

Sigismund waged five successive campaigns against Bohemia, in each one of which he suffered humiliating defeats at the hands of the brilliant Czech military leader Jan Žižka. The Bohemian wars had unwelcome consequences for Hungary in addition to their human and financial cost. They distracted Sigismund's attention from what had been happening in Dalmatia, where his erstwhile rival for the Hungarian crown, László of Naples, had established himself and, in 1409, had sold four of the coastal cities to Venice for 100,000 florins; the remaining ports acknowledged Venetian suzerainty shortly afterwards. After a few desultory attempts to restore Hungarian authority, Sigismund in 1420 accepted the status quo, bringing to an end three hundred years of Hungarian presence on the Adriatic shore. This was not the only territorial sacrifice that Hungary was called upon to make in the interests of Sigismund's imperial objectives; to raise money for military purposes, Sigismund mortgaged to Poland a substantial portion of Szepes County, in northern Hungary on the Polish border, including the three prosperous towns of Lubló, Podolin and Gnézda, together with thirteen market towns populated mainly by Germans; the towns were destined to remain in Polish hands until 1772, when Maria Theresa redeemed them.

In 1389, two years after Sigismund's accession, an event had occurred that not only helped to determine the history of central and southern Europe for the next three hundred years but still casts its baneful influence over the present-day Balkans. At Kosovo Polje, in southern Serbia, the Ottoman Sultan Murad I[11] soundly defeated a combined force of Serbs and Bosnians, establishing in the process a lasting Turkish presence in the Balkans.[12] The collapse of Serbia put Hungary into the front line of Western Christendom in the face of the Ottoman advance. Although the new Sultan, Bayezid I, was initially preoccupied with civil wars in Anatolia, he resumed his father's subjugation of the Balkans by defeating Prince Mircea of Wallachia, who owed allegiance to the Hungarian crown, in 1395. This impelled Sigismund to action. With papal blessing, he launched a crusade against the Muslim invaders and marched south at the head of an army in which Hungarian and French cavalry predominated. In 1396, Sigismund's force confronted the Ottomans at Nicopolis, on the Wallachian/Bulgarian border, where it sustained a disastrous defeat. The Turkish infantry, like the English bowmen at Crécy and Poitiers before them, established complete superiority over Sigismund's French and Burgundian heavy cavalry; their victory was followed by a wholesale slaughter of French prisoners. Sigismund himself escaped and eventually returned to Buda after a roundabout journey lasting several months.

Despite his other preoccupations, Sigismund responded intelligently to the Ottoman challenge. As a first step he won the agreement of the Diet, at Temesvár in 1397, to changes in the rules governing military service. The duties of barons and bishops to supply troops to the crown from their *banderia* (private armies) were clarified and these were henceforth to be supplemented by a militia: every landowner became obliged to provide one light horseman for every twenty tenant holdings on his estate. In return, Sigismund undertook to call on the nobility for personal military service only if his own resources proved inadequate to repel an invasion. A further decree, approved by the Diet in 1435, obliged barons and royal office-holders to supply to the crown three fully equipped and mounted archers for every hundred peasants (*jobbágyok*) in their service: the Diet agreed to ensure that the King disposed of the necessary means to maintain Hungary's frontier defences and to ensure the country's security in general. Sigismund also entrusted an Italian, Filippo Scolari (known to the Hungarians as Pipo Ozorai), with the planning and construction of a fortified defence zone along the 170 kilometre stretch of the Danube between Nándorfehérvár (Belgrade) and Szörényvár (Turnu Severin). Scolari carried out his commission with some skill, drawing on the best contemporary Western practice; the fortresses at Szörényvár, Orsova and Temesvár (Timişoara) were modernised or completely rebuilt. Taken together, these measures brought about a significant improvement in Hungary's military capability: the Ottomans sustained two defeats at Hungarian hands in 1416 and the new Sultan Murad II subsequently agreed to the first of a succession of armistices. During the last years of Sigismund's reign, however, Murad once again increased the pressure and launched a series of raids into Transylvania; in 1428 he captured the new fortress at Galambóc in Serbia.

Transylvania was a source both of strength and of weakness to the Hungarian kingdom. During the twelfth and thirteenth centuries, the northern and central regions of the province had been settled, with the help of royal land grants, by Hungarians and Saxons. Further south, the Székely, who in the aftermath of the 'conquest' had been widely dispersed in the Carpathian Basin, had concentrated during the thirteenth century in the region around Szászsebes (Sebeş); with the arrival of Saxon immigrants, the Székely moved south-eastwards, taking many of their place-names with them, and settled in the area later known as Székelyföld, where they enjoyed free peasant status and a significant degree of autonomy. On and beyond the slopes of the southern Carpathians, however, the relatively sparse population was largely Romanian: the Romanians (or Vlachs), professing the Orthodox Christian faith, lived mainly by sheep-breeding, grazing their flocks on the Carpathian foothills in summer and moving down to the valleys in winter. They paid their taxes in sheep and, in return for their grazing rights, acted as frontier guards, as did their neighbours, the Székely.[13] The leading families of the Hungarians, Saxons and Székely enjoyed noble or quasi–noble status and held their land on a hereditary basis; in addition, Charles I sought to resolve the anomalous status of the Romanian *knezi* (headmen) by admitting them to the nobility as well (if they abandoned their Orthodox faith) and by giving them, as a grant from the crown, formal title to the lands which they already held. The rich pastures of the Transylvanian uplands, its fertile valleys and, above all, its gold, silver, iron and salt mines, made the region a powerful contributor to the growing economic strength of the Hungarian kingdom. At the same time, the geography of Transylvania—its distance from the seat of royal authority and its mountainous terrain—dictated a natural tendency to autonomy, while its population shared with all pioneers and frontiersmen an independent disposition. During the thirteenth and fourteenth centuries Transylvania increasingly took on the character of a kingdom within a kingdom. Stephen V, before his accession, had used Transylvania as a power-base against his father, Béla IV. Charles I, in the interests of stability, allowed the then Voivod (Governor-General), Tamás Széchy, to exercise his authority throughout the region (which had until then been divided into a number of smaller voivodships), a move that ensured that a Voivod of Transylvania would always be the most powerful Hungarian after the king; and when Louis I and Sigismund both endeavoured to extirpate Eastern Orthodoxy from Transylvania, the entrenched Romanian *knezi* proved too strong for them.

In the early 1430s, the Bishop of Transylvania's zeal in attempting to convert the Orthodox to Rome, together with the strengthening influence of Hussite doctrine, contributed to the mounting social unrest which, in 1437, erupted into Hungary's first major peasant revolt. The other ingredients of an explosive situation included the greed of the Church in demanding that the tithe, including arrears, should henceforth be paid in cash rather than in kind—a requirement that imposed an intolerable burden on the peasantry—and, not least, the introduction of financial penalties for the migration of peasants from one landlord to another. Initially the rebels—whose ranks included tenants, new settlers, poor townsmen and some freemen as well as Romanians—achieved some success: in the treaty of Kolozsmonostor, the nobles agreed to the removal of penalties for peasant migration, a modification of tithe payments and an end to the 'ninth' tax. They refused, however, to accept the demand for a peasant assembly, at which every town and village in Transylvania would be represented and which would monitor the nobility's record in respecting peasant liberties. As soon as the Treaty had been concluded, the nobility regrouped for a counter-attack: the Union of Kápolna, or Alliance of Three Nations, brought together the Hungarian, Saxon and Székely nobles and freemen in a solemn compact to retrieve what had been conceded. When, in December 1437, news reached Transylvania of the death in Moravia of Sigismund I, whose sympathies were thought to have lain with the peasants, the nobles decided to suspend negotiations and to put down the rebellion by force. At Kolozsvár in January 1438, the peasants were routed and their leader, Budai Nagy Antal, killed. A wave of punitive executions followed. The rebellion crushed, the nobles of Transylvania were able to concentrate on repelling the continuous series of raids the Turks were mounting on their southern borders.

His inescapable responsibilities as King of the Romans and, from 1433, as Holy Roman Emperor had inevitably distracted Sigismund from his duties to his Hungarian kingdom. He was obliged to travel widely in western Europe. In 1416, for example, he spent four months in England as the guest of Henry V—the only Hungarian king to cross the English Channel—and concluded, in Canterbury, a treaty of alliance; from 1430 he was absent from Hungary for over four years. Sigismund was extravagant: he built a large palace in Buda but seldom used it. The expenses of his imperial role and of his military campaigns fell on the Hungarian as well as on the imperial treasury, hence the mortgage of sixteen towns to Poland. He allowed the internal balance of power to swing back to the barons; at his death, the crown disposed of only fifty-six castles as against the 185 under baronial control. His attempts to mobilise the support of lesser nobles against the greater had no lasting effect. In terms of Hungarian security, however, Sigismund's reign produced positive results. The loss of Dalmatia to Venice, though it caused great anguish at the time, shed an asset Hungary could not defend and had never put to good use. Although his campaigns in Bohemia were wasteful and pointless, he bequeathed to his successors greatly improved defences in the south, whence came the greatest threat; and his military reforms enhanced Hungary's capacity to man them. Hungary was flattered by the reflected glory of the imperial crown; but diminished by Sigismund's religious bigotry and complicity in some of the worst excesses of the papacy's anti–Hussite campaign. Sigismund was held in higher regard, as an accomplished statesman and a worthy Emperor, in western Europe than in his own kingdom.

Hungary in the Fourteenth and Fifteenth Centuries

During the late Middle Ages, Hungary's population increased from about 2 million in 1300 to 3.5 million, or thereabouts (statistics for this period are naturally sparse and unreliable), by 1500. The population was thinly spread: in the mid-fourteenth century, there were only seven inhabitants per square kilometre, compared with twenty-seven in Italy. The majority, probably around 70 per cent, was Hungarian; the remainder included Germans, Slovaks, Croats, Romanians, Cumans and Ruthenians. At the summit of Hungarian society stood up to 400 barons, the *barones regni*, whose status depended on their appointment by the crown to royal office or to the Church hierarchy; most of Hungary's bishops and abbots came from noble families, although it was by no means unknown for outstanding scholars of more humble origins to work their way into and up the ecclesiastical hierarchy. Although royal offices, and the titles which went with them, were not hereditary, landed estates were; in practice, therefore, the largest landowners were the strongest candidates for office and leading positions in the state tended to remain in the same baronial families unless they fell from favour. As we have seen, baronial strength increased significantly during the reign of Sigismund I and the character of local government reflected this. Many of the old royal counties came to be ruled by leading baronial families: by 1407, nine baronial families governed twelve counties between them. By the middle of the fifteenth century, sixty barons owned 40 per cent of all the villages in Hungary; foreign visitors were astonished to find themselves travelling for days on end through the estates of one baronial landlord. In the absence of a standing army, until Matthias Corvinus created one, the barons supplied the bulk of the kingdom's military strength: a baron or bishop who could put more than fifty men into the field was entitled to do so under his own personal standard, hence the term *banderium* ('banner') by which these private armies were known. The king's army at any given time consisted not so much of all existing *banderia* as of those *banderia* whose baronial proprietors chose to put them at the monarch's disposal for the particular purpose or campaign he had in mind; and the barons themselves were under no obligation to fight, except in defence of the kingdom against an invader.

The growth of baronial power not only weakened royal authority but also eroded the independence of the lesser nobility, who numbered about 50,000 or 2 to 3 per cent of the population. Economic necessity drove increasing numbers of lesser nobles into baronial service, as paid members of the *banderia* or as officials in baronial households: bailiffs, stewards, tax collectors or constables. They did not thereby lose their noble status—they could be taxed or judged only by the king— but as servants (*familiares*) of a baron they were obliged to go to war when ordered to do so and to equip themselves for this at their own expense. The relationship known as *familiaritas* became a key characteristic of Hungarian noble society during the fourteenth and fifteenth centuries. Faced with the possibility of sinking, through indigence, into the peasant class, thousands of nobles entered the service of barons who gave them, in exchange for specified services, protection, subsistence and sometimes land. Barons holding office under the crown typically delegated to their *familiares* a major part of their duties, whether tax collection, castle management or the administration of justice; an *ispán* (count) was likely to ensure that his deputy, the *alispán* (vice-count), in effect the chief executive officer of a county, came from the ranks of his *familiares* so that he could be assured of his subordinate's loyalty. Subordinate office-holders could usually expect to be rewarded with a share of the perquisites of the office: in the mid-fifteenth century, for example, one *alispán* received from his superior a moiety of the surplus produce of four villages, six hundred chickens, ten barrels of wine, up to 400 dinars from the fines he had imposed and an annual stipend of 100 florins.[14] Some *familiares* would reside in the castle itself as members of the baronial household; many at least tried to arrange for their children to be brought up and educated under the baronial roof.

The majority of noble *familiares*, however, lived on their own estates, probably in the vicinity of 'their' baronial castle, and carried out local duties on their lord's behalf. They lived off rents from their peasant tenants plus 'the ninth' part of the peasants' produce, which Louis the Great's decree obliged them to collect. This income was frequently insufficient to cover the expense of their military obligations. Many nobles fell into a downward spiral of indebtedness, which reduced them to a standard and style of living little better than that of their own peasants and sometimes worse. Others endeavoured to make something of one of their remaining privileges, namely the duty to attend the national Diet: during the fifteenth century the political consciousness of the lesser nobility increased, fuelled by their financial grievances and by their growing numbers—both consequences, in the absence of a law of primogeniture, of the constant sub-division of noble estates. In this context, a decree approved by the Diet in 1435 on the administration of justice was of some significance: the decree was approved by the Diet 'with the unanimous counsel, deliberation and consent of these prelates and barons and nobles, *representing the whole body of our kingdom* with full powers of those absent' (italics added).[15] This was the first public appearance of the concept, later sanctified by law, that the Hungarian nobility and the Hungarian nation were one and the same, an exclusive definition of nationhood that exercised a baneful influence over Hungary's subsequent social history. Among its promoters was the young János Vitéz, later an eminent humanist and at that time a member of Sigismund's chancellery. The nobility's political clout received a significant boost at the outset of the short reign of Albert I (1437–39), Sigismund's son-in-law and, with his wife Elizabeth, successor: Albert was obliged to accept, at his coronation, obligations to devote all his time to Hungary, to appoint a Palatine only on the advice and with the consent of the Diet, not to appoint foreigners to offices of state, not to alienate royal property and not to require nobles to give military service outside Hungary. Except for those of them who were ordained and educated by the Church, however, members of the nobility were handicapped in the Diet, as in other political contexts, by a low or non-existent level of literacy which put nobles at a disadvantage *vis-à-vis* not only the baronial families and most townsmen but even the wealthier peasants on their own estates.[16]

By the end of the fifteenth century the evolution of the Hungarian noble class had reached a settled state that makes descriptive generalisations possible. It consisted of about 20,000 families, comprising over 3 per cent of the total population—a higher proportion than in any European country except Poland. Within it, there were essentially three strata of wealth and distinction. The upper stratum, of between thirty and forty families, included the barons, who held the principal offices under the crown, and, from the end of the fourteenth century, the 'magnates' who equalled or surpassed the barons in wealth and influence but held no crown appointments. Between them, they owned nearly 30 per cent of the land of the kingdom and an average of over fifty villages per family. The greatest among them, János Hunyadi, owned thirty castles, forty-nine market towns and about a thousand villages.[17] In second place came a stratum of nearly sixty families, owning between them about 10 per cent of the total land area. Below them, in by far the widest and deepest stratum, were the lesser nobility—country gentry rather than aristocracy—of whom the majority had no tenants but worked their own small plot of land; they were nonetheless noble, their status and its attendant liberties assured by their unencumbered ownership of a parcel of land, however small. A noble lacking peasant tenants from whom to exact taxes for the crown was himself liable to tax, but at a reduced rate. A well-to-do peasant might occupy a much larger plot than his noble neighbour, but his tenant status barred him permanently from entry to the noble class, unless he married the daughter of a noble or performed a service for the king that resulted in ennoblement. Occasionally, a commoner owning or permanently occupying land of significant extent might be tacitly admitted to the nobility by the nobles of his county and allowed to claim the liberties and other attributes of their class, pending the outcome of a petition to the king for ennoblement.

Approximately 2.5 million peasants, the *jobbágyság*,[18] constituted the base of the social pyramid. Typically, a *jobbágy* was a free peasant village-dweller who cultivated a portion—a *sessio (telek* in Hungarian)—of the land surrounding his village. Only a minority worked a whole *sessio*; most peasants worked half a *sessio*—usually about 15 *hold**—or less. Although his status was theoretically that of a tenant, a *jobbágy* had security of occupancy of his *sessio* and could bequeath it to his children. He was likely to own, in addition and in his own right, a vineyard and such land as he had himself cleared for cultivation. He could, if he wished and if he had no unpaid debts, migrate from one landlord to another, although landlords were inclined, illegally, to put obstacles in the way of free movement. A *jobbágy* was liable for at least three taxes: a tithe to the Church, a second tithe (the 'ninth') to his landlord on the produce from his vineyard and cleared land, and an annual money tax of between fifty dinars and one florin to the crown. In addition, he was obliged to make 'gifts' in kind to his lord on certain feast days; but he had only a small liability, during the fourteenth and fifteenth centuries, for labour service, since few landlords at that time were actively engaged in agriculture on their own account. A typical *jobbágy* also owned two horses, a wagon, two or three cows and some pigs. In a climate characterised by frequent droughts and harsh

---

* The *hold* was until the mid-twentieth century the Hungarian unit for the measurement of land area; it was the equivalent of 0.57 of a hectare or 1.43 acres.

winters, most *jobbágy* concentrated on animal husbandry rather than arable farming; the Cumans possessed particular skills as cattle-breeders and their heavy steers constituted a valuable export. Barley was grown for brewing and oats for horse fodder; but in many areas the vineyards provided a much more reliable source of income than grain. Although the demand for grain from western Europe was growing, the only means of delivering grain in bulk was by sea, to which Hungary had no ready access; Hungarian wheat became a viable export commodity only with the advent of the railway in the nineteenth century.

The counting unit for the *jobbágyság*, important in the context of liability for military service, was the *porta* (gateway); a *porta* was defined as a gateway large enough to admit a wagonload of hay into the courtyard beyond, which usually denoted a holding worked by at least two *jobbágy* families. We have already encountered the law of 1397, which called for one fully equipped cavalryman from every twenty *portae;* since the cost of providing a soldier and mount was approximately fifty gold florins, the increment to the tax burden was not insignificant. Overall, however, the average Hungarian *jobbágy*, arduous and uncertain though his life undoubtedly was, would have been envied by peasants in most European countries at that time. But there was a rural underclass below the average *jobbágy*, that of the cottars, or landless labourers, whose lot would have attracted no envy from any quarter. The cottars, who often worked for the more well-to-do *jobbágy* as well as for noble landlords, were usually former slaves, often pagan, who had been converted and given what passed for freedom. The usual annual wage for a cottar, in return for a twelve-hour working day, was one gold florin and a rent-free cottage or hut; his employer was also likely to allow him a cow, a pig and twelve bushels of wheat annually to keep himself and his family just above starvation level. Like all *jobbágy*, cottars had the right to migrate but were unable to acquire land, even if plots were vacant or had been abandoned by *jobbágy*, since they had no tools or livestock of their own nor any security against which to borrow. In years to come, as we shall see, their condition was to become much more typical of the Hungarian peasantry as a whole than that of the fifteenth-century *jobbágy*.

There were already ominous developments. The lavish grant by the crown of 'immunity', or abnegation of the royal writ, to a number of large estates handed over the poorer nobility and the peasantry to their landlords without the possibility of appeal. In the wake of the Black Death, and with urban life just beginning to exert a magnetic attraction, barons and noble landlords were concerned to prevent a seepage of labour from their estates; exploiting the law that a *jobbágy* could migrate only after paying his debts, landlords began to raise rents to levels that reduced their tenants to permanent indebtedness and thus tied them to the estate. Many *jobbágy* were forced off their holdings and into cottar status. By the end of the fifteenth century, a second eruption of rural discontent, more serious by far than the Transylvanian revolt of 1437, awaited only a catalyst.

In terms of social status, Hungary's small but growing urban population fell between the lesser nobility and the peasantry. By the end of the fifteenth century about 3 per cent of the population lived in towns, of which Buda was by far the largest, with a population of about 8,000. Under Louis I, Buda had become the royal capital and Sigismund I spent a great deal of money on the enlargement of the palace Louis had built there. By 1437, there were as many as 997 dwellings in Buda, providing 3,276 heatable rooms and stabling for 4,705 horses (one of the advantages of German domination of the city's governance was German thoroughness in recording such matters). As a royal town, Buda enjoyed privileges of which most were probably shared by the thirty-five other towns in Hungary with royal charters: staple rights, the right to elect its own judges, customs privileges, a monopoly of property purchase within the town walls and exemption from the obligation to house royal servants in transit. These privileges were not, however, enjoyed by the much larger number of market towns (*oppida*) in Hungary, which by 1500 were home to around 500,000 people; the market towns were not urban in the strict western European sense but primarily collection centres for livestock and agricultural produce prior to export. Horses, cattle, sheep and pigs accounted for 60 per cent of Hungary's export trade at this time: the livestock was mostly driven on the hoof to Germany, whence it was sold to meet the growing demand for meat in western Europe's expanding cities and towns. Hungary had become Europe's largest supplier of meat and there were fortunes to be made by the foreign entrepreneurs involved in the trade. Wine was the only other significant export that helped Hungary to pay, in part, for rising imports of textiles and luxury goods. Imports accounted for two-thirds of total trade; the deficit was financed by the sale of gold coins, accounting for two-thirds of Hungary's annual production, and silver. This pattern of trade, dictated partly by the appetite of the nobility for imported cloth, jewellery and metal artefacts, was responsible for the very slow and stunted development of crafts and manufactures in Hungary; artisans accounted for only between 20 and 30 per cent of the urban population as against 50 per cent in Bohemia and even higher proportions in western Europe. This deformation continued to handicap Hungary's economy for a further five hundred years.

Growing antagonisms within Hungarian society—between crown and barons as well as between the barons themselves, between greater and lesser nobles, between landlords and tenants, between landed and landless peasants—together with a small population, an under-developed urban economy and the continuing absence of a sense of nationhood, (despite an inchoate Magyar consciousness of being 'different') imposed upon Hungary insuperable handicaps in the control and defence of the immense area over which it had proclaimed its suzerainty. This disparity between aspiration and capacity would be camouflaged for nearly a further century by the talents for leadership and improvisation of a few individuals; but, with hindsight, the flaws were already perceptible.

4

FROM LIGHT INTO DARKNESS

(1444–1526)

János Hunyadi (c. 1407–56)

Until shortly before Sigismund's death in 1437, the Turkish Sultan Murad II had been preoccupied, first, with the suppression of rebellious challenges to his authority by rival princes in Anatolia and then with the ejection of the Venetians, allies of Byzantium, from Salonika and the Morea. By 1432, however, Murad was ready to turn his attention to Hungary and began a series of major raids on Transylvania that yielded substantial booty and large numbers of slaves, possibly as many as 70,000 in 1439 alone. In the same year Murad occupied Serbia, driving its Despot, Djordje (George) Branković, to take refuge in Hungary, where he disposed of considerable estates as the reward for his vassalage to Sigismund. Hungary's buffer against the Turkish advance thus disappeared. In 1440 Murad laid siege to Belgrade, pivot of the Hungarian defensive line established by Scolari and the only major obstacle in the way of a Turkish advance into the Carpathian Basin.

Meanwhile, Albert I's premature death, from dysentery, had plunged Hungary into turmoil yet again. Four months after her husband's death, Queen Elizabeth had given birth to a son, having first, with notable presence of mind and convinced that she was about to bear a son, ordered her lady-in-waiting to steal the Holy Crown and royal regalia from the castle strong-room in Visegrád. The infant prince, aged three months, was crowned Ladislas V, with the Holy Crown, at Székesfehérvár in May 1440. The prospective Regent, Elizabeth, could count on the continuing support of the two leading baronial families, the Garais and the Cilleis; but some barons and most of the untitled nobility found the prospect of a prolonged regency unattractive and were keen, in any case, to assert the principle of election to the throne rather than acquiescing in automatic inheritance. The nobles consequently offered the Hungarian crown to Wladislas III of Poland, who accepted it and was duly crowned Wladislas I of Hungary, also at Székesfehérvár but with a substitute crown which allegedly came from the reliquary of St Stephen I. Civil war ensued, in which Elizabeth bought the support of the Habsburg Emperor and King of Germany, Frederick III, by putting in pawn to him not only the Holy Crown but also the north-western town of Sopron and her own sizeable estates. Although the *banderia* of Elizabeth's baronial allies, reinforced by German mercenaries, achieved initial successes and soon controlled all of western Hungary, in 1441 they sustained a crushing defeat at Bátaszék, in southern Hungary, at the hands of Wladislas's supporters, whose forces had been strengthened by Polish troops fighting for their King. This effectively ended the war. Elizabeth died in the following year, after recognising Wladislas in return for the promise of the succession for her son; the infant Ladislas V survived, as a ward of Frederick III, to claim the throne some years later.

One of the captains of Wladislas's victorious army was János Hunyadi. Hunyadi's origins have been the object of controversy. He apparently came from Romanian (Vlach) stock; there is little evidence for the alternative view that he was a natural son of King Sigismund I. Devoted military service to the crown earned János Hunyadi's father the royal grant of substantial estates in Transylvania and János himself a place at Sigismund's court. It was natural for János to follow his father into a military career; he took his soldiering seriously, serving his apprenticeship as a *familiaris* to several barons—including István Újlaki, whose son Miklós became his close comrade-in-arms—and then as a knight to King Sigismund. He was a member of Sigismund's entourage for a visit in 1431 to Milan, where Sigismund was crowned King of Italy; and it is likely that he used the occasion to learn from leading Italian mercenary commanders. He may also have received instruction in military matters from Filippo Scolari himself; and he certainly studied and imitated the techniques of the Czech Hussite hero, Jan Žižka, including the latter's use of the wagon both as a means of transporting infantry and as a mobile fortress.[1] His early friendship with János Vitéz, a leading humanist scholar and skilled political operator, became important to his later career.

With his younger brother, János Hunyadi fought for Albert I in the successful Bohemian campaign of 1439. Albert recognised the prowess of the two Hunyadis by sending them south to face the Turks as joint commanders of the Scolari fortress at Szörényvár (Turnu Severin) where they introduced a number of tactical innovations, including the posting of scouts deep in Turkish-occupied territory to give early warning of a Turkish advance. In return for further grants of land in Transylvania and eastern Hungary, the Hunyadis also enlarged the mercenary force under their command; this reinforced their growing *banderium* which, as their military reputation grew, members of the lesser nobility were flocking to join. Returning north to join the supporters of Wladislas I against Elizabeth, János Hunyadi, together with Miklós Újlaki, played a leading role in the defeat of the pro-Habsburg forces in 1441. Wladislas rewarded them by appointing the two men joint Voivods (Governors-General) of Transylvania and, in addition, entrusting them with the joint command of the fortress of Nándorfehérvár (Belgrade) and of all the fortifications along the Danube.[2]

Now in his early thirties, János Hunyadi already enjoyed—by virtue of his appointments and the size of his estates—baronial status and the fastest-growing reputation in the realm. He owned over 700,000 *hold* of land in Transylvania, encompassing over a hundred villages, a number of castles and several gold mines. He administered the lucrative royal salt monopoly, another perk from a grateful monarch. He had married Erzsébet (Elizabeth) Szilágyi, who came from a Transylvanian family very similar to his own in status—minor nobility with a strong military tradition—and by whom he had two sons, László and Matthias. Concepts of nationhood and patriotism had yet to emerge in Hungary, as elsewhere in Europe: Hunyadi was essentially an *arriviste* whose motivation in fighting the Turks related to the enhancement of his own and his family's status and reputation, the protection of his vast estates (which covered nearly three million *hold* by the end of his career) and his duty to his king, probably in that order. The service he rendered the kingdom of Hungary and her Christian neighbours was nonetheless of immeasurable value: Hunyadi's victories won for Hungary a further eighty years of integrity and independence.

The Turkish siege of Belgrade in 1440 had not prospered, despite Hungary's preoccupation with civil war. Murad II withdrew his forces through Serbia, where they looted prodigiously, and Hunyadi used the respite, during the summer of 1441, to repair the damage which Belgrade's walls had sustained during the Turkish bombardment. In the following year, however, Murad struck again, this time from Wallachia into Transylvania and the Maros River plain. Taken by surprise and with an inadequate force, Hunyadi was severely worsted in the first encounter; but with characteristic resilience he quickly raised another army and struck back, defeating the Turks near Gyulafehérvár (Alba Iulia). This, the first defeat in a set-piece battle the Turks had sustained during their advance northwards, both established Hunyadi's military reputation and served notice on Sultan Murad that the Hungarians had to be taken seriously. Murad responded by sending a much larger force, of about 70,000 men, into Wallachia under his senior commander in Europe, Sehabeddin; Hunyadi, meanwhile, had raised an army of 15,000, which for the first time included Saxons and Székely. The two armies confronted each other near the Wallachian village of Tirgoviste. Hunyadi seized the initiative and his superior tactical skills outweighed the Turkish superiority in numbers: the Turks were routed, leaving behind 5,000 prisoners and a larger number of dead, half their army according to one account.

Hunyadi's victories put a temporary stop to Turkish expansion into Christian territory. They also had a consequence less beneficial to Hungarian long-term interests: they confirmed Hungary's status as the leading defender of Western Christendom and inspired Pope Eugene IV, among others, to urge Wladislas I to mount a major campaign against the Turks. Now that the Turks had been halted, argued the Papal Legate, Giuliano Cesarini, and Djordje Branković of Serbia (most of whose kingdom was under Turkish occupation), the time had come to drive them out of Europe. With some reluctance, since he feared that Frederick III would take advantage of his absence to install his ward, Ladislas V, on the Hungarian throne, Wladislas bowed to this pressure despite the absence of any promises of support from other Catholic monarchs. Hunyadi spent the vast sum of 32,000 gold florins on assembling a mercenary army of 30,000 men, including Hussite Czechs, and marched south with his king in June 1443; Branković rallied 8,000 Serb troops to Wladislas's banner en route. The Long Campaign, as it came to be known, produced a striking series of victories for Hungarian arms but no lasting results. Having reached and sacked Sofia, Hunyadi's advance was checked at the Rhodope Mountains, which barred the way to Macedonia and whose passes were well defended by the Turks. Winter closed in and the Hungarian column turned for the long march home, with several thousand prisoners and several hundred wagon-loads of loot. The rest of Europe applauded and demanded an encore; Buda hosted a crowd of envoys from Western kingdoms bearing messages of congratulation and expressions of hope that a second campaign would be launched. The fact remained that little Serbian territory had been recovered, to the disappointment of Branković, and no key Scolari fortress had been recaptured. Hungary had achieved as much as could have been expected of one relatively small country, and more; but only a concerted effort by Western Christendom could turn the Ottoman tide, and this was not forthcoming.

Even before Wladislas and Hunyadi reached home, Sultan Murad, who was impatient to deal with a further revolt in Anatolia, had offered the Hungarians a long-term truce. There followed several months of negotiations, of which the course has never been satisfactorily established, culminating in the so-called 'Treaty of Szeged', which remains a matter of controversy between historians to this day. The Pope, represented by Cardinal Cesarini, the Doge of Venice and the Duke of Burgundy, favoured the immediate resumption of hostilities and the launching of a crusade in which the Venetian fleet, to be stationed in the Dardanelles, would play an important part by cutting off all traffic between Europe and Asia Minor. János Hunyadi, doubtful of the feasibility of raising quickly another army of adequate size, favoured a truce. Djordje Branković was eager for any arrangement that might enable him to reclaim his Serbian kingdom. Negotiations, sanctioned by Wladislas, between Branković and the Sultan in Edirne (Adrianopol) revealed that Murad was prepared to offer remarkably generous terms, which included the return to Branković of all the fortresses on Serb territory and the complete withdrawal of Turkish forces from Serbia, as well as a substantial cash tribute to Wladislas. The negotiations continued in Szeged, in southern Hungary, where the Turkish offer was confirmed, apparently in return for a Hungarian undertaking not to interfere in Bulgaria. Wladislas himself had avoided taking a firm position on the question of a truce. He appears to have authorised Hunyadi to sign, in Várad (Oradea), a document embodying the agreements reached at Szeged; but on 4 August 1444, Wladislas pronounced a solemn oath in the presence of Cardinal Cesarini and representatives of the Doge of Venice and the Duke of Burgundy to the effect that, irrespective of whatever agreements had been or might be signed to the contrary, hostilities against the Turks would be resumed before the end of the year, come what may.[3] Wladislas had evidently baulked at disappointing three powerful allies and had doubtless been assured by Cesarini that undertakings given to infidels had no validity and could be broken with impunity. Murad, meanwhile, had departed for Anatolia in the belief that a truce was now in place; and the Turks duly began the evacuation of the Serbian fortresses and the payment of tribute to the Hungarian crown. In accordance with his oath and claiming, quite falsely, that the Turks were in breach of the 'Treaty of Szeged' because the fortresses had not been returned to Branković quickly enough, Wladislas crossed the Danube on 22 September and marched into the Balkans.

János Hunyadi, now reconciled to a further campaign, had met with only indifferent success in raising an army for it. Apart from three bishops the barons, in particular, turned their backs on the enterprise; Hunyadi could muster only 10,000 troops, pressing a further 10,000 into service during the southward march towards Nicopolis. The invading force, increasingly encumbered by wagon-loads of loot, reached Varna, on the Black Sea coast, at the beginning of November. Here Wladislas and Hunyadi were unpleasantly surprised to find that Murad II had either evaded or bribed the Venetian navy and had succeeded in crossing the Bosporus from Anatolia to resume command of his army, which outnumbered the Hungarians by at least two to one and occupied good positions in the Hungarian rear. Despite this, the Hungarians prevailed in the early stages of the battle that ensued. Wladislas, however, insisted on leading a cavalry charge against the serried ranks of janissaries in the Turkish centre. He died in the attack. Wladislas's death threw the Hungarian army into panic and then into headlong retreat; Hunyadi himself was one of the few survivors and suffered the further humiliation of being kidnapped and temporarily imprisoned by Vlad Dracul of Wallachia on his way back to Hungary.[4] Varna set the seal upon Turkish hegemony in the Balkans and ensured the eventual fall of Constantinople.

In a novel but salutary development, the political vacuum created by Wladislas's death was filled by the Diet. This was largely due to the efforts of János Vitéz, who had worked hard to forge an alliance between king and nobility and to enhance the Diet's authority; the Diet now assembled at least once a year and broke the monopoly of political decision-making, which had hitherto rested with the Royal Council. Wladislas had confirmed in 1440 that all laws required the assent of the Diet as well as that of the barons and prelates. Meeting six months after the Battle of Varna but still lacking firm evidence of Wladislas's fate, the Diet now resolved that if Wladislas had not returned to Hungary by 30 May 1445 it would recognise Ladislas V—but not his eventual heir—as King, provided that Frederick III allowed him freely to return to Hungary and also disgorged the Holy Crown and regalia, together with the territory he still occupied in north-west Hungary. In the meantime, governance of the country was entrusted by the Diet to seven 'Captains in Chief', all barons, including János Hunyadi, each administering a geographical region (Hunyadi assumed responsibility for Transylvania and eastern Hungary). Frederick III, meanwhile, had rejected the proposals made to him by a delegation from the Diet, in terms that revealed his objective of ruling Hungary himself during Ladislas V's minority. The Diet riposted in the following year by electing János Hunyadi Regent of Hungary until Ladislas came of age; Hunyadi had rejected suggestions that he might assume the crown himself. The oath administered to Hunyadi on taking office had to be drawn up in Hungarian, since he knew no Latin, and became the first legal document to be drafted in the vernacular.

Hunyadi's priority as Regent was to secure Hungary's western and northern frontiers so that his hands would be free to mount a further campaign against the Turks in the south. A show of military force persuaded Frederick III to accept an armistice, under which he returned the town of Győr to Hungary (while keeping Sopron and Kőszeg) but retained control of Ladislas V and of the Holy Crown. In the north, the Czech mercenary leader Jan Jiškra controlled several Hungarian counties; after fruitless attempts to dislodge him by force, Hunyadi agreed to allow the occupation to continue provided that Jiškra assumed responsibility for internal order in the territory he held—Jiškra was, in fact, one of the seven 'Captains in Chief' appointed by the Diet despite his Czech nationality. The co-operation of the perennially troublesome Cillei family, which controlled Slavonia in the south and also large areas in the west on both sides of the Austria/Hungary border, was purchased by the betrothal of Hunyadi's elder son, László, to a Cillei daughter. None of this betokened the smack of firm government—internal problems were shelved rather than solved and the Diet demonstrated its growing disillusionment with Hunyadi by electing his chief enemy, László Garai, to the office of Palatine; but Hunyadi had at least succeeded in avoiding the civil war into which a vacant throne usually plunged Hungary and in buying time he could use to raise yet another army against the Turks. As usual, Hunyadi's pleas to Western rulers for military or financial support for his forthcoming campaign against the infidel were either rebuffed or unanswered. Pope Eugene counselled postponement but Hunyadi was having none of it and replied to the Pope in forthright language:

… the enemy attacks our neighbours, incites [them] to war against us. We have decided to attack him instead of waiting for him to attack us. We have had enough of our men enslaved, our women raped, wagons loaded with the severed heads of our people, the sale of chained captives, the mockery of our religion … we shall not stop until we have succeeded in expelling the enemy from Europe.[5]

By early September 1448, Hunyadi had succeeded in raising an army of some 16,000 in Hungary, to which the new Wallachian leader, Dan II, added half as many again. Hunyadi's objective was to bisect the Turkish-occupied Balkans by striking down towards Macedonia, Skanderbeg of Albania having promised to join him en route. In order to link up with Skanderbeg, Hunyadi headed for Kosovo, whence the combined force could push further southwards into Macedonia. Sultan Murad II, having been alerted by Branković to Hunyadi's line of march, intercepted the Hungarian force on the very plain—Kosovo Polje, the 'Field of Blackbirds'—that had been the scene of Murad I's victory over Serbia nearly sixty years previously. Skanderbeg and his army had yet to reach the rendezvous. Although Hunyadi had taken up a good position on high ground overlooking the plain and although, as at Varna, the Hungarian and Wallachian forces had the better of the first day's fighting, the second day of the battle was a disaster for Hungary and her ally: the Hungarian cavalry and the entire Wallachian contingent were annihilated, sustaining casualties of up to 17,000 killed or taken prisoner. Hunyadi himself again, as at Varna, managed to escape and reached Serbia; but here he fell foul of Branković, now openly making common cause with the Turks in order to hold on to his newly regained kingdom, who seized and imprisoned Hunyadi in Szendrö (Smederovo). The Hungarian Royal Council eventually negotiated his release; but Hunyadi was compelled to agree to the return to Branković of his confiscated estates in Hungary, to hand over his elder son, László, as hostage and to accept the betrothal of his younger son, Matthias, to Branković's granddaughter, Erzsébet Cillei. Hunyadi's political authority, not least in relation to the barons who had negotiated his release, never recovered from this humiliation.

All Hunyadi's instincts impelled him to seek to avenge his defeat at Kosovo: his reluctance to accept a continuing threat to the kingdom, his concern to protect his estates in Transylvania from a resumed Turkish advance and, of course, his desire to restore his own military reputation. But Kosovo had proved beyond doubt that the Turks would never be defeated by Hungary alone; the Catholic rulers of western Europe maintained their attitude of studied indifference to the threat. Even the Pope (now Nicholas V) was for once counselling caution and the concerns of the Hungarian Diet centred on problems in the north, where Jan Jiškra's mercenaries were on the rampage; Jiškra himself had consolidated his hold over the northern towns and Frederick III continued to hold Ladislas V and a large slice of western Hungary. A truce with the Sultan, whose army had sustained considerable losses at Kosovo, enabled Hunyadi to turn his attention to these difficulties. Military action against Jiškra, prosecuted in a series of campaigns between 1448 and 1451, achieved no more than stalemate. An alliance with his old enemy László Garai, which Miklós Újlaki was also persuaded to join, enabled Hunyadi to exert sufficient pressure on Branković to secure the release of his son László; and on Frederick III to bring about the handing over, at last, of young Ladislas V, albeit into the hands of Hunyadi's leading opponent, Ulrich Cillei. Frederick did not disgorge the Holy Crown. In 1453, however, Ladislas V (1453–57) took the coronation oath before the Hungarian Diet, assembled for the purpose in Pozsony (Bratislava); Hunyadi resigned his regency, receiving in recognition of this act of loyalty (Ladislas had doubtless feared that Hunyadi would try to hang on to power) the captaincy-general of all forces under royal command, the lucrative privilege of administering royal revenues, and the title of Count of Beszterce in Transylvania. Hunyadi's son László became Governor-General of Croatia, Slavonia and Dalmatia—a setback for the Cilleis—and his ally János Vitéz was promoted to head the royal chancellery.

The apparent restoration of János Hunyadi's personal fortunes coincided with the arrival of news that inaugurated the final phase of his remarkable career: Constantinople had fallen to the new Sultan, Mehmed II. Although this event had little strategic significance—Constantinople had been neutralised by the enveloping Turkish presence for many years—its symbolic impact was immense. Byzantium was no more. The Balkan alliances that Hunyadi had painstakingly constructed at once fell apart as local rulers scrambled to make their accommodations with and submissions to the Sultan. Pope Nicholas proclaimed a Crusade; and Hunyadi, in 1454, succeeded in persuading a still reluctant Diet that recruitment to the King's forces had to be intensified: for one year only, nobles agreed to furnish their sovereign with four horsemen and two foot soldiers for every hundred portae on their estates. Later in the year, when the Sultan had launched a probing sortie into Serbia, Hunyadi delivered a boost to Hungarian morale by ambushing and destroying the Turkish rearguard near Belgrade. Brushing aside this minor setback, Mehmed II proceeded, with due deliberation, to make his dispositions for a further assault on Hungary. A formal treaty, in which Branković accepted vassalage to the Sultan in return for territorial security, neutralised Serbia. Mehmed next turned on and defeated Skanderbeg of Albania, depriving Hungary of another potential ally and establishing Turkish dominion over the whole length of the Dalmatian coast. By the beginning of 1456, Mehmed was poised to march on Belgrade, the pivot of Hungary's southern defences.

With the exception of the Pope, Europe looked the other way; so did the majority of Hungary's barons, many of them using an outbreak of plague as their excuse for failing to field their *banderia* in defence of the realm.[6] Hunyadi's alliance with Garai and Újlaki had already fallen apart; they and Ulrich Cillei, while in continuous conflict with each other, were united only in their opposition to the Captain-General. Ladislas V's contribution to the defence effort was to touch Hunyadi for a sizeable personal loan, the last of many, before departing to the safety of Vienna with Cillei. Hunyadi found his only effective ally in Giovanni da Capistrano, an elderly Franciscan friar from Italy, whose passionate sermons proved to be an invaluable recruiting tool. Their combined efforts produced an ill-assorted and ill-equipped army of between fifteen and twenty thousand men, which assembled at Szeged in the early summer. Fortunately, rumours had reached Mehmed II of the despatch of a papal naval force to blockade Constantinople, obliging him (unnecessarily as it turned out) to leave part of his army behind to defend the city; even so, the Turks outnumbered the Hungarians and their allies (mainly crusaders responding to Capistrano's appeals) by at least three to one. Mehmed arrived before Belgrade just ahead of Hunyadi and at once laid siege to the fortress, blasting its walls with cannon newly cast for the purpose and with giant catapults. To forestall a Hungarian attempt to relieve the fortress by water, Mehmed also blockaded the Danube with a barrage of anchored river boats, chained together. Hunyadi decided to tackle this obstacle first and assembled a water-borne assault force which eventually prevailed over the Turkish river fleet after a battle lasting several hours. He was then able to enter the fortress with some 3,000 men who were at once put to work on the repair of breaches in the walls. On 21 July, Mehmed launched a major assault on the fortress, filling its moats with bundles of branches, which the janissaries used as a bridge to reach the breached fortifications. These makeshift bridges turned out to be the Turks' Achilles' heel: on Hunyadi's orders, the defenders on the walls threw quantities of burning material on to the branches, which burst into flame and cut off the janissaries from their main force. The janissaries already inside the fortress were massacred, those approaching it burned to death. The Sultan recalled the survivors to rest and regroup.

On the following day, Capistrano's crusaders, against orders, crossed the river and provoked a skirmish that quickly developed into a pitched battle in which Capistrano himself (aged seventy-one) had no option but to take part. The Turks, weary, surprised and weakened by an epidemic of plague, gave ground; seeing this, Hunyadi led his cavalry out of the fortress and joined battle. The fighting continued until darkness fell, the Hungarian army continuously reinforced by newly arrived crusaders. Mehmed II, himself wounded and unnerved by a mutiny among the janissaries, ordered a nocturnal retreat; when dawn broke on 23 July, the Turkish camp, with all its weapons and stores, was found to be deserted. Belgrade had been saved and the Turkish advance on central Europe halted. Pope Callistus III had ordered Christendom to pray for victory at noon on 22 July: the church bells that had summoned the faithful to prayer rang daily thereafter, in perpetual celebration of Hunyadi's victory, and still do so today.[7] Hunyadi himself did not take part in the rejoicing with which Europe greeted the news from Belgrade; he died of plague during the journey home, at Zimony, on 11 August 1456. Giovanni da Capistrano also died, in Hungary, two months later. The Turks, for their part, concentrated during the next decade on consolidating their grip on the Balkans, subduing Serbia, Wallachia and Albania in turn; Mehmed II strengthened the Ottoman hold on Greece, the Mediterranean islands and Asia Minor. But Hungary, largely thanks to János Hunyadi, was spared Turkish attentions for seventy years.

Hunyadi was not a great general: the defeats he sustained at Varna and Kosovo cost his country nearly as much as his victories gained for it. Nor was he a gifted statesman, as the troublesome political legacy of his regency showed. Hunyadi was, however, a brave soldier and a courageous leader who pursued his struggle against the Turks with single-minded determination despite the paucity of support accorded to him either inside or outside Hungary. He was undeterred by overwhelmingly unfavourable odds and in the last days of his life memorably triumphed over them.

Matthias I Corvinus (1458–90)

On receiving news of János Hunyadi's death, Ladislas V at once appointed his uncle and protector, Ulrich Cillei, to the vacant captaincy-general; but he also put Hunyadi's elder son, László, in command of Belgrade. Cillei made little secret of his intention to settle accounts with the surviving Hunyadis once and for all; when he accompanied the King on a celebratory visit to Belgrade he was murdered on the initiative of László Hunyadi, who had resolved to make a pre-emptive strike on behalf of his family. Early in 1457, Ladislas V took his revenge by summoning the Hunyadi brothers to Buda, having promised that Cillei's murderers would not be punished, and arresting them for high treason. László Hunyadi was beheaded outside Buda castle; when his mother, Erzsébet Szilágyi, raised the banner of revolt against the king, Ladislas V fled to Prague taking Matthias Hunyadi with him as hostage. In Prague Ladislas V, now aged seventeen, suddenly died, possibly of leukaemia, although rumours inevitably circulated that he had been poisoned. Matthias Hunyadi,* who had used his short stay in Prague to good effect by becoming betrothed to the daughter of the newly elected Bohemian King, George Podiebrad, was now free and an obvious candidate for election to the Hungarian throne. He would bring to it not only the lustre of the Hunyadi name but also a lively intellect and, by contemporary standards, a broad humanist education supervised by János Vitéz. In January 1458, Matthias's uncle, Mihály Szilágyi, marched from Belgrade to Pest, surrounded the Field of Rákos, where the Diet was in session, with 15,000 troops and persuaded the assembled nobles that Matthias should be their King. Matthias was duly elected but his coronation had to await Frederick III's eventual surrender of the Holy Crown; with no royal blood in his veins, Matthias needed legitimacy. He also needed a broader and more secure base for his authority than the shifting and ephemeral baronial alliances on which so many of his predecessors—and his own father as Regent—had depended; he set about securing this with considerable courage and, for an eighteen-year-old, political maturity.

Matthias's first, and very risky, move was to distance himself from the group of barons, headed by his mother and uncle, which had secured his election to the throne. Szilágyi reacted quickly, forming an alliance with László Garai and Miklós

---

* Matthias was subsequently given the sobriquet 'Corvinus', after the raven on the Hunyadi family coat of arms, by the humanist historian Bonfini who arrived in Hungary in 1486 and wrote a history of Matthias' reign; Matthias has since been remembered by posterity as Matthias Corvinus.

Újlaki among others to depose Matthias before his coronation; in 1459, the group, now numbering about thirty barons, elected Emperor Frederick III to the Hungarian throne. Matthias arrested and imprisoned Szilágyi, subsequently releasing him only so that he could lead an expedition against the Turks who were harassing Transylvania; the expedition foundered, Szilágyi was taken prisoner and later beheaded in Constantinople. With the help of his future father-in-law, George Podiebrad of Bohemia, and enlisting the diplomatic skills of the indispensable János Vitéz, Matthias then initiated a protracted negotiation with Frederick which, in 1463, finally produced an acceptable outcome. The Emperor, it was agreed, would adopt Matthias as his son and would inherit the throne of Hungary if Matthias were to die without a male heir; for his part, Frederick would hand over the Holy Crown, and by implication forgo any immediate claim to it, in return for a payment of 80,000 gold florins. Having thus outflanked the barons, Matthias—whose coronation, with the Holy Crown, finally took place at Székesfehérvár in 1464—lost no time in dismissing from their royal offices the barons who had opposed him, forging instead a broadly based alliance with the nobility. He also negotiated a lasting truce with Ján Jiškra, who yielded to him the towns he controlled in the north, and imprisoned Vlad Dracul, Voivod of Wallachia, who had sought refuge in Hungary from the Turks but whom Matthias suspected of harbouring designs on Transylvania. Having neutralised these various potential threats to his authority, Matthias was ready to embark on reshaping his kingdom.

Matthias's twin objectives, both designed to reduce the dependence of the crown on baronial support, were to put the royal finances on a sounder footing and to assure the crown of military superiority in the face of any internal challenge. In 1467 he won the agreement of the Diet to a wholesale reform of the taxation system, which a steady accretion of exemptions and immunities over the years had rendered virtually inoperative. In future, every household in the realm, apart from the nobility and the clergy, would be liable for an annual tax of one-fifth of a gold florin. The reform offended important groups, such as the Saxons and the Székely, which had hitherto enjoyed tax exemption; and this contributed to a serious rebellion in Transylvania in the same year which, however, Matthias suppressed without great difficulty, punishing with particular severity the lesser nobility who took part. The new tax, moreover, was to be doubled in time of war and was supplemented by regular subsidies and forced loans, which bore especially heavily on the towns, whose already slow development was further stunted as a result. By these means Matthias gradually increased royal revenue from about 200,000 gold florins at the time of his accession to the unprecedented level of nearly a million by the end of his reign, putting the royal treasury once again on a par with those of France and Burgundy as it had been in the days of Béla III.

Matthias's financial exigencies had important consequences for Hungary's Jewish community. Like most kings of Hungary since the late thirteenth century, Matthias had confirmed at his coronation the privileges granted to the Jews by Béla IV. During the intervening century and a half, Hungarian Jews had continued to enjoy better treatment than Jewish communities in other European countries, including those under temporary Hungarian rule such as Austria, Silesia and Bohemia. During periods of anarchy, Jews tended to suffer more than most as their involuntary role in society as moneylenders and pawnbrokers inevitably made them unpopular; as soon as royal authority had been restored, however, Hungary's rulers invariably perceived their interest to lie in protecting a community that made a disproportionately large contribution to tax revenue. Conflicts of interest occasionally arose when a ruler's need to curry favour with a particular urban community outweighed his interest in maintaining Jewish rights; both János Hunyadi and Ladislas V, for example, released the citizens of Pozsony (Bratislava) from their obligation to repay loans owing to Pozsony Jews. In general, however, Hungary's chronically indigent kings took good care of the goose that laid the golden eggs. Characteristically, Matthias Corvinus adopted a more systematic approach to this question. The office of 'Jew judge of the whole kingdom' had lapsed in the 1440s, although local 'Jew judges' remained. In 1476 Matthias created the new office of 'Jewish Prefect', which carried with it considerable prestige: a place at court, a small militia to enforce his rulings and a private gaol in Buda in which to incarcerate the disobedient. Although the Jewish Prefect's duties included that of presenting directly to the king petitions and grievances from the Jewish community, his main role was that of tax–farmer: informed by the Royal Treasurer of the total sum Jews in Hungary were required to contribute in tax, the Jewish Prefect had the invidious task of allocating the liabilities of each Jewish community and ensuring payment. This innovation brought about a massive increase in the Jewish contribution to the crown's revenues: from 4,000 to 20,000 gold florins during Matthias's reign.

The expenses Matthias had to meet, however, had also risen to unprecedented levels. The defence of Hungary's southern borders, continually harassed by Turkish raids, was a constant drain on resources. Matthias's efforts to build up a military force under exclusively royal control were as expensive as they were impressive. Beginning with a small contingent of 500 Czech mercenaries loaned to him by his father-in-law, Matthias gradually assembled Hungary's first significant standing army (subsequently christened the 'Black Army') of around 28,000 Hungarian, German, Polish, Czech, Serb and Swiss mercenaries. This gave the crown a formidable instrument of policy, both inside Hungary (where barons were now forbidden to recruit mercenaries of their own) and beyond its frontiers; but at about 30 florins per year per mercenary, the standing army could stand at full strength only for relatively short periods.

With the same objective of strengthening central authority, Matthias significantly improved the machinery of government. The royal chancellery and treasury were no longer staffed exclusively by nobles and bishops; the introduction of men, including a number of foreigners, hand-picked for their brains rather than for their social origins, greatly increased the efficiency of the central administration. Matthias also reformed the judiciary, creating a core of professional judges who served their apprenticeships in the lower courts and local government. Formally, barons and nobles still presided over the central courts but trained lawyers ran them. As a result of the judicial reform, common people were more likely to be given a fair trial and to secure redress against injustices inflicted by a social superior; when Matthias died, the lament 'Dead is Matthias, lost is justice' became common throughout the realm. Despite his need for good relations with the Papacy, Matthias maintained firm control over ecclesiastical appointments, telling Pope Paul II that Hungary would rather forsake Catholicism than give up the crown's right of investiture: János Vitéz became Archbishop of Esztergom (as well as Chancellor) and his nephew, the brilliant Janus Pannonius, Bishop of Pécs. Both these beneficiaries of Matthias's patronage, however, joined a baronial plot in 1471 to offer the Hungarian crown to Casimir, son of the King of Poland Casimir IV; this was partly a reaction to what they saw as an excessive concentration of power in Matthias's hands—in the previous year he had raised taxes in defiance of the Diet's veto—and partly a protest against his apparent neglect of the Turkish threat. Matthias defused the plot without great difficulty (although Casimir junior got as far as invading northern Hungary) and pardoned Vitéz; Pannonius, however, fled to Croatia and died there shortly afterwards.

The reservations Vitéz, Pannonius and others expressed with regard to Matthias's style of kingship were not without justification. 'The king himself is no slave or tool to the law', Matthias was recorded as having said to an Italian humanist, 'he is above it, ruling over it'.[8] Matthias clearly believed in the doctrine of royal absolutism; after 1471 he rarely summoned the Diet and governed his kingdom, from the centre, through the talented group of professional bureaucrats, owing allegiance only to him, which he had assembled. In these matters Matthias was in no sense out of tune with his age; none of his contemporary Christian rulers—Louis XI of France or Henry VII of England, for example—would have found anything surprising in his attitude to monarchy. Matthias's absolutist and centrist approach was, however, at variance with Hungary's idiosyncratic political tradition and social structure. Internal opposition to his style of government never disappeared and Matthias occasionally found himself obliged to make concessions to it. In 1486, for example, he convened a Diet and approved its award of yet further privileges to the nobility; the Palatine, moreover, was henceforth charged with mediation between the crown and the Diet when the nobility believed its privileges to have been infringed, an innovation that significantly dented the absolutist concept. But apart from the abortive plot of 1471 Matthias's authority faced no serious challenge during the thirty-two years of his reign; and, in particular, the barons posed less of a threat to the crown or to the integrity of the kingdom during this period than at any time during the century.

The concerns of János Vitéz and his fellow plotters regarding Matthias's priorities in foreign policy were also understandable. Whereas his father had made the protection of Hungary's southernmost borders and the halting of the Turkish advance towards them his primary objective, while guarding his rear with bribes and compromises to his northern neighbours, Matthias stood this agenda on its head. His intention was to make Hungary the dominant power in central Europe; his personal ambition, to secure election to the imperial throne. A strategy of expansion to the north and west had obvious economic attractions: control of Austria and Silesia would bring the royal treasury the benefits of the lucrative staple rights of Vienna and Wroclaw (Breslau) and, to Hungary, a dominant position in regional trade. In 1469 Matthias invaded Bohemia and in a direct challenge to the reigning king, George Podiebrad,[9] secured his own election to the Bohemian throne by the Catholic nobility. When George died two years later, however, the Bohemian nobility as a whole preferred Wladislaw Jagiello of Poland, heir to Casimir IV, who promised tolerance to the Hussites, unlike Matthias, whose invasion of Bohemia had been dressed up as a Catholic crusade.

Thwarted for the time being in Bohemia proper, Matthias moved into Silesia and seized Wroclaw, which he then succeeded in holding against a besieging force of Czechs and Poles. This victory enabled Matthias to drive a hard bargain in the ensuing peace negotiations: in 1478 the Treaty of Olmütz (Olomouc) confirmed Matthias's suzerainty over Moravia and Lusatia (north of Bohemia) as well as Silesia and recognised him as joint ruler, with Wladislaw Jagiello, of Bohemia. The territorial concessions were valid for Matthias's lifetime only; they could be bought back on his death for the sum of 400,000 gold florins. Meanwhile, Matthias had taken other steps to enhance his own prestige and that of the Hungarian crown. In 1476 he had married Beatrix of Aragon, daughter of the King of Naples, a match that gave the Hunyadi name greater respectability in European royal circles. A year later, Matthias occupied much of Lower Austria and extracted from Frederick III, in return for his withdrawal, a substantial payment of 100,000 gold florins and recognition of his right to the Bohemian throne. Frederick's delay in handing over the money gave Matthias the excuse to invade Austria again in 1480 and, after a campaign that brought the whole of eastern Austria into Hungarian occupation, to besiege and finally capture Vienna in 1485. He entered the city he intended to make the capital of his central European empire in triumph, with Queen Beatrix at his side, and in a grand gesture of reconciliation promised to donate a new roof to St. Stephen's Cathedral. In his own terms, therefore, Matthias had achieved his objective: Hungary was now the dominant power in central Europe and respected as a well-ordered, and increasingly cultivated, Christian kingdom. The Holy Roman imperial crown, however, was not to be his: Frederick III's son, Maximilian, was elected Emperor-elect in 1486. Matthias's conquests may have impressed, but they won him few friends.

Matthias Corvinus was by no means oblivious to the Turkish threat—the Papacy constantly nagged him to do something about it; and he did, indeed, achieve significant military successes against the Turks, notably the recapture of the fortress at Jajce in 1463 and of that at Szabács (Šabac) in 1476. But although he had at his disposal a much larger and better-equipped army than any his father had been able to muster and despite the steady erosion of Hungary's southern defences and border regions, which continued, virtually unchecked, throughout his reign, Matthias never mounted a major campaign against the Turks. There were a number of reasons for this. First, as we have seen, a policy of expansion in central Europe appeared to offer greater economic and financial rewards than campaigns in the now virtually barren Balkans. Matthias, moreover, always conscious of his unroyal origins, wished to carve out for himself equal status among the crowned heads of Europe, by giving those nearest at hand a taste of his strength, rather than acting as their virtual mercenary in defending Christendom against the infidel. Matthias would have been reluctant, in any case, to turn his back on Frederick III, who could be relied upon to stick a knife into it given the opportunity. Above all, Matthias simply did not have the financial resources to contemplate sustained campaigning in the south as well as in the north. By the end of his reign, the peasantry, on whom the main burden fell, were being taxed beyond endurance, as constant migrations and minor insurrections showed. Hungary's towns were relatively small—Buda, by far the largest, had a population of only 8,000 compared with Prague's 30,000—and their capacity to lend money to the crown was limited; even the wealthiest, the mining towns, disposed of only a fraction of the wealth of their Italian and German counterparts.[10] Although Hungarian gold, silver and copper production continued to rise,[11] imports of manufactured goods rose even faster; this not only created an annual deficit of between 200 and 300 thousand gold florins but also imposed a continuing inhibition on the development of domestic industry, which could have provided a new taxable resource. As it was, Hungary's small merchant class preferred profits from commerce to risky investment in crafts and manufactures; the more successful merchants put their capital into land in the hope of acquiring noble status.

The lavish style in which Matthias maintained the royal court succeeded in impressing his peers and contemporaries—palaces in Buda, Visegrád and Esztergom were extravagantly refurbished and at the wedding feast after his marriage to Beatrix twenty-four courses were served from 983 dishes—but it imposed a massive burden on the royal treasury. Even without a major campaign against the Turks, the maintenance and manning of the fortresses on the southern defence line absorbed virtually all the crown's normal revenues. Matthias's northern campaigns and the upkeep of the Black Army were financed by extraordinary taxation and forced loans from the towns and barons. Despite squeezing the kingdom dry, Matthias still bequeathed to his successor debts totalling around two million gold florins. For all these reasons, and in the absence of allies prepared to support him in the field as well as with subsidies, it is probably true that a serious counter-attack against the Sultan was not an option for Matthias. But it is equally arguable that his conquests at the expense of Bohemia and Austria were an expensive mistake: they did not survive him for more than a few years and brought no benefit, economic or political, to Hungary. For all his improvements to the machinery of government and his creation of an effective standing army Matthias, when he died in Vienna in 1490, aged only forty-seven, left his kingdom even less well prepared to face a renewed Turkish threat than he had found it.

The reign of Matthias I Corvinus is not, however, honoured in Hungary primarily for his military achievements, nor even for his administrative reforms, but for the fact that, if only for a short span, he brought Hungary into the mainstream of European humanist culture. Under his inspiration Hungary became, for a time, part of the Italian Renaissance.

Cultural life in Fourteenth and Fifteenth-Century Hungary

Until the reign of Sigismund I, cultural activity in Hungary had been scant; foreign visitors frequently commented on the low level of literacy in the country, even among the nobility, and on the poor quality of the written Latin produced by the small literate minority. Three Hungarian barons, all holding high office under the crown, were unable to attach their signatures to the Peace of Pressburg in 1491 because they could not write their names.[12] Education had been confined largely to aspirants for the priesthood, in cathedral schools; in the fourteenth century rudimentary education spread to some parishes and in the towns merchants began to establish grammar schools in which boys could be taught enough of the 'three Rs' to equip them for careers in trade. Although universities had been founded, by Louis the Great in Pécs and by Sigismund in Óbuda (Old

Buda), they quickly succumbed to inadequate funding. Higher education failed to take root in Hungary as it had done in Bohemia and Poland; if they could afford it, Hungarian students undertook their studies in Cracow, Vienna and Prague as well as further afield in Padua, Bologna, Paris and Oxford. The Dominican and Franciscan monasteries provided the main centres of scholarship and art, producing some illuminated manuscripts and miniatures of high quality; but the overall level of activity could not compare with that in neighbouring countries. There were striking individual achievements, among them the history *Gesta Ungarorum* written in the early thirteenth century by 'Magister P', or 'Anonymus', a member of Béla III's chancellery, and a dramatic account of the Mongol invasion, *Carmen miserabile*, by 'Magister Rogerius' which he produced remarkably soon after the event, in 1244. Very little was written in the vernacular until the fifteenth century: among the few surviving examples are a *Funeral Oration*, translated from the Latin in about 1150, the *Lament of Mary*—also a translation but a particularly fine one—dating from the end of the twelfth century and *The Legend of the Blessed Margaret*, an account of the life of the saintly daughter of Béla IV (after whom the *Margit-sziget*, Margaret Island, in Budapest is now named), written in about 1310. The great breakthrough in written Hungarian came in the 1430s with the first Hungarian translation of the Bible, by two Hussite Hungarian priests whose inventive efforts to expand the limited vocabulary of medieval Hungarian, to accommodate the rich vocabulary of the scriptures, helped to create the literary Hungarian language when it was first printed over a century later.

Sigismund, especially after his election to be Holy Roman Emperor, injected new life into this sparsely featured cultural landscape by bringing to his chancellery in Buda several prominent Italian humanists of whom some, including Pier Paolo Vergerio, spent many years in Hungary and brought the new learning to the royal court. Vergerio, an educationist, taught János Vitéz, who in turn became tutor to the young Matthias Hunyadi.

Both from personal inclination and for reasons of state Matthias built energetically and ambitiously on the foundation Sigismund had created. His patronage brought to Hungary, mostly from Italy, numerous scholars, artists and architects whose presence and works helped him to establish a reputation for the royal court in Buda as a vital centre of humanist scholarship and Renaissance art. Matthias's marriage to Beatrix of Aragon, a cultivated lady with a wealth of Italian connexions, gave added impetus to the process. Galeotto Marzio, a true Renaissance figure who combined scientific with classical scholarship, wrote a valuable and perceptive memoir of Matthias's court; the historian Antonio Bonfini was commissioned by Matthias to write a history of Hungary, *Rerum Hungaricarum Decades*; Matthias gave charge of the royal observatory to the German astronomer and inventor of trigonometry, Regiomontanus (Königsberger), whose pioneering work on navigation, used by Christopher Columbus, was dedicated to his Hungarian patron; Filippino Lippi crafted the altarpiece of the royal chapel—the catalogue of cultural activities, of which these are but a few examples, is long and impressive. Matthias's most conspicuous personal contribution was the foundation of the *Bibliotheca Corvina*, the Corvinus Library, which he built up to be one of the foremost collections in Europe. The library eventually contained over two thousand manuscripts, magnificently bound, which acted as a magnet to attract to Buda scholars from all over Europe for colloquia and seminars, on the Italian pattern. Matthias encouraged the establishment in Buda, by András Hess, of Hungary's first printing press which produced a Latin chronicle of Hungarian history in 1472, five years before William Caxton published his first printed book in England.

This striking upsurge of scholarly and artistic activity encouraged the flowering of indigenous talent in Hungary. Much of this, for example the remarkable work of the artist known only by his initials 'M.S.' and, much later, the historical writings of Forgács and Istvánffy, emerged only after Matthias's death; but one native star that shone during his lifetime was that of János Csezmiczei, known to his contemporaries and to posterity as Janus Pannonius. A nephew of János Vitéz, Pannonius received his education in Italy; he was appointed Bishop of Pécs on his return to Hungary at the age of twenty-four and subsequently served as Matthias's diplomatic envoy to the Papacy. His Italian contemporaries acknowledged him to be one of the leading Latin poets of his time. His epigrams, both the profound and the bawdy, were as widely quoted as his elegies were admired. Although he died relatively young, following his condemnation to exile for treason, Pannonius fathered humanist poetry in Hungary; most of his works circulated in Hungarian translation and although they represented a literary genre soon to be largely eclipsed by the Reformation they stimulated a new level of native poetic activity. On a more pedestrian level, the Hungarian notary János Thuróczy produced, in 1488, a synthesis of existing chronicles concerning the history of Hungary, the *Chronica Hungarorum*. Humanist learning provided a useful instrument of royal policy. In his constant campaign for acceptance by the crowned heads of Europe, Matthias was well served by the elegantly drafted correspondence which Vitéz's well-drilled chancellery churned out. The literary skills of Vitéz and Pannonius could also be put to good use in a propaganda role, as Matthias's efforts to justify, to the Papacy in particular, his incarceration of Vlad Dracul ('the Impaler' and the model for the fictional Dracula) demonstrated; a poem by Pannonius detailing Vlad's unpleasant habits reached many influential readers outside Hungary.

In the longer term, Matthias's undoubted achievement in bringing the Renaissance to Hungary produced few lasting results. As an exercise in public relations it succeeded brilliantly and temporarily changed European perceptions of Hungary. Some cultural residue remained, but in most respects Hungarian society rejected the transplant. The 'Hungarian Renaissance' had little domestic impact outside the royal court, where the chancellery remained a busy workshop of humanist scholarship under Matthias's two Jagiellonian successors, and the ecclesiastical hierarchy, many of whose members actively encouraged art and learning in their sees; but the barons and nobility remained, for the most part, unimpressed—secular patronage of the arts and scholarship did not become significant for a generation. Possessing neither a university nor a cathedral, Budapest had little chance of joining Prague, Cracow and Vienna as a major centre of intellectual activity in central Europe. Matthias's proudest legacy, the Corvinus Library, was to be destroyed within fifty years. The university he had founded at Pozsony (Bratislava) disappeared even more quickly. As soon as Matthias Corvinus had been interred at Székesfehérvár on 24 April, 1490, Hungary turned in upon itself in another spasm of self-mutilation.

FROM LIGHT INTO DARKNESS (1444–1526)

Towards Mohács

Medieval Hungary's last thirty years were marked by the destruction of the centralised authority Matthias Corvinus had established, by a massive revival of baronial power and by renewed tension between the barons and the lesser nobility. Both barons and nobles made common cause, however, in ensuring that Matthias would be succeeded by a weak ruler whom the Royal Council and the Diet could control. This ruled out two of the leading claimants to the succession: Matthias's natural son, János Corvinus, who would have continued his father's policies; and, despite Matthias's 1463 agreement with Frederick III, his son Maximilian I (who would succeed Frederick as Emperor). Instead, the Diet plumped for Wladislaw Jagiello, co-ruler with Matthias of Bohemia, who was crowned Wladislas II of Hungary in September 1490. Maximilian Habsburg, outraged by this breach of the promise made to his father, at once invaded Hungary and occupied much of the western part of the country. After prolonged negotiations, he was persuaded to withdraw by the promise of both the Hungarian and the Bohemian crowns if Wladislas died childless, together with the restitution of the Austrian provinces seized by Matthias and a payment of 100,000 gold florins; these arrangements were enshrined in the Peace of Pressburg in 1491. János Corvinus, for his part, received the title of King of Bosnia in return for withdrawing his claim (he subsequently died fighting the Turks); and Queen Beatrix, who had political ambitions of her own, was silenced by a secret and deliberately invalid marriage to Wladislas that Pope Alexander VI declared null and void a few years later. The Royal Council then proceeded to destroy the main surviving instrument of royal power, Matthias's Black Army, by sending it south against the Turks unprovisioned and then, when it perforce resorted to looting, ordering its annihilation by a force of *banderia* led by one of Matthias's leading captains, Pál Kinizsi.

Wladislas II, who either brought with him or very quickly acquired the nickname 'Dobzhe' (the Polish for 'OK') because of his inclination to agree to any proposal put before him, suited the barons and the nobility very well. Power ebbed away from the crown and its revenues shrank. The Diet resolved that half of the money raised for national defence, the special tax or *subsidium* introduced by Matthias I, should now be allocated to a group of forty named barons authorised to raise mercenaries of their own. In addition to their other burdens, the towns and the peasantry were thus compelled to finance baronial private armies. The new arrangements also had the effect of increasing the power of the wealthiest barons, downgrading to the level of untitled nobility those excluded from the *subsidium* windfall and widening the gulf between the greater and lesser nobility. The lesser nobility, commanding as they did a majority in the Diet, also profited from the weakness of the crown. Excluded from the Royal Council by the barons, shortly after Wladislas's accession, the Diet won royal assent in 1500 to a law by which the four barons and four bishops who made up that body would in future be joined by sixteen representatives of the nobility. In 1504 the Diet ruled illegal any tax levied without its express consent and forbade the raising of forced loans under the guise of 'gifts' to the crown. The Diet also demanded a larger say in the perennially vexed question of the succession: when in 1505 Wladislas declined to approve a law prohibiting the election of any foreigner to the Hungarian throne, the Diet demanded his abdication and the election of a leading baron and Governor-General of Transylvania, János (John) Szapolyai, in his place. Szapolyai hoped for the support of King Sigismund I of Poland in his bid for the crown. Wladislas and his supporters at court looked to Emperor Maximilian Habsburg for help: not only, in their view, would a Habsburg succession be preferable to a constitutional victory for Szapolyai and the Diet, but the Habsburgs represented Hungary's only hope of securing military aid against the Ottomans.

In July 1515, a meeting was arranged in Vienna between Wladislas, Maximilian and Sigismund which in many respects determined the future of central Europe. Sigismund promised to support Habsburg dynastic ambitions in Hungary instead of Szapolyai's; Maximilian, in return, undertook to withdraw support from the Teutonic Knights in their hostilities against Poland; and Wladislas agreed to a 'double marriage' that would bind the Jagiellos firmly to the Habsburgs: Louis, Wladislas's heir, was to marry Maximilian's granddaughter Maria and Louis's sister Anne would marry either Maximilian himself or Ferdinand, one of his grandsons. This contract was to result in four centuries of Habsburg rule in Hungary.

Meanwhile, a development of central importance to the future of the nobility—and to the future of Hungary—was in gestation. For several years István Werbőczy, a professional jurist who had been politically active in defence of the rights of the lesser nobility *vis-à-vis* the barons, had been working on a codification of the statute and customary law of Hungary: the *Tripartitum Opus Juris Consuetudinarii Inclyti Regni Hungariae*, known as the *Tripartitum* ('Three-parter') for short. The work had been commissioned by the Diet, with the object of drawing together all the fundamental laws of the kingdom, particularly those that had a bearing on the rights of the nobility and its relationship to the crown. As Werbőczy noted in his preface: 'The laws of Hungary and the edicts of dead kings [are] confused, disconnected and often contradictory, and so liable to give rise to internal dissension, which is more injurious than foreign wars'.[13] Werbőczy, and his fellow nobles who commissioned the study, had a clear idea of the conclusions they wished to emerge from it; and his research duly supported them. They were dramatic. The Hungarian nobility and the Hungarian nation, Werbőczy argued, were one and the same. The Holy Crown, irrespective of who wore it at a given time, was the symbol of the noble community, all the members of which—be they bishops, barons or mere nobles—'enjoy one and the same liberty'. Laws could be made only with the consent and approval of both king and people (i.e. the nobility); there could be no king save by noble election and only the king could confer nobility (this was not strictly true—the Diet had gained a right of veto). A noble was subject only to the authority of the crowned king and could not be arrested or imprisoned without due legal process. Nobles could dispose of their income (but not their land, the essential attribute of their nobility) as they wished but were exempt from 'all services, taxes, contributions, tribute or other obligations save that of military service in defence of the kingdom'. Moreover, the nobility had the right to resist the king should he interfere with the rights and privileges of 'the nation'. None of these elements was new in itself—the Golden Bull had included most of them—but their codification gave them added potency. The main novelty lay in Werbőczy's exclusive concept of 'the nation' which implied the complete absence of rights for all non-nobles, or *misera plebs con-*

tribuens ('the wretched taxed common people') as Werbőczy called them. They, the *jobbágyság*, could not acquire land since all land was in the gift of the Holy Crown. They were nothing. As one Hungarian historian has commented,[14] the *Tripartitum* "buried alive" two and a half million *jobbágy*. It did so because, although Werbőczy's codification never itself formally became law, it was given royal approval by Wladislas II in 1514 and, once it had been printed in Vienna three years later, became the bible of the nobility; indeed, after being republished eleven times during the sixteenth century, it was more likely to be found in a noble household than the Bible itself. The *Tripartitum* determined the self-perception and the behaviour of the Hungarian nobility for the next four centuries. Its malign influence derived added force from the fact that its appearance coincided with the largest peasant revolt in the history of the kingdom.

Even without Werbőczy, conditions of life for the *jobbágyság* had deteriorated sharply. On top of the increased burden of taxation imposed by Matthias's military campaigns and personal extravagance, the recrudescence of baronial and noble power under his successor was bound to have adverse consequences for those who worked the land. In 1492, the Diet had passed a law ruling that peasants could migrate from one estate to another only with the consent of their landlord, which would be withheld if there were debts outstanding. A few years later the Diet imposed a new tax on livestock—including even bees—and required every tenth sheep to be handed over to the landlord; and in 1504 peasants were deprived of the rights of hunting and fowling, a major blow to their standard of living. Because the nobility was keen to profit from the growing demand in western Europe for agricultural produce, labour dues, hitherto relatively light, had been drastically increased by most landlords, sometimes to as much as three days a week, in order to boost output. It was thus against a background of deepening rural misery that Archbishop Bakócz of Esztergom, in 1514, proclaimed a crusade against the Turks.

Bakócz, an intelligent and thoroughly unscrupulous priest, had just been disappointed in his ambition of securing election to the Papacy; he had been engaged in an expensive campaign of self-promotion for two years in Rome. When the vote went to Leo X, Bakócz was given the consolation prize of appointment to be Papal Legate in all of east central Europe with authority to launch a Crusade. He did so, despite the misgivings of most of the barons, who considered it too risky to put arms into the hands of the peasantry and in any case resented the loss of labour from their estates. In the event, it was precisely the peasants who responded to Bakócz's call with the greatest enthusiasm, taking full advantage of a licence to desert the privations of their villages: over 40,000 rallied to the banner, raised outside Pest, of György Székely (more usually known as Dózsa), a soldier from the lesser nobility to whom Bakócz had entrusted the leadership of the Crusade. The barons and most of the nobility had no appetite for a campaign and stayed at home. As Dózsa marched south at the head of a rapidly growing peasant army, Bakócz belatedly heeded baronial concerns, called off the Crusade and instructed the friars accompanying the crusaders to order the peasants back to their villages. This turned an already unruly enterprise into a full-scale revolt. The natural hostility of the peasants towards their landlords, intensified by the latter's refusal to join them in fighting the infidel, exploded into violent rebellion with Dózsa, who made common cause with his men, at its head. Burning and looting as it went, Dózsa's army crossed the Great Plain and reached south-east Hungary, where it laid siege to the fortress of Temesvár. János Szapolyai, Voivod of Transylvania, had meanwhile resurrected the Union of Three Nations, of Hungarians, Saxons and Székelys, and mobilised a noble army to raise the siege. Szapolyai's relatively well-ordered force quickly prevailed over the much larger but raggle-taggle peasant army, relieving Temesvár and ending the rebellion.

The dreadfulness of the sequel surpassed any of the excesses of the peasant revolt itself. His captors chained György Dózsa to a red-hot iron 'throne', placed an iron 'crown', also red-hot, on his head and then compelled some of his leading supporters to eat his roasting flesh before they, too, were executed. Of more lasting malevolence was the vengeful legislation proposed by the Diet in October 1514 and approved by the king: this deprived the peasantry of any right to migration, condemning it to 'perpetual servitude'; imposed a new tax of one gold florin, twelve chickens and two geese annually as compensation for the damage wrought by the rebellion; and established a landlord's right to claim at least one day's unpaid labour every week. The same Diet, as it happened, took delivery of Werbőczi's *Tripartitum*, which provided the ideological and legal underpinning for this punitive legislation: together, they condemned the Hungarian *jobbágyság* to a status not far removed from serfdom which, despite the subsequent repeal of some elements in the new laws and the weak enforcement of others, endured until 1848.

The war of attrition on Hungary's southern borders had meanwhile continued spasmodically, despite the regular conclusion of truces and Sultan Selim's preoccupations with the expansion of the Ottoman Empire in other directions. The Hungarians had not been supine; János Szapolyai in particular had led raids into Bulgaria and Serbia, which hurt the Turks but failed significantly to weaken their grip on the Balkans. The Turks, for their part, overran fortresses in Bosnia in 1512, which brought their occupation forces to the Sava River, part of Hungary's crucial defence line; they cannot but have been aware, moreover, of the steady deterioration of the Hungarian defence system which lack of resources and neglect had brought about. Hungary's weakness was further advertised when Wladislas II, who died in 1516, was succeeded by his ten-year-old son Louis II (1516–26), leaving the governance of the kingdom in the hands of the faction-riven Royal Council. When, therefore, Selim's successor Suleiman ('the Great') sent an ambassador to Buda in 1520 with the offer of a renewed truce he doubtless expected a favourable response: inexplicably, the Royal Council rejected the offer and imprisoned the envoy. Perhaps the Council was concerned that Hungary should cut a brave figure in the eyes of the Western powers who constantly urged it to stand up to the infidel; at all events, its action ensured a robust Turkish response to the insult. This was not long in coming. During a short campaign in the summer of 1521, Suleiman's forces captured, in succession, the fortresses of Szabács, Zimony (Zemin) and, with greater difficulty, Belgrade. János Hunyadi's brave achievement of sixty-five years before was annulled; Hungary's southern defences had been comprehensively breached and the way to the Carpathian Basin lay open. Only the end of the campaigning season and preoccupations elsewhere within the empire prevented Suleiman from advancing down it at once.

The Hungarian kingdom, accustomed as it was to troughs in its fortunes, had seldom been less well prepared for the inevitable renewal of the Ottoman advance or for the national crisis it would bring. Louis II's marriage, in 1521 at the age of sixteen, to Maria of Habsburg—a lady of strong character, sister of the Emperor Charles V and of Archduke Ferdinand of Austria—injected new muscle into the so-called 'court party' and strengthened the Habsburg grip on the eventual succession. But it also further divided the barons and the nobility, some of whom were quite ready to abandon their 'national', anti–Habsburg enthusiasms for the prospect of royal favour and elevation. As Charles V's ambassador to Hungary reported:

If the Hungarians were united, we are told, the richness of their country would enable them to defend it in the face of any enemy. But they are of the worst type in the world, everyone is seeking his own profit and, if he can, lives on the fat of public property. They have no esteem for other countries. Though they feast together as if they were all brothers, surreptitiously they fight each other. There is no case so evil that it should not be won by the bribing of two or three men. They are haughty and proud, unable to command and to obey but unwilling to accept advice. They work little as they spend their time with feasting and intrigues.[15]

This dyspeptic assessment may have been overdrawn but, leaving personal qualities aside, there was no disguising the dire condition of Hungary's economy and finances. Wladislas II and Louis II both resorted to that old standby of medieval Hungarian kings, the regular debasement of the coinage, in order to boost royal revenue. This, as a Hungarian expert has commented, 'had catastrophic consequences; by 1526 it had rendered the long latent but growing economic and political crisis so deep and encompassing that the state seemed to disintegrate even without the intervention of the Turks'.[16] In a despatch to its envoy in Rome, the Royal Council complained that 'Hungary's meagre revenues are insufficient for the defence of such an extensive line of border fortresses … 32,000 golden pieces [florins] are needed every year to pay the bans of Croatia and to supply the country's castles … while [other fortresses] absorb incredible sums each year'.[17] The Ambassador's reaction, all the more remarkable since he was a bishop, was to note that 'Hungary's only refuge is friendship with the Turks'. In 1525 the Diet chose that of all moments to accuse the Fuggers, the German family of financiers that funded the Hungarian mining industry, of swindling the crown. Louis's officers arrested the Fuggers' representative in Buda; royal decrees froze the family's assets in Hungary and ordered an examination of their accounts. In retaliation the Fuggers, who as a family matched the power of most contemporary kingdoms, having enlisted the support of the Emperor and Pope Clement VII, threatened to close down Hungary's mines and put an end to the export, which they controlled, of Hungarian gold, silver and copper. In a humiliating climb-down, Hungary was obliged to withdraw its accusations and to pay substantial damages to the Fuggers. This was just one instance of the apparent determination of the Hungarian court and the Hungarian Diet to alienate all their friends when they needed them most; just at the time, indeed, when Hungarian envoys were touring the kingdoms of Europe with pleas for financial and military assistance against the Turks. The King of Poland, Sigismund, offered to include Hungary in a peace treaty he was negotiating with Suleiman: Louis ignored him. Venice made Hungary an offer of alliance: Louis rejected it on the grounds that Venice had failed to pay an old debt to the Hungarian crown. Small wonder, then, that Hungary was left to face the Turks alone. To be fair to Louis and his advisers, western Europe would almost certainly have abandoned Hungary in any case (as it would in the future, too); but Hungary perversely provided it with excuses for turning its back.

Suleiman, meanwhile, had forced the Knights of St John on the island of Rhodes to surrender after a long siege (they moved to Malta) and had quelled a revolt against Ottoman rule in Egypt; he was ready to contemplate the next significant expansion of his empire. Although an influential group of advisers at the Ottoman court had been lobbying for some time in favour of prosecuting the next phase of the *gaza* (holy war) by sea rather than on land—partly to protect Turkish trading interests against Western, especially Portuguese, naval depradations and partly to challenge the Christian monopoly of maritime discoveries— Suleiman found compelling reasons for resuming expansion northwards into Europe. In the Habsburg Emperor, Charles V, he saw his principal rival for mastery of the known world; and his concerns over the growth of Habsburg power, already aroused by the 'double marriage' agreement of 1515 that assured the Habsburgs of the Hungarian succession, were sharpened by Charles's decisive victory over Francis I of France at Pavia in 1525. Francis, Suleiman's natural ally, had subsequently smuggled from captivity an appeal to the Sultan for his intervention to curb Habsburg hegemony. At the same time, a serious mutiny of janissaries in Istanbul (Constantinople) reminded Suleiman of the political risks involved in keeping a standing army inactive and deprived of loot for too long. Reports from scouts and spies, moreover, made Suleiman aware of Hungary's continuing weakness and failure to reinforce or even adequately to maintain the southern fortresses. All these factors argued for a renewed assault on Hungary. At the end of 1525 Suleiman ordered the mobilisation of his armies in southern Europe: on 23 April, 1526 he led a force of some hundred thousand troops northwards from Istanbul.

Historians continue to argue about the real nature of Suleiman's intentions towards Hungary. The traditional view has been that the Sultan, driven by the spirit of *gaza*, was determined to engage in a trial of strength with Charles V, the leader of Christendom, and to occupy as much as possible of the territory, including Hungary, that stood between them. Suleiman's subsequent campaigns of 1529 and 1532, which took him to the gates of Vienna, are adduced as evidence in support of that view. Against this it has been argued that Suleiman wanted no more than to prevent Hungary from falling into Habsburg hands; his preferred objective was to secure its submission as a vassal state so that it would constitute a compliant buffer between the two empires. Adherents to this view maintain that Hungary lay beyond the geographical limit of manageable direct Ottoman rule: lines of communication with Istanbul were simply too long; and that occupation of the whole country would have imposed an unacceptable drain on Suleiman's treasury. This assessment might be held to attribute to Ottoman policy a greater degree of rationality than it displayed in some other contexts; but, on balance, it is more plausible than the traditional interpretation and is supported by Suleiman's subsequent treatment of Transylvania. The significance of the controversy lies in its implications for a judgement on Hungarian policies at the time. If Suleiman was hell-bent on conquest, Louis II and his Royal Council were justified in rejecting Turkish offers of a long-term truce such as the one Suleiman's envoys put forward in 1520; but if the offers were sincere the Hungarians, knowing as they did from bitter experience that they could expect no assistance from the rest of Europe, might have been wiser to accept vassalage in preference to virtually certain military defeat. But this conclusion is easier to reach with hindsight than it would have been at the time. It was no light matter for a Christian monarch, with his due share of self-esteem, to contemplate a deal with Islam; military defeat, moreover, seemed by no means a certainty: Hungarian victory over the Turks in a skirmish at Jajce in 1524 boosted confidence in Hungarian arms. Rightly or wrongly, therefore, it was probably inevitable that the Diet assembled on the Field of Rákos, outside Pest, at the end of April, 1526 should have approved Louis II's conduct of policy during the previous year and ordered preparations for a defensive military campaign. A month later, the Royal Council decreed that the noble levy should assemble at Tolna on 2 July and mobilised the *banderia*. Although the Turkish force had by now penetrated beyond Belgrade, these calls to arms met with only a minimal and grudging response, even in the southern regions most directly threatened. Many barons, especially those opposed to Habsburg influence, looked the other way; the lesser nobles were reluctant to leave their estates at harvest time. Only a few hundred had assembled at Tolna by the appointed day; and when Louis II rode out of Buda on 20 July, he headed a force of only 4,000 men.

Slow mobilisation and mutinous behaviour on the part of the barons, the majority of whom refused to embark on a pre-emptive march south until the King could lead them himself, enabled the Turks to cross first the Sava River and then the Drava virtually unopposed, depriving the Hungarians of the only natural lines of defence remaining to them. The fortresses of Pétervárad, Újlak and Eszék had succumbed to the Turkish advance with only minimal resistance. The Hungarian mobilisation, however, had at last begun to gather some momentum and by the time Louis reached Mohács on 23 August his army numbered some 25,000 men with further contingents of Bohemian and Polish mercenaries expected at any time. The Voivod of Transylvania, János Szapolyai, had meanwhile been ordered to conduct a diversionary operation through Wallachia in order to compel Suleiman to detach part of his force to protect his right flank. This would have been an intelligent strategy if it had been initiated sooner and then carried through; in the event, Louis countermanded Szapolyai's orders at the last minute and summoned him to Mohács; Szapolyai consequently spent the whole of this crucial five-week period marching and counter-marching without at any time engaging the enemy. At Mohács, command of the Hungarian force was divided between Archbishop Tomori of Kalocsa and János Szapolyai's brother, György. As reports arrived of the continuing Turkish advance, Louis was bombarded with conflicting tactical advice. Some favoured a reversion to traditional Hungarian frontier tactics: the creation of a scorched-earth zone behind which the defenders could withdraw, sucking the invader in and attacking when his supplies were low. Others argued for a static defence at Mohács, tempting the Turks to exhaust themselves against well-prepared positions before subjecting them to a massive counter-attack. The issue was decided by the speed of the Turkish advance: a strategic retreat would have been transformed into a rout by the pursuing Turkish cavalry and there was no time to prepare elaborate defensive positions. The only course open to Louis, despite his justified misgivings, was to risk everything in a pitched battle at Mohács.

During the morning and afternoon of 29 August, the Hungarian army, positioned across the width of the small Mohács plain with a stream at its back, watched Suleiman's screen of scouts and light cavalry and then his main force of about 60,000 cavalry and infantry (some units having been dropped off during the advance to garrison fortresses and protect supply lines) arrive on the battlefield. At about four o'clock, while the Turkish troops were still in movement, Louis reluctantly acceded to Tomori's request to attack before the enemy's deployment had been completed. The first line of Hungarian cavalry hurled itself against its Turkish counterpart and made good progress, with infantry following up behind, until it came up against the main contingent of crack Turkish infantry, with the janissaries at its core. The Turkish artillery, positioned behind a fold in the ground and invisible to the charging Hungarians until the last minute, fired a massive salvo and, although most of its shot passed over Hungarian heads, this, together with disciplined volleys from the muskets of the janissaries, brought the advance to a virtual standstill. Tomori then ordered flanking movements by Hungarian cavalry contingents; these had some initial success but failed to get behind the Turkish artillery and infantry in sufficient numbers to make a decisive impact. Tomori therefore called up the remainder of the Hungarian force, led by the King. As the first line had done, it charged full tilt against the Turkish centre and met with the same devastating response. Suleiman now ordered a counterattack on both flanks, a pincer movement that quickly succeeded in enveloping the entire Hungarian army. The ensuing slaughter was virtually total: very few, mainly mercenary infantry, escaped. Over 20,000 of those whom Louis had led to Mohács perished there, including twenty-eight barons and over five hundred nobles. Tomori and György Szapolyai were killed. King Louis, wounded, fell from his horse while attempting to cross the stream in the Hungarian rear and died there. The battle had lasted barely three hours. Suleiman the Great, whose casualties amounted to no more than 3,000, marched on to Buda, loaded his river galleys with everything of value in the city—including the entire Corvina Library, every statue, candelabra and church bell—and led his troops southwards again to their winter quarters. Deprived of its King, its ruling caste, most of its Church hierarchy and many of its landowners, the medieval kingdom of Hungary had been mortally wounded. It would bleed for a further fifteen years and then expire.

Could this catastrophe have been prevented? Arguments over the rights and wrongs of Hungarian tactics at Mohács itself are surely irrelevant. Once a Turkish sultan had decided to use his formidably large, disciplined and well-equipped army to subjugate Hungary—whether or not with the intention of conquest and occupation—the outcome of a pitched battle in which Hungary stood alone against the invader, wherever it were to be fought, could not be in doubt. It has been argued by some Hungarian military historians that Hungary's main southern line of defence should have been established along the Sava or even the Drava River rather than along the more distant 'Scolari line', running west and east of Belgrade, which it was beyond Hungary's capacity effectively to maintain and hold. From the logistical viewpoint, there is clearly force in this contention although its feasibility in practice is open to question.[18] Politically, however, it could never have been a realistic option since it would have left most of Croatia, an integral part of the Hungarian kingdom since the twelfth century, beyond the defensive pale; no Hungarian ruler could have been expected to contemplate this. The hard truth is that unless Hungarian society had developed very differently, the human and economic resources of the Carpathian Basin together with Transylvania were adequate for the defence of that relatively compact region but of little, if anything, beyond it. The fundamental weakness of the Hungarian kingdom had been disguised at critical junctures by the outstanding abilities and courage of a few individuals, the two Bélas, Louis I and the two Hunyadis among them. But medieval Hungary's periods of ascendancy and expansion had alternated with troughs of misrule and internal division. If one of these troughs were to coincide with a challenge from a powerful and determined foe, the essential vulnerability of the kingdom would inevitably be exposed. The southward extension of Hungary's borders at the end of the eleventh century had already contained the seeds of the disaster at Mohács over three hundred years later. The era of the Árpáds, Anjous, Hunyadis and Jagiellos had nevertheless given the Hungarian kingdom the experience of greatness, for which a certain nostalgia lingered among its people during the succeeding centuries. To few other peoples does their medieval past mean so much.

Part Two

THE HABSBURG KINGDOM

5

HUNGARY DIVIDED

(1526–1711)

Civil War (1526–41)

The Mohács disaster left Hungary prostrate. For the next fifteen years, the dying kingdom became a battlefield over which the Turks and the mercenary armies employed by the two rival claimants to the Hungarian crown sporadically fought and pillaged. The Diet, or what was left of it after the slaughter at Mohács, assembled at Székesfehérvár on 10 November and elected János (John) Szapolyai, Voivod of Transylvania, to the throne. His coronation, with the Holy Crown, took place on the following day. Szapolyai, having failed to join battle at Mohács—whether by design, as his opponents claimed, or because of royal mismanagement—now commanded the only viable Hungarian fighting force. Even before the battle, his power-base in Transylvania, his personal wealth and his vast estates had given him formidable authority and influence; *vis-à-vis* his Habsburg rival, his Hungarian nationality was a powerful asset. The rival claim of Ferdinand Habsburg, King of Bohemia and Archduke of Austria, rested on his marriage to Anne, daughter of Wladislas II, and that of his sister, Maria, to the late King Louis II. It had the support of a small number of barons, led by the Palatine István Báthory, for whom the harsh lesson of Mohács had been that Hungary could not hope to withstand the Turks without a foreign ally; they attended a Diet in Pozsony at which, on 17 December, Ferdinand was elected King of Hungary. Each side now set about winning support against the other. John I, as Szapolyai had become, convened a Diet in Buda early in 1527 that loyally voted to donate to him one tenth of all personal property to fund defence against the Turks; it declared contact of any kind with Ferdinand to be treasonous. Ferdinand, displaying remarkably advanced public relations skills, despatched to his sister Queen Maria seventy-nine personally signed letters appealing for support, which she was asked to date and distribute to all barons and bishops; he also let it be known that supporters of John I who switched their allegiance could expect to be rewarded handsomely with money and advancement. In a final throw before resorting to force, Ferdinand offered John I 300,000 florins for his abdication. When this was indignantly rejected, Habsburg mercenaries, paid for by the Fugger family, marched into Hungary and entered Buda in August, 1527: two months later, Ferdinand was crowned in Székesfehérvár with the Holy Crown, which had been filched from John by a turncoat baron. It was symbolic of the complete collapse of morale in Hungary that the coronations of both John I and Ferdinand I were performed by the same bishop, of Nyitra: similarly, it was not uncommon at this time for nobles with two sons to play safe by sending one to each of the rival courts.

Driven by Ferdinand's military success to seek temporary refuge in Poland, John I sought to enlist foreign allies. Henry VIII of England politely declined to involve himself in Hungarian affairs but Francis I of France promised financial support if John would resume hostilities against France's permanent enemy, the Habsburgs. Welcome though this was, it could not by itself solve the immediate problem of ousting Ferdinand's troops from Buda. John was now obliged to think the hitherto unthinkable: after agonised deliberation and reference to holy scripture, he despatched a Polish emissary, Jerome Laski, to Constantinople with instructions to seek military assistance from the Sultan. Suleiman, already allied with Francis I as an insurance against Habsburg expansion, proved surprisingly amenable. By the new year (1528), Laski was able to return to Poland with a signed treaty in which Suleiman graciously 'restored' the kingdom of Hungary to John I and promised military aid against Ferdinand in due course; unusually, no tribute was demanded of the Hungarians. John returned from Poland to eastern Hungary, where he rallied significant support. In 1529 Suleiman kept his promise by leading a large Turkish army into Hungary and, with a good eye for dramatic effect but little respect for Hungarian feelings, met John I with considerable pomp on the blood-soaked field of Mohács. John kissed the Sultan's hand—an act for which he was subsequently excommunicated by Pope Clement VII—and presented him with a ring that had belonged to Matthias Corvinus. A member of John's entourage[1] recorded agreement between John and Suleiman that 'we be allowed to live by our own laws and that we may retain the country in peace, without having to pay tribute or accept [Turkish] sovereignty'. John had nevertheless embarked on a risky course that could have turned popular opinion, and the nobility, against his cause; fortunately for him, Ferdinand's mercenaries had engaged in such unbridled rapine and looting that hatred of the Habsburgs eclipsed aversion to an accommodation with the infidel. Suleiman marched from Mohács to Buda, recaptured the town, presented John I with the Holy Crown, which Turkish troops had 'liberated', and went on to besiege Vienna, where the city's defenders managed to hold out until the approach of winter compelled Suleiman to withdraw. His next attempt to lay siege to the Habsburg capital, in 1532, was frustrated by the heroic and successful defence of the fortress of Kőszeg, which stood in his path, by Miklós Jurisics and a Hungarian garrison of just forty men.

There followed a decade during which the Sultan devoted his attention to problems more central to Turkish interests, in Persia and North Africa, and which was marked in Hungary by inconclusive campaigning and half-hearted negotiation. Ferdinand attempted to supplant John I in Suleiman's favour by opening negotiations with the Porte, without success. Aloise Gritti, the Venetian whom Suleiman had appointed to govern Buda in John I's interest, turned his coat, opened negotiations with Ferdinand and paid for his treachery with his head. John himself made overtures to Ferdinand when, with the Turks temporarily out of the frame, Habsburg troops began to gain the upper hand. The nobility, mean-while, exasperated by the continuing devastation of their estates by rival merce-nary bands, brought increasing pressure to bear on the two Kings to compose their differences. The result was the secret Treaty of Várad (1538) which promised the Holy Crown to Ferdinand if John were to predecease him, even with an heir; if Ferdinand and his brother, the Emperor Charles V, were both to die first, the crown would remain with John and his heirs. Ferdinand relinquished his claim to Transylvania and undertook to defend Hungary against the Turks; John gave up his claim to Croatia and Slavonia. This compromise lasted only as long as it took John to marry Isabella of Poland and produce an heir, János Zsigmond. Two weeks later, John I was dead, the last Hungarian to wear King St Stephen's crown. After hesitating for two months, Queen Isabella took it upon herself to repudiate the treaty of Várad and arrange for the election and coronation of her infant son.

In the autumn of 1540 two emissaries arrived in Constantinople. The first, the aged István Werbőczy, came on behalf of the Szapolyai party to inform the Sultan of the infant János Zsigmond's election (at a hurriedly convened Diet in Buda) to the Hungarian throne and to seek his help against the latest Habsburg invasion. The second, none other than the same Jerome Laski who had previously inter-ceded on behalf of John I, now came on behalf of the Habsburg party to inform the Sultan of the Treaty of Várad, under the terms of which the succession should pass to Ferdinand. Understandably infuriated by this revelation of his protégé John I's clandestine, albeit abortive, agreement with Ferdinand, Suleiman II's reaction was none the less considered and deliberate. In the following summer, he led his army northwards and by August 1541 had encamped beneath the walls of Buda; a Habsburg force which had been about to lay siege to the town melted away. Precisely on the fifteenth anniversary of the Battle of Mohács, the Sultan received in his camp a large delegation of leading Szapolyai supporters and announced that János Zsigmond would be permitted to rule the lands east of the River Tisza, including Transylvania, but as a vassal of the Porte and for an annual tribute of 10,000 florins. While this was going on, Turkish soldiers entered Buda, ostensibly as sightseers, and quietly took over the town, beginning an occupation that was to last until 1686.

Suleiman II had evidently concluded that he could not expect to hold the whole of Hungary against the Habsburgs: supply lines and marching distances from the heartland of the Ottoman Empire to north-west Hungary were simply too long, with a typical transit time of between six and eight weeks. He had therefore opted for a tripartite division of the country. Ferdinand would be con-fined to the northern and north-western regions; subject to their good behaviour, János Zsigmond and his mother would rule in the east, essentially over a Turkish protectorate; the remainder of Hungary—a triangle with one tip resting on the confluence of the Drava and Tisza Rivers—would be occupied and absorbed into the Ottoman Empire. This was the most economical solution to the problem of neutralising the Habsburg threat to Turkish interests, which required the denial of southern Hungary, Transylvania and the Balkans to a hostile power. During the next four years, Suleiman consolidated the Turkish military presence in the zone of occupation by establishing garrisons in Pécs, Siklós, Székesfehérvár, Esztergom, Visegrád, Nógrád and Hatvan. Ferdinand made two half-hearted attempts to regain Buda but eventually had to reconcile himself to holding only what he already had. In 1547, in the first Peace of Edirne, a five-year truce was agreed. Suleiman recognised Ferdinand, de facto, as ruler of the crescent of territory later known as Royal Hungary; in return, Ferdinand recognised János Zsigmond as ruler of eastern Hungary, including Transylvania, and agreed to pay Suleiman a tribute of 30,000 florins a year.

The delineation of divided Hungary, as it was to remain for nearly a century and a half, had now been virtually completed. There was one dramatic postscript. The principal adviser to John I during the last years of his life had been György Martinuzzi, known then and since as Brother György. A friar from Croatia, Brother György rose to become Bishop of Várad and then Royal Treasurer; despite his origins, he had a deep commitment to the ideal that gave the Szapolyai party its *raison d'être*, that of restoring unity to Hungary under a single crowned head. On his deathbed, John I had entrusted to Brother György the care of his Queen, his heir and his realm. In a decade of virtuoso statecraft, Brother György did everything possible to advance the cause of a reunited Hungary. Although he accepted, on Queen Isabella's behalf, Suleiman II's offer of the eastern lands to János Zsigmond, he did so only to buy time for the development of his longer-term strategy; he saw in Ferdinand Habsburg Hungary's only hope of confronting the Turkish threat as a united kingdom. In secret overtures to the Habsburg party it was agreed that Ferdinand would 'invade' Transylvania, unopposed, and present the Turks with a *fait accompli*. Ferdinand, short of funds as ever, sent a suspiciously small army: 7,000 mercenaries under General Castaldo. Brother Gyorgy and Castaldo then presided over the conclusion of the Treaty of Gyulafehérvár (1551) in which Queen Isabella, on behalf of her infant son, renounced the Holy Crown in favour of Ferdinand and recognised his descendants as heirs to the Hungarian throne; she accepted in return a Silesian dukedom and a Habsburg bride for János Zsigmond, together with 140,000 florins for herself. Despite feverish diplomatic activity by Brother György, the Sultan smelt a rat; while Castaldo, suspicious of Brother György's placatory contacts with the Turks, arranged his assassination. Suleiman's revenge was swift and comprehensive: in 1552, two Turkish armies, under the Grand Vizier and the Pasha (Governor) of Buda, rolled up virtually all the Habsburg defensive positions on the southern border of the territory controlled by Ferdinand—Ipolyság, Drégely, Szécsény, Hollókő and Veszprém among them—and also added to the Turkish-occupied zone most of the land between the Tisza and Transylvania by taking over Temesvár and Szolnok. Only the town of Eger, in a heroic thirty-eight-day defence by its small garrison and the townspeople under István Dobó, defied the Turks until the onset of winter brought the punitive campaign to an end.[2]

After handing over the Holy Crown to Castaldo, Queen Isabella and János Zsigmond had moved to their new estates in Silesia and thence to Isabella's native Poland. In 1556 the Sultan instructed the Diet of the eastern kingdom to recall and reinstate them. As a result of the last Turkish campaign, their kingdom now consisted virtually of Transylvania alone. Thus began a period of over a century during which Transylvania, a vassal state but at least free from foreign occupation, became the focus of Hungarian aspirations for independence and the custodian of Hungarian culture. The character of the new mini–state was partly defined by the impact of the Reformation.

The Reformation in Hungary

Throughout western and central Europe during the sixteenth century, religion was the object of intense enquiry, debate and often conflict. Disgust with the trough of superstition and greed into which the Church of Rome had fallen found expression in the preaching and writings of several remarkable individuals, among them Martin Luther, Ulrich Zwingli and John Calvin, whose views and beliefs found an unprecedentedly wide audience thanks to the rapid development of printing. The Protestant movement for reform reached Hungary shortly after the publication of the Reformation's manifesto and statement of Lutheran belief, the Confession of Augsburg, in 1530. Partly because of a widespread belief that the disasters recently inflicted on Hungary represented God's judgment on the arrogance and materialism of its Catholic Church; partly because Protestant use of the vernacular had great appeal; but mainly on the strength of the simplicity and directness of its doctrine, the Reformation in Hungary gained ground with astonishing speed. As the years passed, resentment against foreign domination, whether Habsburg or Turkish, gave the movement even greater momentum. By 1600, nine-tenths of the Hungarian population had abandoned Catholicism and had embraced one or other of the reforming creeds.

Although Lutheranism was the vanguard of the Reformation in Hungary, as elsewhere, Calvin's doctrine of predestined election seems to have held particular appeal for Hungarians. Lutheranism, with its German liturgy and literature, remained strong in the largely German-speaking towns and among the nobles of north-west Hungary; but elsewhere, and especially in the eastern lands and Transylvania, Calvinism had by the 1570s overhauled it. The Calvinist confession benefited from the energy and organisational talents of its leading disciples in Hungary: the principal founder of Hungary's Calvinist Reformed Church, Péter Juhász in Debrecen, and his co-believers Gáspár Heltai and Bishop Ferenc Dávid in Transylvania. The Unitarian movement, which denied the Trinity, also prospered, especially among the Székely in Transylvania; even the Anabaptists, whose radical views on political society disqualified them from official recognition, gained a significant following. In 1584, there were over 500 Protestant preachers in Transylvania and only ten Catholic priests.[3]

The Reformation, combined with the advent of the modern printing press, had a dramatic impact on the level of cultural activity, both religious and secular, in Hungary. The first printed book in Hungarian appeared in 1533 (a translation of St Paul's epistles by Benedek Komjáti); János Sylvester's translation of the New Testament followed in 1541. It took some time for the first complete Hungarian Bible to materialise but when it did, in 1590 in Gáspár Károlyi's translation, it had a powerful effect on both the currency and the quality of the Hungarian language. In the same year another Calvinist, Balázs Fabricius, published the first Hungarian-Latin dictionary; Mátyás Bíró had already completed the first Hungarian Grammar, in 1538. The vitalisation of the vernacular had wider consequences:

elementary education took a stride forward and produced a demand for printed Bible stories, histories, travellers' tales, poetry and even fiction, which the new presses at Pápa, Kolozsvár and Debrecen did their best to meet. Higher education expanded with the foundation of Calvinist seminaries at Pápa, Nagyvárad, Debrecen and Sárospatak.[4] The period can be said to have given birth to Hungarian literature, in the poetry of Péter Bornemisza and his pupil, Bálint Balassi. Bornemisza, a scholar of noble birth who took holy orders in the Lutheran Church, preached tirelessly against the monarchy, the nobility and the Catholic Church. One of the poems in his 'Book of Songs' voiced the frustration and anguish of many Hungarians:

> I'm being hunted and chased by those boastful Germans, I have
> been near trapped and snared by those Turkish pagans.
>   When, pray, shall fair Buda be once again my dwelling? I have been
> so wearied by those Hungarian nobles,
>   They have rendered our homeland forsaken and godless. When,
> pray, shall fair Buda be once again my dwelling?[5]

Balassi, whose family gave protection to Bornemissza when the latter was on the run from charges of *lèse majesté*, crammed into his forty-year life a sequence of amorous and military adventures beside which the life of Lord Byron looks almost insipid. His love poems, usually inspired by his latest tempestuous romance, make him the father of Hungarian lyric poetry; they were the crowning, if belated, achievement of the Hungarian Renaissance. Despite his conversion to Roman Catholicism in the last decade of his life, Balassi's religious poetry, in which man stands face to face with God to conduct a dialogue with Him, is also imbued with the spirit of the Reformation. Bálint Balassi was killed during the Hungarian relief of Esztergom in 1594.

For a time it looked as if this new surge of activity might also act, at grass-roots level, as a yeast for political and social improvement. The Reformation brought the Church closer to the people and made social grievances more audible; the common people were able to read for themselves or have read to them printed polemics against the Habsburgs, the Catholic Church and the barons. But the essential condition for all these positive developments was the period of relative peace and stability Hungary enjoyed between 1547 and 1593: when Hungary once again became a battleground with the onset of the Fifteen Years' War,* the reform movement and all the activity which it had generated slowed down and even regressed. Only in Transylvania was the momentum to some extent sustained during the seventeenth century.

The Catholic Church, it seemed, had no answer to the Protestant advance. The dispatch from Austria in 1560 of a token force of a dozen Jesuits made no impression on the new religious landscape. Meanwhile, the whole Catholic hierarchy remained in place and retained its seats in the Diet, presiding over only a small rump of the faithful. The great majority of Catholic parishes had been taken over by Turks or by Protestants; their parishioners had deserted to the new confessions in droves, accompanied by a significant number of priests and monks. The first

---

* See Chapter 6.

Catholic printing press was not set up until 1578, by which time the Protestants disposed of seven. The influence of the Church over its fellow estates, the nobility and the towns, evaporated, leaving the monarchy more directly exposed to their demands. The Habsburg rulers tried, of course, to stem the Protestant tide and to protect their Roman Catholic faith in Hungary as in their other realms. Ferdinand I attempted on three occasions to pressure the Diet into approving decrees condemning 'heresy' and imposing Catholic censorship on printed materials; the Diet rebuffed his efforts, consenting only, in 1556, to exile Anabaptists. Maximilian II, although personally sympathetic to the Reformation, supported the Catholic hierarchy in Hungary in its vain attempts to root out 'heresy'. The more aggressive religious policies of Maximilian's successor, Rudolf II, were partly responsible—as we shall see—for goading the Hungarian people into active insurrection against Habsburg rule. The Catholic hierarchy nevertheless assumed, with the arrogance born of centuries of unchallenged authority, that the wheel would turn and that its time would come again: to the misfortune of the Protestant majority, the hierarchy was right.

There is no tidy or wholly satisfactory way of depicting divided Hungary in the sixteenth and seventeenth centuries or of recounting chronologically the course of events during the one and a half centuries of division. The three regions of the country—the Turkish-occupied zone (approximately 120,000 sq. km), Royal Hungary (117,000 sq. km) and Transylvania (90,000 sq. km)—at once acquired strikingly different characteristics; and the focus of events shifted between the two unoccupied regions with great rapidity. In the occupied zone, by definition, very little happened apart from the slow and inexorable process of decay; that process none the less deserves attention since it left scars that far outlasted the occupation itself. Transylvania, despite its status as a Turkish protectorate, carried for nearly a hundred years the hopes of all Hungarians who shared the ideal of a reunified and independent realm; kept alive a distinctively Hungarian culture; and for half a century operated virtually as an independent European power. Royal Hungary continued its indigenous development in directions that profoundly affected the future Hungarian nation; and eventually produced, in the War of Independence, the strongest challenge to Habsburg hegemony to be mounted until 1848. Each of the three regions, therefore, deserves separate treatment, even at the expense of an orderly narrative.

Occupied Hungary

Although it lasted for nearly 150 years, the Turkish occupation of central and southern Hungary evinced a curious quality of impermanence. This may have been due to its strictly limited objective: the denial to the Habsburgs of territory the occupation of which by a hostile power would have threatened the whole Turkish position in the Balkans which was, in turn, vital to the security of Constantinople. It was a purely military, rather than an imperial, strategy. Perhaps, too, the character of the occupation conveyed the first faint indication that Ottoman power had already reached and passed its zenith. This was not, however, readily apparent to contemporaries; nor did the oddities, viewed with hindsight, of the occupation regime in any way diminish the burden on those obliged to live under it. Outwardly, occupied Hungary conformed to the established pattern of Ottoman imperial rule. It was governed from Buda, the senior of the four *vilayets* (provinces) into which the occupied zone was divided, by a Pasha (Governor) whose office gave him a high ranking in the Ottoman hierarchy; the *vilayets* were sub-divided into *sandjaks* (districts), administered by Beys (Commissioners), which replaced the Hungarian counties. Hungarian landlords were dispossessed, all land passing into the ownership of the Ottoman state: 80 per cent of it was then leased to Turkish officers and officials, in parcels of a size appropriate to their rank, while the remainder—the best—was managed by agents on behalf of the Sultan.

The great majority of the nobility did not wait to surrender their estates to the occupiers but migrated to Royal Hungary or Transylvania, sometimes accompanied—willingly or not—by their peasant tenants. There was a similar exodus from the royal towns, which lost their privileges. The peasants who remained may not have experienced a drastic deterioration in their already low quality of life: taxation increased, a poll tax on non-Muslims supplementing the existing household tax and tithe on agricultural produce, but labour dues were not exacted by the new landlords. The peasantry remained liable, as in the past, for unpaid labour on public works such as fortifications and road maintenance. Taxes were paid to the Turkish landlord, who then passed the revenue on to a state tax–farmer, holding back as much as he thought he could get away with. As an insurance against corruption and the establishment of local fiefdoms, Turkish policy favoured a rapid turn-over of military commanders and civilian officials: there were, for example, ninety-nine Pashas of Buda during the 145 years of its occupation. This had serious implications for the peasantry: a landlord had no interest in the development of an estate of which his custodianship would be brief, but every interest in squeezing as much revenue out of it as possible before his recall or transfer. If he ruined his tenants and cottars in the process, that was a problem for his successor. This phenomenon was in large part responsible for the widespread agricultural degradation that marked the years of occupation.

Peasants living in the border regions—on both sides of the divide—fared worst of all. Not only did they suffer the theft of livestock, destruction of crops and loss of life that resulted from the almost continuous border raids, in both directions, which persisted even during periods when the Habsburgs and the Sultan were formally at peace; but they were also vulnerable to tax demands from both sides. Dispossessed Hungarian landlords made forays into the occupied zone in order to extort dues, in both cash and kind—especially wine—from their former tenants, whose uncertainty about the future and perverse attachment to the status quo ante often disposed them to pay up. A curiosity of the occupation was the agreement between the Habsburgs and the Sultan, formalised in the second Peace of Edirne, that each side would, in effect, squeeze as much tax revenue out of the occupied and border zones as it could and then split the proceeds on a fifty-fifty basis. After the Fifteen Years War (1591–1606) the occupation zone became increasingly permeable. As the Turkish presence in what had by now become a virtual wasteland was reduced, so former Hungarian landlords became bolder in laying claim to the peasant inhabitants and produce, such as it was, of their erstwhile estates.

Life in the towns of central and southern Hungary, which had always lagged behind those of the north and west in size and vitality, stagnated or died during the occupation. Because it was the centre of the Turkish administration and because its remaining burghers continued to maintain municipal records, most is known about the situation in Buda; but the situation in Esztergom, Szeged and Pécs is unlikely to have been very different. The Hungarian and German population of Buda shrank from 8,000 to 2,000 during the early years of occupation and then continued to decline, at a slower rate: by 1627 only fourteen Christian families remained.[6] The Turkish military garrison numbered around four thousand, serviced by about a thousand civilian officials, traders and craftsmen; both the military and the civilian elements included Greeks and Serbs of the Orthodox Christian faith as well as the Muslim majority. The Turks initially appointed István Werbőczy, of all people, to act as Chief Justice for the Hungarian community and as liaison officer between it and the occupying power. He lasted only a few months: the Turks became so exasperated by his pedantic defence of Hungarian law and custom that they poisoned him in 1541. The Hungarian community did, however, retain the pre-occupation institutions of municipal government including the town council; but their function did not extend much beyond the implementation of Turkish orders and regulations. These flowed principally from the *kadi* (judge) who, under the Pasha, headed both the judicial and the administrative apparatus of the occupation. Although the Turks regarded the Christian faith with contempt, they tolerated its observance: Protestants and Catholics shared the church of St Mary Magdalen from which they were, however, obliged to remove all its statuary.[7] The Jews of Buda were permitted to maintain three synagogues. The Christian and Muslim cultures seem to have co-existed quite peacefully: pork and wine were on sale in the Hungarian stalls; lamb, sherbet and coffee in the Turkish. For Hungarian shopkeepers and craftsmen, however, trade withered for lack of demand; increasingly, they turned to agriculture for their livelihood, wintering livestock within the town walls and cultivating fruit and vegetables outside them, although existing vineyards rotted as the demand for wine fell away. Seen from a distance by the approaching traveller, occupied Buda had a superficial appearance of romantic elegance: slender minarets pierced the skyline, offset by the Byzantine domes of mosques, baths and storehouses. Closer acquaintance obliged travellers to revise first impressions. As temporary occupants—individually if not collectively—the Turks had little incentive to concern themselves with the physical maintenance of the town and no funds to spend on it. The minarets were hastily constructed appendages to existing Christian churches, now converted into mosques; the domes crowned existing medieval thermal bathhouses. Municipal services such as fire-watching were neglected; fires were consequently frequent and the town suffered extensive damage in 1578 when the powder-house exploded. Buildings that fell into disrepair were left to decay further. Visiting travellers noted unburied corpses in the streets. One of them, Hans Dernschwamm, recorded: 'Houses collapse one after the other. Nothing new is built, except for shelters against rain and snow. Larger halls or rooms are subdivided into cells with walls improvised of stone, clay and wood to resemble stables. They filled up the cellars with rubbish, since they do not need them. No one is owner and master in his own house'.[8]

To one group of Buda's citizens, however, the Turkish occupation brought positive benefits: the Jews. When the occupation began, the Jews had little incentive to join the migration to Royal Hungary, where the first half of the sixteenth century had been marked by vicious outbreaks of anti–Semitism. Most of them therefore stayed—as did the smaller Jewish communities in the other towns of occupied Hungary. In the 1580's there were eighty-eight Jewish families, or about five hundred individuals, in Buda, accounting for about 20 per cent of the town's Hungarian population.[9] The Jews were accorded freedom of worship, communal organisation and a degree of judicial autonomy in return for certain duties to the occupiers; the Turks appreciated the Jewish talents for commerce and finance and in general ensured conditions in which they could be usefully exercised—in trade on the Danube, for example, which continued to flourish during the occupation. By 1683 the Jewish community in Buda and Pest had grown to about 1,000 members, including a number of immigrants from Royal Hungary; it had prospered, as generous donations to Jewish charities in the Near East showed. The Pasha of Buda regularly intervened on the Jewish behalf in cases in which Jews had been wronged by Hungarians. The Jews repaid Turkish tolerance and support by taking an active part in the defence of Buda against Habsburg armies during the Habsburg rulers' sporadic attempts to recapture the town. When Leopold I's general, Charles of Lorraine, finally succeeded in 1686, many of those Buda Jews who had not made their escape to Belgrade and Constantinople were slaughtered by the victorious imperial troops and their synagogues put to the torch.

The temporarily improved situation of urban Jews nevertheless represented the only patch of light on a canvas of otherwise unrelieved darkness. The Alföld, already depopulated by the Fifteen Years' War, became the *puszta*.[10] Much of south-west Transdanubia suffered a similar fate: the 11,000 households of Somogy county had been reduced to 106 by 1671.[11] Turkish neglect of drainage and flood control created hundreds of square kilometres of marsh and swamp in both regions, which became breeding grounds for disease including *morbus Hungaricus* (typhoid fever). In a phenomenon that was to be of great significance for Hungary's future, the deserted villages emptied by migration, warfare, abductions into slavery and disease were gradually reoccupied by non-Hungarians from neighbouring regions: Serbs came from the south to settle in the cattle-breeding areas of the Alföld, Croats from the south west into the empty villages of Transdanubia and Romanians from Wallachia into the eastern lands. A Hungarian historian[12] has nevertheless argued that the overall reduction in the population of Hungary during the sixteenth century has almost certainly been exaggerated. Many villages were deserted because their inhabitants had fled, with their livestock, into nearby forests and hills to escape marauding soldiery; tallies of peasant numbers were routinely falsified, downwards, by the nobility in order to reduce their tax liability. When these factors are taken into account, the truth seems to be that the population of Hungary stagnated, at a level of about four million, during a period in which populations in the rest of Europe were increasing rapidly. It is equally beyond question, however, that in the zone of Turkish occupation a marked and real population decrease took place; and that its ethnic balance changed to the disadvantage of the Hungarians. As we have seen in earlier chapters, Hungary had never been an ethnically homogeneous society. One of the troublesome legacies of the Turkish occupation was a significant enhancement of its heterogeneity.

Transylvania

The Turkish occupation of the eight counties east of the River Tisza in 1556 had recast Transylvania as a compact Principality, comparable in size to the two neighbouring Turkish protectorates of Moldavia and Wallachia and possessing a clearcut political structure markedly different from that of Royal Hungary. When Queen Isabella returned from Poland at Turkish behest to rule Transylvania during the minority of her young son, János Zsigmond, she made effective use of the strong centralised authority her late husband, John I Szapolyai, had built up. Already by far the greatest landowner in the kingdom, he had added to his estates those of the vacant bishoprics of Transylvania and Várad and diverted all tithes to the royal treasury. Even in combination, the wealthiest noble families of Transylvania—who typically disposed of no more than fifty villages apiece—posed no threat to this consolidation of power. The Transylvanian Diet, on which the 'three nations'—nobles, Saxons and the Székely—were represented, numbered among the delegates in its single chamber all holders of royal office and a number of other royal nominees, together with a single delegate nominated to represent the interests of all Transylvania's urban municipalities; it was unlikely, therefore, to give the crown much trouble. Queen Isabella never found it necessary to consult the Diet over the appointment of senior officials, even when they were foreign, or to seek its backing in her negotiations with foreign powers. The strength of central authority in Transylvania easily survived its only significant internal challenge, which came from the Székely. Over the centuries, the Székely tribes had outgrown the border territories they defended in return for their tax–free status as freemen; they resented the breakdown in their traditional way of life that the shortage of land had caused. They rebelled in 1562, in 1571 and again in 1575. The Habsburgs offered moral but no practical support to the rebels and István Báthory, now ruler of Transylvania, suppressed the revolts without great difficulty; in retribution, the Székely—other than those of noble rank—were deprived of their free status and reduced to that of taxable peasants.

In the conduct of Transylvania's external relations, the rulers of the Principality faced a complex task. The Transylvanian role in the long struggle for the reunification of Hungary will be described in a later chapter; but in order to fulfil that role Transylvania had to maintain its own separate identity *vis-à-vis* Royal Hungary and the Habsburgs, an objective that sometimes called for political accommodation as well as straightforward self-defence. Princes of Transylvania admittedly enjoyed an advantage in that, for so long as the Turks held Buda, Habsburg troops could not reach the Principality during the winter months. The Turkish Sultan, however, was a jealous suzerain: Gábor Bethlen received an explicit warning from the Grand Mufti that, even were he to win the Hungarian crown, 'we shall never allow Transylvania to be unified with Hungary. Transylvania is Sultan Suleiman's invention and the property of the Mighty Sultan ... We do not give to anybody else what belongs to us'.[13]

Transylvanian rulers had to be careful to avoid giving the Porte, to which they owed allegiance and to which in the last resort they could turn for protection, an excuse to jerk the leash. Just such an excuse could have been offered in 1570 when János Zsigmond decided to defuse tension between Transylvania and the Habsburgs by giving up the title of King of Hungary he had inherited from his father. Under the Treaty of Speyer, the Habsburg King of Hungary, Maximilian I, recognised János Zsigmond as 'Prince of Transylvania and Sovereign of Parts of Hungary'. The expression 'Parts of Hungary' referred to the Hungarian counties lying east of the River Tisza; after 1571, the Prince of Transylvania continued to be *'dominus partium Hungariae'* and the counties concerned were known as 'the Partium' for short. In the treaty, János Zsigmond acknowledged Habsburg suzerainty over the Principality, which meant that if he were to die without an heir Transylvania would become part of the Hungarian kingdom. János Zsigmond did in fact die, without an heir, only a year later; but the Transylvanian Diet which, like the Turks, was unaware of the Treaty of Speyer, elected István Báthory, chief adviser and mentor to the late Prince, to succeed him as ruler. Maximilian, cheated, invaded Transylvania but suffered immediate defeat, the first successful challenge to Habsburg hegemony. Maximilian sustained further humiliation when, in 1575, Báthory won election to the throne of Poland, a prize Maximilian had himself coveted. Although he subsequently ruled from a distance, devoting more time and effort to his Polish kingdom than to the Principality, István Báthory nevertheless succeeded in further strengthening central authority in Transylvania before his death in 1586.

Remarkably, the combination of a strong ruler and a compliant Diet created in Transylvania a degree of religious liberty and toleration which, in sixteenth-century Europe, the Principality shared only with Poland. Already in Catholic Queen Isabella's time, the Diet had determined that 'everyone should keep the faith he wishes'. János Zsigmond granted freedom of worship to Calvinists and Unitarians, himself embracing the Unitarian creed. In 1568 the Diet decreed that 'a village shall be allowed to keep any preacher, whose preaching pleases it … because faith is a gift of God'.[14] From that year the Catholic, Lutheran, Calvinist and Unitarian faiths were accorded equal recognition in Transylvania, while Orthodox Christians and Jews enjoyed full freedom of worship. István Báthory, a staunch Catholic, endeavoured to restore the primacy of the Roman creed and invited Jesuits into Transylvania; but they were permitted to remain only if their purpose was to teach rather than to proselytise (they were eventually expelled for allegedly failing to observe this condition). Báthory's departure to Poland brought the brief Catholic revival to an end. In a ruling that was extraordinarily progressive for its time, and which had important social as well as religious implications, the Diet declared in 1588 that serfs should not be compelled to follow the religion of their landlord but should enjoy freedom of conscience, a notable and pioneering breach in the principle of *cuius regio, eius religio* ('follow the faith of your master') that applied in most of Europe.

Gábor Bethlen, who was elected Prince of Transylvania in 1613 after serving as chief adviser to his two predecessors, István Bocskai and Gábor Báthory, consolidated this tradition of toleration and turned it to the economic advantage of the Principality by encouraging the immigration of Protestant merchants, craftsmen and miners from Germany and Bohemia. Bethlen had assumed power in unpromising circumstances. The Principality had been devastated by the Fifteen Years' War and the short ascendancy of the unstable and extravagant Gábor Báthory (1608–13) had impeded Transylvania's recovery. Bethlen nevertheless restored and strengthened central authority remarkably quickly; princely power reached its apogee while he held office and Transylvania flourished under his rule. A mercantilist commercial policy enriched both the Principality and its ruler, who greatly enhanced his revenues by creating for himself monopolies in whichever sector of import or export trade happened to be flourishing at a given time. Bethlen put these revenues to good use, endowing the first Transylvanian academy at Gyulafehérvár and making his palace there a notable centre of patronage of scholarship and the arts. At his instigation, the Diet ruled in 1615 that the greater part of fines imposed on individuals for religious transgressions should be devoted to building or maintaining churches and schools; Bethlen also imposed a severe penalty—a fine of 1,000 florins—on landlords who prevented the children of their serfs from attending school. Transylvanian theological students were encouraged to further their studies abroad, especially in England; John Milton commented: 'Nor is it for nothing that grave and frugal Transylvania sends out yearly from as far as the mountainous borders of Russia, and beyond the Hercynian wilderness, not their youth but their staid men, to learn our language and our theologic art'.[15]

Bethlen was the founder of Transylvania's short period of European statehood, giving the Principality a sound economy, an effective standing army and an efficient administration. Shortly after his election, he had described Transylvania as 'a holy alliance of the three nations [Hungarians, Saxons and Székely] in times of peace and war for the preservation of our country [Hungary]'.[16] As we shall see, Bethlen followed István Bocskai in making Transylvania an effective guardian of the cause of Hungarian reunification and independence; but he also created a respected European state, a party in its own right to the Treaty of Westphalia, which in 1648 ended the Thirty Years' War. Contacts between Transylvania and England were particularly close: many students and scholars returned from their studies in England fired with zeal for the Puritan ethos and, under the inspiration of János Tolnai, determined to give their country more and better schools in which teaching would be in the vernacular, and a more democratically organised Church. Although Gábor Bethlen's eventual successor, after the brief reign of Catherine of Brandenburg, György I Rákóczi (1593–1648), had little enthusiasm for educational or social reform, his remarkable widow, Zsuzsanna Lorántffy, became an active patron of the culture of the Reformation. Puritan scholarship and pedagogy continued to flourish in the Principality throughout a period of great political and military activity. There were close scholarly links with England—János Tolnai founded the Puritan League in London to campaign for educational reform in Hungary—and with the Dutch United Provinces; the leading educationist of his age. the Bohemian scholar Joannes Comenius (Jan Komensky), taught for four years in Sárospatak's Protestant Collegium (where mementos of his stay can be seen today); János Apáczai Csere, preacher and scholar, collated for Hungarian readers the scientific and philosophical landmarks of the sixteenth and early seventeenth centuries, including the ideas of Copernicus and Descartes, in his *Hungarian Encyclopaedia*, published in Utrecht in 1655, a work of sufficient significance to be banned by the imperial censor as late as 1803.

The century of virtual Transylvanian autonomy had thus been characterised by more than the Principality's leadership of the struggle for Hungarian unity and independence (which the next chapter will recount). It had been a period of striking advance in the development of Hungarian scholarship, literature and education; above all, in the flowering of the Hungarian language in response to these stimuli. This does much to explain passionate Hungarian resentment against the amputation of Transylvania (along with other territories) from the rest of Hungary in the Treaty of Trianon of 1920 and its award to Romania.* Transylvania had offered a beacon of hope and pride to all Hungarians during one of the darkest periods of their history.

Royal Hungary

The arc of territory that after 1527 became the Habsburg realm of Royal Hungary embraced Slavonia (northern Croatia) at its southern extremity and Debrecen on its eastern border. Pozsony (Pressburg, Bratislava) became its capital. Geography thus dictated that during most of the sixteenth and seventeenth centuries, Royal Hungary's 1.2 million people suffered even more grievously than their fellow Hungarians in Transylvania and the Turkish zone from the ravages of war: from Turkish invasions and Habsburg counter-offensives, from the Thirty Years' War and from successive rebellions against Habsburg rule. Political and social developments in this northern third of the country were none the less crucial to the future of the whole since, once the Turks had finally been driven out and Transylvania brought to heel, they determined the fortunes of reunified Hungary for the next two hundred years.

This is an appropriate point at which to attempt, briefly, to unravel the complex skein of titles and possessions the Austrian house of Habsburg, in the person of Ferdinand I, contributed to the fabric of the history of Hungary. As Archduke of Austria, Ferdinand ruled the so-called Hereditary Lands, comprising upper and lower Austria, Styria, Carinthia, the Tyrol and Istria. As King of Bohemia, he ruled the Lands of the Bohemian Crown: Bohemia itself, Silesia and Moravia; and as King of Hungary, Ferdinand now ruled the Lands of the Hungarian Crown: Hungary (or, rather, that part of the kingdom unoccupied by the Turks), Transylvania (in theory) and Croatia. At the same time, the Austrian and Spanish branches of the Habsburg dynasty between them monopolised, from the reign of Albert II (1438–39) onwards, the title of German Emperor, elected ruler of the 'Holy Roman Empire of the German Nation'. The term 'Holy Roman Empire' described an amorphous conglomeration of German states and city-states, of which Saxony, Brandenburg, Bavaria and the Palatinate were the most significant. The degree of control the Emperor of the day could exercise over this amoeba-like entity, subject to periodic sub-division in the absence of a law of primogeniture and a kaleidoscope of shifting rivalries and alliances, varied with the personality of the ruler but was seldom more than tenuous. It should be borne in mind, however, that until the demise of the Holy Roman Empire in the early nineteenth century, Hungarian affairs had only a partial claim on the attention of those kings of Hungary who wore the imperial crown, since they were obliged, not infrequently, to give priority to the problems, not only of their Bohemian lands but also to those—and they were many—of their German Empire. Moreover, in the European context the term 'empire' can be applied only to the Holy

---

* See Chapter 13.

94

Roman Empire until 1804, when Francis I assumed the title 'Emperor of Austria' and thus made it possible to refer to a 'Habsburg Empire'.

Ferdinand I and his successors ruled Royal Hungary through a Regency Council, which he established in Pozsony. Unlike the Hungarian Royal Council, which it replaced, it was not headed by the Palatine, an office the Habsburgs deliberately left unfilled during the second half of the sixteenth century lest it should become a focus for Hungarian particularist aspirations. In effect, the Regency Council took its orders from the Habsburg Aulic Council (*Hofrat*), on which Ferdinand offered the Hungarians two seats (the offer was rejected on the grounds that acceptance would appear to signify Hungarian acquiescence in the loss of the country's independence). Similarly, the Hungarian treasury and chancellery were subordinated to their Habsburg Court equivalents, the *Hofkammer* and *Hofkanzlei;* after 1556, the Court Military Council (*Hofkriegsrat*) took control of imperial defence policy, including the defence of Hungary.

The Hungarian Diet, however, was an institution with which the Habsburgs were obliged to come to terms. After 1608 it consisted of two Chambers, the Upper (*felső tábla*) in which barons and bishops sat; and the Lower (*alsó tábla*), to which each county sent noble delegates and in which the towns were accorded a single vote between them. Holders of hereditary titles, who sat in the Upper Chamber as of right, could, and sometimes did, choose to stand for election to the Lower Chamber instead. Legislation resulted from discussion by both chambers of a royal proposition, followed by a sometimes lengthy dialogue, in written correspondence, between the Diet and the ruler; the resulting agreement, if any, was embodied in a royal decree that had the force of law. But the ruler held strong cards—the right to make grants of land from the royal estates and Hungarian dependence on Habsburg leadership against the Turks—and the Habsburgs bypassed this disputatious and drawn-out legislative process whenever they could. Both Chambers of the Diet, but the Lower in particular, were zealous exponents and defenders of Hungarian customary law, to an extent that exhausted the patience of Ferdinand's successors, Maximilian I and Rudolf I. There was one important issue, however, on which the Diet could not be bypassed: money. Tax collection lay in the hands of the county administrations and thus in those of the *ispáns*. The Habsburgs were chronically short of funds and hard put to meet an annual defence bill of a million florins, of which revenue from Hungary accounted for approximately half. Ferdinand, who was to leave debts of over 7.5 million florins, tried to prevail upon the Diet to vote taxes for six years at a time; the Diet refused to go beyond two years and maintained this position against all royal threats and entreaties. On a related issue, that of peasant migration, the Diet also had its way, in practice if not in form. Since virtually the whole burden of taxation fell on the peasantry, the nobility remaining exempt, the rulers had a clear interest in creating circumstances in which the peasants could improve their lot and consequently their capacity to pay taxes. The only means by which a peasant could better himself was by moving from one landlord to another, from one plot to a more productive one; during a period of serious labour shortage, the landlords—especially the poorer ones—had an interest in preventing this. On four occasions during the sixteenth century, the Diet reluctantly agreed, at royal insistence, to permit migration; but the relevant laws were hedged around with conditions and restrictions and were, in any case, never applied in practice. As we shall see, during the sixteenth and seventeenth centuries peasant bondage became tighter rather than looser.

During the same period, politics and economics combined to strengthen still further the dominance of the barons *vis-à-vis* the other strata of Hungarian society. Ferdinand I introduced, and his successors continued, the practice of buying the allegiance of leading Hungarian families with the grant of hereditary titles, which were inherited by all the descendants of the original grantee. The decimation of the baronial class at Mohács, which the heads of only three baronial families survived,[17] was therefore quickly made good: by 1601, forty barons were receiving royal invitations to attend the Diet's Upper Chamber and by 1649 this number had risen to 120.[18] A dozen or so leading baronial families held a monopoly of state offices and *ispán*-ships . The award of a hereditary title often carried with it a handsome addition, from the royal domain, to the recipient's estates. On these, another development was taking place that exacerbated the deformation of Hungarian society. During the second half of the sixteenth century, agricultural prices in western Europe rose dramatically, by as much as 300 to 400 per cent, while the price of manufactured goods, such as cloth, remained relatively stable; the balance of trade thus moved sharply in Hungary's favour. The landowning nobility, and especially the barons, reacted to this happy situation by developing their demesne ('home') farms; these expanded rapidly, partly through clearing and enclosing uncultivated land, partly through encroachment on to vacant peasant plots and common land, occasionally through forcible eviction. Instead of relying on their tenants to support them with dues of cash or produce, the landlords entered the farming business on their own account in order to profit from favourable price levels. An immediate consequence of this was an increase in labour dues, or *robot*; landlords needed free labour more than they needed tenant produce. Although laws of 1514 and 1548 had fixed the level of *robot* at fifty-two days a year, these were widely ignored in practice: by 1570, two days of *robot* per week was normal and three days not uncommon. The extent to which the peasants could themselves profit from the advantageous level of prices was thus extremely limited. When a radical change in the overall situation at the end of the sixteenth century brought stagnation to European economies and a drastic fall, of up to 50 per cent, in agricultural prices, the lot of the peasantry remained parlous but for partly different reasons. Baronial and noble landlords reacted to the crisis by substituting self-sufficiency and local market domination for export trading, which had in any case been hard hit by the alteration in European trading routes in favour of bulk water-borne freight. Tenants were commonly obliged to sell their produce only to their landlord, at artificially low prices, and often to buy from him commodities, such as wine, they did not produce themselves. During the seventeenth century, levels of *robot* continued to increase: three or four days a week, or the whole of every other week, became the norm and during harvest time there were no limits.

The change from largely passive to active management of Royal Hungary's estates by their baronial and noble landlords had the effect, over a period of two centuries, of reducing the great majority of the peasantry to serfdom. The annexation to demesne farms not only of common land but also of peasant holdings

became increasingly common. The fifteenth century trend towards the commutation of labour dues and payment in kind into cash payments was reversed as inflation, throughout Europe, reduced the value of money. Most peasants found it
impossible to meet their obligations for *robot*, pay their *muneralia* (compulsory gifts
of produce to their landlord) and their taxes while saving their families from starvation: as an alternative to the death penalty for disobedience, they were obliged
formally to renounce their right to migrate and to take an oath of perpetual obedience to their lord. Werbőczi's condemnation, in the *Tripartitum*, of the *misera
plebs contribuens* to virtual expulsion from human society became the reality: the
European phenomenon that became known as the 'second serfdom' developed in
Hungary into 'perpetual serfdom'. This took place, towards the end of the sixteenth century, against a background of unremitting natural and man-made disaster. The 'Little Ice Age' caused widespread flooding, the failure of crops and near
famine. Hungary suffered five major epidemics of plague and smallpox during the
seventeenth century, three per generation. The Habsburgs' mercenaries and their
Turkish adversaries marched and counter-marched through the borderlands, leaving devastation in their wake. Mass abductions by the Turks in the border regions
exacted a heavy toll: in 1596 10,000 peasants in Szabolcs county were driven
south into slavery and a similar fate befell Sopron county ten years later. The
decline in revenue from the one-florin war tax, levied on every household in
Royal Hungary, provides a grim indicator of the population drain caused by
abductions and epidemics: in 1590 the tax yielded 240,000 florins but in 1604
only 65,000 florins.[19] Even a wealthy baron, István Illésházy (who later fell foul of
the Austrians), was moved to write: 'Would that the Lord had not let me live and
I could have departed this loathsome world long ago; happy are those who have
died in the grace of God and have not experienced these horrors'.[20]

For all except the barons, magnates and the wealthier nobles—much of the
lesser nobility had been reduced to peasant status—the late sixteenth and most of
the seventeenth centuries were a time of unrelieved misery in the Royal Hungarian countryside. Lady Mary Wortley Montagu passed through Hungary in January
1717, on her way to Constantinople where her husband had been appointed British Ambassador to the Porte. Describing her journey through former Royal Hungary in a letter to her sister, she wrote on 30 January: 'We continu'd two days
traveling between [Komárom] and Buda, through the finest plains in the world, as
even as if they were pav'd, and extreme fruitfull, but for the most part desert and
uncultivated, laid waste by the long war between the Turk and Emperour, and the
more cruel civil war occasion'd by the barbarous persecution of the protestant
Religion by the Emperour Leopold … Indeed, nothing can be more melancholy
than traveling through Hungary, reflecting on the former flourishing state of that
Kingdom and seeing such a noble spot of Earth allmost uninhabited'.[21]

The situation in the towns was little better. Although the market towns enjoyed
a short period of prosperity during the sixteenth century as a result of the boom
in cattle prices, the royal towns stagnated or declined. Many of their privileges
were suppressed by the Habsburgs, who lost no opportunity of putting them at a
commercial disadvantage in relation to their Austrian counterparts; in 1581, for
example, Rudolf I ordered the closure of the weekly market at Győr in order to
eliminate competition with Vienna. As if that were not enough, the Hungarian

barons and nobles who now dominated the economy developed craft workshops and breweries on their increasingly self-sufficient estates, undercutting the guild-controlled and consequently more highly priced urban craftsmen and brewers. In self-defence, royal towns bought up farmland and vineyards in order to reduce their dependence on the great estates and increase their self-sufficiency; burghers became farmers and a number of them entered the nobility by the land-owner-ship route. The virtual ban on peasant migration prevented any population move-ment from the countryside to the towns and froze urban populations at a low level; in 1600, the average town in Royal Hungary housed 3,000 people at a time when the population of Prague had reached 50,000. In the period of disorder fol-lowing Mohács, several towns expelled their Jews in order to escape the repay-ment of debts; some of the expellees settled on baronial estates and managed their finances, many more emigrated to the Turkish zone where their talents were respected. In short, Royal Hungary at this time exemplified the judgement of two Hungarian historians, that 'in East-Central Europe, the period from the sixteenth to the eighteenth centuries cannot be regarded as an era of transition from feudal-ism to capitalism but rather a peculiar, belated feudalism. Medieval conditions, instead of waning, were consolidated'.[22]

The lesser nobility, from whom in earlier times some defiant reaction to Hun-gary's manifold misfortunes might have been expected, had disintegrated as a political class. Those with estates of moderate size, perhaps including a couple of villages, continued to form the backbone of local administration; they provided the deputy *ispáns (alispánok)*, judges, lawyers, tax collectors and county treasurers. Some nobles were reduced by debt or some other misfortune to the status of *familiaris*, serving a baron in an administrative or military capacity in return for bed, board and a small wage; others made a precarious living as soldiers in the frontier fortresses. The majority, however, were reduced to the status of peasants or even serfs. This resulted from the massive dilution of the nobility during the sixteenth and seventeenth centuries. The Habsburg rulers were profligate with patents of nobility, often issuing them unaccompanied by grants of land so that they amounted to little more than certificates of exemption from taxation; barons, after pocketing a fee for manumission, were happy to promote the aspirations to nobility of their peasant tenants as a means of keeping them on their estates when labour was in short supply. During the seventeenth century, most counties regis-tered as many as 500 new members of the nobility. The growth of the noble class not only made it much less effective politically than had been the case when the entire nobility attended meetings of the Diet: it also compounded the burdens of the *misera plebs contribuens* by increasing to an absurd level—nearly 10 per cent in Royal Hungary—the proportion of the population that was tax-exempt.

The Habsburgs nevertheless succeeded in provoking successive spasms of resist-ance from the seemingly lifeless body of divided Hungary. Their impatience with Hungarian exceptionalism, their reluctance to accept that Hungary's history and traditions entitled it to any form of special treatment and their failure, for a cen-tury and a half, effectively to protect Hungary from Turkish depredations stirred the dying embers of Hungarian pride and lit the flame of insurrection.

6

THE STRUGGLE FOR INDEPENDENCE

(1547–1711)

The Fifteen Years' War

The barons who had supported Ferdinand I against János Szapolyai in the contest for the Holy Crown had been motivated, along with their expectation of personal reward, by the belief that the Habsburgs represented Hungary's only hope of protection against the Turks. The Habsburgs' success or lack of it in fulfilling this role was consequently a major factor in determining Hungarian acquiescence in or opposition to foreign rule. When the Habsburgs not only failed to expel the Turks from Hungarian soil—leaving little doubt that they regarded Royal Hungary merely as a convenient buffer zone for the protection of Austria and Bohemia—but also embarked on policies of religious oppression and economic exploitation, the scene was set for insurrection.

Hungarian disillusionment did not set in immediately. Ferdinand I initiated an ambitious programme of fortification, the *Militärgrenze*, which by 1562 had established fifty-five fortified strongpoints along the border between Royal and occupied Hungary. One of the reasons for this essentially defensive—and, as some Hungarians saw it, defeatist—strategy was the absence of a Habsburg standing army. Ferdinand and his immediate successors disposed of sufficient funds only to engage mercenaries, who refused to campaign in the winter months, which was precisely the period during which the Turks were most vulnerable. Doubts concerning the strength of Habsburg determination to defeat the Turks were increased when, in 1566, Sultan Suleiman launched his seventh invasion of Hungary and besieged the fortress of Szigetvár, just north of the Drava River and 30 kilometres west of Pécs. The defence of Szigetvár was led by Miklós Zrínyi (Nikola Zrinski in Croatian), who owned most of the land surrounding the fortress, with about 2,500 men under his command;[1] he held out against Suleiman's force of over 100,000 troops and 300 guns for nearly six weeks before leading the few hundred survivors of the garrison out through the breached walls to die in hand-to-hand combat with the Turks. Throughout the siege, messengers had been sent north to Emperor Maximilian, commander of the sizeable Habsburg mercenary force encamped near Győr, urging him to relieve Szigetvár: he refused to budge. The fall of Szigetvár was not, however, an unmitigated disaster: the ageing Sultan Suleiman succumbed to a stroke towards the end of the siege, which lasted long enough to compel the Turks, who had lost some 20,000 men, to withdraw southwards before winter set in. Zrínyi's heroism frustrated Suleiman's last campaign despite Habsburg lack of zeal for a confrontation with the invader.

Confrontation was nevertheless forced upon Rudolf I when, smarting from a minor reverse to Turkish arms in Croatia, the Turkish Grand Vizier[2] declared war in 1593; his troops invaded Royal Hungary, quickly occupying Veszprém and Várpalota in the initial engagements of what was to be known as the Fifteen Years' War, or Long War. The Habsburg armies, commanded initially by the Archduke Ernst and then, more successfully, by Archduke Matthias (to whom Rudolf had delegated responsibility for most Hungarian affairs) and consisting of a mixture of German mercenaries and Hungarian troops drawn from baronial private armies, enjoyed some early successes but failed to take Buda. In 1594 the tide turned again when the Turks seized the major fortress of Győr, which guarded the approach to Vienna; but at this point the Turks were confronted with a new adversary—their own protectorate, Transylvania. As soon as the war had begun, Grand Vizier Sinan invited the Prince of Transylvania, Zsigmond Báthory (nephew of István, the late King of Poland), to join the Turks in their onslaught against the Habsburgs. Zsigmond, a weak and indecisive twenty-one year-old, employed his usual tactic when faced with a difficult problem—he adopted it four times in eight years—that of temporary abdication. It was left to his chief adviser, István Bocskai, to resolve the issue. Bocskai's upbringing, as a page at the court in Vienna, had given him a deep respect for Habsburg power and grandeur. Convinced that alliance with Austria represented Hungary's only hope of salvation, Bocskai routed the pro-Turkish faction in Transylvania and persuaded Zsigmond to join the Christian League which the Habsburgs were forming to contribute soldiers and money to the anti-Turkish cause. Resuming his office, Zsigmond complied; in 1595 the Transylvanian Diet voted to join the League as part of a deal by which Zsigmond recognised Rudolf I as King of Hungary in return for the latter's recognition of him as hereditary Prince of Transylvania. One part of the bargain failed to prosper: the homosexual Zsigmond's marriage to the Habsburg princess Maria-Christina was unhappy and unconsummated.

The Turks were now faced with a war on two fronts and the problem was compounded by an alliance of convenience between Zsigmond of Transylvania and his fellow Turkish vassal, Michael of Wallachia. A combined Transylvanian-Wallachian force, led by Bocskai and Michael, soundly defeated the Turks at Djurdjevo and overran a number of Turkish forts along the Maros River; the diversion helped the Habsburg general Mansfeld to capture Esztergom, the fortress that held the key to Buda. In the following year, however, the Turks, led in person by their new Sultan Mehmet III, launched a devastating counter-attack: Eger fell and in the autumn of 1596 the Turks annihilated a Habsburg and Transylvanian force at Mezőkeresztes in the longest and fiercest battle of the war.

Mezőkeresztes did not, however, bring the war to an end. It dragged on for a further ten years; both sides suffered reverses but none so severe and lasting as those sustained by the ordinary Hungarian people, both in Royal Hungary and in Transylvania, across whose land the war was fought. Both the kingdom and the

Principality were devastated. Those market towns that survived absorbed the deserted villages in their hinterlands. As had been the case after earlier periods of disaster, Slovak, Romanian and Serb immigrants moved in to populate the wasteland: by the end of the seventeenth century, the Magyar-speaking proportion of the population of Hungary as a whole had declined from about 80 per cent to around 45 per cent.[3] Transylvania—where, as we shall see shortly, there were additional problems—lost half of its population and most of its not inconsiderable wealth. The survivors faced famine and starvation.[4]

By 1604, the chemistry of despair was working both in Royal Hungary and in Transylvania to produce a reaction. Despite some earlier imperial successes, including the recapture of Győr in 1598, the Turks launched a successful counter-offensive in 1600, which led to the occupation of Nagykanizsa, the strategically vital fortified town that linked Royal Hungary with Slavonia. By this time, the Habsburgs had virtually eliminated direct Hungarian participation in the conflict: Hungarian frontier troops had been largely replaced by German mercenaries, who were considered to be more reliable, and no Hungarian baron was entrusted with a military command. Hungarians were thus obliged to watch their country bleed from an inconclusive war in which the maximum Habsburg objective appeared to be the protection of Vienna rather than any desire to liberate occupied Hungary. The Habsburgs compounded their indifference to Hungarian interests by using the war to enrich themselves at Hungarian expense. Not only were Hungarian barons and nobles squeezed out of the business of supplying the imperial armies with victuals and other necessities in order to give Austrian merchants a monopoly; but when István Illésházy, an entrepreneurial baron, objected to the practice he was charged with treason and, despite being found not guilty by a Hungarian court, condemned to death by Vienna and forced to flee to Poland. Illésházy's estates were confiscated and used to pay off Rudolf I's debts. This episode inaugurated a spasm of institutionalised theft by the Habsburgs: several other Hungarian barons faced spurious charges of treason trumped up to justify the confiscation of their estates. It was at this inauspicious moment, finally, that the Counter-Reformation—long in preparation in Rome—made its first militant appearance in Hungary. The reconversion of Protestant Royal Hungary, by persuasion rather than coercion, was still to come; but already in 1604 the imperial governor of the town of Kassa (Košice), General Belgiojoso, sequestrated and reserved for Catholics the town's Protestant churches, confiscating the property of pastors and members of their congregations who resisted; the outrage was repeated in other towns. In the same year, probably at Rudolf's instigation, Archduke Matthias, in an act of flagrant contempt for the largely Protestant Hungarian Diet, inserted into a law which it had already approved an additional Clause 22 which made illegal, and an act of treason, discussion by the Diet of any religious matter. The military occupation of Hungary, occasioned by the Fifteen Years' War, had thus brought about a change in the character of Habsburg rule, from suzerainty to oppression.

István Bocskai and the Haiduks

In Transylvania, meanwhile, events had taken place that were to bring matters to a head. Zsigmond Báthory had abdicated, for the last time as it turned out, in

1599; István Bocskai, his hitherto pro-Habsburg adviser, retired to his own estate in the Partium, in Bihar county. The move brought Bocskai face to face with the ravages of the war, particularly the devastation inflicted by the constant passage of mercenary troops, and with the increasingly ugly characteristics of Habsburg rule. Bocskai began to think in terms of reorientating Transylvania towards the Turks and, with their support or at least acquiescence, making the Principality a base from which Hungary's independence might be regained. Rashly, Bocskai committed these thoughts to paper, in a correspondence intercepted by the Austrians. The imperial general, Basta, led a punitive expedition into Transylvania, where he found an ally in Michael of Wallachia who had fallen out with Zsigmond Báthory a few years before; Transylvania, already ruined by war with the Turks, descended into anarchy as German mercenaries, Vlachs and rebellious Székely tore it apart. General Basta carried all before him, disposed of his allies (Michael of Wallachia was assassinated) and initiated a reign of terror. Basta himself described the condition into which Transylvania had by now (1603) fallen: 'The changes and wars have turned the country into a desert. The boroughs and villages have been burned, most of the inhabitants and their cattle killed or driven away. In consequence, taxes, excise, bridge and road tolls yield but little, the mines are deserted, there are no hands to work'.[5] It was in this situation that Gábor Bethlen, a young Transylvanian who, like many others, had sought refuge in Turkish-occupied territory, approached István Bocskai with the proposal that he, Bocskai, should put himself at the head of armed insurrection against Habsburg rule.

Bocskai, already in a receptive frame of mind, accepted Bethlen's proposal; and led the haiduks into Hungary's history. The haiduks were a product of the nightmarish closing decades of the sixteenth century in Hungary. Evicted or defaulting peasants, escaped serfs, deserters from the border fortresses, even bankrupt nobles—the haiduks were too numerous to be called outlaws but they lived outside the pale of feudal society. They were willing to fight for whoever could pay them. Bocskai rallied a few hundred haiduks to his standard in Bihar county and then persuaded a further 5,000, who were for the time being part of General Basta's mercenary army, to change sides and fight for the independence of Hungary: 'to defend Christianity, our country and dear homeland, and especially the one true faith [i.e. Protestantism]'.[6] The captains in Bocskai's ragtail army called upon their fellow nobles to join them: 'We owe it to our dear country and nation ... to rise all together and live or die together'.[7] These appeals represent the earliest evidence that a concept of Hungarian nationhood, independent of social class, was in gestation: Habsburg tyranny was to be its midwife. This imparts to Bocskai's rebellion a significance transcending its immediate results. Nationhood had yet to emerge as an ideal distinct from religious conviction or the resentment of the poor against the rich, which were the principal motivations of Bocskai's followers; but a seed had been sown.

Not surprisingly, Bocskai's disorganised and untrained force sustained initial reverses at the hands of General Belgiojoso; but the haiduks rallied remarkably quickly, occupying first Debrecen and then Belgiojoso's base, Kassa. Unsuited to set-piece battles against a trained and disciplined force, the haiduks showed a natural aptitude for guerrilla warfare: by the end of 1604, Basta had been evicted from Transylvania and during the following summer Bocskai liberated Pozsony,

Győr and Komárom. The haiduks raided lower Austrian, Moravian and even Silesian territory. Controlling much of Royal Hungary as well as Transylvania, Bocskai was in a position to dictate terms. He had by now been elected Prince of Transylvania by the Transylvanian Diet and 'Prince-Protector of Hungary' by the Hungarian Diet sitting at Szerencs (the barons and nobles assembled at Szerencs, acting in character, also demanded punishment of the haiduks for indiscipline and the return of fugitive serfs to their landlords); the Turks offered Bocskai a crown, which he accepted as a gift while declining the title of king. Bocskai incorporated his demands of Rudolf I in fifteen articles, of which the most important stipulated: religious freedom for Hungarian Protestants; the revocation of the notorious 'Clause 22'; the expulsion of Jesuits from Hungary; the appointment of a Palatine; Hungarian administration of Hungarian financial and military affairs; the exclusion of the Catholic hierarchy from offices of state; and an end to bogus treason trials as a tool of extortion.

The Peace of Vienna, concluded by Bocskai and Archduke Matthias (on Rudolf's behalf) in 1606, met all these demands save that for the expulsion of Jesuits. In addition, the agreement laid down that a peace settlement should be reached with the Turks; restored to their owners estates that had been illegally confiscated; withdrew all decrees that ran counter to the traditional laws of Hungary; and granted semi–noble status to the haiduks by which, like the Székely, they received land and exemption from feudal dues in return for military service when required. Transylvania was enlarged by the cession of three counties from the Partium. Rudolf recognised Bocskai as Prince of the independent Principality of Transylvania during his lifetime, but the title was to revert to the Habsburg king's gift on his death—which in fact occurred shortly after the agreement had been signed. Finally, as required by the Peace of Vienna, the Fifteen Years' War was brought to an end by the Peace of Zsitvatorok which, in effect, declared the costly and devastating conflict to have been a draw: the Habsburgs achieved the commutation of their annual tribute to the Sultan into a one-off payment of 200,000 florins, thus casting off their quasi–vassal status, but the Turks retained Nagykanizsa, Eger and Esztergom.

Rudolf had no intention of honouring the Peace of Vienna; indeed, before signing it he had drawn up a secret abjuration of his consent on the grounds that it had been extorted under duress.[8] Archduke Matthias, who had negotiated the deal, had little enthusiasm for it either; but he humoured the Hungarians, in whom he saw a useful lever with which to prise Rudolf from the imperial throne, on which Matthias would then replace him. Matthias's plan succeeded. When Rudolf refused to implement the provisions of the Vienna agreement, the haiduks resumed their insurrection; the Hungarian barons demanded and secured Rudolf's abdication of the Hungarian crown, electing Matthias II in his place in 1608. In the same year the Hungarian Diet translated most of the provisions of the Peace of Vienna into law. With his eye on the imperial crown, Matthias refused to accept the exclusion of the Catholic hierarchy from public office; but he did agree to give the Diet the final say on issues of war and peace, to endorse the election of István Illésházy to the office of Palatine and to restore the Holy Crown to Hungarian keeping. Although the Peace of Vienna and the laws of 1608 were eroded and partially neutralised as time went on by the pressures of Habsburg absolutism, they nevertheless represented an important landmark in Hungary's development and a valuable set of precedents for a people adept in the use of precedents. The new laws maintained and strengthened Hungary's claim to special treatment among the lands ruled by the Habsburg Monarchy; they established, for Hungary, the principle of religious freedom and ensured that Hungary would once again— for the time being, at least—be governed by Hungarian officers of state through the Hungarian Diet, and a Hungarian treasury. István Bocskai's achievement, of which he did not live to see the fruits, was substantial.

Counter-Reformation

When Rudolf I, by now deranged, died in 1612, Matthias succeeded him as Holy Roman Emperor. His chief minister, Cardinal Khlesl, had already decided that the Hungarian Estates should no longer be encouraged by Transylvania to defy the Habsburg monarch's absolute authority. He therefore threw down a challenge to István Bocskai's successor, Gábor Báthory, by invading the Principality in 1611. Although Transylvania was in turmoil, suffering violent internal divisions as a result of Báthory's erratic rule, the invading force sustained a heavy defeat. Cardinal Khlesl thenceforth concentrated on weakening the Hungarian Estates by dividing them, using the formidable resources of the Counter-Reformation for the purpose: by far its most effective instrument in Hungary was Cardinal Péter Pázmány. Pázmány was, by any standards, a remarkable man. Born into a Protestant noble family, he converted to Roman Catholicism while a pupil at the Jesuit college in Kolozsvár (the pedagogical reputation of this recent foundation was such that it attracted Protestants as well as Catholics); he entered the Society of Jesus and became a university teacher in Graz, where his literary and oratorical talents soon attracted attention. He made rapid progress up the ecclesiastical hierarchy, culminating in his appointment in 1616 to be Archbishop of Esztergom and Primate of Hungary. Pázmány preached and wrote not only in Latin but in Hungarian—superb Hungarian, elegant but clear, which earned for his sermons a place in the literary development of the language. His political allegiance, moreover, was to the people of Hungary as well as to the Habsburg monarchy; although his successful prosecution of the Counter-Reformation served the interests of the latter, he was also concerned to protect Hungarians from Habsburg self-interest. He conducted a revealing personal correspondence with the Princes of Transylvania, commenting in a letter to Gábor Bethlen that 'we [the Hungarians] are squeezed between two powerful Empires like a finger between folding doors'; he nevertheless opposed Bethlen's policy of military confrontation with the Habsburgs, explaining to Bethlen's successor, Prince György Rákóczi I (according to one authority): 'I should like to have this little stock of Hungarians spared for better times and to prevent them from destroying one another. Providence may one day have mercy upon us and save us from our natural foe, the Turk'.[9] While disagreeing with Bethlen's tactics, Pázmány remained very much aware of the value of Transylvania to the cause of Hungarian reunion and independence, to which he was deeply committed; he opposed the election of the pro-Habsburg Palatine, Miklós Eszterházy, and once commented that 'when she [Transylvania] ceases to exist, the Austrian will promptly spit under our collar'.[10]

Given his personal qualities and his political stance, it is not surprising that under Pázmány's leadership the Counter-Reformation made remarkable inroads into Protestant Hungary. By 1630, a large proportion of the barons had returned to the Catholic fold, taking their peasants and serfs with them on the principle of *cuius regio, eius religio*. Life returned to the monasteries. Especially after early Habsburg successes against their Protestant foes in the Thirty Years' War, Royal Hungary became, once again, a Catholic Habsburg realm. The predominance of the Catholic faith in western Hungary to this day is in large part Péter Pázmány's legacy; so is Budapest's foremost university, the Eötvös Loránd Tudományegyetem, which began life as the university founded by Pázmány in Nagyszombat (Trnava) in 1635. According to one Hungarian historian 'all Hungarians, Catholics and Protestants alike' mourned Pázmány's death in 1637.[11]

Gábor Bethlen, György Rákóczi I and the Thirty Years' War

In Transylvania, meanwhile, the newly elected Prince, Gábor Bethlen, had been watching the early successes of the Counter-Reformation and the erosion of the Peace of Vienna in Royal Hungary with concern. Unlike Pázmány, Bethlen regarded the Habsburgs rather than the Turks as the main obstacle to Hungarian reunion and independence; he had twice been obliged to spend periods of exile in Turkish territory to escape, first, General Basta's reign of terror in Transylvania and then the paranoia of the Prince whom he had served as chief adviser, Gábor Báthory. In view of his Turkish connexions, Vienna greeted Bethlen's election to succeed Báthory (who had been murdered by haiduks) in 1613 with suspicion and hostility, a reaction that soon turned out to be justified. For Bethlen (whose success in restoring order and relative prosperity to Transylvania has already been recounted)* came to power with a wider objective than the sound governance of the Principality: he aspired to restore the unity of Hungary under his own leadership and, as a devout Calvinist, to protect the Protestant faith. Protestantism in central Europe had come under severe threat since the elections of Ferdinand II—ruler of Austria since 1596—to be King of Bohemia in 1617 and King of Hungary one year later. A fanatical Catholic, Ferdinand quickly provoked unrest in Protestant Bohemia by imposing a series of discriminatory measures; in 1618, the Bohemian nobility rose up in rebellion against their new king. In this situation, the perception of Habsburg vulnerability combined with religious conviction to impel Gábor Bethlen towards involvement in what was to become the Thirty Years' War, the series of bitter conflicts that devastated much of Europe until the Peace of Westphalia brought hostilities to an end in 1648.

Having prepared the ground with a vigorous propaganda campaign that won him important allies including the newly elected Palatine, Zsigmond Forgách, and György Rákóczi, Bethlen led his army into Royal Hungary in September 1619. Like István Bocskai before him, Bethlen achieved remarkable initial success. Before the end of the year—and before the rest of Protestant Europe had rallied to the support of the Bohemian rebels and their chosen ruler, Frederick V of the Palatinate—Bethlen had conquered northern Hungary, seized Kassa and Pozsony

* See pages 92–94.

(where he captured the Holy Crown), invaded Austria and joined Count Heinrich Thurn's Bohemian force before the gates of Vienna. Assessing—probably correctly—that a siege of the city would be beyond the capacity even of the combined armies, Bethlen then withdrew, to the disappointment of his supporters. At its meeting in January 1620, the Diet nevertheless offered Bethlen the title of King of Hungary, and later in the year, having formally deposed the Habsburgs, elected Bethlen to the throne; Bethlen declined the crown on both occasions, perceiving that in Hungary he could not expect to enjoy the virtually absolute power of which he disposed in Transylvania. He did, however, accept and adopt the style 'Prince of Hungary'. Meanwhile, Ferdinand II, bolstered by his recent election to the imperial crown, had been mobilising support from the League of German Catholic Princes; he bought time for this by concluding a nine-month truce with Bethlen, who was running short of funds and welcomed a pause in the campaign. The tide now began to turn against the Protestants, who could not match the swelling Catholic war chest. In November, Ferdinand inflicted a crushing defeat on the Bohemians on the field of the White Mountain, near Prague. Six months later, imperial forces recaptured Pozsony. The fortified town of Kőszeg surrendered to Ferdinand. Although he still controlled most of Royal Hungary and continued to chalk up victories (one of which took the life of the senior Habsburg commander, Count Bucquoi) Bethlen decided that it was time to negotiate: following the battle of the White Mountain the Hungarian barons, chronically inconstant in their political as in their religious loyalties, had begun to mend their fences with Ferdinand. Bethlen's support among the nobility was beginning to melt away. On the last day of 1621, Bethlen and Ferdinand II concluded the Peace of Nikolsburg: Bethlen renounced the title 'King of Hungary' (which he had never used) and returned the Holy Crown to Ferdinand, gaining in return Transylvanian sovereignty over four Hungarian counties (in addition to those ceded in the Peace of Vienna), amnesty for his Hungarian supporters, and confirmation of the Peace of Vienna. Bethlen nevertheless regarded the agreement as no more than a breathing-space in his campaign against Habsburg hegemony and at once began to assess the opportunities provided for it by the Thirty Years' War, now well under way.

By the spring of 1623, Bethlen was ready to prepare for a second campaign against Ferdinand; it turned out to be singularly ill-timed. Just a week before Bethlen led his army out of Gyulafehérvár, the Catholic League's commander, Count Tilly, had routed a large Protestant force under the Duke of Brunswick in the battle of Stadtlohn on 6 August. Bethlen pressed on regardless, occupied Kassa, captured Nagyszombat and laid siege to the fortress of Hodonin in Moravia, neutralising the sizeable imperial force within. It now became clear that, as a result of Stadtlohn, he could expect no help from the Protestant Union and he sensibly decided to quit while he was ahead. Two weeks of negotiation at Hodonin resulted in a further truce, until September 1624, together with an undertaking by Ferdinand (which he obviously had no intention of honouring) that he would not lead foreign troops into Hungary. After two years, however, Bethlen was ready to resume his anti–Habsburg offensive once again, knowing that he would be doing so without active Turkish support: in 1625 Ferdinand II and Sultan Murad IV had renewed the Peace of Zsitvatorok, which precluded Turkish involvement in the war. Bethlen enhanced his own and Transylvania's standing by means of a shrewd political marriage: he sought and won the hand of Catherine, younger sister of the Elector of Brandenburg, a leading member of the Protestant Union. The marriage began a year, 1626, that confirmed Transylvania's place on the European stage as an independent state. When news reached the Protestant leaders that Bethlen had once more led his army out of Transylvania for his third campaign against Ferdinand, they ordered Count Mansfeld to march from Silesia to support him. The two armies succeeded in linking up in northern Hungary just before Count Wallenstein, the Catholic commander, arrived after forced marches to confront them. What could have been one of the great battles of the Thirty Years' War was in fact an anti–climax: both Mansfeld's and Wallenstein's mercenaries were too weary to fight and Bethlen's force, though fresher and skilled in mobile warfare, lacked the fire power for a set-piece engagement. Both armies turned round and headed for home.

Just a few weeks after this non-event, ironically, Charles I of England signed at Westminster the protocol that formally admitted Transylvania to the Protestant alliance, joining the Dutch United Provinces, Denmark and England. Three weeks later, Bethlen, isolated once again on the eastern fringe of the theatre of war, renewed the Peace of Nikolsburg with Ferdinand; and in 1627, at Pozsony, concluded a definitive peace treaty with the Emperor. Although he toyed with plans for an alliance with Gustavus Adolphus of Sweden directed against Poland, the Pozsony treaty in fact marked Bethlen's withdrawal from the war: in 1629 he died, in Gyulafehérvár. His last acts were to ennoble all Transylvania's Protestant ministers; and to enjoin his eventual successor, György Rákóczi, not to permit the return of the seven counties to Ferdinand after his death. Although Bethlen's campaigns had raised the European standing of his remote Principality, they had done little to further his primary aim of winning independence for a reunited Hungary. Ferdinand's grip on Royal Hungary, strengthened by the success of the Counter-Reformation, remained as strong as ever; the barons saw no profit in resistance and vied, as usual, for royal favour. Bethlen's achievement lay more in his creation, in Transylvania, of an environment (described in the previous chapter) in which Hungarian culture, and specifically Hungarian Calvinist culture, could develop in security from the counter-reforming offensive.

Bethlen's widow Catherine, who succeeded him briefly as ruler, thought it her duty to return to Ferdinand the seven Hungarian counties the Peace of Nikolsburg had ceded to Transylvania for Bethlen's lifetime only. The haiduks who had been settled in the counties concerned thought otherwise and rose in rebellion as soon as Catherine's intention became known. The pro-Habsburg Palatine of Royal Hungary, Miklós Eszterházy, marching to suppress the revolt, saw an opportunity to bring Transylvania to heel at the same time; but a Transylvanian force advanced to meet him, defeated him soundly and obliged him to withdraw. Shortly afterwards the Transylvanian Diet, concluding that Transylvanian interests would be better protected by a more forceful ruler, elected a Hungarian Protestant baron, György Rákóczi, to be Prince in Catherine's place. Despite Bethlen's dying injunction, Rákóczi saw no advantage in flouting the otherwise advantageous Peace of Nikolsburg and ceded the seven counties, but only in return for assurances from Ferdinand that haiduk rights and liberties would be respected.

Rákóczi proved to be a sound and effective ruler but he did not share Bethlen's passionate commitment to the reunification of an independent Hungary; in advancing Transylvanian interests for their own sake—and he did so with success—he hoped at the same time to add further to his and his family's already considerable wealth and estates. Having declined, shortly after his election, an offer of alliance from Sweden, he responded positively when the offer was renewed in 1643. In 1644, accordingly, György Rákóczi invaded Royal Hungary in order to divert Ferdinand from his support of Denmark against the Swedes. After an initial reverse Rákóczi, like Bocskai and Bethlen before him, succeeded in overrunning most of Royal Hungary—obliging Ferdinand to recall an army from Holstein—and invaded Moravia, linking up with a Swedish force near Brno.

At this point the Turkish Sultan, for reasons that remain obscure, either decided that his Transylvanian vassal had become too big for his boots or, perhaps, feared that Rákóczi was courting eventual defeat, which would lead to Transylvania falling into Habsburg hands. Turkish pressure obliged Rákóczi to desert his Swedish ally and conclude a separate peace with Ferdinand in the Treaty of Linz (1645). The terms of the treaty reflected Ferdinand III's eagerness to neutralise the Transylvanian irritant. The King confirmed the principle of freedom of religion for all his (Hungarian) subjects, their right to use their churches freely and the return to their congregations of churches that had been sequestrated; the agreement also forbade interference with the religious observance of the peasantry, a defeat for the principle of *cuius regio, eius religio*. Of the seven counties that had shuttled back and forth between Royal Hungarian and Transylvanian sovereignty, Rákóczi gained for himself and his heirs Szabolcs and Szatmár; the other five, three of them west of the Tisza in northern Hungary, were ceded to him for his lifetime only. The requirement that the treaty be subject to ratification by the Diet, to be convened within three months, enhanced that body's authority. In return, György Rákóczi undertook to dissolve his alliances with Sweden and France, to refrain from interference in the affairs of Royal Hungary and to lead his troops back to Transylvania.

The greater part of Transylvania's territorial gains from the Treaty of Linz was short-lived: György Rákóczi I died in October 1648, necessitating the return·of the five Hungarian counties to the Habsburgs. Two weeks later, Transylvania's inclusion, as an independent state, among the parties to the Peace of Westphalia served as a permanent memorial to Gábor Bethlen's and György Rákóczi's achievement in winning a place for their small Principality on the international stage. The cause of a reunited and independent Hungary had not been significantly advanced in practical terms, although the Princes had kept the ideal alive. It did not prosper, however, in the decade (1648—58) during which Rákóczi's son and successor, György Rákóczi II, ruled in Transylvania. The younger György's territorial and dynastic ambitions brought the Principality to its knees. Encouraged by his successful subjugation of Wallachia and Moldavia, György Rákóczi II set his sights on the Polish crown (despite his Protestant faith), which he hoped to secure by intervening in the ongoing war between Poland and Sweden, as the latter's ally. His invasion of Poland in 1657 not only failed militarily but also infuriated his liege-lord, the Sultan—or, to be accurate, the Grand Vizier Ahmed Köprölü, with whom power in Istanbul now lay. They decided to put an end to the indiscipline of the Rákóczis once and for all and sent a Tartar force to confront Rákóczi on Polish territory; the Transylvanian army was all but annihilated and although György Rákóczi himself escaped he found on returning home that he had been deposed on Turkish orders. Unsurprisingly, his appeals to Ferdinand III for support against the Sultan fell on deaf ears. Pressing home his advantage, the Grand Vizier sent a Turkish army against Transylvania, which rapidly recaptured all the forts along the Maros River that had fallen to Bocskai sixty years previously and, in 1658, sacked the Principality's capital, Gyulafehérvár. Rákóczi, to his credit, fought on but met his death defending Nagyvárad in 1660. The subsequent installation by the Porte of a puppet Prince, Ákos Barcsay, to rule a devastated Transylvania marked the end of the Principality's existence as an independent force in European politics. As the previous chapter showed, however, there were enduring reminders of Transylvania's flowering.

The Peace of Westphalia (1648), which brought the Thirty Years' War to an end, and the collapse of Transylvania ten years later, made possible a much more vigorous imposition of Habsburg absolutist rule on Royal Hungary. Between 1652 and 1660 the number of Habsburg troops in Royal Hungary increased from 4,000 to 18,000.[12] Since their only deployment against the Turks consisted of a half-hearted and unsuccessful expedition in 1661, under General Montecuccoli, to stem the continuing devastation of Transylvania, the primary purpose of their presence was clearly to intimidate the Hungarian Estates. The Treaty of Linz proved to be no protection against the rigours of the Counter-Reformation, which rapidly conquered the western counties; by 1670, Protestantism had been virtually eliminated from the counties of Sopron and Vas. Austrian exploitation of the economy, at the expense of the Hungarian nobility, intensified with the creation, in 1651, of the *Kaiserliche Ochsenhandlung*, a company backed by imperial capital to establish a monopoly of Hungarian cattle exports. Hungarian cattle-dealers, faced with ruin, attempted to divert their exports to the Adriatic port of Buccari, in a region controlled by Miklós Zrínyi, Bán of Croatia, and his family: the resulting clashes between imperial troops and Zrínyi's own private army inaugurated a new phase in Hungary's struggle for independence.

Resentment, Conspiracy, Repression

Hopes that Leopold I, who succeeded Ferdinand III as King of Hungary in 1657 and as Emperor three years later, would adopt a less passive policy towards the Turks were short-lived. The fortresses along Royal Hungary's southern borders continued to be starved of both men and *matériel;* the Turks continued to infiltrate the border regions and to abduct thousands of Hungarians and Croats into slavery every year. Miklós Zrínyi, a baron and soldier-poet from a Hungarian-Croatian family, became the voice of Hungarian frustration with the Habsburg rulers' wilful neglect of the interests of their Hungarian kingdom and subjects. In his epic poem, 'The Sziget Disaster' (*'Szigeti veszedelem'*), Zrínyi sought to evoke Hungarian national pride by recounting, in powerful verse, the heroic defence of Szigetvár by his great-grandfather and namesake.* Two of his prose writings, 'Reflections on

* See page 99.

the Life of King Mátyás' and 'Remedy against the Turkish Opium',[13] unpublished during his lifetime but circulated widely in manuscript, were of seminal importance in developing the concept of Hungarian nationhood. Zrínyi argued for the creation of a Hungarian national army, drawn from all strata of society, to take up the struggle against the Turks, blaming the Mohács disaster on the reluctance of the nobility to arm the peasantry; his own army consisted largely of freed peasants, reflecting his profound belief in the necessity of reconciliation between the estates of the realm. Rather than playing the Turkish card against the Habsburgs, as the Princes of Transylvania had tried to do, Zrínyi favoured alliance with the French, although he also toyed with an ill-conceived plan to offer the Hungarian crown to György Rákóczi II. Above all, he believed that Hungarians should resume responsibility for their own destiny rather than relying on the Habsburgs to fight their battles for them. 'See', he wrote in 'Remedy against the Turkish Opium', 'I am calling: see, I am shouting! Hear me, Hungarians! Here is the danger, here the consuming fire ... We, the descendants of the glorious Magyar race, must go to our deaths if need be for our wives, our children and our country'.[14]

Miklós Zrínyi himself set a powerful example, translating his own rhetoric into effective action. Having built a new fortress, Zrínyi–újvár on the Mura River, to serve as his operational base, he launched an offensive against the Turks in 1664, overrunning all the Turkish forts along the Drava river and destroying the strategically vital bridge at Eszék. Zrínyi then marched north to lay siege to the Turkish-held fortress of Kanizsa. His military superior, the Habsburg commander-in-chief General Montecuccoli, neither encouraged nor discouraged Zrínyi's initiative but refused to despatch troops to support him when the siege of Kanizsa failed and the Turks, on the counter-attack, destroyed Zrínyi–újvár. Ordering Zrínyi to retreat, Montecuccoli concentrated on defending the approaches to Vienna and inflicted a heavy defeat on the Turks when they overreached themselves by pursuing Zrínyi as far north as Szentgotthárd. Instead of exploiting this rare success against Turkish arms, Leopold I chose this moment to sue for peace, which he secured in the Treaty of Vasvár (1664). The treaty amounted to a humiliation for Hungary: the Turks were to retain all the Hungarian territory they had occupied so far, with the gratuitous addition of the fortified towns of Várad and Érsekújvár, the latter situated less than 100 kilometres south east of Pozsony. Transylvania would remain under Turkish suzerainty—Leopold recognised the Turkish puppet-Prince, Apafi—but both Habsburg and Turkish troops were to be withdrawn from the Principality. The Turks agreed to destroy their fortress at Székelyhíd, south of Várad; but Leopold, for his part, undertook to ensure that Miklós Zrínyi's stronghold, Zrínyi–újvár, was not rebuilt. From the Habsburg viewpoint, the unfavourable terms of the Treaty of Vasvár could be justified by the need, as Leopold saw it, to sate Turkish appetites so that he could concentrate on meeting the threat from France. Seen through Hungarian eyes, the treaty represented a deliberate attempt to weaken Hungary, as a prelude to the final destruction of the Hungarian constitution. When, in 1664, Miklós Zrínyi died in a hunting accident, shortly after the conclusion of the treaty, rumours of his assassination by Habsburg agents quickly gained currency.

The Treaty of Vasvár dismayed the Hungarian Estates: even those Catholic barons who had sought to further their material interests by toadying to the Habsburgs were finally disillusioned. One faction, led by the Palatine, Ferenc Wesselényi, favoured putting Royal Hungary under Turkish protection on the Transylvanian model so that Hungary, like Transylvania, could maintain its own laws and customs, together, of course, with the privileges of the nobility. Others agreed with a baron, Ádám Forgách, who ridiculed the pro-Turkish party: 'Those who want lords like the Turks are likely to come off like the frogs who elected the stork to be their king'.[15] Those who opposed the Turkish option canvassed the arguments for putting Hungary under the protection of Louis XIV of France; but geography argued powerfully against this alternative. A Catholic baron, Ferenc Nádasdy, expressed the Hungarian dilemma in a pamphlet which he published in 1668:

Our protector [Vienna] obviously knows that the Turks will tear us apart unless we submit. Now we desperately cry out and say: 'Either protect us or let us submit!' But the answer is threatening: 'We do not let you submit'. And of protection no mention is made, since there is nothing they could protect us with … Look and judge, Christian World, what is the soul that wilfully lets this be so, and even promotes this by suitable action.[16]

The bitter disillusionment and anxieties of the Hungarian Catholic establishment found expression in an unfocused and disorganised conspiracy that had the broad objective of finding a foreign protector for Hungary. The conspirators included not only Palatine Wesselényi (who died before the conspiracy reached its denouement) but also Miklós Zrínyi's brother, Péter; the Catholic Primate and Archbishop of Esztergom, György Lippay; the Lord Chief Justice, Ferenc Nádasdy; and Hungary's greatest landowner, Ferenc Rákóczi. At various times between 1665 and 1670, the conspirators made contact with the court of Louis XIV, with the Polish court, with the Doge of Venice, with the newly established Rhenish Federation and even with the Turkish Grand Vizier, Ahmed Köprölü, with offers of annual tribute in return for protection. There were no takers: nor, as Ferenc Rákóczi found when he attempted to raise the banner of revolt in northern Hungary, did a group of thoroughly unpopular barons attempting to put Hungary under foreign protection enjoy any significant support. At this point two of the leading conspirators—Péter Zrínyi and his brother-in-law Ferenc Frangepán—lost their nerve, fled to Vienna and threw themselves on the mercy of Leopold I. Leopold, unimpressed, ordered the arrest of all those involved; reports from his agents as the conspiracy developed had kept him fully informed of their identities and activities. Through the intercession of his mother, Zsófia Báthory, Ferenc Rákóczi won his freedom in return for a 400,000 florin ransom; but Zrínyi, Frangepán and Nádasdy were executed in April 1671.

The so-called 'Wesselényi conspiracy' had only one practical result: the provision of a pretext for savage reprisals against the Hungarian nobility and the Protestant Church. The imperial authorities confiscated the estates of any nobleman remotely connected with the conspirators. In 1673 Leopold suspended the Hungarian constitution and entrusted the governance of Hungary to a small Directorate of six members, of whom only three were Hungarian, headed by Johann von Ampringen, Grand Master of the Teutonic Order. Such political autonomy as remained to Hungary evaporated overnight; so did religious freedom. Bishop Leopold Kollonics, one of the king's leading advisers on Hungarian affairs and the most hostile to Hungary, seized the opportunity to prosecute the Counter-Reformation with redoubled vigour: he instigated a wave of arrests of Protestant ministers who were then force-marched to the Adriatic coast, shipped to Naples and sold there as galley slaves.[17] In a spiteful move, which was to rebound against it, the imperial high command dismissed two-thirds of the Hungarian soldiers who garrisoned the border fortresses, claiming that they were unreliable; the imperial troops who replaced them plundered the Hungarian towns and villages through which they passed. From 1672, the counties were made responsible for maintaining the imperial mercenaries quartered on their territory; this requirement, accompanied by a swingeing increase in the war tax and the introduction of a tax on personal consumption, imposed a crushing burden on the tax–paying peasantry. Habsburg policy already reflected the advice given to Leopold I by the Jesuits: that Hungarian behaviour had released him from the undertakings given in his coronation oath and that he was no longer obliged to treat Hungarians as human beings. Leopold recorded his own view: 'Most Hungarians are suspect, unfaithful and disobedient; and whenever misfortune and danger are at their height, then they create the gravest annoyances. It would be best to get rid of them and to leave them to their own kind'.[18]

Inevitably, this tightening of the screws on the Hungarian population generated a reaction. A rebellious underclass came into being, made up of dismissed soldiery from the border region, fugitive serfs, refugees and vagabonds; they adopted with pride the name by which the nobility contemptuously referred to them: *kuruc*, which recalled the crosses worn by György Dózsa's crusading peasants in 1514 and also echoed the Turkish word for 'rebel' (*khurudsch*). Some members of the nobility saw in the *kuruc* a weapon that might be used against the Habsburgs in defence not only of Hungarian interests but of their own endangered privileges and liberties; one of them, István Petróczy, wrote the *'kuruc* proclamation', which circulated in 1673: 'Our eyes are full of tears, when watching the sorrowful nightfall of our decaying dear fatherland and nation, since there has never been on earth a nation strong enough to have defeated our beloved one ... Understand, true Hungarians, make yourselves believe that the Germans hate the whole Hungarian nation *sine discretione religionis* [regardless of religion]'.[19] *Kuruc* bands initiated a series of guerrilla actions, which at first had little more than nuisance value but which soon attracted the attention of the Habsburgs' foreign enemies, the Turks and the French, who both promised support, passing their message via the Transylvanian court. When a leader of the *kuruc* movement emerged, in the person of Imre Thököly, Leopold had to take it more seriously.

Imre Thököly and the Kuruc: Liberation and Retribution

At the age of fourteen, Imre Thököly had witnessed the death of his father, a newly created noble on the fringe of the Wesselényi conspiracy, in the punitive siege by imperial troops of the family castle at Árva in northern Hungary, in 1671. There have been varied assessments of his character[20] but no disagreement about his qualities of leadership, even at the age of twenty when he led the *kuruc* in their first major offensive, in north-east Hungary. Within two years, all imperial troops, now nicknamed *labanc* by their enemies,[21] had been driven from the region and by 1680, the year of his election to be commander-in-chief of all the *kuruc*, Thököly controlled all of upper Hungary. Here he established what amounted to

1 and 2. Two views of medieval Buda: one looking east, with the royal palace on the right (1); and one west, with the palace on the left (2). Béla IV built the first fortress on Castle Hill in 1247.

3. The relief of Belgrade in 1456, János Hunyadi's last and greatest victory over the Turks. Capistrano, the warrior Dominican friar, is depicted left of centre, brandishing a Christian banner.

4. Matthias Corvinus enters Buda after his election to the throne by the Diet in 1458; however, he had to wait six years for his coronation.

5. Fraknó Castle, near Sopron in western Hungary. Strongholds like this were the basis of both royal and baronial power in medieval Hungary.

TRISTE RVDVS VISEGRADI

Danubius

6. The castle at Visegrad, on the Danube Bend north of Buda. Charles I established his court here in 1321; it was enlarged and used as a summer palace by Matthias I.

7. The Mongol invasion of 1241, as portrayed in a German sixteenth century woodcut.

8. The dreadful end of György Dózsa, leader of the peasant revolt of 1514; he is bound to a red-hot iron 'throne' whilst an iron 'crown', also red-hot, is forced on to his head.

9. Ferdinand I of Austria, the first Habsburg king of Hungary, crowned in 1527. He had to make do with only a third of his new kingdom—Transylvania became a Turkish protectorate and the rest of Hungary was under Turkish occupation.

10. Gábor Bethlen, Prince of Transylvania (1613–1629), who established Transylvania as the heartland of Hungarian Calvinist culture.

11. István Bocskai, Prince of Transylvania, leading his haiduks in rebellion against Habsburg rule in 1605.

12. Charles of Lorraine and Jan Sobieski of Poland relieve Vienna from Siege by the Turks, 12 September 1683.

13. Led by Charles of Lorraine and Prince Eugene of Savoy, the armies of the Holy League expel the Turks from Buda; their final assault, on 2 September 1686, was assisted by the explosion of the Turkish armoury, as shown here.

14. Ferenc Rákóczi II, Prince of Transylvania and leader of the continuing Hungarian struggle for independence from the Habsburgs, arrives at the Diet of Ónod (1707) that declared Joseph I deposed and Hungary an independent state.

15. Maria Theresa is crowned Queen of Hungary in Pozsony, 1741; from 1758 she was accorded the title 'Apostolic King of Hungary'.

16. Joseph II, who because of his refusal to be crowned King of Hungary—in order to avoid taking the Coronation Oath—was known to Hungarians as 'the king in a hat'.

17. Joseph's successor, Leopold II. His premature death robbed Hungary of an intelligent and sympathetic ruler.

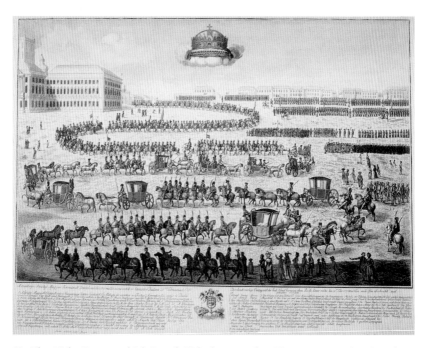

18. The Holy Crown, which Joseph II had removed to Vienna, returns in triumph to Buda immediately after his death in 1790.

a mini–state, with its own coinage bearing the inscription *'Pro Libertate et Justitia'*. He married astutely: Ilona Zrínyi, Ferenc Rákóczi's widow, brought to the *kuruc* cause the immense wealth of the Rákóczi estates. Thököly had also played his diplomatic cards with skill: the promises of support he had successfully solicited from both Louis XIV and Sultan Mehmet IV may not have amounted to much in practical terms but they served thoroughly to alarm Leopold I, already concerned by the ominous growth of French military power. Leopold decided to make a tactical withdrawal. At a specially convened Diet in Sopron in 1681, he restored the Hungarian constitution and the office of Palatine, reconfirmed the Peace of Vienna,* rescinded von Ampringen's appointment, granted partial religious freedom—though restrictions remained on Protestant observance in public—and withdrew the punitive taxes that had been imposed in 1672. Disaffected nobles were promised an amnesty and the restoration of their confiscated estates if they deserted the *kuruc* cause: most of them did so.

The pace of events now increased. Despite noble defections, Imre Thököly and the *kuruc* commoners fought on, in a civil war that, in the opinion of a nineteenth century Hungarian historian, 'for cruelty and mercilessness stands alone in the history of Hungary';[22] *kuruc* propaganda now placed less emphasis on the struggle for religious freedom—partially restored at Sopron—and more on Hungary's aspiration to independent statehood, under Turkish 'protection'. Moral support came from as far away as England, where the Tories dubbed the Whigs 'Teckelists' in mocking reference to the latter's enthusiasm for Thököly's cause. In 1682, Sultan Mehmet 'appointed' Thököly to be King of Hungary: Thököly modestly declined the title but agreed to be styled 'Prince of Upper Hungary'. The Sultan evidently believed Thököly to be stronger than he was, for in 1683 he judged the time to be right for a final showdown with the Habsburgs. He sent the Grand Vizier Kara Mustafa north at the head of a huge army,[23] their right flank protected, as they approached Vienna, by Thököly's force of about 20,000 *kuruc*. Kara Mustafa laid siege to the Habsburg capital in mid-July. Pope Innocent XI, meanwhile, had brokered an alliance between Leopold I (who had deserted Vienna when the siege began) and the King of Poland, Jan Sobieski; he also persuaded Louis XIV to moderate his attacks on the Empire until the infidel had been turned back from the gates of Christian Europe. Kara Mustafa should, perhaps, have been concerned by these developments and also by the news that Imre Thököly had sustained a rare defeat, at the hands of the Habsburg commander-in-chief, Charles of Lorraine, at Pozsony; evidently unperturbed, however, the Grand Vizier settled down to a leisurely siege, concentrating on the elaborate mining of Vienna's walls.[24] He delayed his assault too long. On 12 September 1683, Charles of Lorraine and Jan Sobieski appeared opposite the Turkish left flank at the head of a largely Polish army of about 70,000 men; storming its ill-prepared defences, the relieving force overran the Turkish encampment and drove the Turks into headlong retreat.

Led first by Charles of Lorraine and then by Prince Eugene of Savoy, the army of the Holy League chased the Turks back into Hungary, inflicting a series of defeats on Kara Mustafa's still sizeable but battered force. The Grand Vizier him-

* See page 103.

self sped southwards, hoping to exculpate himself before the Sultan by blaming his subordinates (many of whom he executed) for the disaster at Vienna. Mehmet IV was unmoved: his enforcer intercepted Kara Mustafa in Belgrade, garrotted him and delivered the severed head to the Sultan in a bag. The Austrians and Germans, meanwhile, continued their advance. Imre Thököly's authority crumbled as his *kuruc* deserted to Leopold in droves; Thököly himself escaped the rout, only to be captured by the Pasha of Várad, who hoped to use him as a hostage. In June 1686 Charles of Lorraine stood before Buda at the head of 65,000 men; after a tough two-month siege, during which the Turkish armoury exploded and caused widespread devastation in the town, the final assault began at 6 a.m. on 2 September. By seven o'clock in the evening the Turks had, after 145 years, been expelled from Buda.

The Turks did not yield their conquests easily—the war continued for a further thirteen years; but although they occasionally succeeded in stemming the tide of the Habsburg advance, for example by recapturing Belgrade in 1690, the outcome was seldom in doubt. A symbolic Turkish defeat near Mohács in 1687 caused Mehmet IV to be deposed by his brother Suleiman. In the same year, Habsburg forces invaded Transylvania, the Principality's Diet seizing the occasion to declare Transylvanian independence from the Turks and to place Transylvania under imperial protection. Thököly made his last entry into Transylvanian history in 1690 when, after the death of Mihály Apafi, he led an invading force of Turks and Tartars against the Habsburg occupiers and claimed the title of Prince; Louis XIV of France, now waging war against the League of Augsburg (which included the Habsburg monarchy), had encouraged him to do so with promises of subsidy and recognition. Thököly's remarkable wife, Ilona Zrínyi, had earlier distinguished herself by holding the fortress of Munkács for two years against a besieging Habsburg detachment, an episode that left a lasting impression on her young son, Ferenc Rákóczi II, who shared the privations of the siege. After spending five years in confinement in an Ursuline convent in Austria, Ilona was eventually able to rejoin her husband, who had negotiated her release in exchange for a Habsburg general whom he had captured two years earlier, in Serbia in 1694; but although his Turkish allies fought on, Thököly's personal cause was lost and he never returned to Transylvania. Thököly and his gallant wife spent their remaining years in impoverished exile in Turkey. In the aftermath of Thököly's downfall, Leopold I affirmed Habsburg sovereignty over the Principality in the *Diploma Leopoldina*, in which he assumed the title of Prince of Transylvania; although the *Diploma* also recognised the 'three nations' (Magyars, Saxons and Székely) and their religious liberties, it in fact marked the end of Transylvania's existence as a quasi–independent Principality and ensured its continued separation from Hungary. Transylvania was henceforth ruled from Vienna.

Meanwhile, the Turkish war continued to ebb and flow. A Habsburg army under Louis of Baden smashed the main Turkish force at Szalánkemén, at the confluence of the Tisza and Danube Rivers, in 1691, killing 20,000 Turks including the Grand Vizier; and after further fluctuations of fortune, Prince Eugene of Savoy delivered in 1697 what turned out to be the *coup de grace* at Zenta bridge over the southern Tisza, which French sappers had built for the Turks. The Sultan thereafter allowed the British Ambassador to the Porte, Lord Paget, to convey peace terms to Leopold. Under the resulting Treaty of Karlowitz (1699), in the negotiation of which Hungarians were permitted to play no part, the Turks recognised Habsburg sovereignty over the whole of Hungary and Transylvania, retaining only a small slice of territory between the rivers Tisza and Maros, in the Temesvár region, in which they were forbidden to station troops. After one hundred and fifty-six years, the Turkish occupation of Hungary was over.

As we have already seen,* 'liberation' spelt disaster for the Jews of Buda; and so it did for the great majority of Hungarians throughout the land. No sooner had Buda been relieved than General Caraffa, the Habsburg military governor, set up a military tribunal in Eperjes, in northern Hungary, and used it as an instrument of retribution and extortion. Sixteen of Thököly's leading supporters were executed and many more deprived of their personal wealth and estates. The example of the Eperjes assizes triggered a reign of terror throughout Hungary, conducted by local military commanders. In the shadow of these reprisals, the Diet assembled in Pozsony in 1687 in response to Leopold's summons. Grateful for the expulsion of the Turks but numbed by its aftermath, the Estates assented to the constitutional changes which Leopold demanded. Succession to the Hungarian crown would henceforth be hereditary in the Habsburg male line unless that were to die out: the elective principle was thus virtually buried; the Diet surrendered the right of resistance to a monarch enshrined in Andrew II's Golden Bull; and the coronation oath would in future omit any guarantee of religious freedom. As the Diet dispersed, Cardinal Kollonics, Leopold's principal adviser on Hungarian matters, launched his administrative plan to convert Hungary into a model province of the Habsburg lands. The boast attributed to Kollonics that he would 'make of the Hungarian first a slave, then a beggar and finally a Roman Catholic' may have been apocryphal; but of his profound hostility both to Hungarian disaffection and to Hungary's over-privileged nobility there could be no doubt. It found expression in the *Neo-acquistica Commissio*, a department of the *Hofkammer* (Treasury), the ostensible purpose of which was to restore estates to owners who had been forced by the war to abandon them. In order to secure restitution, land-owning families were obliged both to produce detailed documentary proof of ownership—which, in the circumstances of the time, they were often unable to do—and to pay a massive fee (10 per cent of the value of the estate claimed). In practice, therefore, the Commission dedicated its efforts as much to confiscation as to restitution, to the benefit of the imperial treasury and of those whom Leopold chose to reward for their loyalty. The Commission's work also had a more sinister dimension: in its own words, 'Hungarian blood, which makes people inclined towards unrest and revolution, should be mixed with German blood so as to assure trust and love towards their natural hereditary king'.[25] To this end, Germans were settled on Hungarian estates, which their rightful owners were prevented from reclaiming. The policy of Germanisation also included the towns, although in some cases this merely involved restoring the status quo ante; Buda became, once again, a German-speaking town, while towns such as Várad, Eger, Székesfehérvár and Esztergom acquired new German majorities. Nor were Germans the only beneficiaries of Vienna's resettlement policy: when Leopold's armies had

* See page 90.

failed to dislodge the Turks from Serbia, the Orthodox Patriarch of Péc, Arsenije Črnojević, led some 30,000 of his fellow Serbs northwards into Hungary where, in some cases, Hungarians were evicted from their holdings to accommodate them. Unlike the Hungarians, the newly arrived Serbs enjoyed complete freedom of religious belief as well as exemption from the tithe. These privileges had originally been offered by Leopold as an inducement to persuade the Serbs to rise up against the Turks, in support of the Habsburg army;[26] the Serbs had not responded to this appeal but pocketed the promised privileges anyway. Szentendre, a small town on the Danube north of Buda, became—and remained into the nineteenth century—a virtual Serbian enclave and an episcopal see of the Orthodox Church; its cathedral and several rather fine Orthodox churches still stand there.

While these prongs of the Kollonics administrative plan affected primarily the landowning classes, its financial prong bore most heavily on the peasantry, the *misera plebs contribuens*. On Kollonics's recommendation, the court in Vienna set Hungary's annual tax contribution at 4 million florins—double the existing rate and one-third of the tax revenue from all the lands of the monarchy. This liability was to be shared between the nobility and clergy (1.25 million), the towns (250,000) and the peasantry (2.5 million). The Palatine, Prince Pál Eszterházy, argued on behalf of the Estates that they could contribute no more than one-thirtieth of the total rather than one-third (he evidently recognised that to insist on the continued exemption of the nobility from taxation would be a waste of breath). After some haggling, Leopold conceded that the nobility and the towns should contribute 250,000 florins each and the peasantry 3.5 million, a crushing burden. In order to escape it, many peasants—if they could not afford to purchase patents of nobility—divested themselves of plots and livestock, becoming voluntary landless cottars. Initially, responsibility for tax collection lay with the army, a punitive arrangement that enabled the collectors not only to extort more than was due but to loot and plunder into the bargain; the eventual transfer of the collection process back to the counties, after 1696, enabled the nobility to cheat in their turn. As if a disproportionate share of the tax load was not enough, the peasants also bore the brunt of the Habsburg army's depredations. Not for the last time in Hungarian history, an army of 'liberation' had become an army of occupation. Vienna made Hungary liable for over 50 per cent of the cost of maintaining it and for the provision of living quarters, rations and fodder for 44,000 men and 12,000 horses.[27]

Ferenc Rákóczi II and the War of Independence

During the closing years of the century, religious persecution, economic exploitation and the devastation wreaked by unpaid and hungry Habsburg mercenaries provoked an inevitable reaction. In north-eastern Hungary, and particularly in the relatively prosperous wine-growing region of Tokaj where the pickings were richest, the misery of desperate peasants produced sporadic insurrections culminating, in 1697, in the occupation of Tokaj and Sárospatak castles. Two veterans of Imre Thököly's campaigns, Tamás Esze and Albert Kis, had already spent two years in the region trying to mould an organised rebellion out of inchoate discontent. They identified the ideal leader for it in the young Ferenc Rákóczi II, hereditary *ispán* of Sárospatak county and the greatest landowner in the north east—and indeed in all Hungary—having inherited estates covering nearly 2 million *hold*.[28] As the descendant of four Princes of Transylvania, son of a leading participant in the 'Wesselényi plot' (Ferenc Rákóczi I, who died in the year of Ferenc II's birth) and of the redoubtable defender of Munkács castle, Ilona Zrínyi, Ferenc Rákóczi II's anti–Habsburg credentials seemed impeccable; but they took some time to materialise.

When, ten years earlier, Munkács had finally succumbed to the Habsburg force besieging it, Ilona Zrínyi, her son Ferenc and daughter Julia had been taken to Vienna, where the two children were made wards of Cardinal Kollonics. Julia was packed off to a convent, Ferenc to a Jesuit school. Ferenc Rákóczi was apparently mature for his twelve years, not outstanding intellectually but possessed of great personal charisma and very conscious of his social rank. He did his best to integrate into his new environment, learning German and adopting the Viennese style of dress. After making a Grand Tour of Italy and Germany, he incurred Leopold's displeasure by marrying without permission, at the age of eighteen, into a well-connected German princely family;[29] despite the suspicions that, in view of past history, the name of Rákóczi inevitably attracted, the Emperor nevertheless allowed Ferenc to take his bride and his new title of Prince back to his estates in Hungary, where imperial agents kept a close eye on them. Conscious of this surveillance, Rákóczi rebuffed the approaches of the leaders of the Tokaj uprising in 1697 and kept his distance from the insurrection; indeed, he over-reacted, rushing to Vienna to protest his loyalty to the Emperor in person and offering to exchange his Hungarian estates for equivalent property in Austria or Germany as a guarantee of his good intentions. Leopold professed to be reassured, but when Rákóczi returned to Hungary Kollonics's spies went with him. Back on his estates, Rákóczi underwent a radical change of heart, which owed a great deal to his close friend, the *ispán* of neighbouring Ung county, Count Miklós Bercsényi. Bercsényi, who had fought with distinction against the Turks and held the office of Royal Commissary-General of upper Hungary, was Rákóczi's senior in years and his superior in intellect; he believed passionately in the cause of Hungarian independence but from a strictly aristocratic viewpoint, namely that the barons of Hungary should be allowed to run the country in their own way without foreign interference. Rákóczi soon came not only to share this view but, with the zeal of the convert, to wish to translate it into action. In north-east Hungary, the two men could see the raw material of rebellion all around them in the anger of pillaged and impoverished villages; and in the bitterness of the former *kuruc* and peasants who had taken their families and livestock into the hills and forests to escape the attentions of tax collectors and marauding mercenaries. Especially in eastern Hungary, resentment against the persecution of Protestants was profound and widespread.

The opportunity to catalyse this bitter discontent arrived with the outbreak, in 1701, of the War of Spanish Succession, which pitted France against the Habsburg monarchy in contention for the Spanish throne. Rákóczi composed a letter to Louis XIV soliciting his support for an armed uprising in Hungary, entrusting it to an apparently sympathetic Walloon officer in the imperial army, Captain Longueval, for delivery to Paris. Longueval delivered it instead to the imperial court in Vienna. Bercsényi managed to escape to Poland but Rákóczi was arrested and incarcerated in the same cell in the fortress of Wiener Neustadt from which his uncle, Péter Zrínyi, had been led to execution thirty years before. With the connivance of an Austrian officer, who paid for it with his life, Rákóczi escaped and eventually joined Bercsényi in Warsaw.

During eighteen months of exile in Poland, Rákóczi and Bercsényi fired off a succession of appeals for support to the crowned heads of Europe but with little success. England, the Netherlands and Poland had already declared for the Habsburgs in the war; Russia and Sweden had their hands full with a war, the 'Northern War', of their own. Only Louis XIV agreed to provide limited support, which at its peak eventually amounted to a financial subsidy of 50,000 livres per month—sufficient to pay 5,000 soldiers—and the secondment of ninety army officers to help with military training; but this still lay some way ahead. It took the arrival in Brezán (where the exiles had been given refuge by a Polish noble-woman) of two emissaries from Tiszahát—Mihály Pap, from the lesser nobility, and György Bige, a former *kuruc* lieutenant—to bring Rákóczi to the point of action: they assured him that 'our countrymen are ready, they lack only a leader'.[30] When reports from other intermediaries, including Tamás Esze, confirmed this claim, Rákóczi sent Esze back to Hungary with a red banner bearing the slogan *Cum Deo pro patria et libertate*. With Bercsényi, he signed a manifesto to the Hungarian people, dated 'Brezán, 6 May 1703', calling upon all who loved their country, and wished to regain its liberty, to take up arms against the cruel empire which had besmirched its honour and robbed it of salt and bread:

Arise, all of ye, for your country and take up arms for the sake of the widows, orphans and helpless poor. Those who do so and their descendants shall be exempt from all taxes and seigneurial burdens in perpetuity, and shall be granted liberty. If an entire community rises as one and is willing to fight for its liberation, the village shall be granted perpetual freedom in common and its renown will be remembered by generations to come.[31]

Shortly after signing this appeal, Rákóczi left Brezán, arriving on Hungarian soil at Verecke (where the Magyars had entered the Carpathian Basin eight centuries before) on 7 June 1703. Only a few hundred poorly armed and undisciplined peasants awaited him; but within days, as the Brezán manifesto became more widely known, Rákóczi's neo-*kuruc* army numbered thousands, including Slovaks, Ruthenians and Romanians as well as Hungarians. Of Hungary's and Transylvania's ethnic groups only the Serbs—the Habsburg fifth column—and, of course, the Germans, stayed away. The free town of Debrecen, prosperous from cattle trading, declared for Rákóczi in July and became the main commissariat for the rebellion, supplying the *kuruc* with firearms, swords, clothing and harness.

Rákóczi and Bercsényi had timed the insurrection well: by midsummer 1703, the exigencies of the war with France had drained Hungary of Habsburg troops: apart from those garrisoning the border forts, only three and a half regiments of infantry and three of cavalry, about 6,000 men in all, remained.[32] Rákóczi's force outnumbered them within weeks: by November, it had grown to 30,000, nine-tenths Calvinist according to Rákóczi himself. Nagyszombat, Pozsony and, by the year's end, all of western Hungary fell to the *kuruc*.

The Brezán manifesto's promises of freedom for serfs and exemption from taxation and *robot* for peasants who joined the *kuruc* explained the phenomenally rapid growth of the rebel army. As early as August 1703, Rákóczi had also issued the Patent of Vetés (Szatmár county), which laid down that the wives and children of serfs who had rallied to the scarlet banner should not be liable for rent or services during the absence of their husbands, although they would be expected to share the burden of provisioning the rebel force. None of this greatly enthused the nobility, most of whom also reacted negatively to the open threat in the appeal for noble support that Rákóczi had issued at Namény in July, 1703: 'If their [the nobles'] persons or goods suffer the force of arms, fire and steel, they should blame it only on their lack of patriotism and their German-mindedness'.[33] The nobility resented the exodus of labourers from their estates and harboured traditional misgivings about arming the peasantry.

In January 1704, Rákóczi published a second manifesto, addressed this time not to Hungarians but to 'all the princes and republics of the whole Christian world'; it came to be known by its opening words, *'Recrudescunt inclytae gentis Hungarae vulnera'* ('The wounds of the renowned Hungarian people have opened afresh') and was printed in German, French and Dutch as well as Latin and Hungarian.* It listed twenty-one Hungarian grievances against the Habsburgs which had constrained the Hungarian people to take up arms. The manifesto rejected, for Hungary, the hereditary principle, insisting on the Diet's right to elect its monarch; it maintained the nobility's right of resistance to the crown, as enshrined in the Golden Bull; it disavowed, in their entirety, the proceedings of the Diet of 1687; and it protested against the exclusion of Hungarians from the governance of their country, for example in the negotiation of the Treaty of Karlowitz. Unlike its predecessor, therefore, this manifesto set out the agenda of the Hungarian nobility rather than that of the common people.

There were in 1704 good reasons for doubting whether the early military successes of the *kuruc* could be maintained: by inflicting a decisive defeat on a large French and Bavarian force at Blenheim (Höchstädt), Marlborough, the English commander, prevented the French from linking up with Rákóczi's *kuruc* and from mounting a joint siege of Vienna. With Bavaria effectively out of the war, Leopold could afford to reinforce his beleaguered rearguard in Hungary. This change in the military balance nevertheless took time to materialise and most of the nobility, impressed by Rákóczi's continued success in reducing Habsburg strongholds, concluded during 1704 and 1705 that their interests would be best served by joining the rebellion with a view to controlling it. They succeeded. By the end of 1705, twenty-five of the *kuruc* army's twenty-six generals were nobles: they included eight counts, seven barons and ten nobles of lesser rank; General János Bottyán alone represented the lower orders in the *kuruc* high command.[34] Their army now numbered 100,000, composed of ninety-one regiments of infantry and fifty-two of cavalry, together with artillery and auxiliary units. A peasant insurrection had become a national rebellion.

The death of Leopold I in May 1705, reminded the Hungarian Estates that although his successor as Emperor, Joseph I, had been crowned King of Hungary

---

* The manifesto, although published in January 1704, was symbolically dated '7 June 1703, Munkács' since its purpose was to set out the case for the rebellion which had begun on that date.

in 1690, he had not been elected by the Diet and that Hungary consequently lacked a legitimate ruler. A Diet therefore assembled at Szécsény in the autumn. Attended as it was by six bishops, thirty-six barons, twenty-five lesser nobles representing the counties and several spokemen for the towns, it demonstrated the now national character of the independence movement. The Diet declared its refusal to recognise Joseph I as king, maintained its right of election and elected Ferenc Rákóczi II 'Governing Prince of Hungary' (he had already, in 1704, been elected Prince of Transylvania). It formed a 'Confederation of Estates', imitating Poland, to be led by a Senate of twenty-five members dominated, naturally, by the barons. The Diet demanded the restitution of Hungary's liberties and the recognition of Transylvania as a sovereign state. The Szécsény Diet marked the graduation of the *kuruc* movement to something resembling organised statehood. Although it as yet levied no taxes, it mobilised revenue from customs duties, estates confiscated from nobles loyal to the Habsburgs and the mines: it issued its own coinage, in copper, and set up an Economic Committee to manage it. It established state workshops to produce arms and uniforms for its large army, which in 1706 acquired its own manual of army regulations, based on a French model. Plans were drafted to improve Hungary's schools and to establish a postal service. But the mismatch between the ideals and objectives of the common *kuruc* on the one hand and those of his noble commanders on the other had begun to emerge. In taking up arms under Rákóczi's *'pro libertate'* banner, the peasants and the serfs had sought to fight for an improvement in their conditions of life: for relief from oppressive taxation, for protection against marauding mercenaries and for greater respect on the part of landlords for their dignity as human beings. They now found themselves fighting a war that seemed more directed towards the restoration of *noble* privileges and liberties; and their initial enthusiasm was further cooled by the spectacle of Prince Ferenc Rákóczi's elaborate court, complete with its bodyguard of the young noble elite. Already in 1706 Miklós Bercsényi was moved to remark: 'We have lost the love of the common people'.[35]

Before his death, Leopold I had agreed, with considerable reluctance, to accept an offer from his English and Dutch allies to mediate between his government and Rákóczi and to try to broker a settlement; the allies had a clear interest in bringing to an end a conflict that had by now tied down in Hungary 30,000 Habsburg troops that could be better employed in fighting the French. Rákóczi, for his part, had become concerned by his continued failure to enlist a foreign ally (even Louis XIV had drawn the line at a formal alliance with rebels) and by an ominous improvement in the Habsburg military performance: the new Austrian commander, Herbeville, had inflicted a heavy defeat on the *kuruc* at Zsibó and János Bottyán's siege of Sopron had failed. Rákóczi was ready to discuss terms. The negotiations dragged on through 1705 and 1706. Joseph I, however, was sufficiently encouraged by developments in the war against the French—Marlborough's victory at Ramillies and Prince Eugene's at Turin, both in 1706—to eschew concessions; in particular, he refused to recognise Ferenc Rákóczi as Prince of Transylvania. One of the intermediaries, the English Ambassador in Vienna, entertained little hope of a successful outcome: 'I dare think', he noted, 'that the intention of this [Habsburg] Court is to have very little regard to the privileges of that [Hungarian] Kingdom, laying hold of this occasion to establish a Despotic power there which they have aimed at, and to which the People of all kinds are very averse, especially in the hands of the Germans, to whom they have an extreme Antipathy'.[36]

By 1707, the mediators had reached a dead end. In a final effort to win Louis XIV's open and wholehearted support, Rákóczi called the Diet to Ónod, where it formally declared Joseph I deposed and Hungary an independent state; by thus shedding, technically, the status of rebels the *kuruc* hoped to win not only French but possibly other foreign support. Preoccupation with money dominated the remainder of the Diet's proceedings; in the absence of taxation, funding for the huge *kuruc* army threatened to dry up. The Diet's resolution reflected the acuteness of the crisis: it introduced *general* taxation, from which only serving *kuruc* and their families—but not the nobility—would be exempt. There were sops to landlords, including the promise of compensation from state funds for the loss of serfs; but only the force of Rákóczi's personality and the summary execution of two of his opponents *pour encourager les autres* secured the resolution's passage. Once away from Ónod, the barons began to grumble. It was the beginning of the end.

Although Rákóczi and his closest aides, most of them drawn from the lesser nobility, did their best to ensure respect for the Patent of Vetés by landlords, their success was patchy. Landlords frequently resorted to eviction to rid their estates of the families of serving *kuruc;* immune from taxation and *robot*, they were a burden landlords could well do without. The threat of such evictions was used by the nobility to recall their serfs from the ranks of the *kuruc* army. The *kuruc* themselves resented being paid in the new copper coinage, which many tradesmen refused to accept. These factors and the social tensions to which they gave rise began to erode support for Rákóczi. Outside Hungary, too, the tide began to turn against him. France, ever harder pressed in the war, suspended all financial aid to the *kuruc* cause after 1709; forced to consider peace negotiations with Joseph I, Louis XIV felt obliged to shed the embarrassment of support for the independence movement. In 1707, Peter the Great of Russia had hoped to persuade the French to mediate in his Northern War against Charles XII of Sweden; and had offered Rákóczi an alliance in order to win Louis XIV's favour. Once he had defeated the Swedes at Poltava in 1709, Peter no longer needed French mediation and consequently lost interest in the Hungarians. All these developments sapped *kuruc* morale and military performance. Rákóczi suffered a serious defeat at Trencsén in August 1708, at the hands of the Austrian general Heister despite a *kuruc* superiority in numbers on the battlefield of nearly two to one. Further defeats followed; and an epidemic of plague swept through the *kuruc* army which, by the end of 1709, had been penned into the north-east corner of Hungary.

The Habsburg army, however, was in no better state. General János Pálffy, a Hungarian loyal to the crown whom Joseph had appointed in September 1710 to command his forces in Hungary, reported to the *Hofkriegsrat* in November that his army, some 45,000 strong, had been decimated by hunger and the plague; and that discipline had broken down. In November, Pálffy sent a personal note to Sándor Károlyi, commander-in-chief of the *kuruc* army—whom he had known personally in happier times—proposing negotiations on a peace settlement. Károlyi showed Pálffy's note to Rákóczi, who still entertained hopes of an alliance with Peter the Great of Russia that would transform *kuruc* fortunes; he therefore instructed Károlyi to send a temporising response. But the succession of *kuruc* reverses continued: the fortress of Eger surrendered to Pálffy's troops at the end of November and Eperjes followed suit shortly afterwards. When Pálffy, sympathetic to the plight of the *kuruc*, renewed his proposal for peace talks, the response was sufficiently positive to encourage him to transfer his headquarters to Debrecen, armed with full powers from the Emperor to negotiate; his first meeting with Károlyi took place on 21 January 1711. Rákóczi had by then left for Poland, to pursue his dream of a Russian alliance; but he returned briefly at the end of the month to meet Pálffy personally and to sanction the continuation of negotiations. Before setting off once more for Poland, Rákóczi briefed his military commanders on the talks with Pálffy and authorised Károlyi to continue them.

By mid-March the two commanders, driven forward to an accommodation by the pitiable condition of their men, had reached broad agreement. To give proof of his good faith, Károlyi took an oath of allegiance to Joseph I, privately with only Pálffy present; he then left for Poland to brief Rákóczi. Apart from seeking clarification on one point, Rákóczi appears to have been sufficiently receptive to the heads of agreement to order an assembly of the Confederation to discuss them at the end of April. Károlyi, however, mindful of the fact that the ceasefire, which had been agreed for the duration of the talks, was due to expire on 7 April, summoned the Confederation to meet at Szatmár as soon as he had returned to Hungary. The Confederation did so; it approved the peace terms negotiated with Pálffy and called upon Rákóczi to return. Rákóczi's response was to dismiss Károlyi from his command and to issue, from Poland, an appeal to the Confederation to continue the struggle: Vienna's promise of amnesty, he claimed, should not be trusted and the peasants should not be consigned once more to servitude. Even Ferenc Rákóczi's immense personal prestige, however, could not overcome the war-weariness that had settled over Hungary; the *kuruc* were already drifting back to their villages. The Confederation voted to conclude a peace agreement and to accept the promised royal amnesty. The death of Joseph I on 17 April did not derail the process. The Peace of Szatmár was signed on 30 April 1711, bringing to an end a war that had lasted eight years, in which 85,000 men had died in battle and during which some 400,000 souls had perished from famine or plague. The agreement was brief: Ferenc Rákóczi and his followers would have their estates restored to them if they swore allegiance to the crown within three weeks; all the *kuruc* would benefit from a general amnesty; the King (Charles III, as yet uncrowned) would respect the rights of Hungary and Transylvania and would listen to the legitimate grievances of the Estates; the existing laws on religion would remain in force. On 1 May, on the field of Majtény near Szatmár, 12,000 *kuruc* paraded before the two commanders-in chief (Károlyi had ignored his dismissal). After swearing an oath of allegiance to the late King Joseph, they laid down their battle standards but kept their arms.

During the eighteenth and nineteenth centuries, the view took root, reinforced by the memoirs Rákóczi himself composed in exile, that Sándor Károlyi had betrayed his Prince and the cause of independence by negotiating with Pálffy behind Rákóczi's back. The foregoing account should make it clear that this was not the case. Indeed, the events which led up to the Szatmár agreement detract more from Rákóczi's reputation than from Károlyi's. Rákóczi's obsession with the possibility of a Russian alliance—which, to be fair, Peter the Great had done nothing to discourage—blinded him to the appalling privations and exhaustion of the *kuruc*, as of their opponents; as it turned out, Peter needed Habsburg neutrality in his war against the Turks—which broke out during the summer of 1711—and after keeping Rákóczi dangling for several months declined to lend him support of any kind. Rákóczi felt unable to accept a peace that did not hold out some prospect of social improvement for the common people; and he insisted to the last on independence for Transylvania, a stipulation that owed as much to his *amour propre* as Transylvania's elected Prince as to wider political considerations. These objectives were neither trivial nor ignoble; but the *kuruc* had lost the war and the terms Károlyi negotiated with Pálffy were, in the circumstances, far from harsh—indeed, Pálffy's moderation exposed him, too, to charges of disloyalty. Rákóczi could not, nevertheless, reconcile himself to this outcome. After Peter I had rebuffed him in Poland, he sought refuge in England, where he was refused permission to land at Hull; he enjoyed a better reception in Paris, where his inconstant ally Louis XIV treated him with honour and where he entered a monastery for a time to reflect on his fate and that of his country. When Paris tired of him, Rákóczi accepted the hospitality of the Sultan, hoping that from Turkey he might, like Imre Thököly, re-enter the history of his homeland. It was not to be: Ferenc Rákóczi II died in self-imposed exile at Rodostó in 1735.[37]

If the Habsburg monarchy had been less well served by its English and Dutch allies in the War of the Spanish Succession, Rákóczi's independence movement might have succeeded in achieving at least some of its declared aims; but without a foreign ally of its own, more committed and active than France, its chances of success had always been small. For all its initial zeal and—until the fortunes of war turned against it after 1706—remarkable *esprit de corps*,[38] the *kuruc* army was unlikely to prevail against the more disciplined and better-equipped Habsburg forces. The movement was weakened, too, by the social divisions within it. For all his genuine sympathy with the plight of the common people and sincere aspiration to improve their lot, Rákóczi remained a prisoner of his own class, a firm believer in its privileges and right to govern. From the nobility's point of view, indeed, the Peace of Szatmár did not represent a total defeat in so far as Charles III undertook 'to maintain and hold sacred and inviolate the rights, liberties and immunities of the kingdom of Hungary and Transylvania',[39] which meant the rights, liberties and immunities of the noble class. The Diets of 1712 and 1715 translated this promise into laws that defined the relationship between the Hungarian nation (namely the nobility) and the monarchy for the next hundred years and more. Albeit at immense human cost, Rákóczi's War of Independence established Hungary's right to be treated by its Habsburg monarchs with, at the very least, circumspection; it put a high price tag on any repetition of the oppression of Leopold I's reign. Ferenc Rákóczi helped Hungary to emerge from the trough of the seventeenth century with some notable battle honours and a degree of self-respect.

7

HABSBURG RULE AND NATIONAL AWAKENING

(1711–1825)

The independence struggles of the seventeenth century had failed to win for Hungary liberation from Habsburg rule or reunification of the lands of the Holy Crown. They had, however, ensured that Hungary, together with Croatia/Slavonia and Transylvania, would not easily be relegated, as Bohemia had been, to the status of mere provinces of the Habsburg monarchy. Hungary had established, albeit at immense cost, her right to be different. During the eighteenth century, this right had to be defended against a more direct and intrusive style of monarchical rule: again, there was a price to be paid but this time in terms of economic development rather than in human blood. The policies Vienna sought to pursue in Hungary were usually well intentioned and based on a rational assessment of where the kingdom's best interests lay; individual Hungarians often played an important role in their formulation. But the spasm of malicious violence that had followed Hungary's liberation from the Turks, and the attentions of Cardinal Kollonics, had made the establishing of mutual trust between the ruled and their rulers difficult, perhaps impossible. Hungary was nevertheless spared, for nearly a hundred years from 1711, armed conflict on her own soil, her longest period of peace since the Middle Ages. This made possible the construction of the framework of a modern state—a framework still filled, however, by a largely feudal society—and, towards the end of the century, the flowering of an indigenous national culture. The history of eighteenth-century Hungary, unlike that of eighteenth-century England, France or Prussia, is not remarkable for great events, victories or achievements; its interest lies in the emergence of all the factors—political, social and cultural—that were to bring about the cataclysms of the two centuries that followed.

The Eighteenth-century Habsburgs—Absolutism and Reform

Charles III (1711–40)

The Peace of Szatmár and the Diets of 1712, 1715 and 1722–23, taken together, comprised an accommodation between the Habsburg rulers and their indigestible Hungarian kingdom that embodied most of the elements of the later Compromise of 1867.* Since the terms of this accommodation defined the relationship between Hungary and the Habsburgs until that later one, and in some respects beyond it, they deserve examination. They provide a benchmark against which the constitutionality of the subsequent behaviour of both parties can be judged.

King Charles III (the Emperor Charles VI), a cautious, deliberate ruler who had succeeded his brother Joseph I in 1711, had two reasons for establishing a modus vivendi with the Hungarians. The first was his need for a stable situation in Hungary that would allow him to concentrate on consolidating his hold on the new additions to the lands of the Monarchy, in the Netherlands and in Italy, which had accrued from the Treaty of Utrecht (1713). The second, and more pressing, was his need to ensure that his own heir—if he succeeded in producing one—whether male or female, would inherit an undivided Monarchy. To this end he had drawn up a law of inheritance, known as the Pragmatic Sanction, which, if it was not to become the trigger for yet another European war, required the explicit approval, in advance, not only of the major European powers but also of the Monarchy's component parts, including Hungary. The Pragmatic Sanction provided that the Habsburg lands were indivisible; that their inheritance should be on the basis of primogeniture in the male line or in the female line if there were to be no male heir; and that, in the latter case, Charles's own daughters should have the prior claim over those of the daughters of Joseph I and Leopold I. By enshrining in the Sanction the overriding importance of the unity of the Monarchy, Charles hoped to pre-empt future bids for independence by its individual parts.

As soon as he had been crowned with the Holy Crown, and even before the Sanction had formally been drawn up, Charles III took soundings of the Hungarian Diet on their likely attitude towards the possibility of female succession. True to form, the Hungarian nobles, demanded an impossibly high price, in terms of special constitutional treatment, for their co-operation.[1] Charles, affronted, decided to concentrate on selling the Pragmatic Sanction to less importunate interested parties; he did not approach the Hungarian Diet on the subject again until 1722. By that time, the succession question had ceased to be hypothetical: Charles's only male child had died in infancy but his Empress had borne him a daughter, Maria Theresa, in 1718. Persistent diplomatic activity secured acceptance of the Pragmatic Sanction by Europe's major powers (except Bavaria) and, with less difficulty, by the Austrian hereditary provinces, by Croatia and by Transylvania; Joseph I's daughters, moreover, had renounced their own claims to the inheritance. This left Hungary. In the event, the Diet of 1722–23 proved to be unexpectedly pliable, or perhaps susceptible to the numerous rewards in honours, land and treasure that Charles liberally dispensed. In return for the Diet's unanimous acceptance of the terms of the Pragmatic Sanction (which the resulting law did not, however, mention by name), Charles promised 'to maintain all the said States and Orders [i.e. the nobility] of his hereditary Kingdom of Hungary, and of the Parts, Kingdoms and Provinces thereto annexed, in all Diplomatic [i.e. contained in the Coronation Oath] and other rights, liberties, privileges, immunities, customs, prerogatives, and laws hitherto granted, established, and enacted, and to be enacted ...'.[2] The law placed the same obligation on Charles's successors. The

* See Chapter 9.

effect of embodying the Sanction in Hungarian law was also to confirm the indivisibility, not only of the lands of the Holy Crown (Hungary, Transylvania, Croatia/Slavonia and Dalmatia), but also of these lands from the Austrian hereditary provinces, since they would share a common monarch for so long as the House of Habsburg endured. The defence of these lands against external threat, and the provision of the necessary means for that, were explicitly recognised to be common responsibilities, in terms that were to be of critical importance over a century later. Should the Habsburg line, namely that represented by the descendants of Charles, Joseph I and Leopold I, become extinct, the right of the Diet to elect its king would automatically revive.

During the constant upheavals of the seventeenth century, the governance of Hungary had inevitably been a haphazard process, frequently interrupted by insurrection and war. In theory, however, the medieval duality of Crown and Diet still obtained, with the Court Chancellery acting as secretariat; interaction between the two Chambers of the Diet, and between the Diet as a whole and the monarch, produced laws and decrees that the Chancellery then instructed the county authorities (*főispáns* and *alispáns*) to implement. The more interventionist style of government to which the eighteenth-century Habsburgs, in the spirit of the age, were committed required more sophisticated machinery. Charles III set about creating it. Charles had already moved quickly to impose his authority on his new kingdom (he had been crowned in Pozsony in 1712); he had firmly rejected the Diet's appeal for the reunification of Transylvania and the Partium with Hungary, persuaded the Estates to approve the creation of a standing army of 15,000—to be paid for by the *contributio*, a tax on the peasantry who would also provide the recruits—and excluded Hungarians from the defence or administration of the Bánát of Temesvár, newly recovered from the Turks. When the third Diet of his reign assembled in Pozsony in 1722, Charles presented it with a substantial package of administrative reforms. The Hungarian Court Chancellery was to be upgraded from a secretariat to the prime instrument of royal governance, located in Vienna except when the Diet was in session and consisting of fourteen members—three barons and eleven lesser nobles—nominated by the king; it would be the sole channel for the transmission of royal edicts and instructions to the executive organs in Hungary, the principal guardian of the royal prerogatives and the first source of advice to the king on Hungarian law and custom.

Below the Chancellery, Charles created a new body, the Lieutenancy Council (*consilium regium locumtenentiale*), located in Pozsony and later in Buda, the task of which was to oversee and supervise the execution by landlords, bishops and counties of royal decrees and royally sanctioned legislation. Consisting of twenty-two councillors under the chairmanship of the Palatine, it was divided into five departments responsible for taxes and military provision, ecclesiastical affairs, education, the economy and trade, and miscellaneous matters. As governmental business increased and administration became more complex, the Council's departments increased in number and totalled twenty by the end of the century. Since the councillors—all members of the nobility—tended to be poor attenders, the Lieutenancy Council's work was largely conducted by professional civil servants (many of them, too, members of the Hungarian noble class), necessarily loyal to the monarch on whom they depended for their salaries and pensions. The Council thus constituted Hungary's first organ of modern government, the forerunner of the ministries and departments of the nineteenth century. Although it inevitably attracted the hostility of the counties, which saw it merely as a passive instrument of Habsburg interference, the Council could and did act as a watchdog over Hungarian interests in general and those of the nobility in particular. Councillors became conscientious when those interests appeared to be threatened by a royal decree and the Council's reports to the ruler could include delicate warnings as to its possible consequences. This does not, however, alter the fact that the effect of Charles's administrative reforms was to centralise and strengthen Vienna's grip on Hungarian affairs. This found reflection, too, in the Hungarian Chamber (Treasury), composed of seven barons and eighteen members of the gentry[3] together with a large subordinate staff of Germans and German-speaking Hungarians and Croats. Formally, the Chamber's role was to manage all royal revenues from Hungary that did not depend on the Diet's assent (income from the mines, the salt monopoly, tariffs and the royal estates); in practice, the Chamber was cat's-paw to the Austrian State Treasury and deeply unpopular as a result.

Finally, Charles effected a substantial reform of the judiciary, although the new superstructure still rested on the feudal infrastructure of the manorial and county courts. The existing Septemviral Bench (*tabula septemviralis*) remained the highest court of appeal but its composition was now enlarged to fifteen nobles, under the chairmanship of the Palatine, selected by the King so as to ensure that all regions of the country were represented; it henceforth sat twice a year, in Pest. The King's Bench (*tabula regia*), headed by a member of the gentry representing the King, who also presided over the Lower Chamber of the Diet, comprised seventeen judges and was now to sit permanently in Pest; apart from hearing all appeals of insufficient importance to merit the attention of the Septemviral Bench, the King's Bench heard all criminal cases involving members of the nobility and cases involving disputes over land. The King's Bench sat as a body in the Diet's Lower Chamber. To replace the old peripatetic Assizes, the 1723 Diet established four district courts covering the whole country between them. Hungary now possessed a more centralised and increasingly professional judiciary; but it could not by any means yet be called independent—its verdicts, although grounded in Hungarian law, tended none the less to reflect the royal will.

Charles III's determination to remove from the Diet and arrogate to the crown the regulation of religious life in Hungary adumbrated the purer absolutism of his successors. Two Patents (*Carolina Resolutio*) of 1731 and 1734 confirmed but also drastically restricted the right of Protestants to practise their own forms of religious observance; the Patents confirmed the limited guarantees of religious freedom agreed by Leopold I in 1681 and 1687 but imposed constraints on public Protestant worship, removed the right of appeal to the King against persecution and obliged Protestants to observe Catholic festivals. Most importantly, the first Patent compelled all Protestants aspiring to public office of any kind to take an oath of loyalty that embraced the Virgin Mary and the Catholic saints: this effective exclusion of Protestants from public life was to last for fifty years.* It is a

---

* It is worth noting that in England the Test Act of 1673, which excluded Catholics and

significant comment on the Hungarian situation that the two Patents were resented as bitterly by the Catholic nobility as by the Protestants themselves: they were regarded by the former as an intolerable derogation of the right of the Estates to settle these matters for themselves.

Maria Theresa (1740–80)

Inheriting the crowns of Hungary and Bohemia at the age of twenty-three, Charles III's daughter quickly justified all the efforts he had made to secure the succession.[4] Maria Theresa was, by any standards, a talented and remarkable woman; an unerring judge of character and ability, she won the unswerving loyalty of several outstanding administrators. In Hungary, during the first half of her reign, she used the newly centralised machinery of government created by her father with tact and discretion; Hungary was for a time spared the tightening grip of absolutism the other Habsburg lands experienced.

One reason for Maria Theresa's initially benevolent policy towards the Hungarian Estates lay in their response to an early opportunity to win her favour. Frederick II of Prussia and Charles Albert, Elector of Bavaria, had both seen in the accession of an inexperienced young woman to the Habsburg throne the possibility of rich pickings for themselves and, in the Elector's case, the chance to win her crowns. At the end of 1740 Frederick invaded Silesia, an invaluable increment to Prussia's flimsy economic base. The Elector, with the active support of France, pounced on Austria and Bohemia. Given Vienna's perennially straitened financial circumstances, this double onslaught—which launched the War of Austrian Succession—placed the Empire in real danger. Maria Theresa had only Hungary to turn to: in a dramatic gesture, she appeared before the Diet in Pozsony, dressed in mourning (for her father), and placed herself, the Holy Crown and her children under the protection of Hungarian arms. The Hungarian nobility, flattered by the appeal and susceptible, as ever, to feminine charm, responded generously: the Diet not only voted to supply 28,000 recruits and 4 million florins for the Habsburg cause but also proclaimed a general levy (*insurrectio*) of the nobility offering, in the traditional oath of loyalty, their 'lives and blood' (*'vitam et sanguinem'*) to their sovereign. The Hungarian contribution to the war—particularly that of the hussar regiments—turned out to be decisive: Hungarian and Austrian troops helped to save Vienna from the Elector's advance, captured Linz from the Bavarians, occupied Munich in 1742 and regained Prague (where Charles Albert had in 1741 had himself crowned King of Bohemia) and occupied Munich. Hungary's unexpected solidarity with her erstwhile Habsburg oppressor astonished Europe and encouraged Britain, the United Provinces and Sardinia to ally themselves with Austria; Hungarian hussars helped Austria's new ally, George II of England, defeat the French at Dettingen.[5] Although the peace treaty concluded at Aix la Chapelle in 1748 left Silesia in Frederick II's hands, the threat from Bavaria had been extinguished. A few years later, Hungarian arms played an equally important role in the

---

Protestant Dissenters from all forms of public office, and from the universities, unless they accepted the Thirty-Nine Articles and royal supremacy over the Church, was not repealed until 1828.

Seven Years' War (1756–63): Count Nádasdy's hussars helped to defeat Frederick II near Prague and General András Hadik, heading a raiding force of five thousand light cavalry, briefly held Berlin to ransome, recalling the Magyar raids eight centuries earlier. Although, again, Maria Theresa failed to regain Silesia, she had reason to be grateful to the otherwise exasperating Hungarian estates. Writing in 1774, she referred to Hungary as the nation 'to which I am beholden for being able to preserve the throne of my ancestors';[6] and four years later she wrote: 'I am a good Hungarian and my heart is full of gratitude towards that people'.[7]

Maria Theresa expressed her gratitude in a number of ways. She promised the Diet, inter alia, that the office of Palatine would not be left vacant for more than a year; that Hungarians would be directly involved in the administration of Hungarian affairs; that the decrees of the Hungarian Court Chancellery would not be obstructed by other authorities; and that she would maintain a residence in Hungary. Few of these promises were kept. When the Diet repeated its demand for Transylvania's reunion with Hungary, Maria Theresa summarily rejected it; it had become a Habsburg article of faith that Hungary could be controlled only if its separation from Transylvania were maintained. The relationship between the Hungarian Estates and their sovereign nevertheless continued for some time to be one of mutual respect, sometimes bordering on affection. It was sustained by skilful gestures on Maria Theresa's part: her use, from 1758 onwards, of the title bestowed upon King St Stephen, 'Apostolic King of Hungary'; her creation of the Royal Hungarian Bodyguard, consisting of two young nobles from each Hungarian county; the provision of scholarships to enable ten young Hungarians to attend the Theresianum, the academy she had founded in Vienna to train the nobility for government service; and her foundation of an Order of St Stephen—all this appealed to the Hungarians' lively sense of chivalry, history and *amour propre*. Of more lasting value were the incorporation into the Hungarian kingdom, later in her reign, of the Bánát of Temesvár (part of the Military Frontier Region, most of which remained under direct Austrian control) and of the port of Fiume on the Adriatic coast, giving Hungary its first maritime outlet since the Middle Ages. There is doubtless some truth in the description of Maria Theresa's policy towards her Hungary kingdom as 'an attempt to kill the spirit of nationality by kindness',[8] but there was more to it than that. Maria Theresa remained very aware, throughout the forty years of her reign, of the vulnerability of her throne in a Europe in which the continuing ascendancy of France was now accompanied by the rise of Prussia and the active engagement of Russia in European affairs: she needed Hungary, militarily and financially, to a greater extent than her forebears.

Maria Theresa was also moved by a genuine commitment to the improvement of the Habsburg lands, including Hungary. In one area of her reforming endeavour, that of improving the lot of the Hungarian peasantry, the measures drawn up by her advisers would have carried Hungary well ahead of most European countries if they had been fully implemented. Having tried but failed to work through the Diet on this issue—the Hungarian Estates refused even to discuss anything concerning their serfs—Maria Theresa issued the Urbarial Patent (*Urbarium*)[9] in 1767. The Patent was designed to regulate the size of peasant land holdings and the extent of a peasant's obligations to his lord. It laid down that a peasant family should be entitled to 1 *hold* (1.43 acres) for its home and outbuildings, between

16 and 40 *hold* for cultivation and between 4 and 15 *hold* for pasture[10] (depending on the quality of the land)—together with the right to gather wood from the forests. In return, each family would owe its lord fifty-two days of *robot* per year (or 104 days if draught animals were not used), a cash rent for its land, and one-ninth of its produce, plus a tithe to the Church. These provisions for land tenure were unrealistically generous and encouraged expectations which, in many parts of the country, could not be met, even by a well-intentioned landlord; the standardisation of *robot*, moreover, encouraged landlords to exact the legal maximum. Implementation of the *Urbarium* was, to say the least, patchy, even when Royal Commissioners were brought in to enforce it; but its establishment of a peasant's right to the tenure of land and the introduction of a right of appeal to the sovereign against a landlord's malfeasance were landmarks that foreshadowed the end of the 'perpetual serfdom' to which the Hungarian peasantry had been condemned since 1514. The emergence of the sovereign, in the best spirit of enlightened absolutism, as the peasant's champion nevertheless stored up trouble for the future. If, for any reason, conditions failed to improve, the landlord would be held responsible for obstructing the sovereign's beneficence: retribution might be, and towards the end of the century frequently was, violent. Maria Theresa's motives, and those of her counsellors, in attempting to alleviate the often intolerable burdens of Hungarian serfdom—and those of serfs in other provinces of the Empire—were of course mixed. It made sense to raise the standard of life of that part of the population from which most tax revenue came; as Maria Theresa herself put it, 'the sheep should be well fed in order to make it yield more wool and more milk'.[11] Humanitarian motives were not, however, wholly absent. Maria Theresa is also recorded as having said, after failing in 1764 to persuade the Diet to address the peasant question: 'I must serve justice to rich and poor alike. I must answer my conscience. I do not want to be damned for the sake of a few magnates and noblemen'.[12]

The Diet of 1764–65, which also defied Maria Theresa on the more central issue of taxation,* marked a watershed in her reign. Her considerable patience with the Hungarian Estates exhausted, she henceforth ruled by Patent and decree through the new all-embracing Council of State (*Staatsrat*, created by her Chancellor, Prince Kaunitz), the Hungarian Court Chancellery and the Lieutenancy Council. She never again convened the Hungarian Diet; nor did her son, co-ruler and heir Joseph II after succeeding his mother in 1780. The Diet did not meet again until after Joseph's death in 1790. For twenty-five years, therefore, the Estates lacked a collective voice; their various grievances and concerns were forced, as we shall see, into less constitutional channels of expression.

Among the positive uses to which Maria Theresa put her absolute powers was educational reform. With less than eight schools for every 10,000 inhabitants, Hungary in mid-century lagged far behind not only Western Europe but also the other Habsburg lands. The royal decree *Ratio Educationis* of 1777, drafted largely by a Hungarian, József Ürményi, created three levels of secondary education: national schools for boys destined to become farmers or artisans; grammar schools for future merchants, teachers or soldiers; and academies to prepare future students of juris-

* See page 134.

prudence, theology, philosophy or medicine. The decree established a national curriculum for elementary schools, which all children between the ages of seven and thirteen were now obliged to attend, emphasising history, geography and mathematics. The state replaced the Church as controller of the educational system, which was now organised into nine districts, each under a Director of Education who was answerable to a new state Education Commission. Hungary's only university, founded by Cardinal Pázmány, moved immediately from Nagyszombat (Tyrnau) to Buda, where it occupied the royal castle in which Maria Theresa had promised but failed to reside. The university brought with it to Buda the formerly Jesuit printing press (the Jesuits had been disbanded by Pope Clement XIV in 1773), which was soon producing books in Hungarian as well as Latin. More than any other single measure, the *Ratio Educationis* equipped Hungary to benefit from the Enlightenment and to take her place in modern Europe. Hungary's system of education is today one of the world's best: its roots are identifiably Theresian.

Maria Theresa's absolutist period nevertheless had a darker side. She was a deeply religious but also an incorrigibly bigoted woman. With her express approval, the Catholic hierarchy in Hungary, in alliance with the Lieutenancy Council, conducted a comprehensive campaign of persecution against Protestantism. She refused to entertain complaints from the victims of persecution who, if they attempted *faute de mieux* to communicate with a Protestant ambassador, were liable to be put to death by hanging. Apostates from the Catholic to the Protestant faith faced imprisonment, while Protestant nobles were bribed with greater honours to travel in the opposite direction. An ever wider spectrum of official posts, including even those in county administrations, was brought into the net of the *Carolina Resolutio*. The larger towns denied citizenship to non-Catholics, who were also barred from owning urban dwellings. The Bishop of Eger publicly burned the Hungarian Bible. Protestant schools in the predominantly Catholic western counties of Hungary were closed and churches expropriated. True to the absolutist principle of state primacy in all matters, Maria Theresa nevertheless pursued a notably robust policy towards the Papacy. She refused to allow the promulgation of Papal Bulls without royal vetting and approval and arbitrarily imposed a swingeing tax of 20 per cent on the higher ecclesiastical revenues; she dissolved lax monasteries, reorganised dioceses and imposed a limit on church holidays. Maria Theresa dealt with Hungary's growing Jewish community more leniently than with the Protestants; although she had herself imposed the much resented 'toleration tax' of 2 florins annually from every Jewish soul in the land and approved the expulsion of Jews from Buda in 1746, she also banned the forcible conversion of Jewish children to Christianity and in 1764 ordered the release of Jews imprisoned following a 'blood libel'. Despite the 'toleration tax', eastern European Jews regarded Hungary with favour: the Jewish population increased eightfold, to 80,000, during the second half of the century.

Noble Recalcitrance, Economic Backwardness

Maria Theresa showed great skill in using the prospect of advancement, office or simply favourable regard to attract the upper echelon of the Hungarian nobility to her court in Vienna. Her father had already created the nucleus of a 'court party' consisting of a handful of Hungary's most powerful families—the Pálffys, Eszterházys, Károlyis and Batthyánys among them—and Maria Theresa expanded it by the judicious selection of candidates for the titles of Count and, more rarely, Prince (of the Holy Roman Empire). Indeed, by 1778 Hungarian counts out-numbered barons, by eighty-two to twenty-four. These magnates acquired or built large houses in Vienna, spoke German or French, dressed in the German fashion, intermarried with the Austrian aristocracy and spent less and less time on their Hungarian estates, although most of them held, on a virtually hereditary basis, the office of *főispán* in their home counties. Although their addiction to court life stemmed mostly from hunger for prestige and for the respect of their peers, it usually included a genuinely patriotic element: the desire to win the ear of their sovereign or her closest advisers on behalf of a Hungarian or at least class interest. Hungarian magnates occupied some of the highest offices of state—the Palatinate (until its suspension in 1765), the Hungarian Chancellorship and military com-mands—and used their authority responsibly. But life at court was extremely expensive: a generously staffed town house in Vienna, an elaborate wardrobe for the entire family, the constant provision of entertainment, all this combined to undermine the solvency of even the wealthiest Hungarian families. In addition, the second half of the eighteenth century witnessed a building frenzy among the magnates and wealthier gentry: 219 mansions and manor houses were built in Hungary during Maria Theresa's reign, primarily to impress and entertain royals and notables from Vienna. This compounded the financial difficulties of their owners. A Swiss traveller in Hungary noted that 'there is scarcely a single promi-nent family in Hungary which is free from debt'. He added the jaundiced com-ment: 'Having thus converted the most powerful part of the Hungarian nobility into spendthrifts, debauchees and cowards, the Court has no longer occasion to fear a revolt'.[13] Maria Theresa was happy to give the magnates more rope, and supplement royal revenues into the bargain, by making loans available at 4 per cent interest; they totalled 2.75 million florins by 1781.

The political and financial emasculation of the magnates had the effect of wid-ening still further the gulf between them and their fellow nobles, the gentry. As the magnates, mainly Catholic, became more Germanised, so the gentry, mainly Calvinist, became more emphatically and demonstratively Hungarian. Narrowly focused provincialism, in deliberate contrast with the cosmopolitanism of the magnates, became a virtue. Many members of the gentry never travelled beyond the boundaries of their own county, on which all their activities were centred. With a copy of the *Tripartitum* in every home, they donned the mantle of guard-ians of noble privilege and took advantage of the long years of peace to consoli-date their grip on county administration. Their wealthier members, the *bene possessionati*, dominated the key office of county magistrate (*táblabíró*), to which election was for life and of which there were several hundred in every county. Litigation, fuelled by the property claims and counter-claims that proliferated after the Turkish occupation, had long been the most popular Hungarian hobby[14] and such was the local influence of a *táblabíró* that he inevitably attracted to his office numerous other administrative powers and duties.* It was he who produced

---

* The *táblabírók* were very similar, both in their place in society and in their jurisdiction, to

arcane legal precedents to frustrate, or at least delay, whenever possible, the execution of unpalatable decrees from the Lieutenancy Council; and it was his savage sentences from the bench, sometimes to torture or even impalement for peasant offenders,[15] which gave the word *táblabíró* the status of a curse in peasant lore.

Joseph II's abolition of Protestant civil disabilities and relaxation of censorship (see below) eventually broadened the horizons of the gentry and encouraged the development of a less reactionary mindset in the counties; but Maria Theresa had to deal with a Diet dominated by unreconstructed disciples of Werbőczy. When in 1751 she sought from the Diet an increase in the war tax (*contributio*) and a separate cash subvention in return for the abolition of the general levy, to help meet the expense of the War of Austrian Succession, she met with a flat refusal. The cash subvention, it was argued by nobles of all ranks, would infringe the nobility's exemption from taxation; and the abolition of the general levy, a 'concession' offered by Vienna despite its increasing military irrelevance, would remove the theoretical basis for that exemption. An attempt by the court to impose a tax on Church property proved equally unsuccessful and aligned the Catholic hierarchy in the Upper Chamber with the Protestant gentry in the Lower. The Diet eventually agreed to vouchsafe a modest increase in the war tax for three years only. When Maria Theresa renewed her requests in 1764, this time in an attempt to alleviate the financial crisis caused by the Seven Years' War, the Diet's response was again negative, amounting to no more than grudging acquiescence in a prolongation of the earlier tax increase.

However unreasonable the Diet's attitude must have seemed to Maria Theresa—nowhere else in the Monarchy had nobles succeeded in preserving their exemption from taxation[16]—the Hungarian Estates were fighting to preserve Hungary's right to be different, a right for which so much blood had been shed during the last hundred years. The nobility, so the Diet firmly believed, was the nation: its privileges and liberties, which successive sovereigns, including Maria Theresa, had solemnly sworn to respect, were those of the nation and would be defended to the last. The Diet's intransigence, which had extended to stubborn opposition to any alleviation of the peasants' lot, encouraged Maria Theresa to press ahead with the Urbarial Patent of 1767. Of even greater long-term importance, however, was the impact of both the 1751 and the 1764 confrontations between sovereign and Diet on Vienna's economic policy towards Hungary.

Already under Charles III, the customs duties imposed on trade between Hungary and the other Habsburg lands had been discriminatory in favour of Austria. When Maria Theresa lost Silesia, the Empire's most industrially developed province, to Frederick of Prussia the development of Austrian industry became a matter of urgency and encouraged a protective tariff policy: the Hungarian Diet's dogged defence of noble privilege both provided a political pretext and strengthened the financial argument for much harsher tariff discrimination against Hungary. The Hungarian Estates should pay a commercial price for their continuing tax exemption and benefit Austrian industry in the process. The outcome was a

---

English Justices of the Peace during the same period; but the English JPs were probably less unpopular, despite the occasional savagery of the sentences which they passed.

situation in which Hungarian exports of manufactures, such as they were, to Austria attracted duty five times greater than Austrian manufactures moving in the opposite direction. Since, until the incorporation of Fiume into Hungary in 1779, nearly all Hungarian exports had to transit Austria, Vienna was able to use penal tariffs as a means to deprive Hungary of her best export markets—Venice for cattle, England and Poland for wine—and oblige her to export cheaply to Austria any commodity, most importantly ore, in which Austria was not self-sufficient. By 1770, therefore, Austria had established a near monopoly of Hungarian trade, taking 87 per cent of Hungarian exports and supplying 85 per cent of Hungarian imports. Vienna's policy, moreover, accentuated even if it did not alone cause the deformation of the Hungarian economy. Although the Lieutenancy Council had endeavoured, during Charles III's reign, to stimulate greater industrial activity in Hungary, evoking a response from several magnates who established small iron foundries, textile mills, tanneries and glass or ceramic factories on their estates, Vienna's tariffs strangled these nascent enterprises almost at birth and most were bankrupt by mid-century.

There can be no doubt that, for most of the eighteenth and well into the nineteenth centuries, Habsburg Austria relegated Hungary, in economic terms, to the status of a colony, producing and exporting only those primary commodities and raw materials the hereditary provinces lacked in sufficient quantity: principally cattle, cereals, leather, wool and tobacco. The argument that this constituted just retribution for Hungary's fiscal intransigence is at least open to question. By 1780, Hungary was contributing 5.75 million florins to the imperial revenue, or between 30 and 38 per cent of the total, a disproportionately large share on a per capita basis. The war tax accounted for only just over two-thirds of this sum: the remaining third consisted of revenues from the royal salt monopoly, the crown estates and, by no means least, the mines. This residue also included customs duties; but here the Habsburg bureaucracy routinely cooked the books, entering duty paid at the two most active customs posts handling Austro-Hungarian trade (Pozsony and Magyaróvár) as revenue received from lower Austria rather than from Hungary.[17] But however wrong-headed Habsburg economic policy towards Hungary may have been and however flimsy its justification, it cannot be held solely responsible for Hungary's continuing industrial and commercial backwardness.

We have seen how, in earlier times, urban development in Hungary already lagged far behind that in western Europe; in the eighteenth century it trailed that of Austria and Bohemia as well. In many respects, the royal free towns remained stuck in the Middle Ages. They were administered by a small and often corrupt oligarchy; the guilds still monopolised the crafts and trades, exploiting their journeymen to the limit, maintaining artificially high prices and opposing innovation. Unusually in eighteenth-century Europe, Hungary's urban population increased much more slowly than did the population as a whole. In 1720, the royal free towns accounted for 125,000 souls out of a total of 2.5 million: in 1787, according to Joseph II's census, their population was 352,000 out of 8 million. The market towns grew more quickly, on the back of an expanding agrarian economy; but only the largest among them showed any evidence of an emerging bourgeois class or culture. The civil disabilities imposed upon Protestants carried a significant economic price. Part of the problem lay in the fact that a burgher with ambition set his sights, not on the creation of wealth through commerce or manufacture, but on buying his way into the nobility and sharing the nobility's monopoly of political influence. The fact that the royal free towns commanded only a single vote between them in the Diet was of less significance, since the Diet met so rarely, than the gentry's domination of county administration. In Hungary, as elsewhere in eighteenth-century Europe, ownership of an estate brought greater social rewards than did the establishment of a factory. The conduct of trade was left largely to Serbs, Armenians and Jews. As late as the 1780s, only 1 per cent of the population was engaged in manufacture or crafts. Hungary's ill-developed infrastructure, moreover, inhibited investment and magnified the risks of capital ventures: appalling roads, ill-maintained waterways and a paucity of inns constrained the transport of goods and individual travel alike, particularly during the winter months. A German merchant noted that the entire highroad between Pest and Szeged remained unmade;[18] and an English traveller, John Paget, writing nearly four decades later, could still record that the road from Szolnok to Abony 'has the reputation of being the very worst road in Hungary ... A gentleman, whom I can well believe, assured me that he had occupied sixteen hours in travelling over these ten miles in a light carriage drawn by twelve oxen'.[19]

Habsburg policies undoubtedly prolonged Hungary's economic stagnation. When, in 1782, Joseph II asked the Hungarian Court Chancellery to produce a list of Hungary's manufactures for use in impending trade negotiations with the fledgling United States of America, the responsible councillor explained that Hungary had virtually no factories, just small numbers of craftsmen who met local needs; the customs regime made exporting impossible.[20] At the time of this exchange, Austria had 280 factories producing finished goods, which accounted for 65 per cent of her exports. The English mineralogist and botanist Robert Townson, surveying Hungary's mineral resources in 1793 for the East India Company, noted: 'The ruling principle of the court of Vienna ... is to consider this country as its magazine of raw materials; and as a consumer of its manufactures. Against this principle great complaints are justly made; but as it has no manufactures but of the coarsest kind, which are for home consumption, it is only felt as an evil preventing the rise of manufactures'.[21] Joseph II commented on a proposal that a grant should be made to stimulate textile manufacture in a declining Hungarian mining town: 'Until Hungary is placed in a position equal to that of the other Hereditary Provinces [i.e. shared the same tax status], the Treasury cannot support any handicraft which would curtail the means of subsistence of the Hereditary Provinces'.[22]

Apart from the few enterprising magnates who had launched manufacturing ventures, only to see them bankrupted by Vienna's protectionism, the Hungarian nobility remained largely unperturbed by the indirect economic consequences of its defence of privilege. Despite their progressive impoverishment by the sub-division of small entailed estates, the gentry were content with the picturesque rural squalor[23] of the counties and, above all, with decades of freedom from war; this was the era of the complacent adage: '*Extra Hungariam non est vita—si est vita, non est ita*' ('There's no life outside Hungary—and if there is, it's not really life at all'). The magnates and the wealthier gentry, for their part, were doing well out of agriculture. The steady growth of towns in Austria and Bohemia, and the European wars of the second half of the century, pushed agricultural prices upwards, encouraging landowners to enlarge, and in some cases improve, their estates. Once the empty spaces of the formerly Turkish-occupied region had been filled, enlargement was mostly at the expense of the peasants. Landlords used every kind of pretext to expropriate peasant holdings, to put common pasture under the plough and to confiscate land cleared by their serfs for their own benefit: during the last four decades of the century, for example, the Eszterházy estates expanded by 47 per cent and those of the Széchényi family by 70 per cent.[24] This process inevitably accelerated the impoverishment of the peasantry, despite the *Urbarium*, and the number of landless peasants (cottars) increased; by 1787, cottars accounted for 51.9 per cent of all peasant households.[25]

The improvement of estates, as distinct from their enlargement, was patchy. Most landlords spent the increased revenue resulting from successive wartime agricultural booms on embellishing their family lifestyle rather than on investment. But there were exceptions: the owners of some of the larger estates and their bailiffs heeded the teaching and pamphlets of the remarkable Samuel Tessedik, a Lutheran pastor in the Alföld village of Szarvas, who made the reform of agricultural practice his mission. Tessedik not only taught by example in his native Békés county, draining marshes, building dams, rotating crops, using manure and planting 100,000 acacia trees to bind the sandy soil; he also founded Hungary's first school of agriculture, the Experimental Economic Institute, which by the 1790s had attracted 991 peasant students who were taught in three languages. A county dignitary visiting the institute made the all too characteristic comment: 'Now these bastards know more than we do'.[26] Tessedik's precepts were reflected in the improved performance of a number of estates, which introduced more advanced crop rotation, new crops such as maize and potatoes, proper soil fertilisation and, most importantly, the use of hired labour to replace reliance on the *robot*. These estates were soon producing seven- to eight-fold yields where a four-fold yield had in the past been regarded as optimal, with profits to match: the revenues on Count Amadé's estates, for example, rose from 10,000 florins in 1788 to 800,000 florins in 1809.[27] In general, however, Hungarian agriculture remained backward, inefficient and dependent on the *robot*, for which peasants used their own primitive tools and designated the least productive members of their families. Richard Bright, a Scottish physician who travelled extensively in Hungary in 1815, commented:

Taking a general view of the situation of the peasants, we may be satisfied that it is not only in appearance, but in reality, oppressive. The appearance of oppression constantly imposing on the sufferer a consciousness of his humiliation, is of itself an evil hard to bear; but in the present case there is more than apparent hardship; for, even supposing that the return made to the Hungarian peasant for his labour by his Lord were an ample recompense, still the unlimited demands of service from government would prevent his deriving advantage from it. It is certain that the whole system is bad. Neither the Lord nor the peasant is satisfied.[28]

As Bright noted, the labour dues imposed without limit on the peasantry by the state could be at least as onerous as those owed to the landlord: a peasant could be obliged to spend as much as six weeks away from his holding, carting provisions to the regiments in the Military Frontier zone. A French traveller made a more sweeping and less charitable judgement: 'The Hungarians are naturally indolent and prefer pastoral to agricultural life. Although Hungary is a fertile country, the inhabitants have no idea how to extract the riches of the soil that is theirs to cultivate. Ignorant and superstitious, the Hungarians are bad agriculturalists, and equally little attracted to trade'.[29]

A radical young Hungarian economist, Gergely Berzeviczy, comparing the Hungarian with the Austrian economy in 1797, commented that 'the condition of the Austrian peasant is often superior to that of many Hungarian nobles'.[30] The gulf between landlord and peasant, moreover, remained as deep as ever. Assuming that any innovation or improvement could be designed only to line the landlords' pockets at their expense, the peasants resisted change and demonstrated their distrust and resentment in a series of violent uprisings during the second half of the century, not only in Hungary but also in Transylvania and Croatia where conditions were no better. Economic backwardness and social division constituted two of the factors that created the impulse to reform in the early nineteenth century, an impulse that in turn led to confrontation with Habsburg absolutism.

Joseph II (1780–90)

When the Emperor Francis I died in 1765, it was expected by many that Maria Theresa, mourning her husband and exasperated by her last battle with the Hungarian Diet, would decide to abdicate in favour of her son, Joseph. Her decision not to do so owed a great deal not only to her strong sense of duty to the dynasty and to her subjects but also to her maternal insights into Joseph's personality. 'You are a coquette of the mind', she told him in one of a stream of affectionate but critical letters: 'A *bon mot*, a phrase strikes you, whether in a book or a person, and you apply it at the first opportunity without reflecting whether it is a suitable time'.[31] Like most of Maria Theresa's judgements of people, this one was on target; but Joseph was very far from being a dilettante. He was a man with a mission and a man in a hurry. He gave this definition of his mission in 1763: 'Our deeds must be guided by two principles: first, the absolute power to be in a position to do all possible good to the state, and, secondly, the means to maintain this state without foreign aid'. He saw the absolute power of a monarch as the instrument through which he could apply the rationalist precepts of the Enlightenment to the creation of a modern state and to the betterment of its citizens. His haste derived from the frustrations of spending fifteen years in his mother's shadow, co-ruler in name but deputy in practice. He had made good use of those years, travelling throughout the Habsburg lands—particularly in Hungary—often incognito and amassing an encyclopaedic knowledge of the social and economic circumstances of his future subjects. His impatience to put this knowledge to the service of the state and to remedy backwardness through the power of reason led him to underestimate the intractability of the human material with which he had to work. He lacked his mother's sensitivity and understanding of human nature. The feudal idiosyncrasies of Hungarian society, in particular, were an affront to his intelligence and to his vision of the future. The great Hungarian historian of the eighteenth century, Henrik Marczali, made this judgement:

The importance of Joseph II in the history of the world consists in the fact that he represented the conception of the unified State, which perceived a disavowal of its own existence in the privileges, restraints and classes of medieval society. As its representative, he

fought strenuously against the organisation that had previously predominated in his dominions, and sought the overthrow of the older Hungarian society as one of the principal
objects in his life.[32]

In order to avoid taking the Coronation Oath, which would have obliged him
to confirm noble privileges and liberties, Joseph refused to be crowned King of
Hungary and thus earned the contemptuous sobriquet 'the king in a hat' (*a kala-
pos király*).

Having long been out of sympathy with Maria Theresa's policy in religious
matters (apart from her firm treatment of the papacy), Joseph lost no time in
reversing much of it. His Patent of Toleration (1781) revoked the *Carolina Resolutio*, abolished the Marian oath as a test of eligibility for office and guaranteed
religious freedom for Protestants. Protestants could once again build churches,
subject to minor restrictions that were soon removed, if they could demonstrate
local demand. Protestants could henceforth compete on equal terms with Catholics for appointment to any public office, including even Hungary's highest Court
of Appeal, the *Septemvirale*. Subsequent Patents and decrees closed all the monasteries and nunneries of the contemplative orders, using their assets to fund the
establishment of new parishes and elementary schools, sometimes converting their
buildings into military barracks. The power of censorship was transferred from the
Church to the state and substantially liberalised: a torrent of books, pamphlets and
journals, mostly propagating the precepts of the Age of Reason, ensued. Joseph's
zeal to create a state Church under the direct control of the monarch carried him,
as usual, too far and into the realm of absurdity: a new Commission for Ecclesiastical Affairs vetted sermons, ordered the substitution of shrouds for coffins (to save
wood and boost the textile industry), stipulated the number of candles that could
be lit in churches and laid down orders of service. A deeply alarmed Pope Pius VI
arrived in Vienna to remonstrate but got nowhere. Despite the obsessive and provocative attention to minutiae, so characteristic of Joseph's rule, the Patent of
Toleration and its addenda were of lasting benefit to Hungary: 1,015 new Protestant church communities were established during his reign and the public service
benefited from the availability of a new pool of talent. The foundations of religious life in modern Hungary were established.

To a more qualified extent, Hungary's growing Jewish community was also a
beneficiary of the new religious regime. A Patent of 1783 on the 'systematic
Regulation of the Jewish Nation' did away with the anomalies of their status and
brought them into the national community. Jews were now to be admitted to
royal free towns, permitted to rent land, to engage in any kind of trade or craft,
and to shed the distinguishing marks on their clothing. On the other hand, the
Patent forbade the use of Hebrew or Yiddish other than for prayer, maintained the
exclusion of Jews from mining towns, prohibited the employment of non-Jews by
Jews (although their children could be apprenticed to Christians) and ordered the
abandoning of traditional Jewish beards and dress. When the Jewish community
united in defence of its beards, however, their prohibition was withdrawn.
Although the text of the Patent was replete with disobliging references to the
Jewish character, describing Jews variously as stubborn, treacherous, distrustful and
suspicious, its reception was mainly positive and Jewish immigration into Hungary
increased: Jews returned to Buda and settled in large numbers in Pest, where

Hungary's first kosher restaurant opened in 1783. As often happens, however, the removal of so many restrictions made those that remained even more intolerable. An eloquent petition, in Latin, by the Jewish community to the Diet of 1790 politely requested their removal; but the issue was shelved.

Whereas in religious matters Joseph largely reversed his mother's policies, in the area of social reform he built impressively on the foundations laid by the *Urbarium* and the *Ratio Educationis*. His Patent Concerning Serfs of 1785 removed all remaining restrictions on peasant movement, protected the peasant against eviction by his landlord without legal process and even abolished the demeaning word 'serf' (*jobbágy*). Peasants were henceforth free to marry without their landlord's consent; and the notorious manorial courts were replaced by thirty-eight courts of first instance, with jurisdiction over nobles as well as peasants and subject only to the *Tabula Septemviralis*. The Patent completed the process begun by the *Urbarium* in bringing 'perpetual serfdom' to an end, at least in theory. In education, too, Joseph continued the work begun during his co-regency with Maria Theresa: he lowered the age for compulsory schooling to six years and established penalties on parents for truancy. In the last year of his reign, 464 new elementary schools opened their doors.

Finally, Joseph launched a draconian reform of local administration in Hungary. In 1785 the county system was replaced by one that divided Hungary and Croatia/Slavonia into ten administrative districts (and Transylvania into three), each headed by a Royal Commissioner armed with a detailed brief on his region drawn up by Joseph himself. The formerly elective county and urban offices became salaried posts and county assemblies were banned, as were all the formal trappings of county autonomy; the Commissioners had unlimited powers of arrest and could draw on the services of the network of police informers created by Count von Pergen with Joseph's blessing. The new administrative machinery was animated by a stream of directives and circulars reflecting Vienna's instructions to the Lieutenancy Council, now relocated in Buda: they covered every conceivable aspect of Hungarian political, social, religious and economic life. During the three years 1781 to 1784, the number of documents emanating from the Council increased from 12,000 to 26,000 annually.[33]

By the end of Joseph's reign in 1790, therefore, Hungary possessed the partial framework of a modern state, with some of its benefits, including a structured educational system, and some of its penalties, including a swelling bureaucracy and an embryo secret police. But the framework had been imposed on a society that remained largely feudal, with a stunted economy. This discrepancy was to generate serious tensions.

The year 1784 marked a watershed in Joseph II's reign, as had 1764 in his mother's. Reactions to his early reforms had certainly been mixed. The Catholic hierarchy in Hungary had been incensed by the Patents of Toleration, practising as much non-compliance as they could get away with; the Catholic lay nobility, for their part, regarded the assault on ecclesiastical privileges with apprehension as the possible prelude to an attack on their own. On the whole, however, Hungarian opinion was prepared to give Joseph the benefit of the doubt during the early years of his reign; the Protestants and Jews regarded him with favour and the peasantry with hope. A group of distinguished Hungarians, including Count Ferenc

Széchényi, openly supported 'Josephism' and worked in various capacities, including as members of reforming Committees of the Diet, to promote and implement Joseph's reforms. In 1784, everything changed. For administrative reasons that seemed perfectly sound to him (he needed the space in Pozsony castle for a state-controlled seminary), Joseph removed the Holy Crown of St Stephen from Pozsony to Vienna, doing away with the highly prized noble office of Guardians of the Crown in the process. Appropriately, the transfer was marked by a spectacular thunderstorm. True, Joseph had already removed the Bohemian crown from Prague; but the Holy Crown had immeasurably greater historical significance and its abduction was a classic demonstration of Joseph's lack of political sensitivity. A further demonstration followed a few weeks later: in May 1784, Joseph decreed that German should replace Latin as Hungary's official language. State employees and county officials were given three years to acquire competence in German or face dismissal: 'If anyone does not conform with my desires', Joseph wrote at the time, 'the door is open and he can walk out, whether he be a member of the Chancellery or the humblest clerk in the county organisation'.[34] A postscript to the decree laid down that German would henceforth be the language of instruction, apart from religious instruction, in all Hungarian secondary schools. Once again, Joseph regarded these innovations as perfectly logical steps towards his ideal of creating an administratively homogeneous, centralised imperial state. Hungarians, for their part, saw the decree as an insult to their history and constitution (the Diet's proceedings and all the laws of the Hungarian kingdom were in Latin) and further evidence of a policy of crude colonialism. More importantly, Joseph's decree brought the question of language to the centre of the political stage. Every Hungarian county and many towns fired off long petitions of protest, replete with legal and historical references, expressing total opposition to the imposition of German, differing only on the question of what Hungary's official language should be. Many counties, including all those in Croatia, argued for the retention of Latin on both historical and practical grounds. As many, however, favoured the replacement of Latin by Hungarian. Richard Bright noted the effect of Joseph's language decree: 'The minds of the Hungarians have been called to the subject [of language]; their national pride is aroused; they begin to read with pleasure, in their own tongue, biographical accounts of the worthies of their own country, and dwell with delight on the strains of the Hungarian muse'.[35]

In the event, the decree slowly broke up on the rocks of passive resistance. Unfazed by mounting evidence of widespread discontent in his Hungarian kingdom, Joseph moved unswervingly down his agenda for the creation of the perfect state: his next project was nothing less than the reform of the taxation system on physiocratic principles, which posited the primacy of land as a source of wealth and consequently as the prime or only target for taxation. A thorough census and land survey had to precede reform and Joseph ordered that this should be conducted in Hungary, as elsewhere in the Empire, by military units. This evoked a further storm of protest from the counties: Nyitra county's submission averred that it would rather 'lose our lives and fortune, endure the cruellist torment, than have to grieve for our freedom during our lives'.[36] Not only was the sacred principle of noble exemption from taxation once again under threat, but the chronic shortage of specie in Hungary made the rate proposed—30 per cent on net income for peasants and an unspecified rate on the income of nobles—unrealistic in practical terms. The officers of the engineer corps entrusted with the survey encountered armed resistance in more than one county. A major uprising by 30,000 Romanian peasants in Transylvania, whose demands for the abolition of nobility Vienna at first appeared to encourage before putting down the rebellion by force, made an increasingly nervous atmosphere in Hungary all the more volatile. With his usual tactical ineptitude, Joseph chose this moment to alienate his most active ally, the Freemasons. In Hungary, as in the other Habsburg lands, the Freemasons had done their best to promote support for Joseph's reforms which, especially those directed against the Catholic Church, were wholly in line with their rationalist, anti–clerical beliefs; they had even supported Joseph's decree on the substitution of German for Latin. Joseph's Patent on Freemasonry (1785) now sought to apply his obsessive tidy-mindedness to that movement: lodges were to be permitted only in provincial capitals, advance notice of meetings was to be given to magistrates and lists of lodge members to the police. This drove the most educated and liberal elements of the gentry and embryo professional class into the arms of Joseph's existing opponents among the magnates and in the counties, where outrage at their subordination to the new District Commissioners was already mounting. It was not surprising that when, at the end of 1785, Joseph hinted to the Hungarian Chancellor, Pálffy, that discriminatory customs tariffs could be abolished if the nobility would agree to be taxed, Pálffy felt bound to advise him that such a deal would not be negotiable.

In 1787 Austria's involvement, as Russia's ally, in a new war against the Turks increased the strains in Hungary's relations with her uncrowned king. The large army Joseph sent into southern Hungary to threaten Belgrade soaked up such little grain and fodder as the region possessed after two bad harvests, followed by floods, creating famine conditions for the Hungarian and Croat population. The army, moreover, immobilised by the hesitations of an indecisive commander, remained in the region for long enough not only to blight the land but also to be decimated by malaria. Desperate for funds and new recruits, Joseph found himself obliged to resurrect the county assemblies so that he could order them to raise both an increased war tax and 400 recruits per 1,000 able-bodied males; at a time when the price of food had risen to levels that threatened the needy with starvation, he also imposed a levy of up to 15 per cent on the salaries or pensions of all state employees, past and present. If any friends remained to Joseph in Hungary, he lost them now. News of Belgium's deposition of the Habsburgs and of the revolution in Paris emboldened the counties, which released a further volley of protests. Szabolcs county spoke for most of them: 'If the Emperor wants something from the country, he should hold a Diet. We have no king and the Emperor took away our crown. He has overturned our ancient rights and revoked our liberties'.[37]

Newspapers in the vernacular had begun to appear during the 1780s, with small lists of subscribers but a much larger readership; they not only gave voice to Hungarian discontents but also kept their readers informed of stormy events elsewhere on the continent: *Magyar Kurir* published a draft of the French 'Declaration of the Rights of Man and the Citizen' four days before it was promulgated in the French National Assembly. Newspapers and pamphlets made a significant contribution to the creation of an atmosphere sufficiently explosive to oblige Count von Pergen, Joseph's most trusted adviser, to counsel retreat. Sick, embittered and depressed, Joseph accepted this advice: after first suspending the work of his military surveyors and then promising to convene the Diet as soon as the war ended, Joseph issued on 26 January 1790. a rescript annulling most of his reforms and restoring the status quo as at the day of his mother's death in 1780. All the thousands of Patents and decrees that had overwhelmed the bureaucracy during the previous decade were negated with a stroke of the pen, saving only three: the Patents on Toleration and on Serfdom, and the decree closing the monasteries. Three weeks later, Joseph II was dead. It would be difficult to improve upon Robert Townson's epitaph, a surprisingly elegiac passage from a usually matter-of-fact contemporary observer of the Hungarian scene:

Arbitrary indeed was the government of Joseph; yet no one I think will question the goodness of his intentions, however they may disapprove of his measures. How severe a mortification must it not have been to him, after passing so many sleepless nights in planning for the welfare of his people, to find nothing but discontent and dissatisfaction within their breasts, and this, when the state of his health required the sincere applause of his subjects, the greatest recompense to a patriot king, as a cordial to support his drooping spirits, now oppressed with disease! Yet still complaint. And now every bright hope of public prosperity, through the introduction of his wise political institutions, he found daily decreasing. How willingly he would have obeyed an earlier call of death, which should have rescued him from greater mortifications! Yet, quick as the summons came, it was too slow to save him from the cruel punishment of being obliged to cancel with his own hand the acts of his whole government, and of thus making, on his death-bed, an *amende honorable* to public opinion and aristocratic rights.[38]

Joseph's own epitaph was more succinct: 'Here lies a monarch whose intentions were good, who failed in all his enterprises'.

On the day following Joseph's death, 21 February 1790, the Holy Crown arrived in Buda amid scenes of wild rejoicing and patriotic fervour; it was displayed to the public on the altar of the *Mátyás Templom* on Castle Hill.

Leopold II (1790–92)

It would be hard to conceive of circumstances more difficult than those in which Leopold II succeeded his brother. The Turkish war had gone badly, expenditure in blood and money far outweighing occasional successes such as the capture of Belgrade; Prussia, Turkey's so far passive ally, was massing troops on the Silesian/Austrian frontier; Belgium remained in open rebellion; there was open defiance of the monarchy in Hungarian counties, where the instruments and documents of the land survey had been seized and burned. The assumption of royal weakness in this situation induced euphoria in the upper stratum of the Hungarian gentry (the *bene possessionati*) and in the larger towns: the more radical spirits entertained the notion that Hungary might follow the Belgian example in deposing the Habsburgs altogether. Even before Joseph's death, there had been contacts between disaffected nobles, through Berlin, with Charles Augustus, Grand Duke of Weimar, on whose behalf a very far-fetched claim to the Hungarian crown had been concocted; the Grand Duke's chief adviser, none other than the poet Goethe, sensibly advised him not to pursue it. The gentry now made a great point of wearing

Hungarian dress on all occasions, deriding and threatening those who did not. Townson noted: '...patriots were more than usually attached to their manners and dress; and the moustaches, which, with the polished part of society, were grown out of use, were again introduced'.

Against this unpromising background, Leopold II summoned the Diet to meet in Buda for the first time since 1527. Leopold brought to the imperial throne more than twenty years experience of governing the Habsburg Grand Duchy of Tuscany, where he had been widely respected. He shared much of Joseph's idealism, but in his case it was accompanied by realism, diplomatic skill and sensitive political antennae. Shortly before his accession, Leopold wrote to one of his sisters: 'I believe that the sovereign, even one who has inherited his position, is only the delegate and representative of his people, for whom he exists, and to whom he must devote all his work and care'.[39] He noted on another occasion that it was 'useless to try to impose even good on the peoples if they are not convinced of its utility'.[40] He proved fully equal to the challenge with which the Diet now confronted him.

The radical constitutional programme which the Diet's Lower Chamber proceeded to draw up resulted from co-ordinated exchanges between the counties in which the Freemasons had played an active role; it reflected the views of a small group of leading *bene possessionati* who sat on the Lieutenancy Council or the *Septemvirale*. It amounted to a constitutional take-over by the Diet, which would in future meet annually without royal invitation; the crown would have the power only to delay legislation; a new body, the Senate, would vet all royal decrees for constitutional legality; the Hungarian Court Chancellery would move to Hungary and report to the Diet; there was to be a Hungarian national army; and the medieval 'right of resistance' would be restored to the nobility. A number of delegates argued that Joseph's refusal to be crowned and violations of the constitution had invalidated the compromise agreements reached between Diet and sovereign in 1715 and 1741, had broken the hereditary chain and consequently entitled the Diet to revert to the free election of a monarch. Of social reform, the programme made no mention; indeed, a new draft of the Coronation Oath reversed Joseph's Patent on Serfdom. It amounted to a programme for the noble 'nation' from which most of the Hungarian nation was excluded. With the object of exerting pressure on Leopold, as yet uncrowned, to accept it, the Lower Chamber set about reviving the *banderia*, the private armies that had made medieval Hungarian kings militarily dependent on the nobility; the county gentry, including the poorest, responded with enthusiasm, some of them selling land in order to pay for weapons and elaborate uniforms.[41] The Diet also attempted to wean Hungarian regiments of the imperial standing army from their oath of loyalty to the new Emperor by working on their purely military grievances—Austrian domination of the officer corps, for example, and the exclusive use of German for words of command; the Diet's efforts were rewarded with a steady trickle of desertions.

Before dealing with the Diet, Leopold set about tackling the problems that weakened his position and encouraged Hungarian ambitions. Prussia was the key. On arriving in Vienna from Florence, Leopold at once made contact with Frederick William II to persuade him of Austria's peaceful intentions and settle outstanding differences. The ensuing negotiations resulted in the Reichenbach

Convention (July 1790), by which Leopold undertook to conclude peace with Turkey and Frederick William agreed to allow Austria to suppress the Belgian rebellion, subject to an amnesty, and to restore the former constitution. An armistice with Turkey had been signed by the end of the year and further negotiations, in which Leopold astutely allowed a Hungarian, Count Ferenc Eszterházy, to participate on the Austrian side, produced the Peace of Sistovo under which Austria lost all the territorial gains of the war, including Belgrade. Austrian troops reoccupied Belgium, restoring the status quo; and Leopold wisely rejected an impassioned appeal from his sister, Marie Antoinette, to intervene on behalf of the monarchy in revolutionary France. Leopold was now free to attend to Hungary and to prepare the ground for his coronation.

While giving priority to issues further from home, Leopold, or rather agents acting on his instructions, had not been idle in Hungary in 1790. Royal blessing had been given to the formation of a burghers' militia as a counterpoise to the noble banderia'; although this project soon petered out, and was unlikely to have caused much noble flesh to creep, it at least served to remind the Diet that there were interests other than its own to be accommodated. Of greater concern to the gentry was a wave of peasant unrest after Joseph II's death, evoked by fears that his and his mother's reforms would now be quietly buried by the landlords. A 'Peasants' Declaration' circulated widely in north-east Hungary, expressing violent hostility to the nobility and all in their service but enthusiastic loyalty to the new Emperor. Leopold's agents responded by circulating a leaflet entitled 'Good News for the Peasants' (*Jó hír a parasztoknak*), which represented Leopold as their champion against the nobility.[42] All this, together with rumours that Frederick William of Prussia had divulged to Leopold the names of those nobles involved in contacts with the Grand Duke of Weimar and the arrival in Hungary of large numbers of Austrian troops, had a sobering effect on the Diet. When its leaders demanded changes to the Coronation Oath to reflect their plans for constitutional reform, Leopold refused to budge from the 1712 (Charles III's) version and eventually prevailed, on the understanding that its provisions would subsequently be given the force of law. He showed tact and sensitivity in excluding Austrians from the negotiation on the terms of the oath and in inviting the Diet to nominate its own candidate for the office of Palatine, a gesture the Diet rewarded by choosing Leopold's son, Archduke Alexander Leopold. Leopold II was duly crowned, in Pozsony, on 15 November 1790.

The package of laws deriving, in large part, from Leopold's Coronation Oath received royal approval in March, 1791; it held out the real prospect of a stable, constructive relationship between the Habsburg sovereign and his Hungarian kingdom. Hungary, together with its annexed territories (Transylvania, Croatia and Slavonia) was declared to be 'a free Realm, independent in all the forms of its government (including all its administration), not subject to any other Land or people, and possessed of its own form of State and Constitution'.[43] Legislative authority was vested jointly in King and Diet, which was to be convened at least every three years and within three months following the death of a sovereign. Taxation could not be imposed, nor the price of salt raised,[44] without the Diet's approval; the Crown was to eschew attempts to govern by Patent and decree. Maria Theresa's *Urbarium* was confirmed, as were Joseph II's Patents on serfdom and religious toleration. The Hungarian language was to be taught in secondary schools, colleges and universities, and would in due course become Hungary's official language; but Latin was to remain for the time being.[45] Leopold, however, remained true to the Habsburg tradition in denying the Diet's demand for the reunion of Transylvania with Hungary; and by decreeing the establishment of a separate, 'Illyrian', Chancellery for the Serb population of Hungary he maintained the high-risk Habsburg strategy of using ethnic rivalries as a political instrument (he nevertheless rejected an appeal from the Serbs of the Temesvár region for local autonomy). He had plans for the gradual transformation of the feudal aspects of Hungarian society, in parallel with a transition from absolute to constitutional monarchy. The Diet, for its part, set up nine committees to consider all aspects of social, economic and political reform and to draw up draft legislation for eventual submission to the court. Hungary, it seemed, could at last look forward to a period of wise rule based on dialogue rather than decree and on compromise rather than confrontation. But it was not to be. Leopold II died on 1 March 1792, at the age of forty-four.

Francis I (1792–1835)

Leopold's son and successor, Francis I,[46] was less well equipped than his father to navigate the difficult waters he now entered. A reserved, unimaginative young man of twenty-four, devoted to his own family but unskilled in personal relations outside it, his political vision did not extend much beyond the preservation of the dynasty and, at all costs, stability. The currents with which he had to contend, but of which he had little real understanding, included those unleashed by the French Revolution, both imitative and reactive; the continuing impulse, inspired by the Enlightenment, towards rational reform; and the growing power of the national idea, not only among Hungarians but in the minds of all the many ethnic groups which made up the Monarchy. To Hungary's misfortune, the first of these elements presented itself in a banal and simplistic form at the outset of Francis's reign and exerted a malign influence on the rest of it.

The French Revolution, especially before the eclipse of idealism by terror, attracted ardent admirers in Hungary as in every other country of Europe. Outstanding among them was a senior civil servant, a former secretary to Count Ferenc Széchényi, József Hajnóczi, whose numerous pamphlets and articles in the early 1790s sought to apply the ideals of the French Revolution to Hungary's feudal society; he argued for a new concept of the 'nation', which would include a peasantry liberated from serfdom; for the abolition of the nobility's exemption from taxation; and for the use of the Hungarian vernacular in education at all levels. Among other Hungarian 'Jacobins', as Francophile enthusiasts came to be known, were a number of Hungary's leading contemporary poets and writers, among them Ferenc Kazinczy and János Batsányi. The evil genius of the movement, if such it could be called, was a former Franciscan friar of Croatian origin, Ignác Martinovics who, after teaching natural science at a Franciscan school in Buda, left the order and became professor of physics and chemistry at the University of Lemberg (Lvov). Leopold II had appointed him court chemist, probably for cover purposes, but employed him mainly as a secret police agent to keep an eye on potential subversives in Hungary. Francis I dismissed him from both posts, whereupon Martinovics became a sudden convert to French revolutionary ideas, translating Rousseau into Latin and publishing a number of rather superficial political pamphlets, including an open letter to the Emperor defending the French Revolution. He organised two societies, one called the 'Society of Reformers' in Vienna, designed to attract members of the nobility interested in moderate reform, and a 'Society of Equality and Liberty' in Pest, for the radical intelligentsia. Both groups were given the conspiratorial trappings of secret societies: members knew the names only of those in the same small cell and of their immediate superior in the 'hierarchy'. Apart from calling for the establishment of a republic, the moderate group's programme did not go much beyond that of the 1790 Diet; the radical group placed more emphasis on land reform at the expense of the nobility. Although Martinovics himself corresponded with French revolutionary leaders in Paris—and may, indeed, have been acting as an agent provocateur throughout—there is no evidence that he received funds from France or that he or the members of his societies, who eventually numbered about 300, engaged in any subversive activity apart from radical discussion. The 'Martinovics Plot', as the movement came to be known, conformed to the tradition of Hungarian 'nonplots', which also included the 'Wesselényi conspiracy' of the seventeenth century and the more recent conspiracy to depose the Habsburgs. In deciding to destroy it, Francis's security adviser Count Thugut was motivated more by the desire to create a pretext for the general repression of anti–court sentiment in Hungary than by the apprehension of any real threat to the regime. The repression was savage. In 1794, police in Vienna and Buda arrested over fifty suspected members of the two societies, including Martinovics and his leading collaborators. Secret trials, in which the case for the defence was barely heard, resulted in eighteen death sentences: of those so condemned seven, including Martinovics and József Hajnóczi, were publicly beheaded on Buda's Vérmező ('Bloody Meadow') in the spring of 1795. Of the remaining defendants only six were acquitted; the others, including Kazinczy and Batsányi, received long prison sentences.

The impact of the crackdown on the Hungarian Jacobins spread far beyond their meagre ranks. Together with fears aroused by the French Terror and by peasant unrest in Hungary, it effectively silenced the moderate reformists for thirty years. Many representatives of the 'enlightened nobility', who had ardently supported Joseph II's reforms and who occupied influential positions in public life and in education, were removed from their posts, or pressured to resign, on suspicion of sympathy for the Jacobins. Gergely Berzeviczy, for example, a talented young economist who had belonged to the 'Society for Reformers' but had not been arrested, felt obliged to resign his post in the Lieutenant Council and to carry on his work from his country home. Károly Koppi, a Piarist educationist who advocated the establishment of what would have been Hungary's first school of business studies, lost his post in Pest University because his name had been mentioned in the Jacobin trial. In 1801, Francis made censorship the responsibility of the police and it at once became more severe: journalists were now forbidden to print any news, domestic or foreign, which had not either already appeared in the official government gazette or been specifically approved by the censor in advance. A general ban was imposed on all reading rooms, public libraries and literary reviews. A review by a Censorship Commission of all books published between 1780 and 1792 resulted in the banning of 2,500 of them over a period of two years. Police spies proliferated: anybody giving evidence of intellectual activity found him-or herself under surveillance. Stifled, the reform movement languished. The poet Mihály Csokonai Vitéz lamented: 'Our modest success is dashed in pieces once more. Hardly one or two worthwhile books come out yearly; the printers are confined to prayer-books and almanacs once more. Our theatre has died in its cradle, our best authors have either died or fallen into misfortune, and the rest are silent, with none to rouse them'.[47]

This narrative cannot accommodate even a summary account of the French Revolutionary and Napoleonic Wars. It is sufficient to note that Austria, and therefore perforce Hungary, was at war during eleven of the first twenty-three years of Francis's reign. Despite increasingly severe defeats, culminating in those at Ulm, Austerlitz and Wagram, resulting in correspondingly adverse peace treaties, Austria, sometimes but not always in alliance with Britain and Russia, repeatedly clambered back into the ring like a punch-drunk prizefighter, only to be knocked down again by Bonaparte's military genius. Eventually, after Napoleon's final defeat in 1815, Austria emerged from the Congress of Vienna with her territorial losses largely restored and her acquisitions, such as they were, confirmed;* but exhausted and on the verge of bankruptcy. With war finance and recruitment to the army the dominant issues, it was not surprising that Francis I's relations with the Hungarian Diet progressively deteriorated during these years. The relationship had begun quite well. Francis pleased the Diet by abolishing, in the first year of his reign, Leopold II's deliberately provocative Illyrian Court Chancellery and by agreeing that the teaching of Hungarian should be made compulsory in all secondary schools and institutions of higher education; in return, the Diet voted an increase in the war tax and in military recruitment to meet the demands of the war with revolutionary France (France had declared war less than two months after Francis's accession). The next Diet, in 1796, obediently voted a further 50,000 recruits for the war, together with provisioning for the army to the value of 5.5m florins; but this time there was no quid pro quo—Francis dissolved the Diet without addressing its usual long list of requests and grievances. This was to be the future pattern. The overdue Diet of 1802 agreed to increase the war tax by less than half the amount Francis had demanded; it dissolved with its petitions unread. The Diet of 1805, intimidated by Napoleon's occupation of Vienna and advance to the Hungarian border, agreed to call out the *insurrectio* (noble levy) and to a further increase in Hungarian recruitment to the standing army; but extracted in return a significant concession in Francis's agreement to the conduct of some official correspondence, with the Hungarian Court Chancellery and the Lord Lieutenancy, in the Hungarian language. Meeting in Buda less than two years later, its early summons necessitated by the deepening financial crisis in Vienna, the Diet agreed to consider the Emperor's demands for a higher war tax and for a one-off contribution to expenditure on weaponry only if it were to be

---

* Under the Treaties of Paris and Vienna (1815), Austria lost Belgium and a part of Galicia; but regained Lombardy, Salzburg and the Tyrol; and expanded into Venetia, Istria and Dalmatia.

granted budgetary control of any funds it might vote and if its outstanding petitions were addressed forthwith. A bargain was eventually arrived at under which the Hungarian Estates would make a 'voluntary gift' to the crown of one sixth of their revenue from rents and 1 per cent of their income from other sources, plus the conscription of a further 12,000 recruits, in return for the immediate consideration of outstanding grievances, especially those concerning tariffs. Francis accepted the 'gift' and promptly dissolved the Diet, its petitions unaddressed. In 1808, however, a liberal distribution of honours and titles, ostensibly to mark the coronation of the new Empress, persuaded the Diet to vote 20,000 more recruits and to give Francis contingent authority, for three years, to call out the *insurrectio* without reference to the Diet, the latter concession being of greater constitutional than military significance. Indeed, when the noble levy confronted Napoleon's advance into Hungary at Győr in 1809, its rapid and humiliating defeat made this the last, and inglorious, page in the long history of the *insurrectio*.

A number of factors had combined to ensure that although Francis's relations with the Diet were bumpy during this period, they did not reach the point of breakdown. The Upper Chamber remained loyal throughout; Hungarian magnates continued to occupy several key posts in the imperial administration, including that of Minister of Finance. Even the Lower Chamber was susceptible, in wartime, to appeals to its patriotism; Napoleon's proclamation to the Hungarian people in 1809 urging them to assert their national identity and cast off the Habsburg yoke evoked nothing more than renewed declarations of loyalty to the crown. Hungary, moreover, was fortunate in its Palatines. The Archduke Alexander Leopold, the Diet's choice in 1790, had taken his duties seriously, showing an intelligent and sympathetic interest in Hungarian affairs; sensitive to Hungarian concerns, he acted as an effective mediator between the Diet and the court until his tragic death, in a firework accident, in 1795. To Hungary's good fortune, his brother Archduke Joseph, whom Francis II appointed to succeed Alexander, proved to be equally able and well disposed. On more than one occasion, Joseph dissuaded the Emperor from courses of action that would have provoked the Hungarians into open defiance. Above all, however, Hungarian landowners were doing well out of the war: provisioning of the imperial armies had pushed agricultural prices sky-high and the *bene possessionati*, basking in the more affluent lifestyle their increased estate revenues made possible, were content to forget politics and value stability. Moreover, Francis's relative lack of concern for the peasants' lot made a welcome change from Joseph II's reforming zeal: manorial courts were revived and landlords set about squeezing the maximum in dues and rents from their serfs without interference from above.

Austria's deepening financial crisis soon threatened an end to this uneasy truce. The state debt had risen from 338 million florins in 1789 to 676 million florins in 1811. In the four years from 1807 to 1811 the face value of paper money, in the form of promissory notes unbacked by gold, issued by the imperial government to fill the widening gulf between revenue and expenditure, rose from 450 million to 1060 million florins; the notes circulated at a discount of over 800 per cent. The inflation generated by this reckless printing of money compelled the government, in 1811, to call in all notes and small coins, replacing them with new paper at the rate of one for five; in effect, a massive devaluation or, as many contemporaries saw it, a declaration of bankruptcy. Presenting this to the Hungarian Diet as a *fait accompli*, Francis demanded that Hungary should help to back the new paper currency with gold and, in addition, shoulder responsibility for half the national debt, reducing the deficit by a doubling of the war tax (*contributio*). After several months of argument, the Diet refused and was summarily dissolved. It did not reconvene for thirteen years, a period during which Francis endeavoured, with some success, to extract the funds and recruits he needed directly from the counties, while imperial agents mobilised the discontents of the poorest nobles against the *bene possessionati*. Election-rigging infiltrated imperial placemen into county administrations; counties over which Vienna failed to establish control by this means, and which failed to comply with the ever-increasing demands for money and men, faced the threat—and sometimes the fact—of military coercion. The Hungarian Court Chancellery and the Lieutenancy Council now became mere agents of the all-powerful State Council; censorship became even harsher, effectively blacklisting all foreign literature. A further devaluation of paper currency in 1816, by 60 per cent, eroded such support as remained to the government in Hungary.

These financial pressures coincided, after the end of the war, with a collapse of agricultural prices resulting both from the drop in military demand and from the reappearance of cheap Russian grain. Many landlords, having put every available inch of land to the plough, faced bankruptcy. The peasants, for their part, were suffering from the effects of two disastrous harvests, in 1815 and 1816, and from three successive increases in the state-controlled price of salt; in the immediate post-war years, deaths from starvation in Hungary were numbered in thousands. Vienna's insistence, in 1822, that the *contributio* should thenceforth be paid in silver coin rather than in devalued paper money—in effect, a tax increase of 250 per cent—proved to be the last straw. When royal commissioners with military detachments arrived in the counties to exact payment, violence flared and threatened to become widespread. In Bars county the entire county administration resigned, leaving the royal commissioner with no interlocutor. Against all his instincts, Francis was compelled to recognise that he could extract money from his Hungarian kingdom only by bargaining with the Diet. On 11 September 1825, he summoned the Diet to meet in Pozsony.

Ideas and Peoples

Ideas

So far in this chapter we have encountered the Enlightenment only indirectly: in Maria Theresa's reform of education and Joseph II's Patent of Toleration, for example, and in Sámuel Tessedik's innovations in agriculture. The Enlightenment, defined by Immanuel Kant in the phrase 'Dare to know!' and by the French philosophe Diderot as 'a revolution in men's minds', was the current of thought that swept through western Europe during most of the eighteenth century, using the power of reason to oppose and, if possible, destroy the irrationalities and inhumanities of feudal tradition and religious dogma. Hungary had produced an early practitioner of the rationalist approach in Mátyás Bél, a Lutheran pastor of Slovak origin who compiled an encyclopaedic survey of the history and geography of his country, the *Notitia Hungariae novae historico-geographica*, a small part of which was published—in five volumes!—between 1735 and 1742; its objectivity and scientific attention to detail placed it squarely in the enlightened tradition. In general, however, only the nobility were in a position to become acquainted with the wave of new and challenging ideas: the magnates, from their lengthy sojourns in Vienna—where, despite Maria Theresa's censorship, French literature and thought were freely discussed—and the wealthier Protestant gentry from travel to western Europe and attendance at Protestant universities in Germany, England and the Netherlands. Those younger nobles fortunate enough to serve in the Royal Hungarian Bodyguard brought the new ideas back to Hungary with them after completing their five years of service in Vienna; since the Bodyguard carried out courier duties for the sovereign, carrying imperial despatches and correspondence all over Europe, these young men were also able to compare conditions in more advanced countries with those in their homeland. A significant number of Hungarian magnates both actively engaged in and patronised the arts, including literature and poetry: Count János Fekete wrote poetry in French, sending copies of his efforts to his idol Voltaire, accompanied by several cases of Tokay wine to encourage the great man's good opinion. The historian Peter Sugar has drawn attention to the important role played by noblewomen in nurturing the new thinking in Hungary: with fewer distractions than their husbands, they collected and read the latest works from France—most of them banned by the censor—in the libraries of their palaces and country mansions. By the end of the century, the library of the Csáky family contained 5,160 volumes, 3,600 of them in French, including the complete works of Voltaire and Rousseau.[48] Freemasonry, which flourished in the Habsburg lands, including Hungary, during the later decades of the century (Maria Theresa's late husband, the Emperor Francis I, had been a Freemason), played an important role in spreading the ideas of the Enlightenment; Hungary's twenty masonic lodges brought magnates, gentry and the professional class together and encouraged discussion of the ideals of the American and French Revolutions, to which some lodges required their members to swear allegiance.

The arrival of enlightened thinking and literature in Hungary had a double significance. In the first place, the political ideas of Rousseau and Montesquieu in particular stimulated discussion of the relationships between the Diet and the crown, between the burghers and the nobility and between the nobility and the peasantry. There was something for everyone. The gentry seized on Montesquieu's theory of the division of powers as an implicit condemnation of Habsburg neglect of the Diet; in Rousseau's theory of Social Contract they professed to see a justification of their defence of noble privilege, equating the contract with the Hungarian constitution. Burghers used French ideas to support their demands for the abolition of nobility. Literate peasants were delighted to find in translations of Montesquieu's *De l'esprit des lois* a chapter on slavery that singled out serfdom in Hungary for obloquy. For the most part, this was all special pleading; although it provided fodder for the pamphleteers and compilers of petitions to the crown for redress of grievances, the political philosophy of the Enlightenment did not as yet engender in Hungary a coherent body of reformist political thought.

In another respect, however, the impact of enlightened thinking was immediate and of lasting importance: it inspired interest in and enthusiasm for the Hungarian language. Hungary's political and literary language, used by the educated classes for all purposes save informal conversation, was still Latin, a circumstance unique in Europe.[49] As well as Latin, the magnates spoke German and French; the burghers, mostly German. Hungarian was the language, predominantly, of the middling and poorer gentry,[50] of some townfolk and of the peasants, giving them access to only a relatively limited and largely folkloric literature. György Bessenyei,[51] a member of the Royal Hungarian Bodyguard, a talented writer and the first Hungarian literary champion of enlightened thought in Vienna and subsequently in his homeland, observed in 1778: 'no nation on the globe has ever acquired wisdom and depth before incorporating the sciences into its own vernacular ... every nation has become knowledgeable by [using] its own and never a foreign language'.[52] In a different context, Bessenyei claimed that 'the basis and instrument of a country's welfare is culture ... The key to culture is a national language ... and the cultivation of that language is the first duty of the nation'.[53] Bessenyei attempted to found a 'society of Patriotic Hungarians', with the objectives of cultivating the Hungarian language and its literature, and of promoting progress in science and agriculture; but the project required royal sanction, which Joseph II denied. Bessenyei found an effective ally in Ferenc Kazinczy, an inspector of schools in the Upper Hungarian town of Kassa. Kazinczy, a prolific translator into Hungarian of the works of Goethe, Shakespeare, Molière and Schiller, and a talented poet in his own right, founded Hungary's first literary journals, *Magyar Múzeum* ('Hungarian Museum') and *Orpheus*. After serving a seven-year prison sentence (his death sentence having been commuted) for involvement in the so-called 'Martinovics Plot', Kazinczy led the group of language reformers, who wished to adapt Hungarian to contemporary requirements, against the traditionalists who regarded the language they had inherited as sacrosanct: the debate between them, conducted in many literary contexts, spanned several years. Perhaps Kazinczy's greatest single achievement was to inspire the foundation of, and to nurse through its early years, the literary journal *Tudományos Gyűjtemény* ('Collection of Studies'), which appeared monthly between 1817 and 1843, providing a forum for literary and linguistic debate as well as for the publication of new literary works. In 1822 Francis I punished a censor for passing an article in the journal which the Emperor deemed subversive; *Tudományos Gyűjtemény* was subsequently forbidden to advertise—a prohibition that deprived it of subscription revenues—or to use the postal service for distribution. In general, however, Kazinczy navigated the minefield of censorship with skill and helped others to do the same, laying in the process the foundations of Hungary's national literature and paving the way for the next, more overtly nationalist, generation of Hungarian writers and poets who, he said, 'run where we had to creep'.[54]

A third protagonist of Hungarian, and the most original, was the poet Mihály Csokonai Vitéz[55] who, like Kazinczy, translated into Hungarian from French, English and Greek but considered the production of original work in Hungarian to be the most effective means of promoting the vernacular. Although Csokonai died young at thirty-two—most of his work was published posthumously—the volume and originality of his output has led some twentieth-century Hungarian writers to regard him as the true father of modern Hungarian poetry. It is in his work, too, that the marriage of vernacular language to patriotism and a national ideal is first and most strikingly demonstrated. As the historian György Bárány has argued,[56] the ideas of the Enlightenment and the ideals of German Romanticism combined to identify the vernacular with the fulfilment of a unique national destiny, thus planting one of the cultural roots of modern nationalism. More immediately, growing recognition of the value of the Hungarian language and of its potential created a new sense of national awareness in what Csokonai described as 'this poor country of ours, this poor fatherland, deprived of liberty and under yoke'.[57] The writings of the German philosopher Johann Gottfried Herder encouraged Hungarians to value their 'Hungarian-ness' (*Magyarság*); he warned that smaller peoples must preserve their collective identity or face extinction through absorption by larger ethnic and linguistic groups. Kazinczy claimed with pride that the central idea of his work was 'nothing but Nationalism—that is my idol and not some petty consideration'. Izidor Guzmics, a Herder disciple, declared language to be the prime determinant of nationhood, since the characteristics of a language helped to form national character: recalling the linguistic discrimination of the Emperor Charles V who, according to legend, spoke French to his friends, German to his horse, Italian to his mistress, Spanish to God and English to the birds, Guzmics added, in an ironic reference to the harsh vowel sounds of the Hungarian language, that if the Emperor had known Magyar he would doubtless have spoken it to his enemies.[58]

Already by the turn of the century, however, growing enthusiasm for the Hungarian language had begun to acquire nationalistic overtones. The daily press and numerous pamphlets poured scorn on the claims of non-Magyar-speaking groups to a separate identity. Building on the Emperor's linguistic concession to the Diet in 1805, the counties increasingly framed their administrative decrees and correspondence solely in Magyar; Békés county made the teaching of Magyar compulsory in its infant and primary schools, which were attended by a high proportion of Slovak children. The 'nationality question', which was to exert a malign influence on Hungarian political life for the next century and a half, had been born.

Peoples

According to what can only have been rather a rough and ready census taken in 1720, Hungary's population at that date was little more than 2.5 million (compared with 4 million in the time of Matthias I Corvinus). Over two-thirds of this number lived in what had been Royal Hungary, the northern and western regions of the country. To the south lay the vast area of near-wilderness from which the Turks had been evicted thirty years earlier, inhabited by abundant game, wildfowl, wolves, robber bands and barely half a million Hungarians. Into these neglected lands moved those descendants of the pre-occupation landlords who had survived the extortions of Leopold I's *Neoacquistica Commissio* to reclaim their estates and a larger number of new landlords, many of them foreign, whom the Habsburgs had rewarded with nobility and land for their loyalty in the War of Independence. Both the monarchy, which needed to create a viable tax base, and the landlords, who needed serf labour for their reclaimed or newly demarcated estates, had an interest in repopulating the region as quickly as possible. Vienna also had a political interest in diluting the 'unreliable' Hungarian population with loyal elements indebted to the regime; and an economic interest in raising the level of Hungarian agriculture by importing industrious German farmers. Habsburg agents toured southern Germany advertising the attractions of central and southern Hungary. Tempted by the promise of tax exemption for five years, by initial grants from landlords of seed grain, livestock and cash, together with the possibility of commuting *robot* into a cash payment, immigrants poured in from southern Germany, Bohemia and other Habsburg lands. Thousands were floated down the Danube by boat and then transported to the Alföld and Bánát in ox–carts. Peasants from northern Hungary—Slovaks, Ruthenians and Germans as well as ethnic Hungarians—also moved south in large numbers, although as Hungarian subjects they were offered the less substantial incentive of a tax holiday for three years only.

As we know from earlier chapters, Hungary had never been an ethnically homogeneous kingdom and immigration had already been actively encouraged in the Middle Ages, notably in the aftermath of the Mongol invasions. In the early seventeenth century, Serbs and Romanians had drifted northwards to settle land laid waste by the Fifteen Years' War; and, as we have seen, Serbs arrived in large numbers at the end of that century. By the beginning of the eighteenth century, ethnic Hungarians were already in a minority, accounting for only 44.1 per cent of the population.[59] The repopulation of the Alföld, Transdanubia and the Bánát now made a further and dramatic demographic impact. In the Bánát, part of which had been included in the Military Frontier Zone until its reincorporation into the kingdom in 1779, its Military Governor settled 21,000 Serb and Romanian[60] families in return for the conscription of their young men into the army. Deteriorating conditions in the Turkish-occupied Balkans continued to push Serbs and Romanians northwards into Hungary and Transylvania during most of the century; by 1763, 58 per cent of Transylvania's population was Romanian. Between 1711 and 1780, eight hundred new settlements were established by German immigrants.[61] By 1786, the Hungarian element in a total population of 8.6 million amounted to 3.35 million, or 39 per cent;[62] although the population subsequently grew quite rapidly, the proportion of Hungarians remained at approximately this level. Economically, the repopulation drive proved a great success: in the former occupation zone the clearing and cultivation of virgin land, the draining of marshes, flood management and, in the south and east, the revival of mining progressed so rapidly as to tilt the economic balance of the country away from the north west and back towards the centre.[63] In political terms, however, the repopulation process contained the seeds of disunity and strife.

In view of later chapters in Hungary's story, it is important to note at this point that Hungarians were not the only inhabitants of Hungary in the eighteenth century to develop an awareness of national identity. The Enlightenment awakened not only Hungarian but also Croat, Slovak, Ruthenian, Serb and Romanian interest in their histories and languages. The first shoots of Hungarian nationalism nudged the other ethnic groups in Hungary into sharper consciousness of the fact that, although for the most part they were loyal Hungarians in political terms, their cultural heritage was distinct from that of the ethnic Magyars.[64] For the *Slovaks*, mostly living in the northern region of Hungary (present-day Slovakia), the new Catholic seminary in Pozsony, for which the Holy Crown had had to make way, became the focus of national awareness; one of its students, Anton Bernolák, became the Kazinczy of the Slovak language and another priest, Ignac Bajza, wrote the first novel in Slovak. Bernolák lamented the fall of the Moravian Empire, original home of the Slovaks, and the shouldering aside of the pure Slovak language by Hungarian, Czech and Latin. Protestant Slovak writers, on the other hand, promoted the merits of Czech as a literary language. The law that emerged from the Diet of 1791–92, making it compulsory for Hungarian to be taught in secondary schools and colleges, had a mixed reception among the Slovaks and evoked demands for more teaching of Slovak. The first history of the Slovak people, *Historiae Gentis Slavae* by Juraj Papánek, appeared in 1780. During much of the century, a scholarly but often heated debate proceeded on the question of whether the Slavs, earlier inhabitants of the Carpathian Basin than the Magyars, had been conquered by Árpád's tribes or whether they had graciously invited the Magyars to share their home, in which case they could legitimately be regarded as belonging to the noble Hungarian 'nation'. The Slovak Protestant Ján Kollár, anticipating the emergence of Pan-Slavism, eulogised the spiritual strengths of the Slav peoples and wrote admiringly of Russian achievements. Despite this small cloud on the horizon, relations between Slovaks and Hungarians remained generally good; there were many Slovaks in the ranks of the nobility and some occupied responsible positions in the bureaucracy. Pro-Russian feeling was also strong among the *Ruthenians*[65] of Transcarpathia, in the northeast corner of Hungary, who by 1800 numbered over 300,000. The leading Ruthenian poet, Aleksander Dukhnovich, extolled Russian victories in the Russo-Turkish wars; the Uniate Bishop of Munkács (Mukacheve), Andrei Bachynsky, promoted the use of the Church Slavonic liturgy and the teaching of Ruthenian in elementary schools.

The development of a sense of national identity in *Croatia* had been impeded, first, by the long-drawn-out process of Ottoman withdrawal from the region, which was not complete or final until 1739; and then by the donation of Dalmatia—the country's southern half—to Venice under the terms of the Treaty of Karlovici in 1699. Under Venetian rule, Dalmatia deteriorated into a virtual wasteland, exploited for its timber and other raw materials but otherwise totally neglected. Croatia's northern half, Slavonia, was dominated economically, after the Turkish retreat, by the newly established estates of Austrian and Hungarian magnates and populated by Catholic Croats and Orthodox Serbs who moved in to fill the vacuum left by the approximately 100,000 Muslims who fled southwards into Bosnia as the Turks withdrew. The Croatian Diet, the *Sabor*, made unsuccessful attempts during the eighteenth century to persuade Vienna to transfer to it administrative control of the Military Frontier Region, the Krajina. When these failed, and when the administrative reforms of, first, Maria Theresa and then Joseph II made further inroads into Croatian autonomy, the Croatian nobility decided in 1790 to make common cause with their Hungarian counterparts by surrendering most of the prerogatives of their *Sabor* to the Hungarian Diet (to which, by tradition, they already sent a small number of representatives). This bid to strengthen Croatia's negotiating position *vis-à-vis* Vienna tended to highlight the areas of difference between Croatians and Hungarians rather than their common objectives: the Croats were determined opponents, for example, of proposals to replace Latin by Hungarian as the country's official language. The constitutional alliance with Hungary against absolutism, renewed in 1825, nevertheless postponed the Croatian national awakening, although the first Slavonian (Croatian) grammar had appeared as early as 1767. In Dalmatia, meanwhile, the impact of the Napoleonic Wars had replaced Venetian by, first, Austrian and then, from 1805, by French rule; the short period of French occupation, which lasted until Napoleon's defeat, gave Dalmatia its first experience of enlightened administration, including a system of primary and secondary education and an indigenous daily press. The restoration of Austrian rule after the Congress of Vienna brought this artificially stimulated burst of progress to a full stop; but a seed had been sown that would germinate later in the nineteenth century.

The midwife of *Serbian* national consciousness was the Orthodox Church, which had for centuries kept alive the folk memory of the Serbian medieval hero-kings, Milutin and Stephen Dushan; the first literary works intended for a Serbian readership were written in a combination of Old Church Slavonic and Russian. The pioneer of a purely Serbian literary language, Dositej Obradović, produced numerous works of prose and poetry which reflected the ideas of the Enlightenment. The first Serbian journal appeared in 1792. The Serbs established two secondary schools of their own and a teachers' training college; of even greater significance was the subsequent foundation, in 1826, of a Serbian Academy of Sciences, the *Matica Srpska*, which became the focus for Serb cultural expression. The Illyrian National Congress, which met in Temesvár in 1790 with Leopold II's encouragement (*divisi ut imperes*), showed that the Serbs had moved beyond cultural to political self-awareness and heard the first Serbian demands for regional autonomy, political and religious equality. The extent to which the Serbs, relatively recent arrivals in Hungary, had improved their standing in the Empire was reflected in the composition of the Congress, delegates to which included three imperial generals and twenty-five noblemen. The Congress petitioned Leopold II for the creation of an autonomous Serb territory, under direct rule from Vienna rather than from Buda or Pozsony, which would be carved out of the Bánát and one county each from Hungary and Croatia. Leopold's compromise with the Diet of 1790–91 ensured that the Serbs would be disappointed and would have to be content with Leopold's establishment of an Illyrian Chancellery; even this disappeared in 1792, during Francis I's honeymoon with the Hungarian Diet. Despite these setbacks, however, Serb national feeling continued to strengthen and to take on, as with the Slovaks and the Ruthenians, a Russophile complexion. In 1804, a metropolitan of the Serbian Orthodox Church urged Tsar Alexander I to create a Russian protectorate comprising the area of southern Hungary in which Serbs predominated, Serbia proper and Bosnia.

During the eighteenth century, Transylvania had been tightly reintegrated into the political institutions of the Monarchy; as in Hungary proper, both the Counter-Reformation and the Enlightenment had exercised powerful influence. The most important development in the former principality, however, was the revelation from the 1733 census that the *Romanians* now constituted its largest ethnic group. The acknowledged leader of the Romanian community, Bishop Inochentie

Micu-Klein, petitioned Charles III in 1735 for the appointment of Romanians to public office in Transylvania, justifying this demand not only by the evidence of the census but also by the subsequently notorious 'continuity theory' of Romanian history: 'We are the oldest inhabitants of Transylvania, here since the time of the emperor Trajan', he claimed.[66] A Romanian was, in fact, subsequently appointed to the post of fiscal director of Transylvania. A few years later, Micu-Klein petitioned again, this time unsuccessfully, for recognition of the Romanian community as the 'fourth nation' of Transylvania, alongside the traditional 'nations' of Hungarians, Saxons and the Székely. He made the Uniate Church the institutional focus for Romanian national consciousness; but ultimately overplayed his hand and was forced into exile. The momentum Micu-Klein had imparted to the growth of Romanian self-awareness, however, survived his departure. A Romanian ophthalmologist, Ioan Molnár-Piuariu, published the first Romanian grammar, in Vienna in 1788. In 1791, the Uniate hierarchy submitted a historical memorandum to the court in Vienna resurrecting the Dacio-Romanian 'continuity' thesis and again seeking recognition of Romanians as the fourth 'nation' of Transylvania. Moreover, and perhaps most significantly, the memorandum called for the exclusive or parallel use of the Romanian language for official purposes in districts populated predominantly or wholly by Romanians. Leopold II declined these requests: but the fact of their submission, like those of the Illyrian Congress, was a straw in the wind and a harbinger of problems with which Hungarians were to grapple in the nineteenth century.

It is against this background of slowly emerging national identities within the lands of the Hungarian crown that the ultimately successful campaign of the Hungarian Diet to promote the teaching and use of the Hungarian language throughout the Hungarian kingdom should be watched: the cultural liberation of the Magyar population was unlikely to be welcomed with enthusiasm by a non-Hungarian majority, which would, however, seek to emulate it.

During the eighteenth and early part of the nineteenth centuries, the factors favouring the development of a symbiotic relationship between Hungary and Austria were at least as strong as those foreshadowing confrontation. The Caroline coronation oath, and the versions of it to which Maria Theresa, Leopold II and Francis II professed to subscribe, established the foundation for constitutional arrangements that protected both Habsburg suzerainty and the historic liberties of the Hungarian 'nation', exercised through the Hungarian Diet. The fact that every Habsburg ruler during the period violated the oath (or, in Joseph II's case, ignored it) when the Diet, as it seemed to them, behaved unreasonably, eroded that foundation but did not destroy it. It remained a basis on which compromise could be built. Under Habsburg rule, Hungary acquired a machinery of government that facilitated its emergence as a modern state and in which members of the leading Hungarian noble families played prominent roles: Count Ferenc Eszterházy as Hungarian Chancellor, Count Lajos Batthyány, whose younger brother Károly was appointed tutor to the future Joseph II, as Chancellor and later Palatine. Representatives of the Hungarian nobility were to be found in key positions in the Habsburg bureaucracy and played an important part in framing the major reforms of the period, notably the *Urbarium* and the *Ratio Educationis*.[67] By no means all Hungarian nobles conformed to the stereotype, created by nineteenth-century, and subsequently Marxist Hungarian historians, of Germanised aristocrats squandering the revenues from their estates in the banqueting halls and gaming clubs of Vienna; many of them were effective advocates of Hungarian interests as well as judicious executants of royal policy. We have already seen that the Hungarian Estates as a whole were loyal when it most mattered: to Maria Theresa in 1741 and to the much less popular Francis I during the wars against France, to which Hungary contributed about one million soldiers and thirty million florins.[68] Many prominent members of Hungary's nascent intelligentsia gave enthusiastic support to, and actively worked to implement, the early reforms of Joseph II's reign. It is not difficult, therefore, to identify in eighteenth-century Hungary the elements that made the Compromise of 1867 and the Dual Monarchy possible and workable.

At the same time, the period contained the conditions precedent for the confrontation of 1848–49. The birth and growth of Hungarian national consciousness, enshrined in the Hungarian language, constituted a potentially incendiary factor, all the more so since it coincided with, and indeed helped to foster, a similar self-awareness among the other nationalities of the realm, who together now constituted a majority of the population. Habsburg rulers had already demonstrated a dangerous inclination to play the ethnic card against the Hungarians. But it was in Hungary's constitution, to which Habsburg rulers were obliged to pay at least lip-service if they wished to be crowned, that the greatest potential for conflict lay. The Hungarian nobility's stubborn defence of its ancient privileges, above all its right not to be taxed, had frozen Hungary's political and economic development in a medieval time-warp and prolonged the hardships endured by 90 per cent of the population; it remained a running sore in relations between crown and kingdom. It also bore indirect responsibility, or at least provided the pretext, for Habsburg policies that arrested and deformed Hungary's economic development. At the same time it cannot be disputed that, however selfish its motivation, noble obstinacy achieved for Hungary what no other land of the Monarchy—and few other countries in mainland Europe—had been able to accomplish: effective resistance to absolutist rule and the preservation of respect for a constitution, however flawed. Francis I, who made no secret of his contempt for constitutions in general, found himself obliged to convene the Hungarian Diet in 1825. The outstanding British historian of central Europe, C. A. Macartney, made this unequivocal judgement: 'For good or ill, Hungary owed it to her nobles, and to them alone, that she did not become a German province in the German Reich'.[69] As we shall see, the aftermath of the Napoleonic Wars was not perceived by those who lived through it to be a time of hope. Hungarians might, however, have found some consolation in reflecting on the fortunes of the two nations with whom, in their medieval past, they had shared greatness: Bohemia had been politically neutered by absolutist bureaucracy, its historic institutions reduced to ciphers; while the great nation of Poland had been written off the map of Europe by the three Partitions. For all her troubles, which were many, Hungary had not only survived but had maintained, in defiance of absolutism and the centralised state, her right to be different.

REFORM, LANGUAGE AND NATIONALITY

(1825–43)

The Case for Reform

Few among Hungary's population of 10 million had much to celebrate during the early decades of the nineteenth century. In the slump that succeeded the agricultural boom of the war years, only the largest and best-managed estates came through unscathed. 'A great difference has taken place', one deputy told the Diet of 1825–27, 'between the turn of the century and our present time. Due to high prices, people abroad have switched over to agriculture; consequently, there is no market for Hungarian agricultural products. In the past, we exported Hungarian wheat, but now Russian corn from Odessa conquers the world markets. The prices of agrarian products are so low that they do not cover the expenses of the cultivation of the land'.[1]

Some magnates, especially those who had substituted hired labour for the *robot* and had established mills, sugar refineries or distilleries on their estates, continued to prosper; but many, having borrowed recklessly in order to buy more arable land during the wheat boom, sank into debt. A majority of the gentry found itself in the same predicament. The reforming politician Ferenc Deák told his county assembly in 1845: 'The impoverishment of our country is shown by the fact that there are very few families among the Hungarian nobility who are not in debt, although half a century ago these families were well off'.[2] Miss Julia Pardoe, an Englishwoman who visited Hungary in 1839, recorded this impression: 'From the gorgeous and princely Eszterházy, with his debt of two millions sterling, to the minor Magnate who rattles over the pavement of Pesth behind his four ill-groomed horses, there are not twenty nobles in the country who are not *de facto* bankrupts ... The Hungarian noble sacrifices everything to show, and luxury, and ostentation'.[3]

Defaulting nobles unable to pay the interest on their borrowings, let alone the capital, and the obstacles county officials placed in the way of creditors attempting to collect the money they were owed, did lasting damage to Hungary's financial reputation. The prolonged crisis swelled the ranks of impoverished nobility: prevented by the law of entail from selling their land to raise money, many land-owning gentry disposed of their estates on 'perpetual leases' at a fraction of their value and lived out lives of poverty on small plots of formerly urbarial land. Others abandoned the land for modest salaried positions in the county administrations or for the professions; while many sank to the status of 'sandalled nobility' (*bocskoros nemesek*), the readily bribable noble under-class which the authorities, and conservatives opposed to reform, were wont to manipulate in order to fix elections or disrupt the proceedings of county assemblies.

The collapse of grain prices precipitated a dash for wool, for which European demand remained high. Sheep proved to be the salvation of many estates—wool exports doubled during the 1820s despite its poor quality—but brought ruin to large numbers of peasant families as landlords annexed common pasturage and converted to pasture from arable usage non-urbarial land on which peasants had relied to supplement the meagre income from their urbarial plots. By the 1840s, three-quarters of the land of Hungary was under the direct control of noble landlords (demesne land or *majorság*) leaving only one-quarter (urbarial land), divided into plots of between seventeen and fifty-seven acres, for 620,000 peasant families. The early decades of the century were, moreover, a period during which Hungary's population increased significantly: this resulted in the accelerated sub-division of peasant plots, frequently rendering plots too small to support the feudal dues demanded of the peasant tenant, who was then obliged to abandon his holding (and the dues that went with it) for the lower status of a landless cottar. By 1847, 60 per cent of the peasant population had been registered as landless, a rural proletariat of 920,000 families rendered highly vulnerable, as the cholera epidemic of 1831 showed, to disease and to natural disasters by the still primitive state of Hungary's roads and waterways.

Nor, until the 1830s, was the depressed state of Hungary's rural economy balanced by any surge in urban and industrial activity such as most of Europe experienced during this period. On the contrary, the population of the royal free towns actually declined in relative terms between 1787 and 1837, accounting at the latter date for only 5.09 per cent of the total.[4] The younger generation of burghers, like their contemporaries in the poorer gentry, tended to gravitate towards the professions rather than to commerce or industry; since entry into a profession required knowledge of the Hungarian language, this trend had the effect of blurring and diluting the hitherto largely German ethnic identity of the towns. Despite pockets of enterprise on the larger noble estates, Hungary's industry lagged far behind the other Habsburg lands: by 1830, her production of pig-iron and cast iron amounted to only one-sixth of that of Austria. In 1841, two hundred steam engines were operating in Austria while Hungary could boast only nine. In these circumstances of economic stagnation or decline, Hungary's growing Jewish population made itself indispensable by filling the role that in other countries was filled by the bourgeoisie. By 1842, there were 250,000 Jews in Hungary, providing the majority of factors in the grain and wool trades, competing successfully with the guilds in the craft sector and supplying, through their connexions outside Hungary, much of the financial support for nascent industrial activity as it began to emerge. Inevitably, as elsewhere, Jewish ubiquity, hard work and prosperity inspired jealous hostility, particularly among the conservative burghers of the towns in which Jews settled, in defiance of the law but largely unhindered; their readiness to assimilate and diligence in learning Magyar never-theless won them a high degree of tolerance from most of Hungarian society—although for many liberal reformers Jewish success merely underlined the need for native Hungarians to get their act together.

A general sense that contemporary Hungary was worthy neither of the tri-umphs nor of the tribulations of her past pervaded the literature and, above all, the poetry of these unhappy years. There was a sense, too, that to the poets' gen-eration had fallen the duty and the opportunity of national redemption. Hungary's two national anthems[5] were both written at this time and they both convey these themes. Ferenc Kölcsey's *Himnusz* concludes:

> Pity then, our people, Lord,
> Shaken by disaster!
> From our sea of woes we cry:
> Save Hungary, Master!
> After storms of bygone days
> Favour our endeavour;
> Sins of future, sins of past,
> Are atoned for ever.[6]

While Mihály Vörösmarty, probably the greatest of Hungary's romantic poets, proclaimed in his *Szózat* ('Appeal'):

> In spite of long calamity and centuries of strife,
> Our strength, though weakened, is not spent:
> Our country still has life ….
> It cannot be that all in vain so many hearts have bled,
> That haggard from heroic breasts so many souls have fled![7]

Speaking through the mouth of the seventeenth-century poet-hero Miklós Zrínyi,* Ferenc Kölcsey asked what had become of the nation which had so often triumphed over adversity:

> Wanderer, stop! Its mother's blood was base,
> And now another nation takes its place,
> Weak-headed, heartless, selfish, full of fear,
> The glorious nation that once learned to toil
> And reap heroic laurels as its spoil
> Lives but in name—It is no longer here![8]

Deep pessimism also permeated the poems of József Bajza, who was to become the first director of Hungary's National Theatre:

> Your past was bereft of pleasure,
> Your future knows but need;
> My country, sick past measure—
> Alas, for you I bleed![9]

The authors of these sad lines were not recluses, wallowing in self-indulgent gloom in isolated garrets: they were men of affairs as well as poets, mixing daily with politicians and members of the liberal intelligentsia; Kölcsey, indeed, repre-

* See page 109.

sented Szatmár county in the Diet of 1832–36 until his attacks on feudal privilege went beyond what his noble electorate was prepared to tolerate. Their poetry, and the writings of many of their contemporaries in the (usually) poorer gentry, reflected a mood widespread in their class: it was not just helpless lamentation but a wake-up call to their countrymen. The call gained in urgency from the apocalyptic predictions of the German idealist philosophers concerning the fate of small nations over whom the impersonal forces of history loomed with menace. The poets expressed a widespread but inchoate sense that something had to be done. Patriotic writings both reflected the concerns and inspired the activities of the remarkable group of men that dominated the politics of what came to be known as Hungary's age of reform: István Széchenyi, Lajos Kossuth, Miklós Wesselényi, Ferenc Deák and their allies wrote the greatest pages of their country's history.

The Reformers

István Széchenyi

One of the most eminent magnate families in the country, the Széchényis[10] had given Hungary, over three centuries, a Palatine, a cardinal, several archbishops and a number of her most distinguished soldiers. István Széchenyi's father, Ferenc, an active patron of poets and scholars, had founded the National Museum and established the national library which still bears his name. Born in 1791, the youngest of five children, István grew up in an environment of loyalty and devotion to the Emperor and to the Roman Catholic Church. He was a late developer, unlike his elder brother Pál who greatly impressed Robert Townson with his linguistic skills;[11] István's first language was German, he spoke Hungarian rather badly and embarked on serious study of Latin only in middle age. He joined the army at the age of eighteen and as a young cavalry officer distinguished himself in the Battle of Leipzig in 1813 by his fearless performance of courier duties between the three allied commanders. After the defeat of Napoleon and the Congress of Vienna at which, aided by his good looks and social talents, he thoroughly enjoyed himself, István Széchenyi developed more serious interests. He began to keep a diary (in German), to which he confided his thoughts and emotions with total candour, and, on apparently indefinite leave from his regiment, became a serious traveller, driven by an intense and intelligent curiosity about the workings of countries other than his own. Széchenyi's first visit to England, in 1815, gave him a working knowledge of the English language, profound admiration for English political institutions and social mobility, and a lasting fascination with the gadgetry of the Industrial Revolution. He was impressed by the radical ideas of the Benthamites and by their insistence that old laws and customs, however hallowed, should be discarded if they were no longer useful: the dead should not be allowed to exercise a tyranny over the living. During the course of visits to Newmarket, his love of horses deepened into a passionate interest in the techniques of horse-breeding and in the breeder's testing ground, the racecourse. This and a later sojourn in England, in 1822, together with travels in France, Italy, the Balkans and the Levant, gave him both a keener awareness of his own national identity as a Hungarian and an appalled recognition of the extent of Hungary's backwardness relative to most

European countries. With these reactions went a more critical attitude to the Habsburg establishment and its policies, resulting, it is thought, in unguarded comments that aroused suspicions in Vienna and damaged his chances of promotion in the army. In the early 1820s, Széchenyi began to prepare himself seriously for public life, reading as widely as he could on the history, constitution and laws of his country; he struck up a close friendship with Baron Miklós Wesselényi, the young liberal magnate who led the opposition to the government in the Transylvanian Diet and shared his increasing preoccupation with Hungary's future. Their association was prolific of ideas concerning the need for change and of prescriptions for reform; it helped to equip Széchenyi for his debut on the public stage, in the Diet of 1825.

Istvàn Széchenyi's charm and public confidence masked an exceptionally complex personality. His personal charisma is amply attested. Miss Pardoe, a prolific writer of romantic novels as well as an intrepid traveller, met Széchenyi in 1839:

He has a dark, keen, eagle eye, softening, however, at intervals almost into sadness; heavy eyebrows, finely arched, and in perpetual motion, giving a character of extraordinary energy to his countenance; and one of those full, deep-toned, sonorous voices to which you cannot choose but listen. In common conversation he is fluent and demonstrative rather than logical … In the House [i.e. the Upper Chamber of the Diet] he is earnest, rapid and impassioned; and very graceful in his attitudes and movements … Murmurs of applause universally drown his first words and form an echo to his last …[12]

But throughout his life Istvàn Széchenyi was prone to profound depressions, which eventually eroded his sanity. He frequently contemplated suicide and on more than one occasion attempted it. He was deeply introspective and assumed massive burdens of guilt. He fell in love frequently, usually with married women with one of whom,[13] thanks to the sudden death of her husband, he eventually found happiness. He was a devout Catholic and his religious faith informed his political beliefs. His diaries reveal a constant turmoil of conflicting loyalties, ideas and emotions. He developed a deep affection for Hungary but at the same time despised her: 'Poor little fatherland, how filthy you are!', a place 'where no one in his right mind would want to live'.[14] He believed profoundly in Hungary's destiny as a component of the Empire and remained loyal to the monarchy until the last years of his life; but he recognised, at the same time, that the monarchy and its servants were the main obstacle to the reforms he deemed essential. He remained loyal, too, to his own aristocratic class, believing that 'the continued preponderance of the landowning classes [is] the sole guarantee for the survival of the nation'; 'Our most sacred duty', he declared in a letter to Wesselényi, 'is to change the condition of the fatherland with as little fanfare as possible, and, I believe, can only be accomplished at the Magnates' Table'[15] (i.e. in the Upper Chamber of the Diet). He took an unsentimental view of the lower strata of Hungarian society; but he nevertheless had, for the long term, an inclusive rather than exclusive concept of the Hungarian nation. Convinced that necessary reform could be achieved only by working through the government and with royal sanction, he ultimately lost the confidence of more radical reformers; but his outspoken commitment to reform incurred the suspicion and mistrust of the government and its secret police. The Imperial Chancellor, Prince Metternich, with whom Széchenyi had his first serious discussion in 1825, perceptively warned him of the dangers of running with the hare and hunting with the hounds. Three years later Széchenyi noted in his diary: 'Many think I am proud, others that I am a *radical reformer*, still others that I am an *aristocrat*. I feel the grief of being completely isolated. In fact, I have ruined my relations with everybody'.[16] Despite his neuroses, Széchenyi was a man of remarkable and diverse talents: an unschooled economist, an unapprenticed engineer, an untrained administrator: gifted amateurism carried to heights without precedent in Hungary or, indeed, in most other countries of Europe. He possessed every quality of statesmanship except political acumen.

Széchenyi set out his philosophy and programme for reform in three books that established the agenda for the reform movement in Hungary: *Hitel* ('Credit'), published in 1830; *Világ* ('Light'), 1831; and *Stádium* ('Stages'), published in Germany to escape the censor in 1833. The books represent the first serious Hungarian attempt at self-criticism, long overdue; taken together, they constitute a major landmark in Hungarian history. Given his belief that change could and should stem only from aristocratic initiative, Széchenyi's primary objective was to persuade his own class of the need for reform: this meant that, particularly in the earlier two books, he was obliged to pull his punches to some extent, concentrating on criticism of the existing state of affairs rather than on specific proposals for reform which would only alienate his peers. He tried to encourage the landowners to draw from his critique their own conclusions concerning the changes that were needed; only in *Stádium* did he unveil a legislative programme, and even that only implied, rather than demanded, an end to noble exemption from taxation. Unlike most of his peers, Széchenyi did not blame Hungary's predicament primarily on Austria's discriminatory tariff policy. Instead, he argued that the landowner, as much as the peasant, was a prisoner and victim of Hungary's feudal system. The *robot* labour of his serfs was *gratis* but hopelessly inefficient; the landowner might be exempt from taxation but he could not raise the money to replace the *robot* with hired labour or to modernise his estate. He could not borrow on credit because he could not offer his entailed estates as security; and without credit the feudal structure of *robot*, common pasture and forest, together with commerce-stifling guilds and Hungary's appalling infrastructure, condemned him to eventual ruin. 'We, well-to-do landowners', he declared in *Hitel*, 'are the main obstacles to the progress and greater development of our fatherland'.[17] He repeated this charge in *Világ*. '... we should be indebted to the nobility for maintaining our national existence but, at the same time, the nobility was the chief cause why the Magyar people were the most backward nation in the Christian community'.[18]

The solution, according to Széchenyi, lay in the abolition of entail and the establishing of a legal structure for the provision of credit. This could lead in turn to the substitution of well-motivated hired labour for the *robot* and the redemption of feudal dues and obligations with cash payments. Nobles and commoners should be equal before the law; the estates of extinct families should no longer revert automatically to the crown but help to create a free market in land; peasants as well as nobles should enjoy the right to own land; all guilds and monopolies should be abolished; and a national bank should be established. Széchenyi believed, but for the time being forbore to assert publicly, that a more prosperous nobility, freed from the burden of debt and feudal trammels, would in time be willing to surrender its exemption from taxation; an equitable distribution of the tax load throughout the population would then increase the purchasing power of the peasant smallholder and stimulate the domestic economy, including manufacturing and trade. His proposal, in *Stádium*, that indirect taxes such as tariffs, and tolls on highways and bridges, should be determined by the Diet and should apply equally to all citizens was designed to drive a wedge into the principle of noble exemption; but Széchenyi remained convinced that reform could succeed in Hungary only if it took place gradually, with the acquiescence of government, nobles and commoners alike. He was the consistent advocate of 'the golden mean', which could be realised by the identification of community of interest between the counties and the centre, between Pest-Buda[19] and Vienna.

Significantly, Széchenyi's programme contained no specific proposals for political reform. He was fully aware that social and economic changes were bound to have political implications. He acknowledged this in *Világ*. 'Hungary will be neither happy nor influential unless the common people are taken into the national ranks, unless out of the province perpetually disrupted by conflicting interests and privileges a free country is formed, perpetually united by common interests'.[20] But Széchenyi did not believe that Hungary was yet ready for an expansion of the political 'nation' beyond the nobility; a premature extension of political suffrage would, he believed, be disastrous. Although enthusiastic about most things English, to an extent which invited ridicule, Széchenyi remained cautious about the extent to which English practices, whether political or economic, could be transplanted on to ill-prepared Hungarian soil. There first had to be what he rather vaguely referred to as an 'advancement of public intelligence', by which he meant both education and the process known to the reformers as *polgárosodás* (literally 'embourgeoisement'), a concept that embraced the creation both of a bourgeoisie and of a modern civil society. In this context, Széchenyi attached importance to the nurturing and development of the Magyar language which, he believed, should become the official language for all Hungarians instead of Latin; he urged this partly on utilitarian grounds but also because, despite his loyalty to the Habsburg monarchy, he feared the Germanisation of Hungarian society and culture. Széchenyi made several practical contributions to the realisation of these ideas. Making his political debut in the Diet of 1825, and speaking—in Magyar—as a guest in the Lower Chamber, Széchenyi pledged a year's income from his estates as a contribution towards the foundation of an academy for the cultivation of the Magyar language; others followed suit and the National Academy of Sciences was founded on 3 November 1825. In the same year, Széchenyi established in Pozsony a gentleman's club, modelled on those he had visited in London, where members of the Diet and other leading citizens could meet, exchange ideas and read such Hungarian and foreign newspapers and journals as had been spared by the censor. In order to pre-empt imputations that the institution had been created in imitation of the political 'clubs' of revolutionary Paris, it was called a 'Casino', although games of chance did not officially figure in its activities. Two years later, a larger Casino—which became known as the National Casino—opened its doors in Pest, providing a neutral venue, and a good restaurant, where politicians, merchants and members of the professions could meet and mingle.

Inevitably, the Casinos (others were established in the counties) aroused the suspicions of the authorities; but Széchenyi rightly regarded the breach in Hungary's rigid caste system that they represented as a significant step towards the creation of a civil society. More idiosyncratically, Széchenyi saw horse racing in the same light, as an activity which brought together people from all sectors of civilised society while also encouraging the potentially profitable industry of horse-breeding; on Széchenyi's initiative. Hungary's first horse races took place in Pozsony in 1826 and were subsequently held annually in Pest (where the major flat race of the year is still known as 'the Derby'). These initiatives, which testified to Széchenyi's extraordinary capacity for marrying ideas to action and for getting things done, reflected his belief that if, under the guidance of the magnate class and with the co-operation of the government, Hungary could develop the attributes of a civil society, her future could be bright: the nation 'may rise to any heights, for spiritual and physical powers are latent in its youthful bosom ... It has but two enemies, Prejudice and Conceit'.[21] *Hitel* ended with a clarion call: 'The *Past* has slipped from our grasp for ever but we are masters of the *Future*. Let us not bother then with futile reminiscences but let us awaken our dear fatherland through purposeful patriotism and loyal unity to a brighter dawn. Many think: Hungary *has been;* I like to believe: she *will be!*'[22]

Lajos Kossuth

István Széchenyi and Lajos Kossuth personified the counterpoint of Hungary's progress from stagnation through reform to revolution. Whereas Széchenyi believed that the ruling nobility could be encouraged, by the revelation of its own self-interest, to change its ways and share its privileges without violent constitutional disruption, Kossuth soon became convinced that if Hungary was to be reborn, nothing less than root-and-branch reform would suffice.

Lajos Kossuth came from a long-established family of gentry in Zemplén County, in the extreme north of Hungary. He left the Lutheran gymnasium in Eperjes with a sound knowledge of Latin, Greek, German, French, Slovak and, probably, English[23] as well as Magyar and graduated from the law faculty of the Sárospatak Collegium at the early age of eighteen; after serving his legal apprenticeship in Pest he passed the bar examination in 1823 and returned to his home county to set up a legal practice. In 1827, at the age of twenty-five, he was appointed to the office of *táblabíró* (county magistrate) and then to that of municipal attorney in Zemplén, an ideal springboard from which to launch himself into the politics of the county assembly, where he became a vocal critic of the aristocracy and the government. He achieved local prominence during the cholera epidemic of 1831,* as one of the commissioners appointed to cope with the emergency. Early success seems to have gone to his head: rumours of a liaison with the wife of Count Andrássy, a minor but proven case of embezzlement and mounting gambling debts eroded his popularity and eventually cost him his attorneyship. This turned out to be a blessing in disguise: two local magnates, impressed by young Kossuth's talents and, despite their social status, sharing his liberal views, used their right to appoint an 'absentee's deputy' to deputise for them in the Diet by sending him to Pozsony in 1832 to act as their proxy. As an 'absentee's deputy',

---

* See page 171.

Kossuth sat in the Lower Chamber and had no right to vote; but he could speak, and did so soon after his arrival, vigorously attacking censorship of the press. Fourteen years were to pass, however, before Kossuth became a member of the Lower Chamber in his own right. By that time he had already established a national reputation, as the country's most influential political journalist. He began by inventing, and producing almost single-handed, Hungary's first parliamentary report, the *Országgyűlési Tudósítások* ('Reports from the Diet'), which summarised, on the basis of Kossuth's own notes, speeches made in the Diet. The 'Reports' were produced in manuscript by Kossuth himself and a small team of helpers drawn from the so-called *jurati* or 'Dietal Youth', young lawyers and students, usually from the poorest stratum of the nobility, who attended the Diet under the patronage of their local deputy, sometimes acting as his secretary. The *jurati*, representing a generation strongly influenced by French Liberalism, filled the public gallery of the Lower Chamber to cheer their reformist heroes—especially Kossuth—and barrack the conservatives. Between them, they churned out up to seventy copies of each report, which were despatched to every county and free town in the country and enjoyed an extraordinarily wide readership. Exercising editorial privilege, Kossuth summarised liberal speeches much more fully than those of the government's supporters; but the bias was not extreme. After the dissolution of the Diet in 1836, Kossuth established an alternative vehicle for his views in *Törvényhatósági Tudósítások* ('Municipal Reports') which purported to summarise the proceedings of the county assemblies but were in reality designed to propagate liberal views and to rally the counties behind reformist positions; the government closed it down after two dozen issues.

In 1837, Lajos Kossuth was arrested and charged with sedition. His brilliant conduct of his own defence further enhanced his national reputation but did not save him from a three-year term of imprisonment, which he put to good use by improving his knowledge of English.[24] Soon after his release in 1840, a printer in Pest offered Kossuth the opportunity to edit a daily newspaper, the *Pesti Hírlap* ('Pest News'). The offer, which Kossuth immediately accepted, was apparently inspired by the government; but if Metternich entertained hopes that editorial responsibility would cramp Kossuth's political style and diminish his influence, he could not have been more greatly mistaken. *Pesti Hírlap* became the standard-bearer of the reform movement and, with an eventual circulation of over five thousand and a readership of at least ten times that number, a powerful disseminator of Kossuth's political ideals and beliefs. The full content of Kossuth's political credo will emerge later in this account; but a brief summary would be appropriate at this stage as an introduction to the rift between Kossuth and Széchenyi, which became one of the most dramatic features of the political landscape during the era of reform.

Kossuth, like Széchenyi, was passionately committed to the objective of leading Hungary out of feudal backwardness to take her place as an equal among the nations of modern Europe. He shared most of the ideas for reform which Széchenyi set out in *Hitel*, *Világ* and *Stádium*. For many years, like Széchenyi, he assigned the leading role in the process of change to the nobility—although Kossuth's 'nobility' was the county gentry from which he himself sprang rather than the magnates, whom he attacked without mercy as cat's-paws of Vienna. Unlike

Széchenyi, however, Kossuth did not regard the constitutional status quo as sacrosanct: if Vienna stood in the way of the changes on which Hungary's future depended, Vienna should be defied. Kossuth agreed with Széchenyi on the importance of nurturing a distinctively Hungarian culture and of the crucial role in this of the Magyar language; but whereas Széchenyi believed that Hungary's national minorities could be attracted to Magyardom by the force of example, Kossuth thought it essential that Magyardom should be imposed if necessary. Széchenyi, convinced that only gradual change could be lasting, was prepared to wait to see Hungary evolve into a modern industrial nation once the essential precondition of a civil society had been established. In Kossuth's view, patience and consensus were luxuries Hungary could not afford: he was a tireless propagandist for the rapid development of industry in Hungary and for the concomitant development of a Hungarian, rather than German, bourgeoisie. By 1843, Kossuth had concluded that it did not lie within the power of the nobility alone to lead Hungary forward; his leading article in *Pesti Hírlap* entitled 'Disillusionment' (*Kiábrándulás*) criticised the shortcomings of institutions based on privilege, such as the Diet and the counties, resting his hopes instead on broader 'social movements'. As a leading spokeman of the Industrial Society (*Iparegyesület*) and founder and chief executive of the Protection Association (*Országos Védegylet*), which urged the nation to 'buy Hungarian', Kossuth campaigned energetically for the replacement of Vienna's discriminatory tariff structure—to which, unlike Széchenyi, he attributed most of Hungary's ills—by a protective tariff wall behind which Hungary's infant industry could grow to maturity. In this Kossuth was influenced by the German economist Friedrich List, father of the *Zollverein* which protected the German states from an influx of cheap British manufactures; although List himself, perhaps more realistic than Kossuth in assessing Hungary's economic potential, described the latter's tariff proposals as 'sanguine, overconfident and damaging'.[25]

Kossuth lacked both Széchenyi's intellectual depth and his clear-eyed pragmatism; he certainly lacked Széchenyi's self-doubt. As a master of both the spoken and the written word, however, Kossuth had no equal among his contemporaries (Széchenyi's oratory and prose tended to be complex and discursive). Kossuth's bleak view of Vienna's intentions towards Hungary turned out to be more soundly based than Széchenyi's belief that enlightened self-interest would dispose the court to take a benevolent view of Hungary's efforts to stand on her own feet. But, in turn, Széchenyi's fears that confrontation with Vienna could result only in disaster for Hungary were tragically vindicated in the ashes of Kossuth's brave but over-confident defiance. The increasingly bitter war of words between these two remarkable Hungarians did not extinguish generosity: it was Lajos Kossuth who, in a public speech in 1840, gave István Széchenyi the accolade by which posterity has remembered him: 'The greatest among Hungarians'.

Although Széchenyi and Kossuth dominated Hungary's era of reform—and Kossuth went on to become Hungary's undisputed leader in revolution and war while Széchenyi was confined to an asylum in Döbling—the blurring of social boundaries and the invigorating prospect of change attracted into public life a number of highly able men with liberal or radical views, mostly from the educated gentry, who greatly enhanced the quality of political debate. Miklós Wesselényi has already been mentioned; his belief in the necessity for constitutional as well as social change brought his close political alliance with Széchenyi to an end, although their personal friendship survived. Wesselényi's great personal bravery in rescuing victims of the catastrophic flood in Pest in 1838 intensified the hostile public reaction to his arrest on charges of treason shortly afterwards; imprisonment destroyed his eyesight, his health and with them his political career. Ferenc Deák, another leading member of the liberal opposition in the Lower Chamber, brought wisdom, moderation and encyclopaedic knowledge of the law to the reformist cause; he was to become one of Hungary's foremost statesmen in a later chapter of his country's history. On the more radical wing of the reform movement, József Eötvös used his literary talents to advance his belief in strong reforming government from the centre, as opposed to Deák's—and Kossuth's—faith in the counties as the agents of change; his novel *The Village Notary (A falu jegyzője)* was a devastating attack on the backwardness, obscurantism and corruption of county administrations. Among those to whom Eötvös's championship of the *misera plebs contribuens* against the nobility had strong appeal was a young poet and pamphleteer, Sándor Petőfi, whose tragically brief life has been an inspiration to every succeeding generation of Hungarians.

The Reforms

The Diets, 1825–44

The Hungarian Diet, perhaps because the experience of being alternately ignored and provoked by Habsburg monarchs acted as a stimulus, had by 1825 developed into a relatively sophisticated political institution. Miss Pardoe, who attended several of its sessions in 1839–40, was greatly impressed by the orderliness and efficiency of its proceedings and called it 'an oasis of liberty' in a 'desert of despotism'.[26] A Diet began with a joint session of the Upper and Lower Chambers, usually in the presence of the King, at which the Palatine read out the royal propositions and rescripts. The members of the Lower Chamber then retired to debate these, not in formal session but in so-called 'district' or 'circle' meetings (*kerületi ülések*)[27] at which the Personalis[28]—the crown appointee who normally presided over the Lower Chamber—was not present. Debate could consequently be less inhibited than in formal session and increasingly it was at these 'district' meetings that the real business of the Lower Chamber came to be conducted. On the basis of the debate, the secretary to the Chamber drew up 'acts', or counter-proposals to be addressed to the King. These 'acts' were then read out in a formal session of the Lower Chamber, approved by acclamation and embodied in a message to the Upper Chamber, whither it was conveyed by a deputation. The message now became the object of negotiation, frequently protracted, between the predominantly conservative Upper Chamber and the predominantly liberal Lower Chamber; if and when a compromise text resulted—and sometimes it did not—the agreed version became a 'representation' to the King who, in due course, conveyed his reaction to it, often a veto, in a rescript. The court naturally did its best to influence the proceedings at every stage, both through the influence of the Palatine and the Personalis and through the activities of secret police, who also operated the so-called 'Black Cabinet' in the central post office, which opened and monitored the correspondence of politically suspect deputies. Although the Lower Chamber routinely adopted a self-denying ordinance at the outset of each Diet, vowing not to accept offers of preferment or other inducements from the court, the King's representatives were frequently successful in bending the views of invariably impoverished deputies. Despite these attentions, however, this basically undemocratic bicameral assembly, representing only five per cent of the population and operating within the framework of an absolute monarchy, conducted its business in a remarkably open and 'democratic' manner, under the eyes of an invariably packed public gallery to which, as Miss Pardoe noted, 'all respectably-dressed persons' were admitted. The constraints of the political and social environment notwithstanding, the Hungarian Diet, at least after 1830, approached the English parliamentary model more closely than the majority of contemporary European representative institutions.

We have seen, in the previous chapter, that financial exigencies and the threat of impending war obliged Francis I to mend his fences with the Diet by convening it in 1825. This did not turn out to be a 'reforming' Diet, but it did establish important preconditions for future change. Francis renewed, for example, the crown's obligation to convene the Diet every three years and to make no innovations in taxation or military recruitment without the Diet's consent: the constitutional arrangements agreed by Leopold II in 1791 but ignored by Francis for over thirty years were thus reaffirmed. The reports on possible reforms prepared by committees of the 1790–91 Diet had already been outdated: the new Diet set up a commission to revise them and draw up an agenda of reform for the next Diet, which would be due to meet in 1830. In the meantime, the 1825 Diet accepted minor but significant innovations which pointed the way towards the future: it was agreed that nobles working urbarial plots should be counted among the *misera plebs contribuens* and that a financial census should be carried out, two precursors to the reform of Hungary's harshly inequitable taxation system. Finally, as noted in the previous section of this chapter, it was at the 1825 Diet that Count István Széchenyi proposed and achieved the foundation of an Academy to standardise and promote the Magyar language. The 1825 Diet also won royal assent to a law which placed some modest limitations on the use of Latin in official correspondence, another harbinger of more radical change in the following decade; the language issue, however, is sufficiently complex and controversial to deserve separate treatment later in this chapter.

In 1830, the July Revolution in Paris, which installed Louis Philippe on the French throne, encouraged the Belgians to rise against the Dutch and, later in the year, the Polish nobility to rebel against Russian rule. A tempestuous summer prompted Francis I to reconvene the Hungarian Diet in order to obtain more manpower for the imperial army. The Upper Chamber, apart from a small opposition group led by Miklós Wesselényi, and the more conservative elements in the Lower, all nervous that social unrest might spread to Hungary, were quite ready to vote funds for the 48,000 recruits requested by Vienna. A majority of the Lower Chamber, however, inspired and advised by Wesselényi, succeeded in extracting two significant concessions from the court in return for their support: a formal explanation from the President of the Imperial War Council as to why the new recruits were needed and an undertaking from Francis (which he did not honour) that Hungarian officers would be appointed to the command of Hungarian regiments and to the General Staff—tacit recognition that the Diet had a right to participate in the discussion of foreign policy and of military affairs. As we shall see, there were also further concessions from the crown on the language issue.

Although it sat for only three months, the 1830 Diet gave those in both Chambers who were opposed to the government an intimation of their own potential strength and an opportunity to lay their plans for promoting reform. Change was in the air. The taxation census had been carried out in 1829—and would reveal that by no stretch of the imagination could the tax burden on the peasantry be increased—and the work of the Diet's commission on the agenda for reform was nearing completion. The publication of Széchenyi's *Hitel* in 1830 and of *Világ* a year later acted as a powerful stimulus to political discussion. Literacy by this time was by no means confined to the nobility: Hungary's tally of one schoolteacher to approximately eleven hundred inhabitants, a respectable level for a predominantly rural country, implied a significant degree of literacy among commoners and a substantial readership for political literature. The writings of Thiers, Lamartine and Hugo were available in Magyar translation, as were De Tocqueville's *De la démocratie en Amérique* and Spark's *Life of George Washington*. Hungarians began to travel to the United States of America—one of them, Sándor Farkas Bölöni, published an enthusiastic account of his travels of which two editions were sold out in a year (1834)—and the United States began to overtake England and France as the democratic ideal. Széchenyi contributed to the general mood of excitement in a whirlwind of diverse activities: to his active involvement in the establishment of the Academy of Sciences, in the Casino movement and the promotion of horse racing, he added leading roles in the foundation of the Association for Animal Husbandry, in the formation of Hungary's first fire insurance company, in the campaign for a permanent bridge linking Pest with Buda, in the construction of the first National Theatre and in the development of steam navigation on the Danube; the first steamship, *Franz I*, financed by Széchenyi in partnership with British shipbuilders, began to ply between Pest and Vienna in 1830.

Two major events in 1831, moreover, helped to heighten an atmosphere of mounting restlessness which prompted both the Palatine and the Chief Justice of Hungary to warn Vienna that revolution might be brewing—an absurd exaggeration. The first was Russia's defeat of the Polish uprising which, under Czartoryski's leadership, had briefly dethroned the Romanovs in Warsaw. The Polish nobility's bid for freedom had evoked widespread sympathy in Hungary, expressed in declarations of solidarity by thirty counties; its collapse brought large numbers of Polish refugees into northern Hungary, where most of them found a ready welcome in the homes of the local gentry. The second event, linked to the first, was a major epidemic of cholera that Polish refugees apparently brought with them, the bacterium having been imported into Poland by Russian troops transferred from Central Asia. The impact on northern Hungary, in particular, was devastating: in the country as a whole, over half a million people fell sick and of these nearly half—one in twenty-five of the population—died. The government closed the frontier with Poland and imposed draconian restrictions on local movement, which brought daily life to a halt, prevented the annual migration of poor peasants from the north-east to work in the harvest on the Alföld and threatened to add famine to the epidemic. In desperation, the peasantry resorted to violent insurrection, fuelled by rumours that the bismuth and chloride of lime distributed by the authorities (who, as we have seen, included Lajos Kossuth on this occasion) as prophylactics were in reality poisons designed to decimate the peasantry so that their land could be used by the nobility for pasture. The uprising, eventually suppressed by armed force in a welter of reprisals including 119 executions, both alarmed the conservatives and injected greater urgency into the reformers' call for the abolition of serfdom. The collapse of the Polish revolution, the liberals also argued, had been due in part to the failure of the nobility to win the support of the peasantry by promising emancipation; the Russians had been able to mobilise the peasants against their masters and Hungarian landowners should draw the appropriate conclusion.

The cholera epidemic necessitated a twelve-month postponement of the Diet which had been due to meet in 1830: this gave the counties more time to debate and formulate instructions to their deputies and more time for the political yeast of *Hitel* and *Világ* to work. (*Stádium*, suppressed by the Lieutenancy Council in 1832, did not arrive in Hungary, from Germany, until 1833, when the Diet was already in session.) The outline of a coherent programme of reform at last began to emerge from discussion in the county assemblies. Most counties echoed Széchenyi's call for changes in the feudal structure: for the abolition of the *robot*, of the 'ninth' (the landlord's right to a ninth part of their peasants' produce) and of the manorial courts; for the redemption of feudal dues and services by voluntary agreement between landlord and serf; and for legal recognition of the peasant's right to be a freeholder. At this stage, there was little support for the abolition of entailment. For the first time, however, the reformers' programme began to acquire a political dimension. Most counties demanded an expansion of the political 'nation' to include some or all of the common people; Ferenc Kölcsey called for 'a nation of ten million free men instead of one consisting of seven hundred thousand demoralised souls'.[29] A few went further, proposing representation of the gentry in the Upper Chamber or even, in one case, the Upper Chamber's abolition. Of greater concern to Vienna were the numerous demands for greater Hungarian autonomy: for the surrender by the royal government to the Diet of control over foreign trade, tariff policy, education, religion and mining. When it eventually assembled in Pozsony in December 1832, the Diet did not lack an agenda.

In the event, the 'Reform Diet' of 1832–36 turned out to be something of an anti–climax, its sobriquet justified more by its aspirations than by its achievements. The government succeeded in luring the two Chambers into a lengthy wrangle over urbarial issues and, by active lobbying and lavish bribery in the counties, in securing changes to deputies' instructions that drew their reformist teeth; Ferenc Kölcsey, for one, resigned his seat in protest. When the Lower Chamber, under Deák's leadership, finally persuaded the Upper Chamber to accept a package of relatively moderate urbarial reforms, Francis I vetoed most of it. The eventual outcome consisted of a number of changes that ameliorated the feudal system but did not begin to dismantle it: regularisation of the *robot* enabled a peasant to give priority to his own plot when the season demanded it, to migrate without his landlord's consent if he owed him nothing, and to be judged by the county rather than the manorial court in disputes with his own landlord. The medieval structure nevertheless remained in place. More substantial changes were enacted, and approved, on other fronts: the Partium was to be rejoined to Hungary; and a law on language, as we shall see, took Magyar further along the road to national pre-eminence. All proposals for political reform were smothered by the prolonged urbarial debate.

Széchenyi's expectations from the Diet, of which he had a generally low opinion, were probably modest. He once wrote: 'The Germans write much, the French talk much, the English do much' and in this as in many other matters, his affinity was with the English. During most of the 1830s he spent less time in the Diet than in engaging in an ever wider range of practical activities. His most cherished project was the construction of a permanent bridge linking Pest with Buda.

By the 1830s, Pest–Buda had already acquired many of the attributes of a capital city. Napoleon's 'continental system', which excluded British exports from mainland Europe, increased the importance of the Danube as a commercial artery and that of Pest as one of its principal ports; the town began to flourish. An 'Embellishment Plan', approved by Joseph II and supervised by an 'Embellishment Commission' under the chairmanship of the Palatine, Archduke Joseph, transformed the layout of the town and, over a period of three decades—especially after the disastrous flood of 1838—authorised the construction of a large number of imposing buildings, both public and private. Pest's only link to Buda, however, and thus to western Hungary, remained the pontoon bridge which the increase of river traffic rendered increasingly inconvenient and impractical. In 1832, Széchenyi founded the Pest–Buda Bridge Society to rally support and funding for the construction of a permanent replacement for the pontoon and sought technical advice in England. There, he recruited a prominent engineer, William Tierney Clark, to design a bridge and a Scotsman, Adam Clark (no relation), to oversee its construction. The Diet approved his plans in 1836 and Széchenyi formed a holding company, financed by a Viennese banker, to administer funding. William Clark had already designed Hammersmith Bridge, across the River Thames in London, and a smaller version of similar design at Marlow in Buckinghamshire; these were the models for the bridge which he visualised for Pest–Buda—a suspension bridge supported by massive chains.[30] Archduke Karl ceremonially laid the foundation stone of Pest–Buda's future Chain Bridge (*Lánchíd*) on 24 August 1842 and Széchenyi thereafter took a close personal interest in the construction process; he seems to have used it as a form of therapy to escape from political concerns and from his depressive illness. Sadly, that illness was to deprive him of the satisfaction of witnessing his project's completion.

The Chain Bridge was by no means Széchenyi's only project. He had identified the milling industry as a natural bridge between an agricultural and an industrial Hungary; after a thorough examination of milling in other European countries, and in the United States, he formed the Pest Milling Company, in which he was a major shareholder and chairman of the board. He also worked to promote the silkworm industry (which was doomed in Hungary by the reluctance of peasants to forgo the tobacco smoking which killed the silkworms, the original victims of passive smoking). He founded the Pest rowing club. Most importantly, he accepted appointment by the government to be royal commissioner for regulating navigation of the lower Danube. The appointment may have been intended by Metternich to divert Széchenyi from unwelcome political activities and, if so, it succeeded to some extent: Széchenyi was fascinated by the engineering challenge of widening the Iron Gates—the rocky outcrops that narrowed the Danube just beyond the point at which it crossed Hungary's southernmost frontier into Turkish territory—and by the other construction projects that opening up the lower Danube would involve. The enterprise also had a significant political dimension: the possibility that steamships might be able to carry bulk freight between Central Europe to the Near East, via the Black Sea, rang alarm bells in London, ever sensitive to competition in maritime trade, and in Saint Petersburg, where any southward extension of Habsburg influence would be unwelcome. Széchenyi's efforts to overcome these apprehensions and to win international support for the project were time-consuming and ultimately unsuccessful; the scheme in any case stuttered to a halt in 1837 for lack of funds. The 1830s were nevertheless the high noon of Széchenyi's reputation and popularity. His writings had established the agenda for reform; his commercial and cultural activities had demonstrated in the most effective possible way that change was not only possible but beneficial; while his travels around Europe in connexion with his various projects had helped to promote Hungary's national identity. After 1840, his energies were to be absorbed by his defence of a gradualist, consensual approach to reform against the more radical policies promoted and personified by Lajos Kossuth, which he perceived to contain the seeds of disaster. But for the time being István Széchenyi's standing with the liberal nobility and with commoners alike approached the heroic; his portrait was everywhere to be seen.

Even before the dissolution of the 'Reform Diet', however, events were conspiring to confront Széchenyi with a tragic dilemma. Francis I died in 1835, to be succeeded as Emperor of Austria by Ferdinand I (Ferdinand V of Hungary), an epileptic weak in mind and body. Effective power passed to a Council of Regency (*Staatskonferenz*), dominated by Metternich and Kolowrat; and the office of Hungarian Chancellor was held at this time by the arch-conservative Count Fidel Pálffy, who spoke no Magyar and whom Széchenyi described as 'worse than an Austrian minister'. The proceedings of the Diet, relatively anodyne though they were, had been enough to persuade the council that Hungary needed a firmer hand than Francis had seen fit to apply. The arrest of Miklós Wesselényi, in violation of his immunity as a member of the Diet, was followed at the Diet's conclusion by harsh measures against members of the young *jurati;* their leaders were charged with treason and sentenced to varying terms of imprisonment, the most severe being the ten-year sentence imposed on young László Lovassy, whose incarceration in the notorious Spielberg prison destroyed his sanity. Kossuth, who had spoken out as much as he dared in Lovassy's defence, was (as we have seen) himself arrested a year later, in 1837. Under the impact of these events, the reform movement began to polarise. Széchenyi, alarmed by what he saw as a dangerously volatile interaction between Kossuth's rhetoric and the Diet's public gallery, had in 1835 addressed to Metternich a rather demeaning exculpatory 'memorandum' which stressed his own attachment to the monarchy and attempted to demonstrate that the promotion of moderate reform and loyalty to the Empire were entirely compatible. Széchenyi's decision at this time to blackball Kossuth's application for membership of the National Casino gave further evidence of a tendency to overreact to perceived threats to the realisation of his ideals; but he sincerely believed that the political behaviour of Kossuth and his supporters endangered such reforms as had already been achieved and, more importantly, those that could be accomplished in the future by persuasion and moderation.

Kossuth's arrest and trial, which concluded in early 1839 with the imposition of a three-year prison sentence, inevitably exerted a powerful influence on the preparations for the next Diet (1839–40), which a pressing need for army recruits obliged Ferdinand to convene in accordance with the constitution. During the previous Diet, a new face had come to the fore of the liberal group of deputies, that of Ferenc Deák, who was destined to become one of his country's greatest statesmen. Devoted to his family estate at Kehida, in Zala county, but not very good at managing it, Deák was in many ways a typical representative of the Hungarian country gentry. He had come to politics by the usual route of legal practice, having served his county as *táblabíró* and as a member of the county judiciary; he succeeded his elder brother Antal, to whom he was devoted, as a deputy for Zala county in 1833. His strengths lay in the depth of his commitment to social and political reform; and in the forensic skills he could deploy in promoting it. An English visitor, John Paget, who heard Deák speak in 1835 recorded his impressions: 'Deák is one of the best speakers and has one of the most philosophical heads in the Diet. Heavy and dull in appearance, it is not till he warms with his subject that the man of talent stands declared'.[31] These were qualified by a tendency to morbid pessimism and a strong aversion to decision-making; if Deák could find a good argument for postponing a decision, he used it. He never married ('Honest men marry, wise ones don't', he once said)[32] and, despite his growing prominence in national politics, found his greatest pleasures in the slow rhythm of village life.

In 1838, Deák made his first venture in a role he was to make his own, that of mediator; but his attempt to strike a bargain with the Regency Council, whereby the Diet would suspend its endless repetition of grievances in return for royal respect for the Hungarian constitution, fell on deaf ears in Vienna. A storm of protest in the counties against the imprisonment of Wesselényi and Kossuth triggered a new wave of arrests and prosecutions; while in Pest the influence of the young radicals steadily increased. When the Diet opened in Pozsony in June 1839, the atmosphere deeply concerned Széchenyi, who noted that 'the lower estate and the youth are dissatisfied with the progress of reform and demand more and more in their reckless intemperance'. Matters were not improved by the refusal of the government to allow one of the deputies returned for Pest county, Count Ráday, who faced prosecution for his support of Wesselényi and Kossuth, to take his seat; the Lower Chamber refused even to discuss the royal propositions to the Diet until Ráday had been admitted. Fearing prorogation of the Diet and a further setback for the reform process, Ferenc Deák, with Széchenyi's help, eventually persuaded the Count to stand down. Metternich, meanwhile, had been sufficiently concerned by the prospect of serious unrest in Hungary, at a time when the international situation required calm within the Empire, to initiate a change in the government's strategy. Pálffy had been replaced as Hungarian Chancellor by the more emollient Count Anton Majláth; and the reactionary Chief Justice Cziráky, who had sworn never to cross the new Pest-Buda bridge rather than pay a toll, was also removed. Metternich next encouraged a young conservative magnate, Count Aurél Dessewffy, to introduce in the Upper Chamber a government-sponsored programme of very moderate reform, designed to attract support away from the opposition, now led in the Upper Chamber by Count Lajos Batthyány. The new strategy foundered, however, on the refusal of Batthyány's group, now numbering about forty, and of the liberal majority in the Lower Chamber under Deák, to consider any government proposals for reform until the unconstitutional trials of Wesselényi, Kossuth and their supporters had been set aside. On this issue, the Diet won its first clear-cut victory over Vienna for half a century: in May, 1840, Wesselényi, Lovassy, Kossuth and others regained their freedom. In return, the Diet approved the enlistment of 38,000 new recruits for the imperial army. This cleared the way for an intensive spell of legislative activity, which marked a major step forward in the reform process. It also constituted a watershed in the development of the Diet as an institution, justifying the assessment of a leading historian of the period, George Bárány: 'The prevalence of an essentially moderate leadership in the chamber of deputies and the takeover by a new generation in the chamber of magnates meant that modern party politics and parliamentarian tactics could make their first appearance in the feudal Diet of Hungary'.[33] This was an environment in which Lajos Kossuth would thrive.

In all, the Diet of 1839–40 enacted fifty-five new laws, many of them in the sphere of social reform. The feudal bonds binding serfs to landlords were loosened by a law that enabled individual peasants, as well as peasant communities, to escape feudal dues and services in perpetuity by payment of a fixed cash sum. Ferenc Deák noted that the law involved no compulsion: 'Its effects may be slow, but they will be sure, and its consequences will be great and irreversible'.[34] With Hungary on the threshold of her Industrial Revolution, restrictions on the establishment of factories were removed; but a timely law on child labour limited its use to nine hours a day for children under sixteen and prohibited the hire of children under twelve in factories where their health might be endangered. Laws on bills of exchange and bankruptcy put in place the first ingredients of a modern commercial infrastructure. Enabling legislation opened the way for the construction of the Pest-Buda bridge, of Hungary's first railway line and of the National Theatre. Efforts to secure the complete emancipation of the Jews succeeded only in part (and were opposed by Széchenyi, perhaps reflecting the anti-Semitic views of his wife); but a new law did allow Jews to settle where they wished, except in mining towns, to own property and to engage freely in any occupation—a significant step forward. On one of the most emotive issues of the day, however—the removal of all remaining disabilities from Protestants and, in particular, the vexed question of the religious upbringing of the children of mixed marriages between Catholics and Protestants (which the Catholic Church recognised only if they had been conducted by a Catholic priest)—the Diet failed to move the government from its support for the conservative Catholic hierarchy. Attempts to reform criminal law and to improve prison conditions were equally unsuccessful (Deák's comment that '… in this country the gaols are not places of rehabilitation but schools for crime' has a modern ring). Taken as a whole, and despite its failures, this Diet showed that progress could be made with the acquiescence of Vienna and the conservative magnates, provided always that it proceeded step by modest step and that the case for it was skilfully and persuasively presented. That these conditions were met owed much, not only to Deák's political talents, but also to the sympathy and mediatory skills of the Palatine, Archduke Joseph.

Széchenyi may have been tempted to conclude that the outcome of the 1839–40 Diet, in which he had played an active role, vindicated his belief in the possibility of 'quiet reform'; if so, his satisfaction was short-lived. Lajos Kossuth's appointment to the editorship of *Pesti Hírlap*, less than a year after his release from prison, soon led to the onset of open hostility between the two dominant figures of Hungary's age of reform. Széchenyi had already evinced symptoms of hypersensitivity on political issues, a clouding of judgement that perhaps foreshadowed his eventual mental breakdown; before the Diet had opened, for example, he had denounced the staging in Pest of József Katona's historical drama *Bánk Bán*, set in medieval Hungary, on the grounds that it might give offence to Germans and trigger a political reaction. Now, he read successive issues of *Pesti Hírlap*, and in particular Kossuth's colourfully written editorials, with mounting concern. After only seven issues of the newspaper, Széchenyi took it upon himself to advise the Palatine to censor it more strictly; after a few more, he not only began to criticise Kossuth in public but composed a diatribe of book length—nearly four hundred pages—denouncing *Pesti Hírlap* and its editor in remarkably intemperate terms. Even before its publication, in June 1841 under the title *The People of the Orient* (*A Kelet Népe*) Széchenyi's most prominent supporters—Lajos Batthyány, Ferenc Deák, József Eötvös, Count Gyula Andrássy—tried to restore his sense of proportion, arguing that one newspaper could not destabilise a nation and that Kossuth himself would benefit rather than suffer from the publicity which Széchenyi's attacks were generating. Unmoved, Széchenyi persisted in his accusations: Kossuth's inflammatory editorials were stirring up social conflict, traducing every responsible authority, inviting anarchy. The Hungarians, a people of the Orient surrounded by more sophisticated races and nations, had to be educated before they could flourish; the arousal of primitive emotions could be no substitute for the exercise of reason and the quiet promotion of measured change. Széchenyi's aristocratic hauteur showed through in his mockery of Kossuth's espousal of projects for the intellectual improvement of the common people. For all its shortcomings, however, *The People of the Orient* transcended polemics: even those contemporaries who disagreed with him recognised it as Széchenyi's personal testament, a last appeal for peaceful change within a framework of order, a final warning against the perils of radicalism. The tones of desperation which pervade *The People of the Orient* perhaps stemmed from Széchenyi's perception that the tide of events was already sweeping Hungary past the quiet waters of gradualism and into the rapids.

Language and the Nation

During the last decade of the eighteenth century and the early years of the nineteenth, the issue of extending the official use of the Magyar language had moved to the centre of political debate with remarkable speed. We have seen (in the previous chapter) that the Diet of 1790–91 made the teaching of Magyar compulsory in secondary schools and colleges; in 1805, Francis I had approved a law that permitted the submission of petitions to the crown, by the Diet or Chancellery, in Magyar as well as Latin and obliged the Lieutenancy Council to respond in Magyar to communications addressed to it by the counties in that language. The county administrations, meanwhile, had gone much further on their own initiative. The Pest county assembly resolved to use only Magyar in its records and correspondence and to oblige every town and village to employ at least one Magyar-speaking schoolmaster; in Békés county, the teaching of Magyar was made compulsory in infant and elementary, as well as secondary, schools. Newspapers and pamphlets began to eulogise the merits of the Magyar language and to pour scorn on those who could not or would not speak it. Demands for the ever wider use of Magyar featured in the opening response of every Diet to royal propositions. Royal approval of the 1825 Diet's laws to establish the Academy of Sciences and further to restrict the official use of Latin has already been noted; several magnates in the Upper Chamber followed Széchenyi's example in addressing that Diet in Magyar, one of them going so far as to demand the exclusion from elementary schools of children whose parents had not taught them Magyar. The pace quickened in the Diet of 1830, which secured the approval of laws making knowledge of Magyar an essential qualification for public office and for the conduct of legal practice; for the first time, the messages of the Lower Chamber to the Upper were drafted in Magyar. The law on language for which the 'Reform Diet' won royal sanction extended the frontiers of Magyardom still further: the Magyar text of laws published both in that language and in Latin would be authoritative; high court decisions on lawsuits conducted in Magyar should be couched in Magyar; registers of births, marriages and deaths in parishes where sermons were preached in Magyar should be maintained in the same language. By degrees, Magyar was supplanting Latin as Hungary's official language. The court in Vienna did not see this process as threatening imperial interests; indeed, the court found convenience in an issue on which concessions could safely be made to the Hungarian Diet, thereby easing the passage of measures on money and recruitment. When the language issue began to cause division and unrest in the Hungarian kingdom, Vienna did not repine: coping with the ethnic minorities who together comprised a majority would keep the Hungarians busy and divert them from more dangerous ambitions. As yet, however, the Habsburg regime forbore actively to encourage the ferment the language question was beginning to engender.

There was, of course, a perfectly respectable case to be made for the promotion of Magyar without resorting to Herder's German romanticism or to mystical concepts of 'the Nation'. Hungary had retained Latin as the language of politics, law and administration for longer than any European country, a dead language, attuned to feudal precepts and practices, adaptable to more modern circumstances only with difficulty and contortion. The majority of the common people, moreover, could not understand it; it was thus wholly inappropriate to an era in which an expansion of the political 'nation' had entered the agenda. As a replacement for Latin, German had been tried and shown to be politically impracticable. Magyar, the language of Hungary's largest ethnic group, represented the only sensible option. Sound government required that it should at least be understood by all the governed even if, in certain regions of the realm, the language of the local ethnic majority had to be employed in parallel with Magyar. Effective administration, whether central or local, could not be carried out in several languages at once; even in the technologically advanced twenty-first century, this creates serious problems for federal and international bodies. The political question, therefore, was: in how wide an area of an individual's life should the use of Magyar be required by law and how much licence should there be for linguistic and cultural diversity?

For most members of the liberal intelligentsia, including Lajos Kossuth and his supporters, the language issue was inseparable from that of nationhood and patriotism. The first champion of the Magyar language, Ferenc Kazinczy, went so far as to favour 'expelling from my fatherland all those who enjoy living on Magyar bread and air and yet refuse to learn Magyar'. Without going to this extreme, Kossuth firmly believed that all those who enjoyed the benefits of the Hungarian constitution—benefits that should of course be extended more widely—should accept that they were members of a Hungarian nation in which the Magyar language ruled in every sphere of public life, whatever language they might choose to speak in the privacy of their homes. In his first leading article in *Pesti Hírlap*, Kossuth defined the bargain: 'On the one hand, we should demand the acceptance of our nationality and, on the other hand, let us give them the benefits of our Constitution … All non-Magyar elements should be welded together with us by the flame which is ignited and kept alive by the Hungarian Constitution'.[36] Much later, he declared: 'I shall never recognise, under the Holy Crown of Hungary, more than one nation and nationality, the Magyar'.[37] The question of language was thus being extended far beyond the practicalities of government: willingness to learn Magyar and to accept its primacy had become the touchstone of loyalty to Hungary, the precondition of membership of the Hungarian nation. No less a figure than the Palatine, the Archduke Joseph, told the Hungarian Diet in 1843: 'When every fraction of the Hungarian people lays claim to a separate individuality, the general welfare of the country is threatened. I belong to those who think that every inhabitant of Hungary, whatever his language may be, while he enjoys the rights, the privileges and the benefits of the Magyar Constitution, should consider himself a Magyar'.[38] Kossuth and his allies believed that an inescapable corollary of this view was the denial of the right of non-Hungarian communities to claim a nationhood of their own. In part, this reflected an exaggerated awareness of the vulnerability of the Hungarian nation, vastly outnumbered and therefore threatened by Germans on the one hand and by Slavs on the other. According to the pro-Kossuth journal *Társalkodó* ('Social Forum'), echoing the writings of Johann Gottfried Herder: 'The cause of Magyarisation is, simultaneously, the cause of unification in our country. Our country, from the point of view of language, is a true Babel. If we cannot change the course of things, and the country cannot be united through Magyarisation, sooner or later the German or Slav elements will assimilate our nation and even our name will be forgotten'.[39]

On the language question above all, István Széchenyi's wisdom and vision raised him above his contemporaries. As his promotion of an Academy of Sciences had shown, he was as fully seized as any of his contemporaries, including Kossuth, of the value and importance of the Magyar language as a vital component of Hungarian nationhood. In *Hunnia* ('Hungary'),[40] a book written just after *Stádium* but published posthumously, Széchenyi declared: 'The greatest treasure of Hungarians is their national idiom; this is the only safeguard of their entity as a nation, for no nation can exist without a national language. Hungarian progress depends on loyalty to the dynasty and on the promotion of national characteristics predetermined, however, by the free development of the language'.[41] Széchenyi's championship of Magyar as the national language, however, was qualified and nuanced. Magyar should replace Latin, but no more than that; non-Hungarian nationalities should be allowed to use their own languages for all but administrative purposes and their cultures should be protected. Széchenyi shared Kossuth's fears for the survival of the Magyar race but drew the opposite conclusion from them. In *A Kelet Népe*, he argued against confrontation with peoples who outnumbered the Magyars even in Hungary: 'Is it sober tactics if we, the lesser weight, ceaselessly collide with the boundlessly greater weight? ... Do not force the Magyar language by flame and sword ... otherwise you cannot prevent your own destruction by flame and sword'. He proposed a *modus vivendi*:

You [the non-Magyar 'nationalities'] have another country outside our boundaries. But we have nowhere but here. But you do not possess a Constitution; we do possess one. Therefore we should conclude a treaty of peace, the main features of which should be these: we let you speak Slovak, German, Romanian, Greek, Latin, French, even Sanskrit in family circles ... but Magyar should be exclusively the language of public affairs.[42]

On the surface, this statement had much in common with Kossuth's position; but Széchenyi also believed passionately that assimilation into Magyardom could occur only voluntarily, by mutual attraction; it could not be imposed by legislative fiat. In a remarkable address to the eleventh plenary session of the Hungarian Academy of Sciences in 1842, Széchenyi attacked the notion that assimilation could be achieved simply by compelling non-Hungarians to speak Magyar: '... speaking is by no means a sentiment, the sounding of a tongue is by no means the beating of a heart, and thus he who speaks Magyar even most eloquently is not yet a Magyar'.[43] The address also showed that Széchenyi's views on language and nationality owed much to his deeply held religious beliefs: love for one's neighbour, he argued, is an essential ingredient of national identity: 'Do not do that to others which you would not accept wholeheartedly from others'. Nationalism should not be confused with the higher virtue of patriotism: 'This is the main reason why Magyar patriotism is less respected on the stage of the world, why the purest Magyar civil virtue cannot excite sympathy and cannot form a favourable opinion outside Hungary'.[44] Policy towards Hungary's 'nationalities',[45] Széchenyi concluded, should be informed not by emotion but by moderation, caution and patience.

The debate over language has deserved a full summary because its outcome exercised a significant and baneful influence on Hungary's future. The insight and political sensitivity of Széchenyi's views on the subject put him ahead of his time: his prescriptions are relevant in many parts of the world over one and a half centuries later. His speech to the Academy, in particular, earned him the praise and gratitude of leading figures among the 'nationalities': but only contumely from his fellow Hungarians, including even Miklós Wesselényi. The liberals supported Kossuth virtually to a man. Széchenyi's career as a leader of the reform movement—though not as a public figure—was effectively over, his political credit exhausted. He could be said to have been the first casualty of the language and nationality issue; but there were many more to come.

Already in the 1830s, there were among the 'nationalities' a few advocates of separation from the Hungarian kingdom which, it was argued, had been created not simply by Magyars but by all its historical inhabitants, Croats, Serbs, Slovaks, Saxons and Romanians among them. The Croats had maintained their opposition to the replacement of Latin by Magyar and had challenged the assumption of their subordination to Hungary. Count Draskovich argued in 1832 that Croatia, as an allied rather than a conquered state, should not have to defend her rights and privileges in the Hungarian Diet but should deal directly with the court in Vienna; he demanded the restoration of the prerogatives Croatia had voluntarily surrendered to the Hungarian Diet in 1790.* A remarkable young intellectual, Ljudevit Gaj, now took up the running for Croatia. Gaj had already accomplished, as a young graduate in Pest where he fell under the influence of the Slovak nationalist Jan Kollár, the not inconsiderable feat of devising a standard Croatian orthography. Like his Hungarian contemporaries, he regarded language as an essential component of nationhood. There were three distinct Croatian dialects, spoken almost exclusively by the peasants: the nobility and burghers spoke Italian, German, Hungarian or Croatian and, for all official purposes, Latin: Gaj chose the dialect closest to the Serb language, reflecting his commitment to the unity of all southern Slavs and his admiration for the Serb linguist, Vuk Karadžić, who had already published a standard dictionary of the Serbian language in 1818.[46] As Ferenc Kölcsey had done for Hungary, Gaj also wrote a Croatian national song, 'Still Croatia Has Not Fallen', which achieved great popularity; anticipating Lajos Kossuth by eight years, he established a newspaper, the *Croatian News*, and led the agitation in Croatia against the Hungarian Diet's law (1827) making the teaching of Magyar compulsory in Croatian secondary schools. These were the components of the 'Illyrian movement', aspiring to the creation of an Illyrian nation comprising Croatia, Slovenia, Serbia and Bulgaria (the latter two still nominally under Turkish suzerainty). Vienna was not blind to the political opportunities this development might create. As early as 1791, Prince Kaunitz, the Austrian Chancellor, had declared: 'The more apparent and well-considered the attempts at securing the unity of Hungary, Transylvania and the Illyrian nation, the more recommended and necessary is the principle of *divide et impera*'.[47] But although Vienna adopted a benevolent attitude towards 'Illyrianism'—Gaj was received by Count Kolowrat, who gave him permission to publish his newspaper—there was as yet no disposition to act on Kaunitz's advice. The Hungarian Diet, for its part, reacted to the growing ferment in Croatia with irritated exasperation rather than apprehension: of Hungary's other 'nationalities', only the Slovaks, under Kollár's inspiration, reacted strongly against the steady advance of Magyar, demanding the establishment of Slovak libraries and reading rooms in predominantly Slovak

* See page 155.

regions—the Serbs and Romanians, for the time being, had different preoccupations. There were calls in the Diet of 1832–36 for the severing of all ties with Croatia on the grounds that Croatians were failing to pay their fair share of the taxes demanded of the Hungarian kingdom as a whole. Even the moderate Ferenc Deák, speaking in the 1839–40 Diet, envisaged the possibility of separation: if the Croats considered 'it a sacrilege to bear their part of the tax burden in even the same proportion as Hungary, the desire would involuntarily be kindled in his breast that the tie should cease to be, though this would hardly be to the advantage of either Croatia or Hungary'.[48]

Lajos Kossuth, writing in *Pesti Hírlap* in 1842, proposed complete independence for Croatia. In Croatia itself, political views had begun to polarise between Gaj's Illyrian nationalists and the conservative Church and nobility; this led to violent clashes, in the elections of 1845, between the 'sandalled nobles' of the Turopolje region and the 'Illyrians'. Although the seeds of crisis were germinating in Croatia, however, they had not been fully recognised when the Diet assembled in Pozsony in May, 1843, after elections dominated not by the language issue but by that of Protestant disabilities and the continuing problem of the religious upbringing of the children of Protestant-Catholic marriages.

Except on two issues, the reform movement did not prosper in the Diet of 1843–44, partly because it lacked the leadership of Deák, who had refused to accept instructions from his county assembly to vote against taxation of the nobility and resigned his seat.[49] When the county administration tried to resolve the problem by staging a second election, in which thousands of 'sandalled nobles' were bribed to vote for Deák and his stand against noble tax exemption, Deák still refused to serve, on the grounds that the election had been corrupt. In the Diet, where the liberals held only a narrow majority in the Lower Chamber, most of their usual demands—for the redemption of tithes, for general taxation, for the abolition of entailment, for the mandatory redemption of feudal services, for the right of commoners to own land and to hold public office—won acceptance in principle in the Upper Chamber but no commitment to implementation and, in any case, fell victim to the royal veto. The Diet did, however, achieve full equality of rights for Protestants, including the legitimation of mixed marriages; and it secured the King's assent to a law which finally installed Magyar as the official language of the Hungarian state and nation.

Croatian deputies to the Pozsony Diet raised the temperature of the debate on the language question by insisting on addressing the Lower Chamber in Latin, a last act of defiance against a law that made Magyar the sole language of debate in the Diet, although non-Hungarians would be permitted to use Latin for a further six years. Henceforth, documents issued by the Chancellery, the Lieutenancy Council and the courts would be in Magyar only (although non-authoritative translations into the first languages of each of the 'nationalities' were to be made available); Croatia, Transylvania and the Partium were obliged to accept documents in Magyar but could respond in Latin if they so wished. Magyar was to be the language of instruction in all Hungarian secondary schools except non-Catholic church schools, which could continue to use the local vernacular; in Croatia and the other 'annexed territories', Magyar was to be taught as a curricular subject.

As it finally stood, the new law on language was neither draconian nor unreasonable; but it impinged on areas of particular sensitivity, such as the language of instruction in secondary schools and the use of Magyar in religious services. So far as debates in the Diet were concerned, it made obvious sense, in the days before the invention of simultaneous translation technology, for a legislature to have one official language and for that to be the native tongue of the overwhelming majority of its members; the six–year grace period for non-Magyar speakers— including the Croatian representatives—was generous. Requirements for the written translation of government and legal documents safeguarded the transparency of the legislative and legal processes. But the language question merely provided a context for deeper passions and wider aspirations: on the Hungarian side, a measure of arrogance and insensitivity, stemming in part from a paranoid fear that the Magyar identity would be gobbled up by the Slav or German Molochs; on that of the 'nationalities', a degree of particularism quite incompatible with the early development of a modern state. It was not long before these emotions and ideals engendered a degree of volatility Vienna found alarming and to which the *Staatskonferenz* was bound to react.

9

OPPOSITION, REVOLUTION AND WAR

(1844–49)

The Growth of Opposition

Although the Hungarian Diet's campaign to promote the official use of the Magyar language had, after fifty years, been crowned with success, its efforts to secure an end to Vienna's discriminatory tariff policies—to which Lajos Kossuth and many of his fellow liberals attributed Hungary's economic backwardness—had made no progress. Kossuth helped to draft a memorandum to the Commercial Committee of the 1843–44 Diet that deplored Hungary's quasi–colonial status and the obstacles to economic development represented by the guilds and feudal laws which, for example, made it impossible for commoners to purchase land on which to build factories. The memorandum made sensible and specific proposals for reform: exemption from medieval guild regulations for factories in royal free towns and government subsidies for new ones; the establishment of a technical college in Pest; the drafting of a law to protect patents; the transfer to the Diet of responsibility for tariffs and customs regulations; and the granting to Hungary of the right to conclude her own foreign trade agreements (an aspiration with greater political appeal than practical sense). The rejection of these proposals by the government provoked the foundation of the Protection Association (*Védegylet*), of which Kossuth was appointed manager, with a salary; the board of directors included a number of liberal magnates (but not István Széchenyi). The association, which proposed to campaign for tariffs that would protect Hungarian rather than Austrian industry and to encourage a boycott of Austrian manufactured goods, enjoyed great popularity but little practical success. Bolstered by a declaration of support from the Diet's Lower Chamber, the association quickly attracted 60,000 members, set up 146 branches nationwide and collected 100,000 promises from individual citizens not to buy Austrian goods for six years; but Hungary's infant industrial economy could not yet support a 'Buy Hungarian!' campaign—it was noted that even the lapel badges distributed by the association were made in Vienna. Despite its early promise, the Protection Association's activities soon petered out. Undeterred, Kossuth took the lead in establishing the Commercial Society and the Society for the Establishment of Factories, which campaigned not only for industrial development but also for the building of a rail link between Pest-Buda and the port of Fiume, which would enable Hungarian exports to be shipped directly to western Europe without transiting Austria. Both organisations were short-lived and cost Kossuth most of his savings.

Irrespective of the success or failure of these endeavours, Metternich and his colleagues in the Council of Regency found it intolerable that Hungarians should presume to trespass on areas of policy—tariffs, trade and industry—reserved to the royal prerogative. Abandoning the more emollient approach he had adopted in 1843, Metternich took the offensive: in July 1844, he 'arranged' Kossuth's removal from the editorship of Pesti Hírlap and then tried, but predictably failed, to buy Kossuth with the offer of a post with a pro-government journal. The Hungarian Chancellery was stiffened by the appointment of the conservative Count Apponyi to the Vice-Chancellorship. Finally, in February 1846, Metternich adopted the Josephine strategy of despatching 'administrators' to those Hungarian counties that had proved persistent in their defiance of the government and support for the liberal opposition. The 'administrators', instructed to disable the authority of the counties and with troops at their disposal, packed meetings of county assemblies with bribed 'sandalled nobles', ejected supporters of the opposition with armed force and compelled assemblies to draw up instructions for their deputies to the Diet that conformed with government policy. These activities persuaded Kossuth and other prominent liberals that opposition to the government and its sponsor-ship of disorder could not succeed unless the forces of opposition were organised and united behind a common programme. Count Lajos Batthyány agreed to chair a central opposition committee but Ferenc Deák, cautious as ever, at first declined even to discuss a liberal manifesto, on the grounds that a written programme would divide rather than unite the opposition. In 1846, two events persuaded Deák to change his mind. A rebellion by the Polish nobles of Galicia against Aus-trian rule ended in the massacre of over a thousand noblemen at the hands not of imperial troops but of the Galician peasantry, whose hatred of their landlords may have been exploited by Austrian officials: this accelerated the polarisation of the Hungarian political class into those whose fears of a peasant uprising nearer home propelled them into the arms of the government and those for whom the Gali-cian tragedy increased the urgency of social and economic reform in Hungary. Metternich naturally gave encouragement to moves within the Hungarian Diet towards the formation of a Conservative Party: in a memorandum to Count Apponyi, now promoted to be Hungarian Chancellor, Metternich visualised the purpose of the new party as being to 'unite the conservative element throughout the country, to integrate them into the political life of the nation, and to co-ordi-nate their activities in electing deputies and officers of local government'.[1] This was the second event that persuaded Deák to join Kossuth, Batthyány and others in drawing up a statement of the opposition's objectives, but he remained unen-thusiastic and distanced himself from the rising level of opposition activity. Simi-larly, István Széchenyi held aloof from the Conservatives; but he did accept the post of Commissioner for Transport in the Lieutenancy Council, thereby placing himself firmly in the government camp.

The framework of a liberal programme had been established five years earlier, in a resolution carried in the Szatmár county assembly that came to be known as the 'Twelve Points'; since most or all of these featured in virtually every opposition declaration until 1848, they deserve a summary. Szatmár County demanded: the abolition of entail; mandatory redemption of all feudal dues and services, to be compensated by payments from a fund to which emancipated serfs would contribute over a thirty-year period; the establishment of a land bank and land register; recognition of the right of all citizens to own property and to hold office; taxation of the nobility; the abolition of guilds and monopolies; the abolition of censorship and freedom of the press; universal education, to be funded by the sale of church lands; representation of all the people in the Diet; abolition of feudal courts and the introduction of trial by jury; and separation of the judiciary from the executive. These proposals formed a basis for discussion by 1,200 delegates at the first national conference of the opposition, which opened in Pest on 15 March 1847; Kossuth chaired a drafting committee, which eventually produced a Statement of the Opposition, to be approved at a second conference in June. Committee wrangling and Deák's caution had eroded the clarity and radicalism of Szatmár's 'Twelve Points', particularly on the important question of the redemption of feudal dues. But the statement laid heavy emphasis on one issue that Szatmár had not addressed, that of national independence: while reaffirming adherence to the terms of the Pragmatic Sanction approved by the Diet in 1723, it also demanded respect for the famous passage in Law X of 1790, which had been included in Leopold II's coronation oath and declared Hungary to be free, independent in its government and not subordinate to any other state or nation.* Most of the other Szatmár points found a place in the statement, including general taxation and the abolition of entail; the statement also demanded that Magyar should be the language of instruction in all state schools, whatever the race or religion of their teachers and pupils. The statement's call for the introduction of all these reforms in Austria and Bohemia, as well as in Hungary, as a condition of Hungary's continued membership of the imperial family of nations, marked the debut of an issue which was to acquire great significance in future years.

Deák's fear that a written programme would be divisive proved to be well founded. The opposition was, in fact, already divided: between the liberal gentry, led by Kossuth, who regarded county autonomy as the only reliable guarantee of freedom in the new Hungary, and the intelligentsia, which favoured a strong central government capable of forcing through reforms unimpeded by county conservatism or inertia. The Statement of the Opposition provoked a further split, when radicals disappointed with its more cautious passages formed their own group, which came to be known by the name of the café in which they habitually met, the Pilvax in Pest. The Pilvax group, which styled itself 'Young Hungary' and of which the young radical poet Sándor Petőfi was the acknowledged leader, included many of the leading writers and intellectuals of their time: János Arany, the great lyric poet; Mór Jókai, whose novels won critical acclaim throughout Europe; Mihály Tompa, the populist poet; the peasant writer and polemicist Mihály Táncsics; and the historian Pál Vasvári, who rallied students to the radical cause. These were powerful pens which, in a nation increasingly addicted to the written Magyar word, gave strength and passion to the liberal cause (the works

* See page 145.

that flowed from them will be given more attention in a later chapter). The hard core of the Pilvax group was the 'society of Ten', formed by Petőfi in 1846 from young writers who shared the ideal of a free and independent Hungary united by a pure Magyar culture.

The programme on which supporters of the new Conservative Party, led by Count Emil Dessewffy, fought the elections to the Diet of 1847 consisted largely of a recital of traditional values and virtues, but made some concessions to the climate of reform; it championed freedom of speech, the reform of the civil and penal codes, the removal of discriminatory tariffs and the provision of credit for landowners. It did not, of course, call for the mandatory redemption of feudal dues or for the taxation of the nobility. Thanks in part to the activities of the 'administrators', the Catholic Church, the secret police and perhaps above all the impact of the Galician uprising, conservatives nevertheless did rather well in the 1847 elections, ousting several leading members of the opposition in their home counties, Ferenc Deák and József Eötvös among them. National attention focused on the election in Pest county, where Lajos Kossuth, standing for election for the first time, campaigned on the agreed opposition platform. It was in this election that the traditional colours of Hungary's medieval kings, which were to be those of the modern Hungarian nation, made their first reappearance, in the red, white and green feathers sported by Kossuth's supporters. To the strength of Kossuth's oratory was added the power of considerable sums of money put at the disposal of his campaign by liberal members of the Upper House, including Lajos Batthyány, to pay for a lavish succession of political banquets and the printing of campaign literature: these resources resulted in an impressive victory for Kossuth, who defeated his conservative opponent by 2,948 votes to 1,314. Elsewhere, however, only a third of Hungary's counties—those in which the gentry rather than the magnates and the Church owned most of the land—remained loyal to the opposition cause.

The reading of the royal propositions at the opening of what was to be Hungary's last feudal Diet, on 11 November 1847, showed that Metternich's strategy of alternating repression and concession remained in place: the government programme pre-empted most of the opposition's demands and threw in for good measure the abolition of customs barriers between Austria and Hungary. Kossuth, determined that the opposition should not be thrown off balance as Metternich hoped, succeeded in persuading the Lower Chamber to insist on the usual discussion of grievances—first among them the appointment and conduct of the 'administrators'—before addressing the royal agenda. When this course had been rejected by the Upper Chamber, as it invariably was, the Lower Chamber decided to dispense with the usual address to the throne and to get on with debating issues of substance, including the mandatory redemption of feudal dues and taxation of the nobility. This produced one important decision: the acceptance in principle (albeit with no provision for implementation) of mandatory redemption, subject to financial compensation to landowners by the state. When, after over three months of discussion, Kossuth proposed that the unconstitutional appointment of county 'administrators' should be formally condemned, his motion fell, by a single, Croatian, vote. Széchenyi, now sitting as a deputy in the Lower Chamber for the express purpose of opposing Kossuth, contributed significantly to this outcome with persuasive interventions in favour of moderation; when Kossuth sought to reintroduce his motion, Széchenyi accused him of inciting rebellion. This was a reckless overstatement: in his very first speech to the Diet as a deputy for Pest county, Kossuth had firmly denied the existence of any conflict between Hungarian and Austrian interests, affirming that 'the complete development of constitutional life in Hungary is perfectly compatible with the Austrian connexion'.[2] Apart from the Jacobin-inspired radicals, no member of the opposition was at this stage calling for, or even contemplating, a break with Austria, simply for greater autonomy within the Empire and greater freedom of action in the ordering of Hungary's internal affairs.

In the early weeks of 1848, indeed, there seemed every reason to expect that although the process of reform in Hungary would continue, it would do so at a pace and within bounds dictated by Vienna and its allies in the Hungarian Upper Chamber rather than by the liberal opposition. The long tradition of alternating friction and accommodation between the Austrian government and the Diet would be maintained, or so it appeared from the limited perspective of Pozsony. So far as Hungary was concerned, only in the coffee houses and lecture halls of Pest were there echoes of the expectations of cataclysm, which had by now become widespread in western Europe as a whole. Abroad, there was a general sense that the life expectancy of the Holy Alliance against change and of the alliance of the bourgeoisie, fearful of revolution, with reaction had already been exceeded. As long ago as 1831, Victor Hugo had written prophetically of 'the dull sound of revolution, still deep down in the earth, pushing out under every Kingdom in Europe its subterranean galleries from the central shaft of the mine which is Paris'.[3] Observers with insight recognised that the political and social structures of the early nineteenth century, preserved by artifice for so long, could no longer bear the strains placed upon them by nationalism and by the Industrial Revolution. In January, 1848, Alexis de Tocqueville exclaimed to the Chamber of Deputies in Paris: 'Do you not feel the earth of Europe trembling once more! Do you not feel the wind of revolution in the air!'[4] One of the very few strokes of good fortune in Hungary's history lay in the fact that her Diet happened to be in session when the storm broke.

News of the revolution in Paris reached Pozsony on 1 March 1848, a week after Louis Philippe's abdication. The immediate reaction was a run on the banks, in the expectation that the Bank of Vienna would fail; on 5 March, a Sunday, crowds attempting to storm the State Bank in Pest, in order to exchange their paper money for silver, had to be dispersed by a cavalry squadron from Buda. In Pozsony, Lajos Kossuth—whose second attempt to persuade the Lower Chamber to call for the dismantlement of the regime of the 'administrators' had failed as recently as 27 February—displayed the sure political instinct and gift for seizing the moment that István Széchenyi lacked: on 3 March he presented to the Lower Chamber the draft of an address to the throne that incorporated all the components of the Statement of the Opposition. For good measure, Kossuth declared that full responsibility for the Empire's dire financial situation lay with the government in Vienna; and demanded an autonomous financial regime for Hungary. The Palatine, Archduke Stephen, sensing that in just forty-eight hours the tide had turned dramatically against the government, left Pozsony for Vienna so that the

Upper Chamber would be unable, in his absence, to take delivery of Kossuth's address to the throne, which was duly adopted by the Lower Chamber with over-whelming acclaim on 4 March. In response to the Palatine's tactic of evasion, the Lower Chamber also resolved to send the address directly to King Ferdinand, bypassing the Upper House altogether.

Meanwhile, just as Victor Hugo had predicted seventeen years before, the reper-cussions of revolution in Paris were spreading throughout Europe. The mid-1840s had been marked by bad harvests, widespread industrial unemployment and a sharp increase in food prices; as the Galician uprising in 1846 had shown, the peasantry had reached the end of its endurance and many European cities, includ-ing Vienna, were teeming with refugees from the stricken countryside seeking work in the factories. The Empire's chronic financial crisis had deepened further during the two preceding decades: by 1847, interest on the state debt amounted to 45 million gulden, only slightly less than the entire imperial revenue from direct taxation.[5] In Austria, the growing middle class and the intelligentsia were seething with frustration with the constraints imposed by the regime on industrial enterprise and free expression. News of the Paris revolution, of insurrections in Munich and Berlin and, not least, reports of Kossuth's speech in the Hungarian Diet on 3 March provided the catalyst for action: on 13 March, against a back-ground of violence and arson in the working-class suburbs of Vienna, the Austrian Estates sent a large delegation to the Hofburg palace to petition for urgent reform. The delegation was urged on its way by a mass meeting of students, ablaze with enthusiasm after a public reading of Kossuth's speech by one of their number who had obtained the text from Pozsony. By late evening, the Archdukes acting on behalf of their enfeebled brother Ferdinand had given in: the dismissal of Met-ternich, the resignations of Counts Sedlnitzky (chief of police) and Apponyi (Hungarian Chancellor) and the abolition of censorship were announced in quick succession.

The Palatine, Archduke Stephen, now hurried back to Pozsony in order to convene the Hungarian Upper Chamber which, in a state of shock following the news from Vienna, accepted Kossuth's address to the throne, without discussion, on 14 March. The Diet resolved to send a joint delegation, from both Chambers, to present the address to the King in Vienna; on the following day, the delegation, arrayed in the magnificent national dress of the Hungarian nobility, embarked on the Danube paddle steamer *Franz Karl* for the short journey upstream to the imperial capital. Crowds lining the river bank cheered their departure; they cheered the red, white and green pennant flying from the steamer's masthead; and they cheered the sight of not only Lajos Kossuth standing on the deck but of István Széchenyi close by him. Széchenyi declared to his diary on that day: 'I must support Louis Batthyány and Kossuth! All feelings of hatred and antipathy and even ambition must be silenced'—even if they were, as he feared, risking 'the complete disintegration of Hungary'.[6]

The Revolution of 1848

News of the insurrection in Vienna did not reach Pest, via a Danube steamboat, until 14 March; but events there had already developed their own momentum.

Earlier in the month, Kossuth had suggested to the Opposition Circle, which was in effect his constituency liberal party in Pest, that it should send to the Diet in Pozsony a petition, based on his speech of 3 March, which would heighten pressure for the presentation of his address to the throne. Sándor Petőfi's 'Society of Ten' eagerly accepted the task of drafting the petition which, under the heading 'Twelve Points' became the manifesto of 'Young Hungary'. It demanded:

- the abolition of censorship and freedom of the press
- government by an independent Hungarian ministry, residing in Pest-Buda and responsible to parliament
- a parliament elected by universal suffrage, to meet annually
- civil and religious equality
- equality of taxation
- the abolition of feudal burdens
- the formation of a National Guard
- trial by jury
- the foundation of a national bank
- the formation of a national army and the withdrawal of foreign (i.e. Austrian) troops from Hungary
- the freeing of political prisoners
- the reunion of Hungary and Transylvania.

The society planned to distribute printed copies of this programme—which went significantly further than Kossuth's speech in its demands—and to canvass support for it at the annual fair on St Joseph's Day, 19 March. Forty thousand peasants from all over the country were expected to converge on the Field of Rákos, on the outskirts of Pest, for this event: like their contemporaries elsewhere in the Empire, they had endured two successive bad harvests—Bihar County had reported over 81,000 cases of starvation in 1847—and would be receptive to radical oratory and demands for reform. The political stage was thus set for Sándor Petőfi's brief but dazzling appearance at its centre.

Petőfi, the son of an innkeeper turned itinerant butcher, had arrived in Pest in 1844, aged twenty-one; since leaving school he had scraped a living as an actor in various theatres; a short spell in the army had been curtailed by ill health. Poetry had flowed from his pen since his schooldays. A number of his poems, combining unvarnished realism with soaring lyricism, had already been published in literary journals, with one of which he now secured a post as assistant editor. His political radicalism sprang from his direct experience, during his wanderings through northern and eastern Hungary, of the brutish poverty and deprivation of the countryside; his populism, from his observation of how the human spirit was so often able to rise above it. But Petőfi's status as Hungary's national poet, to which he laid claim already during his short lifetime, rested on much more than his passionate championship of reform and defence of the oppressed; nor did it depend on, although it was certainly enhanced by, the drama of a hero's death on the battlefield at the tragically early age of twenty-six. Like Mozart's, Petőfi's genius defies rational analysis or explanation. His poetry embraced every known genre and explored new ones. During the course of only seven years (1842–49) he wrote about 900 poems, as well as plays, novels and translations. His populist (*népies*) works looked with an unsentimental but deeply sympathetic eye on the life of the village and the peasantry, drawing some of its inspiration from the folksongs and rhymes he heard during his travels. His long narrative poem, *János Vitéz* ('John the Hero'), treats a romantic theme—the rise to greatness of a young man born in poverty and sustained through heroic adventures by loyalty to his first love—in the language of everyday life, quite unlike the high-flown abstractions of the Romantic poets who preceded him. His love poems, nearly all addressed to his wife, Júlia, also brought the theme of love down from the clouds and treated it in settings with which ordinary people could empathise. One of the best-loved, '*Szeptember végén*' ('At the End of September') contains these lines:

> ... Still young in my heart burn the hot flames of summer,
> Whence spring in its glory has never yet fled,
> But see, my dark hair shows the first tints of autumn;
> The hoar-frost of winter has smitten my head.
> The petals are falling, and life is fast fleeting,
> Sit here, my beloved, sit here on my knee!
> Will you who have now laid your head on my bosom
> Tomorrow not weep at the graveside for me?[7]

Petőfi's poems describing the Alföld, the Great Plain, a region Hungarians had not hitherto thought of as beautiful or romantic, gave them an enduring, if melancholy, national image:

> The winds grow weary now, and at dusk they die again;
> Pallid mists arise and settle on the plain,
> Half-covering in grey
> The brigand on his way,
> Whose snorting steed now carries him towards his nightly bed–
> At his heels a wolf, and a crow above his head.[8]

Sándor Petőfi's poetic vision and style were directly related to his political radicalism. In 1847 he wrote to the poet János Arany: 'After all, the poetry of the people is the only genuine poetry. Let's make this poetry predominant in the realm of literature. When the people are prominent in poetry, they are very near to power in politics....To heaven with the people, to hell with aristocracy!'[9] Once he had settled in Pest, Petőfi's daily contact with other radical writers, poets and students brought politics to the core of his art. His output was prodigious, his skill in the use of everyday Magyar in poetic expression unmatched; within two years, he had become Hungary's most popular poet and a household name. As noted earlier, he was also the acknowledged leader of the Society of Ten and of the Pilvax group as a whole. On 11 March 1848, he wrote a poem that ended:

> The gentry have waxed fat on us
> For long years past,
> But now it's our turn; let our dogs
> On them grow fat.
> So toss them with your pitchforks in
> The dung and mud,
> And there the dogs can make their meal
> Of bones and blood...[10]

Although other stanzas of the poem draw back from violence and enjoin reconciliation, this vein of Petőfi's writing did not commend itself to the liberal gentry. Another poem, composed two days later on 13 March, made a much greater impact and attracted universal acclaim. Petőfi's 'National Song' (*'Nemzeti Dal'*) became just that: the poetic anthem of the revolution and of the war that followed:

> Rise up, Magyar, the country calls!
> It's 'now or never' what fate befalls...
> Shall we live as slaves or free men?
> That's the question—choose your 'Amen'!
> God of Hungarians, we swear unto Thee,
> We swear unto Thee—that slaves we shall no longer be![11]

On 15 March, elated by the news from Vienna that had reached Pest on the previous evening, Petőfi and other members of the Pilvax group toured the medical and law faculties of the university, where the 'Twelve Points' were declaimed and Petőfi recited his 'National Song' to enthusiastic crowds of students. Both texts were then taken to a nearby printer, where large numbers of copies were reproduced, in defiance of censorship, and distributed to the growing throng. After addressing a crowd of several thousand in front of the National Museum (contrary to legend, Petőfi did not recite his 'National Song' on this occasion), the young radicals led a march to Pest's Town Hall, where a frightened council readily agreed to endorse the 'Twelve Points'. A Committee of Public Safety—on which 'Young Hungary' secured only four seats out of thirteen—was constituted on the spot and the nucleus of a National Guard formed from the existing civic guard. Later in the afternoon, the committee led a crowd of some twenty thousand across the pontoon bridge to Buda and burst into the offices of the Lieutenancy Council to demand the abolition of censorship and the release of political prisoners: like the municipal council in Pest, the Lieutenancy Council caved in without argument. There turned out to be only a single political prisoner: Mihály Táncsics, the peasant populist and scourge of landlords. He was carried in triumph back to Pest, where a gala evening at the National Theatre brought the first phase of the Hungarian revolution to a rousing conclusion.

Meanwhile, the Diet's deputation, steaming up the Danube from Pozsony to Vienna and unaware of events in Pest, had been making preparations for negotiating acceptance of its address to the throne. There was general agreement among the delegates that, given the revolution in Vienna, the Diet's demands should go beyond the relatively moderate terms of the address; but the address could not be amended without the authority of the whole Diet. Széchenyi suggested, and Kossuth at once agreed, that the solution to this dilemma lay in pre-drafting the King's response to the address and including in this Rescript royal assent to such additional proposals as the delegates wished to make. Drafting of the Rescript began on board the *Franz Karl* and continued after debarkation in Vienna, where the delegates were welcomed as heroes by crowds of up to 100,000 citizens, their triumphal progress through the streets of the capital pausing at intervals to allow Kossuth to make a speech. The final version of the Rescript provided for the endowment of the Palatine, Archduke Stephen, with imperial plenipotentiary authority, which meant that his approval of legislation would require no other royal sanction; for the immediate formation of a Hungarian national government; and for the appointment of Count Lajos Batthyány to head it as Prime Minister. Széchenyi expressed strong reservations over the latter two demands, on the grounds that they would amount to an unnecessary humiliation of the monarchy and store up trouble for the future. As usual, he was right: but, also as usual, he had failed to recognise the political imperatives of the moment. Széchenyi nevertheless played a full part in trying to persuade, first, the Palatine and then members of the *Staatskonferenz* to accept the Rescript. The Palatine, Archduke Stephen (mockingly nicknamed 'Rákóczi' by the Viennese court on account of his unconcealed sympathy with most things Hungarian), quickly recognised the necessity of granting the demands embodied in the Rescript in order to avert further damage to the authority of the Crown; the *Staatskonferenz* took longer to convince, although first reports of events in Pest proved helpful to the Hungarian case.

At an embarrassing audience on the afternoon of 16 March, the Hungarian delegation had been obliged to watch their King, Ferdinand, pleading with the Palatine in childish language not to take his throne away. Late that night, the Palatine was able to inform the Hungarians that the Rescript had been signed. On the following morning, however, it emerged that the text signed by Ferdinand omitted any reference either to the appointment of Batthyány to head a Hungarian government or to the expeditious approval of legislation passed by the Diet. Palatine Stephen persuaded Ferdinand to authorise him to make good these omissions in his capacity as imperial plenipotentiary, without referring the matter back to the *Staatskonferenz*, an act for which he was subsequently rebuked and for which he would not be forgiven. The Hungarian delegation, meanwhile, exhausted but triumphant, had re-embarked on its paddle steamer to Pozsony, where the immense task of translating into legislation all the momentous provisions of the Rescript awaited it. Writing to his secretary in Pest after reaching Pozsony, István Széchenyi made a generous admission:

My policy was certain … but slow. Kos[suth] staked everything on one card, and already has won more for the nation than my policy could have produced over perhaps twenty years! If there is no reaction, and if we prove to have more patriotism than envy and more civic virtue than vanity … well, I believe we Hungarians may yet achieve something—and something great![12]

The Diet now embarked on a period of hectic activity, with Lajos Kossuth as its main driving force. Lajos Batthyány, as Prime Minister, submitted his list of proposed cabinet appointments to the Palatine: it included, among others, Kossuth, as Minister of Finance; Széchenyi, as Minister of Public Works and Transport; József Eötvös, as Minister of Education; Colonel Lázár Mészáros (who was serving with the imperial army in Italy), as Minister of War; and Prince Pál Eszterházy as 'Minister at the King's side', whose role was intended to be that of mediator between the King and the Hungarian ministry, but who regarded himself as Hungary's foreign minister. Of the whole cabinet, only Kossuth was not a landowner. By 23 March, a number of major laws had been prepared for submission to the crown. The crucial legislative act, Law III, on which to a large extent the others depended, required the King, or if he were absent from Hungary, the Palatine to exercise royal executive power only through a ministry that was to have responsibility 'for all questions which hitherto fell, or ought to have fallen, within the competence of the Hungarian Court Chancellery, the [Lieutenancy] Council, the Camera [Treasury] (including the mines), and in general all civil, Church, fiscal, military and in general all questions of defence'.[13] Other laws provided for: the creation of a National Assembly to replace the Diet, to meet annually; the establishment of a national bank; the formation of a National Guard (but with a high property qualification, to avoid arming the peasantry); general taxation; the abolition of entail; the reunion of the Partium and, if its Diet agreed, of Transylvania with Hungary; and an end to censorship, subject to safeguards to protect the monarchy and its servants from public attack.

Two draft laws caused immediate difficulties. The first provided for the almost complete emancipation of the Jews, including their enfranchisement subject to a property qualification: when this became known in Pozsony, local artisans immediately launched a violent pogrom, which spread within a few days to Pest, Székesfehérvár and several other towns. Unlike the poet Vörösmarty, who declared that 'the sacred name of equality has never been a more monstrous lie than now', Kossuth reacted to the pogroms with unbecoming pragmatism: '...prejudice exists', he told the Diet, 'and against its blindness, as the poet said, "even the gods fight in vain"'; and later: 'To legislate now concerning the Jews would be equivalent to throwing masses of this race victims to the fury of their enemies'.[14] The draft law was withdrawn, testimony to the growing strength in Hungary, as in several other European societies, of jealous hatred of the Jews. Problems also arose from the law abolishing feudal dues and services, making peasants the owners of the land they occupied. Kossuth bounced this through the Upper Chamber when only a few magnates were present; it contained a vague reference to financial compensation for landlords but no clear indication of how this was to be funded. Consternation among the nobility over the prospect of losing their serfs without being given the means to hire labour encouraged the *Staatskonferenz* to send the law back for revision. In a separate Rescript, the *Staatskonferenz* attempted to claw back all the derogations from the royal prerogative—and from the Pragmatic Sanction—that the new Hungarian laws implied: it insisted on the preservation of the supervisory powers of the Hungarian Chancellery; restricted the Palatine's plenipotentiary powers to the lifetime of the current incumbent, Archduke Stephen; rejected the Hungarian ministry's claim to dispose of revenues raised in Hungary; and reserved to the King the right to commission army officers and deploy troops. For good measure, the Rescript demanded that Hungary should assume responsibility for over 25 per cent of the state debt.

This counter-attack from Vienna provoked a wave of mass demonstrations in Pest as soon as news of it arrived on 28 March. The Committee of Public Safety, now with a National Guard numbering over 6,000 at its disposal, resolved that any further delay in royal approval of Hungarian legislation should be countered by revolution and a declaration of independence. The streets of Pest sprouted barricades; Petőfi harangued a crowd of thousands from the steps of the National Museum. Although the ferment in Pest strengthened Kossuth's hand, *vis-à-vis* both the Upper Chamber and Vienna, the main reason for the court's complete climbdown on 31 March lay elsewhere. Revolution had triumphed in Milan and in Venice; Cracow was in rebellion; a delegation from Prague hoped to achieve for Bohemia what the Diet's delegation had achieved for Hungary; and the

Empire's strongest military force, under Count Radetzky, already mauled by Italian revolutionaries and eroded by desertions, was bottled up in the Quadrilateral, the group of fortresses in Lombardy that guarded the Alpine passes. With the Empire apparently about to crumble, the constitutional niceties of Austria's relationship with Hungary became less significant. The *Staatskonferenz* therefore withdrew all its objections to the new Hungarian laws, saving for the Crown only its military prerogatives—and the exercise even of these became subject to the counter-signature of the 'Minister at the King's side'. For the time being, Hungary was left to her own devices. On 1 April, Kossuth was able to declare to the Palatine: 'The nobility, this first-born of the fatherland, has decided to share with all others the treasury of rights and liberty. Instead of privileged classes, Your Highness is now surrounded by a free nation, one that has become master of its fate and future'.[15]

In the few remaining days of its existence, the last feudal Diet worked hard to put the finishing touches to the new constitutional structure to which Vienna now appeared to be reconciled. On 11 April, Ferdinand V appeared at Pozsony in person to dissolve the Diet and give his sanction to the body of legislation which came to be known as the April Laws. The thirty-one laws incorporated all the provisions already summarised, with some important additions. The new National Assembly, of which the Upper Chamber would retain its traditional composition, would meet annually in Pest, not Pozsony; bills were to be given royal sanction before the end of the session in which they had been presented; the King retained the right of dissolution, but a new Parliament had to be convened within three months. The Lower Chamber, consisting of 446 deputies, would be elected on a significantly expanded franchise—of all male citizens over twenty years of age, without serious criminal convictions and owning urban property to the value of at least 300 florins or approximately six to eight *hold* (eight to twelve acres) of rural land. The franchise law had the effect of excluding all those dependent on a wage for their livelihood, the great majority of the peasantry and all Jews, but it was nevertheless more generous than Britain's 'Great Reform Act' of 1832 and enfranchised about 25 per cent of Hungary's adult male population. In county elections, however, the franchise would still be restricted to the nobility, a restriction designed to prevent the take-over of county assemblies by a non-Hungarian nationality in counties where Hungarians were in a minority. Compensation to landowners for the loss of serf labour would come from the new Credit Bank. Magyar was to be the official language of all Hungary: in one of his last speeches before the Diet's dissolution, Kossuth declared:

The true sense of freedom is that it bestows the benefits of freedom not on one caste as a kind of privilege but on all the inhabitants of the country regardless of language or religion. It is indispensable to the unity of the country that Hungarian be the diplomatic language of public life—and I believe that the Hungarian nation by extending, on this basis, Hungarian freedom to all its citizens without difference and by frankly confessing to the principle of honouring the use of each nationality's own language in its internal and clerical affairs ... shall have strengthened the Hungarian nationality...[16]

The law on language nevertheless exempted Croatia from the provision that Magyar should be official language of county assemblies and gave the Croatians a higher level of representation in the new National Assembly.

The April Laws laid the foundations of the modern Hungarian state. They dismantled and interred most of the institutions of feudalism, even if they could not erase the feudal mentality—and even if the conservatives consented to the burial only from fear of violent revolution. In terms of personal liberty, civil rights and freedom of expression they brought Hungary to the level of parity with most European states and ahead of some; they established the essentials of that 'civil society' István Széchenyi regarded as the precondition of further political and economic advance. It has been argued[17] that the April Laws did no more than restore to Hungary her traditional rights, which the Habsburgs had progressively usurped since 1526; the case is not without historical foundation, although laboriously expressed in true Magyar legalistic style. The fact remains that in less than quarter of a century Hungary had progressed from being little more than a backward, stagnant province of the Empire to becoming a vital, reformed and all but independent state, well able to speak to Vienna on equal terms and to command the influence appropriate to a country the territory of which accounted for nearly half that of the Empire. To Széchenyi belongs the credit for the awakening; to Kossuth, that for the achievement.

In describing the events that culminated in the passage of the April Laws, I have followed historiographical convention in using the term 'revolution': but was it, in reality, a revolution? Ferdinand V remained King of Hungary; he was protected by law from public defamation; only the radicals, a tiny minority, challenged the institution of monarchy or the Habsburg succession; the King retained the right to appoint and dismiss senior officials and senior members of the Church hierarchy; the declaration of war and the commissioning of officers remained within his sole prerogative; he could still suspend (for a limited time) and dissolve Parliament; and, as before, only he could grant titles of nobility and pardons. Above all, the Hungarian nobility remained firmly in control of their nation's destiny. This degree of continuity is incompatible with any commonly accepted definition of 'revolution': events in Pest, Pozsony and Vienna in March, 1848, cannot be equated with those in Paris a few weeks earlier. To say this is not to diminish, in any way, the achievement of the Hungarian liberal opposition; it is, rather, to enhance it, by illuminating the comparative restraint of the Hungarian leaders in a situation in which, for once, they had the upper hand. The April Laws were the product, not of a revolution, but of yet another adjustment of the Austro-Hungarian relationship—albeit a massive one. Like earlier such adjustments, that of April, 1848 contained in its imperfections the seeds of its eventual collapse. The 'common affair' of defence identified by the Pragmatic Sanction in 1723, with which the related policy areas of finance and foreign policy were now in practice inextricably linked, could not be smoothly discharged by the two Ministries of War, two Ministries of Finance and two 'Foreign Ministers' which, in effect, the 1848 accommodation sanctioned. Nor, as Széchenyi recognised, could a corpus of thirty-one laws in which the sole, and indirect, reference to the 'nationalities' was the requirement that Magyar should be the official language for all, offer a secure foundation for such a heterogeneous state as Hungary had become.

Hungary's 'nationalities' had at first welcomed the March events with great enthusiasm. On 21 March several thousand Serbs rallied in Újvidék (Novi Sad) to express support for Hungary's defiance of Vienna; one of their future leaders,

Djordje Stratimirović, took part in the demonstration wearing a red, white and green cockade. There were similar rallies in the Military Border Region, by Romanians in Transylvania and by Slovaks in the north west. This positive reaction reflected, of course, a general expectation among the national minorities that what the Hungarians had secured they, too, could achieve. Within days of Vienna's concessions to the Hungarian Diet, the Serbs demanded recognition of a separate Serb nation, the use of Serbian in their internal administration, an annual national congress and the abolition of conscription for military service in the Military Frontier Region (where Serbs were in the majority). The Slovaks made similar demands. The Romanians, both in Hungary and in Transylvania, called for national recognition. The Croatian Diet, the *Sabor*, urged on by a mass demonstration in Zagreb on 25 March, addressed a petition to King Ferdinand seeking complete autonomy within the Empire as a Triune Kingdom of Croatia, Slavonia and Dalmatia; the abolition of the Krajina (Military Frontier Region); recognition of Croat as its official language; the satisfaction of a number of specific demands based on the Pest 'Twelve Points'; and the appointment of a certain Colonel Josip Jelačić as Bán. Unknown to the *Sabor*, King Ferdinand had already met this last request two days before, at the suggestion of the *Staatskonferenz;* ostensibly, Jelačić's appointment was intended to boost the morale of the large Croatian contingent in Radetzky's beleaguered army in Lombardy—Jelačić had become something of a Croat national hero as a result of a daring retaliatory raid against the Turks in Bosnia. The King's advisers, however, and in particular the Minister of War, Count Latour, had a hidden agenda: Jelačić's reputation for Magyarphobia made him a tempting candidate for the highest Croatian office, in which he could be expected to cause problems for the importunate Hungarians. Further honours awaited Jelačić when he arrived in Vienna a few days later for a royal audience: promoted to the rank of Field Marshal, he was given command of the Military Frontier Region and, in all probability, a hint from Latour that Vienna would be indulgent with regard to the uses to which he might wish to put his new authority. Without such a hint, it seems unlikely that Jelačić would have ventured, as he did on his return to Zagreb, to proclaim himself President of a virtually autonomous Croatia; to assume authority over Slavonia and Hungary's port, Fiume; to forbid his officials to communicate with Budapest; and to break off relations between Croatia and Hungary. When Hungary's new Council of Ministers, under Lajos Batthyány's chairmanship, held its first meeting on 12 April, in Pozsony, the Croatian threat of secession was high on its agenda.

Croatia, however, was by no means the only problem that confronted Batthyány and his colleagues at this meeting and during the weeks which followed. In May, at Karlóca in the Military Frontier Region, a congress of 8,000 Serbs declared the creation of an autonomous Serbian province, the Vojvodina, extending over much of southern Hungary and taking in even parts of Slavonia and Croatia. The congress elected an Executive Committee (*Glavni Odbor*), under the chairmanship of Djordje Stratimirović, to administer the new province: before long the committee had gained control of most of it, evicting Hungarian officials in order to do so. Meanwhile, in Transylvania, an even larger congress of 40,000 Romanians had assembled at Balázsfalva to support a petition to the Transylvanian Diet and to the Emperor demanding the redemption of feudal dues without compensation, a

Romanian national parliament, Romanian representation in the Diet, Romanian schools and a Romanian militia. Like the Serbs, the Romanians formed an Executive Committee and, going further, a National Guard. In northern Hungary, the Slovaks called for Hungary to become a federation, of which an autonomous Slovak region with its own administration and university would be a member.

The Hungarian Ministry's response to these developments was unyielding; indeed, it is not evident that Batthyány, Kossuth and their colleagues had a clear appreciation of their seriousness. The new government persisted in the view that the April Laws benefited the 'nationalities' as much as the Hungarians and should be an inspiration to gratitude and loyalty rather than to sedition. It would certainly have been unreasonable to expect a ministry that had just succeeded in winning autonomy for the Hungarian kingdom willingly to preside over the fragmentation of that kingdom into a number of self-administering provinces, each using a different language for official and educational purposes—a prototypical Yugoslavia without a monolithic Party to hold it together. Sympathy towards such a recipe for chaos and division would have amounted to an abdication of the government's newly acquired national responsibilities. At this stage, moreover, Vienna had showed no disposition to encourage any national movement other than that of the Croats. The fact remains that *if* Batthyány and Kossuth had found it possible to offer at least symbolic concessions to the 'nationalities', such as minor cabinet posts for representatives of each of them, they might have averted a looming tragedy: but to suggest this is, perhaps, to project the painfully acquired political wisdom of a later century on to a situation in which inexperienced politicians were encountering new problems with few precedents to guide them. As it was, a Romanian delegation to Pest-Buda (the seat of Hungarian government since 14 April) received only an admonition to be content with the freedom Hungarians had won for them. When, in April, the Serb leader Stratimirović told Kossuth—more in sorrow than in anger—that if Serbs could not win from Hungary sympathy for their aspiration to independence they would have to look to Vienna, Kossuth coldly remarked that 'in that case, the sword must decide between us'.[18] As for the Slovaks, the government dismissed their agitation as a pan-Slavic plot: it issued warrants for the arrest of their three leaders—Štúr, Hurban and Hodža—and appointed commissioners to administer the northern counties in which Slovaks predominated, an extraordinary imitation of Habsburg practice. Only Széchenyi had the vision to foresee the consequences of the government's attitude. Earlier in the year he had questioned the complacent assumption that the 'nationalities' would happily assimilate into Magyardom in return for their new constitutional liberties: 'It is generally said that common liberty will weld us together. But if the Slavs and the Germans will say the same, and we number less than they do, who will finally assimilate whom? The six million Magyars will assimilate the sixty million Slavs, or vice versa …?'[19]

Agitation among the 'nationalities' took place against a background of more general unrest during the weeks following the passage of the April Laws. As usual, the righting of some wrongs rendered those that remained all the more intolerable. Strike action in the towns against working conditions and low wages was accompanied by unrest in the countryside resulting from disappointment with the law on peasant emancipation, of which the practical implications were just beginning to sink in.[20] This social volatility encouraged the government, first, to demand from Vienna the return to Hungary of all Hungarian regiments stationed elsewhere in the Empire; and then, when this demand was rejected, to press ahead with the formation of a National Guard, for which the April Laws provided and which became the country-wide successor to the Pest National Guard formed by the Committee of Public Safety during the March days. Despite Hungary's flat refusal to assume responsibility for 25 per cent of the interest on the imperial state debt, as Vienna had requested, the King raised no objection to the creation of ten National Guard battalions, nor even to the subordination of the imperial Commanding-Generals on Hungarian territory (including, in theory, Jelačić as Bán of Croatia) to the Hungarian Ministry of War. Batthyány also persuaded Ferdinand to empower the Palatine, Archduke Stephen, to appoint a plenipotentiary to bring Croatia to heel; the Palatine chose General Hrabovsky, commander of Pétervárad fortress, for the task but the general proved powerless in the face of Jelačić's continuing defiance. There was at this point a certain confluence of interest between the monarchy and the moderate wing (led by the Prime Minister) of the Hungarian Ministry. In mid-May, renewed violence on the streets of Vienna prompted the evacuation of the court to Innsbruck. In Pest, a mob led by 'Young Hungary' marched across the pontoon bridge to Buda to demonstrate against the Austrian garrison commander, Baron Lederer, whose guards opened fire and killed at least one student, wounding many more; Lederer subsequently fled to Vienna but Batthyány refused to give way to radical demands for reprisals against the garrison. The radicals, still led by Petőfi, thereupon demanded that the people should be armed to defend the revolution; and that Batthyány should be replaced by Kossuth, who had taken care to keep his lines open to the left wing. Both the King and his Hungarian Prime Minister, therefore, found themselves under pressure and with a common interest in avoiding any further deterioration in the Austro-Hungarian relationship. When the Palatine and József Eötvös travelled to Innsbruck at the end of May, ostensibly to invite the King to open the new Hungarian Parliament in July, they found Ferdinand amenable. Accepting the invitation, the King also responded courteously, if vaguely, to the Hungarian suggestion that he should seek refuge from Vienna's turbulence in Buda rather than in Innsbruck; he further agreed, at the Palatine's urging, to order Jelačić to abandon his planned convening of the Croatian *Sabor* and to come to Innsbruck to negotiate with Batthyány.[21] In defiance of the royal injunction, Jelačić opened the *Sabor*, in Zagreb, on 2 June. A week later, on 10 June, Ferdinand authorised a Rescript suspending Jelačić from the exercise of all his official responsibilities; and, in a different matter of equal importance to the Hungarians, ratified the decision of the Transylvanian Diet to reunite Transylvania with Hungary.

Events were nevertheless conspiring to ensure that this encouraging *rapprochement* between Hungary and the Court at Innsbruck would be short-lived. Serbs in southern Hungary were already taking the region, and its frontier, out of Hungarian control. Reacting to this, Batthyány had on 16 May initiated recruitment to a 'regular' National Guard, henceforth known as the *Honvéd*, with a view to allowing it to grow into a permanent national army; there was no property qualification for enlistment. On 24 May, a 'national congress' of Serbs had elected the nationalist Metropolitan of the Serbian Orthodox Church, Rajačić, to be their

Patriarch; proclaimed the Vojvodina an independent province loyal to the House of Habsburg; and voted for an alliance with the 'Triune Kingdom' of Croatia. By mid-June fighting had broken out in Slavonia between Serbian rebels and units of the *Honvéd*. Jelačić led a combined delegation of Croats and Serbs to Innsbruck in a bid to secure royal blessing for the two new self-proclaimed autonomous provinces and for the alliance between them. Although such blessing was withheld, Jelačić conducted a sufficiently skilful exercise in public relations to secure the de facto retention of his office of Bán of Croatia. This marked a turning point. The Austrians were not only increasingly exasperated by the cockiness of the Hungarian Ministry but also more confident of their capacity to do something about it. On 17 June Kossuth, as Minister of Finance, arranged with the Hungarian Commercial Bank of Pest for the issue of government 5 per cent bonds, purchasable only with specie, to cover the eventual issue of bank notes to a total value of 12.5 million forints, in order to fund the *Honvéd*.

The independent issue of paper money went far beyond the provisions of the April Laws and infringed the monopoly of the Austrian State Bank. For conservative Austrian ministers, already smarting from the reunion of Transylvania with Hungary, suspicious of the formation of the *Honvéd* and very far from reconciled, in any case, to the April Laws themselves, this was an open provocation (although they had taken good care to ensure, in April, that Kossuth would inherit a virtually empty treasury). A minor but significant victory for Radetzky over the Piedmontese carried the promise of better news from Italy. Jelačić, for his part, used his visit to Austria to secure the continuing patronage of his supporters, Count Latour and Baron Kulmer chief among them. His efforts were rewarded by a belligerent memorandum from Latour to the Hungarian government, which reached Batthyány's cabinet on 4 July: it threatened that unless an immediate accommodation with Croatia could be negotiated, Austria would be compelled to end its 'neutrality' towards Hungary. Latour also demanded that Hungary reimburse the Austrian treasury for the 150,000 gulden it had remitted to Jelačić for the payment of his troops (which in theory constituted part of the imperial force stationed in Hungary); and, for good measure, condemned Kossuth's bank note issue. Batthyány responded robustly, pointing out that a renunciation of 'neutrality' was meaningless since the sovereign of Austria and Hungary could not wage war on himself.

This exchange took place on the eve of the first session of Hungary's new National Assembly[22] which, after all, was opened by the Palatine, Ferdinand having chosen to be 'indisposed'. The Assembly's Lower House continued to be dominated by the land-owning gentry, with a leavening of urban bourgeoisie, clergy and a handful of peasants; Mihály Táncsics, who had been borne in triumph from Buda's gaol on 15 March, was returned by two constituencies. The Conservative Party had been eliminated but the radicals were present in sufficient strength to influence the debates. Once various administrative questions had been settled, the main issue confronting the Assembly was that of how it should respond to Ferdinand's request for 40,000 recruits to reinforce Radetzky's army in Italy. The moderate majority in the cabinet favoured compliance, on the grounds that the terms of the Pragmatic Sanction should be honoured and that Austrian goodwill would be needed as the crisis in relations with Croatia and the Serbs deepened; the radicals strongly opposed military aid to the suppressors of the Italian revolutionaries, with whom they would have preferred to make common cause. Kossuth inclined increasingly towards the radical view, while remaining loyal to the government. In his opening speech in the debate on finance and defence on 11 July, he skilfully buried the Italian issue in an avalanche of rhetoric about Hungary's own defensive needs: 'Gentlemen! The fatherland is in danger!' Kossuth urged the Lower House to vote for the creation of a national army of 200,000 troops and for the raising of 42 million forints with which to pay and equip them. He asked, without mentioning Italy, that 40,000 soldiers should be recruited immediately, thus making it possible for the government to meet the royal request if necessary. The House passed a resolution incorporating all Kossuth's proposals. In subsequent cabinet discussion it was agreed to recommend to the Assembly that the required reinforcement for the imperial army in Italy should be provided, but that strings should be attached: troops would be made available as soon as Hungary's own territorial integrity had been assured, law and order restored in the frontier regions and in Croatia, and Austrian support for legality and justice—in Italy as well as Hungary— guaranteed. The House approved a resolution on these lines on 22 July, only thirty-six radicals voting against it. Only three days later, Radetzky's crushing victory over the Piedmontese at Custozza made the issue of reinforcement irrelevant. The debate on defence moved on to the equally divisive question of whether the 200,000 new recruits should be allocated to the imperial regiments stationed in Hungary or to the *Honvéd*: Széchenyi and Mészáros, the Minister for War, favoured the former alternative against Kossuth and the radicals who argued passionately for the latter, with most of public opinion on their side. The balance of the eventual compromise strongly favoured Kossuth's position. Another resolution, approved unanimously by the House on 3 August, signified a further drift to the left: in a clear violation of the Pragmatic Sanction, this declared that if the Austrian government were to become involved in war against the Frankfurt Congress, it should not count on Hungarian support.[23]

Like planets in contrary orbits, Austria and Hungary were once again drifting apart. Radetzky's triumph in Lombardy, following hard on the snuffing out of insurrection in Prague by Prince Windischgrätz, had transformed morale in Vienna. Ferdinand and his Court returned to the capital amid general celebration, the remaining embers of working-class unrest were doused and Vienna recovered its poise. In Hungary, dire financial necessity compelled Kossuth to prohibit the export of silver to Austria; when the imperial treasury forbade banks throughout the Empire to accept Hungary's newly issued two-florin notes, Kossuth retaliated by making Austrian notes circulating in Hungary illegal tender, yet another violation of the spirit of the Pragmatic Sanction. István Széchenyi, in his most apocalyptic frame of mind and on the verge of nervous collapse, watched the disintegrating framework of the Austro-Hungarian relationship with despair and foreboding: 'The decline and humiliation that Hungary and the Hungarian nation will suffer are unprecedented in history', he wrote in his diary on 7 August.[24] He nevertheless remained true to the government and continued to speak in the Assembly, despite the increasing abuse to which he was subjected by the radicals for his steadfast defence of moderate and loyalist positions.

Széchenyi's fears were given their first vindication when, on 14 August, Ferdinand rescinded the Palatine's plenipotentiary status and specifically his power to ratify laws passed by the National Assembly; this meant that the crucial finance and defence laws of 11 July remained unratified. Lajos Batthyány, hitherto prepared to give Vienna the benefit of the doubt, began to share Széchenyi's pessimism: 'Reaction has now come out into the open', he wrote to a colleague on 18 August, 'and no longer conceals its plans and intentions. Hungary is indicated as the first victim ... at the most we have three weeks before us'.[25] Ten days later, accompanied by Ferenc Deák, he travelled to Vienna in order to secure Ferdinand's sanction for the 11 July laws and, if possible, to have a general negotiation with the Austrian government to resolve outstanding differences. Neither Ferdinand nor his ministers would receive the Hungarians. On 4 September, when Batthyány and Deák were still in Vienna, the Palatine informed the Hungarian cabinet that on 31 August Ferdinand had approved a memorandum from the Austrian government that declared not only the financial and defence laws passed by the National Assembly but the April Laws themselves to be incompatible with the Pragmatic Sanction and destructive of the unity of the monarchy. The memorandum therefore declared all measures introduced by the Hungarian government since March 1848, to be illegal. In a separate Rescript, Ferdinand summoned members of the Hungarian cabinet to Vienna in order to reach an accommodation with Jelačić; Hungary was to desist from making military preparations against Croatia (in fact, there were none); the Austrian Minister of War would take over responsibility for the Military Frontier Region.

The Hungarian cabinet had, in fact, already approved a draft bill prepared by Ferenc Deák that would have offered the Croats very generous terms. It provided for the appointment of Croats to vice-ministerial posts in the Ministries of War, Finance and Commerce and a representative alongside Prince Eszterházy 'at the King's side'; a separate Ministry for Croatian Affairs; for Croatian to be Croatia's official language; and for official correspondence between the two countries to be conducted by each in its own language, with translations enclosed. On 27 August, the cabinet had resolved that 'should it not be possible to come to terms on this basis, the government is ready to accept separation and a mere relation of alliance, retaining Fiume and the Hungarian littoral and thus the possibility of free travel and commerce'. And two days later Kossuth, who had effectively been leading the government even before Batthyány's departure, sent an instruction to the government's commissioner in charge of the defence line on the Drava, László Csányi, to:

contact the Croats and—if they are really prompted by national and not by reactionary aspirations, if they don't want to be fools and act as the hand that retrieves the chestnuts from the fire for reaction—ask them to tell what they wanted. We grant Croatia everything, even separation—may they go and may we remain good friends—but we are not bargaining with reaction ... Tell them to be reasonable—if they want to secede, let them, we wish them freedom and happiness—but tell them not to involve our two countries in bloodshed and misfortune for the sake of foreign reaction.[26]

He added that in a few days Deák's draft bill 'will be submitted to the house along with the alternative that if the Croats don't like it, they can secede, but Fiume is ours, that we'll give nobody'.[27]

Although these projected concessions testify to Hungarian readiness to negotiate a generous settlement in good faith, they were overtaken by events and not made public until it was too late. It is doubtful, in any case, that Jelačić would have found them attractive. His objective, as set out in a resolution of a Croatian Congress in May, was 'to contribute ... to the restoration of a ... strong and free Austrian State and to promote successfully the consolidation of the throne'.[28] Jelačić's primary commitment was not to Croatia per se but to the Emperor and the dynasty: at a meeting with Batthyány in Vienna on 24 July, at which the Hungarian Prime Minister had hoped to negotiate a settlement, Jelačić's first demand had been that Hungary should surrender its Ministries of War and Finance to Vienna. The Bán was not so much Vienna's dupe as its willing agent, eager to undermine Hungarian independence as much for Austria and the monarchy as for Croatia. On 31 August, having received a green light from Vienna and in the knowledge that 20,000 Croatian troops had been released from Radetzky's army, Jelačić occupied Fiume. Four days later, Ferdinand revoked his Rescript of 10 June and formally restored Jelačić to all his offices and honours.

On 4 September, as soon as the Palatine had informed the Cabinet of Ferdinand's Rescripts dated 31 August, they and the Austrian government's memorandum were read to the Lower House. Kossuth, in complete command of the situation and now the acknowledged leader of his nation, proposed that the House should address a manifesto to the peoples of Europe and that the Assembly should despatch a delegation to Vienna to address their King. One hundred members, of both Houses, were deputed to make the journey. While they were still steaming up the Danube Kossuth, in an act of extraordinary confidence or rashness, ordered that five-florin notes should be issued to the value of 61 million florins, unsecured apart from the promise of an eventual government loan; these were the first 'Kossuth notes', which served as Hungary's remarkably successful currency for the next twelve months. In Vienna, the Hungarian deputation presented to Ferdinand an address that opened by declaring that:

Hungary is no dominion that has been won by the sword, but a free country, whose constitutional liberty and independence have been sealed and confirmed by your Majesty's coronation oath. The laws which were consecrated by your Majesty's royal assent on 11 April fulfilled the heartfelt desires that the nation had long entertained; and the nation, tranquil and loyal as of old, borrowed fresh strength from liberty, and stood ready to defend your Majesty's throne against the dangers which threatened it from various quarters.

The address went on to ask the King to order his military forces in Hungary to defend his Kingdom against Serbian insurrection and Croatian invasion; to liberate the Croatian people from tyranny; and to express his confidence in the Hungarian government by coming to Hungary.[29] Ferdinand's response, read in a quavering voice, merely undertook to 'preserve the laws, territorial integrity and rights' of his Hungarian kingdom and to give the matters laid before him appropriate consideration. The Hungarians bowed and withdrew. When their paddle steamer, now decorated with red flags, arrived in Pest it was greeted by cheering crowds. During the deputation's absence, Széchenyi had suffered a complete nervous breakdown and had made several attempts at suicide. He foresaw 'blood and blood everywhere. Brother will be slaughtered by brother, one race by another, irreconcilably and insanely ...'.[30] He blamed himself for the disaster he was convinced would now overtake Hungary: 'I alone have pushed my nation into misery … O, my God, have mercy on me'. On 7 September, Széchenyi was admitted to a mental asylum in Döbling, on the outskirts of Vienna; he was thus fated never to witness the completion and eventual inauguration of his most cherished project, the Chain Bridge (*Lánchíd*) linking Pest with Buda. Three days later Lajos Batthyány, who had returned to Pest with the parliamentary deputation, resigned from the premiership; and on 11 September Jelačić led a Croatian army across the Drava River into southern Hungary. Hungary was to be at war for the next twelve months.

It has been necessary to describe the events of the spring and summer of 1848 in some detail because an understanding of what actually happened during those extraordinary months is essential to an understanding of the Austro-Hungarian relationship, not only during the war that followed but during the years leading up to the historic Compromise of 1867. In particular, the question of Austrian good faith requires examination. Was Austrian acquiescence in the April Laws and Hungarian independence a sham from the beginning? Were Batthyány, Széchenyi and the other moderate liberals led by the nose throughout? These and other questions raised by the Hungarian experience in 1848 can, as is usually the case in history, be answered in terms only of probabilities rather than certainties. It is not necessary to postulate, as some have done,[31] the existence of a malign 'camarilla' in Vienna in order to show that some members of the imperial court and of the Austrian government saw in the April Laws a disastrous precedent that threatened to transform the Empire into no more than a loose federation, incapable of holding its own against the other Great Powers and vulnerable to, in particular, Russian ambitions. Széchenyi's original apprehensions, before the apparent success of the April conjuring trick dazzled his judgement, were soundly based: too complete a triumph would invite retribution. But it does not follow that in conceding as much as it did in April, the imperial administration had, as it were, its fingers crossed behind its back or harboured then the conscious intention of clawing back the April Laws as soon as opportunity offered. In April, the monarchy's priority was to save the Empire: the April Laws seemed a reasonable price to pay for pacifying a major part of it. As soon as the main danger had passed, thanks to Radetzky and Windischgrätz, second thoughts surfaced and the full implications of Hungary's virtual independence began to sink in. Croatian autonomy was no more palatable to Vienna than Hungarian, for the same reasons; but to some, notably Latour and the Croatian Baron Kulmer, Jelačić represented an irresistible instrument with which to bring the Hungarians to heel. In all this, of course, the feeble-minded monarch was no more than a passive signer of Rescripts. But none of the above alters the fact that the case so eloquently advanced in the address of the Hungarian parliamentary deputation was incontrovertible. Ferdinand's Rescript of 31 August represented a gross betrayal and perhaps the most pernicious example, in the 300 year-old Austro-Hungarian relationship, of the Habsburg propensity for observing the Hungarian constitution—for which the monarchy reaffirmed its respect at every coronation—only when it suited its own interests. As in comparable circumstances in the past, however, even the royal *volte-face* in 1848 made no more than a small dent in the fundamental loyalty of the overwhelming majority of Hungarians to the wearer of the Holy Crown. This was to prove an important factor in the coming war.

The War of Independence

While Jelačić was leading a force of about 30,000 men across the Drava River at three crossing points, Batthyány's resignation—in which his cabinet joined him—had plunged the capital into political crisis. The Palatine, Archduke Stephen, announced that in the absence of a government he intended to assume sole executive power on a provisional basis; when the Lower House unanimously repudiated this move, the Palatine asked Batthyány to form a new government. Batthyány did so, but omitted Kossuth from the new cabinet because the latter's success in winning the support of the House for his finance and recruitment bills had convinced the Palatine that Kossuth would lead the country to disaster if given the chance. The omission was meaningless. Kossuth, with demonstrating crowds on the streets of Pest behind him and with his own daily newspaper, 'Kossuth's Journal' (*Kossuth Hírlapja*), in which to broadcast his views, did not need a seat in the cabinet in order to dominate the Lower House. When news of Jelačić's invasion arrived on 12 September, Kossuth led the House into a whirlwind of legislative activity, much of it designed further to relieve urbarial burdens in order to encourage the peasantry to resist the invaders. When Batthyány persuaded the Palatine to take command of the meagre forces facing Jelačić, Kossuth immediately proposed, successfully, that the House should appoint three parliamentary commissioners to oversee his conduct of the defence, an important precedent. He also persuaded the House, on 15 September, to send a delegation to the Austrian parliament to enlist its support for the Hungarian cause (in the event, the Slav majority in the *Reichstag*, supportive of the Croats and Serbs, refused to allow the Hungarians to enter the building); and, more importantly, to set up a committee to advise the Prime Minister on national defence. The radical complexion of this committee of six members, forerunner of the National Defence Committee that was to be Hungary's wartime government, reflected the rapid drift to the left in the capital and the increasing irrelevance of Batthyány's moderate cabinet. The Palatine, despairing of a peaceful outcome to the crisis, resigned on 23 September; regarded by the court as a traitor and by the Hungarians as a deserter, Archduke Stephen spent the remaining twenty years of his life in exile in Germany.

Among the Emperor's ministers there were those, such as Baron von Wessenberg, who believed that events in Hungary threatened to spiral out of control; on their advice, Ferdinand appointed Count Franz Lamberg to be royal commissioner in Hungary and Commander-in-Chief of all imperial army units in Hungary, with instructions to arrange an armistice with Jelačić and to restore relations between Hungary and Austria on the basis of the Pragmatic Sanction. Kossuth publicly condemned Lamberg's appointment as a violation of the Hungarian constitution, since it had not been endorsed by Batthyány as Prime Minister; and ensured that posters announcing the Count's impending arrival in Pest-Buda received a wide distribution. As a result, when Lamberg reached Buda on 28 September he was recognised while his carriage traversed the pontoon bridge to Pest: an angry mob dragged him out and lynched him on the spot. Batthyány was not alone in recognising this ugly event as a defining moment. After making one final and unsuccessful attempt to negotiate with Jelačić, the Prime Minister resigned, for good, on 2 October. For several weeks, Lajos Kossuth had been behaving as leader of his nation; he was now unchallenged. On 18 September, his editorial in 'Kossuth's Journal' had concluded with this summons: 'To arms, therefore, if you are men: and let the women dig a huge grave in which to bury either our enemies or the Magyar name, Magyar honour and the Magyar nation'.[32] Kossuth then embarked on a marathon recruiting tour of the Alföld, during which thousands obeyed his call to arms and tens of thousands flocked to hear Hungary's new messiah.

Meanwhile, the initially phoney war in the south—in which imperial forces defending Hungary had been reluctant to join battle with the imperial forces invading it—had warmed up. After advancing halfway across Hungary virtually unopposed, Jelačić found his way barred by three infantry battalions and a squadron of hussars loyal to the Hungarian government at Pákozd, on the north shore of Lake Velence only 45 kilometres south west of Pest-Buda. Although outnumbered by nearly ten to one, the defending force of regular and *Honvéd* troops, under General János Móga, prevailed in a pitched battle on 29 September, saving the capital. Vienna chose this moment, while the Croats were licking their wounds during a three-day armistice, to appoint Jelačić to succeed Lamberg as royal commissioner and commander-in-chief of all imperial forces in Hungary. For good measure, Latour issued an order absolving all Hungarian soldiers in the imperial army from their oath of loyalty to the Hungarian constitution. On the same day, 3 October, Ferdinand dissolved the National Assembly *sine die* and proclaimed martial law throughout Hungary. On a motion proposed by Kossuth, the Lower House repudiated the royal proclamation and remained in session: shortly afterwards, the Lower House voted to invest the National Defence Committee with supreme executive authority in Hungary and elected Kossuth to be its chairman.

From this moment, Hungary entered a state of rebellion against imperial rule while remaining, in theory, loyal to Ferdinand V as King of Hungary. Ferdinand, meanwhile, faced problems nearer home. A battalion of imperial grenadiers mutinied in Vienna, in protest against orders to march south to support Jelačić; this sparked a more general insurrection, fuelled by deprivation in the imperial capital's teeming slums. The garrison force of 14,000 troops disintegrated, the mob hanged Count Latour from a lamp-post and Ferdinand, accompanied by his ministers and advisers, fled to Olmütz in central Moravia. General Móga, whose small force had already inflicted a further defeat on the Croats at Ozora, south of Székesfehérvár, pursued Jelačić to the Austrian frontier and eventually, after some hesitation, crossed it and advanced to the Viennese suburbs. Prince Windischgrätz, meanwhile, having restored order in Bohemia, had set about restoring it to Austria. With a newly assembled force of 70,000 men, which included Jelačić's Croats, Windischgrätz intercepted the advancing Hungarians at Schwechat and defeated them after a hard-fought battle in which the *Honvéd* contingent sustained heavy casualties, including a disabling injury to General Móga, who resigned shortly afterwards; on the following day, Windischgrätz moved into central Vienna and wrested control of the city from the insurgents. With the Court in Olmütz, the *Reichstag* in the process of reassembling in nearby Kremsier and the Austrian government in disarray, Windischgrätz was for a few weeks the arbiter of events in Austria: he used them both to build up a well-equipped military force and to arrange for the appointment of his brother-in-law, Prince Felix

Schwarzenberg, to head a new government. That done, his hands were free to deal with Hungary.

Prince Windischgrätz would find waiting for him south of the River Leitha a new Hungarian military commander, whom Kossuth—already exercising virtually dictatorial powers—had appointed on 1 November. Artúr Görgey, a young officer from an impoverished noble family, had resigned his commission in an imperial hussar regiment three years earlier, in order to marry. He then studied chemistry at the Charles University in Prague and graduated with sufficient merit to win appointment to an academic post in the University of Lemberg; instead of taking it up, Görgey returned to Hungary in order to enlist as a volunteer in the new regular National Guard. He fought with distinction against the Croats in the battle of Pákozd but then revealed one of the less attractive traits in his complex personality by denouncing his commanding officer, General Móga, for an allegedly treasonable act in granting Jelačić's request for an armistice; he also intercepted and summarily executed a Hungarian conservative magnate, Count Zichy, who was acting as a courier between Latour and Jelačić. These actions, together with Görgey's proven courage on the battlefield, evidently impressed Kossuth sufficiently to warrant his elevation of the austere, prickly but outstandingly able thirty-year-old to command of the Army of the Upper Danube. Görgey had at his disposal an army made up of three components: predominantly Hungarian regiments of the imperial army, including hussars; the original *Honvéd*, or regular National Guard, battalions; and the battalions raised by, in effect, selective conscription from mid-September onwards. Estimates of numbers made by historians vary considerably, but it is probable that in November 1848. Görgey had up to 100,000 men, at various levels of training, under his command. The chain-of-command and other problems, which inevitably arose from the heterogeneous character of the Hungarian force, were resolved by Kossuth on 27 November, when he declared that since all the disparate elements of the army had in common their sworn loyalty to the constitution, it would henceforth be a united, *Honvéd*, army whatever the provenance of its individual units. Formerly imperial battalions discarded their black and gold flags and replaced them with the Hungarian tricolour. Kossuth's decree could not, however, solve the intractable problem of divided loyalties, which has been admirably summarised by the historian István Deák:

… few soldiers, and even fewer officers, desired to fight. On the contrary, most desperately wished to serve His Majesty well. Some manifested their loyalty to the ruler by obeying his orders; others disobeyed him in what they thought was the ruler's best interest; some marched to defend the constitution granted by the ruler; others marched to destroy the constitution which, they believed, the ruler had ratified under duress; some tried to distinguish between emperor and king, who were one and the same person, and they fought against the first in the name of the second … Only a small minority among the officers and men actually rebelled against the dynasty and endeavoured to put an end to Habsburg rule.[33]

Artúr Görgey himself, as we shall see, personified this ambivalent state of mind in the combatants of 1848–49: he remained loyal both to the King and to the April Laws which, he believed, were threatened by the malfeasance of the King's advisers.

The loyalty issue was further complicated when, on 2 December, Ferdinand V succumbed to pressure from the court (including his wife) and his ministers to abdicate in favour of his nephew, Franz Josef. The main argument for abdication, apart from the manifest incompetence of the incumbent, lay in the convenience of installing a monarch whose hands were not tied by Ferdinand's misguided ratification of the April Laws and other concessions to the Hungarians: the counter-argument advanced by Kossuth and his supporters was that the abdication, to which the National Assembly had not assented, itself violated the constitution and that in the absence of a coronation oath Franz Josef had not become the legitimate sovereign of Hungary. The abdication nevertheless evoked the first indications of a loss of nerve among some members of the National Assembly. In what was to be his last address to the Assembly, the near-blind and ailing Miklós Wesselényi urged its members to recognise Franz Josef as King of Hungary and not to embark on a war Hungary could not win. The nucleus of what later became the Peace Party, grouped around Batthyány and Deák, made its appearance, favouring accommodation instead of confrontation. There could, however, be no accommodation with the monarchy while Kossuth and his radical deputy László Madarász continued to head Hungary's administration. In any case, Franz Josef's inaugural proclamation left no room for compromise: declaring Kossuth and his supporters to be guilty of treason, it ordered Windischgrätz to dissolve the National Assembly and to use as much force as might be needed to bring Hungary to heel. On 13 December, imperial troops crossed the Hungarian border in strength.

In Transylvania, meanwhile, events had reminded the Hungarian leadership that confrontation with Austria had exacerbated rather than overlaid the difficulties it faced from the country's national minorities. The Austrian military commander, Baron Puchner, had in October seized all executive powers, including command of the National Guard, and proscribed the *Honvéd*; he called upon the peoples of Transylvania to demonstrate their loyalty to the Emperor by taking up arms on his behalf. The Romanians, in particular, needed no encouragement; their two regiments of frontier guards, augmented by tens of thousands of insurgents, embarked on a ruthless massacre of Hungarian landlords and officials. Only the Székely stood firm for the revolution, opposing Puchner and the Romanians with a small but equally ruthless force of their own. Despite this, Puchner had by mid-November taken over Kolozsvár, established control of all Transylvania save for one Székely pocket of resistance, advanced into Hungary and threatened Nagyvárad. In an inspired response to this crisis, Kossuth appointed an exiled Polish officer, General Bem, to lead a small army against Puchner and to take command of any remaining forces in Transylvania still loyal to the government. Despite being heavily outnumbered, Bem quickly achieved remarkable success: by January, he had ousted Puchner's army from most of Transylvania and removed the threat that an invasion from the east might complement the imperial advance from the north west. The Romanian problem, however, had by no means gone away and would re-emerge. The monarchy, meanwhile, had abandoned any pretence of neutrality as between the Hungarians and the 'nationalities'. On 15 December, Franz Josef had formally confirmed Rajačić and Stefan Šupljikac in their respective offices of Patriarch and Voivod (leader) of the insurgent Serb nation, which continued to hold down a significant *Honvéd* force in southern Hungary; and promised the Serbs national autonomy when peace had been restored. An attempt by the Slovaks in the north to take advantage of Hungary's difficulties proved less successful; the Slovak nationalist leaders—Hurban, Štúr and Hodža—recruited a small Slovak force to fight with the imperial army, but most Slovaks, keen to defend the April Law on peasant emancipation, chose to join the *Honvéd* instead.

In the face of Windischgrätz's continuing advance towards the capital and shaken by General Perczel's heavy defeat at Mór, only 50 miles west of Pest-Buda, Kossuth announced, on the last day of the most momentous year in Hungary's history since 1526, that the National Defence Committee and the National Assembly would evacuate to Debrecen. All the paraphernalia of government, including the mint and the Holy Crown, were loaded on to trains that took them as far as Szolnok; there, they were transferred to carts for the remainder of their eastward journey. Under pressure from the embryo Peace Party in the Assembly, Kossuth agreed to leave behind a delegation, led by Batthyány and including Deák, which would attempt to open negotiations with Windischgrätz. The attempt failed. Windischgrätz rejected the delegation's request for an armistice and confirmation of the April Laws, insisting on Hungary's unconditional surrender. When this was refused, Windischgrätz arrested Batthyány and ordered his companions to remain in territory under imperial control.

The campaigns of 1849, and the dramatic fluctuations of fortune that attended them, rightly command the interest, even the fascination, of military historians. They are replete with strategic and tactical lessons and have great relevance to the endless debate over the relative weight that should be ascribed, in determining military superiority, to the merits or demerits of individual commanders, on the one hand, and to the quantity and quality of military *materiel* on the other. With the obvious exception of their final outcome, however, the campaigns were of less importance to Hungary's future than the politics of 1849: and it is therefore to politics that this chapter must give priority, limiting its treatment of the campaigns to a brief summary.

The Hungarian Military Council, meeting in Pest at the beginning of January 1849, after Kossuth's departure to Debrecen, decided to abandon the capital, redeploying all its forces in an arc from the north west to the south east as far as the lower Tisza River. Görgey led his Army of the Upper Danube into the north-western hills and vanished; General Perczel marched east to Szolnok in order to bar the way to Debrecen. Early in February, after a forced march through difficult mountainous terrain, Görgey broke through prepared Austrian positions in the High Tatras and joined forces with Colonel (later General) Klapka on the upper Tisza. This compelled General Schlick to lead his imperial troops out of north-eastern Hungary and to join Prince Windischgrätz, who had by then occupied Pest-Buda and was ensconced there awaiting what he assumed to be the inevitable Austrian victory. On 1 April, however, Görgey, having regrouped along the Tisza due west of Debrecen, launched an offensive that produced a string of remarkable Hungarian victories culminating in the relief of the fortress of Komárom and, on 24 April, the recapture of Pest, although four imperial battalions under General Hentzi still held Buda. With Austrian forces in full retreat towards their frontier and Windischgrätz dismissed by the Emperor, Görgey had the opportunity, as he clearly recognised, of continuing his advance north west to the Austrian border and dictating peace terms from a position of strength. Instead, he decided first to lay siege to and recapture the fortress of Buda. This was undoubtedly a strategic error—arguably his only failure of military judgement during the entire war—and historians have blamed him harshly for it. Kossuth, however, who attached political importance to the recovery of Buda and urged Görgey to achieve it, must share the responsibility. In his memoirs, Görgey argues that his army had insufficient ammunition to continue its advance immediately and that he had good reason to believe that Buda could not be held for long; above all, he writes:

... when I acceded to [General] Klapka's proposal to let the reconquest of Ofen [Buda] precede the vigorous prosecution of our offensive operations against the hostile principal army, I did so with the conviction that the attempt to facilitate an agreement between the Austrian Government and the Hungarian Diet *[sic]*, based on the constitution of the year 1848, must have far more chance of success if the fortress of Ofen was previously ours, than if it continued in the possession of the enemy...[34]

In the event, Buda did not fall to Görgey's besieging force for three weeks, by which time Emperor Franz Josef had personally sought and been promised immediate military assistance by Tsar Nicholas I. On 15 June, 200,000 Russian troops under Prince Paskevich, Viceroy of Poland, invaded Hungary. Meanwhile, Baron Julius Haynau, a brilliant commander with a deserved reputation for sadistic brutality,[35] had taken over as commander-in-chief of Austrian forces in Hungary. During June and July, Haynau led his well-disciplined imperial army to a succession of victories, including the defeat of Klapka at Komárom where two Hungarian army corps subsequently remained bottled up in its fortress. On 13 July, Haynau occupied Buda; Russian troops moved into Pest shortly afterwards. Kossuth, with his government and what was left of the National Assembly, had by then retreated to Szeged in the south east, facing virtually certain defeat. The stage was set for the last act of another Hungarian tragedy.

Before examining the factors that made the eventual defeat of the Hungarian revolution inevitable, it is worth adding a few further comments on the war itself. Contrary to popular legend, it was not—until the Russians intervened—a contest between a Hungarian David and an Austrian Goliath. Kossuth's recruiting machine, inherited from the old administration, operated sufficiently well to ensure that the *Honvéd* was not seriously outnumbered during the first half of 1849. In the April offensive, Görgey led about 52,000 troops against 55,000 Austrians; the battle of Nagysalló, the last major Hungarian victory, was fought by 20,000 troops on each side. Although the imperial army initially had the edge in terms of discipline and training, the *Honvéd*, especially under Görgey, made immense strides as the months passed; and the hussars were an important asset. Despite a desperate shortage of weapons during the first months of the war, Hungary's infant armaments industry, centred on Nagyvárad, developed with remarkable speed, partly with the help of foreign engineers recruited in western Europe: by June, 1849, muskets for the *Honvéd* were in surplus, production having reached 500 a day. The Hungarians were, however, handicapped by a serious shortage of artillery and shells, a factor that contributed significantly to the duration of

Görgey's siege of Buda; the *Honvéd* never disposed of more than 500 field guns, whereas in the summer of 1849 it was confronted by 330 under Haynau, 190 under Jelačić and 600 under Paskevich. A further weakness on the Hungarian side lay in the clash of personalities between Kossuth and Görgey. Görgey despised politicians, not least when they attempted to interfere in military affairs; Kossuth, for his part, suspected the general—correctly, on one occasion—of planning a coup against the civil authority. Both men, in their different ways, were incorrigible prima donnas who could never be comfortable sharing the same stage. Kossuth repeatedly attempted to diminish Görgey's authority and prestige by subordinating him to new commanders-in-chief—the inexperienced Vetter, the incompetent Pole Dembinski and the intellectual Mészáros—each of whom lost battles that Görgey, unfettered, might have won; each attempt, however, ended with Kossuth's reluctant acknowledgement that Görgey's strategic talents and leadership qualities made him indispensable (in May 1849, Kossuth even appointed Görgey to be Minister of War in independent Hungary's first cabinet). Against this must be set the fact that the Austrians, for their part, had serious leadership problems of their own until the appointment of Haynau. Overall, in purely military terms and in the short term,[36] there was no reason to regard the Hungarian cause as hopeless. Other factors made it so.

The problem of divided loyalties has been briefly noted. The experience of war did not diminish it. The magnates divided between the traditional conservatives, some of whom served the Austrian government as commissioners in regions controlled by imperial troops, and the newly constituted Peace Party, the influence of which in the Assembly increased as the activities of the radicals tended to polarise opinion in the Lower House. Only twenty-eight members of the Upper House followed Kossuth to Debrecen; with one or two conspicuous exceptions—the Hungarian Primate Hám and the radical Bishop Horváth—the Catholic hierarchy remained loyal to Vienna. Although the gentry supplied the revolution with its leaders and the *Honvéd* with its officers, the level of commitment to the cause at county level remained patchy: about one-third of the deputies to the Lower House kept their heads down on their estates rather than joining the Assembly in Debrecen. Until Haynau's arrival, Austrian administration of Hungarian territory under imperial control was relatively benign and provoked no resistance, active or passive, from the local population. The loyalty problem was most acute, naturally, in the army, in which the great majority of officers had sworn loyalty to Ferdinand V as well as to the Hungarian constitution. Throughout the months of war, there was a steady trickle of desertions from the revolutionary to the imperial camp and little movement in the opposite direction. In February 1849, a whole battalion, consisting largely of Italian troops, deserted from the *Honvéd* after a battle at Kápolna. Görgey, whose own loyalty to the monarchy (in the person of Ferdinand V) remained constant, attempted to steady morale in his Army of the Upper Danube with an order of the day, which he issued at Vác on 5 January: this reaffirmed the army's duty to the crown, its loyalty to the royally sanctioned constitution and its freedom from the taint of party politics; and declared that the army would support a peace settlement if this were to guarantee the constitution and the army's honour. The order infuriated Kossuth, who accused Görgey of treason and sent two political watchdogs to his headquarters to keep an eye on him.

Even Görgey's loyalty to the monarchy was shaken, however, by the so-called 'imposed' or 'March' constitution, which Franz Josef promulgated from Olmütz on 7 March, pre-dated 4 March so that it appeared to precede the dissolution of the Reichstag on 6 March: this proclaimed an indivisible monarchy and subjected Transylvania, Croatia/Slavonia, Fiume, the Military Frontier Region and the Serbian Vojvodina to the authority of central government, thus removing all these territories from Hungarian jurisdiction in defiance of the April Laws. Although never implemented, the March Constitution would have done much to weaken lingering military loyalties to the monarchy had it not been followed six weeks later by Kossuth's announcement of the deposition of the Habsburg dynasty from the Hungarian throne and his proclamation of Hungarian independence. Elected to the high office of Governor-President by the Assembly, Kossuth proceeded to appoint a cabinet headed by Bertalan Szemere, a radical, as Prime Minister. This was further than many army officers—and indeed many Hungarians in all walks of life—could happily go: the enthusiasm that greeted Kossuth's ringing independence speech in the great Calvinist church of Debrecen was tinged with doubt and apprehension. As the months passed, it became ever clearer that the power of even Kossuth's oratory could not engender a wholehearted national commitment to the defence of Hungarian independence. Recruitment became increasingly sluggish; after the Russian intervention had begun, the government's exhortations to the common people to rise against the invader and to implement a scorched earth strategy fell largely on deaf ears. In order to retain the support of the land-owning gentry, Kossuth had deliberately soft-pedalled issues of social and economic reform since confrontation with Vienna had begun in September 1848; the loyalty he commanded among the common people was consequently contingent rather than absolute and began to weaken as the months passed.

The task of mobilising a national commitment to the defence, first, of the April Laws and, later, of independence, naturally gained in difficulty from the fact that a majority of the kingdom's population was not Hungarian. The failure, first, of the Batthyány government and then of the National Defence Committee to make adequate concessions to the aspirations of the 'nationalities' inevitably diminished enthusiasm for the revolutionary cause in predominantly non-Magyar regions of the country. The 'nationalities' also greatly compounded the difficulty of the Hungarian military command in achieving a satisfactory concentration of force against the main enemy, Austria. In the south, Jelačić's army of over 40,000 Croats, most of them battle-hardened in the Italian campaigns, held down a significant *Honvéd* force under Generals Vetter and Perczel. The same Hungarian army had to contend with the gadfly operations of the Serbs under General Todorović, until Perczel settled accounts with them in May 1849, massacring Serbs by the thousand in their stronghold at Szenttamás. In Transylvania, an insurrectionary army of Romanians, under independent Romanian command, added substantially to General Bem's problems and terrorised the local Hungarian population: in January, 1849, 600 Hungarians were massacred in Nagyenyed and the priceless college library and archive put to the torch. Even the Slovak legion made its presence felt from time to time on the northern front. Franz Josef's March Constitution created a perfect opportunity for the Hungarians to wean the 'nationalities' away from their support for the Habsburg cause, since its terms were as destructive of nationalist hopes as of Hungarian achievements. Although the new constitution carved a number of Crown Provinces out of historic Hungary, the degree of administrative autonomy offered to the Croats, Serbs, Romanians and Slovaks turned out to be extremely limited: this was because the definition of 'common affairs' reserved to central imperial authority had been broadened from the traditional areas of finance, defence and foreign policy to include ecclesiastical matters, higher education, internal order, industry and transport. The Saxons were denied a province of their own; and even the Serb Vojvodina was presented as an aspiration rather than an accomplished fact. No less a figure than Bakunin had warned the national minorities in 1848: 'I know many of you put faith in support from the dynasty. The dynasty is now promising the earth to you because it vitally needs you … but will it keep its promises? … I am convinced that it will not … You will see that the Austrian dynasty will not only forget your services, but will take revenge on you for its own shameful weakness'.[37] The March Constitution appeared largely to vindicate this judgement.

Kossuth and his colleagues certainly recognised the existence of an opportunity but, perhaps because the string of Hungarian victories in April appeared to make the matter less pressing, failed adequately to exploit it. Tentative overtures to the Serbs were stillborn because they did not include recognition of an autonomous Serbian Vojvodina, although as late as June 1849, Stratimirović offered to change sides with five battalions if this demand could be granted. Negotiations with the Romanian leaders in Transylvania broke down almost as soon as they had started because Kossuth refused to order a ceasefire while they were in progress. Only on the eve of final defeat did Kossuth offer the Romanians, from Szeged, terms that might have been acceptable: recognition of a Romanian 'nation' in Transylvania, autonomy in education and religious affairs and annual assemblies to discuss them, Romanian as the official and military language and the abolition of all feudal obligations. Although the Russian invasion put an end to discussion of these proposals, the rump National Assembly in Szeged passed a bill on 28 July that offered the same terms, short of territorial autonomy, to all Hungary's national minorities. This was of course too late and, as the 'nationalities' would have seen it, too little, in that territorial autonomy remained their key demand. It is none the less worth repeating that this demand was both unrealistic and unreasonable. It is difficult to dispute the force of the argument Kossuth set forth in a letter to the Romanian leader, Avram Iancu, on 5 July 1849, which deserves to be cited at some length:

That each people should have the right to use its language not only in private life but also in its churches, schools, communities and to expect the support of the State in the development of that language in the interest of civilisation, that I believe and profess. But that there should be several diplomatic [i.e. official] languages in a country, if that country wishes to be one body, and that it should be divided into separate sovereign cantons, that I cannot understand … It is particularly hard to understand in a country where the nationalities of various tongues live not in separate and delimited territories but mixed and blended … to divide a country according to languages, to give each part separate territory and separate political nationality is equivalent to the dismemberment and liquidation of that country … Hungary cannot establish a federation with herself, with the citizens living on her territory. This is impossible—common law, common right, common liberty: this is what the country's constitution offers, this is what the government of the country offers to all. No one can give more than that, for no one can possess more.[38]

The radical Count László Teleki, who served as revolutionary Hungary's Ambassador in Paris, favoured going the whole hog and offering the 'nationalities' membership of a Danube federation of which Magyar Hungary would be the leading member, on the grounds that 'the more we give the minorities, the less we shall have to give to Austria and to absolutism'.[39] But even Teleki insisted that Magyar would have to be the sole official language of the central administration and parliament. It is not inconceivable, given the Szeged bill of 28 July, that a rational and generally acceptable accommodation between the Hungarian government and the national minorities might have been arrived at in cool and patient negotiation; but such a process was out of the question during the war and the end of the war left the Hungarians in no position to initiate it. The arc of active hostility, from north through east to south, with which the Hungarian revolution had to contend contributed significantly to that outcome.

Even with hindsight, it is not easy to determine with certainty whether Austria could have defeated independent Hungary single-handedly, without Russian assistance. It is, however, certain that without foreign support Hungary had no hope of defeating Austria. Franz Josef's public appeal, on 1 May 1849, for Russian military intervention probably reflected an overestimate by the Emperor and his ministers of Hungarian strength. Haynau's succession of victories in the summer of 1849 bear out that conclusion: apart from one inconclusive battle with Görgey at Vác in July, they owed nothing to direct Russian support. Tsar Nicholas, for his part, had been by no means reluctant to intervene, not least in view of the prominent part played by renegade Polish generals in the Hungarian war effort; General Bem had given the Russians a bloody nose in February when a small Russian force had entered Transylvania in response to an appeal from Baron Puchner. Hungary's Declaration of Independence provided a further pretext for action by the leading member of the Holy Alliance. Kossuth, on the other hand, persisted in making a wholly unrealistic assessment of the likely impact of Hungary's struggle—and of the Declaration of Independence in particular—on the governments and peoples of Europe.

When Kossuth joined Görgey for discussions in the palace at Gödöllő, near Pest, on 7 April 1849—and took childish pleasure in sleeping in the bed last occupied by Prince Windischgrätz—he explained to the sceptical general that the rest of Europe was only waiting for Hungary to declare her independence before lavishing aid upon her: Poland would follow the Hungarian example and enslaved peoples everywhere would rally to the cause of freedom Hungary had championed. Görgey attempted to curb this euphoric optimism. Even if Hungary was temporarily strong enough, because of victories accomplished 'only with the utmost exertion of our powers', she would lack the strength to maintain that independence against hostile neighbours. Above all, Görgey argued, Hungary's victories stemmed from the knowledge that her cause was just:

The separation of Hungary from Austria would no longer be a just cause; the struggle for this would not be a struggle *for*, but *against* the law; not a struggle for self-defence, but an attack on the existence of the united Austrian monarchy ... in every neighbouring state a natural ally of our opponents would arise *against us*, THE DISTURBERS OF THE BALANCE OF POWER IN EUROPE. [Italics and upper case in the original.][40]

Görgey's arguments may of course have gained in trenchancy and eloquence from their retelling in his memoirs; but he was none the less right. Kossuth, however, remained unmoved; he even welcomed the news of forthcoming Russian intervention because it would make Hungary's clarion call to the rest of Europe irresistible. With his Minister for Foreign Affairs, Count Kázmér Batthyány, he drafted a 'solemn appeal' to the peoples of Europe, while Batthyány addressed a separate appeal to the English Prime Minister, Lord Palmerston.

These appeals, and lobbying by Hungarian agents in every European capital, fell on deaf ears. In the House of Commons in London, on 21 July, Palmerston explained why:

Austria is a most important element in the balance of European power. Austria stands in the centre of Europe, a barrier against encroachment on the one side, and against invasion on the other. The political independence and liberties of Europe are bound up, in my opinion, with the maintenance and integrity of Austria, as a great European power; and therefore anything which tends by direct or even remote contingency, to weaken and to cripple Austria, but still more to reduce her from the position of a first-rate power to that of a secondary state, must be a great calamity to Europe, and one which every Englishman ought to deprecate, and to try to prevent.[41]

In other words, an Austria deprived of a major component of her Empire—of territory, moreover, that bordered on the Ottoman Empire into which Russian expansion was most to be feared—could not be an effective counter-balance to Russian power. As an English specialist on the issue put it: 'Palmerston believed that the independence of Hungary was quite incompatible with the one essential task which the Dual Monarchy [sic] had to perform—the turning back of the tide of Russian aggrandisement westwards and southwards'.[42] In Paris, the newly installed President, Louis Bonaparte, did not yet feel strong enough to offend Austria (although he would later do so in Italy) and needed the goodwill of Saint Petersburg as well as that of Vienna. Count László Teleki and another Hungarian radical, Ferenc Pulszky, worked hard to promote the Hungarian cause in France and England, but their efforts foundered on the hard realities of balance of power politics. Nor could Hungary look to Berlin, from where Frederick William IV, the scourge of the Frankfurt Congress, had already made Franz Josef an offer of Prussian troops. Like Ferenc Rákóczi a century and a half before, Kossuth looked in vain for an ally; not for the first nor for the last time in her history, Hungary found no friends when she needed them most.

When Kossuth and his cabinet withdrew to Szeged in early July 1849, with the intention of concentrating all their forces there in a last stand against the Austrian and Russian invaders, the end was already near and the outcome obvious to most of the participants. The government's desperate efforts at the last minute to mend fences with the 'nationalities', drawn together by the Law of 28 July, have already been described. The National Assembly approved another important law in Szeged, granting complete emancipation to the Jews, who had supported and fought for the revolution almost to a man: they were now rewarded with equality of rights, including the right to marry Christians in civil ceremonies. This was the Assembly's last legislative act. Görgey, who had bitterly opposed the evacuation to Szeged, preferring to gamble everything on one last victory against Haynau as a basis for a favourable peace settlement, conducted a masterly strategic withdrawal, which brought his army, virtually intact, to the upper Tisza region; from here, to Kossuth's fury, he established contact with the Russian commander, Prince Paskevich, to explore the possibility of negotiating terms that would preserve the April Laws in exchange for the sacrifice of independence. Further military reverses, however, destroyed Hungarian bargaining power. On 29 July, the hitherto indomitable General Bem sustained a serious defeat at the hands of the Russians at Segesvár in which one of his aides, the radical poet-hero Sándor Petőfi, disappeared and was presumed killed. Although keen to bring matters to an early conclusion—his army had been decimated by cholera—Paskevich refused to budge from his insistence on an unconditional Hungarian surrender, even when Kossuth authorised an offer of the Holy Crown to a Romanov. Kossuth then decided on a further withdrawal, this time to Arad, some 60 miles east of Szeged, where Görgey's and Dembinski's armies were ordered to concentrate. Haynau, who had crossed Hungary with remarkable speed, cut off Dembinski's retreat to Arad and forced him to march southwards instead, to Temesvár. Görgey, unaware of this, duly kept the rendezvous at Arad, where he found Kossuth, his cabinet, a National Assembly reduced to twelve members and news that a second, decisive, Russian victory over General Bem had brought the Transylvanian campaign to an end. Bem himself escaped to Temesvár, where he was ordered by Kossuth to relieve Dembinski of his command and take over.

On 9 August, Haynau launched an offensive against Temesvár and broke its *Honvéd* defenders under Bem, who sustained serious injury in a fall from his horse. The Austrians took several thousand prisoners; those Hungarians who escaped, dispersed and headed homewards. When news of the disaster at Temesvár reached Arad, Görgey suggested to Kossuth that he should resign and that he, Görgey, should be entrusted with supreme civil and military authority; he had already warned Kossuth that if there should be no possibility of defeating Haynau—and now there clearly was not—he would surrender to the Russians in order to spare the army further pointless suffering. After some hesitation, Kossuth complied and issued a decree transferring power to Görgey, who thereupon drafted a letter to General Count Rüdiger, commander of the 3rd Russian Army Corps, offering unconditional surrender, but only to Russian, rather than Austrian, units; the Military Council approved the letter, which was then despatched. The rump National Assembly formally declared the war lost and the Assembly suspended. Görgey marched his army to Világos, east of Arad, where the formal surrender was to take place; there, he informed the army of its fate and distributed the contents of the national treasury to compensate for arrears of pay. Görgey later recalled:

... in the twilight of the 13th of August, 1849, General Count Rüdiger ... inspected the Hungarian troops under my command. But the cavalry was dismounted, and had their swords hung on the pommels of their saddles; the muskets of the infantry were piled in pyramids; the artillery was drawn close together and unmanned; the flags and standards— lay there unprotected before the disarmed ranks.[43]

The garrisons of two Hungarian fortresses held out for several weeks longer: Pétervárad surrendered on 5 September and General Klapka marched his troops out of Komárom, with honour, on 5 October. After the main surrender at Világos, Kossuth, in disguise, made his way from Arad to the Turkish frontier, pausing in the border village of Orsova to bury the Holy Crown and regalia which, throughout the war, he had carried with him in a wooden chest. On 17 August, he entered Turkey and exile, initially in the Turkish town of Vidin. Görgey, the only senior Hungarian officer to be amnestied by the Emperor—at the insistence of Tsar Nicholas—was obliged to settle in Carinthia until, after the Compromise of 1867, he was permitted to return to Hungary. He lived in Visegrád until his death in 1916, at the age of ninety-eight, surrounded by the incessant echoes of Kossuth's accusation, from Vidin in 1849, that he had betrayed his country.[44]

The warnings of Széchenyi, Wesselényi and, among others, Görgey had been tragically vindicated. Alone, Hungary could not yet hope to prevail in a confrontation with Austria, bravely though the *Honvéd* fought. In making his declaration of Hungary's independence (and it was very much *his* declaration—there was no irresistible groundswell of popular opinion demanding it), Kossuth hoped to win international support for the revolutionary cause. This simply revealed his ignorance of the world outside Hungary: even Görgey, who was not particularly well-versed in foreign affairs, knew better. The declaration, and the deposition of the Habsburg dynasty, gave a cloak of virtue to the Russian intervention and a pretext for the harsh Austrian retribution that followed Hungary's surrender. The political and human ideals Kossuth aspired to promote were irreproachable. Apart from an excusable tincture of vainglory, his motives and political conduct were entirely selfless, his skills in leadership and organisation phenomenal. His passionate desire to secure a better future for his country and its people nevertheless blinded him to the prosaic fact, so well appreciated by Széchenyi and Deák, that geography and their shared history had condemned Hungary and Austria to an unhappy marriage from which neither party could afford to seek divorce. Kossuth never became reconciled to this, even when equilibrium had been restored to the relationship in 1867.

10

THE POLITICS OF COMPROMISE AND DUALISM

(1849–1906)

Retribution and Neo-Absolutism (1849–1860)

The savagery of Austria's revenge on Hungary for her bid for independence shocked Europe. At Arad, on 6 October 1849, twelve *Honvéd* generals and a colonel were hanged;[1] on the same day, Lajos Batthyány—who had spared no effort to avert the catastrophe and had not subscribed to the Declaration of Independence—was executed by a firing squad in Pest, where he had been incarcerated since January.[2] General Haynau, who retained his plenipotentiary powers in Hungary for nearly a year after Görgey's surrender at Világos, used them to inaugurate a virtual reign of terror. Executions of leading participants in the revolution, by hanging or shooting, eventually totalled nearly 150. Lajos Kossuth and others who had escaped into exile—including Count Gyula Andrássy, the future imperial and royal Foreign Minister—were hanged *in absentia*, their names pinned to the gallows. The dungeons of Austrian fortresses were filled with the 1,765 victims of long prison sentences imposed by courts martial. Surviving officers of the *Honvéd* and about 45,000 of its rank and file under the age of thirty-eight were conscripted into Austrian regiments of the imperial army. Severe punishments were decreed for defiance of the bans on public meetings, on the wearing of Hungarian national dress and on beards cut in the Kossuth style. 'Kossuth' bank notes to the value of 70 million florins were destroyed and swingeing increases in all forms of taxation imposed. Under a provisional constitution decreed by Haynau on 24 October, Croatia (with Slavonia) and Transylvania (with the Partium) were detached from Hungary; and Hungary proper was divided into fifteen military districts. Numbed and dismembered, Hungary for a time fell silent.

By the summer of 1850, Emperor Franz Josef and his advisers were persuaded of the inadequacies of martial law and crude repression as a long-term policy towards Hungary. Tamed and reconstituted, Hungary could again become a significant imperial asset. The Ministerial Council in Vienna resolved that Haynau had exceeded his authority, pensioned him off and transferred responsibility for Hungary to the Minister of the Interior, Alexander Bach. Under the direction of the Prime Minister, Schwarzenberg, who maintained that by her rebellion Hungary had forfeited all her historic constitutional rights, Bach set about moulding the country into a model imperial province. He replaced Haynau's military districts with five Crownlands, having Pest-Buda, Sopron, Pozsony, Kassa and Nagy-várad as their administrative centres, directly subordinate to Vienna; the south-eastern region of Hungary became the Serbian Voivodina and Bánát of Temes. The old Lieutenancy Council was revived, under the unsympathetic chairmanship of Archduke Albrecht. The abolition of tariff barriers between Austria and Hungary not only symbolised Hungary's absorption into the Austrian Empire but, as we shall see in the following chapter, opened the way to her economic recovery and development. German replaced Magyar as the language of government, local administration and education above primary level. A new bureaucracy appeared, staffed for the most part by imported German and Czech officials from Austria, Bohemia and Galicia attired in ornate uniforms that earned them the mocking sobriquet 'the Bach hussars'; their alien presence was leavened by a significant number of Hungarians whose inhibitions over collaboration with their erstwhile enemy succumbed to the offer of generous levels of pay. To restore and maintain order in rural areas, where gangs of former *Honvéd* soldiers roamed, Bach created a gendarmerie (*pandúrság*, later replaced by the *csendőrség*) whose remit covered political as well as criminal offences; the *pandúr* and his successor the *csendőr* became, and remained for the rest of the century, the most feared and reviled figures in the countryside.

Despite its many ugly features, the Bach regime administered Hungary efficiently, helped the country to recover remarkably quickly from the chaos of war and gave it the foundations of a modern economy. Ironically, the nationalities which—especially the Croatians—had made a contribution to Kossuth's defeat received no reward for their efforts. Croatia, the new Voivodina and Transylvania became, like Hungary, components of a centralised Empire: German became their official language, the burden of taxation increased and pleas for greater local autonomy—for example from the Romanians—were rejected by the Emperor as summarily as in the past. Ferenc Pulszky, Kossuth's former envoy to Paris and London, now in exile, was said to have commented that 'the nationalities who were allies of absolutism in the past struggle received as reward the same treatment meted out to the Hungarians as punishment'.[3] Franz Josef's 'Sylvester Patents', named after the date—31 December 1851—on which they were issued, replaced the still-born Constitution of March 1849 and formalised the neo-absolutist administrative practices that had been introduced in the interim; they also confirmed, and gave practical effect to, some of the landmark achievements of the 1848 revolutions, notably land reform, peasant emancipation and the guarantee of equality before the law. Politically, the key provision of the Patents—and from Hungary's point of view the most ominous—lay in their proclamation of uniformity of citizenship within the Empire, to match its financial and commercial integration into a unified whole. This development was clearly at variance with the Pragmatic Sanction of 1723, venerated by Hungarians as the foundation of their right to be different, a right that, in Vienna's view, they had forfeited in 1849.

During the 1850s, Hungary's political alignments gradually settled into a new pattern. Some Hungarians, of course, had been loyal to and prominent within the imperial court throughout the revolutionary upheavals and remained so. Counts Ferenc Zichy and László Szőgyény occupied two of the nine seats on the *Reichsrat* (Imperial Council), the advisory body that, under the new imperial constitution, had replaced the Ministerial Council;* General Ferenc Haller served as Archduke Albrecht's deputy in the Lieutenancy Council; at a later date, Count Ferenc Nádasdy was appointed Imperial Minister of Justice; and Aurél Kecskeméthy advised Alexander Bach on press affairs before accepting the post of censor. For these men, loyalty to the Empire and to the person of the Emperor eclipsed all national attachments and aspirations; to them, the war and declaration of independence had been not merely misguided but treasonous. To their left stood the conservatives, the surviving leaders of the Conservative Party of 1848, including Counts Emil Dessewffy, Antal Szécsen and György Apponyi. The conservatives condemned all or most of the April Laws and hankered after the pre-1848 status quo; but they opposed the detachment of Transylvania and Croatia from the Hungarian Kingdom and the centralisation of government at the expense of the counties. They addressed memoranda to Franz Josef in 1850, 1852 and 1857 calling for the restoration of the old royal institutions of Hungarian government, reunion with the lost territories and lower taxes, which, since the introduction of general taxation in the April Laws, the nobility now had to pay; the Emperor rejected all three. The conservatives retreated to the sidelines, but they were to make one further, crucial, intervention in the political process.

Hungary's political centre of gravity now settled around the redoubtable but uncharismatic person of Ferenc Deák, Minister of Justice in Kossuth's government and, with Batthyány, a member of the ill-starred deputation to Prince Windischgrätz from Pest in January, 1849. Marooned in Pest by Kossuth's declaration of independence in Debrecen in March, Deák had retired to the seclusion of his small, debt-ridden estate at Kehida in Zala County. With Batthyány and Wesselényi both dead, Széchenyi in the asylum at Döbling and Kossuth in exile, Deák had become the only leading member of the reform movement still on Hungarian soil. Steeped in the constitutional and legal history of his country, reflective and an observer by temperament rather than a man of action, Deák returned to the centre of the political stage with some reluctance; he would not have done so at all if the Széchenyi family had not bought his estate in return for an annuity. This enabled him to move to Pest in 1854 and establish himself there in an apartment in the 'English Queen' hotel, which was to be his home for the next twenty years. Deák's strength lay in his unshakeable conviction that the starting point for any resumption of political life in Hungary, and for any further evolution of the tortured relationship between Hungary and imperial Austria, had to be the reinstatement of the April Laws. The laws, passed by an elected Parliament and sanctioned by a properly crowned sovereign, represented the last unbroken link in the chain of Hungary's constitutional history: any forward movement, if it was to be on firm ground and not lead into a quagmire, had to begin there, not in 1847, nor yet in 1849. Until that became possible, Hungary should simply wait and eschew any actions that might appear to legitimise the existing, wholly unconstitutional, situ-

---

* The *Staatskonferenz* had ceased to exist on the abdication of Ferdinand V and accession of Franz Josef.

ation. When, as early as 1850, the imperial Minister of Justice invited Deák to serve on a committee convened to bring Hungarian law and judicial procedures more closely into line with those of Austria, Deák declined: 'After the regrettable events of the recent past', he wrote to Minister Schmerling, 'and in the prevailing circumstances, it is not possible to co-operate actively in public affairs'.[4] This sentence was the cue for the adoption by a majority of Hungary's gentry and professional class of a policy of passive resistance towards the regime imposed by Alexander Bach. Tax payments were delayed for as long as possible, offers of public office declined, the implementation of decrees obstructed by inactivity and collaborators with the government ostracised. In a mood of embittered intransigence, the political nation settled down to await some change of circumstance that would make possible a revival of Hungarian fortunes.

Visits to Hungary by Emperor Franz Josef in 1852 and 1857—accompanied on the second occasion by his new bride, Elisabeth of Bavaria—did little to heal the wounds of 1849 despite the lifting of martial law and the proclamation of a number of amnesties for exiles and political prisoners. The Concordat of 1855 between the Empire and the Vatican, which restored to the Roman Catholic Church a degree of autonomy it had not enjoyed since the Counter-Reformation and revived significant discrimination against Protestants, exacerbated hostility to Vienna among Hungary's largely Protestant gentry. The funeral of the great poet Vörösmarty in the same year provided the occasion for a national demonstration, in defiance of a government ban, in which Deák played a prominent role. Deák and the members of his political salon in the 'English Queen' hotel watched with close attention the continuing deterioration of the Empire's financial situation: the imperial budget for 1855 posted a deficit of 139 million florins and revealed that the state debt had increased by over a billion florins since 1849. While drawing encouragement from these indications of the Empire's potential vulnerability, Deák continued to counsel patience: 'All we can do is cultivate [our nationality] and preserve it where the power of the regime does not penetrate: in the private circle of our social lives'.[5] There were some, however, for whom patience and passive resistance held little appeal and who looked to the exiled leaders of the revolution for a swifter and more dramatic salvation from their country's plight.

Kossuth and the Exiles

Lajos Kossuth, and the five thousand or so officers and soldiers of the *Honvéd* who had followed him from Arad across the frontier into Turkish territory, were first interned in Vidin in northern Bulgaria. The Porte refused repeated requests from Vienna for their extradition. A senior Austrian officer of the imperial army, however, was allowed to visit their camp, armed with offers of amnesty and homeward transport of which nearly 3,500 soldiers took advantage. The Turks subsequently transferred Kossuth himself, with his entourage, to Shumla, where he was eventually joined by his wife and children; and finally to Kütahya in central Anatolia. From his internment Kossuth generated a blizzard of letters, appeals and declarations, which created widespread sympathy in Europe and the United States of America for his cause and for his predicament. The most practical response came from the Americans, in the form of an offer of free passage to the

United States, via England, in the US frigate *Mississippi*, which the Turkish authorities, to Vienna's dismay, allowed him to accept. On 23 October 1851, Kossuth and his family arrived in Southampton, where they were given a tumultuous reception and where Kossuth delivered the first of innumerable public speeches, in excellent English, which made a profound impression first on British and subsequently on American public opinion. Lord Palmerston, defying the wishes of both Queen Victoria and the Prime Minister, Lord John Russell, received Kossuth in London, a contributory factor to his dismissal from the Foreign Secretaryship two months later. In Washington, President Fillmore invited Kossuth to the White House and he addressed both Houses of the US Congress. In the course of a month in England and eight months in the United States, he put his case to over five hundred audiences in the major cities of both countries. His plea was for 'intervention to guarantee non-intervention': when the Hungarian people rose once more to reclaim their independence, the liberal Anglo-Saxon powers should use all their considerable influence to prevent both Habsburg repression and Russian interference.

Kossuth's public relations triumph exceeded all his expectations; it nevertheless achieved nothing. The British government continued to regard the Habsburg Empire as an indispensable component of the balance of power in Europe and would do nothing to damage it; the United States, for its part, had no intention— and little capability—of intervening in the immoral manoeuvrings of Old World power politics. Moreover, Kossuth's expectation that Austria would forfeit British goodwill by supporting Russia's attack on the Turkish Empire in 1853 was disappointed; Austria at first maintained neutrality and then concluded an alliance with Britain and France. Kossuth's hopes now centred on the possibility of finding some profit for the cause of Hungarian independence in the ambition of Napoleon III to strengthen French influence in Italy; the French Emperor, nephew of Napoleon Bonaparte, had offered to help the Kingdom of Piedmont and its remarkable Prime Minister, Cavour, in their bid to break the Austrian grip on northern Italy and achieve victory for the Risorgimento. Kossuth, through intermediaries, suggested an embellishment to this plan by which, in return for efforts to subvert the imperial army and mobilise Romanians and Serbs against the Habsburgs, French and Piedmontese troops would march into Hungary in support of an uprising there.

In May 1859, Napoleon III received Kossuth in Paris and sealed a bargain to that effect. Kossuth immediately announced the establishing of a Hungarian National Directorate—in effect, a government-in-exile—in which László Teleki and General György Klapka were his principal lieutenants; in its first proclamation, the Directory called upon Hungarian patriots to await its signal for an uprising, to make no premature moves and to mend their fences with the nationalities. The Directory also urged Hungarian soldiers serving in the imperial army to desert and to join an army of liberation. Negotiations with the ruler of the newly autonomous provinces of Moldavia and Wallachia—soon to become Romania— produced an agreement by which Prince Cuza would store arms for eventual use by an army of liberation and allow his country to be used as its base; in return, Kossuth undertook that Hungarians would liberate Bukovina from Habsburg rule and help to bring about a federation uniting Hungary with Serbia and Romania.

Austria then gave Napoleon III the *casus belli* he needed by issuing an ultimatum to Piedmont demanding that the kingdom disarm. There followed a messy little war in which both sides were incompetently led, the French and Piedmontese by Napoleon in person; both armies sustained heavy casualties in the two pitched battles at Magenta and Solferino (June 1859) but the Austrians emerged the greater losers. In response to Kossuth's appeal, two Hungarian infantry divisions deserted the imperial army at Solferino. At this point, however, Napoleon lost his appetite for war and at Villafranca offered Franz Josef an armistice under which Austria would cede Lombardy to Piedmont but retain Venice and its province of Venetia. This sudden access of prudence on Napoleon's part—if the war had continued he would have had to tackle the formidable fortresses of the Quadrilateral—dealt a major blow to Cavour and the Risorgimento, but also to Kossuth and his dreams of a liberating invasion of Hungary following a French triumph in northern Italy. Napoleon displayed no further interest in the Hungarian cause and Kossuth's hopes of liberating Hungary on the back of the Risorgimento all but evaporated. They were finally extinguished by the proclamation of the Kingdom of Italy, followed shortly afterwards by the death of Cavour, in 1861. Already during his exile in Turkey Kossuth had toyed with the idea of a confederation embracing Hungary and the Balkan provinces and, as we have seen, the plan resurfaced in the context of his negotiations with Prince Cuza of Romania. Having left London for Turin, where he was to spend the rest of his life, Kossuth now gave further thought to the project, with a view to enlisting the support of the Romanians and South Slavs for a revival of the Hungarian independence movement. An Italian newspaper published his design for a Danubian Confederation in 1862. It envisaged confederal union between Hungary, Transylvania, Romania, Croatia and Serbia, which would be open to accession by other Balkan states and whose foreign and defence policies would be executed by a Federal Council meeting in the capital of each country in turn. Each member-country would be free to choose its own form of government provided that civil liberties—including full male suffrage—were guaranteed. Publication of the plan did immense damage to Kossuth's standing in Hungary, where not only the conservatives but, in particular, the land-owning gentry were outraged by his apparent readiness, as they saw it, to compromise their country's national integrity; the proposal for full male suffrage attracted violent hostility. Even the radical supporters of Hungarian independence found it difficult to defend Kossuth's ideas: although he remained a hero in the eyes of most Hungarians, his subsequent influence over the politics of his homeland was slight.

Marxist historians, in their efforts to build up the Kossuth legend, have tended to exaggerate the actual and potential significance of the activities of the Hungarian exiles.[6] Their undoubted success in public relations was never likely to be translated into political or military achievement on Hungarian soil. Even if a foreign ally could have been found who, unlike Napoleon III, was willing to carry professed sympathy for the Hungarian cause to the point of launching a destabilising war in the heart of Europe, Austria's military grip on Hungary would have been hard to loosen: indeed, one of the reasons for the Empire's poor military performance in Northern Italy lay in the number of crack regiments tied down in the occupation of Hungary. Even after the Austrian had become the Austro-

Hungarian Monarchy, ultimate military control of Hungarian territory remained a vital Habsburg interest that would have been defended at any cost. The exiles, moreover, produced no political programme behind which both Hungarians and the nationalities would have been likely to unite in a renewed struggle for independence. Kossuth and his National Directorate were for a short period the focus of romantic longings in their homeland but they never offered a realistic alternative to the revival of political dialogue with Vienna. When, in 1864, a police informer and former *Honvéd* colonel, Lajos Asbóth, betrayed the entire network of Kossuth's active underground supporters to the authorities, resulting in a wave of arrests and suicides, the movement for independence by direct action—as distinct from those who espoused the independence ideal as a long-term political objective—virtually expired.

Towards a Compromise

Not for the first time, a reverse for Habsburg fortunes abroad, such as the loss of Lombardy represented, combined with a dangerous increase in tension in Hungary to restore some movement to the tortured Austro-Hungarian relationship. Concern had mounted in Vienna over the dire state of imperial finances, the Empire's declining credit worthiness and the drying up of foreign investment. Unrest and a tax boycott in Hungary could only exacerbate this situation. The dismissals of Alexander Bach and Baron von Kempen, the Chief of Police, in August 1859 might have lowered the temperature somewhat had they not been followed almost immediately by the introduction by Count Thun, the imperial Minister of Education and Cults, of the so-called Protestant Patent. This measure made all Protestant ecclesiastical appointments, right down to the level of pastors and schoolmasters, and the agendas of Protestant synods subject to government vetting and approval; it provoked widespread anger in Hungary, and not only among Protestants. Franz Josef had second thoughts; but his withdrawal of the Patent and dismissal of Thun at the beginning of 1860 were forgotten in the outburst of public fury that followed the arrest of Mihály Táncsics and the killing of a student in the break-up of a demonstration on 15 March to commemorate the 1848 revolution. Meanwhile, from Döbling, István Széchenyi had published anonymously a furious attack on a pompous, self-serving memoir compiled for Alexander Bach celebrating the salutary effect of his administration on backward, uncivilised Hungary; in *Ein Blick* Széchenyi denounced absolutism above all for its stupidity and placed the blame for any shortcomings in Hungary's situation squarely on centuries of Habsburg misrule. Suspecting Széchenyi's authorship, police searched his rooms and discovered a manuscript in which Széchenyi compared Franz Josef unfavourably with Nero and held him personally responsible for the Empire's moral and political decline. Knowing that imperial retribution was inevitable, Széchenyi relapsed into a deep depression; on 8 April, he shot himself. During the following days, Hungarians in their tens of thousands flocked to memorial services in his honour and relived the hopeful years of the reform era.

Whether or not in response to this powerful demonstration of popular feeling, Franz Josef on 19 April appointed General Lajos Benedek to replace Archduke Albrecht as Governor-General of Hungary, abolished the division of Hungary into five Crownlands, restored county administration and invited six Hungarians to join an enlarged Imperial Council. Two of them, Counts Apponyi and Szécsen, accepted, signifying a renewed, if temporary, alliance between the Emperor and the conservatives. For the time being, the balance of influence at court had swung towards those who advocated a federal structure for the Empire, with Diets, limited in competence, for each province, and against the Austrian liberals, who argued for a responsible ministry and central Parliament in Vienna. The practical result of this shift emerged in the form of the so-called October Diploma, promulgated on 20 October 1860, which had been drafted by Count Szécsen on the basis of the most recent memorandum submitted to the crown by Count Dessewffy and the Hungarian Conservatives. Optimistically styled 'a permanent and irrevocable fundamental law of state', the Diploma went some way towards restoring, so far as Hungary was concerned, the pre-1848 institutions of government—the Diet and the Hungarian Chancellery. The Transylvanian Diet and the Croatian *Sabor* were also resurrected and both provinces were to have their own chancelleries. The imperial cabinet now included a minister (Count Szécsen) with exclusive responsibility for Hungarian affairs. Magyar was to replace German once more as the language of national and county government, while communities would be free to choose the language of local administration and primary education in their districts. But legislative responsibility for taxation and commercial affairs were reserved to an enlarged *Reichsrat** (Imperial Parliament) and all other financial matters, and control of the police, would remain the preserve of the appropriate imperial ministries. Defence and foreign affairs remained within the imperial prerogative.

Quite apart from their traditional refusal to accept constitution-making by decree, most Hungarians objected strongly to many of the Diploma's provisions, above all to the transfer of control over taxation from their Diet to the *Reichsrat*. The continued separation of Transylvania from Hungary also evoked hostility. The effect of the Diploma, despite the fact that it represented a significant retreat from neo-absolutism, was to unite the political classes behind Ferenc Deák's demand, published in *Pesti Napló* ('Pest Journal'), for the restoration of the April Laws. The demand was echoed in resolutions passed by most county assemblies and the tax boycott—the form of protest that hurt Vienna most acutely—continued, despite the pleas of Hungarian Conservatives for its abandonment. Losing confidence in the conservative federalists, Franz Josef turned again to the liberal centralisers and appointed one of them, Baron Anton von Schmerling, to the imperial premiership in December; on Schmerling's advice, the Emperor summoned Deák and Eötvös to separate audiences just before the new year. Despite a good atmosphere at both meetings—Franz Josef was impressed by Deák's modest bearing and evident sincerity—they produced no concessions from either side.

Schmerling went some way towards the creation of an imperial parliament in the February Patent, an imperial rescript issued on 26 February 1861, which transformed the *Reichsrat* into a bicameral legislature of which the Lower Chamber would have 343 members representing the provincial Diets on a proportional basis; Hungary would have the right to send eighty-five representatives, Transyl-

---

* The body that had previously borne this title, the Imperial Council, was now defunct.

vania twenty-six (a large quota relative to its population, designed to favour the Saxons) and Croatia nine. The accompanying electoral law applicable to Austria, Bohemia and Galicia maximised German and minimised Slav representation. Hungarians found the Patent even more objectionable than the October Diploma. The formal subordination of the Diet to an imperial Parliament amounted to a national humiliation; and suspicions were aroused by a provision in the Patent (Article 13) that authorised imperial ministers to act without reference to the Parliament when it was not in session. The new body would have the right only to examine, not approve, the imperial budget. The centralising thrust of the Patent, its implied treatment of Hungary as a province among others, and the continued removal from the national Diet of its traditional rights with regard to taxation and recruitment, were all abhorrent to the Hungarian nation.[7] The tax boycott continued, accompanied in several counties by arrests of tax–collectors and gendarmes. *Pesti Napló* declared that Hungary would never surrender the rights enshrined in the Pragmatic Sanction and repeated Deák's call for the restoration of the April Laws.

Elections to the Hungarian Parliament, due to convene on 6 April, produced a Lower House unanimous in its loyalty to the April Laws and differentiated only by degrees of radicalism in its response to the February Patent. László Teleki, formerly the Kossuth ministry's envoy to Paris and London and then, in exile, one of Kossuth's closest collaborators, emerged as leader of the irreconcilables. Teleki had been arrested in Dresden while visiting his mistress and handed over by Saxony to the imperial authorities in Vienna; Franz Josef had granted him an amnesty on the understanding that he would refrain from political activity but Teleki claimed this agreement to have had only short-term validity and stood for election to Parliament regardless. His political stance revealed an exile's loss of touch with reality: he urged that Ferdinand V's abdication should not be recognised, that Franz Josef's right to rule should be rejected—along with the October Diploma and February Patent—and that Parliament, rather than sending an address to a sovereign whom it did not recognise, should simply pass a resolution implementing the April Laws and proclaiming equality of rights for all, including the nationalities; it should then adjourn *sine die*. Deák argued for moderation and for retention of the traditional address. On this issue the liberals split into two factions: the Address Party, numbering about 130 members, under Deák's leadership and the Resolution Party of between 160 and 170 members, under Teleki. But before the House had been able to get beyond the discussion of procedure, László Teleki shot himself in his lodging. The reasons for his suicide remain obscure; but it seems likely that after living for over a decade in the sheltered fantasy world of political exile, Teleki simply found it impossible to cope with the stresses and strains of a political environment in which he was out of his depth. Hungarian politics were nevertheless the poorer for the loss of a richly talented idealist and champion of minorities. Kálmán Tisza, Teleki's nephew and a member of Kossuth's revolutionary government, replaced him at the head of the Resolution Party, thus relaunching a political career which was to last until 1890.

Shortly after Teleki's demise, Ferenc Deák began the defence of his own political programme with an appeal for a calm, rational approach: the Lower House should take a firm stand on the basis of the Pragmatic Sanction and the April

Laws but should also put forward, in its traditional address to the crown, incentives for an agreement, including an offer to assume part of the Empire's state debt and acceptance of defence as a responsibility to be shared between the Empire and the kingdom. Franz Josef should be recognised as de facto ruler of Hungary; but Parliament could not enter into negotiations concerning his eventual coronation until representatives from Transylvania and Croatia had rejoined it and Hungary's territorial integrity had been restored. All these points were preceded, both in Deák's speech and in the address it subsequently became, by a résumé of Hungary's history that amounted to a powerful, indeed unanswerable, case for picking up the constitutional chain at the point at which it had last been broken, in 1848. When the issue came to a vote, Kálmán Tisza shrank from the consequences of forcing through his late uncle's insistence on a resolution followed by adjournment; he personally believed, in any case, that Parliament should remain in session. A judicious number of Resolution Party absences allowed the Lower House to approve Deák's draft of an address by a majority of three votes on 5 June. The Address passed through the Upper House virtually without debate and the presiding officers of both Houses presented it to Franz Josef in Vienna on 8 July. Franz Josef's arrogant and provocative response, reminiscent of Ferdinand V's Rescript of 31 August 1848, commanded the Hungarian Parliament to submit proposals for the repeal of the April Laws which, he claimed, constituted an attempt to dissolve the union of Hungary with the Empire; he ordered the Parliament to send its eighty-five representatives to the *Reichsrat*; and asserted, in an unnecessary invitation to scepticism, that 'the incorporation [into the Empire] of the realms of the Crown of St. Stephen is far removed from the intentions of our paternal heart'.[8]

Deák at once recognised that relations with Vienna were about to enter a further period of stalemate and concentrated on preparing a position on which Hungary could rest her case until circumstances favoured a resumption of dialogue. His second draft of an address, which he presented to the Lower House on 8 August, rejected Franz Josef's Rescript and once more rehearsed all the Emperor's violations of the Pragmatic Sanction and the Laws of 1790. The draft asserted that neither the October Diploma nor the February Patent was recognised in Hungary and that no Hungarian representatives would be sent to the *Reichsrat*, the decrees of which had no validity on Hungarian soil. In the only suggestion of an incentive to dialogue, the draft address allowed that certain amendments to the April Laws could be considered, but not until Transylvanian and Croatian deputies had taken their seats in the Hungarian Parliament. In a remarkable peroration, Deák's draft concluded:

The nation will endure hardships if it has to, in order to preserve for future generations the freedom bequeathed to it by our ancestors. It will endure without despair, as our ancestors endured and suffered to protect the nation's rights; for what may be wrested away by main force may be won back with time and good fortune, but what the nation voluntarily surrenders for fear of suffering may not be regained, or only with great difficulty. The nation will endure in hope for a better future and in trust in the justice of its cause.[9]

This classic evocation of the spirit of the Hungarian nation in the struggles of the past three centuries united both Houses of Parliament behind Deák's draft, which was approved unanimously and presented to the sovereign. Inevitably, the address merely confirmed Franz Josef in his decision, already taken in the Council of Ministers, to dissolve the Parliament. On 23 August, Schmerling told the *Reichsrat* that the dissolution had been effected, under threat of force, on the previous day; the Hungarian constitution, he declared, had been forfeited and stood annulled. In Hungary, the whole apparatus of neo-absolutist rule was immediately reassembled in a hail of imperial decrees that proclaimed the dissolution of county assemblies and municipal councils, the appointment of imperial administrators to take over local government, the establishing of military courts and the reimposition of censorship. The reactionary Count Móric Pálffy took over the chairmanship of the Lieutenancy Council. With characteristic overkill, Vienna imposed a similar regime on Transylvania and dissolved the Croatian *Sabor*. During the following months, schoolteachers suspected of disseminating subversive ideas faced savage punishment; and a number of leading editors and writers were imprisoned. The eminent novelist Mór Jókai, who himself served a short prison sentence, commented in 1862: 'The greatest accomplishment of [last year's] newspaperman is what he did not do; his wisest speech, the one he did not print; and his greatest good fortune, that which had not befallen him'.[10]

At the end of 1861, it looked both from Vienna and from Pest-Buda as if relations between Austria and Hungary had settled into one of their not infrequent spells of embittered stasis, steeped in mutual hostility and resentment. But during the next four years, again not for the first time, a number of circumstances combined to propel the two countries towards yet another, reluctant, accommodation. The appointment of Otto von Bismarck to the Minister-Presidency of Prussia provoked anxieties in Vienna for the future of Austria's leadership of Germany, anxieties fully vindicated in 1864 when disputes over Schleswig-Holstein, in the wake of their joint attack on Denmark, brought the two countries to the brink of war. German liberals in Vienna feared that the prolongation of absolutist rule in Hungary might endanger further constitutional progress in Austria and damage the Empire's relations with Britain and France (on this score, at least, they need not have worried). The Austrian bourgeoisie was rightly concerned by the spiralling rise in state debt and by the financial burden the military occupation of Hungary, combined with loss of tax revenue, imposed; martial law in Galicia, in reaction to renewed insurrection in Poland, helped military expenditure to account for nearly a third of the state budget; continuing tension in Hungary, moreover, discouraged foreign investment in Austria and Bohemia. On the other side of the Leitha, successive droughts caused serious hardship and provoked unrest in the Alföld, alarming landowners still struggling to survive the financial consequences of emancipation and in dire need of Austrian credit. Hungarians were disturbed by the news that in the Transylvanian Diet, the Saxon/Romanian majority, further increased by the gerrymandering February Patent, had resolved to send representatives to the *Reichsrat*; if the nationalities were making their peace with Vienna, Magyars might be isolated. The circumstances were therefore propitious for what was to be the last significant intervention by the Conservatives in Hungarian politics, in the form of a memorandum drafted by Counts György Apponyi and Emil Dessewffy, and submitted to Franz Josef in December, 1862, proposing a new framework for the Austro-Hungarian relationship.

The Apponyi–Dessewffy memorandum was informed by its authors' belief, shared by most of their fellow Conservatives, that the security of the Habsburg

Empire and its status as a great power would be best served by the restoration of Hungary's integrity and historic rights. It therefore suggested that 'a coequal dualism, which safeguards both sovereignty and the community of national goals, would satisfy not only the basic requirements of the Pragmatic Sanction but would also break the passive resistance which Hungary's instinct for self-preservation had so far dictated, but which had been detrimental to the Monarchy's chiefest national goals'.[11]

The memorandum proposed that foreign and military affairs should be considered common to the non-Hungarian and Hungarian components of the Empire, administered by imperial ministers responsible to permanent delegations elected by the two parliaments. Hungary would contribute to imperial expenses, assume a proportion of the state debt and accept abolition of the National Guard. All official appointments would continue to be reserved to the imperial prerogative, as would the right to dissolve the Hungarian Parliament. Hungary, however, would regain her territorial integrity by reunion with Transylvania and Croatia and a responsible Hungarian Ministry would be appointed. The Emperor rejected the memorandum in April 1863; but a seed had been sown that would germinate in the following year. Franz Josef may already have been persuaded of the essential sterility of Schmerling's rigid centralism; and the Empress Elisabeth, whose sympathies lay with Hungary, may have added her influence to the other factors that argued for progress towards an accommodation. In the last days of 1864 Baron von Augusz, acting on the Emperor's instructions, called on Ferenc Deák in Pest to explore his ideas on how such progress might be made. Deák provided a written statement, of which the main points saw the light of day four months later in his so-called 'Easter Article' in *Pesti Napló*: they included acceptance of the possibility of some revision of the April Laws—'We shall ever be prepared through the means provided by the law to bring our own laws into harmony with the demands of the complete security of the Empire'[5]—and insistence that constitutional government in the rest of the Empire would be a precondition for any settlement. These proposals, together with a summary of those in the Apponyi memorandum, received further publicity in the Viennese press in May although continuing censorship prevented their publication in Hungary.

Progress towards a *rapprochement* accelerated during 1865. Franz Josef visited Pest in June to attend an agricultural fair, commented on the need to reach a settlement and promised that the Hungarian Parliament would soon be reconvened, a promise fulfilled in September. By then, Schmerling had resigned, military courts had been abolished and the reactionary Pálffy had been replaced as Chairman of the Lieutenancy Council by a moderate, Baron Sennyey. Parliamentary elections in November produced an overall majority for the Address Party—now generally known as 'Deák's Party'—which won 180 seats and could count on the support, on most issues, of the twenty-one conservatives; the potential opposition consisted of ninety-four left-centre members led by Kálmán Tisza and twenty radicals. Shortly before the Hungarian Parliament assembled, the Transylvanian Diet voted for the restoration of union with Hungary and, after holding hasty elections, sent seventy-three deputies to the Lower House in Pest. Franz Josef opened the Hungarian Parliament in person on 14 December; his address from the throne incorporated many of the provisions of Deák's 'May programme' but insisted on amendment of the April Laws as a precondition both of their restoration and of the appointment of a Hungarian Ministry. Parliament's reply to the royal address, drafted by Deák, took the opposite position, arguing that the laws could be amended only by due constitutional process, which meant that the appointment of a responsible ministry would have to come first. Moreover, no legislation could enter into force until Franz Josef's coronation as King of Hungary gave him the necessary authority to ratify it; and there could be no coronation until he had taken the traditional oath to maintain the constitution and observe the laws ratified by his predecessors. Disagreements within the Hungarian Parliament centred on the definition of 'common affairs'. Tisza's left-centre, on the basis of a very strict interpretation of the Pragmatic Sanction, argued that the joint formulation and execution of policy by Austria and Hungary should be limited to the sphere of defence and that, even then, Hungary should have her own army, albeit under a common commander-in-chief. Deák and his supporters adopted a more flexible position, broadening the definition of defence to include foreign affairs and military expenditure. The debate dragged on into the spring of 1866, when the Lower House agreed to elect a committee of sixty-seven members to thrash out an agreed position on 'common affairs'; this committee in turn elected a sub-committee of fifteen to conduct negotiations with Vienna on the issue. Deák declined to chair either body, proposing that Count Gyula Andrássy[12] should lead both.

Meanwhile, the storm clouds that had been gathering over Austria's relations with Prussia thickened with the conclusion of an alliance between Prussia and Piedmont in April; in June, they burst. When fighting flared up once more in northern Italy, Austria was at first victorious—on land at Custozza and in the Adriatic at Lissa—but Prussia, moving in support of its Piedmontese ally, inflicted a crushing defeat on the imperial army at Königgrätz (Sadowa) in Bohemia. By the provisional peace agreement of Nikolsburg, finalised by the Treaty of Prague in August, the Empire ceded Venetia to neutral France, which transferred it to Piedmont, and accepted exclusion from German affairs—the end of Austrian leadership of the German Confederation. On 19 July, Franz Josef received Ferenc Deák for the second time, in order to explore the likely impact of this disaster on progress towards an Austro-Hungarian accommodation. At Deák's urging, the sub-committee of fifteen had accelerated its work in order to present Vienna with a final proposal before the war with Prussia ended; Deák wisely wished to insure against the possibility of an Austrian victory, which might have hardened Vienna's position. In the event, the boot was on the other foot; and Franz Josef evidently expected the Hungarians to exploit Austria's humiliation by adding new demands to the set of proposals that had been published, after approval by the committee of sixty-seven, on 25 June. Making a judgement heavy with implications for his country's future, Deák assured the Emperor that Hungary's demands were no greater after Königgrätz than before it.

Matters now moved rapidly towards a conclusion. From Vienna's point of view, settlement with Hungary had become an urgent necessity; Franz Josef s advisers were agreed on the need to consolidate the Empire in the wake of its ejection from Germany, although they differed on the form consolidation should take. The Prime Minister, Count Belcredi, remained opposed to special treatment for Hungary and argued for the revival of a federal structure for the Empire; the new imperial Minister for Foreign Affairs, the Saxon Baron von Beust, more conscious than Belcredi of the weakness of Austria's bargaining position, favoured a rapid settlement on the basis of the Hungarian committee's draft. Franz Josef, after listening to both arguments, decided in favour of Beust; Belcredi resigned. On 17 February 1867, Franz Josef appointed Count Gyula Andrássy, former revolutionary and exile, to be Prime Minister of Hungary and approved the composition of his ministry three days later. In March, the Lower House began its debate on the draft bill on 'common affairs' that had been approved by the Committee of sixty-seven—in fact, on the interim report of the sub-committee of fifteen which came to the floor of the House unchanged and without any prior attempt to convert it into carefully drafted legislation. The Lower House approved the draft, as Law XII of 1867, on 29 May: 209 deputies voted for it, eighty-nine against and eighty-three abstained: an adequate majority for Deák but falling short of a ringing endorsement of his long campaign to win back the April Laws.

In Vienna, Franz Josef pressured the *Reichsrat* into accepting a German-language version of Law XII virtually without debate. The cavalier approach to legislative drafting in both Parliaments resulted in the survival of significant ambiguities and, more importantly, of numerous discrepancies between the Austrian and Hungarian laws; these were to cause problems in the future. On 8 June, with extravagant pageantry and amid the rich harmonies of Franz Liszt's specially composed 'Coronation Mass', Franz Josef was crowned King of Hungary in the Matthias Church (*Mátyás Templom*) on Buda's Castle Hill. He took the traditional coronation oath, in Magyar, to maintain all the rights and privileges of his Hungarian kingdom and to observe the laws passed by her Parliament. He granted full amnesty to all political prisoners and exiles. Finally, in a striking gesture of reconciliation, he donated 100,000 florins for distribution to the widows and orphans of Hungarian soldiers killed in the War of Independence.

The Compromise (1867)

The Compromise[13] of 1867 restored to Hungary her own laws, as agreed between King and Parliament, in all areas except those designated 'common affairs' and those that continued to be expressly reserved to the sovereign's prerogative. Resting its provisions specifically on the Pragmatic Sanction of 1723 and reproducing the main points of the Apponyi–Dessewffy memorandum of 1863, Law XII recognised that the interrelated areas of defence and foreign policy—including commercial relations and international treaties—concerned both halves of what now became the Austro-Hungarian Monarchy equally and should therefore be administered by 'common' ministers of War and Foreign Affairs. A common Minister of Finance would be responsible for administering their expenditure. The three 'common' Ministers would not be responsible to the two legislatures but to two delegations of sixty members, each elected by their Parliament and meeting alternately in Vienna and Pest-Buda. In order to preserve the principle of the separateness of the two components of the Dual Monarchy, the delegations would meet and vote in joint session only in the event of otherwise irreconcilable disagreement between them; otherwise, they were to communicate with each other only in writing. The Delegations would prepare the annual estimates of expenditure on

19. When Napoleon advanced south from Vienna and briefly invaded Hungary in 1809, the Hungarians confronted him at Győr (Raab), only to be comprehensively routed. This was the last, and ignominious, appearance of the traditional noble levy, the *insurrectio*.

20. Horse racing was one of several aspects of English social culture which Count István Széchenyi imported into Hungary. This was the second race meeting to take place in Pest, in 1827.

21. A view of Pest from Buda, *c.* 1850. Széchenyi's newly constructed Lánchíd (Chain Bridge can be seen in the background; the old pontoon bridge is in the foreground.

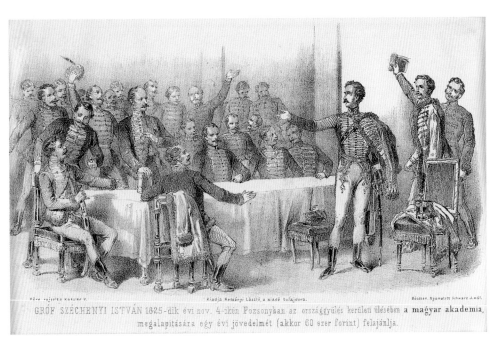

GRÓF SZÉCHENYI ISTVÁN 1825-dik évi nov. 4-kén Pozsonyban az országgyülés kerületi ülésében a magyar akademia megalapitására egy évi jövedelmét (akkor 60 ezer forint) felajánlja.

22. In a committee meeting of the Diet, in Pozsony, Count István Széchenyi pledges a year's income (about 60,000 forints) towards the foundation of a Hungarian Academy of Sciences.

23. The ceremonial laying, by Archduke Karl, of the foundation stone of the Lánchíd (Chain Bridge), the first permanent link between Buda and Pest, in 1842. The project's originator and champion, Count István Széchenyi, is standing at the top of the white-covered steps, among the assembled Hungarian political establishment.

24. Croatian militia units, part of the invading force led by Colonel Josip Jelačić, Bán of Croatia, surrender to the Hungarian revolutionary Generals Móga and Perczel at Ozora on 7 October, 1848—one of Hungary's early victories in the War of Independence (1848–49).

25. The Pilvax coffee house in Budapest, the favourite meeting place for Sándor Petőfi and the members of 'Young Hungary' in 1847–8.

26. Pest, 15 March 1848: the 'Pilvax group' has drawn up its Twelve Points, has had them printed in defiance of the censor and is now declaiming them to an enthusiastic crowd.

27. A deputation from the Hungarian Diet, led by Lajos Kossuth and István Széchenyi, marches through the streets of Vienna on 15 March 1848, to a tumultuous welcome from the Viennese.

28. Lajos Kossuth in full flow in Szeged, during the course of his remarkably successful recruiting campaign for the revolutionary army. The banner's inscription reads 'Long Live Kossuth'.

29. Lajos Kossuth (1802–94), compelling orator and champion of Hungary's independence.

30. Count István Széchenyi (1791–1860), leader of Hungary's reform movement and acknowledged by Kossuth to be 'the greatest among Hungarians', believed that only gradual change could be lasting.

31. Baron Miklós Wesselényi (1796–1850), Széchenyi's close associate and friend until political differences drove them apart, was also the hero of the great flood in Pest in 1838, rescuing numerous flood victims from drowning.

32. Count Lajos Batthyány (1806–49), Prime Minister of Hungary's first autonomous government in 1848. He was arrested by the Austrians while leading a delegation to negotiate an end to the War of Independence and subsequently executed—the revolution's most distinguished martyr.

33. General Artúr Görgey (1818–1916), commander of the Army of the Upper Danube and then commander-in-chief of the Hungarian Army in the War of Independence; a complex and difficult personality but a military genius.

35. Sándor Petőfi (1823–49), hero of the Hungarian independence movement and Hungary's national poet, died on the battlefield in the final weeks of the War of Independence, assuring the iconic status which he retains to this day.

34. Baron Josip Jelačić (1801–59), imperial army officer, appointed Bán of Croatia in 1848. He led, from Croatia, the first military assault on the Hungarian revolution.

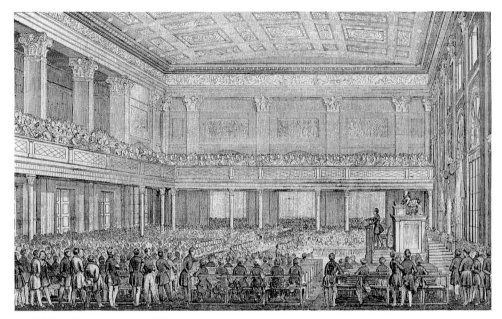

36. The Lower House of the new National Assembly, successor to the Diet, in session in the hall of the Vigadó, in Pest in 1848—the first session of the Assembly after its move from Pozsony.

37. The Hungarian army surrenders to Count Rüdger, commander of the 3rd Russian Army Corps, at Világos in eastern Hungary on 13 August 1849; when surrender became inevitable, General Görgey insisted that it should be to the Russians rather than to the Austrians.

'common affairs' and these would be immune from challenge by either Parliament; revenue to cover this expenditure would be voted by the Hungarian Parliament and by the *Reichsrat* separately. The important question of how such expenditure should be shared out between the two nations was to be determined, for ten years at a time, by two 'quota deputations': the quotas for the first decade under the new arrangements were to be 70 per cent for Austria and 30 per cent for Hungary. As a matter of convenience, the framework of commercial and tariff relations between Austria and Hungary would also be determined decennially, and by the same mechanism. The law expressed Hungary's willingness to negotiate, as one free country with another, acceptance of part of the burden of servicing the state debt—an offer accompanied by disobliging references to the need to save the monarchy from financial collapse and to remedy the consequences of absolutist rule.

Military issues, and the taxation associated with them, had traditionally constituted the most sensitive and volatile element in the Austro-Hungarian relationship: the right of the Hungarian Diet to approve or reject imperial requests for recruits and a war chest had been its main weapon against Habsburg absolutism. Not surprisingly, therefore, the military provisions of the Compromise were the most difficult to negotiate and proved to have the greatest potential for generating problems. Law XII recognised that 'all questions relating to the unitary command, control and internal organisation of the whole army, and consequently of the Hungarian army as a complementary part of the whole army' were reserved to the sovereign's prerogative. Hungary, however, was to retain legislative and executive control of all matters relating to the supply of recruits, periods of service and the territorial distribution and provisioning of troops; the Hungarian Parliament also retained a veto over what the law vaguely described as 'the organisation of the system of defence'. A separate Law on Military Service, introduced in and approved by both Parliaments, provided for a regular army and navy, maintained by conscription, and for two 'home guard' formations, the *Landwehr* in Austria and the *Honvédség* in Hungary; recruits would serve for three years with the colours, seven in reserve regiments and two in the 'home guard'. German was to be the language of command in the common army; but the *Honvédség* could use Magyar and also sport its own flags and insignia. The *Honvédség* could not, however, include artillery units; Franz Josef was determined to deny it the capacity to conduct independent operations. Force strengths, initially set at 800,000, of which Hungary was to provide nearly 330,000, were to be reviewed every ten years by the two Parliaments. Taken together with the renegotiation of taxation and tariffs every ten years, this virtually guaranteed decennial crises. In a significant gain for Hungary, the same law abolished the Military Frontier Region. All these military arrangements became an immediate focus of controversy in both countries. The reference in the Compromise legislation to a 'Hungarian army' attracted the wrath of Austrian generals, while Hungarian opponents of the Compromise attacked Andrássy's failure to secure for Hungary an independent army.

This necessarily dense summary of the constitutional and military provisions of the Compromise of 1867 is an essential prelude to the important matter of assessing its merits and demerits: important, because it was to dominate the politics of Hungary for the rest of the century and beyond. But reference must first be made to a meeting of the new Hungarian cabinet on 17 March 1867, at which Franz Josef presided in person. At this meeting, Count Andrássy and his ministers accepted from their monarch a detailed list, running to twenty-four paragraphs, of all the matters in which ministerial recommendations, whether or not they had been discussed in cabinet, would require the monarch's prior approval (*előszentesítés*) before they could be pursued further. The list included all draft legislation, all senior appointments, financial transactions, matters concerning state property, the draft statutes of new associations and any amendments thereto.[14] Franz Josef doubtless regarded this regulation as a necessary royal safety-catch on the Compromise settlement and there is no evidence that he subsequently abused it; its acceptance by the Hungarian ministers is nevertheless a considerable tribute to the Emperor's personal authority. The 'rule of prior sanction' represented, at the very least, a major hostage to fortune and had the potential to drive a coach and horses through both the April Laws and the Compromise itself. Andrássy and his colleagues presumably accepted it only out of fear that a major row with the monarch at that late stage could place the whole settlement in jeopardy. The Hungarian Parliament was not aware of the agreement when it voted on Law XII on 29 May; had it been so, the voting figures, if not the actual result, must surely have been different. So far as I am aware, the agreement was not made public during the lifetime of the Dual Monarchy; but its existence is relevant to any assessment of the merits of the Compromise as a whole.

Criticism of the Compromise in Hungary centred on 'common affairs' and the means of administering them. In a powerfully worded open letter to Deák published in *Magyar Újság* ('Hungarian News') in May—just before the final vote in Parliament—and widely circulated, Lajos Kossuth attacked the derogation of the April Laws, which now gave Austria the right to interfere in Hungary's finances and defence. Hungary had given away her hard-won defences against despotism, namely the autonomy of the county administrations and the National Guard. Kossuth attacked Deák's failure to exploit Austrian weakness after Königgrätz. Finally, he argued, by binding herself to Austria Hungary was condemned to share that country's fate which, sandwiched as she was between Germany and Russia, could only be tragic. Kossuth concluded: 'If I cannot carry with me to the grave the tranquillising consciousness of success, at least let me be accompanied by hope for the future of my country. I know that Cassandra's role was a thankless one, but remember that she was a true prophetess'.[15] Kálmán Tisza and his left-centre supporters advanced the same criticisms in Parliament and in the press; they had considerable resonance throughout a country that still hankered after the full independence which it had so briefly enjoyed in 1848–49.

Deák's general defence of the Compromise was grounded in a more sober and realistic vision of Hungary's situation than that of his opponents. He argued (in 1867):

If the Monarchy would disintegrate, Hungary could enter into alliance with its smaller neighbours or could become totally independent. But the former would lead to frictions in the area of territorial integrity, while the latter would be good only if we were to have the power and the strength that such an independence requires ... Once we were a large state, but can we stand on our own now, wedged between the Russians and the Germans? ... [No,] we cannot survive without powerful support.[16]

Deák thus accepted the uncomfortable truth to which Kossuth, despite his bitter experience, always closed his eyes: the inescapable mutual dependence of Austria and Hungary. Without Hungary, Austria could not be numbered among the Great Powers; without Austria, Hungary would be at the mercy of the Great Powers. Within the framework of this necessary alliance, Hungary had to persuade Austria that the restoration of Hungarian rights, far from constituting a threat to the security of the Empire, would in fact enhance it. As for 'common affairs', these were a legacy of the Pragmatic Sanction and would in any case constitute essential features of any alliance: since they were unavoidable, it made sense to regulate them properly. In response to Kossuth's criticisms, Deák pointed out that whereas the April Laws had left foreign affairs within the imperial prerogative, their recognition as a 'common affair' and the creation of the delegations gave Hungary a measure of influence over foreign policy which she had not possessed since the sixteenth century. Andrássy and Deák both knew, moreover, but could not argue publicly, that whereas the Hungarian delegation would always—at least until suffrage reform improved representation of the nationalities—be homogeneous and united, the delegation from the *Reichsrat*, consisting of Germans and Slavs, would be vulnerable to wedge-driving, which could make Hungarian influence decisive. Finally, since Hungary had always insisted that constitutional reform must be effected in both components of the Monarchy in parallel, since a constitutional monarchy could not enter into partnership with an autocracy, the Compromise reactivated political reform in Austria and the Emperor's other dominions, giving the Poles and Czechs, for example, the eventual prospect of home rule.

These were powerful arguments. Most members of the Hungarian political class accepted them, either openly if they were 'Deákists' or tacitly if they belonged to the Left-Centre, hence Tisza's reluctance to use his command of superior voting power to defeat Law XII. Most Hungarians indulged in romantic dreams of true independence but only the Radical Left remained loyal to it as a serious objective. The question remains of whether the Compromise represented the best bargain available to Hungary. Deák might have been able to insist on further imperial concessions in the wake of Königgrätz, perhaps in the field of defence; but he was rightly concerned with the durability of the settlement and wished to avoid including in it any ingredients which Vienna might subsequently attempt, in more confident times, to claw back. On balance, his decision not to raise the ante was probably correct and certainly helped to maintain Franz Josef's confidence and his engagement in the negotiation; the Emperor's past conduct indicated that he could easily have lost patience and kicked over the table if pushed too far. Deák's acquiescence, and that of Andrássy and his other cabinet colleagues, in the 'rule of prior sanction' is less easy to defend. At least potentially, it tipped the balance of advantage from the Compromise decisively in favour of the monarch, who, once crowned King of Hungary, could of course lay claim to all the traditional prerogatives the Holy Crown bestowed upon its wearer. Franz Josef was already assured of continuing effective control of foreign policy and defence through the informal cabinet he established, comprising the three 'common' ministers, the Prime Ministers of both governments and the chief of staff of the 'common' army; he listened to advice but made the final decisions. Most important military decisions remained within his prerogative, including even the choice of commanding officer

235

of the *Honvédség*. The 'rule of prior sanction' gave Franz Josef, in addition to all this, a veto over a wide area of Hungarian internal affairs, should he ever wish to exercise it. This constituted a much more drastic retreat from the April Laws than Law XII implied; and here we encounter for the first time the strange, unwritten compact between the crown and the Hungarian political 'nation' that largely determined the course of Hungary's internal politics until the collapse of the Dual Monarchy in 1918. Genuine patriotism and a sincere desire to further the interests of their country had informed the efforts of Deák, Andrássy and their supporters, during the long years of neo-absolutism, to regain for Hungary the rights and privileges, within the Empire, which were enshrined in the Pragmatic Sanction and consecrated by three centuries of troubled history. There were nevertheless boundaries beyond which, as representatives of a political class that had begun to feel insecure and vulnerable, they chose not to venture. It could be said that they needed the Monarch just a little more than he needed them; and one is reminded of the nursery injunction never 'to stray too far from Nurse for fear of meeting something worse'. That 'something', of course, was the complex of looming problems involving the nationalities and a distressed rural underclass.

Some Marxist historians have interpreted what might be called the dark side of the Compromise as a straightforward manifestation of the historical class struggle. Péter Hanák, for example, wrote:

The Hungarian landowning class turned their backs on the revolutionary achievements of 1848 in order to retain their leading role, economically and politically, in the face of the rising middle class, and their rule over the Hungarian people and the other nationalities. The new system did not alter, indeed reinforced, national oppression, even if this was now divided 'more fairly' between the Austrians and the Hungarians.[17]

Even a decidedly non-Marxist historian, László Péter, has expressed a similar view: 'The Settlement enabled the *magyar nemzet* [Hungarian 'nation'] of the land-owning classes and the intelligentsia to secure five decades of dominance over all the other social and national groups in the lands of the Hungarian crown'.[18]

The next chapter will throw more light on this question, as well as exploring the balance of economic advantage, as between Austria and Hungary, resulting from the Compromise. As an interim judgement, it can be said that the leaders of the Hungarian political class—overwhelmingly, the gentry—were prepared to leave in the hands of the Monarch powers of last resort which he deemed essential to the security of the Empire, in return for his unspoken guarantee of the social and political status quo in Hungary. This should not, nevertheless, obscure the fact that the Compromise gave Hungary formal equality of status with the totality of the Monarch's other dominions in an Empire in which she had so recently been an occupied and heavily oppressed province; she regained her historic rights and acquired new influence. As we shall see in the next chapter, the Compromise also gave Hungary a launching pad from which to develop the attributes of a modern European state and from which to address, albeit with uneven levels of commitment and determination, the deepening problems of Hungarian society.

As soon as the Compromise had passed on to the statute book and received royal sanction, Hungary's political map began to settle into a new pattern. The governing party, still known as the 'Deák Party' but also, increasingly, as the 'Party of 1867', became divided by differing levels of commitment to political and social reform. Deák (who had declined the offer of a ministerial post) and Eötvös, at the head of the majority of the party, wished to consolidate the Dualist structures but also to press ahead with the modernisation of Hungary's internal political structure, economy and society; Eötvös, in particular, introduced pioneering measures of reform.* They resurrected many of the policies of the Centralists in the 1840s. The Prime Minister, Gyula Andrássy, and his fellow magnates in the party favoured laissez-faire policies which would best serve further to increase the prosperity of their newly modernised estates; their group was augmented by a number of conservatives who now joined the Party of 1867. In opposition, Kálmán Tisza's Left-Centre Party recovered from its failure of nerve over the passage of Law XII and in 1868 produced a programme, the 'Bihar Points' (named after Tisza's native county) which called for the abolition of the 'common' institutions (the Delegations and three 'common' ministerial posts), the creation of a Hungarian national army and full independence in financial and commercial affairs. The Austro-Hungarian relationship, in the view of the Left-Centre, should not go beyond the personal union created by the fact of a common Monarch. To the left of Tisza's party stood the Extreme Left, now renamed the 'Party of 1848', under the leadership of József Madarász, a former minister in Kossuth's revolutionary administration; the '48–ers' demanded Hungary's complete secession from the Empire, universal male suffrage, the satisfaction of nationality aspirations in a federal structure and improved living standards for the peasantry.

In the 1869 elections the Party of 1867 lost forty-eight seats to the opposition parties but still retained a comfortable majority of eighty-five seats. The impetus for reform, however, had begun to slacken. Deák withdrew into virtual retirement after the elections, making only occasional appearances in the Lower House. József Eötvös died suddenly in February 1871. And later that year Gyula Andrássy left for Vienna to succeed von Beust as joint Minister for Foreign Affairs. From now on, controversy over the rights and wrongs of the 1867 Compromise became virtually the only item on the Hungarian political agenda. As C. A. Macartney has commented, for the remainder of the century and well into the next:

this question dominated Hungarian parliamentary life near-completely. With a single exception [the Christian People's Party] ... no major nation-wide political party made any other question the central plank of its political programme. No election was fought on any other issue ... no other problem was ever treated in Parliament entirely on its own merits, but always with at least an eye on its bearings on the Issue...'[19]

Without its leading liberal thinkers, the Party of 1867 began to drift to the right; with the departure of the Centralists, the increasingly nationalist gentry strengthened its grip on county administrations. Kálmán Tisza, recognising that Franz Josef would never appoint a Ministry committed to the 'Bihar Points', abandoned them; in 1875 he led his Left-Centre Party into union with the Party of 1867, thus creating the Liberal Party, which was to govern Hungary, apart from one brief interval, for the remainder of the life of the Monarchy. Invited to sign his name at the head of the Liberal Party register, Ferenc Deák asked: 'Was I not a liberal until now?' He died a year later; his statue, opposite the building of the

---

* See Chapter 9.

Academy of Sciences in Budapest, bears the inscription 'The sage of his home-land' (*A haza bölcse*).

Foreign Affairs

Count Gyula Andrássy's appointment to the imperial Foreign Ministry in 1871 ensured that, for the first time, the foreign policies of the Empire would take account of specifically Hungarian interests—but without being subordinated to them. Andrássy's career—a radical member of the 1847–48 Diet, a battalion commander in the War of Independence, nine years of exile—gave ample testimony to his Hungarian patriotism. But his wide-ranging knowledge of Europe and the entrée into European society his own noble birth, like István Széchenyi's, gave him were an insurance against a narrow or parochial approach to his new responsibilities. Andrássy possessed exceptional talents, including the ability to charm without leading the charmed to question his sincerity. Tsar Alexander II judged, correctly, that he was 'too proud to deceive'. The British Ambassador in Saint Petersburg assessed him as being 'gifted with great perspicacity, large-minded and liberal views, and the decision of character so necessary to be a ruler of men … he was ever governed by a feeling of justice and honour in the performance of duty'. The Paris correspondent of *The Times* wrote of Andrássy's 'irresistible will at the service of a fertile imagination. He is at the same time a man of great suppleness and patience'.[20] He won the confidence of Franz Josef—no mean achievement—and maintained a close relationship with the Empress Elisabeth, in whom Hungary had found a consistent and sympathetic advocate. He had soon tired of his administrative duties as Prime Minister of Hungary and embraced the opportunity to act on a larger stage. The experience of defeat and exile had led Andrássy to the conviction that Hungary could survive only within the Empire and that the Empire's security was consequently a primary Hungarian as well as imperial interest: he believed that the greatest threat to both lay in Russian expansion and in pan-Slavism, which would incite the Slav peoples of the Empire to tear it apart. The most likely direction of Russian expansion would be southwards, into the Balkans; it was therefore essential that the Turkish Empire's loose hegemony over that region should be preserved.

Shortly after Andrássy's installation in the Ballhausplatz, the League of Three Emperors (*Dreikaiserbund*) formally replaced the Holy Alliance, following the proclamation of the German Empire in defeated France. Although concerned to prevent closer relations between Prussia and Russia which might encourage the latter to assume *carte blanche* in the Balkans, Andrássy made what use he could of warmer personal relations between Franz Josef, Alexander II and Wilhelm I. When Alexander visited Vienna in 1873 for the opening of the World Fair (which embarrassingly coincided with a financial crash on the Vienna Stock Exchange), Andrássy succeeded in negotiating an Austro-Russian commitment to the status quo in the Balkans; neither power would intervene in Balkan conflicts unless impelled by extreme necessity, in which case there would be prior consultation. When, in 1875, Bosnia and Herzegovina rose up against the Turks, triggering a declaration of war against Turkey by Serbia and revolt in Bulgaria, Andrássy, having tried in vain to prevail upon the Turks to defuse the crisis by introducing reforms, succeeded both in restraining the Austrian generals who were eager to join Russia in a Balkan carve-up and, in 1876 at Reichstadt, in buying Russian inactivity from his counterpart, Gorchakov, with a promise of the eventual restoration to Russia of Bessarabia. But Russia was straining at the leash: when the Serbs had been subdued by Turkish arms (in a ceremony replete with historical irony, the Budapest City Council* later presented a sword to the Turkish general responsible), Alexander II did his best to persuade Franz Josef to join him in a crusade to liberate the Balkans from the Turkish yoke. The Emperor, itching to compensate for his loss of Lombardy and Venetia, was sorely tempted. Andrássy, once more, argued for restraint. He not only wished to spare Hungary the destabilising consequences of a probably prolonged and possibly unsuccessful offensive being launched from her territory; but he also wished to avoid the addition to the Empire of more Slav–populated territory, which would further tilt the ethnic balance against both Magyars and Germans and provide fertile ground for Russian-backed pan-Slavism. The secret agreement, concluded in Budapest in January 1877, represented a partial success for Andrássy. It provided that Austria-Hungary would remain neutral in a Russo-Turkish war and could occupy Bosnia and Herzegovina as a reward; Romania, Serbia, Bulgaria and Montenegro would be granted independence provided that they did not combine into a southern Slav state, with or without Russian help. The Tsar's army marched into the Balkans three months later.

The Russian onslaught, which after early reverses promised an early and complete victory for Alexander, provoked anger both in London, as it opened the way to Constantinople and the Dardanelles; and in Budapest, as it threatened to give Russia control of Hungary's main trading outlet, the Danube delta. The British hoped for an anti–Russian alliance with the Empire, unaware that Franz Josef's hands were tied by the Budapest agreement; the Hungarians still thirsted after revenge for Világos. Andrássy turned a courteous but deaf ear to both. His composure did not, however, survive the Treaty of San Stefano—which brought the war to an end in March 1878—when its terms became known. They provided for a greatly enlarged and independent Bulgaria, nominally a Turkish client state but occupied by Russian forces for two years, forces that would clearly put the rest of the Balkans, including newly independent Romania and Serbia, under Russian tutelage; this completely undermined the Budapest agreement and, with it, Andrássy's personal standing. He was rescued by Disraeli, determined to cut back Russia's gains sufficiently to protect British naval control of the Mediterranean, and by Bismarck's agreement to act as honest broker between Great Britain and the Austro-Hungarian Empire on the one hand and Russia on the other. At the Congress of Berlin (June 1878), of which Andrássy was the formal initiator, Russia, isolated, was obliged to agree to a substantial reduction in the size of independent Bulgaria and an earlier deadline for its evacuation by Russian troops; in return, Russia only gained Bessarabia, already promised at Reichstadt. Austria-Hungary received the largely unwelcome (to Andrássy) gift of the right to occupy and administer, but not annex, Bosnia and Herzegovina; this would assist the pro-

---

* Budapest had been created by the union of Pest, Buda and Óbuda in 1873—see Chapter 11.

tection of Croatia and Dalmatia from a Serb attack but would also carry heavy economic penalties. For Britain, the ebbing of the Russian tide was reward enough; although it subsequently emerged that Disraeli had succeeded in wheedling Cyprus out of the Turks on the side.

Taking stock after the Congress of Berlin, Andrássy concluded that its logical sequel should be an alliance between the Monarchy and Prussia that would provide a sturdy insurance against a revival of Russian ambitions in Europe. He had, indeed, always regarded Prussia as Austria-Hungary's natural ally against Slavdom; and the good personal relationship that had developed between him and Bismarck during the Congress reinforced this inclination. Bismarck had been thinking along similar lines. Prussia needed a continental ally: France was ruled out by political antipathy and military weakness and Russia had entered one of its periodic spasms of domestic turmoil. He therefore listened to Andrássy's overtures in 1879 with sympathy; and when he visited Vienna in 1879 the Dual Alliance was concluded, despite Wilhelm I's strong reservations. The treaty bound each party to come to the aid of the other in the event of a Russian attack and to remain neutral in the event of attack by another country unless Russia aided that country. Bismarck's attempts to obtain a contingent promise of Austro-Hungarian support against France were unavailing. On the day following the signature of the Dual Alliance (which became the Triple Alliance three years later when Italy joined it), Andrássy tendered his resignation to Franz Josef. He was in poor health and unsettled by the novelty of unpopularity. After their violent disagreements over the Balkans, the Emperor was not sorry to see him go. Returning to his estates in Hungary, Andrássy continued to warn his fellow magnates in the Upper House against Russian ambitions and subversion; he died in 1890.

Andrássy regarded the conclusion of the Dual Alliance as the crowning achievement of his career. It was, indeed, the logical consequence both of Alexander II's overplaying of his hand in the Balkans and of Andrássy's fear of the Slav threat both to Hungary and to the Empire as a whole. The Alliance nevertheless contained the seeds of tragedy for Andrássy's homeland, a point which has to be made as we return from the broader context of European politics to the history of Hungary that is the focus of this narrative. In attacking the Compromise, Lajos Kossuth had predicted that it would 'hold in store for us no other glory than that of being the stake upon which the Austrian eagle will be burned—and of ourselves burning'.[21] He remained convinced for the rest of his life that Austria would be destroyed in a conflict of the Great Powers and that Hungary would be dragged down with her. Svetozar Miletić, a Serb deputy in the Hungarian Lower House, had warned Andrássy as early as 1870 of the dangers of an alliance between the Dual Monarchy and Prussia: if it comes about, he presciently warned, 'this Austrian-Prussian alliance will certainly not secure the peace of Europe; on the contrary, the alliance of the Russian and the French states which will be necessary is going to conceal the seeds of a new world war and thus it is going to threaten our very existence'.[22]

Dualism, combined with the alignment with Prussia and thence with a united Germany, locked Hungary into the alliance of Central Powers with whom she went down to defeat and subsequent dismemberment in 1918; and that in turn determined her eventual alignment, in the quest for revision, with Nazi Germany and the double tragedy in which that resulted in 1945. Had he been able to fore-see the future, Andrássy would nevertheless have replied that, given her geographical situation and her limited resources, Hungary had nowhere else to go. The concept of a Danubian Confederation had attractions and would resurface from time to time during the years ahead. But its advocates never explained satisfactorily how Austria was to be reconciled to Hungary's secession from the Dual Monarchy; nor how the Hungarian political class was to be persuaded to embrace union with the southern Slavs. The events for which Andrássy's occupancy of the Ballhausplatz would be remembered only served to underline, once again, the inescapable truth that the destinies of Austria and Hungary were inseparable.

The Politics of Dualism (1875–1906)

The domination of Hungarian politics after 1875 by constitutional issues, or 'issues of public law' (*közjogi kérdések*) as they were known, pushed most social and economic issues off the political agenda, pressing though many of them were. Such legislative initiatives as were taken in Parliament during the remainder of the century and the early years of the next were mostly directed towards the further consolidation of the political and social status quo. The matters that gave rise to the most violent controversy, those concerning Church-State relations and the army, were functions of the permanent debate over Hungary's relationship with the other half of the Monarchy. This gives the political history of the period a curiously one-dimensional quality and renders a narrative account of it almost superfluous. A description of the political environment, however, is necessary to an understanding of the developments recounted in the next chapter.

When he took over the premiership from Baron Wenckheim in 1875, after leading his new Liberal Party (*Szabadelvű Párt*) to a crushing victory in the summer elections, Kálmán Tisza might have said that he had three priorities: stability, stability and stability. Hungary certainly needed political stability in order to encourage the return of foreign investors who had, so far as they could, withdrawn their capital after the financial crash of 1873, thus contributing to the subsequent recession. To Tisza and his Liberal colleagues, a prerequisite of stability lay in the continuing political hegemony of the magnates, gentry and upper bourgeoisie; and in the socio-economic domination of the country by the Magyar race. Both objectives required retention of the goodwill, or at least neutrality, of the monarch, Franz Josef, and the continuation of the tacit compact with him into which the Hungarian nation had entered in 1867. The electoral law of 1874 had already provided Tisza with a sound foundation on which to build: by erecting a complex web of property and other qualifications for the franchise, Law XXXIII (1874) restricted suffrage to approximately 14 per cent of the population, a proportion that progressively diminished as taxation eroded small land-ownership while the population grew. By the turn of the century, only 6 per cent of the Hungarian population possessed the right to vote. Until 1913, moreover, there was no secret ballot: some cities and towns acquired it in that year, but voting in the countryside remained open for the lifetime of the Dual Monarchy. Careful definition of constituency boundaries and distribution of seats ensured that regions likely to favour the opposition parties, particularly the newly renamed

Kossuth-ite '1848 and Independence Party', elected a disproportionately small number of deputies; ironically, this disadvantaged constituencies that were largely Magyar in their ethnic composition whereas geographically peripheral constituencies with minuscule electorates filled a large number of parliamentary seats.

Kálmán Tisza, a highly talented political manager who, in all areas save that of the manipulation of people, elevated laissez-faire to a universal principle of life, moulded the Liberal Party into a formidable political machine; it maintained its monopoly of power for thirty years. Its members, christened 'the Mamelukes' for their blind obedience to 'the General' (as Tisza came to be known) heeded the advice of their party's President, Frigyes Podmaniczky, who told them: 'My sons, you should stick to voting and refrain from thinking—thinking is bad for you and the nation will not benefit from it, either'.[23] The composition of Parliament as a whole broadly reflected that of its largest party: about one-third of its members owned large estates, most of the remainder coming from the ranks of the impoverished gentry who now dominated the bureaucracy, and a small number from the professional classes. Of the 333 Liberal deputies elected in 1875, 176 were former county magistrates. Apart from the magnates, who were well represented, most Liberals owed their selection, and their majorities, to Kálmán Tisza personally and gave him their total allegiance. In return, to an increasing extent, they were allowed to enrich themselves by peddling their political influence in the new environment of finance and commerce. The expanding railway network offered particularly rich pickings; a law designed to prevent conflicts of interest served as little more than window-dressing and even if charges were brought, accused members of Parliament were almost invariably acquitted. Elections in about half of Hungary's parliamentary constituencies were rigged in favour of the ruling party as a matter of routine. The British historian R. W. Seton-Watson has documented the various means by which this was achieved, although his accounts are intemperately worded and his indignation overdone.[24] Gerrymandering was none the less rife: in the elections of 1896, twelve constituencies had electoral rolls of fewer than 500 voters while in eleven the rolls exceeded 5,000. Tisza also strengthened the governing party's control of the Upper House: an Act of 1885 introduced a stricter property qualification for membership, which had the effect of excluding nearly five hundred poorer or absentee magnates, and created a category of 'life peers' to which nominations, up to a limit of fifty, were in the hands of the Prime Minister.

Unedifying though much of it was, parts of the Hungarian political landscape under Dualism were less reprehensible. Partly as a defence against foreign criticism and sometimes because local circumstances made corrupt practice difficult, the Liberal machine abstained from manipulation in a significant number of constituencies: government ministers were occasionally defeated in them, as even the Prime Minister discovered when he stood in Debrecen in 1878. Public opinion could in any case make itself felt through channels other than the ballot box, not least through the written word, always a powerful and effective weapon in Hungary. Freedom of the press remained untrammelled and many editors and journalists were uninhibited in their castigation of those in power. The citizens of Budapest had twenty-one daily newspapers to choose from by 1900, with a combined readership of over a million; nationwide, in addition to numerous newspapers and journals in Magyar, there were 150 in German, forty-four in Romanian and eleven in Slovak.[25] The impact of press criticism and revelation, as well as personal intrigue and even, on occasion, actual political issues ensured that the party lines drawn by a parliamentary election did not remain rigid until the next one. The Liberal Party was not as monolithic as Tisza would have wished and rebellions did occur on the back benches. The magnates, whose local power and influence gave them immunity from Liberal gerrymandering, had their own agenda, which often differed from that of the government: in particular, they demanded protection for agriculture in the form of tariffs and subsidies, lower taxes and the restoration of some feudal rights. These priorities drove them, over time, towards the nationalist Independence Party, via Count Albert Apponyi's 'Moderate Opposition Party', which became the 'National Party' (*Nemzeti Párt*) in 1892. The '1848 and Independence Party' (*Negyvennyolcas Függetlenségi Párt*), usually known simply as the Independence Party, had been formed in 1874 by the union of the '1848 Party' with the left wing of the Left-Centre Party, which refused to follow Kálmán Tisza into merger with Deák's Liberals; its programme acquiesced, with varying degrees of enthusiasm, in the continuation of the 'personal union' of Austria and Hungary but demanded the abolition of the common ministries and the delegations. The Independence Party also stood for an independent Hungarian army, diplomatic service and national bank, together with an autonomous customs regime. The more radical wing of the party, the former '1848-ers', took a strongly nationalist line, even favouring recovery of Hungary's former dependencies in the Balkans in order to enlarge the market for Hungarian products; they professed to champion the small farmer and the craftsman against the new capitalism. The National Party, standing some way to the right of the Independence Party, supported the institutions of the Compromise, except for the joint State Bank, but demanded the use of Magyar in the training and command of Hungarian regiments.

Tisza thus had to contend with both a conservative and a radical opposition; in alliance, they would constitute a potent threat. In the meantime, denied the possibility of a fair contest at the polls, the opposition parties were obliged to resort to the only weapon available to them, abuse of Parliament's flaccid rules of procedure, which made it all too easy to disrupt parliamentary business by filibuster, demands for roll-calls and other time-wasting tactics. The spectacle of Parliament tying itself into procedural knots combined with routine corruption at constituency level to create a deep and widespread cynicism with regard to the political process, which contributed further to the stunting of Hungary's political development. One of the stranger phenomena produced by this unhealthy political climate was the increase in the frequency of duelling by politicians. At a time—the late nineteenth century—when duelling had been virtually extinguished outside military circles in most countries of Europe, it flourished in Hungary as the recognised, although illegal, means of settling personal disputes and real or imagined matters of honour. Fencing and pistol shooting were popular and useful accomplishments; Hungary's continuing eminence in both sports at Olympic level is a legacy from this period, in which the trappings of neo-feudalism enjoyed a revival. As the opportunities for personal enrichment by politicians increased, so did occasions for attacks on their conduct. As András Gerő has perceptively commented:

'An increasing sensitivity to personal honour went hand in hand with the loss of public decency'.[26]

During the final decade of the nineteenth century and the first years of the next, three issues, two of them in the area of 'common affairs', subjected the Compromise to severe strain and at one stage threatened to destroy it. The first crisis arose over questions of Church-State relations, to be followed in quick succession by crises concerning economic relations and, most seriously, the army. Church-State relations in Hungary were still in practice governed by the Concordat of 1855 (despite Hungary's release from it following the 1867 Compromise), which gave the Roman Catholic Church—claiming the allegiance of 49 per cent of the population—powerful influence over questions of marriage, divorce and the registration of births, marriages and deaths, as well as a substantial slice of the educational system. The Church refused to recognise mixed marriages unless the parties promised to bring up their children as Catholics; and civil marriage did not yet exist. Gyula Szapáry, who had succeeded Kálmán Tisza as Prime Minister and leader of the Liberal Party in 1890, saw in this limitation of personal freedom an issue that might restore the unity of his increasingly faction-ridden party. Franz Josef had nipped in the bud earlier attempts to legalise civil marriage by using his right to veto, or withhold 'presanction', from draft legislation for the Hungarian Parliament. Szapáry now tried again, ran into violent opposition from the Church to which Franz Josef bowed, and resigned in 1892. To succeed him, Franz Josef appointed Sándor Wekerle, despite the fact that Wekerle, a successful and talented Minister of Finance, was known to be as committed to the reform of Church-State relations as Szapáry. Wekerle went the whole hog, submitting bills providing not only for compulsory civil marriage but also for state registration of births, marriages and deaths and the removal of all remaining practices discriminating against Jews.

Given the strength of public opinion behind the bill in a country in which tension was already running high on other issues, Franz Josef flinched from using his veto; Wekerle's bill passed through the Lower House but the Catholic magnates and bishops in the Upper House threw it out. Wekerle successfully played the resignation card and in June, 1894, the Upper House retreated. With great reluctance, Franz Josef sanctioned the whole package of religious reform at the year's end but took his revenge on Wekerle, who had successfully faced him down, by dismissing him. A legacy of the episode was the formation by Counts Nándor Zichy and Miklós Eszterházy of the Catholic People's Party (*Katolikus Néppárt*), dedicated to clawing back Wekerle's reforms—which had attracted favourable comment throughout Europe—and to promoting the agrarian interests of the magnates; its programme, published in 1895, was designed to attract the smallholders and artisans of the countryside, together with the rural intelligentsia—the schoolmasters, pharmacists and priests. The programme condemned the new capitalism, both industrial and agrarian, favoured compulsory Sunday attendance at church and called for a ban on female and child labour. The sympathetic attitude of the People's Party towards the nationalities—an element in its nostalgia for an imagined rural Utopia—proved to be a major electoral liability; its allegations of exploitation of defenceless minorities by bankers and financiers also carried undertones of anti–Semitism. The People's Party joined the Independence Party and Apponyi's National Party in opposition—the embryo coalition that was to defeat the Liberals in 1905.

In succession to Wekerle, Franz Josef appointed one of Transylvania's *ispáns* who had already made a name for himself locally as a scourge of the nationalities, Dezső Bánffy. Once installed in Budapest, Bánffy turned the Prime Minister's office into a centre for the systematic repression not only of national minorities but also of Hungary's infant but rapidly developing labour movement. The Independence Party, in particular, made Bánffy's downfall its first objective and attempted to exploit the opportunity provided in 1897 by the third decennial renegotiation of the financial and commercial provisions of the Compromise. Bánffy and his ministers had, in fact, reached an agreement with Vienna that was by no means unfavourable to Hungary: it provided for an increase in agricultural tariffs, which would please the magnates, for Hungary's full equality of status with Austria in the joint State Bank and for a more equitable division of income from the Monarchy's customs and excise. In return, Hungary's share of 'common expenses' would rise for the second time, from 32.5 per cent to 34.4 per cent. The Independence Party made this concession the excuse for a sustained campaign of parliamentary obstruction, demanded full economic independence for Hungary and made it impossible for Bánffy to secure a majority even for the national budget. In Austria, meanwhile, the parliamentary chaos resulting from the government's concessions to the Czechs on the use of their language had made ratification of the economic agreement with Hungary as impossible in Vienna as it was in Budapest. To resolve the impasse, the two governments negotiated what came to be known as the 'Ischl proviso', under which existing economic arrangements would remain in place until 1903; if ratification of the new agreement had not taken place by then, the existing arrangements would remain in force until one side or the other repudiated them. This understanding, however defensible on grounds of common sense, clearly violated the constitution by bypassing the two parliaments, as the Independence Party and their allies were quick to point out; the Ischl proviso also outraged the increasingly nationalist magnates in the Liberal Party many of whom, led by Count Gyula Andrássy (Junior), defected to the opposition benches. Bánffy, no longer able to command a majority, resigned, making way for a more subtle politician, Kálmán Széll. Széll, an able financier and husband of Ferenc Deák's adopted daughter, succeeded in persuading Vienna and the Hungarian Parliament to accept the new economic agreement, which would last until the end of 1907, on the basis that Hungary possessed 'the legal status of an independent customs area' but chose voluntarily to prolong the customs union with Austria. This soothed the nationalist sensitivities of the Independence Party and the Liberal defectors, most of whom—including Apponyi's National Party—now returned to the fold.

Crises over the Church and the economic negotiation had revealed irritants in the Austro-Hungarian relationship that could endanger the viability of the Compromise. The Compromise, after all, with its many illogicalities, complexities and textual discrepancies, could work only if both sides willed it to do so; if the will of either side, or both, were to weaken, there were abundant pretexts for disruption. On the Hungarian side, for reasons which the next chapter will explore, nationalist sentiment had become increasingly pronounced and prickly; while the

Austrians, stiff-necked as ever, were less and less ready to engage in the give and take the Compromise demanded. Two funerals generated ill feeling. Although Franz Josef allowed the body of Lajos Kossuth to return to his homeland after his death in Turin in 1894, he refused, not unreasonably, to give the funeral the status of a state occasion; Bánffy's government acquiesced in the ruling and sent no official representative to the ceremony. The Municipality of Budapest, however, defiantly proclaimed three days of official mourning, during which the entire capital was draped in black; but while the bells of all Protestant churches tolled, those of the Catholic churches remained silent. Four years later the Empress Elisabeth, whom Hungarians idolised and regarded as their champion at court, was murdered by an Italian anarchist on the shore of Lake Léman. Her body was brought back to Vienna, to lie in state in the chapel of the Hofburg under a coat of arms inscribed 'Elisabeth, Empress of Austria'; a heated Hungarian protest secured the addition of 'Queen of Hungary' but, for lack of space, no seats were allocated to the Hungarian delegation to the funeral ceremony in the Kapuzinerkirche, a decision which Hungarians chose to interpret as a deliberate slight. With Kálmán Tisza's retirement, moreover, the tacit compact between Monarch and Hungarian ruling 'nation' became less tightly managed and more vulnerable to squalls of popular emotion. Tisza's withdrawal from the political stage had itself been prompted by the intractable issue which brought all the problems of the Compromise to a head: the army. Not only to the Independence Party, but to the population at large, the army was a constant and all too visible reminder of the imperfections, from a Hungarian viewpoint, of the 1867 bargain. Within the army, Dualism had no place. Whereas in political contexts Hungary could claim equality in the constitutional partnership with Vienna, in the army Hungarians were subjects of the Emperor on a par with Slovaks, Serbs and Croatians. Two-thirds of the officer corps were Germans; German was the language of command and training. Defenders of the Compromise pointed out that a common army under unified command represented a natural and inescapable consequence of the Pragmatic Sanction and its requirement for common defence; it was as necessary to Hungary as to Austria to provide protection against Russian expansion and pan-Slavism. Critics of the Compromise, however—and on this issue they were in a large majority—regarded the army as a symbol of continuing Austrian domination, a daily reminder of Hungarian weakness. The army's behaviour, in garrison towns throughout the country, did not help matters. The Hungarian press was quick to report incidents such as Lieutenant-Colonel Seemann's exclusion of the Hungarian flag from a military ceremony in Eger with the order 'Away with that old rag!'[27] In 1886, in Budapest, troops had to break up mass demonstrations in the streets against the action of the Austrian garrison commander, General Janszky, in laying a wreath on the grave of one of his predecessors, General Hentzi, who had died defending the fortress of Buda against General Görgey in 1849. When, therefore, in 1889 Kálmán Tisza, acting on instructions from Vienna, introduced a Defence Bill, which among other things, would require reserve officers to take an examination in German, it was assured of a hostile reception. Not only in Parliament but also on the streets of Budapest and other cities, Hungarians reacted with fury and violence. By amending the bill so as to provide for examinations in Hungarian and Croatian as alternatives to German, Tisza eventually succeeded in persuading Parliament to pass the Bill; but the crisis left him exhausted and his party demoralised. Early in the following year, Tisza defied Franz Josef over the question of whether Lajos Kossuth should be permitted to retain his Hungarian citizenship, despite his refusal to register at an Austro-Hungarian consulate, and thankfully resigned.

The army question, justly described by Péter Hanák as 'the Achilles heel of Dualism',[28] soon returned to dominate the political scene and even more dramatically. In 1902 Franz Josef, reacting to an uneasy international situation, decided that the strength of both the common army and the second line forces should be increased by 25 per cent; and the common Ministry of War conveyed its detailed requirements to the Austrian and Hungarian Parliaments. The Hungarian Prime Minister, Kálmán Széll, and his cabinet were not opposed to the increased recruitment and financial provision requested; but the Independence Party, reverting to the time-honoured tradition of the feudal Diet, seized the opportunity to put forward a number of conditions designed to further its objective of restoring a national army to Hungary. Supported by Apponyi's National Party, the Independence Party demanded that the language of command in Hungarian regiments should be Magyar; that their oath of loyalty should be to the Hungarian Constitution; that Hungarian troops should be commanded by Hungarian officers; and that the Hungarian coat of arms should feature in the army's insignia. The government, naturally, rejected these demands; and the opposition then embarked on several months of parliamentary obstruction to prevent the passage of the Army Bill. The demobilisation of serving conscripts was suspended, a necessary measure that nevertheless fuelled popular protest. In June 1903, Széll resigned in frustration and when Franz Josef's first choice for the succession, István Tisza (Kálmán's son), had failed to assemble a cabinet, the Monarch appointed Count Károly Khuen-Héderváry, a former Bán of Croatia, to the premiership. Mounting public indignation and continuing demonstrations in Hungary provoked a harder line from Austria, where leading military figures coalesced around the heir-apparent, Franz Ferdinand, who detested all things Hungarian and of whom C. A. Macartney wrote: 'Towards them [the Hungarians] he had, partly for political and partly for personal reasons, early conceived a veritably pathological hatred which became, perhaps, after his love for his wife, the strongest element in all his emotional make-up'.[29] The prospect of Franz Ferdinand's eventual succession perhaps added an element of desperation to Hungarian behaviour during this period. It was probably as well, at this stage, that Hungary's political leaders remained unaware of the existence of a plan drawn up by the Military High Command, *Fall-U*, for the military occupation of Hungary by troops from other parts of the Empire.

On 17 September 1903, Franz Josef issued from Chlopy, in Galicia, where he was commanding the army during manoeuvres, an order of the day in which he ruled out any derogation of the military prerogatives reserved to the Monarch in the 1867 Compromise:

My army shall remain common and unified, as it is, a strong force in defence of the Austro-Hungarian monarchy against every foe. Loyal to its oath, my armed force will advance further along the road of the strict fulfilment of its duty, imbued with that spirit of harmony which respects every national characteristic, resolves every difference and turns the advantages peculiar to every tribal people to the benefit of the great whole.[30]

The Monarch's order not only made it clear that there would be no concessions to the demands of the Hungarian opposition, it also ground a military boot into the most sensitive Hungarian nerve of all by making it clear that, in the eyes of their supreme commander, Hungarian soldiers merely represented one 'tribal people' among others. Not surprisingly, the 'Chlopy Order', as well as finding a place in history for an obscure Galician village, fanned the flames of Hungarian protest and encouraged a swelling campaign of civil disobedience which recalled neo-absolutist days. Kálmán Széll despaired: 'The clouds of evil times, a heavy, dense, and death-dealing fog has descended upon our nation. Since Mohács no situation has been fraught with greater difficulty'.[31]

In a final attempt to break the impasse, Franz Josef again turned to one of the few Hungarian politicians for whom he had any respect, István Tisza, whom he charged with the premiership and the task of driving the Army Bill through Parliament, come what may. Tisza, who had followed his father* into politics as a Liberal deputy in 1886, brought to his new responsibilities a stern Calvinist faith, iron determination and a deep commitment to the Compromise, rooted in the conviction that in Dualism lay Hungary's only hope of survival. Bludgeoning the opposition with the threat of amendments to the rules of procedure that constituted its only political weapon, Tisza secured the passage of a modified Army Bill that contained a few sops to Hungarian pride: the Hungarian tricolour could fly alongside the imperial standard on military buildings, and Hungarian officers, whose numbers would now be proportionate to those of Hungarian troops, could conduct official correspondence with each other in Magyar. The bruising debate on the bill resulted in further changes to the pattern of Hungarian party politics: Apponyi once again detached himself and his supporters from the Liberals, reconstituting the National Party, which was shortly to merge with the Independence Party; and Bánffy left the Liberal benches to found the New Party. After nearly thirty years in power, the Liberal Party was haemorrhaging. Undeterred, Tisza pushed ahead with his revived plan, which he revealed in a letter to his constituents in Bihar county, to put an end to parliamentary obstruction by tightening up the rules of procedure; a bill to this effect was introduced in November 1904. Tisza secured its passage by a procedural trick (he triggered a snap vote by waving a handkerchief to his supporters)[32] which itself violated house rules. In protest, Gyula Andrássy led a further group of Liberal dissidents into opposition, forming the Constitution Party which, on 19 November, formally allied with the Independence Party, the People's Party, the National Party and the New Party to constitute the Coalition. As if the political process in Hungary had not been sufficiently devalued or her greatest political institution—now housed in a magnificent neo-Gothic building on the Danube's left bank—sufficiently shamed, on 13 December Coalition deputies set about wrecking their new chamber, smashing furniture and ripping off panelling in protest against Tisza's procedural coup.

Tisza nevertheless remained convinced that the country would back his attempt to clean up Parliament and called an election for the end of January 1905. This turned out to be a disastrous misjudgement. Led by Ferenc Kossuth, son of Lajos and now, on the basis of respect for his name rather than for his modest political

---

* Kálmán Tisza died in March 1902.

talents, chairman of the Independence Party, and by Counts Apponyi and Andrássy, the Coalition inflicted a crushing defeat on the Liberals, who won only 159 seats out of 413. Although Tisza immediately resigned, Andrássy, to whom Franz Josef offered the premiership, refused to form a government until demands put forward by the Coalition had been met; since these included an end to the customs union and the replacement of German by Magyar words of command in Hungarian regiments, the Coalition should not have been surprised when Franz Josef reacted by appointing Baron Géza Fejérváry, a former Minister of War and commander of the Royal Hungarian Bodyguard, to be Prime Minister at the head of a cabinet of senior bureaucrats. Outraged by this blatantly unconstitutional act, the Coalition parties proclaimed a national campaign of civil disobedience. They had evidently drawn courage from the fact that the pro-independence tide was now running high, strengthened by the example of Norway's separation from Sweden, which had just occurred; and they may have hoped that Franz Josef would be unnerved by the revolution which was rocking the throne of Tsar Nicholas II in Russia. A five-minute audience with Franz Josef on 23 September showed the Coalition leaders that this hope was misplaced: the Monarch offered no concessions and insisted on fulfilment of the letter and loyalty to the spirit of the Compromise. Fejérváry, who had resigned earlier in the month as the civil disobedience campaign gathered momentum and threatened bloodshed, was reappointed with a remit to implement the programme of electoral reform, which his Minister of the Interior, Kristóffy, had already prepared, and to hold elections on that basis in 1906.

Short of the use of military force, electoral reform was Franz Josef's most potent weapon against the Hungarian 'nation'. Kristóffy's proposals would have more than doubled, to over 15 per cent, the proportion of the Hungarian population entitled to vote and would have brought to an end the monopoly of power enjoyed by the traditional political class for so long; representation of the nationalities in Parliament would have been dramatically increased. But, with the Monarch's and Franz Ferdinand's backing, Fejérváry now went much further, laying before Parliament a plan for full adult male suffrage and a secret ballot. István Tisza summed up the rationale for the Hungarian political establishment's rigid opposition to universal suffrage:

Entire regions of the country would be lost to the national cause and fall easy prey to anti–Magyar subversion coloured by socialism. Two to three hundred Magyar deputies would face between 150 and 200 non-Magyars, and a certain part of the former bloc would be controlled by the agents of the internationalist socialist movement. The rural constituencies would be swept by a demagoguery of the worst kind. The serious, responsible representatives of a national policy would be reduced to a handful.[33]

When the Coalition parties and Liberals alike united in angry condemnation of the government's proposals, Franz Josef ordered the dissolution of parliament; on 19 February 1906, an Austrian colonel at the head of a platoon of Romanian soldiers ushered deputies from the Chamber.

Despite brave calls for the Hungarian nation to exercise its feudal 'right of resistance', to renew the tax strike and to abstain from any activity—such as mailing letters—which might bring revenue to the government, the Coalition had in fact begun to lose its nerve. Hungary had entered her second year of acute economic crisis, deepened by political instability, social unrest in town and country and a continuing wave of strikes which had at times paralysed whole sectors of the economy. Harvest strikes in 1905 had been broken by military force and thousands of arrests. Foreign investment had dried up. Secret negotiations between the Coalition and the Court resulted in an agreement, also secret, on the conditions on which the Coalition could be installed in government. The Coalition agreed to drop its demands concerning the army; to secure the early passage through Parliament of the national budget and recruitment quota; to pass the decennial economic agreement into law; to introduce measures of electoral reform; and to accept the appointment of Sándor Wekerle—who, although a Liberal, commanded wide respect in Parliament for his financial expertise—as Prime Minister. This amounted to almost complete capitulation by the Coalition. Unaware that its hands were now firmly tied, the voters returned the Coalition to power in the elections of May 1906, in which the Liberal Party played no part. In the subsequent renegotiation of the 'economic compromise', Ferenc Kossuth, as Minister of Trade, found himself obliged to accept a further increase in the Hungarian contribution to 'common expenses', to 36.4 per cent, in return for Austrian recognition of the autonomy of the Hungarian customs regime, which nevertheless mirrored that of Austria. This essentially shabby episode did little to assist Hungary's advance towards democracy, particularly since the Coalition's undertaking to introduce electoral reform was honoured, by Andrássy as Minister of the Interior, only to a minimal extent. Hungary's image in Europe also suffered, not least in Great Britain. The deal between crown and Coalition did, however, demonstrate once again—if further demonstration were needed—that the bonds of mutual necessity binding Hungary and Austria could be stretched but not broken; and that the further they were stretched, the stronger the eventual rebound.

11

ECONOMIC ADVANCE IN A TROUBLED SOCIETY

(1850–1913)

Towards a Modern Economy

Just as the symbiosis and the tensions of the Austro-Hungarian relationship dominated Hungarian politics during the second half of the nineteenth century and beyond, so that relationship remained, throughout the period, a major determinant of Hungary's economic development. We have seen* that at mid-century agriculture, dominated by the great estates and deformed by the creation of a large rural underclass, represented almost the sum total of Hungary's economic activity, complemented as it was only by a weak, embryo industrial sector. This remained the case until after the 1867 Compromise; but the preceding neo-absolutist period, the years of the 'Bach regime', was nevertheless a time of important and largely positive economic change.

   In agriculture, the reign of wool came to an end in the 1850s with the recovery of cereal prices; Hungarian landowners, who never did anything by halves, abandoned the sheep for the plough. By 1867, 75 per cent of the country's cultivable land was producing wheat, rye, barley and oats. The Urbarial Patent of 1853 essentially confirmed but also accelerated the implementation of the emancipation of 1848 and cleared the way for the transformation of the larger estates into capitalist enterprises employing wage labour. The building of a national railway system provided a powerful stimulus to agricultural production. The 46–kilometre line between Pest and Vác, which opened in 1846, inaugurated a surge of railway construction in the 1850s, largely financed by Austrian capital, which gave Hungary's principal grain-growing regions direct access to the all-important Austrian market. Szeged and Temesvár via Pest, and Debrecen via Szolnok and Pest, were linked to Vienna. Assisted, in addition, by the customs union between Hungary and Austria that the Bach Regime proclaimed in 1850, Hungary soon achieved a dominant position in the wheat market of central Europe: exports increased threefold from under half a million tonnes in the 1840s to 1.47 million tonnes in the 1860s. But the agricultural market was characterised by violent upswings and

---

* In Chapter 8.

downturns that only the largest estates were able to weather. In the 1870s, railway links between the Mid-West and the eastern seaboard of the United States, together with the development of steam navigation, made it possible for cheap American grain to flood the European market; market prices collapsed and were back to 1840 levels—a fall of nearly 50 per cent—before the end of the century.

This man-made calamity for European farmers—especially harsh for the relatively inefficient Hungarian producer—happened to coincide, in the 1880s, with natural disaster: an outbreak of phylloxera devastated Hungary's vineyards and drove thousands of smallholders into bankruptcy. Kálmán Tisza's hitherto laissez-faire Liberal government campaigned, successfully, for a protective tariff wall around the customs union to save Hungarian agriculture. In the event, Hungarian agriculture found its salvation not so much in protection—the tariffs eventually agreed with Vienna were relatively modest—but in an accelerated effort to modernise and diversify, combined with social regimentation in the countryside. Following the Compromise, Austrian capital had stimulated the mortgage market in Hungary—liberated after 1848 from entailment—and thus enabled the larger landowners to fund the purchase of machinery, the drainage of land and other measures to improve efficiency. By 1871, over 2,000 steam threshing machines were in operation, together with thousands of mechanical reapers and seed-drills. Under the impact of the cereals crisis of the 1870s and 1880s, landowners redoubled their efforts: increased use of animal manure (and the introduction of artificial fertilisers after 1890), the reclamation of flooded land and the cultivation of pasture combined to achieve a steady rise in agricultural production. The cultivated area expanded by one-third between 1873 and 1913, largely as a consequence of waterway regulation and the drainage of marshland; over-specialisation in cereals was corrected by greater attention to potatoes, sugar beet and hemp. Between 1864 and 1913 the production of wheat increased by 285 per cent, of maize by 361 per cent, of potatoes by 750 per cent and of sugar beet by an astonishing 2,165 per cent.[1] Livestock-breeding also made a comeback, the production of cattle, pigs and horses more than doubling during the same period. As we shall see later in this chapter, however, the rather surprising resilience of Hungarian agriculture in the adverse circumstances of the late nineteenth century was achieved partly at the expense of social progress.

Austrian capital and railway construction were also the catalysts, during the 1850s, for the belated development of Hungarian industry. The railways, which benefited from a government guarantee of a minimum return on investment, not only revolutionised the transport and export of agricultural produce; they also, again with the help of Austrian investment, gave a powerful stimulus to the mining of coal and iron ore and, eventually, to the development of heavy industry. Progress was uneven and, until after 1890, considerably less rapid than in the agricultural sector. The basic platform for industrial development was created by the purchase by Austrian companies of the small processing plants established on the great estates during the first half of the century—flour mills, sugar refineries, breweries, glass factories, iron foundries and brick kilns. The Compromise of 1867 encouraged a second wave of Austrian investment and inaugurated the preparatory phase of Hungary's industrial revolution, which did not begin in earnest until the 1890s. By the year of the Compromise, Hungarian production of pig-iron had risen from virtually zero in 1849 to 100,000 tons and coal production had reached 350,000 tons; in parallel, the embryo railway system had grown from 48 to 2,160 kilometres. The Austrian State Railway Company and the Danube Steamship Navigation Company dominated the mining industry as well as rail and river transport. The Austrian State Railway Company's foundry in Transylvania produced, during the decade following the Compromise, 20 per cent of Hungary's pig-iron and was equipped with the country's first Bessemer converter and Martin open-hearth smelter; the introduction of this technology proved to be a crucial element in the launch of Hungary's industrial revolution.

After 1867, however, an indigenous manufacturing base began to emerge, albeit under the aegis of foreign settlers such as Abrahám Ganz and with the backing of foreign capital. Ganz patented and manufactured roller milling equipment for the food processing industry, branching out later into the manufacture of threshing machines and railway rolling stock. In 1873, the establishment of MÁVAG (the Hungarian State Railway Machine Plant) gave Hungary a domestic producer of steam locomotives and steam-powered agricultural machinery. But agricultural processing remained for some decades the strongest sector of Hungarian industry, especially the flour milling to which István Széchenyi had given the first stimulus in the 1840s; fourteen large flour mills had been established in the capital by 1867 and Hungarian flour dominated the domestic market of the Monarchy for the rest of its life as well as becoming a significant export to Germany and other European countries. The financial crash of 1873, which wiped out seventy-four Viennese banks and credit houses, inevitably applied a brake to the growth of Hungarian industry as Austrian investment temporarily dried up; but the pause was short-lived and a resumption of the capital inflow in the 1880s made possible Hungary's long-delayed industrial revolution. Industry in Hungary acquired an increasingly modern profile, dominated by large plants: between 1890 and 1900, the number of industrial companies employing more than twenty workers grew from 1,120 to 2,049, of which twenty-nine had a workforce of over a thousand.

In belated fulfilment of István Széchenyi's prescription, the machinery of credit provision developed in Hungary at a rate, from 1880 onwards, that made possible the explosion of industrial activity in the first two decades of the twentieth century. The banking system doubled in size during that period, from 2,696 credit institutions with assets of 2.6 million crowns to (in 1913) 5,993 institutions with 6,691 million crowns worth of capital assets at their disposal. The five largest banks, which included two survivors from the Széchenyi era—the Commercial Bank of Pest and the First Pest Savings Bank—controlled between them 47 per cent of Hungary's capital resources. The major part of those resources, however, was of foreign origin: in the early 1900s, 80 per cent of Austria's exported capital went to Hungary, while 54.5 per cent of Hungarian state loans, 70 per cent of railway bonds and 54.7 per cent of municipal bonds were held abroad. Forty per cent of shares in the 'big five' banks were in foreign hands. Domestic capital accumulation nevertheless kept pace with the gathering momentum of industrial development: the foreign share of new capital investment, accounting for 60 per cent in 1873, fell to 45 per cent by 1900 and to 25 per cent by 1913.

Once industrial take-off had been achieved, in the 1890s, it accelerated with remarkable speed. The production of steel, virtually non-existent before 1880, reached 427,000 tons in 1900 and had nearly doubled, to 800,000 tons, by 1913; by that date, four shipyards were in operation and the production of steam turbines, tractors and automobiles was well under way. Despite its laissez-faire philosophy, the Liberal government assisted the process in a series of Industrial Acts (1881, 1884, 1890 and 1907), which granted tax holidays to newly established factories, provided duty rebates on imported machine tools (domestic production met only one-quarter of the national requirement) and facilitated state subsidies and interest-free loans.

Native ingenuity injected a uniquely Hungarian element into some important manufactures: Kálmán Kandó's development of the electric locomotive, Tungsram's pioneering use of tungsten in the filaments of electric light bulbs and the invention of the alternating current electrical transformer by the technicians at Ganz were prominent examples. Underpinning manufacture, the mining industry expanded strongly with the introduction of modern techniques: the production of both coal and pig-iron grew by over 400 per cent between 1880 and 1913. Although the food processing industry remained strong—Hungary had become the world's second largest exporter of flour, surpassed only by the United States—it had been overtaken by heavy industry before the onset of the First World War; by 1914, food processing accounted for 38.9 per cent of industrial production by value and heavy industry for 41.2 per cent. Light industry, however, lagged well behind, partly because the customs union put the Hungarian market at the mercy of textile products from Austria and the Czech lands—despite government subsidies for domestic manufacturers. Although the development of the Hungarian industrial economy after 1890 was impressive, contributing 28 per cent of a GNP which, between 1900 and 1915, grew at an annual rate of 8.5 per cent, it still occupied a lowly place in the European league table: gross output per capita by 1913 still hovered around 45 per cent of that of France and Germany, and around 75 per cent of that of Italy and Austria. In 1900, just over 60 per cent of the working population was still employed in agriculture. National income per capita, although it had increased by 61 per cent between 1860 and 1910, was still, in 1913, less than half the average for western Europe. Moreover, although new industrial sectors such as the electrical and chemical were emerging, those related to agriculture and transport predominated to a disproportionate extent. Whereas finished goods accounted for 60 per cent of Hungarian imports in 1913, they made up only 37.8 per cent of her exports. These imbalances made Hungary over-dependent on imports of manufactures in sectors other than the national specialities and encouraged a growing demand, which came to be coloured by nationalist sentiment, for an autonomous Hungarian customs regime under the protection of which Hungarian industry could diversify.

This leads directly to the question, to which Austrian and Hungarian historians have devoted a great deal of attention,[2] of whether the economic dimension of Dualism disadvantaged Hungary or whether she gained from it. It should be obvious from the preceding paragraphs that the inflow of Austrian capital played an indispensable role both in the modernisation of Hungarian agriculture and in the development of Hungarian industry. The most effective incentives to Austrian investment were the Monarchy's common currency and the assurance of political stability Austria's dominant influence in Hungary afforded: it is hardly conceivable that Austrian investors would have rushed as eagerly to put their money into the state and mortgage bonds of an independent and therefore unpredictable Hungary. The customs union brought benefit both to Hungarian agricultural producers, 80–90 per cent of whose exports were absorbed by the Austrian and Czech markets, and to Austrian and Czech industrialists, who were able to export to Hungary products that would have been uncompetitive in the markets of western Europe. It is true that the customs union retarded the development of industries in Hungary, particularly the textile industry, which started a long way behind those of Austria and the Czech lands and were continually smothered by tariff-free imports from those sources; Austrian landowners, for their part, complained of unfair competition from the much larger and increasingly efficient Hungarian estates. The fact remains that both halves of the Monarchy prospered under the economic regime of the Compromise. Between 1850 and 1913, Hungary's net national product (with allowance made for price increases) grew by 500 per cent and Austria's by 400 per cent; and Hungary's share of the Monarchy's industrial production increased by 6–7 per cent—having started, of course, from a significantly lower baseline. It is probable, if not provable, that the economies of both Austria and Hungary developed more strongly within the common market of the Empire than they could have done independently. The only important asymmetry of advantage lay in the fact that whereas Austrian industry prospered at the expense of certain sectors of Hungarian industry, Hungarian agriculture prospered at the expense not only of Austrian and Czech landowners but also of the Hungarian smallholder and peasant: the sustained success of agricultural exports from Hungary's great estates helped to consolidate and perpetuate the inequities of land distribution in the Hungarian countryside and, with that, the increasingly stark inequities of Hungarian rural society.

Hungarian Society under Dualism

The Nobility

Having progressively increased the demesne proportion of their estates, first to maximise their profits from the grain boom early in the century and then to take advantage of the boom in wool that succeeded it, the magnates—unlike the gentry—sustained relatively little economic damage from the emancipations of 1848 and 1853. A few of the less well-managed estates went under, but many more seized the opportunities provided by the numerous bankruptcies of smaller landowners to make their large estates even larger. Between six and seven hundred families owned a quarter of Hungary's arable land: the estates of many counts exceeded 150,000 *hold** in size—Princess Eszterházy's extended to over 516,000 *hold* by 1895. In order to protect themselves against the vagaries of the agricultural markets and potential creditors, the magnates lobbied with some success for the revival of entailment, the abolition of which in 1848 had been confirmed in 1853. Although the classic Hungarian form of entailment, *ősiség* or *avicitás*, was not restored, a number of magnates made use of the Austrian equivalent, *fidei commissa*,

---

* 1 *hold*= 1.43 acres.

under which entailment could be granted by the monarch on a case-by-case basis. By 1867, sixty-four estates had been newly entailed, bringing the total area of 'indivisible and inalienable' land to 2.3 million *hold*.

Although the gentry had supplanted them as political leaders of the nation and, with the Compromise, as the Monarch's principal support and partner, the magnates were careful to maintain a political presence in order to promote and protect their particular interests. In 1848, magnates had made up only 6 per cent of the membership of the Lower House of the Hungarian Parliament; in 1861, their representation had increased to 13 per cent and in 1865 to 16.5 per cent. When the decline in grain prices after 1875 began to eat into the profits of the large estates, magnates were at the head of the neo-conservative agrarian movement, which challenged the priority given by the Liberal government to industrial modernisation and demanded protection for agriculture. Counts Sándor Károlyi, Albert Apponyi and Gyula Andrássy (Jnr) led an amorphous group of the larger landowners in Parliament whose political loyalties were in constant motion but which gravitated increasingly towards the Independence Party and its demand for a national tariff regime. Although a few of them led the promotion of sectional interests, however, the magnates no longer provided leadership to the whole nation as they had before 1848. This by no means diminished their social influence: no bank or company could hope to succeed unless its board of directors included at least one magnate—in 1905, financial and industrial boards claimed the membership of a total of eighty-eight counts and sixty-six barons. Equally, although their patronage of the arts and sciences had dwindled away, magnates continued to monopolise prestigious public offices such as the Presidency of the Academy of Sciences: when Count Emil Dessewffy succeeded Count József Teleki in that office, Sámuel Brassai, commoner and scientist, laid on the irony: 'Here in Hungary, every President has to be an aristocrat. Far from disparaging this custom, I give thanks to God that our nation is so far superior to the English, French, Italian and all others, which have not got aristocrats competent in every discipline, and what is more, so much more competent than their fellow citizens'.[3]

Neo-conservative agrarianism brought some benefit to the countryside, in particular the network of credit, marketing and consumer co-operatives the leaders of the movement inspired in the last years of the nineteenth century—by 1908 there were over two thousand co-operatives in existence, with a membership of over half a million. But although their estates continued to make the greatest contribution to Hungary's agricultural prosperity and to set the pace in agricultural modernisation, the magnates, on balance, retarded the development of rural society and prolonged its feudal character well into the twentieth century.

Whereas, for the magnates, the emancipation of 1853 created opportunities—both for the enlargement of their estates and for the increased efficiency hired labour made possible—for the majority of the gentry it spelt disaster. Deprived almost overnight of the free serf labour on which their small estates depended and compensated, eventually, with indemnity bonds that had to be held for a significant period if they were to realise their face value, the medium and small landowners somehow had to find means for paying the taxes from which, as nobles, they had hitherto been exempt. The Urbarial Patent of 1853 had restored the tithe on vineyards, abolished during the 1848 revolution. They could neither repay existing debts nor provide security against new loans. Bankruptcies became the norm rather than the exception. In 1848, there had been about 30,000 estates of between 200 and 1,000 *hold*—the normal spectrum of gentry land ownership; by 1867, this number had been halved and by 1900 there were only 10,000 estates of that size. In 1890 alone, mortgages on 14,978 farms were foreclosed—a fate that befell 118,000 small and medium farmers altogether between 1876 and 1906. The dispossessed or otherwise ruined could attempt to eke out a living on dwarf hold-ings, alongside their former peasant serfs; they could offer their services to more fortunate relatives; or they could join the army. But they refused to contemplate a new life in trade or industry, occupations unworthy of their gentle birth. By far the most preferred recourse was to the bureaucracy, a respectable occupation adequately remunerated. As soon as the conclusion of the Compromise ended the practice of passive resistance and removed all stigma from state service, job-seeking gentry invaded Pest-Buda in their thousands. The machinery of government expanded to accommodate them, partly as a consequence of increased govern-mental activity in a more modern society, partly as a result of growing administra-tive centralisation and, in great measure, as a politically expedient strategy. When Law XII/1867 was enacted, the bureaucracy numbered about 16,000: this rose to 22,000 by 1872, to 32,000 by 1875, to over 60,000 by 1890 and to nearly 100,000 by the turn of the century. This army of gentleman-bureaucrats, bound by their salaries to loyalty to Dualism, constituted a key component of Kálmán Tisza's political machine—one-third of the Liberal parliamentary party was recruited from their number. Political leadership of the nation now came from those mem-bers of the wealthier stratum of gentry, the former *bene possessionati*, whose estates of 1,000 *hold* and above had survived the economic impact of emancipation and provided sufficient income to support the political careers of their owners.

Inflation of the central bureaucracy went hand in hand with a gradual down-grading of the administrative role of the counties, where the members of the impoverished gentry who had remained in the countryside—either from choice or because they had failed to qualify for the bureaucracy—were strong supporters of the Independence or 1848 Parties and thus represented an unreliable element, to be distanced from the levers of local administration. The county assemblies became largely ceremonial in character, surrendering their powers to executive committees of whose members only half were elected. Thus polarised into ultra-loyalists and permanent oppositionists, the gentry nevertheless shared certain char-acteristics. Chief among these were a sense of deprivation, of enforced betrayal of their family tradition and inheritance and, perhaps above all, of insecurity following the removal of so many comfortable certainties. These emotions were, as we shall see, well reflected in the literature of the time and also informed prevailing atti-tudes towards the nationalities. The greatest beneficiaries of the steadfast refusal of the uprooted gentry to reinvent themselves as bourgeois were the Jews.

The Jewish Bourgeoisie

Treatment of Hungary's Jews during the period of the Bach regime illustrated the curious ambivalence of Austrian policy towards Hungary in general. On the one hand, the annulment of their partial emancipation in 1849 brought with it the reimposition of restrictions on occupation and domicile, a ban on Jewish purchase of land and the imposition of a swingeing fine of 2.3 million florins on the Jewish community as punishment for its support of the cause of Hungarian independence. On the other, Jewish businesses ruined by the war received compensation from the state; the punitive fine was commuted into a 1 million florin contribution from the Jewish community to the establishment of Jewish schools; and a decree of 1851 banned the exclusion of anybody from commercial or industrial activity on religious or ethnic grounds. The Austrians, clearly, were fully alive to the importance of the contribution the Jewish community could make to the economic prosperity of the Empire. This relatively benign environment encouraged Jewish immigration, principally from Galicia: Hungary's Jewish population grew from 343,000 in 1850 to 407,800 in 1857, to 624,700 in 1880 and to 910,000—8.5 per cent of the total population—in 1910. By the latter date, over 23 per cent of the population of Budapest was Jewish. In bringing this growth about, rising immigration was complemented by the high standards of hygiene in Jewish families, which kept infant mortality well below the national average. Among the acts Ferenc Deák and József Eötvös piloted through the Parliament of 1867 was Law XVII, passed unanimously by the Lower House and attracting only four negative votes in the Upper:

1. It is hereby proclaimed that the Israelite inhabitants of the country are entitled to exercise all civil and political rights equally with the Christian inhabitants.
2. All laws, practices and regulations contrary to these present are hereby repealed.[4]

Appropriately, the coping stone of Jewish emancipation in Hungary was set in place through the efforts of József Eötvös's son, Loránd, two decades later: the Law of Reception (the *Recepció*) of 1895 formally acknowledged Judaism as a received religion, alongside Christianity, legalising both conversion to it and mixed marriages. A new synagogue, then and still the largest in Europe, opened its doors on Dohány Street to the congregation of Pest in 1859.

These liberalising measures both acknowledged and encouraged the increasingly important role of Jews in the life of the Hungarian nation and their growing assimilation into the Magyar community. From their traditional roles as the middle-men of the agricultural countryside and the nation's moneylenders, the Jews graduated to leadership of the new capitalism and industrial economy, in which they were the most energetic agents of modernisation. By 1910, 54 per cent of the owners of business establishments were Jewish, as were 85 per cent of the directors and owners of financial institutions and 62.1 per cent of all employees in the trading and financial sectors. Manfred Weiss created and owned Hungary's largest manufacturing enterprise, the armaments and munitions complex on Csepel Island, south of Budapest; Zsigmond Kornfeld dominated the transportation and milling industries; Ferenc Chorin achieved pre-eminence in coal mining, as did Leó Lánczy and several other Jews in banking. The leading figures in the Budapest Stock Exchange and the National Association of Manufacturers were Jewish, as were those in the medical and other professions. Jews, moreover, joined the ranks of Hungary's larger landowners: by 1913, Jews owned 19 per cent of the estates of between 200 and 1,000 *hold* and accounted for over 26 per cent of the salaried employees (agronomists, accountants and superintendants) in agriculture. Jews were less predominant among the petit bourgeois—the artisans, small traders and junior public servants who made up about 12 per cent of the population—but were significantly represented nevertheless. Kálmán Tisza described Hungary's Jews as 'the most industrious and constructive segment of the Hungarian population';[5] in effect, they constituted Hungary's bourgeoisie—only a quarter of all Jews in Hungary were wage-earners.

In the judgement of a leading historian of Hungarian Jewry, Raphael Patai, 'by the end of the nineteenth century, the Jews as a group had achieved a power position in Hungary unmatched by their co-religionists in any other country'.[6] They owed their achievement not only to their talents, skills and work ethic but also, by contrast with other non-Magyar ethnic groups, to their readiness—indeed, eagerness—to be assimilated into the Magyar culture. We have already seen* how knowledge of the Magyar language and willingness to use it had come to be the most important test of Hungarian patriotism and of loyalty to the Hungarian nation. Lacking, until the advent of Zionism, a national ideal of their own and, unlike the Slavs, with no alternative motherland to turn to, the Jews had no reason to resist the adoption of the Magyar language as their own; on the contrary, assimilation into the culture of the nation that had now accorded them equality of rights seemed logical and the natural road to advancement. The Magyars, for their part, saw in the Jews natural and indispensable allies in the defence of Magyardom against encroachment and dilution by the nationalities. Indeed, Jewish families living in the peripheral counties often became pockets of Magyar culture in predominantly Slovak, Romanian or Serbian regions. Jewish schools, of which there were 300 by 1860, offered Magyar as well as German and Hebrew: by 1880, 57 per cent of the Jewish population claimed Magyar as their mother tongue and by 1910 this proportion had risen to 75.6 per cent. In 1861, the Jewish congregation of Pest elected a Magyar-speaking Board, headed by the reforming Jew Dr Ignác Hirschler; rabbis increasingly preached in Magyar rather than in German. The unity of the Jewish community in Hungary, however, became a major casualty of the process of assimilation. The election of a national Jewish Congress in 1868 had the effect of splitting Hungarian Jewry into progressive and conservative camps—later known as the Neologs and the Orthodox—which differed over how far Jewish religious practice, such as observance of the Sabbath, should be adapted to the norms of a Christian society. Internal schism nevertheless did nothing to retard the assimilation process, which was increasingly marked by the conversion of prominent Jews to Christianity. Many Jewish families celebrated the Hungarian Millennium in 1896 by changing their (usually German) surnames to Hungarian equivalents. The Monarch and the Hungarian government were lavish in their gestures of appreciation. Franz Joseph visited the newly opened Rabbinical Seminary in 1877; ennoblements of Jews became frequent—by 1918 there were 346 noble families of Jewish origin, twenty-six of them baronies.

Inevitably, this high profile of success and reward in so many fields provoked a reaction. The Jews never won social acceptance from the gentry: they were

* In Chapter 8.

excluded from county administration and barred from membership of the social and political hub, the National Casino. No member of the gentry would fight a duel with a Jew.[7] A member of the Károlyi family voiced a typically patronising attitude towards the Jews when he commented: 'Just as we keep the gypsies so that they play, we keep the Jews so that they work instead of us'.[8] In the 1870s, the sneers and envy turned into something more ugly. Győző Istóczy, a former county magistrate who had bungled the hearing of a case involving a Jewish plaintiff and lost his post as a result, mobilised the mounting resentment of Jews among the poorer gentry and entered Parliament on the strength of an anti–Semitic manifesto. In 1878, Istóczy proposed the creation of a Jewish state in Palestine to which Hungarian and other Jews could be deported—thus anticipating the Zionism of his fellow Hungarian, Theodor Herzl, by seventeen years and ensuring, incidentally, that true Zionism never attracted significant support from Hungarian Jewry. Istóczy succeeded in creating, by his frequent and well-publicised interpolations in the Lower House, an anti–Semitic lobby that condemned Hungarian Jews as economic parasites, incapable of true patriotism, who were infiltrating the body politic under the guise of assimilation. Istóczy and his supporters called for the revocation of Jewish emancipation, an end to further Jewish immigration, a ban on mixed marriages and a *numerus clausus* to limit Jewish access to higher education.

In this atmosphere, in 1882, a particularly nasty blood libel case in the village of Tiszaeszlár, near Tokaj in eastern Hungary, came to national—and, briefly, international—prominence. The disappearance of a young peasant girl on the eve of Passover was followed by the arrest of the local kosher butcher and fourteen other Jews on charges of ritual murder and, after a long delay, by a much-publicised trial; the case collapsed when the leading witness for the prosecution admitted to having been bribed by the presiding magistrate and the missing girl's body was recovered, unmutilated, from the River Tisza. The acquittal of the falsely accused Jews resulted in anti–Semitic demonstrations of medieval intensity in Budapest and other towns: disorders involving the looting of Jewish shops and attacks on individual Jews had to be put down by troops. Seizing the moment, Istóczy founded the National Anti–Semitic Party in 1883, recruited mainly from the ranks of the Independence and 1848 Parties; it won seventeen seats in the Lower House in the elections of the following year, despite repeated condemnations of its programme by the revered Lajos Kossuth, from Turin. A political commentator noted in 1884: 'Anti–Semitism here among us ... comprises the cry of pain and general dissatisfaction and embitterment over national miseries, decline, impoverishment, the bad administration of justice, the clumsy public services. They cannot beat Tisza, so they beat the Jew'.[9]

The Istóczy phenomenon nevertheless proved short-lived. His Anti–Semitic Party split in 1885 and melted away. An upturn in the economy, and Kossuth's continued warnings against national shame, helped to disperse the poisonous clouds of anti–Semitism; what proved to be the golden age of Hungarian Jewry resumed. István Tisza, when he assumed the leadership of the Liberal Party his father had created, encouraged Jews to enter politics and to overcome the obstructions of the gentry: between 1905 and 1910, the hitherto insignificant number of Jewish members in the Lower House rose to 102; in the Parliament of 1910, they accounted for 22 per cent of the total.[10] Sixteen Jews sat in the Upper House and

Tisza's administration included at least six Jewish ministers. The onset of darkness was only a decade away; but, to quote Raphael Patai once more: 'In no period in their long history did Hungarian Jews feel as much at home in the *haza* [homeland], as much at one with their Christian Magyar compatriots, as much part of the great national endeavour to modernise, to forge ahead, and to become an important cultural entity in Europe, as in the half-century between their emancipation and the end of World War I'.[11]

Peasants and Workers

To a growing rural population sharing a finite area of cultivable land, the Urbarial Patent of 1853—which broadly reaffirmed the emancipation of 1848—brought only patchy relief. Just over 3 million former serfs became owners of their plots, freed from feudal labour obligations; but the plots were small and the land survey of 1869 showed that over half the beneficiaries of emancipation occupied farms of less than 5 *hold*. By the turn of the century, however, landed peasants numbered some 7 million, accounting for 38 per cent of the population, of whom only one third fell into the category of 'dwarf holders' whose plots of less than 5 *hold* could not support a family. At the base of the rural social pyramid, accounting for 24 per cent of the total population and 39 per cent of those engaged in agriculture, were the landless peasants, of whom three-quarters were labourers and the remainder estate servants; this was the rural proletariat, numbering some 5 million. The peasantry as a whole, whether landed or landless, remained vulnerable, as in the past, to fluctuations in agricultural prices, floods, drought and livestock disease, but without the cushion that membership of a feudal community had sometimes provided. While agriculture prospered and the expansion of the railways continued apace, landless labourers had little difficulty in finding work either on the great estates or on construction projects; but with the collapse of grain prices, the increased use of agricultural machinery and, after 1880, the completion of the railway network and of river regulation projects, casual work became hard to find. The typical labourer worked for only between 150 and 200 days a year and earned barely enough to keep himself and his family alive. In the absence of any restrictions on working hours, farm labourers were required to work for sixteen to eighteen hours a day during the summer. Servants on the estates were paid in kind rather than cash and typically lived in stable blocks that bred disease, particularly tuberculosis; infant mortality in the countryside was high—rural destitution made a major contribution to Hungary's positions at the bottom of the European table for life expectancy and at the top of that for the incidence of tuberculosis. During the last three decades of the nineteenth century, the threat of starvation was seldom absent from the Hungarian countryside.

Poor peasants, cottars and labourers showed their desperation in repeated waves of harvest strikes and outbreaks of violence; the south-eastern counties— 'Stormy Corner'—became particularly volatile in the 1880s and 1890s, often keeping disorder on the boil for weeks at a time. Bloody clashes with the gendarmerie were common; the government responded to serious and prolonged unrest with declarations of martial law and repressive action by regular troops. The long-serving Minister of Agriculture, Ignác Darányi, a competent agronomist of otherwise liberal disposition, found it necessary to introduce draconian legislation to discipline the rural population. The Farm Labourers' Acts of 1898 and 1907 banned strikes and labour combination in the countryside; provided for the forcible return of fugitive labourers; subjected the teenage children of estate servants to the discipline, including corporal punishment, of the landlord; and made labourers criminally liable for breaches of contract. At the threshold of the twentieth century, Hungary thus regressed into neo-feudalism. Legislation introducing a measure of sickness and accident insurance for farmhands employed under contract offered some but insufficient compensation. Those peasants and labourers who had the energy and the courage protested with their feet: between 1869 and 1910, 1.25 million Hungarians—predominantly Slovaks and Magyars—emigrated either to the United States or to other European countries and kept their extended families alive with remittances, which by 1902 totalled 100 million crowns per annum and subsequently reached 250 million. Internal migration, mostly to Budapest, offered an alternative escape route from the countryside—less daunting but also less rewarding: between 1880 and 1910, 400,000 peasants and farm labourers migrated to the capital, increasing its population to 880,000 by the latter date.

For most internal migrants, urban industrial wages and working conditions offered some slight improvement over those in the countryside; they were none the less appalling. Wages for unskilled workers, the category into which all the rural poor by definition fell, had to be held down to subsistence level in order to make it possible for industrial employers to offer high wages to skilled workers, of whom the majority had to be attracted from abroad—in 1870, 24 per cent of industrial workers and 33 per cent of transport workers were immigrants, mostly from Austria and Bohemia. During the 1880s, the majority of factories worked a twelve-hour day; in 1910, only 109 out of 5,000 factories offered toilet facilities; seventy-five, canteens; and seven, crèches. Samuel Gompers, founder of the American Federation of Labour (AFL), after a visit to Budapest in 1910, described industrial working conditions there as among the worst in the world. The relatively rapid advance of the educational system in Hungary, however, contributed to the birth and development of a labour movement through which demands for redress could be voiced. Modern industry required a literate workforce and post-Compromise governments responded to the demand. József Eötvös's Public Education Act of 1868 had made elementary education compulsory for all children aged six to twelve or fifteen and gave parochial schools (which then accounted for 13,319 out of the 13,789 elementary schools in Hungary) complete freedom in the appointment of teachers and the choice of their language of instruction. Every village in which there were more than thirty children of school age but which lacked an elementary school was obliged to establish one; the number of elementary schools had risen to 17,000 by 1914. Eötvös's Act, the most advanced educational measure in Europe at that time—compulsory education was introduced in England only in 1882—built on the Maria Theresian foundations laid down in the eighteenth century and established the basis for a modern education system in Hungary. During the last half of the nineteenth century, enrolment in Hungarian primary schools increased seven-fold: from 324,000 in 1849 to over 2.5 million in 1900. The literacy rate rose from 10 per cent in 1842 to 34.4 per cent in 1870 and to 68.7 per cent in 1910; although this compared with an average of around 90 per cent in much of western Europe, it nevertheless represented an impressive increase. Secondary and higher education expanded more slowly; but the basic preconditions for the growth of political consciousness in the working class, both rural and urban, were in place by the last decade of the nineteenth century. As one peasant witness told a High Sheriffs enquiry into rural violence in 1900: 'The rightful demands of the labourers increased because the people of the land study more, know more, see more. How can you blame us? We have learnt how to read and write. We would now like to wear better clothes, eat like human beings and send our children to schools'.[12]

Partly because industrialisation came late to Hungary and partly because industrial workers, especially in the food processing industry, tended to be seasonal, returning to their villages for the harvest season, the Hungarian labour movement was slow to develop. It made a false start soon after the Compromise of 1867: the teaching of Ferdinand Lassalle, imported into Hungary by immigrant skilled workers, inspired the foundation of the General Workers' Association which, under the chairmanship of the veteran Mihály Táncsics, campaigned for universal male suffrage and adult education. Encouraged by the example of the Paris Commune, the association organised its first series of strikes in 1871, in support of the growing demand for a ten-hour working day; the suppression of the Commune, in turn, encouraged the Hungarian government to suppress the Association and to lay charges of treason against its leaders (who were eventually acquitted for lack of evidence). The foundation of the Hungarian Social Democratic Party in 1890, under the leadership of Pál Engelmann, provided a stimulus to the embryo trade union movement, which held its first national congress in 1899; but at the turn of the century, trade union membership totalled no more than 20,000—under 3 per cent of the industrial workforce. The savagery of strike-breaking by the gendarmerie, and occasionally the army, may have deterred potential recruits to the movement: during only three years, 1897–99, fifty-one striking workers were killed and 114 wounded.[13]

The economic downturn of the early 1900s provoked a rise in labour activity and a wave of strikes, mostly in the iron and coal industries but also affecting the countryside, between 1905 and 1907 which, in the latter year, involved 75,000 workers. A mass demonstration in Budapest on 10 October 1907—'Red Thursday'—by over 100,000 workers in favour of universal suffrage[14] and a secret ballot marked the high water mark of the Hungarian labour movement before the First World War; thereafter, its membership and activity diminished, although a further demonstration in 1912 mustered sufficient support to require its dispersal by force, at the cost of four lives. Government and industry had not been wholly unresponsive to the concerns expressed by the trade unions: a factory inspectorate to enforce safety standards had been in place since 1884 and health insurance had been compulsory since 1891, covering 1.1 million workers by 1911. The government introduced compulsory accident insurance in 1907, providing for free medical care for up to ten weeks and paid sick leave for those injured at their workplace. Wage levels remained low for unskilled workers, but the strikes of 1905–07 achieved average increases of 10 per cent. Overall, however, conditions of life for the Hungarian working class, both rural and urban, in the early twentieth century lagged far behind those typical of western Europe and, especially in the countryside, frequently fell to the level of near-destitution.

The Nationalities and 'Magyarisation'

The nationalities, as we saw in the last chapter, had gained no advantage from Lajos Kossuth's defeat in 1849. During the 'Bach period', the Croatians, the Serbs of southern Hungary, the Slovaks in the north and the Romanians of Transylvania suffered equally from absolutist, Germanised administration and punitive taxation; inhabiting as they did the economically backward periphery of the Hungarian lands, they did not even share the benefits of inward investment and modernisation that the 1850s brought to Transdanubia and central Hungary. The potential for political disaffection among the nationalities remained high throughout the second half of the nineteenth century. We have seen in chapter 8 how the national consciousness of the Serbs, Slovaks and Romanians grew, before the 1848 revolution, alongside that of the Magyars themselves. Not only the political hegemony of the Magyars, which the Compromise consolidated, but also the extent to which the nationalities were economically disadvantaged increasingly tinged their new cultural awareness with envy and resentment. With the exception of the Serbs in agriculturally rich southern Hungary, the nationalities lived in regions in which the hilly or mountainous terrain and poor soil made them unsuitable for the production of grain, where the main profits from agriculture were to be found. The distribution of land, moreover, was even more inequitable in these regions than in the countryside of western and central Hungary. Peasant holdings were barely large enough for family subsistence: in Transylvania, 72 per cent of them were of 5 *hold* or less, accounting for only 29.5 per cent of the land area of the province. A comparable situation existed in Croatia, in the Slovak and in the Ruthene regions. The larger and medium-sized estates belonged overwhelmingly to Magyars. Hungary's leading economic historians, Professors Berend and Ránki, concluded: 'It is no exaggeration to say that the lack of adequate land for the non-Magyar peasants was the main, if not the exclusive, reason for their destitute condition and the principal motivating force behind the development of nationalism among them'.[15] Although geography and mineral resources favoured the development of industry in the Slovak region, the other non-Magyar regions lagged far behind the rest of the country in industrial development and were bound to the quasi–colonial status of suppliers of raw materials to Magyar factories. Although demographic and economic pressures were relieved to some extent by emigration, they remained acute well into the twentieth century.

Following Bach's dismissal in 1859, the leaders of Hungary's reviving political life were fully conscious that the problems of the nationalities constituted a major item of unfinished business left over from the reform and revolutionary periods. József Eötvös's parliamentary committee on nationality rights recommended to Parliament in 1861 that basic civil and political rights should be guaranteed to every citizen, regardless of nationality or religion; and that, in addition, ethnic communities should be given freedom to use their mother-tongues in the administration of their counties and municipalities—although Magyar should continue to be the language of central government and Parliament. Franz Josef dissolved

Parliament before the Eötvös report could be considered; but Ferenc Deák gave a firm undertaking: 'We shall not forget that the non-Hungarian [non-Magyar] inhabitants of Hungary are in every respect citizens of the country and we are prepared sincerely and readily to secure to them by law whatever their own interests or that of the country demands'.[16]

After the conclusion of the Compromise, Deák redeemed this promise in the Nationalities Act of 1868 which declared in its Preamble that '… all the citizens of Hungary politically constitute one nation, the indivisible, unitary Hungarian nation, of which every citizen of the country is an equal member, whatever his nationality…'. The Act, which was largely a development of Eötvös's 1861 report, provided that although the official language of central government and legislation would be Magyar, all laws would in future be published in all the languages used in Hungary; that in county assemblies there could be a second official language of debate and record if one-fifth of their members so wished; that members of county assemblies could debate in their mother-tongue; and that communities and parishes could choose the language in which they wished to transact their business. This essentially liberal approach was reflected in the Act's provisions concerning education, including recognition of the obligation of the state 'to ensure that citizens living together in considerable numbers, of whatever nationality, shall be able to obtain instruction in the neighbourhood in their mother-tongue, up to the point where higher academic education begins'.[17]

The political consciousness of the nationalities, however, had already developed beyond the point at which they could be satisfied by concessions, however generous, on the language issue alone: because the Nationalities Act contained no recognition of the right of the nationalities to even a limited measure of political autonomy, their representatives in the Lower House opposed it to a man. A counter-proposal, introduced by Romanian and Serb deputies, for a reorganisation of the counties on an ethnic basis with full political and cultural autonomy provoked equally unanimous condemnation by the Magyar majority: even Lajos Mocsáry, the liberal deputy who had been the most outspoken in defending nationality rights, attacked the proposal on the grounds that it would amount to the dismemberment of Hungary. The deputies representing national minorities (except the Serbs) thereupon quit the chamber—a tactical error which removed from Parliament the only group with an interest in monitoring the implementation of the Nationality Act or in protesting against defiance of its provisions.

The rejection of the Nationalities Act by the elected representatives of the ethnic minorities can now be seen as one of the defining moments in the history of modern Hungary. That the deputies were properly reflecting the views of the communities from which they came was confirmed by the foundation, in 1868 in Turócszentmárton, of the Slovak National Party, which championed territorial autonomy for the Slovak region; by repudiation of the Nationalities Act and a demand for an autonomous Serb-dom by a conference of the Serb Liberal Party in Nagybecskerek, in southern Hungary, in 1869; by the decision of the newly founded Romanian National Party of Transylvania, in the same year, to boycott the national Parliament; and by rejection of the recently concluded compromise agreement between Hungary and Croatia (see below) by the Croatian National Party in 1871. These acts of defiance, though not in themselves particularly damaging or threatening, contributed to a strange transformation in the attitudes of the Magyar political nation towards the nationalities, a transformation that found immediate expression in the policies of the Liberal government and in those of its successors well into the twentieth century. A substantial proportion of the Magyar gentry, although they loyally gave their support to Deák and Eötvös in Parliament, harboured serious misgivings concerning what they deemed the over-generous provisions of the Nationality Act—while drawing some comfort from the fact that responsibility for implementation of the Act, or lack of it, would lie mainly with the predominantly Magyar county assemblies and officials. Magyar attitudes now hardened further. It became a settled objective of the Hungarian government to restrain the developing national self-awareness and identities of the minorities, to nudge them towards assimilation into Magyardom and to promote the widest possible knowledge and use of the Magyar language, still regarded as the most reliable criterion of integration with and loyalty to the Hungarian state. Magyar perceptions of the nationalities were perhaps further distorted by the lingering bitterness of defeat in 1849, by the gentry's subsequent impoverishment, and by revived fears of Pan-Slavism and German hegemony. Paranoia would not be too strong a description of some of the rhetoric that accompanied Magyarising policies and which did as much long-term damage to relations between the Magyars and the national minorities as the policies themselves.

The closure, in 1874, of all three gymnasia in the Slovak region, on the pretext that they engaged in pan-Slavist propaganda, provided an early manifestation of these policies. It was followed, a year later, by the dissolution of the *Matica sloven-ská* (Slovak Cultural Institute) and the confiscation of the museum and library which the *Matica* had established. In 1879 came the first of a series of Education Acts designed to increase the number of Hungarians who could claim Magyar as their first language: the teaching of Magyar became compulsory in all primary schools, irrespective of whether they operated under the aegis of a church or under that of the state. At the same time, teacher training colleges were required to ensure that their students could teach Magyar. Gymnasia, from 1883 onwards, had to give all their pupils sufficient instruction in Magyar to ensure that they could 'master it adequately'; and in 1891 even kindergartens were brought into the net, with a requirement that Magyar should be taught to their infant pupils. By 1900, 12,223 primary schools, out of the national total of 16,618, 189 gymnasia out of 205 and virtually every kindergarten had been completely Magyarised, in the sense that all instruction was conducted in the Magyar language. In 1907, the new Coalition government, which included members of the Independence Party, once champion of the rights of the nationalities, found even this outcome inadequate: Albert Apponyi, as Minister of Education, secured the passage of a law that increased the compulsory weekly quota of Magyar language teaching in non-Magyar schools to thirteen hours—nearly half the curriculum; and empowered the state to regulate the contracts and salaries of all teachers employed in non-state schools, so that under-performance in the teaching of Magyar could be penalised.[18] Schools were required to display the Hungarian coat of arms and to fly the Hungarian flag on appropriate occasions. To the extent that it infringed, in varying degrees, the rights of the churches (under whose auspices most primary schools operated) or contravened the provisions of the Nationalities Act, the constitutionality of all this legislation was questionable; all the more regrettable, therefore, that between 1878 and 1901 there were no representatives of the minority national parties in Parliament to challenge it—even the Serbs had no representative after the arrest and imprisonment of Svetozar Miletić in 1875 for supporting Serbia in her war with the Turks. Lajos Mocsáry, a consistent champion of nationality rights who had left the Liberals in protest over this issue in 1874 to found the Independence Party, was ejected from the Lower House, and later expelled from his own party, for arguing that the Nationalities Act should be observed. On the nationality question, the collective mind of the Magyar majority remained completely closed.

Magyarisation—an ugly word for which there is no effective substitute—was by no means confined to the school classroom. It left its imprint on most areas of national life, whether through legislative action or social pressure. The electoral law of 1874 raised the property qualification for enfranchisement to a level that disadvantaged the nationalities, whose holdings of land were typically smaller than those of the Magyars. Since only holders of a Hungarian university degree could apply for entry into the senior level of the bureaucracy or into the judiciary, and since all instruction at Hungary's two universities was conducted in Magyar, these careers were open only to Magyars by birth or assimilation; the same restriction applied, in effect if not by law, to the legal and medical professions. The government rejected numerous applications for the establishment of new gymnasia in the non-Magyar regions, although the Romanians succeeded in establishing five, together with six teacher training colleges—a tribute to their persistence and to the support given to them from Bucharest. Among the nationalities only the Croats had their own university, founded in 1874 in Zagreb, largely through the efforts of the nationalist leader, Bishop Strossmayer. As a Hungarian writer commented in the late 1870s, with the Slovak region particularly in mind, the schools and the bureaucracy together constituted a big machine, into which 'one feeds a Slovak child on one side, and on the other out comes a Hungarian gentleman'.[19] When, thirty years later in 1906, R. W. Seton-Watson, the Scottish publicist and campaigner for minority rights, asked Professor Lajos Láng, the economist and former government minister, where Magyarisation was leading, Láng replied (according to Seton-Watson): 'We shall just go on till there are no Slovaks left'.[20] In purely statistical terms, the policies of Magyarisation achieved a remarkable success. Between 1850 and 1910, approximately two million Hungarian citizens became, at least in terms of their claimed first language, Magyars: they included about 700,000 Jews, 500,000 Germans, 400,000 Slovaks, 150,000 Romanians and 150,000 South Slavs. Fewer Magyars than members of the nationalities joined the swelling tide of emigration and this assisted the re-establishment of a Magyar majority in the country as a whole. Assimilation progressed particularly rapidly in the cities and towns: Budapest, where in 1848, 75 per cent of the inhabitants had been German-speaking, had become 79 per cent Magyar by 1900 with a population three times the size. By 1910, Magyars accounted for 77 per cent of the total urban population and for just over half the population of Hungary as a whole.

The policies known collectively as Magyarisation have understandably generated a great deal of heat, both among their contemporary opponents and supporters and, subsequently, among historians and writers. Seton-Watson wrote of 'a policy of repression which is without any parallel in civilised Europe'.[21] One of his contemporaries, C. M. Knatchbull-Hugessen, author of the standard constitutional history of Hungary in English, defended the Magyars against 'trial by newspaper' and 'condemnation without investigation', stoutly asserting:'Nothing can hold Hungary together but the Magyar idea and the development of Magyar culture. Magyars created Hungary, formerly the "bulwark and shield of Christendom", and none but Magyars can preserve it'.[22] An account of the language debate during the Vormärz period has already been given; but it is perhaps worth recapitulating some of its elements in this later context. If Hungary was to remain a viable unitary state within the Dual Monarchy, she required one official language for the conduct of state business; the Diet of 1843–44 had already secured this in all essentials. It followed that all Hungarian citizens, of whatever ethnicity, should be given at least the opportunity to acquire that language; and it was reasonable that citizens aspiring to a career in politics, the bureaucracy or the judiciary should be required to do so. A policy that made knowledge of Magyar an essential qualification for state service but at the same time gave non-Magyars no opportunity to acquire it would have been at least as reprehensible as excess of zeal in the opposite direction. In terms of everyday life, knowledge of the language of the largest ethnic group, Magyar, was virtually essential for anybody engaged in the professions, in commerce, in industry or in any other occupation that involved routine social contact. For this reason, a high proportion of those who assimilated into Magyardom did so voluntarily, because they wished to succeed in their chosen occupation; Hungarian Jewry provided the outstanding example of this process, but it extended to all immigrants—typically, skilled industrial workers—who had chosen to seek employment in Hungary. It also applied to large numbers of internal migrants, who found that in an urban industrial environment knowledge of Magyar was essential if they were to understand and retain their factory employment. The great majority of those who assimilated voluntarily would have wished their children to have at least as many opportunities as their parents. It would be difficult, therefore, to make out a case against the provision of instruction in the Magyar language in all schools as a compulsory subject; and since Magyar is a difficult and idiosyncratic language, it made a great deal of sense to begin the learning process as early as possible, in kindergartens where these existed. The post-Compromise legislation on the teaching of Magyar simply built on legislation already passed by the Diet and sanctioned by the sovereign before 1848.

So far, so good. The utilitarian argument, which is also an argument for equality of opportunity, becomes more difficult to sustain when it is applied to legislation designed to make Magyar the *sole* language of instruction throughout the educational system, from kindergarten to university; or, for example, to the 'Lex Apponyi'[5] of 1907, which gave the teaching of Magyar a disproportionately dominant position in the overall school curriculum. And it cannot be applied at all to measures of what might be termed 'aggressive Magyarisation' such as the suppression of non-Magyar cultural institutions, or the Act of 1898, which required all towns and villages to Magyarise their names and local authorities to ensure that gravestones were inscribed only in Magyar. Above all, the Nationalities Act of 1868 had simply not been implemented in counties—the majority—where Magyars controlled the local administration and the county assembly; indeed, there is no evidence that the Act was observed anywhere in the country. Cultural aggression or deliberate inertia cannot easily be justified; but an attempt must be made to explain them. Events and circumstances had combined to create in the Hungarian ruling class—the aristocracy and gentry—an acute sense of insecurity and vulnerability. Paradoxically, their devoted cultivation of a language that has no near relatives and in which most non-Magyars found it difficult to achieve fluency may have increased their sense of isolation. Throughout the nineteenth century, they were constantly aware of having become a minority in their own country—around 39 per cent in 1800 and about 46.5 per cent in 1851. Having discovered their own cultural identity, expressed in Magyar literature and poetry, only within the last hundred years or so, they were obsessively concerned with its survival in the face of potential encroachment by other languages and cultures—the German and Slav in particular—representing much larger ethnic groups. This deep-seated fear led them to exaggerate—as did, in reaction, their opponents—the importance of language as a criterion of nationality and national allegiance, an error against which István Széchenyi had warned them. R. W. Seton-Watson recalled a conversation with József Kristóffy, Minister of the Interior in the unelected Fejérváry government and advocate of universal suffrage, who told him that 'Magyarisation … was only possible on economic lines, through factories or railways, etc. In the schools, it was a hopeless failure, because the children simply did not learn.[23] He therefore favoured the mother tongue in all state schools, though with Hungarian as a compulsory subject'.[24] Kristóffy echoed Széchenyi's belief in mutual attraction as the only sound basis for assimilation; but during the Dualist period this view continued to be confined to a very small minority. More typical were the views of the historian Béla Grünwald, who wrote in the 1880s that Hungary's non-Magyar peoples were 'not capable of an independent advancement' and that it was 'the destiny of Magyardom to assimilate them, to absorb them into a superior people'; this would fulfil the Magyar 'duty to humanity, to elevate them as if we were the champions of civilisation'.[25]

Magyar apprehensions, and overreaction to them, were concentrated on the peripheral regions of the country inhabited by minorities, which could in theory look to neighbouring co-ethnic states for protection or even intervention: the Slovaks to Russia, the Romanians of Transylvania to the Romanian Kingdom and the Serbs of southern Hungary to the Serbian Principality (Croatia, with its historic constitutional link to Hungary but emerging aspiration to independence, fell into a rather different category). But although, during the three decades following the Compromise, the nationalities had ample grounds for grievance and sufficient political awareness to encourage their expression, their national movements remained relatively subdued and, with the possible exception of the Romanians, certainly did little to justify Magyar hysteria. The Slovaks, as we have seen, became the earliest victims of forceful Magyarisation. The Slovak National Party, founded in 1868, won three seats in the 1869 elections but subsequently succumbed to official harassment and boycotted elections after 1872. Between 1870 and 1914, about one million Slovaks emigrated permanently, most of them to the United States; and, as already noted, approximately 400,000 chose to assimilate into Magyardom, many of them achieving eminence in the Church and the professions. Serbian nationalism, led by Svetozar Miletić and Mihajlo Polit, became vocal during the years immediately following the Compromise: Miletić thundered against the Nationalities Act and the restoration of the Military Frontier Region to Hungary in his newspaper, *Zastaba* ('The Standard'); and founded a semi–secret society, the *Omladina*, which sought to promote a closer connexion between the Serbs of Hungary and the Serbian Principality. In 1875, Miletić overstepped the mark by attempting to raise money and recruits in support of Serbia's war with Turkey; his arrest, sentence to five years' imprisonment and the dissolution of the *Omladina* followed. In his absence, the government succeeded in engineering the election to the Patriarchate of the Serbian Orthodox Church of a compliant Bishop, Ivačković, who was able to calm nationalist tempers. The Serbian *Matica* (Cultural Institute) continued its activities unhindered, an indication that the government detected no cause for concern in the mood of the Serb community.

The Romanians of Transylvania maintained a higher profile, staging a mass demonstration in 1868 to demand autonomy for Transylvania. This became the main plank in the platform of the Romanian National Party, which came into being in 1881, and the message of Ion Slavici's nationalist newspaper *Tribuna*. Romanian nationalists dreamed of union between an autonomous Transylvania and the now independent neighbouring Kingdom of Romania. Slavici also founded, in 1891, the 'League for the Cultural Unity of All Romanians', which promoted the Romanian cause throughout Europe, with considerable success. In 1892, the National Committee of Romanians sent a sizeable delegation to Vienna, armed with a Memorandum of Grievances for submission to Franz Joseph. Although the Monarch refused to receive the Romanians, their action obliged the Hungarian government to assert its authority; and this marked a turning point in relations between the Magyar centre and the nationalist periphery. Fifteen members of the Romanian National Committee were arrested and sentenced to five years' imprisonment; the Romanian National Party was subsequently dissolved but succeeded in surviving underground. Magyarisation made little, if any, progress among the Romanians of Transylvania, whose development into a force to be reckoned with was encouraged by the emergence of a distinctively Romanian bourgeoisie and by the surprisingly rapid growth of an indigenous banking system—by 1914, 152 of the 200 non-Magyar-owned banks in Hungary were Romanian and these, like the Tatra Bank in the Slovak region, actively supported the economic, cultural and political activities of the local ethnic majority. Among the Romanians, as among the other nationalities, the indigenous bourgeoisie was not separated from the common people by the social barriers that characterised Magyar society; all groups made common cause in hostility towards Magyar, and sometimes Jewish, landowners and industrialists. Ominously for the Hungarians, the Romanian government began to take an active interest in Transylvania: when, in 1883, Romania concluded secret defence agreements with the members of the Triple Alliance, she requested a moderation of Hungarian educational policy in Transylvania as part of the deal. The 'Congress of Nationalities', which assembled in Budapest during the summer of 1895, provided a further warning to the Hungarian government that, after more than two decades of relative quiescence—except in Transylvania—nationalist aspirations were reviving. Romanian, Slovak and Serb delegates united in demanding, to the fury of the Magyars, a reordering of the county system along ethnic lines and universal suffrage.

Meanwhile, in Croatia, events had been following a not dissimilar pattern but within a different constitutional framework. In 1868, the Hungarian Parliament had approved a law redefining the relationship between Hungary and Croatia in the light of the 1867 Compromise. The Croatians had attempted, unsuccessfully, to negotiate a separate deal with Vienna, bypassing the Hungarians; and had boycotted Franz Joseph's coronation in Buda in protest against the snub he had administered to their delegation. The newly appointed Bán of Croatia, Baron Rauch, then succeeded in creating, through 'administrative methods', a majority in the Croatian *Sabor* for the pro-Hungarian Unionist Party; the negotiation of an agreement, known in Croat as the *Nagodba*, ensued. This mini–Compromise, while reaffirming Hungary's and Croatia's community of statehood, accorded to Croatia complete autonomy in her internal affairs and official status for the Croatian language. Croatia would be represented by forty deputies in the Hungarian Parliament. in which they could speak in their own language, and in the Delegation on 'common affairs'; a Croatian would hold a position in the Hungarian government as head of a Ministry of Croatian Affairs. The financial provisions of the *Nagodba* gave rise to prolonged controversy: although Croatia was required to contribute only 6.44 per cent of the Hungarian share of the 'common affairs' budget of the Dual Monarchy, the agreement obliged her to earmark 55 per cent of her fiscal revenues to the 'common affairs' budget of Hungary-Croatia, leaving only 45 per cent for domestic expenditure. The future status of Fiume (Rijeka), which Austria had awarded to Croatia during the War of Independence, also became a focus of disagreement—finally settled in Hungary's favour after the Hungarians had, allegedly, tampered with the text of the *Nagodba*, which was submitted to Franz Joseph for final sanction. Croatian opponents of the agreement argued, with justice, that it gave Croatia less autonomy in relation to Budapest than the 1867 Compromise had given Budapest in relation to Vienna; they also took strong exception to the provision that future Báns of Croatia were to be appointed by the Monarch on the recommendation, not of the Croatian *Sabor*, but of the Hungarian Prime Minister.

Croatian politics, and the swelling Croatian nationalist movement, were subsequently defined by degrees of opposition to the *Nagodba*. One of the fathers of Croatian nationalism and founder of the National Party, Bishop Joseph Strossmayer, hoped to bring about the creation of an autonomous Croatian state within the Monarchy, converting Dualism into Trialism, which would become the hub of a union of the Southern Slavs—a revival of Gaj's Illyrian ideal. The key element in Strossmayer's plans, which divorced them from reality, lay in *rapprochement* and close union between the Catholic Croatians and the Orthodox Serbs, both within Croatia—where the Serbian minority was later enlarged by Croatia's absorption of the former Military Frontier Region—and in the neighbouring Serbian nation itself. Strossmayer's rival for the leadership of Croatian nationalism, Ante Starčević, took a more hard-headed view, campaigning for complete independence from Hungary, the reduction of Croatia's links with Vienna to that of sharing a common monarch, and stout defence of Croatian identity against encroachment by the 'inferior' Serbs. Although the National Party and Starčević's Party of Right commanded widespread support, their electoral successes in the 1870s were repeatedly frustrated by the packing or dissolution of the *Sabor* by successive Hungarian-nominated Báns. An outbreak of rioting in Zagreb in 1883, caused by the imprudent replacement of Croat by Croat/Hungarian insignia in the Department of Finance by its Magyar director, led Kálmán Tisza to suspend the Croatian constitution and appoint a Royal Commissioner to restore order. When this had been achieved, with the use of troops, Tisza appointed one of his cousins, the young Count Károly Khuen-Héderváry, to be Bán. Khuen-Héderváry proved to be a skilful politician: he cajoled or bludgeoned the National Party into acceptance of the *Nagodba* and for twenty years used it very much as his cousin used the Liberal Party in Hungary—as a political machine with a permanent majority in the *Sabor*, assured by the routine rigging of elections. Khuen-Héderváry also proved to be adept at exploiting the endemic hostility between Croats and Serbs in order to retain control of both communities. Beneath the surface, however, national aspirations continued to grow in strength. The Party of Right, despite a split caused by the formation, by its radical wing, of a Party of Pure Right, which demanded equality of status within the Monarchy for a massively enlarged Greater Croatia, commanded more popular support than bogus election results revealed; and a new reforming movement, the *Omladina*, led by young intellectuals who had studied abroad, stood ready to seize the political initiative whenever Khuen-Héderváry's grip on Croatia slackened. The appointment of Khuen-Héderváry to the Hungarian Premiership in 1903 was to give them, and the Parties of Right, their opportunity.

The riots throughout Croatia in 1903 against Hungary's refusal to adjust the financial clauses of the *Nagodba* inaugurated a decade during which relations between the Magyar ruling establishment and the nationalities went from bad to worse. This created the political psychology that ensured that the eventual dissolution of the Hungarian Kingdom awaited only a catalyst. First, however, Franz Josef's refusal to receive a delegation of Croats, wishing to plead for clemency towards the rioters, brought about an unexpected but temporary *rapprochement* between Croatia and the Hungarian opposition parties, which were soon to form the Coalition Government. Meeting in Fiume in 1905, forty members of the Dalmatian *Sabor* adopted a Resolution offering solidarity with the Hungarian parties in their current dispute with Vienna in return for Hungarian support for the reunion of Dalmatia with Croatia; the Resolution also declared: 'The Croats and Serbs of Dalmatia will work shoulder to shoulder as blood brothers in national and political questions and will endeavour … to realise as soon as possible the union of Dalmatia with Croatia and Slavonia'. Two weeks later, a meeting of twenty-six Serbian deputies endorsed the Fiume Resolution.

Once in power in Budapest, however, the new Coalition Government—or, rather, its Minister of Commerce, Ferenc Kossuth—lost no time in destroying this potentially favourable political climate: an Act introduced in the spring of 1907 making Magyar the sole operational language throughout the state railway system, including its Croatian sector, outraged the Croats and triggered public demonstrations calling for complete separation from Hungary. In the elections of 1908, the Nationalist (Unionist) Party was annihilated; the new Serbo-Croat Coalition and the Party of Pure Right, both now hostile to Hungary, dominated the new *Sabor*, taking seventy-nine out of eighty-eight seats between them. The Bán, Professor Tomašić, dissolved the assembly and held new elections, on a significantly enlarged franchise, which, however, produced an only marginally better result from the government's viewpoint; this *Sabor* went the way of its predecessor. Meanwhile, the patience of the Hungarian government had been exhausted by the opposition of Croatian Serbs to the annexation of Bosnia-Herzegovina by Austria-Hungary in 1908:* over fifty Serb politicians were accused of political incitement, of whom thirty-one, after trial in Zagreb, received prison sentences of up to twelve years. Serious allegations, widely publicised in the west European press and subsequently confirmed, that the prosecution case had been based in part on forged evidence combined with the severity of the sentences seriously to damage Hungary's reputation. Subsequent elections in Croatia produced consistently nationalist majorities—the enlarged electorate proved difficult to manipulate—and the Bán's traditional resort to repeated dissolutions of the *Sabor* brought the machinery of government in Croatia to a standstill. István Tisza brought about a reduction of tension in 1913 through concessions on finance and the retraction of the 'railway language' law. Outside the bureaucracy, however, few Croatians any longer saw the future of their nation as lying in permanent union with Hungary. Some dreamed of an independent 'Greater Croatia': more, of union with Serbia.

The Hungarian government's rearguard action against resurgent nationalism was also fought in Transylvania and most notoriously—thanks to R. W. Seton-Watson—in the Slovak region. In 1906, seventeen Romanians and eleven Slovaks received prison sentences for political activities; in the following year thirteen Romanians and thirty-three Slovaks met the same fate. To the credit of the Hungarian judiciary, which managed to maintain its independence despite the ambient political tension, the majority of sentences were relatively light, typically to two to three months' imprisonment. But the Slovaks arrested in 1906 included Father Andrej Hlinka, a Catholic priest and a member of his local municipal council; his active support of a candidate of the revived Slovak National Party, the principal demand of which was that the Nationality Act of 1868 should be implemented, earned him a prison sentence of two years. In 1907, his parishioners in the village of Csernova rioted in protest against the consecration of a new church, for which Hlinka had helped to raise the money, in their priest's absence in gaol. The situation grew out of hand, the gendarmes panicked and fifteen villagers were killed; thirty-nine more were subsequently charged with acts of violence and sentenced to prison terms of up to three years. Seton-Watson, who had 'adopted' the Slovaks as the most harassed victims of Magyarisation, secured wide publicity for the Hlinka case and for the Csernova massacre, which became the centrepiece of his book *Racial Problems in Hungary*, published in 1908. Among the many voices raised in protest against Hungarian policies towards the nationalities was that of Leo Tolstoy. There can be no question but that recollections of the Csernova killings and other well-publicised incidents in this troubled period of relations between Magyars and non-Magyars lingered in the minds of those whose task it was to be to redraw the map of central and eastern Europe in 1919. This unhappy outcome could perhaps have been averted if the Liberal Party had found it possible to grant

* See Chapter 12.

a limited degree of autonomy—perhaps similar to that accorded to Croatia in the *Nagodba*—to defined regions in which non-Magyars were in an overwhelming majority, with appropriate guarantees for the rights of the Magyars who also lived there. In particular, the establishment of a larger number of non-Magyar gymnasia—subject to the retention of the compulsory teaching of Magyar—and institutions of higher education, together with tolerance of non-Magyar cultural institutes, would have done much to reduce tensions and to channel the aspirations of the nationalities inwards, rather than outwards towards irredentist neighbours. Given the prevailing psychology of the Magyars, however, it would have taken a statesman of at least Ferenc Deák's stature to carry through such a policy; and although Dualist Hungary was well versed in the black arts of political management, statesmanship was in short supply. As a contemporary observer and historian of the period, Gusztáv Gratz, noted: '... the growth among the Magyars of an extravagant self-esteem coincided with manifestations of greater activity among the nationalities of Hungary; this created an even more glaring disparity between the fine dreams of the Magyars and bitter reality, leading inevitably to renewed clashes, and to intensified antagonism, between the Magyars and the nationalities'.[26]

Intellectual and Cultural Life

During the second half of the nineteenth century and the early years of the twentieth, as we saw in the previous chapter, Hungary progressed from defeat and subjection, through rapprochement, to compromise and finally to uneasy, faintly inglorious but increasingly prosperous partnership in the Dual Monarchy. The changes in fortune and national mood that characterised this progression were fully reflected in Hungary's culture, and above all in her poetry and literature, which flourished as never before and arguably as never since. In Hungary, from the reform era onwards, political engagement and aesthetic achievement had usually been complementary rather than mutually exclusive; poets and writers were widely read and appreciated precisely because much of their work was relevant to contemporary issues and problems.

When the War of Independence came to its tragic end in 1849, Hungarian poetry rested on the pillars of two men of genius: Mihály Vörösmarty, whose epics and lyric poems acted as a link with Hungary's deepest literary roots; and Sándor Petőfi, whose death on the battlefield assured him the status of national poet, to which his passionate lyricism in any case entitled him. Both voices had been silenced by the defeat of 1849 (although Vörösmarty, broken by the experience of life as a fugitive, lived for a further six years). Three of Petőfi's comrades in the 'Society of Ten'—János Arany, Mihály Tompa and Mór Jókai—survived the revolutionary war and its savage aftermath to create, with other writers of great talent, a remarkable revival of literary activity in Hungary. After the nightmare years of the early 1850s, during which intellectual life in Hungary was virtually extinguished and many of those writers who were not in prison emigrated, the voices of the survivors were heard once again. Arany, the tenth child of poor peasant parents in the southern Alföld, had established his reputation shortly before the revolution with an epic poem (which eventually became a trilogy), *Toldi*, which recounts the adventures of a young, impulsive aspirant to knighthood in the time of Louis the Great. Like much of Arany's work, the completed trilogy dwelt on the theme of crime—in Toldi's case, double manslaughter—and retribution; an intended second historical trilogy, of which Arany completed only the first part. 'The Death of Buda' (*Buda halála*),[27] had a similar emphasis. In the most famous of his many ballads, 'The Bards of Wales' (*A walesi bárdok*), which Arany composed for the occasion of Franz Josef's first visit to Hungary after the War of Independence, King Edward I of England is driven insane by his guilt for the massacre of the defiant Welsh bards (cf. the 'martyrs of Arad')—a none too subtle warning to Hungary's ruler:

> Let drum and fife now come to life
> And let the trumpets roar,
> To rise above that fatal curse
> That haunts me evermore!'
> But over drums and piercing fifes,
> Beyond the soldiers' hails,
> They swell the song, five hundred strong,
> Those martyred bards of Wales.[28]

Although in its content Arany's poetry reflected his anguish over Hungary's defeat, the remarkable but restrained beauty of its language and the elegance of its structure won instant acclaim and helped to restore Hungarian pride. Arany's duties as Secretary-General of the Academy of Sciences for twelve years did not constrain a prolific creativity that gave Hungary, as well as epics, lyrics and ballads, some of the best translations of Shakespeare into Magyar.

Petőfi and Arany both represented the 'populist' or 'folk' trend in Hungarian literary expression (both adjectives are inadequate translations of *népies*), which aspired to speak both for and to all the people of the land rather than simply to the educated elite; it drew on popular legend and frequently used popular rather than refined language. Mihály Tompa, the second highly talented survivor from the 'Society of Ten', belonged to the same tradition. A Calvinist minister, Tompa's despair over Hungary's defeat was leavened by determination to keep the flame of independence alive. In 'The Bird, to its Young' (*A madár, a fiaihoz*), he exhorted his fellow writers to remain in Hungary and to resume their work:

> How long, despondent birds, with silent throats
> Will you sit grieving on the withered bough?
> Have you, perchance, forgotten all the notes
> That you were taught in happier times than now?
> [...]
> Bring forth your fairest songs of recollection
> Of foliage and blossoming of yore!
> Sing of the future, and in resurrection
> This wasted soil may blossom forth once more.[29]

The response of the third survivor from Petőfi's immediate circle to Hungary's defeat and humiliation was quite different: Mór Jókai set out simply to entertain his countrymen, to divert them from the despondency of the Bach years with recollections of a romantically idealised past and visions of a better future. His medium, the short story and the novel, was a relatively new one in Hungary and he became its master. His themes were varied: the virtues of the liberal gentry of the reform era in 'A Hungarian Nabob' (*Egy magyar nábob*), the possibility of reconciliation with Hungary's Austrian neighbours in 'The New Landlord' (*Az új földesúr*), the revival of Hungarian patriotism in 'The Baron's Sons' (*A kőszívű ember fiai*) which recalled the heroism of the *Honvéd*, the unacceptable face of capitalism in 'Black Diamonds' (*Fekete gyémántok*) and modern urban man's vision of return to a simpler, more natural life in 'The Man with the Golden Touch' (*Az aranyember*). Jókai's genius as a story-teller and the skill with which his plots were constructed won him a large audience outside Hungary—internationally, he is probably Hungary's best-known writer. His output was prodigious—he died (in 1904) shortly after completing his 202nd book; and although the quality of his writing deteriorated sharply after his entry into politics in 1875, as a deputy in Tisza's ruling Liberal Party, his standing as a national figure and father of the Hungarian novel had already been assured. Until the 1867 Compromise restored Hungarian morale, however, Jókai's inventive optimism remained the exception. More typical of the times were Imre Madách, whose masterpiece 'The Tragedy of Man' (*Az ember tragédiája*) found mankind doomed from the first to an unending sequence of disasters and unavailing struggle; and Zsigmond Kemény, a Transylvanian noble whose historical novels set in his homeland were steeped in pessimism—the weight of his depression eventually drove him insane. By no means uniquely, Hungary's period of greatest national tribulation produced some of her greatest literature and poetry.

After 1867 the national mood changed, and with it the dominant trend in Hungarian writing. Instead of reflecting national grief or, in Jókai's case, trying to assuage it, Hungary's writers turned to criticism or gentle mockery of the new society created by *embourgeoisement* and Dualist politics. Realism succeeded romanticism. Kálmán Mikszáth excelled in depicting rural life and in exposing the pretensions of the impoverished gentry from which he came—'The Gentry' (*Gavallérok*), a 'long short story' describing a lavish country wedding of which every detail turns out to be based on fraud or fakery, is a classic of its kind. First-hand experience of Liberal machine politics transformed Mikszáth's gentle satire into outspoken criticism, of which 'Two Elections in Hungary' (*Két választás Magyarországon*) is a striking example. In keeping with a long Hungarian tradition, Mikszáth combined literary activity with journalism and wrote a daily, often scurrilous, column on the personalities and proceedings of Parliament. In general, however, the last quarter of the nineteenth century fell short of its predecessor in literary distinction. There were exceptions, including the lyric poetry of János Vajda and the novels of Géza Gárdonyi; but growing urbanisation and the faster pace of life in a more industrialised economy brought about changes in public taste, which turned increasingly towards the short story and the theatre. By 1900, 475 periodicals were being published in Hungary, most of them providing ample space for short-story writers. The traditionalist weekly 'New Times' (*Új Idők*) and, from its foundation in 1890, the more adventurous literary journal 'The Week' (*A Hét*) provided a forum both for established writers, among them Jókai and Mikszáth, and relative newcomers such as Sándor Bródy and Zoltán Ambrus, both of them accomplished and serious exponents of the short-story genre. Budapest had also become one of the great centres of theatre in Europe. Until the turn of the century, 'folk plays', in which the small dramas of village life were interspersed with popular folk songs and dances, constituted the staple and preferred offerings to theatre audiences. After 1900, the theatrical scene was dominated by Ferenc Molnár and his imitators; a master of stagecraft, Molnár produced a stream of romantic comedies, many of which won acclaim on the stages of western Europe and the United States. He was also a distinguished writer of short stories and novels, many of them—such as the classic 'The Paul Street Boys' (*A Pál-utcai fiúk*) and 'The Hungry City' (*Az éhes város*)—containing serious criticism of the new urban society and the deprivations of the urban poor.

In Hungary as elsewhere in western Europe, the coarsening of popular cultural taste that had marked the closing years of the nineteenth century produced a reaction, which in Hungary centred around the foundation, in 1908, of the literary journal *Nyugat* ('West'). *Nyugat's* creators—Ignotus,* Ernő Osvát and Miksa Fenyő—wished to bring Hungary into the mainstream of west European culture and *vice versa;* they encouraged young Hungarian writers and also brought to Hungarian readers the works of leading writers and thinkers from outside Hungary, sometimes before they had achieved fame in their own countries. *Nyugat* quickly became a cultural institution, though much reviled by conservatives and nationalists; during its first decade of publication, its name was inseparable from that of one of its most regular contributors, Endre Ady. In both his poetry and his prose, Ady became during his relatively short life (1877–1919) one of Hungary's greatest writers and certainly the most controversial; his original use of language and novel imagery also made him an almost uniquely difficult writer, but the raw power of his emotion invariably forced its way through the complexity of its expression. Born in eastern Hungary to Calvinist gentry parents of very limited means, Ady, after completing his studies at the local *gimnázium* at Zilah, entered the law faculty of the Collegium in Debrecen; but journalism attracted him more than the law and he left the Collegium without graduating. He soon became editor of a journal, the *Nagyváradi Napló*, in the town of Nagyvárad** and revealed both his talents as a writer and a fearlessly radical spirit. He was constantly involved in local controversy and taken to court on more than one occasion for defamation: he attacked his main targets, nationalism and clericalism—and those whom he identified as their local representatives—with unremitting ferocity. His career in Nagyvárad came to an end, not as the result of a libel action, but because he fell in love with a married lady, Adél Diósi, and followed her and her husband to Paris in 1903; in many of Ady's poems, Adél appears as Léda, the inversion of her name.

Paris captured Ady although it did not dazzle him—he was never uncritical of anything deserving of criticism; but it also heightened even further his awareness of the shortcomings of his native Hungary. As Paris correspondent of the *Budapesti Napló* he not only reported on events in Europe but also, more frequently, commented on Hungarian events and society, usually to their detriment; István Tisza was his favourite target. He nevertheless remained profoundly attached to his homeland, and above all to its language; he returned regularly to visit his mother, and the stark contrasts between rural destitution in Hungary and the vibrant cul-

* The *nom-de-plume* of Hugo Veigelsberg.
** Now Oradea, in Romania

ture of Paris were thus constantly refreshed in his mind. His national debut as a poet came in 1906, with the publication of 'New Poems' (*Új versek*); these 'new songs for new times', as their first stanza described them, created a sensation that was renewed annually between 1908 and 1914 with the publication of successive volumes of poetry. The attention that they commanded testified to the central importance of literature and of language in Hungarian life, especially when they were mobilised to serve a contemporary cause or philosophy. During these years, Ady became *Nyugat*'s star contributor. His poems gradually supplanted prose in his creative output, but were infused with the same passion and the same themes:

> When will we join at last together?
> When will our voices speak out loud?
>
> Magyar or not—it does not matter—
> We are the crushed, oppressed, and cowed.
> How long must we be ruled by blackguards,
> Poor, chicken-hearted millions, we?
> How long must the Hungarian people
> Like caged and captive starlings be?
> Hungary's miserable beggars
> We've neither bread nor faith for fare;
> But all will come to us tomorrow
> If we but wish, if we but dare![30]

Although it frequently recurred, political and social protest did not completely dominate Ady's poetry, which was as much concerned with his own personal destiny, his inner torments and passions, his relationship with God and with his premonitions of death; his self-indulgent egotism, indeed, attracted as much hostility from his contemporaries as did his alleged betrayal of his homeland. Even his severest critics, however, could not dispute the originality of his language and of his symbolism; he enlisted for his art the entirety of the Magyar language, from its earliest ecclesiastical usage, through the sixteenth and seventeenth centuries and into its eighteenth-century reinvention. His last years were clouded by a final breach with Adél—although he married a young admirer in 1915—and by the ravages that alcoholism and incompletely cured syphilis inflicted on his health. He died in Budapest at the age of forty-two. A fellow *Nyugat* contributor, the novelist Zsigmond Móricz, wrote of Ady: 'No one will ever be able to measure his impact on the entire youth of our time ... Ady was himself the focus of passions that were burning in the minds of masses; his poetry became thus the searchlight and the flamethrower ... and where his words fell the seeds of new powers were cast in the souls of men'.[31] Ady's small circle of friends included a fellow journalist, also from eastern Hungary, Gyula Krúdy. Krúdy was as innovative in the writing of prose as Ady in poetic composition. A short story writer and *feuilletoniste* of genius, Krúdy introduced the prose-poem into a language perfectly suited to the genre. He captured atmosphere, such as that of wartime Budapest in August 1917:

Oftentimes I think this city is like a cheap hotel in a back alley where the window shades are forever pulled down tight, never a loud word escapes into the night, the piano player has gone to bed long ago, the desk clerk is nodding off; but when the police raid the place they find a travelling salesman bricked into the wall, a woman choked to death by pillows, and a small child squatting in the unused summer stove. And yet, in the summertime,

Budapest asleep has a certain feminine fragrance ... I readily agreed with those painters who depicted Budapest as a female with big eyes, a Near Eastern nose, peach bloom on her neck, her feet white after her Good Friday bath; a woman who is voluptuous but hard-working, who can laugh lasciviously but who observes morality; who bestows flirtatious looks but carefully locks the front door; a woman desired by many, but rarely possessed'.[32]

Unlike Ady, Krúdy had no interest in 'abroad', nor in politics or social reform; he kept his distance from the rarefied air of *Nyugat*. A minute observer of Hungarian life, especially that of the capital, Krúdy's descriptive writing has a dream-like quality, which is mesmeric even in translation. In his most famous stories, *Szindbád*, the visitor from afar, guides the reader through a dream world that extends beyond Hungary into the Orient and beyond the present into the past, every scene painted from a palette of the most delicate colours.

The greatest treasures of Hungary's culture lay in her poetry, novels and belles-lettres, of which this study can accommodate only a very few outstanding examples. Alongside literature, music was the other great pillar of Hungary's cultural achievement. For the greater part of the nineteenth century Ferenc (Franz) Liszt, Hungarian by birth (just—Doborján was within a kilometre or two of the Austrian border and is now Raiding in Austria), joined the ranks of the great European composers, drawing inspiration for some of his works from Gypsy versions of Hungarian folk music; he made a massive contribution to pianoforte repertoire, in concertos, sonatas and études, setting at the same time new standards of virtuosity as a performer. Liszt was the first President of Budapest's Academy of Music, which had been founded in 1875. Both before and after the War of Independence, Ferenc Erkel produced a succession of operas on national themes—the musical counterparts of the historical epics of Vörösmarty, Petőfi and Arany. But the two names associated with a uniquely Hungarian musical tradition are those of Zoltán Kodály and Béla Bartók who, towards the end of the period with which this chapter is concerned, had begun to make the collections of Hungarian folk music which inspired so many of their later compositions. Like Endre Ady, they were innovators; and, again like Ady, they sought uniquely Hungarian originality in the roots of the past. 'We must isolate the very ancient', Bartók wrote, 'for this is the only way of identifying the really new'. Again like Ady, they rebelled against bourgeois philistinism. When Bartók's first opera, *Duke Bluebeard's Castle*, baffled and disconcerted the critics, he railed in a letter to Kodály against 'this Hungarian herd of cattle'; 'from now on', he continued, 'I won't bother with them'.[33] Kodály agreed: 'Let asses be asses, let us take our culture out of this country, let them drown in their merry widow and jános vitez [sic]'.*

Hungary was perhaps less rich in original talent in the visual arts than in literature and music—at least until the emergence of the avant-garde school of painting after 1910. The naturalist Mihály Munkácsy and, much later, the expressionist Tivadar Csontváry Kosztka (who was driven to insanity by unsympathetic criticism) won international reputations; but few other Hungarian artists attracted favourable attention outside their country. A number of gifted painters were nevertheless working in Hungary at the turn of the century, most of them preferring

---

* *Vitez János* was the title of a contemporary musical by Pongrác Kacsóh based on Petőfi's eponymous epic poem, less well-known than Franz Lehár's famous *The Merry Widow*.

to work in artists' colonies in the countryside, *en plein air*, rather than seeking attention in the showcase of the capital. Among them, József Rippl-Rónai, János Vaszary and Károly Ferenczi shared a determination to break away from the sentimental romanticism of which Munkácsy had been the leading exponent. Against the background of the contemporary countryside, their realism led inevitably to a generally pessimistic mood, often movingly conveyed; their landscapes tended to portray the death of nature more than its rebirth. They shared with Endre Ady, Gyula Krúdy, Béla Bartók and Zoltán Kodály the desire to distil the essence of Hungary and to give it artistic expression.

In the wider context of intellectual activity, the last years of the nineteenth century and the first years of the twentieth were marked, despite the unpromising political backdrop, by a remarkable upsurge of achievement in the natural and social sciences. Loránd Eötvös (son of József) held the Presidency of the Academy of Sciences for much of the period and, while Professor of Physics at Budapest University (which now bears his name), invented the torsion pendulum that played an important role in Einstein's subsequent work on relativity; his tenure of the Education portfolio in Sándor Wekerle's ministry was short but distinguished. Hungarian scientists and engineers were establishing new frontiers in numerous branches of scientific endeavour: Tivadar Puskás, who invented the telephone exchange, in electronics; Theodor von Kármán in aeronautics; Sándor Ferenczi and Lipót Szondi in psychology; György Lukács in philosophy; and Oszkár Jászi, founder in 1910 of the Citizens' Radical Party, in sociology. The foundation of the Society of Social Sciences (*Társadalomtudományi Társaság*, generally known as 'TT') and its journal 'Twentieth Century' (*Huszadik Század*) provided a focus for intellectual creativity in all fields; the society organised extra-mural adult education classes in Budapest which, although they did not attract a large following, played some part in the development of the Hungarian social democratic movement. The educational pyramid that supported this pinnacle of academic achievement had by 1914 become broader and more substantial: four new universities—at Debrecen, Pozsony (Bratislava), Kolozsvár (Cluj) and the Technical University in Budapest—complemented Budapest University and were attended by 13,000 students. In 1895, Loránd Eötvös had established a college, bearing his father's name, modelled on the École Normale Supérieure in Paris, which became a focal point for Hungary's intellectual élite in the humanities and social sciences. Illiteracy had been reduced from 68 per cent of the population in 1870 to only 33 per cent in 1917; attendance in secondary education had more than doubled during the same period (1870–1914). Thanks to the efforts of a succession of talented Ministers of Education—as well as József and Loránd Eötvös, Antal Csengery, Ágost Trefort and Albin Csáky made important contributions—public education at all levels matched or surpassed western European standards by 1890. The gymnasia, in particular, offering a rigorous curriculum in classics, mathematics, literature and history, attracted teachers of the highest quality and helped to develop many of the minds that gave Hungary such intellectual distinction—and eleven Nobel Prizes—in the twentieth century. Although, therefore, her politics and society remained sadly flawed, the quality of Hungary's cultural and intellectual life now entitled her, at the turn of the century, to be considered on terms of equality with most other European nations. Given the unpromising condition of the country only sixty years before, this was a remarkable development.

A Modern European Capital

Hungary could also claim to match or surpass most other European countries in the size and elegance of her capital city. As John Lukács noted in his brilliant and evocative 'historical portrait' of Budapest at the turn of the century:

Foreign visitors arriving in that unknown portion of Europe, east of Vienna, were astounded to find a modern city with first-class hotels, plate-glass windows, electric tram-cars, elegant men and women, the largest Parliament building in the world about to be completed.[34]

On 22 December 1872, Franz Joseph had sanctioned laws formalising the union of the cities of Pest and Buda to create the capital city of Hungary, Budapest (the town of Óbuda had already been merged with Buda in 1849); and establishing a new united municipal authority. The Budapest City Council held its first meeting, in the Vigadó on the Pest embankment, on 25 October 1873. The council was responsible to a Municipal Assembly of 400 members, of whom half were elected by enfranchised citizens and half selected by the city's 1,200 highest tax–payers from among their number; this curious arrangement was actually more progressive than it looked, since it enabled the Assembly to be leavened with members from outside the classic Liberal establishment—bringing in, for example, Jewish bankers and factory-owners. The Assembly in turn elected, from a list of three candidates approved by the King, a Lord Mayor, whose role as government representative was not dissimilar from that of the Palatine in pre-Dualist Hungary; a Mayor, the city's chief executive officer; and two Deputy Mayors to assist him. The City Council itself, an executive body, consisted of the leading officials of the municipality. Each of the city's nine districts elected its own District Chairman and Council. Budapest was fortunate in its choice of Mayors and the Assembly sensible enough to allow them, by re-election, long terms of office: the capital's first Mayor, Károly Kamermayer, remained in office for twenty-three years from 1873 and his most distinguished successor, István Bárczy, for twelve years from 1906. Both were men of outstanding administrative ability; given Budapest's extraordinary rate of growth, they needed to be. In 1869, the combined population of Pest and Buda had reached 280,249—an increase of over 62 per cent since 1850. By 1900, Budapest was home to 717,681 inhabitants and by 1913 to 930,666. By 1910, Budapest had become the eighth largest city in Europe, with a rate of population growth matched only by Berlin. Immigration, both from the Hungarian countryside and from other Habsburg lands, accounted for most of the increase; internal migration was driven partly by higher levels of wages in the capital than elsewhere and also by the demand for female labour, particularly in domestic service—in 1900 there were 1071 women in Budapest for every thousand men. At 5 per cent of the country's total, the population of Budapest was not disproportionately large; but at 9 per cent of the total, the remainder of Hungary's urban population, strictly defined, was disproportionately small, a telling comment on the unevenness of her economic and social development. Budapest claimed 18 per cent of the industrial workers of the country and 28 per cent of her factory workers.

Three-quarters of Budapest's working population were employed in industry and trade, a tenth in the government and municipal bureaucracy; the remainder were divided between various other 'white-collar' occupations and domestic service. By the turn of the century, Budapest had already developed clearly defined industrial districts: heavy industry in the north, along the Vác highway (where much of it still is today); food processing and milling in the south, close to the Danube quays; locomotive, rolling stock and machine tool manufacture in Kőbánya to the east; shipbuilding, textiles and tobacco processing in Óbuda, to the north west. From the 1860s until 1900, when Minneapolis overtook her, Budapest had been the largest milling centre in the world, a position she owed both to advanced engineering and to the city's excellent access to transportation. By 1900, Budapest had become, by a handsome margin, the largest port on the 2,000–mile length of the Danube; eleven railway lines converged on the capital, carrying 275 million tonnes of freight annually. A rapidly expanding suburban rail network (the *HÉV*) carried workers from the outlying districts to the mills and factories; by 1900, the public transport system as a whole was being used by 200,000 passengers a day. Conditions in the working-class dormitory districts, however, remained dire until well into the twentieth century. Particularly to the north and east, Pest was ringed by a virtual shanty town in which long, single-storey barrack-like buildings were the most permanent structures; streets were unpaved, drainage and water supply primitive in the extreme. Although by 1890 67 per cent of the residential accommodation in Budapest enjoyed the benefit of piped running water, communal sanitation remained the norm in workers' dwellings for many years more. An ambitious municipal housing programme made a considerable impact on the problem—under Mayor Bárczy, 4,816 new apartments were built between 1909 and 1913—but could not keep pace with the rate of population increase. Beyond the dormitories and shacks, the capital was served by an outer ring of market gardens and vineyards, populated and worked largely by migrant peasants from the countryside; far from being submerged by metropolitan sprawl, this agricultural ring actually increased in size as the capital grew—vineyards within the municipal boundary covered 355 acres in 1900 and 401 acres ten years later. Produce from the capital's hinterland and from further afield stocked five covered markets, including the Great Market Hall (*Nagyvásárcsarnok*)—recently (in 1996) restored to its former splendour.

This was the infrastructure of a city growing into one of the most imposing and elegant capitals in Europe. Its architectural profile benefited from exceptionally rigorous and strictly enforced building regulations, which had been introduced after the disastrous floods of 1838 and were regularly updated. By the year of the Compromise, Budapest already possessed a number of distinguished public buildings, including the Academy of Sciences, the Vigadó and the huge synagogue on Dohány Street; a tunnel had been constructed under Buda's Castle Hill to complete the east-west transport axis that Széchenyi's Chain Bridge had begun. After 1867, the Prime Minister, Gyula Andrássy, convened a commission to advise on the future development of the capital. This produced two important results: the creation of a Municipal Public Works Council (*Közmunkatanács*), modelled on London's Metropolitan Board of Works, and a project for the construction of a two and a half-kilometre long boulevard, inspired by the Champs Elysées in Paris, to link the City Park (*Városliget*) with the city's heart. This boulevard, initially christened Sugár Avenue and subsequently renamed Andrássy Avenue, was completed in 1884. From 1870 onwards the Public Works Council, under the energetic chairmanship of Baron Frigyes Podmaniczky, put out to tender a number of major architectural and construction projects that transformed the face of the capital. The Great Ring (*Nagykörút*) described an arc around central Pest, linking the radial spokes of what are now Andrássy, Rákóczi and Üllői Avenues. The Margaret Bridge (1876), Franz Josef Bridge (1896) and Elizabeth Bridge (1903) relieved the over-burdened Chain Bridge. The first green—later yellow—electric trams plied the Great Ring in 1887, the beginning of an extensive network; a funicular from the Buda embankment to the top of Castle Hill had been operating since 1870 and a cogwheel railway up into the hills on the Buda side since 1874. Architecturally, neo-Classicism and neo-Baroque predominated, leavened by Ödön Lechner's 'secessionism', a rather self-conscious Hungarian variant on Art Nouveau, which characterised the new buildings of the Gresham Insurance Company, the Postal Savings Bank, the Geological Institute and the Museum of Applied Art. One of the most successful products of these years of public building boom was undoubtedly Miklós Ybl's Opera House, which opened its doors on Andrássy Avenue in 1884.

An occasional disproportion as between scale and function could be observed. The vast Royal Palace, of which the rebuilding and extension were completed in 1905, very rarely housed the Monarch; the new Parliament Building, completed in 1902, had the distinction at the time of being the largest in the world but housed deputies elected on one of Europe's narrower franchises; and the volume of business carried on in the Budapest Stock Exchange hardly justified its status as the largest exchange building in Europe. All three buildings could be seen as expressions of confidence in the future rather than reflections of present attainment. In 1892, the twenty-fifth anniversary of Franz Josef's coronation, Budapest had been granted the status of 'capital and royal seat' (*székesfőváros*); the view that the Monarch should invest this title with reality by transferring the Monarchy's centre of gravity from Vienna to Budapest was not confined to the city fathers. The vast neo-Gothic Parliament Building asserted the permanence of Hungary's political autonomy and her determination to preserve it. The Stock Exchange proclaimed the confidence of Hungary's captains of finance and industry that the upward trajectory of the country's economy would be maintained and that Budapest would surpass Vienna as the focus of investment in central Europe.

This mood of patriotic self-confidence, sometimes manifested in assertions of Magyar superiority and frequently shading into hubris, found its ideal expression in the Millennial Exhibition and celebrations of 1896—the thousandth anniversary of the 'conquest' of the Carpathian Basin by Árpád's Magyar tribes. On 8 June, a vast ceremonial procession, 1,700 horsemen strong, paraded before Franz Josef and his consort Elisabeth, ever popular in Hungary, on Castle Hill and then escorted the royal pair across the Margaret Bridge to the new Parliament Building, of which enough had been finished to accommodate the inaugural ceremony. The Monarch wore the uniform of Colonel in Chief of Hussars; the nobility perspired under every scrap of ceremonial dress and ornament it could muster. The Holy Crown was unearthed from its vault and displayed in the Parliament's central hall. On the Buda side, roasting oxen revolved on spits in the Vérmező

Park, the centrepiece of a mass picnic; in Pest, a huge fair and exhibition engulfed the Városliget, part of which was (and still is) filled by a scaled-down replica of a Transylvanian castle, Vajdahunyad, which served as a showcase for historic Hungarian architectural styles. Franz Josef conducted an endless series of opening ceremonies: the Gallery of Fine Arts, the Museum of Applied Arts, the Palace of Justice, the bridge that bore his name and, not least, the European continent's first underground railway which ran (as it still does) the length of Andrássy Avenue, from what is now Vörösmarty Square to the City Park. A Millennial Monument at the park end of the avenue had been commissioned by Parliament but, for a number of reasons, took twenty-three years to complete.* At the Millennial Exhibition, Hungarians saw their first (French) cine-newsreel; and a film recording Franz Josef's visit inaugurated the development of Hungary's own film industry, which had a remarkable future before it.

One of the best Hungarian histories of the period, by Gusztáv Gratz—a founding member of 'TT' and later a minister in two governments—contains this perceptive passage:

[The Magyars] were better at knowing what was desirable than what was practical; they tended to regard as real that which they only yearned for. They willingly surrendered themselves to that optimistic view of the facts which appeared to support their secret hopes and wishes and equally willingly closed their minds to those uncomfortable perceptions which could disperse the misty clouds of their illusions ... The Magyars erected towering structures from their hopes and longings without conducting a careful appraisal of their foundations.... They became ever less able to discern the dangers which threatened their existence; and if they did discern them, they turned with a shrug to other matters, in order thereafter quietly to continue weaving their web of dreams.[35]

The effulgence of Budapest encouraged this collective state of mind. In the heady, triumphalist atmosphere of the capital, aspiration was all too easily mistaken for achievement. Celebration of the distance Hungary had undoubtedly travelled since 1849 tended to obscure from view the great distance that remained to be covered if self-image was to be matched by reality. The new splendour of the capital, with its boulevards and newly widened streets lined with elegant and imposing buildings, both public and private; its vibrant intellectual and cultural life, reflected in the theatres, concert halls and cabarets, pulsing through six hundred coffee houses and expressed in over twenty newspapers—including Hungary's first tabloid, 'Evening' (*Az Est*); the declamatory rhetoric of a Parliament obsessed with national *amour propre*—all this diverted attention from the problems and tensions of a country the capital had in many ways outgrown. Unrest in the countryside and frustration among the nationalities seemed distant from the bustle and elegance of a flourishing capital city. So absorbing were events on the metropolitan stage that neither actors nor audience were eager to concern themselves with what might be happening outside the theatre, beyond the municipal boundaries—much less with developments, however ominous, beyond the frontiers of Hungary.

---

* The monument consists of a colonnade of symbolic and historical statuary curving round the eastern edge of a large square (Heroes' Square), in the centre of which stands a tall column surmounted by a statue of the Archangel Gabriel; around its foot cluster equestrian statues of Árpád and his fellow Magyar chieftains.

12

WAR AND REVOLUTION

(1906–19)

The Last Years of Peace (1906–14)

With hindsight, the period of eight years before the outbreak of the First World War can be identified as Hungary's last opportunity to begin, at least, to resolve the problems of ethnic discord and social backwardness that were slowly corroding the integrity of the kingdom. The opportunity was largely wasted, both by Wekerle's Coalition government and by the administration under István Tisza that succeeded it in 1910. The Coalition produced a few useful measures of social reform, including the extension and centralisation of health insurance and the introduction of compulsory accident insurance for industrial workers; but overdue reforms in the crucial area of rural labour, including a ban (in 1907!) on the corporal punishment of adult labourers, were offset by harsh sanctions against strike action by agricultural workers and a guarantee to landowners that the army would be used to suppress labour unrest. A derisory gesture towards electoral reform, introduced by Gyula Andrássy (jnr.) in 1908 in token fulfillment of the government's pledge to Franz Joseph,* was nevertheless more than his coalition partners from the Independence Party were prepared to swallow and he was obliged to withdraw it: the franchise remained frozen until 1913. The policies of the Coalition towards the nationalities were, if anything, more repressive than those of previous Liberal governments. Albert Apponyi's discriminatory Education Act of 1907, the notorious—if well-intentioned—Lex Apponyi, has already been mentioned;** the tally of arrests and prison sentences among the national minorities for alleged agitation against the state remained high. Since the parties represented in the Wekerle cabinet had little in common except their opposition to the now defunct Liberal Party, the break-up of the Coalition was only a matter of time. The final rupture occurred over the issue of the common National Bank, the charter of which was due to expire in 1910. The radical wing of the Independence Party, led by Gyula Justh, demanded an end to this legacy of the 1867 Com-

---

* See page 250.
** On page 266.

promise and the creation of an independent Hungarian National Bank: Ferenc Kossuth and Albert Apponyi opposed this attempt to erode the fabric of the Compromise and argued that Hungary, as the weaker economic component of the Dual Monarchy, gained more than she lost from partnership in a common Bank. Justh led his faction of the Independence Party out of the Coalition, which thereupon collapsed.

Hobbled by its secret compact with Franz Josef and by its internal differences, the Coalition had provided woefully ineffectual government. Partly in reaction to this, the Coalition years were marked by the birth of new political parties. Already in 1906, András Achim, a farmer from Békéscsaba in the perennially turbulent eastern region of Hungary, had founded the Independent Socialist Peasant Party, standing for land reform, universal suffrage and measures to protect small farmers and agricultural labourers. The following year saw the creation of the Christian Socialist Party, to give a political voice to the more right-wing trade unions that opposed class struggle and internationalism but also capitalism and the financial pre-eminence of the Jews. The Social Democratic Party restructured itself as the '48 Social Democratic Party. Of greater significance was the foundation in 1909, by István Nagyatádi Szabó, a well-to-do peasant farmer from Somogy county, of the '48 and Independence National Farmers' Party, to be known more succinctly as the Smallholders' Party (*Kisgazdapárt*); this stood for universal suffrage, a secret ballot and the sale or lease of land from the great estates to competent peasants with holdings too small to be viable. In the continuing absence of meaningful electoral reform, the emergence of new parties intended to defend or promote the interests of sectors of the population yet to be enfranchised had little direct political significance; but they did betoken a rising level both of political con-sciousness and of frustration with the status quo, of which the existing political establishment would have done well to take note. Of much greater immediate importance was István Tisza's creation, early in 1910, of the National Party of Work (*Nemzeti Munkapárt*):[1] this brought together members of both the old Lib-eral Party (dissolved by Tisza in 1906) and the Constitution Party (which Andrássy had just dissolved in order to leave its members free to join Tisza).

Since István Tisza was to dominate Hungarian politics, both in and out of office, for the remainder of the life of the Dual Monarchy, his beliefs and person-ality deserve more attention than they were accorded in an earlier chapter of this book.* What István Tisza lacked in the subtlety that had made his father such a skilful party manager, he more than made up in force of character and strength of purpose. His policies stemmed from two deep convictions, from which he never deviated and which he never compromised. The first was his belief in the mission of the Magyar nobility, both aristocracy and gentry, to lead the nation, preserving both its unity and its Magyar character. This belief determined his resolute oppo-sition both to any significant extension of the electoral franchise and to political, as distinct from cultural, concessions to the nationalities. His attitude towards the peasantry, informed by his experience of managing his estate at Geszt in Bihar county, was kindly and patriarchal: they were children, whom the nobility had a duty to protect from evil influences. Peasants, he wrote in 1912, were 'incapable

* See page 248.

of exercising their political rights, unreliable from the standpoint of national unity, enlightenment and human progress, and easy targets for non-Hungarian national, as well as clerical or agrarian demagogy'.[2] His view of the nationalities, too, was essentially benevolent but patronising: their loyalty to the Magyar state, which alone could protect their best interests, must be secured by force of example on the part of Magyar people, not by oppression. Drawing again on his experience of rural society in Bihar county, Tisza was convinced that the relatively peaceable relationship that prevailed there between Magyar and Romanian could be replicated in all regions with significant national minorities. He opposed both excesses of Magyar chauvinism and minority nationalist agitation with equal strength.

Tisza's second core conviction was that Hungary's vulnerability and relative weakness made preservation of the Compromise and of the institutions of Dualism, including the common army, her foremost national interest. As a young Deputy, he told the Lower House in 1892: 'This small nation is placed at what is perhaps the most exposed spot in Europe, in the path of immense danger and the ambition of great powers. This small nation has had to defend civilisation and freedom against Islam throughout centuries, and it now confronts the same task against Slav absolutism, threatening the culture of all Europe'.[3]

Tisza fought with fierce determination any influence or tendency that might weaken either the unity of the Hungarian Kingdom or its status as an equal partner in the Dual Monarchy. His concern for Hungary's survival inclined him towards caution rather than assertiveness in dealings with her neighbours—his only area of agreement with the heir to the throne, Franz Ferdinand, who detested all Hungarians but the Calvinist, nationalist Tisza more than any.[4]

Károly Khuen-Héderváry, whom the Monarch had recalled to the premiership following Wekerle's resignation, formed a caretaker cabinet and dissolved Parliament. In the elections that followed, in June 1910—elections which, as it turned out, determined the composition of the Hungarian Parliament for the remainder of its existence within the Dual Monarchy—Tisza led his new Party of Work to an electoral triumph, winning 256 seats out of 413. Since the Prime Minister remained in office at the sovereign's pleasure, Khuen-Héderváry nevertheless continued to serve, with a small cabinet of bureaucrats, supported in the Lower House by Tisza and his new majority. A new Army Bill, increasing Hungary's recruitment quota by 40,000 men and military expenditure (mainly on the navy) by 50 per cent, almost immediately plunged Parliament into a rerun of the 1903/04 crisis. As before, Andrássy and Apponyi attached a political price tag to approval of the bill, demanding Magyar words of command in Hungarian regiments of the common army and equality of Hungarian with Austrian flags and symbols. Other opponents of the bill argued that the projected increase in naval expenditure was designed only to reinforce the hegemony of the Monarchy's German ally. István Tisza, in vigorous support for the bill, defended both the expansion of the common army and the German alliance without which, he argued, the burden of military expenditure would be even greater.

Tisza argued in vain. Resorting to its old tactic of filibuster and procedural obstruction, the opposition, reunited by the crisis, staved off passage of the bill for over a year. Khuen-Héderváry, in despair, twice resigned during this period, eventually to be replaced in the premiership by László Lukács in April 1912. Two successive Speakers of the Lower House having also succumbed to the frustrations of trying to bring order to a bearpit, Tisza engineered his own election to that office, determined both to save the military security of the Monarchy and to salvage the reputation of Parliament. Such was Tisza's unpopularity on the streets, however, that his election immediately triggered the largest demonstration by urban workers Budapest had yet experienced. On 23 May, another 'Bloody Thursday', demonstrators demanding universal suffrage and an end to 'class rule' clashed with police and troops in the capital: six of their number were killed and 182 wounded. Over three hundred arrests were made. Undeterred, Tisza forced the Army Bill through the Lower House on 4 June by refusing to recognise opposition speakers and suspending further debate. On the following day, having survived an attempt by an enraged opposition Deputy to shoot him (the would-be assassin's shots missed Tisza and wounded only himself), Tisza expelled leading obstructors from the chamber, formed a 'parliamentary guard' to enforce the Speaker's rulings and reintroduced the rules of procedure that he had tricked the House into approving in 1904 but which the Coalition government had in the meantime revoked. When the opposition declared a parliamentary boycott, Tisza took advantage of the opportunity to secure the passage of emergency legislation for implementation in the event of war. This provided for government censorship, severe constraints on trial by jury, and the appointment of government commissioners to take over local administration from the elected county authorities.

The conduct of the opposition parties had provided abundant justification for firm action by the Speaker. Against the background of a volatile and threatening international situation, the Hungarian Parliament had already delayed by a year measures unquestionably essential to the security of Austria-Hungary, of all the Great Powers the least well prepared for war. As one Deputy recalled:

Until the outbreak of the world war, we carried on with politicking as if we had lived on an island in the middle of the Pacific Ocean. Very few people could see beyond Vienna. There was a great deal of incredible naiveté in judging foreign affairs and, while global military preparations increased and tension among European powers grew, we considered it a great national victory if we could slow down or obstruct the Monarchy's armament.[5]

István Tisza's methods, however, although they achieved their immediate objective, inflicted permanent damage on both the health, already frail, and the reputation of the parliamentary process in Hungary. Procedural improvements could achieve only so much: what the Hungarian Parliament needed was a complete change of culture, a shift of priorities away from constitutional sparring with Vienna and towards the improvement of the conditions of daily life for the Hungarian people. Only radical electoral reform could have brought this about, reform to which Tisza—despite occasional prods from Franz Josef—remained adamantly opposed. The Lukács government took a small step in the right direction in 1913, when Parliament and the Monarch approved a bill that enlarged the electorate by enfranchising self-employed men of thirty and over with elementary education and others who satisfied various property qualifications. The introduction, in the same bill, of the secret ballot in municipal constituencies reflected Tisza's belief that the urban artisan was less likely than the peasant to be led astray by agitators. Since the outbreak of war in 1914, and subsequent internal developments, prevented the reform from being put to the test in an election, it is difficult to calculate the degree of change it was intended to bring about. According to one estimate, based on the census of 1914, the bill would have given the vote to an additional 0.4 per cent of the population. Other calculations are more optimistic.[6] It is, however, beyond doubt that the projected effect of the reform would have been insignificant and intentionally so; even Lukács's Minister of Justice felt obliged to resign in protest. For so long as the Lower House represented only a small fraction of the population and mostly comprised representatives of only one social stratum, the real problems of the country—the frustrated aspirations of the nationalities and the deprivations of the peasantry—would remain neglected and the future of the nation, therefore, clouded.

Two further events defined the two poles of Hungarian politics for the remaining five years of Dualism. István Tisza decided that Parliament had been sufficiently tamed to make it possible for him to leave the Speaker's chair; when Lukács resigned in June 1913, amid allegations of financial impropriety, Tisza bowed to Franz Josef's will and took over as Prime Minister. Impressed by Tisza's handling of the Army Bill, the ageing monarch believed that he had at last found a Hungarian politician he could trust; the relationship of mutual confidence that now developed between the two men became important for Hungary. Less than a year after Tisza's appointment, and following the death of Gyula Justh, the two factions of the Independence Party came together as the 'United Independence and 1848 Party', under the leadership of Count Mihály Károlyi. Károlyi had been elected to the Lower House in 1910, bringing with him qualities in which the political establishment of his time was notably deficient: a social conscience and moral courage. Born into the second richest land-owning family in Hungary, Károlyi as a young man demonstrated both keen intelligence and intellectual curiosity, as well as a taste for high living and reckless extravagance. His uncle Sándor, an unorthodox magnate who founded the agricultural co-operative movement, introduced Károlyi to the works of Marx and these made a profound impression on him. He travelled widely in Europe, meeting a number of trade unionists and left-wing intellectuals—including Sidney and Beatrice Webb—and visited the United States. When he entered the Lower House in 1910 as a member of the Independence Party, he already had much more knowledge and experience of the world beyond Hungary's borders than most of his political contemporaries and certainly more than István Tisza, whose leading opponent he soon became. The two men actually fought a duel in 1912, after Károlyi, angered by the forced passage of the Army Bill, had insulted Tisza and provoked a challenge; the fight was stopped when Károlyi sustained the first cut, but no reconciliation followed.

István Tisza's appointment to the premiership brought with it *ex officio* membership of the Common Ministerial Council, the small group which, under the sovereign's chairmanship, had become and remained the key policy-making body of the Austro-Hungarian Monarchy. Besides the Prime Ministers of Austria and Hungary, the council included the three Common Ministers—for Foreign Affairs, War and Finance—and, usually, the chiefs of staff of the common army and navy. Tisza thus became directly involved, for the first time, in foreign policy and strategic issues, at a time of rising tension in Europe. Tisza was ill-prepared for this new responsibility but keenly aware of its importance. Hungary, he declared in his inaugural speech as Prime Minister, had been thrown on to the scales of world history and her weight could determine the world's fate.

Hungary's reappearance on the international stage, for the first time since 1848/49—or, arguably, since Transylvania's exploits in the seventeenth century— makes it necessary to clarify the limits of this narrative. It cannot, for example, accommodate an analysis of the causes of the First World War, on which there is already a vast literature.[7] The course of the First World War itself and the campaigns on the eastern, Balkan and Italian fronts in which Hungarian soldiers fought and died can, equally, be accorded only sparing attention. And although the war made Hungary and Austria more than ever mutually dependent and the internal affairs of each state more relevant to the other, specifically Austrian developments must continue to be beyond the scope of this volume. Unless this account remains firmly rooted in Hungary, it will risk losing its way and taxing the patience of the reader. It will therefore concentrate on directly Hungarian contributions to the course of events and on the direct impact of those events on Hungarian politics and society. A brief résumé of events in central and southern Europe after 1906 is none the less essential even to this limited purpose.

Baron Lexa von Aehrenthal, who became the Dual Monarchy's Foreign Minister in 1906, brought with him from his previous post as Ambassador in Saint Petersburg a belief in the desirability of agreement with Russia on recognised spheres of influence in the Balkans; and the conviction that the Monarchy should pursue a more active foreign policy if its prestige was to keep pace with that of the Russian and German Empires. Aehrenthal therefore seized with alacrity upon an off-the-cuff suggestion by the Russian Foreign Minister, Izvolsky, in July 1908, that if Austria-Hungary were to support a revision of the Straits regime that prevented the passage of Russian warships through the Dardanelles, Russia would support the annexation of Bosnia-Herzegovina—the Turkish provinces that the Congress of Berlin had authorised the Monarchy to occupy but not annex.* Annexation, Aehrenthal perceived, would consolidate the Austro-Hungarian position in the Balkans, make possible the full integration of Bosnia-Herzegovina into the Monarchy with the concomitant benefits of a constitution and enlightened administration, and serve to warn off neighbouring Serbia, already seething with hostility towards the Monarchy over a tariff war, ostensibly designed to protect Hungarian pig and cattle farmers but in fact intended to strangle Serbia's military procurement programme. After a further discussion with Izvolsky, still conducted in very general terms, Aehrenthal therefore went ahead, in October, with his side of the projected bargain, giving Russia and the other Berlin Treaty powers only forty-eight hours' notice of the annexation; this left Izvolsky humiliated, infuriated and empty-handed. The Monarchy's allies, Germany and Italy, resented Aehrenthal's high-handed behaviour; Britain and France reacted with anger and suspicion; Serbia was enraged and Serbian nationalism greatly inflamed. Despite privately expressed misgivings, the German Emperor nevertheless made clear his unconditional backing for Austria-Hungary, thereby forcing Russia to back down and putting the Monarchy permanently in his debt. Aehrenthal's supposed coup finally buried the ever-fragile Austro-Russian Entente and put the Monarchy's

---

* See page 239.

relations with Serbia beyond repair; it also condemned the Monarchy to client status in relation to its German guarantor. The subsequent appointment of the pan–Slav, anti–Habsburg Baron Hartwig to be Russian Minister in Belgrade; the foundation of the Serbian nationalist organisation *Narodna Odbrana* ('National Defence'); the formation in 1911, by a group of extremist members of *Narodna Odbrana*, of the semi–secret terrorist group *Ujedinjenje Ili Smrt* ('Union or Death'), otherwise known as the *Černa Ruka* ('Black Hand'); and, finally, the brokering by Russia of a military alliance between Serbia, Bulgaria and Greece—the Balkan League—all combined to eliminate any possibility of a peaceful consolidation of Austro-Hungarian influence in the Balkans.

In October 1912, the small Balkan kingdom of Montenegro, having first joined the Balkan League, launched the First Balkan War with an attack on Turkey, in which she was quickly joined by her three new allies. By the spring of 1913, the League had achieved a striking victory: Greece had occupied Salonika, Bulgaria had grabbed Adrianople, while Serbia had at last secured a maritime outlet by seizing the port of Durazzo in newly independent Albania on the Adriatic coast, as well as doubling her territory and population by occupying large swathes of land hitherto occupied by Turkey. Confident and flushed with success, Serbia lost no time in persuading Greece, and later Romania, to join her in turning on her recent ally, Bulgaria. In an effort to avoid war on two fronts, Bulgaria struck first; but when Romania, having characteristically waited to make sure that she would be joining the winning side, stabbed her neighbour from the north, Bulgaria went down to defeat. The Treaty of Bucharest, which ended this Second Balkan War, rewarded Greece with Kavalla and Crete, Romania with Silistria on the Black Sea coast and Serbia with a substantial slice of Macedonia. Throughout the nine months of Balkan war, the Monarchy had been able to exercise virtually no influence on the course of events in its own backyard, apart from securing international recognition for the independent state of Albania which, it was hoped, would constitute a barrier to Serbian expansion westwards; even there, however, Serbian troops remained in defiant occupation. Serbia had grown powerful and arrogant. Terrorist activity by the 'Black Hand' and agitation by 'National Defence' in Bosnia-Herzegovina had increased to an alarming level. Germany, by giving demonstrative approval to the Treaty of Bucharest, had shown callous indifference to the Monarchy's worries over Serbian expansion. This was the situation when István Tisza, two months into his premiership, began to take an active interest in the Monarchy's external relations.

Tisza's two immediate predecessors had adopted a generally cautious approach in foreign policy matters. Wekerle had expressed strong reservations over the annexation of Bosnia-Herzegovina in 1908; both his Coalition government and its Party of Work successor under Lukács did their best to block significant expenditure on the Monarchy's new province. In the wake of the First Balkan War, when the Austrian military led by the redoubtable chief of staff, Baron Conrad von Hötzendorff, were pressing strongly for a preventive war against Serbia and for Serbia's annexation to the Monarchy, Lukács voiced the traditional Hungarian opposition to any increase in the Monarchy's Slav population: 'If [this] proposal is realised, the result will be trialism. The Slavs would be in the majority, which would mean the end of Dualism'.[8] Tisza strongly shared this view. The other fixed point in his approach to foreign policy was his unshakeable belief in the importance to Hungary of the Monarchy's alliance with Germany. 'It is the Hungarian nation', he wrote in 1912, 'that supports our intimate alliance with the German Empire, more directly perhaps than even the Austrian Germans. This is the cornerstone of our entire policy; we remain true to and proclaim the endur-ing principle … that the Hungarian nation must carry out its historic mission shoulder to shoulder with the great German nation in true political solidarity'.[9]

From his temporary retirement, Tisza had supported the annexation of Bosnia-Herzegovina in 1908. In office in 1913, he called for a tough line against Serbia's refusal to respect Albania's borders or to quit the port of Durazzo, affirming in a letter to Count Berchtold (who had succeeded Aehrenthal as the Monarchy's Foreign Minister in 1912) that the Albanian issue would show whether Austria-Hungary was still a viable power or whether the Monarchy had fallen into 'laugh-able decadence'.[10] Tisza supported Berchtold's ultimatum to Belgrade, which brought about Serbia's withdrawal from Durazzo and Albania in October 1913, but opposed Conrad's renewed call for Serbia's annexation. The views Tisza expressed on foreign policy in the Common Ministerial Council often owed a good deal to the influence of Baron István Burián, an experienced diplomat and former common Finance Minister, whom Tisza, on taking over as Prime Minister, had appointed to be his adviser on foreign affairs and Hungary's 'Minister at the King's Side'. Burián, for example, was probably behind the hare-brained scheme Tisza promoted, unsuccessfully, in 1913 for joining Russia in military action against Turkey, in return for Russian help in cutting Serbia down to size. As he became more experienced in external issues, however, Tisza increasingly made his own judgements.

The crisis years of 1913 and 1914 found the Triple Alliance in less than perfect health. Austria-Hungary, though entirely loyal to the Alliance, chafed against Ger-man indifference to her Balkan concerns. Italy's loyalty had become increasingly suspect as she worried over the vulnerability of her ports and coastline to British naval power. But of most concern to Tisza, and to Hungarian interests, was the position of the Triple Alliance's secret partner, Romania. King Carol, while refus-ing to strengthen Romania's commitment to the Alliance by making it public, endeavoured to use it as a lever with which to extract concessions for the Roma-nian minority in Hungary, and particularly in Transylvania. There was lively con-cern in both Vienna and Berlin that Budapest's perceived intransigence on the nationality question might cost them an ally which, although of uncertain fibre, would be of key strategic importance in the event of war with Russia. In an attempt to ensure that Romania remained on board, Berchtold despatched a heavyweight envoy to Bucharest in the person of Count Czernin, a protégé of Franz Ferdinand who was tipped to become Foreign Minister when the heir-apparent succeeded Franz Josef. Tisza reluctantly approved Czernin's appointment, despite his reputation for being anti–Magyar, on condition that he made no attempt to interfere in Hungarian affairs; Tisza also undertook to negotiate a com-promise arrangement with the leaders of the Romanian minority. He did, indeed, make the attempt, in discussions with the Romanian nationalist leaders Teodor Mihály and Iuliu Maniu; but concessions in the educational and religious fields, even the promise of increased Romanian representation in the Lower House, fell far short of the aspiration of the Romanian leaders for significant political auton-omy. Their hopes were in any case centred on the eventual accession to the throne of Franz Ferdinand, whom they knew to be sympathetic to their cause.[11] With Tisza's comment that 'the Magyar stomach cannot digest' the Romanian demands, the negotiations lapsed. In March 1914, Tisza attempted to bypass the Romanian nationality issue by arguing, in a memorandum addressed to Franz Josef and Ber-chtold, that it would be in the interests of Germany, as well as in those of the Monarchy, to make Bulgaria their principal Balkan ally, both to isolate Serbia and to check the vacillations and importunities of Romania, where Czernin had made little or no progress. He was able to advance a diluted version of this argument directly to Kaiser Wilhelm when the two men met in Vienna later in the month. Disingenuously, given that negotiations had already been broken off, Tisza made much of his efforts to conciliate Hungary's Romanians, for which he was being strongly attacked in his own Parliament; favourably impressed by Tisza's forceful personality and expository powers, the Kaiser described him afterwards—to the fury of Franz Ferdinand—as 'a real statesman'.

Although he did not know it, Tisza's instinct that Romania should be written off as a lost cause, in favour of Bulgaria, was fully vindicated in June 1914, when, during a visit by the Russian Tsar and Tsarina to the Romanian port of Con-stanza, King Carol gave a secret oral undertaking to Nicholas II that his country would not enter a war as an ally of Austria-Hungary. During the same visit, the Russian Foreign Minister, Sazonov, made a provocative excursion into Transylva-nia in order to demonstrate support for the Romanian population there. Before Budapest and Vienna were able to digest the implications of Russia's more forward policy in the Balkans, the course of world history was changed by the assassina-tion of Archduke Franz Ferdinand and his wife during a visit to Sarajevo, on 28 June 1914.

Tisza learned of the Sarajevo assassinations while on holiday on his estate in Bihar county. After rushing back to Budapest and thence to Vienna, he lost no time in addressing a memorandum to Franz Josef which, like his conduct in the weeks that followed, showed that his judgement of foreign affairs had reached maturity. Both in the memorandum and at the subsequent meeting of the Com-mon Ministerial Council on 7 July, Tisza argued passionately against using Franz Ferdinand's murder as a pretext for immediate retaliation against Serbia—as Con-rad and others were urging on a receptive Franz Josef. Tisza pointed out that there was as yet no proof of Belgrade's complicity in the crime, without which Euro-pean opinion would condemn Austria-Hungary for starting a war that was bound to spread, involving first Russia and then other powers. Romania could not be trusted even to remain neutral; Bulgaria, a potential ally, had not yet recovered from her recent defeat. Tisza urged that the Monarchy's first step should be a dip-lomatic note making stern but not unreasonable demands of Serbia; if these were rejected by Belgrade, the note should be followed by an ultimatum. Only if Serbia refused to comply with the ultimatum should war be declared, as a last resort.

From the first, Tisza's was a lone voice in the Ministerial Council. Against him, it was argued that delay would give the Russians time to marshal the Balkan states against the Monarchy and that, in any case, the Serbs understood only the lan-guage of armed force. The Kaiser, too, weighed in on the side of an immediate declaration of war, before Russia's plans for enhanced recruitment and armaments could gather momentum. In the face of pressures that would quickly have overwhelmed a lesser man, Tisza held firm. On 8 July he addressed a second memorandum to Franz Josef. After reiterating his earlier arguments against hasty action—'... an attack upon Serbia would conjure up war with Russia and thus world war ...'—he continued:

I therefore by no means intend to plead for our quietly pocketing these provocations; and I am ready to shoulder all consequences of a war caused by a refusal to comply with our just demands. But I believe Serbia should be given an opportunity of avoiding the war at the cost of a diplomatic defeat, and a very serious one, no doubt. Should nevertheless war be the outcome, it should be made obvious to all the world that we are merely acting in just self-defence.[12]

The pro-government daily in Budapest, *Az Újság*, echoed Tisza's views on 10 July, arguing for patience and against 'a hussar-like policy provoking war, which would gamble with our and Europe's peace'.[13] In the meantime, however, Berchtold had skilfully deployed with Tisza the argument to which he was most vulnerable: after claiming that the Kaiser had already delivered a stern warning to King Carol against intervention by Romania, Berchtold went on to say that further vacillation in Vienna 'would be taken in Berlin as a sign of weakness, which would not be without an impact upon the Monarchy's position within the Triple Alliance and upon Germany's future policy'.[14] Tisza began to waver. When, on 12 July, Franz Josef accepted Tisza's case against the annexation of Serbian territory, agreed that an alliance should be concluded with Bulgaria and concurred with Tisza's insistence that the Monarchy's case should be impressed upon west European, and particularly British, public opinion, Tisza gave ground. On 14 July, he agreed that an ultimatum—without a preceding note—should be despatched to Belgrade, giving Serbia forty-eight hours to comply with its terms. Later in the day he explained to the German Ambassador in Vienna that despite his earlier advice he was now convinced of the necessity for action: 'It was very hard for me to come to the decision to give my advice for war, but I am now firmly convinced of its necessity, and I shall stand up for the greatness of the Monarchy to the utmost of my ability'.[15]

Tisza's statement to the Hungarian Parliament on the following day was moderate in tone: 'War is a very sad *ultima ratio*, which should not be used until all other means are exhausted but, naturally, every nation and state, if it wishes to remain what it is, has to be prepared to be able and willing to fight a war if necessary'.[16]

During those critical July days, Tisza had faced an agonising dilemma. His earnest desire to avoid war if at all possible stemmed from his fear that Romania would pounce on Transylvania, transforming the nationality problem into a crisis. In a manuscript note to Franz Josef attached to his memorandum of 8 July, Tisza envisaged a situation in which, after the outbreak of war, the Monarchy's main force would have to be deployed against Russia, leaving the Transylvanian frontier thinly defended: '... the Romanian army will enter Transylvania, there will be insurrections in the regions inhabited by Romanians, and our army fighting against Serbia will be attacked on the flank and in the rear. The certain defeat of that army will open the way for the enemy towards Budapest and Vienna, and decide the entire campaign'.[17] On the other hand, like Gyula Andrássy (Snr) before him, he continued to place his hopes for Hungary's survival on, above all, the German alliance. Berchtold's subtle insinuation that, if Austria-Hungary failed to act against Serbia, the alliance would be weakened persuaded Tisza to give ground. If his original advice had been accepted, Serbia would almost certainly have responded in a way which would have robbed the Monarchy of a *casus belli;* and Europe would have been given a reprieve, albeit of uncertain duration. But in reality Tisza had no chance of winning the argument: Austrian and German minds were made up. Berchtold argued that failure to act against Serbia would be regarded in Europe as a clear 'renunciation of our Great Power position'.[18] Berchtold's wife, a Károlyi, told her family—as Mihály Károlyi later recalled—that 'poor Leopold could not sleep on the day when he wrote his ultimatum to the Serbs, as he was so worried that they would accept it. Several times in the night he had got up and altered or added some clause, to reduce this risk'.[19] Berchtold himself reported to Franz Josef on 14 July: 'The text of the Note [i.e. the ultimatum] to be sent to Belgrade which we have agreed upon today is such that the possibility of war should be counted on'.[20]

If Tisza had stuck to his guns, Franz Josef in all probability would have dismissed him—and would have had little difficulty in finding a suitable successor since the majority of the Hungarian political class favoured a tough line against Serbia. In May 1914, Mihály Károlyi had taken a different view, telling a meeting of the Hungarian Delegation: 'I want a foreign policy in which we have a free hand and are not sycophants of German imperialism … We are simply an exponent of German policies. We should draw nearer to France and Russia and thus enforce our Balkan interests'. And Endre Ady, in an article published in the same month, wrote: 'We like the civilised West, but we do not like and do not want the Germanic West, and we have better things to think of than Vienna, the junkers and Pomerania'.[21] But these views, the authentic voice of Kossuthism, attracted virtually no backing outside the radical intelligentsia; the parliamentary opposition, apart from Károlyi's wing of the Independence Party—and Károlyi himself was in the United States at this critical moment—united behind the government in support for military action. Four weeks to the day after Franz Ferdinand's assassination, despite an accommodating Serbian response to Vienna's ultimatum and in full awareness of all the likely consequences, Austria-Hungary plunged Europe into war. It is impossible to dissent from Alan Sked's judgement: 'Of all the issues concerning the outbreak of the First World War, this one at least is totally uncontroversial: the Austro-Hungarian ultimatum to Serbia was deliberately designed to start a war. It did not begin by accident'.[22] For this, István Tisza and the Hungarian political class must bear their share of the responsibility.

Hungary at War (1914–18)

Like the other eventual belligerents, Hungary greeted the outbreak of war with enthusiasm. In Budapest, as in other European capitals when their turn came, the bands played, flowers were thrown to marching soldiers, cheering and weeping crowds thronged the capital's railway stations to wave off departing troop trains. Hungarians sang and hummed the new smash hit, 'Just wait, just wait, Serbia you dog!' 'At last!' exclaimed Apponyi on behalf of the opposition in Parliament. With the exception of the socialist daily *Népszava*, muffled by the threat of closure, the entire press rallied behind the government in vociferous support for the war. An opportunity to settle accounts with the Southern Slavs, backed by mighty Germany, was to most Hungarians a dream come true. Only the Social Democrats and Oszkár Jászi's newly formed Radical Citizens' Party dissented—and neither party was represented in Parliament.

This euphoria was short-lived. Successive defeats at the hands of the underrated Serbs and a disastrous campaign against the Russians in Galicia quickly brought home to the peoples of the Monarchy the harsh realities of modern warfare. Of all the combatants, Austria-Hungary was the least well prepared for war, partly because of the Hungarian Parliament's relentless opposition to increased recruitment to and expenditure on the common army without political concessions. In 1914, the Monarchy spent less on defence than any of the Great Powers—only 25 per cent of the military budgets of Germany and Russia, 33 per cent of those of Britain and France. The Imperial and Royal Army, in contrast to its dazzling uniforms, was poorly armed and poorly housed; the supply of ammunition was inadequate even for training, let alone combat. By the end of 1914, only four months into the war, the Monarchy had sustained losses of over 800,000 men—killed, wounded or captured—on the Eastern Front and of nearly 50,000 in the Balkans. During the first three months of 1915, costly and, for the most part, unsuccessful offensives against the Russians in the Carpathians added a further 800,000 names to the casualty lists, bringing the Monarchy's total losses in less than a year of war close to the 2 million mark: of these, Hungary's share amounted to over 40 per cent. Over ninety years later, these figures have lost none of their power to appal. Very few Hungarian families were spared.

Almost from the first, a sharp deterioration in the conditions of daily life, in Hungary as in Austria, accompanied the anguish of personal loss. Resorting to the printing presses to meet its share of rapidly escalating military expenditure, the government fuelled inflation with massive emissions of paper money, of which the circulation had doubled after seventeen months of war. The government imposed eight compulsory war loans on a largely needy population. The loss from the countryside of both men and horses sharpened the impact of poor harvests in 1914 and 1915. By mid-1916, the cost of food had trebled while the average wage had only doubled. The rationing of many food items began in 1915; early in 1916, bread and flour were added to the list. Between 1914 and 1917, the price of household goods had increased by 268 per cent, that of clothing by 1,230 per cent; expenditure on food accounted for between 60 per cent and 80 per cent of an urban worker's weekly wage. The fact that the situation in Austria, deprived by battle of her Galician harvests, was even worse brought small comfort to Hungarians; but it did generate considerable tension between the two governments. During the early months of the war, Tisza, in order to protect Hungarian landowners, repeatedly vetoed a lowering of the Monarchy's tariff wall, which would have made possible the import of cheap grain from neutral countries; he even prevented the municipality of Vienna from importing cheap meat from Argentina 'until conditions in the meat markets here [in Hungary] make this import convenient to us'.[23] Tisza rejected repeated Austrian requests to bring Hungarian rations down to Austrian levels, in order to increase the size of the common pool; and insisted on retaining for Hungary up to 20 per cent of the grain imported from (as yet) neutral Romania; Austria secured 50 per cent and the common army the remainder. He made no secret of giving absolute priority to the needs of the Hungarian people once those of the army had been met and for this he was bitterly attacked by the Austrian government and press. A German visitor to Hungary in 1916 commented on the 'inextinguishable hatred in Vienna against Hungary and a similarly deep loathing in Budapest against Austria'.[24] Austrian protests would have carried more weight with contemporaries and with posterity had Austria's past conduct evidenced a more tender concern for Hungarian interests and welfare. The situation in Hungary, in any case, soon became sufficiently grave to justify Tisza's priorities. Hunger riots were commonplace by 1917; and in 1916 the government found itself obliged to establish a Grievance Committee, with executive powers, to act as a safety valve to mounting unrest in militarised factories and workshops. Tisza did not scruple to use the greater leverage accorded to Hungary by the exigencies of war to drive a hard bargain when the economic dimension of the 1867 Compromise came up for its decennial renegotiation in 1916; while accepting the Austrian request for renegotiation every twenty years instead of every ten, Tisza secured a major reduction in the Hungarian share of the Monarchy's common expenses, from 36.4 to 34.4 per cent over this longer period. This success, however, was soon to be rendered academic.

The Romanian problem, in one form or another, continued to be a central preoccupation for István Tisza throughout the first three years of war, until the Russian Revolution in 1917 deprived Romania of her main potential ally. Already in September 1914, following a report from Count Czernin in Bucharest that Romanian neutrality could be assured by the grant of political autonomy to Transylvania and the transfer of part of the Bukovina to Romanian sovereignty, Tisza was subjected to renewed pressure from both Vienna and Berlin. He raised no objection to the second condition but refused adamantly to consider the first. He also rejected a German request that he should at least appoint a Romanian minister to his cabinet and remained unmoved by accusations from Berlin that his obduracy would put the entire war effort of the Central Powers into jeopardy. When leaders of the Romanian community rejected his further offer, published in November, of concessions in public education, the right to use the Romanian language in official contacts and, once again, electoral reform to increase Romanian representation in Parliament, Tisza decided to travel to Berlin to defuse what had become a crisis within the alliance. Deploying all his considerable powers of advocacy, Tisza succeeded in persuading Kaiser Wilhelm, Chancellor Bethmann-Hollweg and German ministers that the solution to the Romanian problem lay not in giving way to blackmail from Bucharest but—here Tisza revived his earlier theory—in playing the Bulgarian card. If Bulgaria were to be brought into alliance with the Central Powers, as Turkey already had been, Romania would be—in both senses of the word—neutralised and Serbia isolated. The Kaiser was convinced and at once adjusted German policy accordingly. An Austrian diplomat present at the discussions reported: 'Count Tisza made an excellent impression upon the Emperor, the Chancellor, and I think upon [Chief of Staff] Falkenhayn as well, by his businesslike, self-confident, calm and extremely clever behaviour'.[25]

At a stroke, Tisza had both removed German interference in Hungary's nationality problem and achieved the wider strategic objective for which he had long argued. It nevertheless took a further year to secure the Bulgarian alliance and during that time Tisza remained apprehensive of a Romanian invasion of Transylvania, with some reason. Following the rejection of his November offer to the Romanian leaders in Hungary, a leading Bucharest daily had editorialised: 'Today it is already too late for reform. We want Transylvania and we shall have it'.[26]

Tisza's concerns became more acute after Italy had been bribed, with promises in the Treaty of London (April 1915) of massive territorial gains, to desert the Triple Alliance and join the Entente. He addressed a memorandum to Burián—whose appointment as the Monarchy's Foreign Minister, in succession to the increasingly limp Berchtold, he had engineered early in 1915—in May: 'An Italian and Romanian attack would be terribly dangerous. Please take the necessary military precautions for a possible Romanian attack as well … this is even more important than defence of the Italian border. A Romanian invasion would cut off our vital forces more quickly than an Italian one. And consider also the effect on the Balkans'.[27] Especially since a joint offensive with Bulgaria in October 1915 had resulted in the removal of any further threat from Serbia, Berlin remained deaf to the Monarchy's concerns regarding Romania until Tisza's worst fears were realised in August 1916 when, after concluding a secret treaty with the Entente, Romania declared war on Austria-Hungary and invaded Transylvania with a force of half a million troops. They were opposed by a force of only 34,000. But, once faced with a concrete threat which, at least in the Kaiser's view, could cost the Central Powers the war, the Germans acted quickly and decisively. A strong German force under General Mackensen, transferred from the Western Front, drove northwards from the territory of the Central Powers' new ally, Bulgaria, and within a few weeks had occupied most of Romania, including Bucharest. The invasion of Transylvania collapsed and the Romanian army sustained extraordinarily heavy casualties. In reaction to the crisis, Kaiser Wilhelm assumed supreme command of all the forces of the Central Powers, thereby formalising the Monarchy's status as the junior partner in the alliance. This humiliation, together with the fact that Transylvania had been saved only thanks to Germany, seriously damaged Tisza's political standing, both in the alliance and in the Hungarian Parliament—where, however, the size of his majority rendered him invulnerable.

István Tisza's control of Parliament and the fact that he continued to enjoy the full confidence of Franz Josef enabled him to govern Hungary, from 1914 until 1917, virtually single-handed. In many respects he succeeded, through sheer force of personality, in making Hungary the dominant partner in the Monarchy. Inevitably, hubris began to infect his conduct and his pronouncements. A letter to Burián reflected his mood at the end of 1915: 'Unless one is quite blinded by prejudice, it is impossible not to see from the experience of this war that not only the natural energies of the Magyar race, but also the strong structure of the Hungarian national state form the greatest force in the Monarchy, the stoutest pillar of its European position'.[28] Tisza found time to score constitutional points off Vienna whenever an opportunity occurred. In October 1915 he persuaded Franz Joseph, over fierce Austrian opposition, that the Monarchy's coat of arms should be described as 'the joint coat of arms of the two states of the Austro-Hungarian Monarchy' rather than as simply 'the joint coat of arms of the Austro-Hungarian Monarchy'. He argued, this time unsuccessfully, that since Hungarian soldiers were winning the lion's share of medals for bravery in the war (this was true), the factory that minted the medals should be located in Hungary rather than Austria. He brushed aside repeated attempts by opposition parties to win the franchise at least for soldiers who had served at the front—men prepared to die for their country should be entitled to vote in it. Tisza argued that suffrage should be regarded as a civic duty, not as a reward; moreover, 'the idea of granting soldiers the vote leads to universal suffrage … I consider the introduction of universal suffrage in Hungary a national disaster'.[29] It was nevertheless to Tisza's credit that both the Hungarian Parliament and the Croatian *Sabor* continued to function throughout the war, unlike the Austrian *Reichsrat* whose sittings had been suspended *sine die*. Tisza also succeeded in protecting the people of Hungary from the excesses of martial law by resisting the transfer of civil authority to the army that had occurred elsewhere in the Monarchy. He insisted that powers of local administration remained in the hands of the Commissioners appointed under the emergency laws approved by Parliament before the war. But although Tisza ensured that the constitutional damage inflicted by the exigencies of war was much less in Hungary than in Austria, he also continued to stifle all proposals for political or social reform. He ignored the extent to which the social chemistry of a war which, for the first time, involved every segment of society, was increasing the pressure for change. His pride in making Hungary the most effective and reliable partner, as he saw it, in the alliance with Germany also blinded him to the limits of the Monarchy's capacity to fight on. When death had finally claimed his protective sovereign, Franz Josef, in November 1916, these two failures of political vision were to bring Tisza's premiership to an end.

The professional core of the Monarchy's common army had been virtually wiped out by March 1915, when the surrender of the key Galician fortress of Przemyśl to the Russians provided a tragic postscript to Conrad's disastrous offensives. A new, raw conscript army was taking its place but as yet lacked training, effective equipment and combat experience. At this stage, Tisza was capable of taking a relatively realistic view of the Monarchy's situation. When Italy joined the Entente, he revived the suggestion that peace proposals should be advanced before Italy could attack her former ally. A few weeks later, the Hungarian cabinet enjoined the Common Ministerial Council to 'decide, within the limits of reason and taking into consideration our military and economic strength, how long we can remain at war';[30] Tisza subsequently told the council that Hungary could continue for only eight months. The remarkable success of the Central Powers' summer offensive on the Eastern Front—in which the depleted and exhausted Austro-Hungarian army played only a minor role—subsequently extinguished all talk of peace for the time being; but the even greater success of General Brusilov's counter-offensive a year later, costing the Central Powers over half a million men, revived it. In July 1916, Mihály Károlyi led twenty-six deputies out of the Independence Party to form the 'Independence and '48 Party' (usually known as simply the 'Károlyi Party'), which put peace without annexations and universal suffrage at the head of its programme.

The presence in the Hungarian Parliament, for the first time, of a party openly committed to ending the war gained in significance when Charles IV (Emperor Karl I), a well-meaning but indecisive young man, succeeded to the Habsburg throne on the death of his great-uncle, Franz Josef, in November. On 22 November, the day after his accession, Charles undertook to exert every effort 'to put an end to the horrors and sacrifices of the war at the earliest possible moment'.[31] Even before Franz Josef's death, Tisza had alienated Charles by bombarding the heir with hectoring memoranda and briefings about Hungary's history and special status; Charles also regretted having allowed himself to be bullied by Tisza, immediately after his accession, into submitting to early coronation (on 30 December) as King of Hungary—Tisza had been determined to see the coronation oath administered before Charles could develop inconvenient ideas about the reform of Dualism to Hungary's disadvantage. By the spring of 1917, the two men were on a collision course. Charles not only favoured exploring the possibility of a negotiated peace—and had taken an ill-fated initiative himself through his Belgian brother-in-law, Prince Sixtus, which infuriated the Kaiser when he later learned of it—but, unnerved by the March Revolution in Russia, wished to defuse political tensions in Hungary through social and franchise reform. Tisza, by contrast, encouraged by the military collapse of Russia and the defeat of both Serbia and Romania, set his face ever more firmly against anything short of final victory— strengthened in his determination by mounting indications that the Entente, if victorious, would set about dismantling the Dual Monarchy and 'liberating' its minorities. At a meeting of the Common Ministerial Council in March, he argued against defeatism and urged his colleagues to keep their nerve; in April, he enjoined Czernin—whom Charles had appointed Foreign Minister in place of Tisza's ally, Burián—to maintain 'a steady nerve—... play the game to the end with sang-froid. Let there be no sign of weakness ...'.[32] Tisza remained equally adamant on the issue of electoral reform: when, at the end of April, Charles urged him to extend the franchise, Tisza offered only early implementation of the anachronistic 1913 package of reforms. 'I am not going to sacrifice the peace of the Monarchy and Hungary in order to support Tisza', Charles then declared; and ten days later asked Tisza to resign. Tisza immediately complied; but took his parliamentary majority with him into opposition, determined to frustrate all government proposals of which he disapproved.

Count Móric Eszterházy, whom Charles IV appointed to head a government consisting of members of the former opposition parties, found himself a prisoner of Tisza's parliamentary battalions and resigned after three months in a state of nervous collapse. The veteran Wekerle, who succeeded him, had little more commitment than Tisza to electoral reform. The Suffrage Bill which the Jewish radical Vilmos Vázsonyi, now Minister of Justice in the Wekerle administration, introduced in December 1917, would have enlarged the electorate to a reasonably respectable (for the time) 20 per cent of the population; but relentless opposition from Tisza and the Party of Work not only eroded this proportion to 13 per cent but also delayed passage of the mangled remains of the bill for nine months. In order to keep Wekerle in power at all, Charles found himself obliged to bolster the government with the promise of an independent Hungarian army—an extraordinary concession to the '48-ers. Meanwhile, however, the popular mood in Hungary was changing in ways that made the deliberations of the Lower House virtually irrelevant. Although the success of Germany's unrestricted submarine warfare and the unexpected victory of the Central Powers over Italy at Caporetto (October 1917) kept hopes of victory alive, living conditions for the civilian population of the Monarchy during the winter of 1917/18 were worse than ever. Wekerle's introduction of price controls did little to curb inflation or the black market. At the turn of the year, a strike movement in Vienna, where conditions were even worse than in Budapest, spread to Hungary where the demand from the streets for an end to the war became ever louder. The award to Hungary of 5,000 sq. km of Romanian territory in the Treaty of Bucharest did little to improve popular morale, especially after the German Kaiser, meeting Charles IV at Spa in May, had punished the latter for his indiscreet peace feelers by bullying him into closer political, military and economic union between the German Empire and the Monarchy.

The prospect of a customs union with Germany was particularly unpopular in Hungary and increased support for Károlyi's call for an end to the German alliance. In the spring of 1918, the Hungarian minister in charge of food supply admitted that the state could feed neither the army nor the civilian population— per capita consumption of flour had already fallen by a third of that pre-war and meat consumption by over half; yet another bad harvest met only 53 per cent of the country's requirements, while the acute shortage of coal threatened to bring industry and the railways to a standstill. Idle troops, moreover, had become a threat to internal stability. By 1918 Austro-Hungarian units, totalling about half a million men, faced the enemy on only two fronts—the Italian and part of the Balkan: twice as many soldiers were on sick leave or stranded in railway sidings, while tens of thousands had simply left their regiments and headed for home. They were joined on the streets by several hundred thousand former prisoners of war whom the Bolshevik regime had released from camps in Russia. A mutiny in the Austro-Hungarian fleet at Cattaro was followed by another by the army garrison in Pécs, which Honvéd and hussar units suppressed, inflicting heavy casualties on the mutineers. The use of the army against striking workers in the MÁVAG plant in Budapest, in June 1918, precipitated a general strike in the capital and the formation of a Workers' Council on the Soviet Russian pattern—the first manifestation in Hungary of direct political action by the urban working class. In Parliament, meanwhile, Tisza's relentless pressure had forced Wekerle into two successive resignations and into the appointment of increasingly right-wing cabinets. With Tisza in the role of puppet-master, Mihály Károlyi and his small party constituted the only genuine parliamentary opposition and the only group whose views came close to reflecting the realities of life outside the chamber of the Lower House.

The failure of a last Austro-Hungarian offensive on the Italian front in June 1918, in effect signified the Monarchy's final defeat, although it took a further three months for this fact to sink in and to be acknowledged. As late as 21 September István Tisza, despatched by his sovereign to the Balkans to assess the political situation, was blustering in Sarajevo: 'What do these impertinent fellows [a delegation petitioning for the union of South Slavs] think? Do they reckon with Hungary's collapse? Perhaps, but Hungary is sufficiently strong to demolish her enemies before she perishes'.[33] Thereafter, the pace of events and the speed with which the Dual Monarchy fell apart were breathtaking. The nationalities, even allowing for the harsh internal disciplines imposed upon them, had remained remarkably quiet during the war: moreover, hundreds of thousands of Croats, Slovenes, Serbs, Poles, Romanians, Ruthenes, Czechs, Slovaks and even Italians had fought loyally and bravely in the army of the monarch in whose lands they had been born. At least until the death of Franz Josef, *Kaisertreue* had been an important factor in holding this heterogeneous, polyglot army together; even in the last weeks of the war, it never completely disintegrated—it took the forces of the Entente two weeks to defeat the Austro-Hungarian army on the Italian front in the final battles of October 1918. Moreover, the successive defeats of Serbia and Romania, and the collapse of Russia, had robbed the nationalities of any certainty that the war would bring about the fulfilment of their aspirations. Their champions and representatives abroad, in the capitals of the Allied Powers, had nevertheless been working steadily throughout the war to bring this about—as we shall see in the following chapter. Once the Central Powers, their defeat certain, had begun to sue for peace, the nationalities moved rapidly and in an almost matter-of-fact manner to detach themselves from the dying Monarchy and assert their independence.* On 16 October, Charles IV published a manifesto proclaiming Austria to be a federal state 'in which each racial component shall form its own state organisation in its territory of settlement', while maintaining 'the integrity of the lands that belong to the holy Hungarian Crown'—a qualification Wekerle secured only by threatening to suspend deliveries of Hungarian flour and grain to Austria. On the following day, István Tisza rose from his seat in the Lower House to declare: 'I will not play with words. I must acknowledge the truth of what Mihály Károlyi said in his speech yesterday. We have lost the war'.[34] News of this admission, from the leading advocate of carrying the war to a victorious conclusion, quickly spread throughout the Monarchy, to devastating effect; it was soon followed by an order from Charles IV releasing all officers of the common army from their oath of allegiance and permitting them to join the armies of the nations that now made up the federal state of Austria. István Deák has recorded one of the extraordinary scenes that followed, as the armies of the Monarchy melted away: '… the 104th Field Artillery Regiment of Vienna carried on the fight until 3 November 1918. For another ten days the regiment held together and then, to the music of the regimental band and under the regimental flag, the colonel commander bade farewell to his troops. Each national group then marched off towards its new fatherland'.[35]

On 20 October, the Hungarian Parliament endorsed the decision of Wekerle's cabinet to revoke Law XII of 1867—the Compromise—but to maintain the personal union, in accordance with the Pragmatic Sanction, between the newly federal Austrian state and the Hungarian Kingdom. Wekerle resigned three days later, this time for good. On 24 October, Gyula Andrássy, appointed to the office of common Foreign Minister, which his father had filled with such distinction, but destined to hold it for only a few days, despatched a note to the United States government accepting all the conditions for peace laid down by President Wilson and requesting an immediate armistice. The Monarchy's war was over.

* See Chapter 13.

On the following day, the Károlyi Party, the Social Democratic Party and the Radical Citizens' Party combined to form a National Council, under Károlyi's chairmanship: the council's first manifesto demanded full independence for Hungary, the immediate conclusion of peace, an end to the alliance with Germany, the introduction of universal suffrage, land reform and self-determination for the nationalities. Hungary now had an alternative government. A large crowd, crossing the Chain Bridge to demonstrate on Castle Hill in support of the National Council, was turned back by police fire which killed three and wounded seventy of its number. Further afield, a Romanian National Council in Bukovina declared its secession from the Monarchy; a Czecho-Slovak Republic was proclaimed in Prague; and, in Zagreb, the *Sabor* announced the creation of an independent state of Croatia-Slavonia within the new federation of South Slavs. Within the space of a few days, and long in advance of any peace settlement, the Dual Monarchy had disintegrated.

On the last day of October 1918, three events combined to form a significant punctuation mark in Hungary's history—it was still much too early, as it turned out, to speak of the end of an era. The Austro-Hungarian fleet in the Dalmatian port of Pula, commanded by an Admiral Miklós Horthy, surrendered on the orders of Charles IV, not to a member of the Entente but to the Yugoslav National Committee. Later in the day, a group of soldiers broke into István Tisza's family villa in Pest and, after a short argument in the hall about responsibility for the war, shot Tisza dead in front of his wife and niece. Tisza had been warned that his life was in danger but refused to flee: 'I wish to die upright, the way I have lived'. His strength of purpose and force of personality entitle him to be remembered as a considerable statesman; but the rigidity of his opinions and the narrowness of his vision deprived him of a claim to greatness. He personified, albeit in an extreme, even distorted form, the Magyar will to survive. Survival could be assured, he believed, by institutional stasis: by maintaining, through strict limitations on the franchise, the political dominance of the Magyar aristocracy and gentry; and by the vigorous defence of Dualism and its institutions against every foe and detractor. The war artificially prolonged his mandate; it also generated social and political currents which exposed the inadequacy of his policies. The third event of moment on 31 October 1918 was the appointment, by Archduke Josef acting as Charles IV's vicegerent, of Count Mihály Károlyi to be Prime Minister.

Revolutions and Counter-revolution

In appointing Károlyi to head a new government, Archduke Josef was merely formalising a virtually accomplished fact. On 30 October, when it had become known that Count János Hadik, rather than Károlyi, had been asked to form a cabinet, supporters of the National Council occupied the main public buildings in Pest, including the railway stations and telephone exchanges, and thronged the streets around the Hotel Astoria which the council had made its headquarters. White asters, on sale for All Souls' Day, became the badge of what was now a revolution—soldiers pinned them to their caps, civilians sported them in their buttonholes. Young members of the Galileo Circle, imprisoned by the Wekerle government for revolutionary activity, were released from their cells by the crowd;

demonstrators tore down the imperial coat of arms from the walls of government offices. Similar demonstrations took place in Debrecen, Miskolc and Szeged. Having taken over the premiership from Hadik, Károlyi put together a cabinet in which members of his own party—and social class—predominated, including only two members of the Social Democratic Party, which already controlled the streets, and two Radicals, one of whom was Oszkár Jászi. Archduke Josef administered to the new ministers the usual oath of loyalty to the constitution and hence to the crown; but on the following day, at Károlyi's urgent request, Charles IV agreed to release him and his colleagues from their oath—faced with mounting pressure from the streets for the proclamation of a republic, Károlyi had to free his government from this encumbrance.

Popular enthusiasm for Károlyi stemmed principally from the belief that. given his political record and open sympathy for the Entente, he would be able to conclude peace more quickly and on more favourable terms than any other political figure. An armistice covering the Italian front had already been negotiated and was signed in Padua on 3 November: Austro-Hungarian forces were to be withdrawn from South Tyrol, Croatia, Istria and Dalmatia—terms that reflected the Italian interest in establishing a substantial presence on the eastern shore of the Adriatic. This armistice did not, however, appear to apply to the southern front and Károlyi therefore hastened to open negotiations in Belgrade with the French commander of Entente forces in the Balkan region, General Franchet d'Esperey. The terms eventually agreed on 13 November were harsh. Károlyi nevertheless accepted them in the belief that they had only temporary validity pending an overall peace settlement: Hungary undertook to withdraw her troops from the eastern two-thirds of Transylvania and from a large area of southern Hungary, including the Bánát, to behind a line running from Varasd in the west, through Pécs and Szeged, to Arad in the east. Hungary's standing army was to be limited to eight divisions, including two of cavalry, and the forces of the Entente were to have the right of free passage through all Hungarian territory. Romanian, Serbian and French troops moved in to occupy the evacuated areas almost immediately. Large numbers of military and civilian evacuees began to converge on Budapest. With the armistice signed, Károlyi was free to attend to internal matters, including the future form of the Hungarian state. Charles IV's abdication, on 13 November, 'of all responsibility in the conduct of state affairs' and recognition in advance of whatever decision Hungary might make regarding her constitutional future, greatly eased Károlyi's task. On 16 November, the Lower House of the Hungarian Parliament, its composition unchanged save by deaths and resignations since the elections of 1910, dissolved itself; and the Upper House, while fighting shy of dissolution, adjourned its sittings *sine die*. In the afternoon, in the hall beneath the great dome of the Parliament Building, Hungary was declared to be an independent republic. Károlyi later recalled that during the ceremony one speaker, spotting a *Honvéd* veteran of 1849 in the audience, told him: 'That which you fought for seventy years ago has now been won—Hungary's independence'.[36]

In January 1919, the National Council—now numbering twenty-four members—elected Károlyi to the Presidency of the Hungarian Republic and he, in turn, appointed Dénes Berinkey Prime Minister. The inclusion of four Social Democrats in the new cabinet better reflected the realities of the political situation but complicated the task of social and economic reform by deepening the divisions within the government. On land reform, the most urgent issue in terms of maintaining popular support for the government, the divide lay between the Károlyi Party, the Radicals and the Smallholder minister Nagyatádi Szabó on the one hand, all of whom wished to divide the large estates into holdings large enough to support a family; and, on the other, the socialists who wished to convert the estates into co-operatives rather than enlarge the class of independent peasant farmers. The law eventually approved by the National Council in February provided for the expropriation of all secular estates of over 500 *hold*, and of church estates of over 200 *hold*, and their division into holdings of between 5 and 20 *hold*, depending on soil quality, and allocation to landless peasants either on perpetual lease or for mortgage-assisted purchase. Landowners were to be compensated with state bonds. Mihály Károlyi personally inaugurated the redistribution programme by dividing up his own vast estate—although it was heavily mortgaged to the banks—and allocating holdings to the landless peasants who worked on it.[37] This symbolic act was worthy of a soundly conceived and balanced measure which, although at least seventy years overdue, should have stood a reasonable chance of success; so adverse was the prevailing political and economic environment, however, that the ceremony at Kápolna remained a unique instance of implementation. Elsewhere, the reform was either obstructed by defiant landlords or swept aside by peasants who arbitrarily occupied estates irrespective of their size and opposed any form of compensation. Good intentions were more salient than concrete results in another field, that of electoral reform. A new electoral law ratified by the National Council in March extended the franchise to all literate men over twenty-one, and women over twenty-four, who had held Hungarian citizenship for at least six years; this measure enlarged the electorate to about 9 million, approximately half the adult population. For the time being, however, the reform remained untested: the internal situation was simply too volatile to permit elections to be called without risking civil war.

On 19 January 1919, Harold Nicolson, then a junior British diplomat attending the Paris Peace Conference, made this entry in his diary: 'An Englishman just back from Kolosvar [*sic*] in Transylvania comes. He said that Buda Pest was heading rapidly towards Bolshevism with Károlyi at the helm. He thinks that Bolshevism when it comes will be shortlived and that a white reaction will follow … The peasants have sown nothing this autumn'.[38] This was a remarkably accurate prediction. The Károlyi regime already faced mounting opposition from both right and left. The petty bourgeoisie and poorer gentry, many of them demobilised officers, opposed land reform, feared the consequences of wider suffrage and were outraged by the occupation of Transylvania and the south, for which they blamed Károlyi's acceptance of d'Esperey's armistice terms. This element of the population, which enjoyed the support and tacit co-operation of much of the civil service, found its representation in several political organisations that emerged in the wake of the Monarchy's defeat and disintegration. The Association of Awakening Hungarians (*Ébredő Magyarok Egyesülete*, or ÉME) had similar objectives to the Hungarian Association of National Defence (*Magyar Országos Véderő Egylet*, or MOVE), which was led by a staff officer in the *Honvédség*, Captain Gyula Gömbös. Count István Bethlen, a Transylvanian landowner, headed the National Unity

Party (*Nemzeti Egyesülés Pártja* or NEP), which brought together former members of the parliamentary right and held the radical intelligentsia responsible for Hungary's current misfortunes. These groups, which broadly shared a platform favouring military dictatorship, punishment of Jewish financiers and industrialists who were perceived as having profited from the war, and an anti–Bolshevik alliance with the Entente powers, found their main enemy not in Károlyi's government, which they dismissed as limp and ineffectual, but in the newly founded Communist Party of Hungary (*Kommunisták Magyarországi Pártja* or KMP), led by a young journalist and former prisoner of war in Russia, Béla Kun. The first issue of the KMP party newspaper, *Vörös Újság* ('Red News'), which appeared on 7 December 1918, called for the destruction of capitalism, for the abolition of private property and for government by workers' councils modelled on the Russian Soviets. The Communists, with fewer more than 30,000 members country-wide by the end of 1918, as yet posed no threat to the dominance of the left by the Social Democrats; but the defeat in cabinet of the latter's prescription for land reform, together with the emergence of organised reaction on the right, created the possibility of co-operation between them. For the time being, however, the two left-wing parties were at loggerheads. At the end of January 1919, the predominantly Social Democrat Workers' Council of Budapest voted to expel all Communists both from the council and from trade union organisations. On 20 February, a mob attack on the offices of the Social Democrat organ, *Népszava*, for which the Communists were thought to be responsible and in which a number of police were killed or wounded, gave the government grounds for taking action against both its left-wing and its right-wing opponents. Kun and over thirty other leading Communists were arrested and imprisoned, although they enjoyed a privileged status in gaol which allowed Kun, for example, to edit *Vörös Újság* from his cell. At the same time Károlyi banned MOVE, obliging Captain Gömbös to flee to Vienna.

In the event, it was not internal opposition from left or right that decided the fate of the Károlyi regime but the Entente. Despite urgent recommendations to the contrary from two successive missions from the Peace Conference in Paris,* both led by Americans (A. E. Taylor and A. C. Coolidge), the Entente powers refused to end the economic blockade of their defeated enemies or to give any signal of support for Károlyi and his government. Living conditions in Hungary consequently continued to deteriorate and disillusionment with Károlyi's capacity to protect Hungarian interests quickly deepened.

A stark revelation of the impotence of Károlyi's government came in the last weeks of 1918. Oszkár Jászi, newly appointed Minister for National Minority Affairs, had endeavoured to persuade the Romanians of Transylvania of the merits of his plan for a confederation, modelled on Switzerland, of ethnically homogeneous cantons; the Romanian cantons, Jászi proposed, would be administered by the Romanian National Assembly in Transylvania. The Romanian leaders rejected this offer: local autonomy within a Hungarian state would no longer suffice—like the other nationalities, the Romanians now demanded nothing less than union with their neighbouring motherland. On 1 December, therefore, the Romanian

---

* The Peace Conference had opened on 18 January 1919: see Chapter 13.

National Assembly in Gyulafehérvár proclaimed union with the Kingdom of Romania; and Romanian troops rapidly advanced beyond the armistice line to occupy the territory secretly promised to King Ferdinand in 1916 in return for his neutrality. Events in both north and south followed a similar pattern. In Slovakia, the Entente acceded to pressure from the Czechs in agreeing to an armistice line well to the south of the linguistic divide; and in Újvidék (Novi Sad) the Serbian National Council proclaimed the union with Serbia of the southern Hungarian counties occupied by Serbian troops. In the belief that these illegal *faits accomplis* would soon be set aside by a final peace settlement, which alone could determine Hungary's permanent frontiers, Károlyi made no attempt to oppose them by armed resistance—although, given the paucity of Entente forces in the region and the fact that Romania's advance had outstripped her supply lines, such resistance might well have been effective.

On 20 March 1919, a Colonel Vyx, of the Allied Military Mission in Budapest, acting on instructions from the Peace Conference in Paris, called on Károlyi to present a formal note signed by the Commander of the Allied Army of Occupation, General de Lobit. The note redefined the area of eastern Hungary and Transylvania which Romanian troops were authorised by the Conference to occupy, drawing a new demarcation considerably to the west of the line which they had already reached: it extended from Szatmárnémeti in the north, through Nagyvárad to Arad in the south, handing to the Romanians all of historic Transylvania, including purely Magyar areas of significant extent, together with a slice of Hungary west of the Transylvanian border. Moreover, the note prescribed that to the west of the new demarcation line a further swathe of Hungarian territory, including Debrecen and Szeged, would become a neutralised zone, to be evacuated by Hungarian and occupied by Entente forces. These provisions reflected the ambition of Entente statesmen in Paris, and of the French leaders, Prime Minister Clemenceau and Marshal Foch in particular, to use Romania as an ally against Bolshevik Russia and as a base from which an Allied offensive against the Bolsheviks could be launched; the neutralised zone was designed to protect the Romanians from Hungarian actions that might interfere with these objectives and to provide a possible assembly area for Allied troops deployed to pursue them. The devastating political impact of this communication was compounded when Colonel Vyx added an oral statement to the effect that the new demarcation line should be regarded as a political frontier between Hungary and Romania; and hinted that hostilities against Hungary would be resumed in the event of her noncompliance with the terms of the note. Vyx subsequently denied having spoken in these terms; the evidence that he did so is none the less compelling.[39] Vyx may well have failed to grasp the full political implications of the issues in which he, a soldier, found himself involved.

Károlyi now faced a cruel dilemma. Capitulation to the Entente's new demands would risk provoking a violent reaction from a middle class already frustrated by the government's passivity in the face of the steady encroachment into Hungarian territory of Czech, Romanian and Serb forces. Defiant rejection of the Vyx note would risk the renewal of hostilities by the Entente. Although Károlyi nevertheless inclined towards the latter course—and the terms of the Vyx Note were indeed formally rejected on 21 March—he had no confidence in the capacity of the government, despite its more social-democratic complexion, to rally the nation behind it. Only a wholly socialist government, he believed—rightly or wrongly—could do this and raise an army. Had Károlyi, as President of the Republic, tried to unite the country in protest against a patently unjust imposition (as Béla Kun was soon to do) he might have succeeded—his popularity with the peasantry had already recovered following the land reform. He chose not to make the attempt. Instead, he passed the cup to the Social Democrats. Having summoned Prime Minister Dénes Berinkey and his cabinet, Károlyi put it to them that since their trust in the Wilsonian principle of self-determination had been betrayed by the Entente, they should make way for a Social Democratic government which, given Communist co-operation, could restore civil order and raise an army. He, Károlyi, would continue to serve as President. No member of the cabinet dissented from this proposition; the government placed its collective resignation in Károlyi's hands. The Social Democrats, however, were already pursuing their own agenda; on 21 March they reached agreement on the amalgamation of their party with Kun's Communists, creating the Socialist Party of Hungary, with the objective of seizing power from the liberals. Learning of this, Károlyi resigned the Presidency and shortly afterwards left Hungary. He later explained: 'I made this sacrifice, instead of assuming the cheap martyr's crown of arrest, to avoid a massacre of citizens, to prevent the useless shedding of blood on the streets of Budapest, and to save the country from the worst horrors of a civil war'.[40]

The socialist press published a proclamation over Károlyi's signature in which he announced his resignation and the transfer of power 'to the proletariat of Hungary'. Károlyi may or may not have signed this proclamation personally—he later denied having done so. This does not alter the fact of his abdication, nor that of the capitulation of Hungary's second liberal revolution—whose leaders showed less courage and political skill than their political forebears had displayed in 1848. The Entente must nevertheless bear most of the responsibility for their failure, and hence for Hungary's introduction to Communism and for the counter-revolution that followed.

The last act of the Berinkey cabinet had been to order the release of all imprisoned Communists. Within an hour of leaving his cell, Béla Kun had seized the reins of power and set about forming the Revolutionary Governing Council (*Forradalmi Kormányzótanács*). During the next four months, he succeeded in imposing on Hungary—now renamed the 'Hungarian Federal Socialist Republic of Councils' (*Magyarországi Szocialista Szövetséges Tanácsköztársaság*)—the complete Leninist agenda of expropriation, nationalisation, regimentation and terror. Fortunately for the Hungarian people, implementation of the torrent of decrees and ordinances that poured out of the Revolutionary Council was at best patchy, especially outside the capital; but, however misguided or downright malign its purposes, the new regime demonstrated remarkable administrative energy and, in certain respects, considerable political skill. Kun himself, a former prisoner of war in Russia where he had directed the political indoctrination of his fellow prisoners, was driven by hunger for the approval of his hero and mentor, Lenin: indeed, he seems to have set out to prove that Lenin's precepts could be realised even more completely and successfully in Hungary than in Russia. Like Lenin, Kun was a small man of unprepossessing appearance but a talented and tireless orator; having installed the Social Democrat Sándor Garbai as President of the Revolutionary Council, he took for himself the People's Commissariat of Foreign Affairs but directed from this office every aspect of the Council's policies. Social Democrats and Communists shared the other People's Commissariats between them. A young Communist named Mátyás Rákosi filled the post of People's Commissar for Production. Significantly, the Revolutionary Council's first decree, issued on 21 March, proclaimed martial law and the death penalty for resistance to the new regime; the replacement of the existing judicial system by Revolutionary Tribunals followed four days later. The existing structure of central and local government was replaced by a hierarchy of village, town and district councils at the apex of which a National Congress of Workers', Soldiers' and Peasants' Councils would be responsible for 'the regulation and direction of all important questions in the life of the State' and which would embody 'the dictatorship of the proletariat'.[41]

Béla Kun and his colleagues lost no time in exercising the arbitrary powers of what Kun himself candidly described as 'a dictatorship of an active minority on behalf of the, by and large, passive proletariat' which would have to 'act in a strong and merciless fashion at least until such time as the revolution spread to the other [European] countries'.[42] Parroting Lenin, Kun proudly declared: 'I know of no difference between moral and immoral acts: I recognise only one standpoint, whether a thing is good or bad for the proletariat'.[43] In this spirit, the Revolutionary Council nationalised all private housing, limiting adult accommodation to one room per head and billeting zealous proletarians in bourgeois homes to report on the activities of the occupants. Industrial, mining and transport enterprises employing more than twenty workers were nationalised and their boards replaced by Workers' Councils chaired by a 'production commissar'. Banks, too, were nationalised and bank deposits frozen. The state appropriated, without compensation, all estates of over 75 *hold*—not for redistribution to the landless peasantry but for conversion into co-operatives and, in the case of the largest estates, state farms. The racecourses of Budapest were put to the plough for the production of vegetables, horse racing having been denounced as a pastime for aristocrats. The state took over and secularised all schools and universities, abolishing religious instruction and banning religious symbols. An ordinance of the People's Commissariat for Education declared: 'All utterances and actions in school or outside it directed against Society as a whole (human rights, existing regulations etc.) or revealing a lack of faith, lack of will-power, or a deficient sense of socialistic self-discipline, solidarity and collaboration will be punished'.[44]

The Academy of Sciences, denounced as a 'reactionary institution', was closed down; thirty-seven professors at the University of Budapest were dismissed from their posts. Rigorous censorship gave the Revolutionary Council complete control of the press, which it used to whip up revolutionary enthusiasm and to encourage belief in the imminence of world revolution. Ration cards, without which food could not be legally purchased, were issued only to members of trade unions, obliging members of the professions to form unions or starve. A new electoral law enfranchised all men and women over eighteen years of age but disenfranchised 'exploiters', namely any employer of labour—including peasant smallholders who employed a single farmhand. More creditably, the regime introduced an eight-hour working day, gave women equality of pay with men and reinforced the system of unemployment benefit established by Károlyi. But Sándor Garbai did not exaggerate when he proudly announced to the National Congress of Councils, elected on a one-party list basis in April 1919, that 'within three months, the greater part of the existing institutions have been destroyed'.[45]

For the first few weeks following its seizure of power, the Communist regime enjoyed a honeymoon with the middle as well as with the working classes. Kun's early proclamations to the Hungarian people skilfully exploited mounting resentment at the behaviour of the victorious Allies, denouncing 'the imperialism of the Entente, whose intention was and is to rob Hungary of its food supply, its industrial raw materials, and all the conditions of existence, by dismembering its territory'.[46] The public offer of alliance with the Russian Bolsheviks was regarded as a deserved and appropriate rebuff to the Entente. Hungary's intellectual élite flocked to serve in the new cultural directories. Zsigmond Móricz, Mihály Babits, Árpád Tóth and Gyula Juhász worked in the Directory of Writers, Béla Bartók, Zoltán Kodály and Ernő Dohnányi in the Directory of Music. Gyula Krúdy accepted a commission from the regime to write about the socialist transformation of the countryside. Sándor (later Sir Alexander) Korda agreed to direct appropriately uplifting films. This level of support from Hungary's cultural heroes made a strong impact on the public at large. As economic and social conditions deteriorated, however, initial enthusiasm for the Kun regime quickly evaporated. Patriotic Hungarians were irked by the new government's ban on the playing of the national anthem and on the display of the national tricolour rather than the red flag; the destruction of statues of national heroes was rightly seen as wanton vandalism. Despite statutory wage increases and rent reductions, inflation, fuelled by the Károlyi government's reckless issues of paper money which Kun emulated, continued to spiral out of control. The country at large became conscious of the extent to which the industrial working class of Budapest had hijacked its destiny. The peasantry, already alienated by the suspension of Károlyi's distributive land reform, seethed with resentment at the procurement of food for the towns by armed force. This in turn generated anti–Semitism in the countryside, since a large majority of the members of the Revolutionary Council was Jewish. When the National Congress of Councils assembled for the first time, in June 1919, the regime was disconcerted to find itself the target of a barrage of criticism from rural deputies: a delegate from Veszprém complained: 'Impossible people have been coming into the country districts.... The agitators came in like a swarm of locusts and have upset everything.... The agitators went out to the villages, and each one began by advising us to turn the church into a cinema'.[47]

When some provincial delegations staged a demonstration against 'the bureaucracy of the Councils and abuse of power by the Revolutionary Councils', Béla Kun, loyal in all things to Leninist practice, closed the Congress down and replaced it with a Central Executive Committee. By no means the least of the sources of the regime's growing unpopularity, especially among the intelligentsia, was its use of terror to compel obedience and root out suspected disloyalty. Tibor Szamuely, nominally a People's Commissar for Education, presided over a 'Red Terror', which claimed nearly 600 lives during Kun's short tenure of power. Szamuely, like Kun a former prisoner of war and propagandist in revolutionary Russia, presided personally over mass executions in Dunapataj and Kalocsa; in

Budapest, he directed the activities of terrorist detachments of which the most feared were the leather-jacketed, red-scarved 'Lenin Boys' led by a sailor thug, József Cserny. As in Lenin's Russia, 'defence of the revolution' provided a cover for corruption, personal revenge and gratuitous sadism. By the midsummer of 1919, the Revolutionary Council's credit outside the radicalised urban working class was all but exhausted.

Whether the apparatus of dictatorship would have enabled the Kun regime to survive its growing unpopularity for much longer remains an open question because, as in the case of the Károlyi revolution, it was the Entente that decided its fate. As soon as the Revolutionary Council had been formed, in March, Kun addressed a note to the Peace Conference in Paris assuring it of the new regime's peaceful intentions towards all countries and inviting the conference to send a mission to Hungary. In doing so, Kun displayed one of his more notable political talents, that of playing for time: his objective in this case was to forestall a knee-jerk reaction by the Entente to the rejection of the Vyx note, and he succeeded. Although the French pressed for immediate offensives against Hungary by Czech and Romanian troops, the Conference's Council of Four* decided to accept Kun's invitation and to send the South African General Smuts to Budapest to assess the situation and put forward new proposals. Smuts arrived in Budapest on 4 April and stayed less than twenty-four hours, never leaving his train, which was parked in the Eastern Railway Station. In two meetings with Béla Kun, the general renewed the proposal in the Vyx note for a neutral zone to separate Hungarian from Romanian forces but offered new demarcation lines—which would not be regarded as political boundaries—more favourable to Hungary, and the lifting of the Allied blockade in return for Hungarian co-operation. Kun made a counter-proposal, for a conference on boundaries in Prague or Vienna (which he saw as a route to international recognition for his regime) but with the reservation that Romanian troops must first withdraw to the east of the Maros River. Concluding that Kun should not be taken seriously, Smuts returned to Paris. Ten days later, with the tacit acquiescence of the Allies, the Romanians resumed their westward advance; and the Czechs invaded from the north, occupying Salgótarján and the industrial suburbs of Miskolc. Kun at once set about enlarging Hungary's Red Army (as it was now called) by conscripting all non-commissioned ranks of the former Austro-Hungarian army and accepting the services of the large number of former officers who volunteered to fight Hungary's invaders. The Social Democrat Commissar for War, Vilmos Böhm, made a brilliant appointment in designating Colonel Aurél Stromfeld, a war veteran and former professor at the Military Academy, to be his chief of staff and, effectively, commander of the Red Army: within a few weeks, and despite sustaining a humiliating defeat on 1 May in the face of a renewed Romanian advance to the Tisza, Stromfeld had transformed a demoralised rabble into a disciplined fighting force of some 200,000 men.

On 20 May, the revitalised Red Army, its morale high in defending Hungarian soil, launched an offensive towards the north east which shattered the right flank

---

* The Council of Four, which succeeded the Council of Ten in directing the work of the conference, consisted of the Presidents of the United States and France and the Prime Ministers of Great Britain and Italy.

of the Romanian line and, wheeling left, drove the Czechs out of northern Hungary. By the end of the month, the Red Army had captured Kassa (Košice) and occupied a substantial slice of Slovakia, threatening Pozsony (Bratislava); alarmed, the Peace Conference in Paris addressed a telegram to the Revolutionary Council demanding an immediate halt to the Hungarian advance and offering discussions with a representative of the Kun regime. Receiving no satisfactory response, the conference sent two further telegrams to the council on 13 June: they combined a punitive sanction with a tempting offer. In their first message, the Allied Powers declared:

1. That the frontiers described in the accompanying telegram are to be the frontiers permanently dividing Hungary from Czecho-Slovakia and from Romania.
2. That the armed forces of those States must immediately cease hostilities and return without avoidable delay within the national frontiers thus laid down.[48]

The frontiers 'thus laid down' were those worked out by the specialist committees of the Peace Conference, which had just been approved by the conference's Supreme Council; they reappeared, virtually unchanged, in the Treaty of Trianon. As we shall see in the next chapter, the telegram thus removed any chance that Hungary might be able to secure some mitigation of the treaty's terms before it was imposed. The second telegram, however, held out a powerful incentive to compliance: if the Red Army withdrew as ordered by the Allies, 'Romanian troops will be withdrawn from Hungarian territory as soon as the Hungarian troops have evacuated Czecho-Slovakia'.[49]

At this juncture, Béla Kun's nerve deserted him. Recovery of Hungarian territory east of the Tisza would do much to ease the critical food shortage, which was causing hunger riots in the counties; and a Romanian withdrawal would supply the regime with a propaganda victory to offset the Red Army's retreat from Slovakia. Moreover, the forces of counter-revolution appeared to be gathering strength: right-wing groups had succeeded in organising, from Vienna, strike action by railwaymen in Sopron and Székesfehérvár. There was growing disorder in the countryside, which kept Tibor Szamuely's armoured train, his mobile instrument of terror, fully occupied. Kun decided to accept the Entente's offer in principle but continued for several days to haggle over the details. This cost Hungary her last chance of securing a Romanian withdrawal. On 23 June, Marshal Foch, his patience exhausted, presented the Revolutionary Council with an ultimatum requiring the Red Army to cease hostilities by the morning of the following day and to withdraw from Slovakia to the original demarcation lines by 28 June. The ultimatum gained in force from the coincidence that on 24 June the Danube Flotilla mutinied and shelled Budapest's Hotel Hungária, occupied by several People's Commissars, while in the Ludovika Military Academy, officer cadets took up arms against the regime; both mutinies were of short duration but helped to unnerve Kun and his colleagues.

On the council's behalf, Böhm now agreed to comply with the Foch ultimatum provided the Romanians drew back from the Tisza. The Red Army's withdrawal began on 30 June: by 4 July, its evacuation of Slovakia had been completed. The process of withdrawal, following hard upon the euphoria of advance, broke the Red Army's morale; Colonel Stromfeld resigned in protest against the council's capitulation. The Romanians, moreover, refused to fulfil their part of the Entente's offer and dug in on the banks of the Tisza. Kun, in desperation, ordered the demoralised Red Army to launch an offensive against the Romanians; predictably, this collapsed after a few days and by the end of the month a successful Romanian counter-attack had driven the Red Army into full retreat. Böhm, despatched to Vienna to explore the Entente's position, found that it had hardened dramatically. The Allies now stated that the Romanian advance would be halted only if the Revolutionary Council resigned, to make way for a more broadly based government whose authority did not depend on the exercise of terror. On 1 August, with Romanian forces only 100 kilometres from Budapest, the council decided to comply. Kun and his principal colleagues (including Rákosi) boarded a train for Vienna, where the Austrian government had promised them political asylum but where his presence soon became an embarrassment. Expelled from Austria, Kun made his way to Moscow and later became a senior functionary in the Communist International; he perished in the purges of the 1930s. Rákosi lived to become a notorious ruler of his homeland. Tibor Szamuely attempted to cross the Austrian border illegally and shot himself when apprehended. The Hungarian people's first experience of Communism had lasted for only 133 days: thirty years later, they were to find that the characteristics of a Communist regime had changed very little in the interim.

Despite its brevity, the Béla Kun experience made a profound impact on the Hungarian national psyche. It instilled a hatred of Communism and, by association, a deep hostility to the Soviet Union which, twenty years later, helped to account for Hungary's tolerance of right-wing extremism, apparent indifference to the horrors of Naziism and popular acquiescence in the eventual occupation of Hungary by Nazi Germany. Communism was perceived to be the greater evil, Stalin's Russia the greater threat. Károlyi's abdication in favour of the Communists, moreover, tainted the cause of democratic liberalism, thenceforth equated with weakness, and partly accounted for the predominantly reactionary complexion of Hungarian politics during the inter-war period.

Most leading members of the right-wing groups that had opposed the Károlyi regime had left Budapest for Vienna, or in some cases for occupied Szeged, as soon as Béla Kun seized power; and they had not been inactive thereafter. Count István Bethlen, leader of the National Unity Party (NEP), having reached Vienna in disguise and on a forged passport, at once set about uniting temporary exiles of similar views under a single umbrella, that of the Hungarian National Committee, later known as the Anti–Bolshevik Committee (ABC). Bethlen enlisted into the ABC former members of the Constitution Party, including Counts Andrássy and Pallavicini, Captain Gömbös and other members of MOVE, a few former members of Károlyi's party and members of his own NEP including Count Pál Teleki. Bethlen and the ABC established close relations with the Entente's missions in Vienna and endeavoured to interest them, without success, in various projects for armed intervention in Hungary to overthrow the Communist regime. In April 1919, the ABC decided to transfer its operations to Szeged, where right-wing elements were coalescing around Count Gyula Károlyi, Mihály's ultra-conservative cousin; the committee first provided itself with funds by means of a daring and successful robbery of the Hungarian Legation in Vienna, which had received large sums in cash from Soviet Russia for the financing of subversive activities in Austria. Colonel Cunninghame, head of the British Military Mission in Vienna, assisted the committee by obtaining visas for twenty of its members to travel to Szeged through Serbia. Bethlen himself remained in Vienna as representative of the 'provisional government' Gyula Károlyi had formed in Szeged on 5 May, but returned to Budapest after the collapse of the Communist regime at the beginning. of August.

In Budapest, Bethlen found that the government of Social Democratic trade unionists under Gyula Peidl, to which Kun's Revolutionary Council had handed over power before dissolving itself, had just been ousted at gun-point by István Friedrich, a former businessman, and a group of right-wingers. The Peidl government, during its five days in office, had repealed most of the decrees and ordinances of the Kun regime, in effect restoring the Károlyist status quo. Friedrich and his colleagues now set about turning the clock back much further, to the pre-Károlyi period. All land sequestrated for redistribution was returned to its original owners; social benefits, including unemployment benefit, were abolished at a stroke; wages were reduced; the institutions of central government and county administration were restored to the wartime pattern. The process of revenge for two revolutions began with the imposition of over seventy death sentences and the dismissal of sympathisers with either revolution from their posts, mostly in the universities. Charges were laid against Béla Bartók and Zoltán Kodály among others. In Szeged, the 'cabinet' formed by Gyula Károly declared its support for Friedrich; and Admiral Miklós Horthy, Gyula Károlyi's 'Minister of War', proclaimed the autonomy of his 'Hungarian National Army' of about 30,000 officers and men and led them north from Szeged into Transdanubia. Meanwhile, on 4 August, Romanian troops had entered and occupied Budapest.

The occupation of Budapest inaugurated three nightmare months that equalled in horror and misfortune the darkest periods of Hungary's troubled history. In the areas under their control—over half the country—the Romanians embarked on a systematic programme of looting, expropriation, deportations and terror. In scenes that would be reproduced a quarter of a century later in the Soviet Zone of defeated Germany, trains were loaded with industrial machinery, agricultural produce and cultural artefacts to be sent on their way to Romania. Only the courageous intervention of an American member of the Allied Military Mission, General Bandholtz, saved the National Museum and its treasury from looting. Arbitrary executions by Romanian troops claimed hundreds of Hungarian lives. At the same time, in western Hungary, Admiral Horthy's National Army had initiated a 'White Terror'. Armed detachments, usually led by junior officers, scoured the countryside for known or suspected supporters of the Kun regime; Jews were assumed automatically to have had Communist sympathies and the pogrom returned to Hungarian towns and villages. In Siófok, on Lake Balaton, over 200 victims were tortured and executed. In Kecskemét, in early November, a similar number were flayed or buried alive, some meeting a swifter death by hanging. In the village of Diszel, near Tapolca, Jewish children were flung into wells. Estimates of the toll taken by the White Terror vary between 2,000 and 6,000 lives; it certainly far exceeded its Red predecessor both in the number of its victims and in the cruelty of its methods. During the first three months of counter-revolution, over 70,000 suspected collaborators or sympathisers with the Kun regime were imprisoned or interned, many of them Jewish.

By October 1919, the Peace Conference in Paris at last awoke to the fact that Hungary had descended into anarchy and that if a peace settlement were to be concluded, civil order would first have to be restored and a government put in place with which the conference could negotiate—it correctly regarded the Friedrich government as unrepresentative and impotent. The Conference accordingly despatched a British diplomat, Sir George Clerk, to Budapest to secure an end to the Romanian occupation and the formation of a representative government. After three weeks of hard negotiation, Clerk persuaded the Romanians to withdraw from all Hungarian territory west of the Tisza, any further withdrawal to await a peace treaty: Romanian troops began to evacuate Budapest on 14 November. Two days later Admiral Horthy, mounted on a white horse, led units of his National Army into the capital. Addressing an assembly of city dignitaries in the square before the Royal Palace, Horthy berated them for dishonouring their country and the Holy Crown, for clothing Budapest 'in red rags': but, he grandly pronounced: 'We shall forgive this sinful city'. By the last week of November, Clerk had brokered the formation of a coalition government of right-wing parties—the Christian National Unity Party (*Keresztény Nemzeti Egyesülés Pártja* or KNEP) and the Christian Agrarian Labourers' Party (*Keresztény Földmíves Párt*)—under Károly Huszár, with token representation in the cabinet for the Social Democrats, the Liberals and the Smallholders, who were allocated one seat each. On 25 November, Clerk recognised the new government in the name of the Peace Conference and conveyed an invitation from Clemenceau for the despatch of a Hungarian delegation to Paris. After over a year in limbo, the way was now clear for Hungary to rejoin the community of European nations. The terms on which she could do so had already been decided in her absence; but they had yet to be formally revealed.

Part Three

TRIPLE TRAGEDY AND REBIRTH

13

THE ROAD TO TRIANON

(1914–20)

During the half century following the end of the First World War, Hungary sustained three tragedies which would have destroyed a less resilient nation: a crippling and unjust treaty, occupation by Nazi Germany and the imposition of a brutal Stalinist regime. Hungary survived, to be reborn in 1989 as a free and democratic state.

The Treaty of Trianon—that part of the Paris Peace Settlement that dealt with Hungary—constituted the most severe reverse sustained by the Hungarian nation since the Battle of Mohács in 1526. Its consequences and the quest for its revision dominated Hungarian politics, and largely determined Hungary's foreign policy, for a quarter of a century after its signature in 1920. To this day, its legacy is a source of passion and dispute in Hungary's relations with her neighbours and a partially coded theme of Hungarian domestic politics. The background to the treaty and the factors that helped to shape its terms consequently merit separate treatment, a brief departure from the largely chronological narrative to which this volume is devoted.

Towards a New Europe

Controversy within the Entente over the post-war future of the Austro-Hungarian Monarchy lasted for nearly as long as First World War itself. It was assumed, after the formation of the Yugoslav Committee in London in 1915, that Croatia would detach herself from Hungary in order to join some kind of federation of South Slav peoples; and that Poland would once again become a unitary state. Until 1918, however, there was no consensus in favour of the actual dismemberment of the Monarchy. There were strong arguments for allowing the Monarchy to remain in being, albeit in a federalised form comprising, perhaps, three autonomous states of Austria, Hungary and Bohemia. Allied statesmen saw the Monarchy as a continuing barrier against both Russian expansion into Europe and a renewed German *Drang nach Osten*. Moreover, the British in particular entertained hopes of detaching the Monarchy from its German ally and concluding a separate peace: this objective would not be advanced if the Monarchy were given reason to see the conclusion of peace simply as the prelude to its own dismantlement. When President Wilson addressed Congress in December 1917, on the United States' entry into the war, he declared that 'we do not wish in any way to impair or rearrange the Austro-Hungarian Empire'. The same message was conveyed in the secret talks on a possible separate peace, which began in Copenhagen early in 1917 and resumed in Geneva, between General Smuts and Count Mensdorff, towards the end of the year: 'nobody in London', Smuts assured Mensdorff, 'desired the destruction of Austria-Hungary'. At the beginning of 1918, the British War Cabinet approved the Prime Minister's view that after the war 'Austria-Hungary should be in a position to exercise a powerful influence in south-east Europe'. Lloyd George spoke in similar terms in the House of Commons on 9 January.

These reassuring professions were at some variance with the promises made by the Entente during the world war to nations whose support or neutrality it wished to secure. The secret Treaty of London (1915) made over to Italy, in return for her declaration of war on the Central Powers and on the assumption of eventual Allied victory, large areas of Austro-Hungarian territory including Trentino and south Tyrol, Trieste, Gorizia, Istria, northern Dalmatia, most of the Dalmatian islands and a protectorate over Albania. The terms of this treaty soon leaked, in Petrograd, and were in any case published by the Bolsheviks in 1918; the prospect of losing northern Dalmatia to Italy injected new fighting spirit into Croatian units of the Austro-Hungarian army, which helped to defeat the Italians at Caporetto. Serbia's government-in-exile was promised Austria-Hungary's recently annexed province of Bosnia-Herzegovina, together with southern Dalmatia and the Entente's good offices in bringing about union with Croatia in a federation of South Slavs. In 1916, Romania, for her part, was promised the whole of Transylvania, the Bánát and the Bukovina in return for her entry into the war—although the Allies subsequently claimed this agreement to have been invalidated by the Treaty of Bucharest (1918), in which Romania concluded a separate peace with the Central Powers after the disastrous failure of her invasion of Transylvania. The Allies drew a distinction between the complete dismemberment of the Austro-Hungarian Monarchy and the cavalier use of its peripheral territories as the currency of international bribery. But even if the Monarchy was to be allowed to survive an Allied victory, to serve as an insurance against revived German or Russian ambitions, a significant reduction in its territorial extent—including that of historic Hungary—was preordained.

There were, moreover, increasingly strong influences working within and alongside the Entente for the complete break-up of the Monarchy after its defeat. These consisted both of leading personalities from the national groupings within the Monarchy who saw in the war their best hope of national independence; and of their active sympathisers within the political establishments of the Entente. As early as the autumn of 1914, two seasoned Croatian campaigners for independence from Hungary, the former newspaper editor Frano Supilo and local politician Dr Ante Trumbić, were lobbying in London to promote the concept of a South Slav (Yugoslav) federation. With the help of Robert Seton-Watson, whom we have already encountered and of whom more below, they gained access to both the British Prime Minister, Asquith, and to the Foreign Secretary, Sir Edward Grey; they won no promises of support but sowed seeds of sympathy for the

Yugoslav idea. In April 1915, the Yugoslav Committee was formally constituted in London, under the chairmanship of Dr Trumbić, with the objective of promoting the post-war creation of a single Yugoslav state, uniting the Serbian, Croatian and Slovene peoples in a federation of equals. This concept took a major step towards realisation in 1917 when, at the Conference of Corfu, the Serbian government-in-exile under Nikola Pašić reached agreement with the Yugoslav Committee on the establishment of a 'Kingdom of Serbs, Croats and Slovenes', under the Serbian Karadjordjević dynasty. Meanwhile, the protagonists of an independent state of Czechs and Slovaks had been equally active and with even greater success. Tomáš Masaryk, a Czech professor of philosophy and future leader of his people, was hard at work within a month of the outbreak of war lobbying in Paris for an independent Bohemia, which would incorporate the predominantly Slovak regions of Hungary. In a memorandum to the British Foreign Office, Masaryk added the requirement for a corridor, to be carved out of western Hungary, to link the new state with the future Yugoslavia. This plan, amounting as it did to the dismemberment of the Austro-Hungarian Monarchy, went further than the Allies, in 1915, were as yet prepared to go; but in the following year Masaryk, having formed the Czecho-Slovak National Council in Paris, persuaded the French Prime Minister, Aristide Briand, that the Monarchy should indeed be broken up and won his support for the creation of an independent Czecho-Slovak state. When, in January 1917, the Allies replied to President Wilson's invitation to state their war aims, they included as one of their objectives 'the liberation of the Italians, as also of the Slavs, Romanians and Czecho-Slovaks from foreign domination'. Despite this implied endorsement for the separation of Bohemia from Austria and of Slovakia and Transylvania from Hungary, the Allies nevertheless continued to encourage Austrian feelers concerning the possible conclusion of a separate peace. In November, Mihály Károlyi, still opposition leader in the Hungarian Parliament, conveyed to the Allies through the British Legation in Berne a possible basis for a peace settlement under which the Monarchy should become a confederation of four states: Austria, Hungary (retaining Slovakia and Transylvania), Bohemia and Yugoslavia (including Croatia). The Hungarian left, evidently, was already at this stage prepared to accept the loss of Croatia.

In their campaigns to promote the claims of their peoples to independence after the war, Masaryk, Supilo, Trumbić and their colleagues were greatly assisted by two British experts on east-central Europe, Wickham Steed and R. W. Seton-Watson. The two men met several years before the war, when Steed was serving as correspondent of *The Times* in Vienna, where Seton-Watson, a young Scot of independent means, was engaged in research into Austrian history. Seton-Watson's interests soon broadened into a study of the Austro-Hungarian Monarchy as a whole and he became proficient in several of its languages. As we have seen,* he also developed a profound antipathy to the Magyars and became the self-appointed champion of those peoples whom he perceived as victims of Magyar discrimination and oppression. Steed, who subsequently became Foreign Editor and then Editor of *The Times*, fully shared Seton-Watson's views and used his considerable influence to promote them. In October 1916, Seton-Watson founded a

* On pages 242 and 273.

journal, *The New Europe*, through the columns of which British and other European academics, and the future leaders of, in particular, Czecho-Slovakia and Yugoslavia promoted the cause of the replacement of Austria-Hungary by a conglomeration of independent nations. At about the same time, the British Prime Minister asked the Foreign Office to prepare a memorandum suggesting a basis for an eventual territorial settlement in Europe. As the following excerpts indicate, the response coincided with, and probably reflected, the views of Seton-Watson and his co-thinkers. As a basic principle, the memorandum laid down 'that no peace can be satisfactory to this country unless it promises to be durable, and an essential condition of such a peace is that it should give full scope to national aspirations as far as practicable. The principle of nationality should therefore be one of the governing factors in the consideration of territorial arrangements after the war'. On the future of Austria-Hungary, the memorandum opined:

If the situation should be one which enables the Allies to dispose of its future, there seems very little doubt that, in accordance with the principle of giving free play to nationalities, the Dual Monarchy, which in its present composition is a direct negation of that principle, should be broken up, as there is no doubt that all the non-German parts of Austria-Hungary will secede.

The memorandum recommended that Romania should be given 'the Roumanian portion of Transylvania'; but went on to state: 'If Hungary is, however, to be an independent State with any chance of vitality it would be inexpedient to deprive it of territory beyond that which is necessary in order to conform to the principle of nationality'.[1] Although the memorandum was never formally approved as a statement of policy, it is unfortunate that this last recommendation had little influence on the thinking of those who eventually framed the Treaty of Trianon.

In 1914, British or French experts on east-central Europe and the Balkans were few and far between. The small group of officials, journalists and academics—no more than half a dozen—with knowledge and direct experience of the region consequently exercised a disproportionately significant degree of influence and enjoyed remarkable ease of access to policymakers at the highest level, from the Prime Minister downwards. In the country of the blind, the one-eyed man is king. Seton-Watson's expertise and his powers of advocacy are unquestioned; but his passionate dedication to the twin causes of helping to create independent Czecho-Slovak and Yugoslav states sometimes clouded his judgement and afflicted him with political tunnel-vision. He became over-excited when events did not go his way. In late 1915 and early 1916, he waged an abusive campaign against the British Foreign Secretary, Sir Edward Grey, for favouring Italian over Yugoslav interests in Dalmatia and for failing to support aid to the retreating Serbian army. 'I have found out Grey in his rotten and perfidious policy', he wrote to a friend, 'and am preparing a philippic against him'.[2] When the 'philippic' appeared, in a leading journal, it claimed that 'official Germany has long known that his [Grey's] honest aimlessness and naive obstinacy make him one of their greatest assets'.[3] The intemperance of these judgements sometimes crept into Seton-Watson's pronouncements further from home. In a newspaper interview he gave during a visit to neutral Romania in 1915, he said: 'What Prussian militarism is for us, Magyar hegemony is for you: these are the principal obstacles to European progress ... you with the Serbs must put an end to the brutal and artificial domination of the

Magyar race over all its neighbours'.[4] From time to time and sometimes at crucial junctures, Seton-Watson's emotions impeded his capacity for dispassionate analysis; the fact that he and Wickham Steed were in a position to significantly influence Allied policy compounded the misfortune for Hungary towards which that policy was now pointing.

The publication in Germany, in 1915, of Naumann's treatise on *Mitteleuropa* had already raised the spectre of the union of Germany with Austria-Hungary in a monster state stretching from the Baltic to the Adriatic. Following the publication of Charles IV's rash offer, in a letter to Clemenceau, to support France's 'just claims to Alsace-Lorraine' in return for a separate peace on acceptable terms, Charles was obliged to face the Kaiser's fury at a meeting in Spa in May 1918, and to sign a convention committing Austria-Hungary not only to long-term political alliance but also to military, customs and economic union with Germany. This removed any prospect of the conclusion of a separate peace between the Allies and the Monarchy. Noting Austria-Hungary's relegation to the status of a German satellite, the American Secretary of State Lansing suggested in a memorandum to President Wilson that the United States should consider whether she should or should not 'favour the disintegration of the Austro-Hungarian empire into its component parts ... giving recognition to the nationalities that seek independence'.[5]

The shift in Allied policy away from preservation of the Monarchy in some form and towards its dismemberment was now rapidly consolidated. On 3 June, the Supreme War Council declared its sympathy for the national aspirations of the Czechs, Slovaks and Yugoslavs; and Allied governments endorsed the final resolution of the Congress of Oppressed Nationalities, which had taken place in Rome a few weeks before. On 28 June, the United States government declared that 'all branches of the Slav race should be completely freed from German and Magyar rule'. This unequivocal statement owed much to the direct influence of Tomáš Masaryk who, during a visit to the United States, had also succeeded in winning the approval of the émigré Slovak leaders there for the union of Czechs and Slovaks in a single state. France now recognised the Czecho-Slovak National Council as the legitimate representative of the Czech and Slovak nation and as trustee of a future Czechoslovak government; the British and United States governments followed suit a few weeks later. When, therefore, Mihály Károlyi, in the name of Hungary's new ruling National Council, sent a message of greeting on 31 October to the Slovak National Council in Turócszentmárton, it elicited the cool response that 'the Slovak National Council, having joined Czechoslovakia, would welcome a collaboration of the Czecho-Slovak Republic with the Magyar People's Republic on an international basis'.[6]

On 28 October 1918, the Czecho-Slovak National Council in Prague proclaimed the foundation of the Czechoslovak Republic, an act quickly ratified by the Slovak National Council in Turócszentmárton. On the following day, the *Sabor* in Zagreb declared the independence of Croatia and her intention of joining a Yugoslav federation. A month later, the Serbian National Council, meeting in Újvidék (Novi Sad) announced the incorporation into Serbia of the southern Hungarian counties occupied by Serbian forces. And on 1 December 1918, the Romanian National Assembly in Gyulafehérvár proclaimed the union of Transylvania with the Kingdom of Romania. Masaryk, in the meantime, had succeeded in using the Ruthenian community in the United States to persuade the Ruthenians of north-east Hungary that their future lay in the new state of Czechoslovakia. These spontaneous defections from the Monarchy, and from the Kingdom of Hungary, had been made possible and accelerated by the commitment of the victorious Allies to the independence of their ethnic components. The birth of this commitment, in the last year of the war, had several midwives. They included President Wilson and his Fourteen Points, of which the Tenth called for the 'autonomous development' of the peoples of Austria-Hungary; the leaders in exile of the Czech, Slovak, Croatian and Serbian peoples; and the small but influential group of advocates of the dismemberment of the Monarchy who helped the national leaders towards the realisation of their aspirations. By formally relegating the Monarchy to the status of a second-rate power, the German Kaiser also played his part. These influences combined to ensure that, when the Paris Peace Conference assembled in January 1919, Hungary already faced the certain loss of Slovakia, Croatia and, in all probability, southern districts inhabited predominantly by Serbs: all these territories, subject to the Holy Crown for nearly a thousand years, had in effect already become components of new states whose creation had been formally sanctioned by the Allies.

The case of Transylvania, well-head of Magyar culture and a symbol for centuries of Hungary's independence, was a little different. Having concluded a peace treaty with the Central Powers as recently as May 1918, following her comprehensive defeat, and having re-declared war on Germany on 9 November, Romania nudged her way into a share of the spoils at the last minute: a National Council of Romanian Unity, chaired by Take Ionescu, was formed in Paris only in September. As we have seen, however, the Romanians of Transylvania[7] had already taken matters into their own hands, proclaiming union with the motherland and welcoming the return of the Romanian army following Károlyi's acceptance of d'Esperey's armistice terms in Belgrade. Since the Peace Conference would inevitably apply the principle of ethnicity in determining Transylvania's future, Hungary could hope for no more than some mitigation of Romania's *fait accompli*. Given the turmoil Hungary underwent during the last months of 1918, it is perhaps unsurprising that the realities of the situation were insufficiently recognised by her leaders or people. The advent of Kun's Communist regime, moreover, deprived Hungary of the chance of making her voice heard in Paris while treaty drafting was in progress—and Kun spurned the opening provided by General Smuts's mission for the despatch of a Hungarian delegation to Paris. But a Hungarian presence in Paris could not have altered this inescapable fact: that by the end of 1918, before the Peace Conference opened and before the drafting of what emerged as the Treaty of Trianon had even begun, Hungary was destined to lose over half the Kingdom and most of her non-Magyar population. The task of the Peace Conference was to ensure that the precise definition of this transfer of territory and people would be conducive to the preservation of peace in east-central Europe; and that it would be seen to respect the principles of natural justice.

The Peace Treaty

The Supreme Council of the Peace Conference decided at an early stage of its deliberations that the task of drawing up recommendations for the delineation of the new frontiers of the defeated powers, in the light of the claims made upon them by the victors, should be delegated to committees of officials of the four principal Allies, advised by acknowledged experts on the regions concerned. The junior British diplomats serving on, respectively, the 'Romanian and Yugoslav Committee' and the 'Czecho-Slovak Committee' were Allen Leeper, a talented official with strong Romanian sympathies, and Harold Nicolson, who later wrote a brilliant account of the work of the conference, based on his own diaries.[8] Nicolson frankly admitted that his feelings towards Hungary were not neutral: 'I confess that I regarded, and still regard, that Turanian tribe with acute distaste. Like their cousins the Turks, they had destroyed much and created nothing. Buda Pest was a false city devoid of any autochthonous reality. For centuries the Magyars had oppressed their subject nationalities. The hour of liberation and of retribution was at hand'.[9] The expert whom the British officials consulted most was, of course, Seton-Watson, now engaged full-time in editing *The New Europe* and living in Paris, with Wickham Steed, to maximise the influence of their journal on the proceedings of the conference. Nicolson recalled: 'Allen Leeper and myself never moved a yard without previous consultation with experts of the authority of Dr. Seton-Watson, who was in Paris at the time'.[10] Nicolson confessed that he went to the conference 'overwhelmingly imbued with the doctrines of *The New Europe*', to which he had devoted careful study. These were unhappy auguries for Hungary, deprived by revolution of a voice in Paris.

Two further factors militated against objective treatment of the question of Hungary's future frontiers. First, the two territorial committees drew up their recommendations independently, on the basis of their respective terms of reference; there was thus no monitoring of the aggregate impact of their proposals. To quote Nicolson once more: 'The Committee on Rumanian Claims', for instance, thought only in terms of Transylvania, the Committee on Czech Claims concentrated upon the southern frontier of Slovakia. It was only too late that it was realised that these two entirely separate Committees had between them imposed upon Hungary a loss of territory and population which, when combined, was very serious indeed'.[11] Second, this flaw in the structure of the conference was compounded by confusion over the nature of the conference's end-game. At least some members of the committees believed that they were preparing a bargaining position that might be modified in negotiation with the defeated powers before a Peace Treaty was finalised. In the event, there was no negotiation; and the committee's recommendations consequently found their way into the treaty virtually unchanged.

In drawing up frontiers, the United States' officials and advisers gave clear priority to the principle of ethnicity, endeavouring to ensure that the new borders conformed as closely as possible to the ethnic map of the regions concerned. The British, in the spirit of *The New Europe*, attached prime importance to the economic and strategic viability of the new states to whose birth they were committed. Nicolson noted in his diary on 2 March 1919: '... Then examine frontier from Komorn [Komárom] to Jung [Ungvár]. The very devil. The Yanks want to go north along the ethnical line, thus cutting all the railways. We want to go south, keeping the Kassa-Komorn lateral communications, in spite of the fact that this will mean putting some 80,000 Magyars under Czech rule'.[12]

The French, with an eye to maximising their influence in the region after the settlement, favoured satisfying virtually any demand the successor states (as they were now beginning to be termed) cared to advance—a position that in practice usually aligned them with the British. The Italians concerned themselves almost exclusively with squabbles with the Yugoslavs over division of the Balkan spoils. If a particular issue had to be put to a vote, therefore, the Anglo-French position tended to prevail over the American; this, again, was unhelpful to Hungary. Even if, moreover, Hungarian representatives had been present in Paris during the short gestation period of the committee's recommendations, they could not have shed their country's greatest handicap—the status of defeated enemy. Sir Eyre Crowe, the senior British official who served on both committees, was later quoted by Lloyd George as having stated at a committee meeting:

When we come to face these ethnographical difficulties it makes a great difference whether they arise between the Roumanians and the Hungarians who are our enemies, or between the Roumanians and the Serbs, who are our Allies. In the first case if it were found to be impossible to do justice to both sides, the balance must naturally be inclined toward our ally Roumania rather than toward our enemy Hungary. At the same time this principle must not be carried too far, for our ultimate duty is to produce a condition of things likely to lead to permanent peace.[13]

The reports of the two territorial committees on Hungary's future frontiers were considered at a single meeting of the conference's Council of Foreign Ministers on 8 May 1919; the council commended them to the Supreme Council of the Conference without amendment. The Supreme Council, in turn, approved the committees' recommendations on 12 May; apart from a brief and inconclusive exchange about Hungary's western frontier with Austria, there was no discussion. The minutes of the meeting baldly state:

(d) Remaining frontiers of Hungary

After a short statement by M. Tardieu* the frontiers of Hungary, as laid down in Annexure A, were accepted. (The meeting then adjourned.)[14]

The effect of 'Annexure A' was to award to Romania the whole of Transylvania, a significant strip of Hungarian territory to the west of the Transylvanian border and the eastern half of the Bánát; to Yugoslavia, all of Croatia/Slavonia, the western half of the Bánát and most of the Bácska (the triangle of territory north of Újvidék bordered by the Danube and Drava Rivers); to Czechoslovakia, all of the predominantly Slovak and Ruthene regions of northern Hungary, plus a strip of Hungarian territory south of the ethnic borderline; and to Austria—in response to a claim that was a poor reward for her former ally's consistent loyalty to the Monarchy—a slice of western Hungary including the town of Sopron.[15] The implications of these awards included: the reduction of Hungary's area by two-thirds, from 282,000 to 93,000 sq.km; the reduction of Hungary's population by

---

* The French Chairman of the 'Romanian and Yugoslav' Committee.

over half, from 18.2 to 7.9 million; the confiscation from Hungary of two-thirds of her railway, road and canal networks, together with approximately 80 per cent of her forests and mines; and—perhaps more importantly than all these losses— the transfer of over three million ethnic Magyars to Czechoslovak, Romanian, Yugoslav or Austrian rule.[16] It was on this last aspect of the emerging peace settlement, in so far as it concerned Hungary, that criticism rightly concentrated.

The obsessive concern of the Entente powers to give their new creations, the Successor States, frontiers they would be able to defend against the perceived menace of Bolshevik Russia—and even, at the time, Communist Hungary—had the effect of leaving Hungary herself virtually defenceless against any future foe. Hungary lost most of the security of her historic natural frontiers—mountains and rivers—leaving only a few stretches of the Danube and Drava Rivers as natural lines of defence. (The new frontiers, incidentally, bisected the areas of twenty-four flood-control authorities, exposing Hungary to serious flood risks on the lower reaches of her rivers—a danger increased by mindless deforestation in Czechoslovakia and Romania.) The Peace Treaty, moreover, limited her defence forces to an army of 35,000 volunteers, without tanks, heavy artillery or aircraft, together with gendarmerie and police forces of 12,000 each. The Successor States along Hungary's borders, by contrast, could muster a combined army of 500,000. To ensure that military would be matched by economic weakness, the massive loss of natural resources which the treaty imposed was to be accompanied by open-ended financial reparations lasting for thirty years from 1921 and payments in kind, of coal and livestock, to Italy, Yugoslavia and Greece. Taken together, the effect of these provisions was to make future Hungarian governments dependent on alliance with a major power if they were to fulfil their basic duty of ensuring the security of their citizens.

It was nevertheless the ethnic aspects of the peace settlement, in so far as it concerned Hungary, that attracted the greatest criticism. As early as March 1919, while drafting was still in progress, Lloyd George had warned against the long-term dangers of imposing too harsh a peace on Germany. His memorandum on 'Some Considerations for the Peace Conference' declared:

> What I have said about the Germans is equally true of the Magyars. There will never be peace in South-Eastern Europe if every little state now coming into being is to have a large Magyar Irredenta within its borders. I would therefore take as a guiding principle of the peace that as far as is humanly possible the different races should be allocated to their motherlands, and that this human criterion should have precedence over considerations of strategy or economics or communications, which can usually be adjusted by other means.[17]

Flushed with the excitement of nation-making, the disciples of *The New Europe* chose to ignore this wise precept, most conspicuously in four aspects of their delineation of Hungary's proposed new frontiers. In three of them, the future transport systems of the Successor States were given priority over ethnic considerations. The Csallóköz, an island of territory between Komárom and Bratislava bordered by the Danube and Little Danube with a predominantly Magyar population, was awarded to Czechoslovakia purely to give her newly acquired river port (Bratislava) a hinterland. Similarly, Czechoslovakia acquired an almost entirely Magyar-populated strip of territory in the south of Slovakia solely because it contained an east-west railway line. Romania acquired the strip of land west of Transylvania containing the mainly Magyar towns of Arad, Nagyvárad and Szatmár on the basis that it contained a north-south railway line linking the two ends of her new territory. In the fourth case, strategic considerations took priority: Yugoslavia was awarded territory in southern Hungary, including the Bácska, simply to provide her capital, Belgrade, with a protective territorial cushion. Lloyd George's attempts to reinstate the priority of the ethnic principle over other factors continued in 1920, when the conference's terms had already been conveyed to the Hungarian government; he argued in one of the last meetings of the Conference of Foreign Ministers and Ambassadors (which had replaced the Supreme Council), on 3 March, that there would be no peace in central Europe if it were discovered that 'a whole community of Magyars had been handed over like cattle to Czechoslovakia and to Transylvania [sic], simply because the Conference had refused to examine the Hungarian case'.[18] He urged revision of the treaty, should Hungarian objections be sustained, prior to its impending imposition. The French, of course, opposed him; but so did his own Foreign Office, the Foreign Secretary, Arthur Balfour and subsequently Lord Curzon, firmly maintaining that the verdicts of the experts should stand. Lloyd George could only secure the agreement of his Allies that if boundary commissions were to discover, in laying down frontiers on the ground, that serious injustice had been inflicted on any party, it would be open to them to report accordingly to the League of Nations.

The truth was that by this stage 'conference fatigue' had set in with a vengeance: statesmen already exhausted by the mental and physical demands imposed by four years of war, followed by over a year of argument across the peace-making table, were understandably disinclined to unravel one of the most complex and arcane components of an overall settlement that was, after all, primarily concerned with the disarming and punishment of Germany. In January 1919, William Beveridge, who was visiting Budapest with an Inter-Allied Relief Mission, recorded in his diary Mihály Károlyi's bitter complaint at the failure of the Peace Conference to respond to his repeated telegrams about a peace settlement; and recalled his response:

I found myself explaining to him and others, as tactfully as possible, that I did not think that the Entente had any particular dislike for Hungary, or any deliberate intention to harm, in leaving them so long unnoticed; the Entente Governments had many more important things to think about than the fate of 10,000,000 people in Hungary, and Hungary must wait her turn for political attention.[19]

Harold Nicolson's diary contains a revealing entry for 7 May 1919:

There is a row about our not having invited the Hungarians to Paris at the same time as the Austrians. The French say that the Conseil des Trois had decided that such an invitation should be sent, and that the British cancelled this decision. It was rather my fault, as we had heard that Béla Kun had fallen.* *Anyhow, doesn't matter much.*[20]

As we have seen (page 315) the Hungarians did eventually receive their invitation to Paris, conveyed by Sir George Clerk in Clemenceau's name on 25

---

* He had not, yet.

November 1919. We have also seen (page 312) that the Hungarian delegation to the Peace Conference would inevitably be confronted with a *fait accompli*: Clemenceau's telegram of 13 June to the Kun government left no room for negotiation, despite the fact that its promise of Romanian withdrawal from Hungarian territory had not been honoured. When the delegation, led by Count Albert Apponyi and including, among others, István Bethlen and Pál Teleki, arrived in Paris on 6 January 1920, it was handed a draft treaty of which the terms were virtually identical with those of the reports of the two territorial committees, prepared eight months earlier. In response, the Hungarians submitted a number of memoranda, taking issue with the draft treaty on historical, demographic, economic and legal grounds, of which Apponyi gave an oral summary in his address to the Supreme Council on 16 January.* Making the focus of his speech the transfer to foreign rule of half the Hungarian population, including (he claimed) 3.5 million Magyars, Apponyi demanded plebiscites in the regions of Hungary affected, in accordance with Wilsonian principles. Recalling Hungary's historic role over ten centuries in protecting Europe from threats from the east, he warned the Council 'that with such artificial enactments as are contained in the Conditions of Peace, the establishment of a peaceful political situation in this much-suffered part of Europe, so important from the point of view of general peace, is hardly possible. Only the stability of this territory is capable of guarding central Europe from dangers constantly menacing it from the East'.[21] The Council heard Apponyi out in silence; there was no subsequent discussion. Apponyi and most of his delegation returned to Budapest two days later. There followed a curious interlude during which secret contacts took place between Hungarian representatives and the new Secretary-General at the Quai d'Orsay, Maurice Paléologue, designed to explore the possibility of giving France uniquely privileged influence in the Hungarian economy in return for French assistance in bringing about a revision of the Peace Treaty terms to Hungary's advantage. In March 1920, these contacts were upgraded to an official, though still secret, negotiation. Hungary was prepared to offer France a lease on all her railways; a contract to build a commercial port on the Danube; and a majority shareholding in the Hungarian Credit Bank. In return, Hungary expected to secure, through French good offices, the retention of predominantly Magyar territories due to be awarded to Czechoslovakia and Romania, the protection of Magyar minorities in Transylvania and other concessions. These bizarre exchanges, which eventually petered out without concrete result and need not, therefore, be further recorded, reflected the level of desperation in Budapest as the full implications of the treaty terms sank in.

The machinery of the conference, now under the chairmanship of Etienne Millerand, who had replaced Clemenceau as French Prime Minister in January, nevertheless ground on. The conference's formal response to Hungary's representations came under cover of a letter from Millerand to Apponyi on 6 May 1920. Its tone was harsh, its content uncompromising. Dismissing Apponyi's references

---

* There is a fuller account of Apponyi's address to the Council, and of subsequent events in Paris, in the present author's monograph, *Mihály Károlyi and István Bethlen: Hungary*, in the series *Makers of the Modern World: the Peace Conferences of 1919–23 and their Aftermath* (London, 2009–10).

to the consecration of Hungary's frontiers by a thousand years of history, the letter brusquely stated: 'A state of affairs, even when millennial, is not meant to exist when it has been recognised as contrary to justice'.

Apponyi's demand for plebiscites received equally short shrift:

The will of the people was expressed in October and November of 1918 at the collapse of the Dual Monarchy when the populations, oppressed for so long, united with their Italian, Roumanian, Yugo-Slav and Czecho-Slovak kindred. The events occurring since that epoch constitute so many proofs the more of the sentiments of the nationalities formerly subjected to the Crown of St. Stephen. The tardy measures taken by the Hungarian Government to satisfy the need felt by the nationalities for an autonomy is not able to create any illusion; they do not change at all the essentials of historical truth: notably, that during long years all the efforts of Hungarian policy were directed to stifling the voice of the ethnical minorities.

The Conditions of Peace—the terms handed to the Hungarian delegation in January—were declared to be 'definitive': 'Consequently, the Allied and Associated Powers expect a declaration from the Hungarian Delegation within ten days … giving them to understand that they are authorised to sign the Treaty as it stands'.[22]

This deadline was not met. Apponyi's delegation returned to Budapest on 19 May and, having recommended to the National Assembly that Hungary had no choice but to sign an unjust treaty, resigned in acknowledgement of their failure. Two relative nonentities, the Minister for Public Welfare and the Hungarian Ambassador to France, signed the Peace Treaty for Hungary in the Grand Trianon Pavilion in the grounds of the Palace of Versailles on 4 June 1920. Having done so, both men immediately retired from public life. In Hungary, flags flew at half-mast—they were to remain at half-mast until 1938—and the country entered a state of national mourning: in the slogan carried by the angry crowds demonstrating in Budapest and other cities, 'Nem, nem, soha!' ('No, no, never!'), revisionism was born.

In many respects the task that had faced the Peace Conference, that of giving precision to new frontiers already drawn by events, could not have been completed with justice or in ways conducive to a peaceful future for east-central Europe. The major transfers of territory, already determined by a combination of popular will and military occupation, could have been reversed or significantly modified only by the use or threat of force by the Allied Powers against the successor states: this was inconceivable. Even with regard to the aspects of Trianon most open to criticism, those that placed so many Magyars under alien rule, the conference had only limited discretion. The fate of the Magyar-speaking Székely, for example, living for centuries in the south-east corner of Transylvania adjacent to Romania, had been determined by history and geography; it was not susceptible to revision by diplomats or cartographers. The same applied to many ethnic islands of Magyars in Transylvania, Slovakia and the Bánát. Plebiscites, which the Hungarians vainly requested, might have modified the outcome—particularly in Slovakia, where enthusiasm in Turócszentmárton for union with the Czechs was less marked than in Prague—but only at the margins. Too much should not be read into the outcome of the one plebiscite that was eventually held, in Sopron and a few neighbouring villages, resulting in a substantial majority against incorporation into Austria; it was possible, in that case, to draw the new frontier around the loyal districts. But a plebiscite could not have helped the Székely in Transylvania or the Magyars in Pozsony and Kassa. That said, the fact remains that in the relatively limited areas in which its deliberations could make a difference, the decisions of the conference were on balance unjust and gratuitously injurious to Hungary. They sowed seeds of bitterness and resentment that would eventually poison Hungarian public life and endanger peace in the region. Even Seton-Watson conceded, if only temporarily, that the settlement was 'unduly severe to the Magyars'. Nevertheless, in acknowledging the evident injustice of an outcome in which Versailles cost Germany only 10 per cent of her territory against the 66 per cent of which Trianon formally deprived Hungary, a caveat must be entered: the major part of Hungary's losses stemmed not from the Peace Conference, nor even from the defeat of Austria-Hungary in war, but from the policies which for three-quarters of a century had made Hungarian rule unpalatable, sometimes intolerable, to the non-Magyar nationalities of Hungary. Those policies helped to ensure the eventual victory of the national idea in a kingdom whose heterogeneous ethnicity had been determined by geography, migration, historical accident and, in her medieval past, over-ambitious expansion; and they must, therefore, bear much of the responsibility for the kingdom's dissolution.

14

HORTHY'S HUNGARY

(1920–42)

The Regency

The note in which Sir George Clerk conveyed the Peace Conference's formal recognition of the Huszár government on 24 November 1919 contained a comprehensive—and optimistic—list of conditions on which continued recognition was dependent:

This recognition is subject, naturally, to the conditions that the Provisional Government undertakes to hold elections without delay, to maintain law and order in the country, to commit no aggressive action, to respect the provisional frontiers of Hungary pending their final definition in the Peace Treaty, and to guarantee to every Hungarian national full civil rights, including those of a free press, free right of assembly, freedom to express political opinions and a free, secret, impartial and democratic election based on universal suffrage.[1]

Elections to the new National Assembly, which took place in January 1920, were held on a franchise less generous than that decreed by the Károlyi government but less restrictive than in any previous parliamentary election in Hungary: nearly 75 per cent of the population over twenty-four years of age, or 40 per cent of the whole, could now vote, and in secret. Competing for their support were the new Christian National Unity Party (*Keresztény Nemzeti Egyesülés Pártja–* KNEP) and an enlarged Smallholders' Party (*Országos Kisgazda és Földműves Párt–* OKFP). The Parties of National Work (István Tisza's creation) and National Independence (1848) had melted away. The Social Democratic Party was driven from the hustings by a concerted campaign of terrorism by right-wing groups, led by the Association of Awakening Hungarians (ÉME), and by the internment of several of its key members on charges of threatening public order; as a gesture of protest, over 70,000 of its supporters, in Budapest alone, returned spoiled ballot papers. When an additional round of elections in the territory just vacated by Romania had been taken into account, the Smallholders emerged victorious with ninety-one seats as against the KNEP's fifty-nine.

Hungary now had an elected parliament and a government recognised as legitimate, but lacked a head of state. The two main political parties agreed that Hungary should once again become a monarchy, in order to regain the constitutional continuity interrupted by the liberal and Communist revolutions. Most members of the KNEP remained legitimist and loyal to Charles IV, proposing that the Archduke Josef should act as Palatine until circumstances were propitious for Charles's return to Hungary. Most Smallholders, however, and other self-styled 'free electors', believed that Hungary should break the Habsburg connection; and that the National Assembly should be free to bestow the Holy Crown on whomever it wished. The Allied Powers influenced the debate by informing the Hungarian delegation in Paris that:

the restoration of a dynasty personifying, in the eyes of their subjects, a system of oppression and domination of other races, in alliance with Germany, would not be compatible with the principles for which they fought nor with the results the war has allowed them to achieve in the liberation of peoples bound hitherto to servitude; ... a restoration of this kind ... would be neither acknowledged nor tolerated by them.[2]

This pre-emptive veto impelled the National Assembly towards a compromise. The throne would remain vacant for the time being and a regency would be established, following the historical precedents of János Hunyadi and Lajos Kossuth. The powers to be vested in the Regent would fall some way short of the monarchical: although he would appoint prime ministers and ambassadors, sign treaties and, if he found fault with a new law, send it back (once) to the National Assembly for reconsideration, he could not declare war nor end it, make grants of nobility or intervene in the judicial process. The Regent, moreover, could be impeached by the National Assembly. There were only two credible candidates for the office: Count Albert Apponyi, already seventy-four and too committed to a Habsburg succession for Allied tastes, and Admiral Miklós Horthy. Horthy was the obvious choice and sufficiently confident to extract from the National Assembly the promise of an extension of the Regent's powers before agreeing to stand: he asked for the right to adjourn, suspend or dissolve the Assembly; to order, as Supreme War Lord, the deployment of the army outside Hungary to meet a genuine threat; and to grant amnesties. The Assembly agreed to meet these demands (it eventually did so on 7 August) and on 1 March elected Miklós Horthy to the Regency almost unanimously—an outcome to which a heavy military presence in and around the parliament building may have contributed.

Miklós Horthy had been born in 1868 into a Calvinist* family of lesser nobility, which owned a medium-sized estate around the village of Kenderes in the Alföld. After entering the Imperial and Royal Navy as a cadet, he enjoyed a naval career of considerable distinction, serving for five years as an aide-de-camp to Emperor Franz Josef and subsequently, in 1917, distinguishing himself in command of a flotilla in the Battle of Otranto, in which he was seriously wounded. A year later, at the early age of fifty and despite his lack of seniority in the rank of captain, Horthy's combat record and reputation as a stern disciplinarian catapulted him into promotion to be commander in chief of the imperial navy with the rank of rear admiral. After only a few months in this position it fell to him, as we have seen, to preside over the surrender of his fleet to the new state of Yugoslavia. The key to Horthy's remarkable rise in the navy lay in his spell as an imperial ADC, a

---

* Although his mother was a Roman Catholic.

position in which he became well known to the Archduke and future Emperor Karl, and in the qualities which made him acceptable to the court. He was good-looking, with an impressive physique that complemented his distinction as an athlete—he excelled at fencing, tennis and equestrian sport—and possessed exceptional charm of manner. Although of no more than average intelligence, at best, Horthy had a remarkable facility for languages and spoke six fluently—German, French, English, Spanish, Italian and Croatian—in addition to his native Magyar. These assets equipped him very well, at least on the surface, to fill the office of Regent: Horthy had an imposing and attractive presence. The office would also benefit from his virtues of personal honesty, straightforwardness, devotion to his family and modest lifestyle.

Other aspects of Horthy's persona, however, augured less well for his conduct of high office. In place of an intellect, Horthy had acquired a small collection of *idées fixes* which predetermined his approach to any given issue. Thomas Hohler, the British Minister in Budapest who, as a naval officer, had known Horthy before the war, described him as 'a man of sterling honesty but of no great cleverness: he has no suppleness of mind, and when he gets hold of an idea, it crystallizes within him into a principle'.[3] His nationalism, perfervid and blinkered even by Hungarian standards, blinded Horthy to the possibility of shortcomings, past or present, in the conduct of his fellow countrymen. Loyalty to his own class, equally, made him complicit in, instead of condemnatory of, the appalling crimes committed by officer bands during the White Terror. His sense of class exclusivity made him notoriously indiscreet, since there could be no secrets between gentlemen. Bitter hostility to Communism, understandable in anyone who had experienced or even witnessed from afar the mad months of the Kun regime, in Horthy festered to an extent that poisoned his view of Social Democrats and even of the urban working class in general. Class loyalty and hatred of the left combined to lead him, only two weeks before his election to the Regency, to protect from justice the officer who had murdered the editor of the Social Democratic newspaper *Népszava* and one of its journalists. As was commonly the case during the inter-war years, Horthy's anti–Semitism went hand in hand with his anti–Bolshevism; but it did not exceed the norm for his class and generation. Indeed, Horthy enjoyed the society of rich, assimilated Jews whom he regarded as honorary Magyar gentry. Twenty years as virtual head of state inevitably increased Horthy's self-regard to the point of vainglory; but they also bred in him a degree of intuitive political sense, which on occasion served his country well. Miklós Horthy was often stupid, usually decent, rarely wicked; he was a true conservative, determined to restore the pre-revolutionary status quo and to arrest further change.

At his last audience with his King and Emperor, Charles IV, in November 1918, Admiral Horthy, after reporting the surrender of the Imperial and Royal Fleet at Pula, had vowed that he would not rest 'until I have restored your Majesty to his thrones in Vienna and Budapest'.[4] The arrival in Budapest, in June 1920, of a secret letter to the newly installed Regent from Charles, announcing his intention of returning to Hungary and requesting that appropriate preparations should be made, therefore caused Horthy considerable anguish. The anti–Habsburg majority in the National Assembly fully reflected sentiment in the country at large; the Allied Powers had made their position abundantly plain; and Hungary's neighbours, now engaged in forming the Little Entente, had warned that they would regard a Habsburg restoration as a *casus belli*. Horthy decided to ignore the letter; and a second letter, which Charles asked Horthy to publish, suffered the same fate. Undeterred by Horthy's silence, Charles IV, disguised and travelling on a false passport, arrived in Szombathely on Easter Saturday 1921, gathered a group of legitimists around him and drove to Budapest to confront Horthy. Count Pál Teleki, whom Horthy had appointed Prime Minister in July, urged Charles not to proceed with the venture, but without success. Horthy, too, when Charles appeared before him in the Royal Palace, urged him to return to Switzerland immediately; despite his acute embarrassment, Horthy was unmoved by Charles's threats (indictment for treason) and bribes (the title of Prince and the two highest imperial decorations), maintaining throughout the encounter that the time would not be ripe for a Habsburg restoration for several years. After obstinately sitting tight in Szombathely for ten days, while hostility to his presence mounted both in the National Assembly and outside Hungary, Charles eventually returned to Switzerland on 5 April, leaving behind him a manifesto that Pál Teleki foolishly agreed to publish—an act which cost him the Premiership.

Undeterred by this fiasco, Charles made a second attempt to regain the Hungarian throne six months later, this time by force. Arriving in Sopron by air on 20 October, accompanied by the Empress Zita, he succeeded in rallying to his cause a significant number of army officers and, as he advanced towards Budapest, scores of loyalists swelled the ranks of his miniature army; the towns of Győr and Komárom declared for Charles. By 23 October, Charles had reached the Budapest suburb of Budaörs and Horthy, unnerved, felt obliged to declare martial law in the capital. The tide turned when the legitimist General Hegedűs, whom Charles had sent ahead to suborn the Budapest garrison, was nobbled by Count István Bethlen—now Prime Minister—and persuaded that if Charles persisted Hungary would face war with the Little Entente. Hegedűs changed sides and support for Charles in the army began to evaporate. After a brief exchange of rifle fire between the Carlists and a scratch force of right-wing youths assembled by Captain Gömbös to defend the government, Charles agreed to an armistice that provided for his surrender in return for a guarantee of his personal safety and an amnesty for his supporters, other than the legitimist politicians who had accepted portfolios in the 'government' which Charles had formed in Sopron. After spending a week under house arrest in Tihany, on Lake Balaton, Charles and Zita embarked in Baja on the British river monitor *Glow-worm* and passed out of history into exile. Charles died six months later, at the age of thirty-four, in Madeira.

On 6 November, Count Bethlen guided through the National Assembly a law (No. XLVII of 1921) abrogating the Pragmatic Sanction and thereby deposing the Habsburg dynasty; this finally broke the constitutional ties that for three hundred years had bound Hungary and the Austrian house together. Although in theory the Hungarian throne remained available for occupation by election, the Regency now came increasingly to be accepted as a permanent institution and Horthy as its occupant for an indefinite term. Charles's double folly enabled Horthy to preside over the rebuilding of Hungary from a much stronger personal position. Its impact on Hungary's international situation, however, was seriously damaging: in the wake of Charles's first adventure, in April 1921, Czechoslovakia and Romania concluded a treaty of mutual assistance, which was followed, two months later, by a similar agreement between Romania and Yugoslavia. Both treaties, backed by France, were openly directed against Hungary as an insurance against revisionism. Hungary now found herself surrounded on three sides by the Little Entente.

Consolidation (1920–31)

There was a certain shabbiness in Hungarian politics during the inter-war period that requires some explanation. The First World War had deprived Hungary, like most other European countries, of the better part of a generation that would have enlarged the pool of talent in politics as in other occupations and professions; as it was, political talent remained in short supply throughout the period. Of Hungary's inter-war politicians, only István Bethlen, Endre Bajcsy-Zsilinszky and perhaps Count Kuno Klebelsberg measured up to Hungary's pre-1914 political tradition. Small men rose to the top. Revolution and counter-revolution had, moreover, driven Hungarians of proven or potential distinction into exile. One of them, the radical Oszkár Jászi, passed this harsh judgement:

The brain of the unhappy country has been destroyed. The four or five thousand men who represented European ideals and culture among us are either languishing in the prisons, or interned, or starving in exile, or if they are still in their homes they never know when they will be insulted in the street or even dragged out of bed by some gang of 'Awakening Magyars'. Even the better public opinion in Hungary was always indescribably flabby and backboneless. Even in normal circumstances it was a very rare event for anyone to take a stand for his convictions. Neither economic, nor moral, nor religious conditions favoured real spiritual independence. How much less now under the White Terror! Now it needs courage not to howl with the wolves but merely to keep silent and wait. Almost all serious thought is now silenced in unhappy Hungary, and the Horthy regime has wiped out the achievements of the last quarter of a century.[5]

Jászi's assessment, written in 1923 and imbued with the bitterness of exile, proved to be over-pessimistic: Hungary's cultural life, and especially her literature, retained its vitality and innovativeness during the Horthy years. Public life, however, was barren and often squalid. The injustice of Trianon compounded the bitter humiliation of military defeat, eating like a canker into both national morale and public morality. Two threads ran through every segment of the political spectrum save for the socialist left: revision (of Trianon) and anti–Semitism. Hungary's quest for revision, ending in a further national tragedy, will be recounted in the next chapter; the prevalence of anti–Semitism, relatively mild and merely distasteful in some political quarters, vicious and criminal in others, will be explored later in this one. For the present, in following the politics of Horthy's Hungary, it is sufficient to bear in mind that these two themes were ever present—distorting perceptions, warping judgements and obscuring realities.

Count István Bethlen had been Horthy's first choice for the post of Prime Minister in 1920 when Huszár's successor, the politically unknown Simonyi–Semadam, had fulfilled his thankless task of occupying the post during the signature of the Treaty of Trianon and thus assuming historical responsibility for Hungary's enforced acquiescence in it. Bethlen, however, failed to form a cabinet and Pál

Teleki took office in his place. As we have seen, Teleki's poor judgement during Charles IV's bid for restoration brought his premiership to an early close; it had been marked principally by the passage through the National Assembly of the notorious *Numerus Clausus* law of 1920 which, by ruling that the ethnic composition of the university student population should correspond to that of the national population as a whole, aimed to reduce the number of Jews entering higher education and thence the professions. On 14 April 1921, Bethlen accepted reappointment to the post of Prime Minister; he was to hold it for ten years, during which he brought about the internal consolidation and international rehabilitation of Hungary. 'Consolidation' (*konszolidáció*), the label attached then and since to Bethlen's decade in office, really amounted to an attempt to recreate pre-war Hungary. Bethlen was the direct political heir of Kálmán and István Tisza. Although genuinely committed to parliamentary government, his belief in democracy was heavily qualified:

Real democracy grants a leading role to the educated and cultured element. Any political system that tries to negate this principle does not deserve the democratic label, for it merely engenders demagoguery and mob rule ... Democracy is a political form suitable only to rich, well-structured and highly cultured countries ... In countries where the above conditions are absent ... democracy easily degenerates into ruthless political conflict, because the complete freedom of speech and assembly are potent instruments of misguiding the masses.[6]

The nobility, in Bethlen's view, was uniquely qualified to take the leading role in government:

The Hungarian aristocracy and landed nobility ... belongs among the strata with the greatest wealth, most independence, most extensive culture, the broadest vision, and with contacts abroad resulting from its knowledge of foreign languages; it also has the greatest resilience. Therefore, it is best able to hold its ground in the face of pressure, whether it come from above, the shelves [sic] of power, or from below, using the terroristic devices of demagoguery.[7]

Like Horthy, Bethlen was firmly opposed to land reform (Trianon had deprived him of his own extensive estates in Transylvania), as to anything that would weaken the position of the natural ruling class; he also shared Horthy's virulent hatred of Communism. Bethlen's pragmatism, however, saved him from classification as a mindless reactionary. Although a passionate revisionist, he realised that Hungary's cause would be best served by patience and by playing her hand long; and although, like many of his class, he regarded Jews with distaste, he recognised the vital role they would have to play in rebuilding the Hungarian economy and took care, therefore, to ensure that the *Numerus Clausus* law, which he inherited from Teleki, was applied with great leniency when it was applied at all.

Immediately after taking office, Bethlen set about achieving three objectives: ensuring the government's control of the National Assembly, making that control permanent and neutralising the political left. He began, in January 1922, by joining the Smallholders' Party* in order to take over its leadership and bring about a merger with the KNEP; this was accomplished in the following month with the

---

* Bethlen had been elected to the National Assembly in 1920 as a non-party candidate.

creation of a new Unity Party (*Egység Pártja*) under the nominal presidency of the veteran Smallholder Nagyatádi Szabó with the radical rightist Gyula Gömbös as executive Vice-President. This soon became a 'government party' on the Tisza pattern, packed with co-opted civil servants; the installation of Unity Party members in key posts in county administration further enmeshed executive and legislature, creating the conditions for authoritarian rule. Bethlen next took steps to ensure that the government's majority in the Assembly would be immune from the uncertainties of the ballot box. His first attempt to force through the National Assembly a law replacing the existing 1920 franchise with its much more restrictive predecessor of 1913 foundered in the face of unexpectedly strong opposition, led by Albert Apponyi. Bethlen therefore persuaded the Regent, who was in sympathy with his objective, to dissolve the Assembly so that the 1913 franchise could be reintroduced by decree; this manoeuvre was given a fig leaf of propriety by a specially convened Constitutional Commission, which ruled that since the 1920 franchise had been introduced by decree it could be replaced in the same manner. The new decree reduced the proportion of the adult population entitled to vote from 40 to 28.4 per cent, a result achieved by raising quite drastically the residence and educational qualifications for suffrage; the decree also deprived all émigrés of the right to return to Hungary to vote and banned anybody who had been removed from his civil service or professional post for 'unpatriotic conduct' from standing as a candidate. Of even greater significance was the abolition of the secret ballot in 195 of Hungary's 245 parliamentary constituencies. From now on, only 24 per cent of the electorate, mainly residents in the capital and the eleven autonomous municipalities, would be able to vote in secret; the majority would once again be vulnerable to threats and pressure. As one historian has noted, '… as the forthcoming and subsequent elections were vividly to demonstrate, the open rural ballot facilitated the exercise of sufficient coercion (short of terror) and corruption (including voting the dead) to assure the Government Party a permanent and safe majority, one easily produced by the potent trinity of landlord, gendarme and village notary'.[8] With breathtaking cynicism, Bethlen remarked that the secret ballot 'was not compatible with the Hungarian people's open character'. Although, in 1920s Europe, Hungary's franchise was not uniquely restrictive, Hungary was certainly alone in actually regressing, both by shrinking the franchise and by curtailing secrecy of the ballot. The new system nevertheless achieved its objective of maintaining in power a government party, under various names and of varying political complexions, for the next twenty-two years.

In the 1922 elections, the Unity Party won 143 of the Assembly's 245 seats, polling 64 per cent in those constituencies where voting was open; but in the urban constituencies, where the secret ballot had survived, the 'government party' garnered only 27 per cent of the votes. The Social Democrats, with twenty-four seats, became the largest party in an opposition divided by the pact Bethlen had negotiated with the Social Democrat leader, Károly Peyer, in December 1921. Under the agreement, the Social Democratic Party (SDP) agreed to abstain from attempts to unionise civil servants, railwaymen and post office workers; from agitation among miners or the rural labouring class; from alliance with the liberal opposition in the Assembly; and from political strike action. The Social Democrats also agreed to use its international contacts in support of the government's foreign policy objectives. In return, the SDP was accorded the same rights of association and assembly as other political parties, together with the expectation of a limited number of parliamentary seats; the restitution of all confiscated and requisitioned property; an amnesty for Social Democrats serving prison terms or awaiting trial for political offences; and freedom to publish the party newspaper and other literature, subject to the same constraints as those applied to other political parties. The SDP thus exchanged activism for recognition. As the Communist Party had already been banned—Mátyás Rákosi, arrested during a mission from Moscow, was serving an eight-year prison sentence—Bethlen had now achieved another precondition of consolidation: disarming of the left and removal of the threat of organised labour unrest. In 1926, Bethlen put the finishing touch to the restoration of Hungary's pre-1914 political system with the re-creation of a bicameral Parliament: membership of the revived Upper House was to be a mixture of hereditary members (members of the Habsburg family resident in Hungary), members taking their seats *ex officio* (bishops, judges and other dignitaries), members elected by local administrations and professional corporations and forty members appointed by the Regent. It was to be, in other words, a profoundly conservative body—an insurance against the unlikely eventuality of accidents befalling the government in the Lower House.

The Government did not, in fact, invariably enjoy a smooth ride in the Lower House. Despite their weakness in numbers, the opposition parties—the Octobrists (Mihály Károlyi's political heirs), the Democrats led by Vázsonyi, and the Social Democrats—were vocal and active, to an extent which obliged Bethlen in 1924 to reintroduce István Tisza's rules of parliamentary procedure,* which he had himself opposed when Tisza introduced them. Nor was the 'government party' as monolithic as Bethlen might have wished: in 1923 Gyula Gömbös, in protest against Bethlen's foreign policy (see below), led a group of fellow rightists out of the Unity Party to form the quasi–fascist Hungarian National Independence (Racial Defence) Party (*Magyar Nemzeti Függetlenségi (Fajvédő) Párt*), known as the 'Race Defenders Party' for short. Bethlen, who had already instigated judicial proceedings against the 'Awakening Hungarians' for anti–Semitic atrocities, succeeded in winning Horthy's full support for a tough line against the extreme right. In August 1923, Horthy was forthright with a group of 'Awakening Hungarians' who called on him to protest against Bethlen's policies: 'We must have order in this country and I will make sure of that. I will order that all troublemakers are fired on, and if the trouble is caused by right-wingers, for me the only difference will be that I will issue the order with a heavy heart, [whereas] I would enthusiastically order fire on left-wing trouble-makers'.[9]

In demonstrating to Horthy that Gömbös—towards whom the Regent had retained a comradely affinity from Szeged days—was engaged in disreputable activities including secret contacts with the German extreme right, Bethlen further strengthened his own position and gained Horthy's complete confidence. This helped him to trounce both the left and right opposition in the 1926 elections, which gave 177 seats to the 'government party' and in which the 'Race Defenders' won only three and the Social Democrats fourteen seats, a loss of ten

* See Chapters 10 and 12.

despite the urban secret ballot. This outcome confirmed Bethlen's total mastery of the political situation and owed a great deal, not only to chicanery at the hustings and the encouragement of defections from the opposition with promises of office, but also to the success with which Bethlen had matched consolidation at home with Hungary's rehabilitation abroad.

Political consolidation would be worth little unless it was accompanied by the recovery of financial solvency and renewed access to the foreign capital that had always been vital to the Hungarian economy. Bethlen's first step towards the realisation of these aims had been taken in May 1921, when Hungary submitted her application for membership of the League of Nations. Consideration of the application was delayed both by Hungary's dispute with Austria (and the League) over the Burgenland and by the inevitable opposition of the Little Entente (Czechoslovakia, Romania and Yugoslavia); but the League eventually approved Hungary's admission in September 1922. The way was now open for Hungary, no longer a pariah state, to set about seeking remedies for her parlous financial and economic situation. Bethlen had very few cards in his hand but he played them skilfully. Having first deliberately stimulated inflation in order to make it easier for landowners and industry, both stricken by the war, to clamber out of debt, Bethlen and his Finance Minister, Tibor Kállay, were able to argue in London, Paris and Rome that unless inflation could be halted by means of foreign loans, Hungary would be unable to pay the heavy financial reparations imposed upon her by the Treaty of Trianon. In making this case, Bethlen played effectively on the sense of guilt that undoubtedly lingered in Western capitals for having made what was already recognised to have been, so far as Hungary was concerned, a bad and unjust peace. Although France, supported by her clients in the Little Entente, at first insisted that a significant portion of any loan should be earmarked directly for reparations payments, Bethlen, in a diplomatic *tour de force*, succeeded in persuading the Little Entente to forgo this condition in return for an undertaking that Hungary would not pursue policies of revision but would seek to normalise relations with her neighbours. In giving this undertaking, Bethlen must certainly have had his fingers crossed behind his back. The outcome, a medium-term loan of 250 million gold crowns at a swingeing 7 ½ per cent interest, to be used solely for reconstruction under supervision by the League and the Reparations Commission, was considerably less than Hungary had sought but proved sufficient to enable Bethlen to eliminate the budgetary deficit in 1924. Inflation—which had reduced the value of paper crowns against the gold crown from 10:1 in 1919 to 18,400:1 in 1924—came to a halt. Most importantly, this loan opened the way for a massive influx of foreign loans and investment into Hungary which, as we shall see later in this chapter, created the conditions for her remarkable economic recovery.

In 1925 an extraordinary episode occurred which could have derailed this encouraging process; the fact that it did not throws an interesting light on the political morality of the period. It emerged that two or three years earlier a plot, of which Bethlen himself was certainly aware, had been hatched in Budapest to forge Czechoslovak, Romanian and Yugoslav currencies in order to finance revisionist activity in the Little Entente countries and sabotage their economies. The forged notes were to be printed in the Military Cartographical Institute, with the full knowledge and approval of its Director, Count Pál Teleki,* Bethlen's predecessor as Prime Minister, and with the active involvement of Budapest's Chief of Police, Imre Nádosy. With a legitimist nobleman, Prince Lajos Windischgraetz, acting as intermediary, German right-wingers including General Ludendorff took an interest in the project and succeeded in diverting it to the forgery of French francs instead of Little Entente currencies. The counterfeit notes were to be deposited in savings banks throughout Europe and the receipts, which were negotiable, used to raise funds for revisionist organisations. On this basis, the plot went ahead. In December 1925, a Hungarian officer, Colonel Jankovich, travelling on a diplomatic courier's passport, arrived in The Hague with a suitcase containing 10,000 forged 1,000–franc notes; the forgery was exposed as soon as Jankovich attempted to pass the first note.[10] Despite the ensuing international scandal and a formal but inconclusive investigation by the French authorities, there were no repercussions whatsoever, nor any interruption in the flow of foreign loans to Hungary. Calls within Hungary for Bethlen's resignation quickly petered out when he played successfully on fears of a lurch either to the left or to the right if he were to be replaced. Even the League of Nations was unfazed by Hungarian chicanery: in 1926, only a few months after the scandal broke, the League brought its oversight of Hungary's finances to an end and passed full control to the National Bank of Hungary. Early in the following year, the League also dissolved its Military Control Commission in Hungary, which had been responsible for ensuring that the Hungarian armed forces did not exceed the limits laid down in the Treaty of Trianon. This completed Hungary's rehabilitation as a sovereign and independent European nation—although she remained burdened with financial reparations and by constraints, now unpoliced, on her military capacity.

Bethlen's patient pursuit of political and economic stability had created the preconditions for what had always been his principal goal: a concerted effort to achieve revision of Trianon and recovery of the lost territories. He now felt able to espouse this objective openly and, less openly, to address its corollary: rearmament. In order to pursue these aims, Hungary needed an ally. Germany's Foreign Minister, Stresemann, was unwilling to participate in or connive at any activity that might compromise his long-term policy of rebuilding normal relations with the Entente. Neither Britain nor France, two of the leading architects of Trianon, could be expected to aid or abet its revision; and the third architect, the United States, had withdrawn from Europe into isolation. That left Italy, where the advent of Mussolini's maverick Fascist regime had for the time being put that country outside the European mainstream. Bethlen's two meetings with Mussolini in Rome in March 1927, revealed a common interest in breaking up the Little Entente (the Duce had ambitions in the Balkans) and paved the way for the signature, in April, of a bilateral Treaty of Friendship and Co-operation. This ended Hungary's total isolation in Europe, a diplomatic achievement of considerable significance. Mussolini also agreed, at Bethlen's request, secretly to ship to Hungary, via Austria, a quantity of Austro-Hungarian arms left behind in Italy at the end of the First World War. Several railway-wagon loads of machine guns and spare parts, declared as agricultural machinery and ostensibly destined for Poland,

* Count Teleki, in addition to his political interests, was a distinguished geographer.

duly arrived in Austria from Italy in December; but a routine inspection by Austrian customs officers exposed the fraud and Hungary once again found herself at the centre of a public scandal, enthusiastically stoked by the Little Entente. Bethlen, however, rode out the storm without much difficulty; an investigative commission appointed by the League found that an illegal transaction had indeed taken place but that it was of no great significance. Rearmament nevertheless remained a top priority for Bethlen's government. In 1925, the Hungarian army was only 22,000 strong, well below the Trianon limit of 35,000 professionals, and poorly equipped. Horthy wished to entrust Gyula Gömbös, who rejoined the Unity Party in 1927 after the heavy defeat of his 'Race Defenders' in the elections of the previous year, with the task of rebuilding Hungary's military capacity; Bethlen reluctantly acquiesced, on the understanding that Gömbös would confine his activities to the military sphere. In 1928, Gömbös dissolved his 'Race Defenders Party' and took up the post of Under-Secretary of State in the Ministry of Defence. A year later, Gömbös became Minister of Defence with the military rank of general. This appointment had important and fateful consequences, in both the medium and the longer term. Gömbös regained direct access to the Regent, of which Bethlen had succeeded in depriving him, and was able to restore the influence over Horthy to which the latter was always susceptible from old comrades of Szeged days; this was to result in Gömbös's accession to the premiership three years later. Secondly, Gömbös seized the opportunity that his new responsibilities afforded of beginning to rebuild the Hungarian officer corps in his own radical-right, pro-German image; this was to contribute significantly to the tragedy that enveloped Hungary in 1944. In the short term, however, Gömbös appeared to justify the confidence Horthy had placed in him: by 1930, the army's strength had increased to 57,000 men, including thirty-one squadrons of cavalry, and by 1932, when general conscription was introduced, Hungary could field a force of 85,000, including two armoured squadrons, and possessed the rudiments of an air force.

In the meantime, Hungary had acquired another ally, and in an unexpected quarter. Lord Rothermere, the British press baron, dazzled by the charms of Princess Stefania Hohenlohe and moved by her laments for despoiled Hungary (although the Princess was in fact Austrian), launched a revisionist campaign in the *Daily Mail*. The newspaper's issue on 21 June 1927, was dominated by a feature article, 'Hungary's Place in the Sun', which argued for the return to Hungary of predominantly Magyar frontier regions, in the interests of European security; at the same time, Rothermere founded the 'Hungarian Revisionist League' which stressed Hungary's importance as the West's champion and defender against Bolshevism. The gratitude of the Hungarian public verged on hysteria: an editorial urged that Rothermere should be offered the Holy Crown and when he visited Budapest with his son, Esmond, tens of thousands packed the streets to welcome them as conquering heroes. Although Rothermere's campaign was in some ways welcome to Bethlen, offsetting as it did Hungary's two recent public relations setbacks, it also created problems for him. The members of the Little Entente clung even more closely to each other and to France, extending and reinforcing their mutual treaties in June 1928. Moreover, Rothermere was preaching the wrong kind of revisionism. Bethlen's objective was nothing less than the re-creation of the 'lands of the Holy Crown'—historic Hungary—albeit in a quasi-federal form. Restoration of the Magyar-speaking border areas would be a useful start but Bethlen did not wish the belief to take root that this would constitute an adequate revision of Trianon. In a government memorandum circulated in May 1929, Bethlen laid down that the primary aim of the government's foreign policy was to restore the *integrity* (in the sense of 'wholeness') of Hungary: those who wished to limit the revisionist movement to ethnic frontiers 'forget that this assumption precludes in advance any serious prospect of revision if occasion arises in an unforeseeable political constellation'.[11] This was Bethlen's characteristically opaque way of saying that a bird in the hand was not necessarily worth two in the bush. But his grand design—a campaign for revision supported by Italy and, in due course he hoped, by Germany, and backed by a credible threat of military force—foundered when the shock-waves of the financial crash on Wall Street in 1929 hit Europe in 1930 and 1931. The collapse of agricultural prices and the calling in of her swollen inventory of short-term loans plunged Hungary into an acute economic crisis that had immediate political repercussions. The government's deflationary measures provoked widespread civil unrest and a wave of strikes which culminated, on 1 September 1930, in a mass demonstration in Budapest in which several hundred workers and police were injured. Terrorist activity, perpetrated by both left-wing and right-wing extremists, increased alarmingly: it peaked on 13 September 1931, when a Communist agent* blew up the railway bridge at Biatorbágy as the Vienna express was crossing it, killing twenty-two passengers and seriously injuring seventeen more.

These events encouraged Gömbös to challenge Bethlen, both publicly and in the Crown Council Horthy had convened on 20 February 1931 to discuss the crisis. Gömbös skilfully fanned Horthy's own concerns about the alleged growth of Jewish influence over the economy and the absence of sufficiently tough government policies to curb violence on the streets and hysteria in the press. Horthy's confidence in Bethlen had already waned; it was further eroded by strong disapproval of the latter's torrid *affaire* with the Countess Széchenyi and by the discovery that his Prime Minister was holidaying with the Countess on the Venice Lido just when the full force of the financial crash hit Hungary in July. Despite the consequent demise of a relationship of mutual trust that had endured throughout his term as Prime Minister, Bethlen managed to hold on and to continue his attempt to cobble together new loans from abroad to stave off national bankruptcy. He succeeded only in Paris, where in August the French government backed a one-year loan of £5 million on the unspoken understanding that Hungary would adopt a more conciliatory policy towards the Little Entente. Bethlen, whose 'government party' had already sustained unaccustomed losses in the June elections, had no appetite for this; nor did he relish trying to steer the government through a crisis that seemed certain to deepen further. He therefore tendered his resignation, and that of his cabinet, recommending to Horthy that his Finance Minister, János Teleszky, a converted Jew, should be appointed in his place. 'So long as I sit in this chair', Horthy responded, 'a Jew will never be Prime Minister in Hungary'.[12] Instead, Horthy called on the francophile ultra-conservative Gyula Károlyi to take over from Bethlen. Bethlen anticipated only a short break from the burdens of office and expected to be recalled when the financial crisis had

---

* Or, possibly, a deranged individual with no political affiliation.

passed. He made no move to vacate the Prime Minister's official residence until the continuing virulence of hostility towards him, voiced in Parliament from both right and left, persuaded him to make a dignified withdrawal into the role of *éminence grise*. Although he lacked the breadth of vision that would have entitled him to be remembered as a statesman, Bethlen had nevertheless served his country well; his patient pragmatism steered her back from outcast status to acceptance as a member of the international community—still not entirely respectable, perhaps, but credit-worthy and offering, before the crash, a stable environment for foreign investment. On a political landscape so depressingly devoid of talent, Bethlen was the only man of sufficient stature to represent Hungary effectively on the European stage; the encomia and eulogies which marked his tenth anniversary as Prime Minister, shortly before his resignation, were not unmerited.

The Drift to the Right (1931–39)

The pressures and dilemmas of the economic crisis soon overwhelmed the modest capacities of Count Gyula Károlyi, who resigned after only a year in office. In replacing him, Horthy allowed himself to be guided by his own instincts but he had also taken note of the fact that in a by-election in August 1931, his own brother-in-law, the Agriculture Minister Emil Purgly, had been defeated in an open ballot by the right-radical Tibor Eckhardt, leader of the new Independent Smallholders' Party, an anti–Semitic nationalist and graduate of the 'Szeged school'. Instinct and observation both prompted Horthy to send for Gömbös.

Gyula Gömbös has already crossed these pages more than once but now merits a closer look. Although he claimed noble descent, Gömbös came from Swabian peasant stock, the son of a village schoolmaster. He served as a junior staff officer throughout the First World War and subsequently, as we have seen, became prominent in the counter-revolutionary movement. If anyone can be said to have embodied what was pretentiously called 'the Szeged idea' (*a szegedi gondolat*), it was Gömbös. The components of the 'idea' included extreme Magyar nationalism, strong hostility to the Habsburg dynasty, racial (as distinct from merely social) anti–Semitism, fervent anti–Bolshevism and a vaguely socialist (but not Marxist) political programme, of which the centrepiece was land reform, to break the dominance of the land-owning class. He headed two of the numerous right-wing organisations that sprang up after 1918: the Hungarian Association of National Defence (MOVE) and the pagan-romantic Etelköz Association (EKSz). In Szeged, Gömbös had put forward Horthy's name to command the National Army—hence the enduring bond between them. His radical-right activities brought him into contact with the nascent National Socialist party in Germany. Given this background and the absurdly ambitious ninety-five point right-radical programme Gömbös had drawn up, Horthy considered it prudent, in offering Gömbös the premiership, to impose certain constraints on his conduct of the office: Gömbös, in accepting the post, consequently agreed to allow the existing Lower House—dominated by Bethlen supporters—to run its full term; to abstain from further discriminatory legislation against the Jews; and to put land reform—to which Horthy remained strongly opposed—on the back burner.

Steeped though he was in rather cracked right-radical ideology, Gömbös revealed in office an unsuspected vein of pragmatism. His ultimate goal remained the creation of a unitary fascist state in Hungary; but he was prepared to move towards it gradually and, in order to avoid alienating the Regent, an essential ally, to abide by the conditions Horthy had imposed upon him, at least until new elections fell due. Gömbös realised that without the co-operation of the Jewish financial community, his government would have no hope of weathering the economic crisis that had engulfed Hungary. He therefore abjured, at least in public, his anti–Semitism, proclaiming in his inaugural speech as Prime Minister: 'I say openly and sincerely to the Jews that I have revised my point of view. Those Jews who acknowledge a common fate with the nation I regard as my brothers, just like my Magyar brothers'.[13] Future co-operation was formalised in a secret protocol signed by one of Gömbös's close associates, G. Baross, and the leaders of the Neolog Jewish community; both sides observed it scrupulously thereafter. In order to ensure Horthy's continuing favour, Gömbös secured the passage of a bill empowering the Regent to prorogue Parliament indefinitely and thus to rule without it if he so chose. To appease Bethlen, Gömbös included several leading conservatives in his first cabinet; in return, Bethlen agreed to cede to Gömbös the leadership of the Unity Party, which Gömbös renamed 'the Party of National Unity'. In other respects, Gömbös lost no time in addressing his long-term agenda, including the transformation of the government party into a national 'movement' on Fascist and National Socialist lines. Under the energetic direction of its Secretary-General, Béla Marton, the Party of National Unity penetrated and soon controlled every organ of national and local administration; party stalwarts were appointed to the post of *főispán* in every county, their authority enforced by teams of 'elite fighters' (*élharcosok*) whose numbers rose to 60,000 nation-wide. Gömbös tightened censorship of the press, founded two new party newspapers and authorised extensive surveillance of political opponents, including the opening of mail, the tapping of telephones and the employment of a small army of paid informers. His efforts to mobilise nationalist sentiment were assisted in 1934 by Hungary's involuntary involvement in yet another international scandal—the assassination, in Marseilles, of King Alexander of Yugoslavia and the French Foreign Minister, M. Barthou, for which the Croatian extremist group, the Ustashe, were thought to be responsible. In furtherance of its campaign to destabilise the Little Entente, the Hungarian government had allowed Croatian terrorists to set up training camps on Hungarian soil; and although these had been closed down, and the Croatians expelled, before the Marseilles murders took place, Hungary was nevertheless held to be partly responsible for the atrocity. Gömbös's movement subsequently thrived on the widespread feeling that Hungary had, once again, been unfairly victimised by the rest of Europe. Recruitment to the government party's quasi–fascist youth movement, the *Turul*, flourished; and when twenty-two of the army's most senior officers resigned in protest against a report by the League of Nations implicating Hungary in the assassinations, Gömbös seized the opportunity of replacing them with fellow enthusiasts for the 'Szeged idea' and for closer ties with Germany. Hungary thus acquired a pro-German General Staff, a fact that was to have fateful consequences ten years later.

Gömbös could fairly claim the dubious distinction of having invented the concept of a German-Italian 'Axis' (the term was his) with which Hungary could be closely associated and which would provide the international muscle required for a revision of Trianon. Shortly after taking office in 1932, Gömbös therefore hastened to consolidate Hungary's developing relationship with Fascist Italy, agreeing with Mussolini a project (eventually brought to fruition in 1934 in the Rome Protocols) for a customs union between Hungary, Italy and Austria, a joint intention to accelerate 'the process of disintegration' in Yugoslavia and the firm prospect of continuing Italian support for Hungary's rearmament.* In the following year, after first addressing to the new German Chancellor, Adolf Hitler, a fulsome letter suggesting an alignment of Hungarian and German foreign policies, Gömbös paid a short visit to Berlin where Hitler received him and advised him to concentrate his revisionist efforts on Hungary's northern frontier with Czechoslovakia. Hitler, concerned to divert Hungarian attentions from Romania, for which he had plans of his own, repeated this message when Gömbös paid a longer visit to Germany in 1935. During the course of this visit, after which he described the Nazi leadership as 'a group of exceptionally gifted, able and resolute men',[14] Gömbös gave Göring a formal but secret assurance that within two years he would transform Hungary into a corporate state modelled on the Nazi system and that 'the Jewish question' would be resolved. Making correct deductions from both fact and rumour, Bethlenite members of the Gömbös cabinet warned the Regent that his Prime Minister was on the verge of establishing a dictatorship; Miklós Kállay (Agriculture Minister) and Béla Imrédy (Finance Minister) resigned and the parliamentary opposition redoubled its efforts to obstruct government business. Using the opposition's activities as a pretext, Gömbös persuaded Horthy to dissolve Parliament and to reappoint him to the premiership at the head of a reshuffled cabinet; he then maintained, to Bethlen's fury, that since he now headed a new government he was no longer bound by his earlier undertaking to allow the predominantly Bethlenite Lower House to run its full term. Horthy, bemused and ignoring warnings from his own entourage that Gömbös planned to usurp him, duly decreed that new elections should be held. When they took place in April 1935, the elections plumbed new depths of corruption and intimidation. Gömbös used them to carry out a purge of the Party of National Unity, replacing Bethlenite candidates with his own nominees; the reconstituted government party and its allies emerged with over 200 of the 245 seats in the Lower House, although a subsequent row between Gömbös and Tibor Eckhardt deprived the former of the support of Eckhardt's twenty-five Independent Smallholders, who joined Bethlen in opposition. Gömbös had, however, finally overplayed his hand; the violence that marred the elections and the increasingly impressive strength, in quality if not in numbers, of a united parliamentary opposition, at last persuaded Horthy that Gömbös posed a threat both to his Regency and to the Hungarian constitution. By mid-1936, Horthy had decided to dismiss his former comrade-in-arms from the premiership. He was spared the necessity: Gömbös, suffering from acute kidney disease, died in a Munich clinic on 6 October 1936.

---

* In a virtual repetition of the 1928 incident, the leaked arrival at the Hirtenberg armaments plant in Austria of a consignment of Italian small arms for repair and onward transmission to Hungary evoked a frenzied fluttering in the dovecotes of the Little Entente and a flurry of Western protests; Italy was eventually obliged to take the arms back.

From this point onwards, Hungary's internal politics as well as her foreign policy were increasingly dominated and determined by the combination of her revisionist ambitions with the resurgence of German power on which she would have to depend for their fulfilment. This doom-laden and ultimately tragic phase of Hungary's history will be recounted in the next chapter; but we should first take a closer look at other aspects of Horthy's Hungary, some of which were more to the credit of her remarkably resilient people than were their politics.

The Inter-war Economy

The disintegration of the Monarchy deprived Hungary of the benefits of assured markets and a common currency. When the Treaty of Trianon added humiliation to the pain of military defeat in the First World War, Hungary's economy collapsed in ruins. Industries that had been artificially stimulated by the war, such as metallurgy and textiles, faced bankruptcy as demand suddenly evaporated. Trianon, moreover, had deprived Hungarian industry of many of its traditional sources of raw materials: most of Hungary's iron ore and copper now belonged to Czechoslovakia, the bulk of her timber to Romania. In a country reduced to one third of its pre-war area, its industry suddenly became top-heavy. Since it was concentrated around Budapest, Hungary retained all her capacity for the manufacture of locomotives and railway rolling stock; but retained only 38 per cent of her pre-war railway network. Disposing of a milling industry built up to mill 65 million tons of grain annually, Hungary could now produce no more than 28 million tons on her shrunken area of arable land. Post-Trianon Hungary still possessed nearly a third of her wartime iron foundry capacity; but only 15 per cent of her former iron ore deposits. In 1920, industrial production reached only 30–35 per cent of its pre-war level, painfully climbing to 51 per cent in 1921. Over a third of the workforce was unemployed. Only an infusion of imported raw materials could revive Hungarian industry: and this could be paid for only by increased agricultural exports.

Hungary's agriculture, however, was if anything in an even more parlous state than her industry. During the war years, over half the rural labour force had been called to military service and most draught animals requisitioned; large areas of arable land fell into neglect as a result. In 1920, wheat yields reached only half their 1913 level; the national herd of cattle, pigs and sheep had shrunk to one-third of its former size. The promise of land reform, which might have increased incentives to higher agricultural productivity, remained unfulfilled. Even allowing for Hungary's reduced size, her agricultural exports in 1921 amounted to only 41 per cent of their pre-war level. The drive to push these exports up in order to finance industrial imports was hampered not only by low production but also by the difficulty of finding markets for Hungarian produce. Hungary no longer enjoyed the benefits of a customs union which had given her assured dominance of the Austrian and Czech markets—these were now being swamped by cheap grain from North America; the previously important Russian market had been closed by revolution and civil war. Only Germany and Italy seemed to offer the prospect of the secure agricultural markets Hungary so badly needed.

Despite the fundamental importance of a viable agriculture to any economic strategy for Hungary, Bethlen nevertheless followed István Tisza's example in giving priority to industry. The tariff bill he guided through Parliament in 1924 imposed swingeing duties on industrial imports, including agricultural machinery and implements. Attacked in Parliament by conservative landowners and Small-holders alike, Bethlen commented simply that 'once we make the decision to industrialise the country, we will have to accept the fact that the interests of agriculture will temporarily suffer'.[15] The impact on Hungary's industry of protective tariffs, which averaged 30 per cent, was in general positive but uneven. Heavy industry, now largely dependent on imported raw materials, continued to languish until the rearmament programme of the late 1930s revived it. The textile industry, on the other hand, recovered from its sudden post-war contraction and by 1938 was producing four times more than in 1913, meeting domestic demand in full. The paper and leather industries also thrived behind the new protective barrier. By 1929, on the eve of the Great Crash, Hungary's industrial output exceeded 1913 levels by an average of 12 per cent; whereas agriculture, handicapped by the high cost of imported fertilisers and machinery and lacking the capital resources for essential irrigation, land reclamation and flood control, had struggled to an increase of only 2 per cent. Overall, however, the 1920s were a period of gradual economic recovery, marked by an increase in GNP per capita of 35–40 per cent. This improvement, modest though it was both in relative and absolute terms by contemporary west European standards, flowed in large measure from the short-term success of Bethlen's financial policies.

Bethlen's efforts to secure foreign loans have already been noted in general terms.* The League of Nations' loan of 250 million gold crowns, to which the Bank of England added 82 million on its own account when the National Bank of Hungary was established in 1924, opened the way to a sizeable inflow of foreign capital into a country which was now widely perceived as stable and deserving. A new currency, the gold-based *pengő*, was introduced in 1925 and achieved rapid respectability. Between 1924 and 1931, Hungary secured the equivalent of 1,300 million *pengő* in long-term loans and 1,700 million *pengő* in commercial and short-term credit; during the three years immediately preceding the Crash, thirty-eight loan agreements were concluded, typically carrying an interest rate of around 7 per cent. This inflow enabled the government to post an annual budget surplus after 1925 and to devote substantial sums to badly needed infrastructural investment, particularly in education, public health and communications. But by 1931, Hungary's total foreign debt—excluding very substantial private liabilities—amounted to 4.3 billion *pengő*. The cost of servicing this debt—about 300 million *pengő* annually—accounted for 10 per cent of the national income, or 54 per cent of Hungary's exports by value; 40 per cent of every new loan had to be earmarked for servicing its predecessors. Hungary's economic recovery was dearly bought: by 1931 she had become, per capita, the most deeply indebted nation in Europe.

The combination of indebtedness and dependence on agricultural exports made Hungary uniquely vulnerable to the impact of the financial Crash of 1929 and to the subsequent recession in Europe. The collapse of agricultural prices worldwide cost Hungary 65 per cent of the value of her wheat exports and 50 per cent of the value of her exports of other crops and livestock—across the

* See page 341.

board, export income fell by 70.3 per cent. Domestic demand for manufactures collapsed: industrial production fell by 24 per cent between 1929 and 1933, putting 250,000 workers on to the streets without the life-belt of unemployment insurance or benefits. In the countryside, smallholders, unable to export their produce, faced ruin; property auctions became a familiar feature of the rural scene. Village shopkeepers went bankrupt by the thousand. For landless peasants and their families, starvation was transformed from an ever present threat into grim reality. In grappling with the crisis at government level, Bethlen showed courage and resource. The collapse of Vienna's Creditanstalt, to which the Hungarian banking system was closely tied, in 1931 led at once to the calling-in of loans by foreign creditors and confronted the government with the immediate threat of national bankruptcy. A relatively small loan (£5 million) from France, whom Bethlen had successfully wooed with partially sincere professions of opposition to German assertiveness, and another from the Bank of International Settlements in Basle helped the government to weather the storm; so did Bethlen's draconian measures to cut government expenditure—drastic cut-backs in the bureaucracy, salary reductions for those remaining and a sharp increase in taxation. Controls imposed on the National Bank's foreign currency and gold reserves just before they were exhausted, a moratorium on all interest and capital payments on foreign loans and the subsequent centralisation of loan repayments into a Foreign Creditors' Fund administered by the National Bank eventually brought Hungary into calmer financial waters; but not before Bethlen (as we have seen) had fallen victim to the social consequences, exploited by the radical right, of his austerity policies.

At the height of the economic and financial crisis, in 1931, Bethlen found time to negotiate and conclude three important 'most favoured nation' (MFN) trade agreements, with Italy, Austria and Germany, which charted the course for Hungary's second economic recovery but were also charged with political significance. All three agreements provided for quotas of Hungarian agricultural exports and manufactured imports at agreed premiums over world prices. In 1934, an economic agreement complementing the Rome Protocols between Hungary, Italy and Austria gave Hungary useful guarantees of agricultural exports to her two partners; but this was dwarfed in significance by a bilateral trade agreement concluded in the same year between Hungary and Germany, which had the effect of committing nearly a quarter of Hungary's exports to the German market. The subsequent history of this agreement and its periodic revisions graphically illustrated the dangers inherent in trade agreements between parties of unequal political and strategic weight. Germany, already intent on building up stockpiles of essential commodities, became increasingly exigent in her demands from Hungarian producers and increasingly tardy in her payments, both in foreign exchange and in her exports of raw materials and manufactures. By 1937, Hungary was sending to Germany 20 per cent of her exported beef cattle, 50 per cent of her bacon, 20 per cent of her milled grain, 60 per cent of her seed grain, 50 per cent of her poultry and eggs and nearly 50 per cent of exported fruit and vegetables. Under the renegotiated trade agreement of that year, Hungary was committed to increasing her exports to Germany by 25 per cent; but German exports to Hungary were due to rise by only 10 per cent, an ominous imbalance which left

Hungary dependent on the uncertain factor of Germany's willingness to bridge the gap with payments of foreign exchange. By 1939, after the Anschluss and Germany's absorption of Czechoslovakia, the enlarged Third Reich accounted for nearly 53 per cent of Hungary's entire foreign trade. This potentially dangerous level of dependence on a single export market nevertheless produced significant benefits in the short term. Hungary made a relatively rapid recovery from the Depression; by 1937, both industrial and agricultural production had reached and surpassed 1929 levels. The discovery and successful exploitation of native deposits of oil and natural gas gave a useful fillip to Hungary's chemical industry, which was now able to reduce her import bill by the domestic production of artificial fertilisers. This in turn benefited agriculture. The discovery of rich deposits of bauxite near Veszprém gave Hungary both a new metallurgical industry—her first aluminium smelter came on stream on Csepel island in 1935—and a valuable export commodity: Hungarian bauxite became a key component in Germany's rapidly expanding aircraft industry and in the creation of the Luftwaffe.

Hungary's existing industries, such as locomotive and rolling stock manufacture, revived and prospered; new ones, including telecommunications, electrical instruments and pharmaceuticals, quickly established an international reputation. By 1937, Hungary's imports of finished manufactures had fallen from the 1929 figure of 40.2 per cent of total imports to 26.8 per cent. Unemployment had been virtually eliminated by that date and national income per capita had increased by nearly 10 per cent over the pre-Depression level. It is true that Hungary, still a predominantly agrarian country with a semi–feudal rural economy, continued to lag far behind the countries of western Europe: industrial production per capita, even after the rearmament programme was launched in 1938, reached only 32 per cent of the European average. But Hungary had pulled significantly ahead of her eastern neighbours, with a per capita national income 21 per cent higher than that of Poland and 31 per cent above that of Romania. Her economy was in better balance, and showing greater vitality, than at any time in her history. As we shall see in the next chapter, however, Hungary's new economic dependence on Germany, mirroring the political dependence revisionism brought about, was to lead to national catastrophe.

Hungarian Society between the Wars

The 'Political Class'

During his ten years as Prime Minister, István Bethlen made twenty-nine cabinet appointments; of the appointees, six came from the aristocracy, twelve from the gentry and eleven were commoners. This broadly reflected the composition of the Lower House of Parliament, though erring on the side of generosity to the aristocrats. The great landowners or magnates, owning estates of more than 1,000 *hold*, had shrunk in number since the beginning of the century, partly through the loss of heirs during the First World War and partly through emigration immediately after it; the 745 magnates who remained in 1930 nevertheless owned nearly one-third of the land of Hungary and consequently still constituted a significant political force. Apart from the oldest aristocratic families, the line dividing the magnates from the upper echelon of the gentry, whose members typically owned estates of between 200 and 1,000 *hold*, was becoming increasingly blurred, as was that between the gentry and the wealthier stratum of the urban middle class. These three groups constituted the traditional ruling class of Hungary and continued to dominate both Parliament and the upper levels of the bureaucracy, often combining a civil service career with politics. A brief reference must be made to some bizarre newcomers to the Hungarian 'political class'. These were war veterans who had been inducted into the Order of Gallantry (*Vitézi Rend*), an institution Horthy had invented to compensate for his inability to bestow nobility—a right reserved to crowned monarchs. He may also have hoped to create something resembling a praetorian guard, loyal to his own person and guardians of the patriotic flame. The hereditary title of *Vitéz* was first awarded to military heroes of the First World War but membership of the Order was gradually expanded to include any ex–serviceman deemed to have given distinguished service to his country; by 1931 it had over 4,000 members. As well as indulging the Hungarian penchant (shared with the English, it has to be said) for elaborate dress uniform, the title carried with it 40 *hold* of land for officers and a barely viable 8 *hold* for the non-commissioned—a conscious revival of the medieval link between land tenure and service to the crown. Members of the Order tended to be cold-shouldered by the nobility and gentry as social parvenus; but, without achieving much political significance, the Order did serve as a reliable collective bastion of nationalism—and, of course, revisionism—as well as adding a touch of Ruritania to Horthy's Hungary.

After Trianon, most members of the 'political' class from the lost periphery of Hungary gravitated to the centre with the expectation of taking part in the government of their now much smaller country. Moreover, rather than abandon the Universities of Pozsony and Kolozsvár to the Czechoslovaks and Romanians respectively, the Hungarian government transferred them to Pécs and Szeged; throughout the inter-war period, therefore, Hungary produced significantly more university graduates than she could usefully absorb into the bureaucracy and the professions. In the 1930s, the permanent pool of graduate unemployed provided an ideal recruiting ground for right-wing extremism. Bethlen at first attempted to apply the traditional Hungarian remedy of expanding the civil service in order to meet the demand for gentlemanly jobs: the civil service actually grew during the early 1920s, from around 65,000 to nearly 70,000, to administer a country only one-third of its former size. Although budgetary pressures necessitated a subsequent contraction—to under 43,000 by 1930—this had also to be accompanied by reductions in salary for those who kept their jobs, with consequent discontent. The professional and lower middle class, which staffed the humbler strata of the bureaucracy and the public services, also experienced a steady erosion of its standard of living, losing the vital insignia that distinguished it from the labouring classes below. Andrew Janos quotes a contemporary diarist, writing in 1927—even before the Depression:

Under the inexorable economic pressures of the day the living standard of the civil servants began to slip. At first they had to drop the theatre, the concert, the books, the newspapers and the dinner parties. Then their clothes and shoes began to acquire a more threadbare look. They had to cut the number of courses at mealtime, let go the inexpensive all-round

38. The coronation of the Emperor Franz Josef as King of Hungary on 7 June 1867, with the Empress Elisabeth, adored by Hungarians, at his side; the acclamation is being led by Count Gyula Andrássy, Prime Minister and later Foreign Minister of the Dual Monarchy.

39. Ferenc Deák (1803–76), statesman and architect of the 'Compromise' of 1867 that won for Hungary equal status with Austria in the Dual Monarchy.

40. János Arany (1817–82), Hungary's greatest epic poet and the dominant literary figure of the nineteenth century.

41. Mór Jókai (1825–1904), like Arany, was a member of Sándor Petőfi's radical 'Society of Ten' and became Hungary's leading novelist of the nineteenth century, pioneering the novel as a vehicle for social commentary.

42. Ferenc Liszt (1811–86), born to German parents in western Hungary but a self-proclaimed Hungarian, an allegiance reflected in much of his music; the young man with his elbow on the piano is Count Albert Apponyi, a prominent and controversial figure in late nineteenth and early twentieth century Hungarian politics.

43. Pest and Buda in the 1850s, with Széchenyi's Chain Bridge in the foreground. The formal union of the two cities which created Budapest did not take place until 1873.

44. The Hungarian nobility pay homage to Emperor Franz Josef on the occasion of his visit to Budapest for the Millennium celebrations in 1896—the high point of Hungarian national hubris.

45. Emperor Franz Josef (on the left) and Archduke Frederick taking part in military manoeuvres in Moravia in 1909. They were joined later by Kaiser Wilhelm II.

46. New recruits to the army march off to war on 1 August 1914, escorted through the streets of Budapest by a band and their relatives.

47. An elaborate complex of Austro-Hungarian trenches and bunkers on the Russian front in 1916; by that date, the Monarchy's casualties—killed, wounded or captured—exceeded two million, of which Hungary's share was about 800,000.

48. Budapest, 31 October 1918: the 'Aster Revolution', which established a republican government headed by the liberal Count Mihály Károlyi. White asters, visible here in the soldiers' caps, were on sale to mark All Souls Day and became the symbol of the revolution.

49. Béla Kun's Communist regime, the 'Republic of Councils', which replaced Count Károlyi's irresolute liberal government in March, 1919, buttressed its rule with a 'Red Terror' which claimed several hundred lives. Here a provincial mayor is hanged for alleged 'counter-revolutionary activity': Leninism had arrived in Hungary.

50. Following the collapse of the Kun regime in August 1919, Admiral Miklós Horthy's National Army installed a right-wing government and unleashed a terror campaign of its own against suspected Communists. The 'White Terror' claimed many more victims—of which a high proportion were Jewish—than its 'Red' predecessor.

51. Kálmán Tisza (1830–1902), creator of the Liberal Party and Prime Minister (1875–90); he introduced 'machine politics' to Hungary.

52. Count Albert Apponyi (1846–1933), twice Minister of Religion and Public Education. It fell to him to lead the Hungarian delegation to the Paris Peace Conference in 1919; his passionate opposition to the punitive terms of the Treaty of Trianon was unavailing.

53. Count István Tisza (1861–1918), son of Kálmán Tisza, Prime Minister for two terms (1903–05 and 1913–17). He strongly but unsuccessfully opposed Austria's declaration of war against Serbia in 1914. He was murdered by mutinying soldiers on 31 October 1918.

54. Béla Kun (1886–1939) founded the Hungarian Communist Party and displaced Count Károlyi's liberal government in 1919 to establish the Republic of Councils, which lasted for only 133 days.

55. Admiral Miklós Horthy enters Budapest at the head of his National Army on 16 November 1919. Horthy was elected Regent, and head of state, on 1 March 1920; he was to hold that office for twenty-four years.

56. Three Prime Ministers of the late 1930s: on the left, Béla Imrédy (1938–9, executed in 1946); next to him, in spectacles, Pál Teleki (1920–1 and again 1939–41, when he committed suicide); and on the far right Kálmán Darányi (1936–8, died 1939).

maid, and begin to sell their furniture and jewelry. While the state and the economy were being put on a more stable footing, the better part of our middle class had reached the depth of material ruin.[16]

Given that this stratum of the population contained tens of thousands who had come to post-Trianon Hungary as refugees from the lost territories, living sometimes for years in railway trucks in the goods sidings of Budapest or in abandoned army barracks, it—like the unemployed graduates—constituted a fertile breeding ground for political extremism. One of the manifestations of the discontents of this newly disadvantaged class was anti–Semitism.

The Jews

After Trianon, Hungary's Jews found themselves in an uncomfortably conspicuous and exposed situation. As before, they made up about 5 per cent of the population and they still dominated the financial, commercial and industrial life of the country; in Budapest, where half of them lived, they accounted for over 90 per cent of those engaged in commerce and finance in the capital. But whereas, in pre-war Hungary, they had been welcomed as assimilees into the Magyar fold, valued as the ethnic make-weight that enabled the Magyars to maintain a slim majority over the combined ranks of Slovaks, Romanians, Serbs and Croats, they were now more clearly perceived, in a newly homogeneous country deprived of its other ethnic minorities, as an ethnic minority themselves—a minority, moreover, that possessed or controlled a disproportionate share of the nation's wealth. Even István Bethlen who, although he did not like them, was not in general ill-disposed towards the Jews, complained in 1922:

The Hungarian middle class lost its leading role in the economic area ... The consequence of this has been that commerce, enterprise, financial matters are in hands that were not in harmony with the feelings of the nation, and perhaps still are not to the correct and desirable extent ... we must regain for Christianity the positions we have lost in our economic and cultural life.[17]

The label 'Christian', which between the wars was attached to so many political parties, societies and movements, really meant 'Jews not welcome' or, not infrequently, 'anti–Jewish'. Béla Bangha, a Catholic priest, raised 10 million crowns to establish the 'Christian Press Company', the board of which included several university professors, with the declared objective of 'crushing Jewish rule' in Hungary. The fact that 300,000 Jews had served in Hungarian units during the First World War, sharing proportionately in the 57 per cent casualty rate, tended to be forgotten, along with the fact that 10 per cent of the funds raised in war loans had come from Jewish pockets. Most Hungarians preferred to remember that the war industries, in the management and financing of which Jews had—as in industry as a whole—played the dominant role, had generated massive profits; and that, although the Red Terror had claimed numerous Jewish victims, the leaders of the detested Kun regime, including Béla Kun himself, had mostly been of Jewish origin.

This mood, which determined the anti–Semitic bias of the White Terror and fuelled the subsequent wave of atrocities against Jews by the 'Awakening Hungarians' (EME), ensured the passage through the National Assembly of Law XXV of 1920, the *Numerus Clausus*. The bill originated from a justifiable attempt by the medical faculty of Budapest University to control the flood of enrolments that had resulted from the influx of refugees from the lost territories; other faculties were experiencing similarly acute problems of overcrowding. The proposal was converted into an anti–Jewish measure by the Dean of the University's theological faculty, Mihály Kmoskó, who introduced the concept that university admissions should reflect the ethnic and religious composition of Hungary's population.[18] In 1913, 34.1 per cent of the university's student population had been Jewish, although Jews made up only 5 per cent of the population as a whole; in a Hungary from which other ethnic minorities had virtually disappeared, the principal victims of any move towards a proportional system of enrolment would obviously be the Jews—and this, indeed, was the intention. Pál Teleki, as Prime Minister, put his weight behind the passage of the bill, despite the fact that it clearly violated both the Emancipation Law of 1867 and the *Recepció* of 1895. In its final form, the *Numerus Clausus* law obliged all universities to ensure that the 'proportion of students belonging to the various races and nationalities living in the country corresponds to the proportion of those races and nationalities in the population of the country, or at least reaches nine-tenths of that proportion'.[19] We have seen that István Bethlen, mindful of the importance of the Jewish community to Hungary's economy and financial wellbeing, did his best to mitigate the effects of the *Numerus Clausus;* in 1927, he pushed through a legislative amendment designed to moderate its impact by making parental occupation rather than race or nationality the criterion for proportionality. Although in practice this brought about only a marginal improvement in Jewish admission prospects—Jewish enrolment increased from 8 to 12 per cent—it was sufficient, given the prevailing national mood, to trigger pogroms in several universities, usually led by Gömbös's *Turul* youth organisation; in Budapest alone, 174 Jewish students sustained serious injuries. Bethlen's efforts did little to stem the emigration, which continued throughout the 1920s, of Jewish students to universities outside Hungary, particularly to Vienna, Prague and Brno as well as to Western universities. Since the validation of foreign degrees was difficult in Hungary, these emigrations tended to become permanent, with the paradoxical but happy consequence that the *Numerus Clausus* saved thousands of Hungarian Jews from the Holocaust.

The Jews refused to allow these developments to dent their determined patriotism. They stoutly rejected offers of assistance from Jewish communities abroad and loudly opposed moves, for example in the League of Nations, towards retaliatory measures against the Hungarian government. In 1925, the Hungarian National Jewish Congress proclaimed that 'we want to settle the matter of the *Numerus Clausus* here at home, with our own government and our own legislation … we did not apply, and do not appeal, to any foreign factor and ask for no help: such help, even if it stems from good intentions, we reject'.[20] Vilmos Vázsonyi, addressing the same Congress shortly before his death from a heart attack after being assaulted on the street, spoke for the majority of Hungarian Jews when he declared: 'We are part of the Hungarian constitution, part of the Hungarian nation … We are not Hungarian Jews but Jewish Hungarians … We adhere to our ancestral religion but this fatherland is also ours. We do not give away our fatherland;

we do not give away our Magyardom'.[21] This commendable, if quixotic, loyalty to
the Magyar nation, combined as it was with continuing Jewish dominance of
Hungarian economic life and conspicuous personal prosperity, counted for little
during the rightward drift of Hungarian politics in the 1930s. Kálmán Darányi,
who had succeeded Gömbös as Prime Minister in 1936,* took a familiar line in
his speech at Győr in March, 1938, which launched Hungary's rearmament programme: 'I see the essence of the question in that the Jews living within the borders of the country, due to their specific disposition and situation, but partly also
because of their indifference to the Hungarian race, play a disproportionately
great role in certain branches of economic life'.[22] Therefore, Darányi argued, Jewish influence in culture and other areas of national life had to be reduced 'to a
proper scale'; this would benefit not only Christian society but also the Jews
themselves, since it would draw the teeth of anti–Semitism. Two months later a
new Prime Minister, Béla Imrédy, secured the passage of a bill—Law XV of
1938—that began the implementation of Darányi's threat. This, the 'First Jewish
Law' as it came to be known, ruled that Jews—already barred from public service—could occupy no more than 20 per cent of the professions or of the employees in a business enterprise. Unlike the law introducing the *Numerus Clausus*, the
new law referred specifically to 'Jews' and defined them as those professing 'the
Israelite religion'. As well as doctors and lawyers, all who worked in journalism,
cinema and the theatre were required to establish, in effect, closed shops in their
professions in order to regulate the proportion of Jewish members. The new law
attracted plaudits from the leaders of every Christian denomination; and strong
condemnation from the non-Jewish intelligentsia, including composers such as
Bartók and Kodály, as well as writers and artists. In a letter to the Regent, István
Bethlen warned that Imrédy was causing wounds 'without thinking of the cure.
He is preparing to transform the nearly one million intelligent Jews who live in
our country into desperate internal enemies of the Hungarian nation'.[23] The First
Jewish Law accelerated the haemorrhage to the West of much of Hungary's intellectual and artistic talent. Although Nazi influence in Hungary had already
reached a significant level by 1938, responsibility for the First Jewish Law cannot
fairly be laid at that door. It was the product of specifically Hungarian prejudices,
envies and fears. The infinitely greater disasters that were to befall Hungarian
Jewry during the next six years, however, reflected the total dependence on Nazi
Germany into which Hungary allowed herself to be drawn.

Workers and Peasants

Among the many respects in which Trianon left Hungary top-heavy was the disproportionate size and economic weight of her capital city. Even before Trianon,
Budapest had outgrown Hungary; now, still growing though more slowly, she was
the capital of a country reduced to one-third of its former area. Two-thirds of the
industrial workforce, itself making up only one-third of the wage-earning population, were employed in Budapest. After the brief Utopian interlude of the Kun
regime, the living standards of the urban working class fell back below 1913 levels.

* See Chapter 15.

In 1920, industrial wages dropped by an average of 50 per cent, unemployment and accident insurances were abolished, laws that had introduced holidays with pay and the eight-hour working day repealed. Real wages inched up to 86 per cent of pre-war levels by 1929, only to drop back to about 75 per cent during the Depression. Few workers put in less than a nine-hour day, many worked for over ten; endemic unemployment throughout the inter-war years, together with the effective neutering of the trade union movement by the Bethlen-Peyer pact, virtually eliminated the possibility of protest against harsh conditions. The great majority of urban working-class families lived in a single room with a shared kitchen, often without plumbing and usually without an indoor lavatory. Budapest had the highest incidence of tuberculosis of any European city and the second highest mortality rate; infant mortality averaged 179 per thousand.

Bethlen, however, recognised the key importance of the industrial workforce to the national economy and, once economic stabilisation had been achieved through the attraction of foreign loans and investment, he embarked on a programme of social reform which was not unimpressive for its time. Legislation passed in 1927 increased the period of a worker's entitlement to free medical treatment and sickness benefit from five months to one year; and in 1928 the Bethlen government introduced compulsory social insurance to provide for old age pensions at the age of sixty-five, disability pensions and benefits for widows and orphans. The financial crash and Depression brought the programme to a halt at this point; but it resumed, under Gömbös, in 1935 with the reinstatement of the eight-hour day and in 1937, under Darányi, with the introduction of a minimum wage, a forty-eight-hour week and holidays with pay. Unemployment benefit, however, remained beyond the government's means in the 1930s, as it had been in the 1920s—permanent unemployment levels of between 10 and 20 per cent ruled it out. Hungary continued to lag well behind the West in terms of urban social provision; but in most respects—and particularly, as we shall see, in public education—she stood well ahead of her immediate neighbours.

Bethlen's attempts at social reform did not, however, extend to the countryside, where the situation of the labouring class was even more sombre than that of the urban proletariat. Throughout the inter-war years, approximately half of Hungary's population of 8.7 million depended on the land for their livelihood—55 per cent in 1920, 48 per cent in 1941. They lived in a countryside that had changed very little for a hundred years. Bethlen remained firmly opposed to land reform throughout his premiership, on the grounds that the property of existing landowners should not be alienated: 'Where private property is sacred nobody has a claim to the land, just as nobody has a claim to my coat'.[24] Horthy took the same view, arguing repeatedly that land reform was impracticable because there was not enough land to go round. Pressure from the Smallholders' wing of his Unity Party nevertheless obliged Bethlen to make a gesture in the direction of reform in 1924, by introducing largely cosmetic improvements to Pál Teleki's equally half-hearted legislation of 1920. The net effect of the two laws was to redistribute just over 8 per cent of Hungary's cultivable land, reducing the large estates of over 1,000 *hold* by 14 per cent and the medium estates of 500–1,000 *hold* by less than 6 per cent. Local obstruction impeded the process of redistribution which, to the extent that it was implemented at all, simply increased by tens of thousands the number of non-viable dwarf-holdings of 1 to 5 *hold*. Since Teleki and Bethlen insisted on full compensation to the landlords, most of the recipients of redistributed land were soon driven into bankruptcy by the payments demanded of them.

In 1930, the more fortunate stratum of Hungary's rural population consisted of about 300,000 relatively wealthy peasants owning more than 20 *hold* and a million or so with smallholdings of between 5 and 20 *hold;* outnumbering them by nearly three to one were 1.2 million dwarf-holders, 600,000 labourers tied to large or medium estates and 1.2 million landless day-labourers—hence the popular con-temporary description of Horthy's Hungary as 'the land of 3 million beggars'.[25] The day-labourers, usually working in teams, could expect employment during only half the year—the government's financial straits and the Depression brought to a stop the public works on which they depended when the estates had no use for them; they and their families consequently lived on the brink of starvation. The situation of labourers on the estates was not much better. Gyula Illyés, one of several writers who tried, during the inter-war period, to draw attention to the plight of the rural poor and himself the son of a farm labourer, described a boy-hood visit to the Szerentsés family in a neighbouring village:

The Szerentséses starved in unison and—here at home—quite unashamedly. The family that lived with them also starved. The whole puszta in general could have done with some-thing to eat. Their eyes did not rattle in their sockets from hunger, nor did they clasp their stomachs and howl: they starved quietly and regularly, but they were obviously starving. They gathered mushrooms in the woods and ate them. When there were no mushrooms, they would go out into the estate sugarbeet fields to steal beet-leaves and ate those. For they ate something every day, but it was so little that it probably did not restore the strength they expended in chewing it.[26]

Most peasant families lived in a single room, sharing a kitchen, in earthern-floored single-storey buildings that were also divided into stables and pig-sties; tuberculosis claimed between ten and twelve thousand victims in most years. As late as 1939, two-thirds of Hungary's villages still lacked electricity. Illyés, who carried out careful field research for his book *People of the Puszta*, gives a revealing breakdown of typical peasant incomes. (Conversion into present-day currency is hazardous, but a very rough guide would be to equate 1 *pengő* with 4 new pence.) A farm labourer's contract would provide for a cash payment of between 12 and 40 *pengő* per year, plus sufficient grain to provide each member of a family of five with 0.27 kg of bread daily, 5–6 m^3 of logs for heating and cooking, one or two pigs (but piglets had to be handed over to the estate), two dozen hens and one or two ducks; the family were also given the use of a small plot of land. The family's total income, in cash and kind, might therefore amount to 350–400 *pengő*. A day labourer could expect to earn, again in cash and kind, about 130–50 *pengő* for the five or six months during which he could expect to find work.

For most, there was no prospect of escape from the extreme hardships of rural living. The level of urban unemployment ruled out emigration to the towns or to the capital. The severe restrictions now imposed on immigration by the American authorities closed off the traditional escape route to the United States. Although the right-wing parties professed to be the champions of the peasantry against the landlords, their rise to power after Bethlen's departure brought little relief to the countryside. The Land Settlement Act of 1936 purported to make 400,000 *hold* of land, in viable plots of 8–10 *hold*, available to the landless, but when Hungary's entry into the Second World War, in 1941, brought the programme to a halt, barely half the redistribution had taken place. The peasantry continued to be excluded from the process of social reform that had brought some relief to their urban counterparts: there was no floor to their wage levels and no ceiling to their hours of work. Compulsory health and accident insurance did not apply to the rural workforce. When, in 1938, provision was at last made for pensions for rural workers it was subject to eligibility qualifications, which excluded many. Although significant advances were made during the period in educational provision for the villages, children of the 1.5 million peasants who lived on isolated farmsteads could not benefit. The level of literacy in rural communities nevertheless rose sufficiently to make peasants more aware, by comparing their lot with that of town-dwellers and even, from the accounts of war veterans, with living standards in other lands, of the depths of their disadvantage. Like other sectors of the Hungarian population, the peasantry became increasingly receptive to the strident appeals of political extremism, from both left and right.

Education and Culture

A positive by-product of the siege mentality that informed Hungarian politics during much of the inter-war period was the degree of priority accorded by successive governments to the improvement of the educational system.[27] The younger generation had to be properly equipped to ensure the survival of its mutilated homeland and to carry forward the revisionist cause. The Education Act of 1921 identified as an objective of education policy 'the positive nurturing of the sense of nation'. Hungary benefited from the efforts of two long-serving Ministers of Education: Count Kuno Klebelsberg, who held the post throughout the Bethlen era (1922–31) and the distinguished historian Bálint Hóman, who survived successive changes of Prime Minister from 1932 until Hungary joined the Second World War ten years later. Klebelsberg concentrated his efforts on the development of elementary education, helped by Bethlen's allocation of 10 per cent of the state budget to his Ministry. Over a thousand new elementary schools were built during Bethlen's premiership, with teachers' accommodation to go with them. By 1938, Hungary's elementary schools numbered nearly seven thousand. Elementary education consisted of six years of full-time schooling (from the age of six), followed by a part-time continuation course of three years; by 1938, a 92 per cent attendance rate had been achieved for the first phase, but attendance at the subsequent part-time stage never rose above 30 per cent and was usually much lower in rural areas. In an attempt to make some provision for the continuing education of rural children who had reached the age (twelve to fifteen) at which they could be useful on the farm, Hóman established a network of so-called *népházak*, village cultural centres, of which over 1,500 existed by 1938; considerable efforts were also made to expand the library service. A more effective solution was the extension, in 1940, of the first stage of elementary education from six to eight years, followed by only two years of part-time attendance. Secondary education expanded less rapidly but underwent significant reform: in 1934, Hóman replaced both the 'classical' and the 'modern' *gimnázium* with grammar schools, which covered the whole curriculum, albeit with a continuing bias towards the humanities. The new schools offered a single syllabus for the first four years of secondary education—compulsory Latin and German plus a choice of Greek, French, English or Italian—followed by four years for which pupils could choose between science and Latin. By 1938, 10 per cent of the age group ten to eighteen was benefiting from secondary education on this pattern. As we have seen, Hungary's higher education sector was disproportionately swollen by Trianon and the transfer of universities from Pozsony and Kolozsvár to new homes in Hungary, Pécs and Szeged. Even so, graduates accounted for only 1.2 per cent of the total population by 1940.

Klebelsberg's and Hóman's policies produced impressive results. By 1938, illiteracy at school age had been reduced to 7 per cent. Although this still lagged behind the west European average of 5 per cent, it compared very favourably indeed with levels of illiteracy in other countries of the region: 23 per cent in Poland, 39 per cent in Bulgaria, 42 per cent in Romania and 45 per cent in Yugoslavia. Beyond elementary level, the pupil and student population came overwhelmingly from the middle and upper classes; Hóman did attempt, however, to make higher education more accessible to students from working-class and peasant backgrounds by establishing a state-funded scholarship scheme for the 'underprivileged, industrious and patriotic'. In keeping with its avowedly patriotic mission, the ideological content of the national curriculum was high. At the beginning and end of every school day, pupils recited the 'Magyar Credo': 'I believe in one God, I believe in one Homeland, I believe in one eternal God-given truth, I believe in the resurrection of Hungary'. 'Hungary truncated (Csonkamagyarország) is not a country: Hungary intact is the Divine Will' was another popular mantra. At secondary level, the curriculum included a compulsory course on Hungary's recent history, which attributed 'the so-called dictatorship of the proletariat' under Béla Kun to the disastrous and treasonous policies of Count Mihály Károlyi and his fellow liberals. High priority was given at all levels to the inculcation of 'national consciousness' (nemzeti öntudat) and also to physical education; young males between the ages of twelve and twenty-one were required to join a paramilitary youth organisation, the Levente. Its nationalist slant did not, however, prevent the educational system from producing academic results of a high order, which were eventually reflected in the international prominence of Hungarian physicists, chemists, mathematicians and medical scientists—and in the large number of Nobel Prizes awarded to the alumni, albeit in exile, of the schools and universities of a country of only 8 million people.

An important fact about Horthy's Hungary, which the historiography of the Communist era naturally glossed over, is that the unattractive aspects of its politics—authoritarianism, nationalism, anti–Semitism—did not stifle, and in general did not attempt to suppress, the vitality of its cultural activity. Literature, in particular, flourished as vigorously in inter-war Hungary as it had in any earlier period. Hungarian writers of the 1920s and 1930s exhibited a wide diversity of approach and a high level of talent. A prominent group, for which the literary journal Nyugat continued to provide a focus, continued the pre-war aesthetic tradition. Its leading member, Mihály Babits (1883–1941), edited Nyugat for a quarter of a century until his death, which also resulted in the demise of the journal. A prolific poet, whose masterpiece *The Book of Jonah* warned against acquiescence in fascism—'for silence midst the guilty is a crime'—Babits was also a novelist of note and a particularly brilliant translator; his translation of Dante's *Divine Comedy* won international recognition. Babits's importance in the cultural life of inter-war Hungary was two-fold: as editor of *Nyugat*, he inspired and encouraged a younger generation of poets and writers; and his own work, particularly in its courageous opposition to war, spoke powerfully for the assumption of individual moral responsibility. A leading member of Babits's *Nyugat* circle, Dezső Kosztolányi (1885–1936) was less socially engaged than his friend and mentor; he exemplified, rather, the pre-war tendency to regard the striving towards an artistic ideal of form and expression as an end in itself. Although, like Babits, Kosztolányi was both a poet of great technical brilliance and a translator of distinction, it is probably his novels which have best stood the test of time: *The Lark, Anna Édes* and *The Golden Dragon* are miracles of minute social observation but unburdened by a social message. More loosely associated with the *Nyugat* circle were the poets Gyula Juhász and Árpád Tóth—both inclined to melancholia—the humorous writer and fantasist Frigyes Karinthy and, representing a later generation, Sándor Márai, one of Hungary's most talented modern prose writers and an acute, if rather detached, social observer.

At the opposite end of Hungary's literary spectrum stood the committed radicals and pioneers of the avant-garde. Their doyen was Lajos Kassák (1887–1967), who in his late teens became actively involved in the working-class movement and before the outbreak of the First World War roamed through western Europe as a journeyman locksmith, supporting revolutionary activity where he found it. In this first phase of his literary development, Kassák resembled Maxim Gorky, his poetry overtly political and his prose largely autobiographical. He worked for the Kun regime in the cultural field but nevertheless opposed literary censorship; his association with Kun earned him imprisonment and exile during the counter-revolution, but his disillusionment with the reality of Communism had already turned Kassák away from literary polemics towards avant-garde experiment and surrealism, in the visual arts—in which he displayed great talent—as well as in creative writing. His prose, in particular his massive autobiography *The Life of a Man* and the social novel *Angyalföld** has proved more durable than his poetry, although one of his earlier and stylistically anarchic poems, 'The Horse Dies and the Birds Fly Out', is now seen to have inaugurated a new phase in the development of modern Hungarian poetry.

Whereas Kassák, during his 'political' period, concentrated mainly on the plight of the urban proletariat, his literary contemporary (though eight years his senior), Zsigmond Móricz (1879—1942), was a powerful champion of the rural poor, of whose problems he had direct experience during his childhood in a peasant family. Like Kassák, Móricz was first inspired and then disillusioned by Béla Kun's Republic of Councils, which did nothing to improve the quality of rural life. He was closely associated with *Nyugat*, in which much of his work was published, and even became its co-editor, but he differed from most of the *Nyugat* circle in giv-

---

* A working-class suburb of Budapest.

ing his writing an avowed social purpose. From his earliest published work—the short story 'Seven Pennies' (1908), which won instant acclaim—onwards, Móricz took a wholly unsentimental and often ruthlessly realistic view of the rural society that provided the background to most of his work. He portrayed not only the human virtues adversity could illuminate but also the equally real vices material hardship encouraged. His novels *Pure Gold* and *The Torch* are as devastating in their exposure of the ugly moral impact of deprivation as is the annihilating critique of the rural squirearchy and urban bourgeoisie in *Gentlemen Make Merry* and *Relatives*. Móricz did not employ his considerable creative talent only as an instrument of social criticism; he also completed a huge historical trilogy, *Transylvania*, which centred on the contrasting characters of the Transylvanian rulers Gábor Bethlen and Gábor Báthory, and began, but failed to complete, another about the nineteenth-century outlaw Sándor Rózsa. Among the many other Hungarian writers of the period who regarded their art as having a purpose beyond its own perfection, Margit Kaffka (1880–1918) deserves a mention as a pioneering feminist; her three best-known novels, *Colours and Years, The Years of Mária* and *Stations*, were all concerned with the problems faced by women in contemporary Hungarian society and by their vulnerability to imprisonment in sterile or damaging relationships. Although her life was cut short by the influenza epidemic of 1918, Margit Kaffka remains Hungary's most eminent woman novelist.

There is no objective criterion for the quality of genius. It is possible for a poet or writer to possess originality and great creative talent while still lacking that elusive attribute: most, perhaps all, of the Hungarian writers mentioned in this chapter so far arguably fall into that category. Few would deny the attribute of genius to Sándor Petőfi or to Endre Ady; nor, I believe, to the outstanding literary figure of the inter-war period, Attila József (1905–37). And yet there are problems in assessing József's true stature. The first is that his short life was so scarred by tragedy that it is tempting to believe that metal smelted in such a fierce heat could not be other than the very purest. József, born into the abject poverty of the Budapest slums, lost his father, who emigrated to Romania, in infancy; his mother died of cancer before József reached his 'teens. His elder sister, who then brought him up, married a wealthy lawyer but was soon discarded and young József with her. József, thrown on to his own resources, worked his way through Szeged University until he was expelled for publishing an atheist poem. Seeking a new life in Paris, he fell in with a group of anarchists and Communists and espoused the cause of the oppressed. Fired with enthusiasm, József returned to Hungary and joined the underground Communist Party, for which he worked loyally and energetically during the early 1930s; but his independence of mind—he refused to disavow Freud and anticipated Moscow in arguing for a popular front strategy—became a liability to the Party, which expelled him. Mental breakdown followed and József threw himself under a train in 1937. The second problem attending an assessment of József as a poet is that, despite his enforced break with the Hungarian Communist Party in 1935, the same Party, once ensconced in power after the end of the Second World War and the 'liberation' of Hungary by Soviet arms, could not resist adopting him as the cultural mascot of Hungarian Communism. Endless editions of and adulatory commentaries on the work of Attila József, literary icon of both the Stalinist and post-Stalinist regimes in Hungary, eclipsed the legacy of his contemporaries and create legitimate doubt as to how his reputation—which, in fact, came to life only after his suicide—would have fared without this artificial enhancement. Probably, it would have flourished equally well—quite possibly better—without the tarnish of Communist endorsement. József's descriptive powers and the vividness of his imagery raised him well above his contemporaries; and these qualities, coupled with his compassion for the disadvantaged and his agonised concern for the future of humanity, give his work—six hundred poems written between the age of seventeen and his death at thirty-two—a wholeness that invites the accolade of genius. By 1937 he had an icy premonition of what might befall Hungary: his 'Welcome to Thomas Mann' (the German writer, already a fugitive from the Nazis, was visiting Hungary to deliver a lecture) voiced his fears:

> We just buried Kosztolányi: cureless, dire,
> The cancer on his mouth grew bitterly.
> But growths more monstrous gnaw humanity.
> Appalled, we ask: More than what went before,
> What horror has the future yet in store?
> What ravening thoughts will seize us for their prey?
> What poisons, brewing now, eat us away?[28]

Another late poem, 'A Breath of Air', helps to explain why, despite his adoption by the Communist regime, József was also one of the icons of the 1956 Revolution:

> They can tap all my telephone calls
> (when, why, to whom).
> They have a file on my dreams and plans
> And on those who read them.
> And who knows when they'll find
> Sufficient reason to dig up the files
> That violate my rights.[29]

The art of one of József s contemporaries, Miklós Radnóti, might not have been accorded the international recognition it richly deserved had it not been for his murder, by a Nazi guard, in a Jewish labour battalion in 1944. Following the recovery of his body from the mass grave he shared with twenty-two fellow victims, a notebook containing a number of poems, judged to be among his best, was found sewn into his prisoner's clothing. They included the short poem for which he is best known and which foresaw the manner of his own death, 'Razglednica' ('Postcard'):

> I fell beside him. His body—which was taut
> As a cord is, when it snaps—spun as I fell.
> Shot in the neck. 'This is how you will end,'
> I whispered to myself; 'keep lying still.
> Now, patience is flowering into death.'
> 'Der springt noch auf,' said someone over me.
> Blood on my ears was drying, caked with earth.[30]

The extraordinary range of Radnóti's output during the 1930s, embracing pastoral, neo-classical and expressionist styles, would have ensured his place among

Hungary's great modern poets even if his life had ended less tragically. He shared József's passionate opposition to fascism and championship of the oppressed. Just as '*Razglednica*' foreshadowed his own end, so poems such as those in the collection *Járkálj csak, halálraítélt!* ('Just walk on, condemned one!'), published in 1936, forecast the tragedy that awaited Hungary.

Alongside the conservative aesthetes and the radical avant-gardistes in Horthy's Hungary stood a third school of writers, the Populists (*népi írók*). The Populists, despairing of the ability of Hungary's traditional ruling class to revive the fortunes of their country, looked to the long-suffering peasantry and its 'ancestral strength' (*őserő*) for Hungary's resurrection. They had much in common with the Russian *narodniki* of the nineteenth century; the fact that the movement emerged in Hungary only in the 1920s and 1930s is in itself a comment on the extent of Hungary's social backwardness. Zsigmond Móricz, with his peasant heroes, had in a sense pointed the way; but the Populists mined their common theme in greater depth, basing their novels and poetry on serious research in the countryside carried out either by themselves or by the new group of sociologists who called themselves 'village explorers' (*falukutatók*)—indeed, there was considerable overlap between the work of the writers and the social scientists, exemplified by Péter Veres (1897–1970) whose work spanned both disciplines. An earlier writer, Dezső Szabó (1879–1945), had pioneered the populist vein with his novel *The Village that was Swept Away*, which idealised pre-war village life and attributed all Hungary's ills to politicians, Germans and Jews. Gyula Illyés (1902–83) was probably the most distinguished of the Populist writers and his later work explored broader frontiers both in poetry and in prose. A schoolboy Communist from a peasant background, he fought for the Kun regime on the Romanian front and emigrated to Paris to escape the White Terror—the French language and French literature were of central importance to him for the rest of his life. Returning to Hungary in 1926, Illyés became a regular contributor to *Nyugat* and eventually one of its editors. He was never, however, a typical member of the *Nyugat* circle: driven by a strong sense of mission to expose the deprivations of the peasant world into which he had been born, he used both verse and prose to express controlled anger at the continued backwardness of the Hungarian countryside. Reference has already been made to *People of the Puszta*, the classic of Populist writing. When *Nyugat* folded with the death of Babits in 1941, Illyés helped to found, and edited, a successor literary journal, *Magyar Csillag* ('Hungarian Star'), which adopted a strongly anti–fascist stance and consequently could not survive the German occupation in 1944. Many other voices were raised on behalf of Hungary's 'three million beggars'—those, for example, of László Németh, János Kodolányi, Péter Veres, Zoltán Szabó and Dénes Barsi, editor of the Populist journal *A Kelet Népe* ('People of the Orient'—named after István Széchenyi's famous tract)—but none was more powerful than that of Illyés.

The belief of many of the Populists in the unique qualities and virtues of the Hungarian peasantry, and their hostility towards an urban economy that happened to be dominated by Jews, sometimes degenerated into a misty-eyed nationalism tinged with anti–Semitism. For another group of writers and scholars, however, 'Christian nationalism' was a primary theme and motivation. The concept, shared by many of them, of a Christian-Germanic cultural tradition of which Hungary was part fitted in well with Hungary's growing political and economic orientation towards Germany during the 1930s. Their conservatism, too, accorded with the aversion of Horthy and most of his ministers to radical reform. This vein in inter-war Hungarian literature and thought acquired intellectual respectability from one of its exponents in particular, the scholar and outstanding historian Gyula Szekfű, who edited *Magyar Szemle* ('The Hungarian Review') from 1927 until the German occupation and was co-author, with Bálint Hóman, of the classic five-volume *Magyar Történet* ('Hungarian History'). Szekfű's critique of recent Hungarian history, *Három nemzedék* ('Three Generations'), attributed the catastrophe that had overtaken Hungary to the hot-headed radicalism of Lajos Kossuth and to the obtuse nationality policies of the liberal Dualist governments: adherence to István Széchenyi's principles of gradual reform and the natural, unforced assimilation of the nationalities would have spared Hungary the tragedies which befell her. But as Hungary became, in the late 1930s, locked ever more tightly into Nazi Germany's embrace, Szekfű became highly critical of the Horthy regime and of the racism that was staining Hungarian public life. One of the leading opponents of the cosmopolitan *Nyugat* and its avant-garde sympathies, János Horváth, a founding editor of the conservative literary journal *Napkelet* ('East'), also gave intellectual weight to the 'Christian national' cause. The movement nevertheless owed its considerable popular impact to writers of lesser calibre, whose favoured genre was the historical novel: the works of Cécile Tormay, Ferenc Herczeg, Irén Gulácsy and Gyula Somogyvári summoned up idealised episodes of Hungary's past as an inspiration to a revival of national pride and to national resurrection. Writing of this type tended to pander to the prejudices of the middle class: Magyar nationalism, aggressive revisionism and anti–Semitism.

This necessarily cursory survey of Hungary's culture between the two world wars has concentrated so far on literature because it is primarily in her literature, and above all in her poetry, that Hungary's national identity has always been enshrined and expressed. But writing was not, of course, the only field of cultural activity in Horthy's Hungary. Only the visual arts, never the jewel in Hungary's cultural crown, tended to languish during the inter-war period; many promising young Hungarian artists chose to study and work in Paris and Rome rather than brave the uncertainties of a volatile political climate at home. The naturalist, Nagybánya, and folk traditions of Hungarian painting and sculpture were nevertheless maintained in the newly established artists' colonies at Szentendre and Zebegény. Modernism, moreover, was by no means stifled despite an unfavourable cultural climate, increasingly determined by Hungary's close relations with Nazi Germany; Lajos Vajda, in particular, made a specifically Hungarian contribution to the international Modernist movement. During the war years, and with the significant exception of poster art—an area in which Hungary's artists were and are uniquely talented—the visual arts were sustained only in the privacy of studios until even they were submerged by the cold tide of socialist realism.

Until the Jewish Laws began to bite, Hungarian music flourished during most of the Horthy era. The pianist and composer Ernő Dohnányi, rehabilitated after his support for the Kun regime, presided over a flourishing Academy of Music. Zoltán Kodály and Béla Bartók, also forgiven for their enthusiasm for the Republic of Councils, both enjoyed a period of intense creativity. Kodály, drawing his inspiration increasingly from the Hungarian folk tradition, composed the *Psalmus Hungaricus*, the *Budavár Te Deum* and the opera *Háry János;* Bartók, continuing his tracing of Hungarian music back to its ancient roots, produced his *Cantata Profana* and *Music for Strings* just before emigrating to the United States in 1940 in protest against anti–Semitic legislation. Indeed, the roll-call of artists and scholars who, like Bartók, left Hungary during the 1930s in itself testifies to the richness of the cultural environment they had helped to create. Among the musicians were Fritz Reiner, Georg Solti, George Szell and Eugene Ormandy; among the actors, Paul Lukas and Peter Lorre, not forgetting ZsaZsa and Eva Gabor; among the film directors and producers, Alexander Korda, Adolph Zukor, Michael Curtiz, Emerich Pressburger and Joseph Pasternak; and among the scientists and scholars, Leo Szilard, Jenő Wigner, Edward Teller, János Neumann, Theodor von Kármán and György de Hevesy.* Such a flowering of talent in a small country of eight million people was remarkable; but a small country, equally, could ill afford to lose it.

Hungarian society between the wars, Horthy's Hungary, was deeply flawed. The corruption of its political process; its tolerance of a virtually feudal situation in the countryside and of a degree of rural deprivation that verged on the medieval; its increasingly strident nationalism, explicable if not excusable as a reaction to Trianon; and the pervasive miasma of anti–Semitism, which towards the end of the period crystallised into active persecution—all these deeply unattractive characteristics set Hungary apart from the western Europe to which she so ardently aspired to belong. That many of them were shared by, for example, Poland and Romania is a poor defence. And yet the depiction of Horthy's Hungary in Communist historiography as an obscurantist and frequently vicious dictatorship must be corrected. Despite electoral chicanery and gerrymandering, Hungary retained a viable parliamentary system under which ministers could be called to account and in which political parties could compete. Thanks to the device of the Regency, the continuity of her ancient constitution was preserved. Too many, especially Jews, were forced into emigration; but not, as yet, into concentration camps. Censorship was not severe: until 1938, when Hungary began to lose control of her destiny, 376 political journals competed for the population's attention and support. Cultural activity, as we have just seen, was not only vigorous but extremely diverse.

After Bethlen's withdrawal, the regime became increasingly authoritarian; but, apart from the absence of land reform, Hungary was not, by contemporary standards, ill-governed. The education system developed into a major national asset, as it has remained. Social welfare made significant advances in the urban industrial environment, though virtually absent from the countryside. Despite the paucity of her resources and the economic depredations of the peace treaty, Hungary made a relatively good recovery from the Crash and the Depression. Had the poison of Trianon not been fermenting in the nation's veins, Hungary could have faced the future with some confidence and hope. Instead, she gambled: and lost.

---

*Hungarian scientists played a prominent part in the Manhattan Project which, at Los Alamos (New Mexico) produced the first atomic bomb. During a routine committee meeting the chairman, the Italian physicist Enrico Fermi, was called out to take a telephone call. Looking round the table, Edward Teller remarked to his colleagues: 'Good. Now we can speak Hungarian' (apocryphal).

15

THE FAUSTIAN PACT I: THE PRIZE

(1936–41)

The Drift towards Germany (1936–38)

Small, vulnerable countries have little scope for the pursuit of glorious, or some-times even honourable, foreign policies. Post-Trianon Hungary was both small and vulnerable. The dissolution of the Austro-Hungarian Monarchy had created a power vacuum in central-eastern Europe that would inevitably be filled, in due course, by Germany or the Soviet Union; in the event it was filled by both, in suc-cession. For Hungary, situated at the heart of the vacuum and surrounded in it by the hostile members of the Little Entente, recovery of at least the predominantly Magyar areas of the lost territories was seen as a matter not merely of national honour but of survival. In the preface to a collection of his speeches and writings published in 1933, Count Bethlen wrote that it was impossible to imagine an inde-pendent existence or survival for the Hungarian state within the frontiers laid down by Trianon: if Hungary failed to seize the opportunities offered by what might be a brief respite from conflict, the 'waves of the sea of Slavs to the north and south and of Romanians will close above our heads'. The Hungarian nation would 'sooner or later vanish from the face of this earth'.[1] To non-Hungarians, these apocalyptic predictions may seem hysterical and paranoid; but the fear of ethnic extinction and envelopment by Slavdom had been a recurrent theme in Hungarian history for centuries, as we have seen in earlier chapters, and had deeper roots than mere tactical rhetoric. Bethlen told a London audience in 1933:

It is owing to this [Trianon] that fully one-third of the Hungarians who had lived for ten centuries in Hungary found themselves outside the new borders of this country and under the domination of Czechs, Rumanians and Serbs ... our national grief and pain on this account is, as you may well imagine, immeasurable. For this very reason, among others, the Hungarian nation never can and never will acquiesce definitely and of its own accord in the Peace Treaty of Trianon.[2]

In this, Bethlen spoke for an overwhelming majority of the Hungarian popula-tion. No Hungarian politician could do other than endeavour to give effect, whether by peaceful or other means, to a virtually unanimous national aspiration. When the retired chief of the German High Command, General von Seeckt, visited Budapest in 1927 to advise on the reconstruction of the Hungarian army, he was told by both Horthy and Bethlen that Hungary would in due course re-annex Slovakia by force. Brave words—but both men knew that they would remain empty until Hungary had found an ally sympathetic to her revisionist aims.

The brief summary in the previous chapter of Bethlen's foreign policy as Prime Minister explained the initial choice of Italy, frustrated by her meagre pickings from the Peace Treaty, as Hungary's principal ally. His attempt at a *rapprochement* with the Soviet Union which, like Hungary, had grievances against Romania, had been aborted by Horthy's refusal to countenance relations with the Bolsheviks (he eventually gave way in 1934). When Bethlen had tried to drive a wedge into the Little Entente by wooing Yugoslavia, a courtship initiated by Horthy in 1926 in a speech marking the 400th anniversary of the Battle of Mohács, the endeavour had been quickly smothered by Mussolini, who had his own designs on Yugoslavia, with the offer to Hungary of a more substantial and potentially much more valuable alliance. This, as we have seen, was created by the treaty affirming 'lasting peace and permanent friendship' between Italy and Hungary, which Bethlen and Mussolini signed in Rome in April 1927. The subsequent conclusion, in 1930, of a Treaty of Friendship between Italy and Austria created the prospect of greater security for Hungary in a formal tripartite relationship with both countries; and this was indeed realised in the Rome Protocols, which representatives of the three countries signed in March 1934. These provided not only for a substantial increase in exports to Italy by the two smaller nations but also for continuing political co-operation—all three governments shared an interest in the maintenance of Austrian independence, which Hitler, now in power in Germany, openly aspired to extinguish.

In the meantime, however, the shadow of German power was beginning to fall over Hungary. The rapid growth in both the volume and the imbalance of German-Hungarian trade from 1931 onwards has already been summarised.* The expansion was designed to promote Nazi Germany's political, as well as economic, interests. The brief for the German delegation which travelled to Budapest in February 1934, to negotiate a crucial supplement to the 1931 Trade Agreement, stated: 'Germany's purpose in the treaty about to be concluded consists of tying the Hungarian economy closely and inseparably to the German economy by means of increased exchange of goods'.[3] After making the Hungarians an offer they could not refuse—a substantial premium for their exports over world prices, to be financed by German assets frozen in Hungary by the financial crisis of 1931—the German delegation reported with satisfaction:

... The German delegation gained the impression that Hungary's will to resist the still very strong political pressure of Italy has been strengthened by the advantages offered by Germany in the Agreement. It may be expected that Hungary will not lightly risk the very considerable advantages granted her by Germany and will be mindful of this in her political attitude and also with respect to commercial policy.[4]

Given Gömbös's pro-German views, Germany was to a large extent pushing against an open door. Shortly after his appointment as Prime Minister, Gömbös

* See pages 350–51.

had personally appealed to Hitler to revive agricultural imports from Hungary, making this the touchstone of the further development of Hungarian-German relations: 'We fellow racists of long standing, who hold a common ideology, shall understand and back each other on economic policy as well'.[5]

For so long as relations between Germany and Italy remained cool, however, Hungary—weak though she was—had some scope for manoeuvre between the two, as indeed the German report quoted above implies. Gömbös hoped to win German support for revision at the expense of Czechoslovakia and Italian support for revision at the expense of Romania and Yugoslavia. In 1935, therefore, Gömbös both supported Mussolini's invasion of Abyssinia, voting in the League of Nations against the application of sanctions to Italy, and sought to win Hitler's favour by promising the creation of a fascist regime in Hungary. In 1936, in Rome, Gömbös backed Mussolini's plan to build a tripartite alliance and a customs union on the foundation of the Rome Protocols while Horthy, meeting Hitler for the first time, at Berchtesgaden, echoed the Führer's expressions of contempt for Czechoslovakia and hatred of Soviet Communism. After the meeting, Horthy described Hitler as 'a moderate and wise statesman', well-mannered and reasonable;[6] after Hitler's remilitarisation of the Rhineland, Horthy told the British Minister in Budapest that he admired the Führer for tearing up the Treaty of Locarno.

Mussolini, however, chastened by reverses in Africa and finding a common cause with Hitler in support for Franco in the Spanish Civil War, was now seeking to mend his fences with Germany: Italian support for Austrian independence evaporated, the 'Berlin-Rome Axis' became a reality,[7] Italy withdrew from the League of Nations and joined Hitler's Anti–Comintern Pact.

It was a measure of Hungary's discomfort over these developments, which closed off most of her few remaining options in foreign policy, that she flirted with the possibility of a rapprochement with the Little Entente, with the members of which she shared a growing concern over the rapid growth of German influence and power; but since Hungary could enter into no commitment which would have contradicted the principle of revision, and since the Little Entente could accept nothing less, the project was doomed from the start. Kálmán Darányi, the rather colourless conservative of the Bethlen school who had succeeded Gömbös as Prime Minister after the latter's death in 1936, even tested the water for an improvement in relations with Britain and France. Horthy had already, on his own initiative, addressed a long appeal for support to the new King of England, Edward VIII, who had visited Hungary as Prince of Wales: it elicited a polite acknowledgement but no interest. Darányi now declared, in 1937: 'The Hungarian nation, in undivided unity, wishes to secure the friendship of England, and would welcome the creation of amicable relationships with France, through the recognition of each other's interests'.[8] When the Darányi government stimulated the creation of an Anglo-Hungarian Friendship Society, Berlin was quick to indicate displeasure and a diminution of German support for Hungary's revisionist ambitions. It was clear from this moment that Hungary was going to have to manage the difficult and lop-sided relationship with Germany alone and as best she could; but also that Hungary could look only to Germany for assistance in recovering her lost territories.

When Darányi and his Foreign Minister, Kálmán Kánya—a suave and cynical former diplomat—paid an official visit to Berlin in November 1937, they found that the cloud over Hungarian-German relations had passed. The Germans wanted something: specifically, Hungarian acquiescence in the forthcoming *Anschluss* with Austria and active Hungarian participation in the projected dismemberment of Czechoslovakia. In return, Hitler and Göring told their visitors, Hungary could expect to recover all of Slovakia and, eventually, to enjoy German support for her other revisionist aims; for the time being, however, Hungary should confine her ambitions to Czechoslovakia and mend fences with Romania and Yugoslavia—Germany wanted peace and stability in the Balkans until the impending crises in central Europe had blown themselves out. The immediate response of the Hungarians was politely non-committal, but shortly after the visit Horthy confirmed, in a personal message to Hitler, that Hungary had no agreements on mutual assistance with either Austria or Czechoslovakia. When the *Anschluss* actually took place, on 13 March 1938, the Hungarian government duly congratulated the Führer—the first government to do so—on its 'bloodless execution' and closed the Hungarian Legation in Vienna, a significant caesura in the four centuries of Hungary's relationship with her Austrian neighbour. Hitler's successes, first in the Rhineland and now in Austria, had evoked a marked increase in support for the extreme right in Hungary and growing impatience in the predominantly pro-German officer corps with a government seen to be insufficiently committed to the German cause and slow to address the question of rearmament. Pro-Nazi demonstrations were accompanied by rumours of an impending right-wing coup. Immediately before the *Anschluss*, but in the knowledge of its imminence, Darányi had sought to lower the temperature by announcing, in a major speech in Győr, an ambitious programme of rearmament to pacify the generals; and restrictive measures against the Jews, subsequently enshrined in the First Jewish Law,* to appease the anti–Semites. To enhance Hungary's military capacity, the 'Győr Programme' envisaged additional defence expenditure of 1 billion *pengő* over five years on a reorganised armed force, consisting of three armies, a mobile corps and thirty-two air squadrons disposing of over 200 aircraft—150 of which were ordered from Germany during Göring's visit to Budapest in 1937.

Behind this confident espousal of the fashionable causes of rearmament and repression of the Jews, however, there were already deep concerns in Hungary over the trend of events. Even before the *Anschluss*, Kánya had confided to his Polish counterpart: 'We should prefer the maintenance of Austria's independence rather than the neighbourhood of an eighty-million-strong Germany. Being familiar with the related very resolute intentions of the German National Socialist Government, we have to be prepared for the event that the union of the two German states will sooner or later be consummated'.[9] István Bethlen was more outspoken, warning the Upper House in February that 'if our political system is subjected to a *Gleichschaltung* [bringing into line] in the form of right-wing ideas, we will become Germany's slaves, not her friends. And in that case an independent Hungarian foreign policy will be once and for all at an end'.[10] German behaviour in recent rounds of trade talks had given rise to considerable anxiety on the part of those involved. Germany had ignored Hungary's request that, since world agricultural prices now exceeded the subsidised prices offered by Germany, a greater proportion of Hungary's exports should be paid for in hard currency or

* See page 355.

that, at least, Germany should increase her exports to Hungary of industrial raw materials to assist the expansion of Hungarian manufacturing. The head of a Hungarian trade delegation reported: 'In general the tendency became obvious that Hungary was to be degraded to the level of raw material base'.[11]

Anschluss had now brought a rising, expansionist power right up to the Hungarian border. All too aware of the role of the Sudeten Germans in the impending crisis in German-Czechoslovak relations, the Hungarian government began to eye its own increasingly vocal German ('Swabian') minority of some 500,000 (5 per cent of the population) with some apprehension. The Swabians had been, for centuries, Hungary's least troublesome ethnic minority; their tidy villages, mostly in the south of the country, were models of good order and efficient husbandry. Hitler's rhetoric now made them conscious of their racial heritage. Anxieties over the implications of *Anschluss* for Hungary were sufficiently widespread to bring the Regent himself to the radio microphone: *'Anschluss'* he said, 'means nothing else than the union of an old and good friend of ours, whom the peace treaties had involved in an impossible position, with another old and good friend and companion in arms of ours ... That is all, nothing else has happened from our point of view'.[12] This Panglossian pronouncement gave some reassurance to those who sought it but did not curb the tendency of the Darányi government to appease the extreme right, which had become increasingly strident in the wake of the *Anschluss;* and at this juncture the reader must be introduced to the most bizarre member of Hungary's political *dramatis personae*, Ferenc Szálasi.

Szálasi, born to lower middle-class parents in upper Hungary in 1897, saw active service in the last stages of the First World War and joined the Hungarian army as a junior officer in 1921; he subsequently graduated to the general staff and interested himself in politics. If not clinically insane, Szálasi was, at least, mentally unbalanced. The following passage from one of his speeches provides a good summary of his political philosophy:

It is my conviction that the whole ordering of Europe can be effected only by that little people, despised of the Germans, the Hungarian people, on the Hungarist basic principles evolved through me. He who does not identify himself with my doctrine, who does not recognise me unreservedly as leader and will not agree that I have been selected by a higher Divine authority to redeem the Magyar people—he who does not understand me or loses confidence—let him go! At most, I shall remain alone, but even alone I shall create the Hungarist State with the help of the secret force that is within me.[13]

Szálasi developed a vision of a Hungarian-led federation embracing the entire territory of historic Hungary, from which all Jews and Communists would be expelled. The instrument for the realisation of this vision was the Arrow Cross Party—named after its symbol, although its formal name after 1937 was the Hungarian National Socialist Party—which Szálasi led and which absorbed a number of small extremist right-wing groups. Although the Arrow Cross Party had much in common with the Nazis, in particular its *Führerprinzip*, and attracted similar kinds of people to its ranks, it was not pro-German; Szálasi consistently gave total priority to the promotion of Hungarian interests, a characteristic that did not endear him to Berlin. Moreover, although Szálasi had many characteristics in common with Hitler, he maintained a deep respect for constitutional legitimacy (as, initially, did Hitler), insisting that he would never take power unless invited to do so by the Regent. He must have possessed a certain degree of personal charisma to remain the unchallenged leader of his party for a decade; and there is, indeed, abundant evidence that many contemporaries found his idealism and personal honesty attractive. But C. A. Macartney, the leading historian of this period, surely allowed himself to be carried beyond the bounds of balanced judgement in writing of Szálasi's 'patent sincerity, his purity of soul, the unpretentiousness of his daily life, his unmistakable sympathy for his suffering fellow-men ...';[14] this was, after all, the man who in 1944–45 would preside over and condone, even if he did not inspire, the most bestial pogrom in Hungary's history.

Horthy's position, already strong, had been made virtually impregnable by legislation, introduced by Darányi in 1937, which gave the Regent both immunity from impeachment—thus in effect installing Horthy in that office for life—and the right to name three candidates to succeed him, from whom Parliament would choose one. His sense of constitutional propriety was none the less outraged by an Arrow Cross proposal that he should be proclaimed King. When, therefore, Darányi attempted to tame the extreme right by offering the Arrow Cross a handful of seats in the Lower House in return for a promise of good behaviour—regardless of the fact that Szálasi's committed supporters still numbered only a few hundred—Horthy promptly sacked him and appointed Béla Imrédy to the premiership in his place in May 1938. Imrédy, an ambitious man of Swabian (German) middle-class stock, had been a successful Minister of Finance under Gömbös and subsequently President of the National Bank, a post in which he earned considerable respect in Western financial circles. Imrédy's range of contacts in London and Paris was, indeed, a major factor in the Regent's decision to appoint him Prime Minister; during the closing month's of Darányi's premiership, Horthy had undergone one of his periodic bouts of nerves about the ever closer German embrace and hoped that Imrédy would redress the balance. In this, Horthy was to be disappointed. Initially, however, Imrédy and Kánya, who retained his post as Foreign Minister, pursued a policy that temporarily restored the illusion of Hungarian independence of action. The British were assured that Hungary had no aggressive designs on her neighbours and heavy hints were dropped in London to the effect that a development of Anglo-Hungarian trade assisted by credits would reduce Hungary's dependence on the German market; the British were unimpressed, correctly concluding that the priority which any Hungarian government would have to give to revision would continue to tie her to Germany. At the same time, Hungary renewed her overtures to the Little Entente: these eventually resulted in the agreement signed by the four parties in Bled, Yugoslavia, in August 1938, which established 'recognition by the three States of the Little Entente of Hungary's equality of rights as regards armament, as well as the mutual renunciation of any recourse to force between Hungary and the States of the Little Entente'.[15] Hungary could now forge ahead with the Győr programme of rearmament without incurring protest from her neighbours; and, when the Bled Agreement was published, acquired an alibi with which she could, if she wished, resist German pressure to take an active part in an invasion of Czechoslovakia.

Publication of the agreement coincided with a state visit to Germany by Horthy, accompanied by Imrédy and Kánya, for which the Nazi propaganda machine pulled out all the stops; the launching of the battle-cruiser *Prinz Eugen* in Kiel provided a ceremonial focus for the visit, which was also the occasion for extensive talks, on Helgoland, between the Hungarians and the Nazi leadership. The visit encapsulated all the elements of Hungary's dilemma, which was to become increasingly painful and acute in succeeding years: it was the genesis of the Faustian pact with Nazi Germany which was to destroy her. On the one hand, Hungary's leaders were determined to redress the injustice of Trianon by bringing as many ethnic Hungarians as possible back into the national fold: on the other, even if they had the wherewithal to pursue this objective by military means—which, in August 1938, they did not—they wished to avoid the damage to Hungary's national reputation which would result from acting as Germany's accomplice in acts of armed aggression. The Bled Agreement predictably infuriated the Germans who, for political more than military reasons, wished to have a partner in their projected action against Czechoslovakia. The Hungarians initially maintained that it would be two years before they would dispose of adequate forces and armaments to invade Slovakia; but when Hitler and Ribbentrop stated forcefully that non-participants could expect no reward—'he who wants to sit at the table must at least help in the kitchen', Hitler remarked—the Hungarians began to waver. Horthy, having enraged Hitler by warning him that British sea-power would be decisive if German action against Czechoslovakia resulted in a wider conflict, ended by asking weakly whether Hitler could not at least postpone action until the spring. Kánya reduced his estimate of the period needed to achieve military readiness from two years to two months: and also told Ribbentrop that it would always be possible for Hungary to disavow the Bled Agreement. After this demeaning performance, Imrédy took a bolder line on his return to Budapest in an interview with a British journalist: 'The key words of Hungary's foreign policy', he said, 'are peace and justice; and if any conflict breaks out in Europe Hungary's aim will be to remain neutral'.[16] When the interview was reprinted in the Budapest evening tabloid *Az Est*, the Germans delivered a protest: the Hungarian government meekly served a suspension order on *Az Est*.

The Prize (1938–41)

Although Hitler now accepted, reluctantly, that Hungary could not be expected to join in military action against Czechoslovakia, the Hungarians' irresolution and patent desire to get something for nothing made a deeply unfavourable impression on him—'spineless dogs', he called them[17]—and strongly influenced his subsequent treatment of Hungary. When Imrédy and Kánya had a further meeting with the Führer shortly before the Munich conference, Hitler told them that this was Hungary's last opportunity to join Germany in settling the Czechoslovak problem: 'if she did not, he would not be in a position to put in a word for Hungarian interests'.[18] Imrédy prevaricated; but Hungary did address formal demands to the Czechoslovak government, on the eve of Munich, for the restitution of the predominantly Magyar regions of Slovakia. This proved insufficient to move the Western or the Axis powers to address Hungarian concerns at the Munich conference table: the Munich Agreement, which sanctioned German annexation of the territory now known as the Sudetenland, merely enjoined Hungary (and Poland) to resolve outstanding territorial issues in direct negotiation with the Czechoslovak government but to consult the four parties to the agreement if no resolution could be achieved in three months. When the resulting negotiations with Czechoslovakia, in Komárom, had broken down after only four days, the Hungarian government, perhaps emboldened by the pusillanimity of the Western powers at Munich and by the disinclination of Britain and France to engage in further consultation, abruptly changed tack: Darányi, now Speaker of the Lower House, was despatched on a confidential mission to seek German support for a Hungarian invasion of Slovakia—an extraordinary reversal of roles. Even more extraordinary was the size of the price Darányi had been authorised to offer in return for German support: Hungary's accession to the Anti–Comintern Pact,* her withdrawal from the League of Nations, a ten-year economic agreement and, even, the dismissal of Kálmán Kánya—whom the Germans, especially Ribbentrop, detested—from the Foreign Ministry.

Such was Hungarian desperation at the prospect of seeing Slovakia's Magyar territory slip from her grasp. Hitler, unsurprisingly, retorted that Hungary had been given her chance and had spurned it: 'Whereas we ... had prepared ourselves to stake everything we had and had also suffered loss of life, Hungary constantly stated that she insisted on her rights but did not wish to achieve these by aggressive means. The moment had passed'.[19] The Hungarian offer nevertheless impressed Hitler sufficiently to move him to agree to mediate, with Italy, on the Hungarian-Czechoslovak dispute; after three weeks of intensive diplomatic activity in Rome, Prague, Budapest and Berlin, Ribbentrop and Count Ciano, the Italian Foreign Minister, meeting in the Belvedere, Vienna, announced on 2 November 1938 what became known as the First Vienna Award. The Czechoslovak government had been bullied into agreeing to the transfer to Hungary of 11,927 sq. km of Slovakian territory, with a population of between 860,000 and a million people of whom between 57 per cent (the Czech figure) and 86 per cent (the Hungarian figure) were Magyar. Hungary regained the towns of Kassa (Košice), Ungvár and Munkács; Horthy, mounted on his white horse, led a triumphal procession of the entire Hungarian Parliament into Kassa. National jubilation was tempered, however, by intense disappointment that the Czechoslovaks had been allowed to retain Bratislava (Pozsony, the Hungarian Parliament's ancient seat) and Nyitra. Crucially, that part of Ruthenia (eastern Slovakia) that would have given Hungary a common frontier with Poland, remained in Czechoslovak hands; it at once became Hungary's next target for revision.

Ruthenia had only a small Magyar population—minuscule after the transfer of Ungvár and Munkács to Hungary; before the transfer, even Hungarian demographers could not produce a figure higher than 10 per cent. The irresistible attraction to Hungary of this eastern appendage to Czechoslovakia lay in its frontier with Poland: acquisition of this frontier through the absorption of Ruthenia would open up the possibility of a new geopolitical axis, running from Warsaw through Budapest and Belgrade to Rome, which would split the Little Entente and balance, without conflicting with, the north-south axis of Berlin-Vienna-Rome. In November 1938, therefore, Hungary prepared and began to canvass

---

* The agreement concluded in 1936 by Germany and Japan (joined later by Italy) in which each party undertook not to assist the Soviet Union in an attack on the other.

support for the annexation of Ruthenia by force. The project immediately encountered major obstacles, including strong German opposition: Hitler, already contemplating the eventual subjugation of Poland, wished to use Ruthenia, with its large Ukrainian population, as a base from which to promote the cause of Ukrainian independence from Soviet Russia. Poland, for her part, rejected a Hungarian proposal for a joint invasion of Ruthenia, offering only participation by irregulars; and Rome obediently joined Berlin in warning Budapest that action against Ruthenia would put the First Vienna Award in jeopardy. Hungary backed down and demobilised but did not give up. Imrédy now concentrated on impressing Hitler with Hungary's good behaviour: the Swabian minority was given permission to form its own political party, the pro-Nazi *Volksbund*, and Kálmán Kánya, *bête noire* of the Germans, was eased out of the Foreign Ministry to make way for the more emollient and pro-German Count István Csáky. When the Italian Foreign Minister, Count Ciano, visited Budapest in December, Csáky informed him, for German as much as for Italian ears, that Hungary would accept an invitation to accede to the Anti–Comintern Pact and would subsequently quit the League of Nations. Both undertakings were fulfilled in 1939, in February and April respectively. When Csáky visited Berlin in January 1939, he promised Hitler, for good measure, that Hungary would rearm, encourage good relations with Romania and Yugoslavia, limit her revisionist aims to predominantly Magyar regions, conclude a ten-year economic agreement with Germany and, perhaps most significantly to Nazi ears, set about resolving the 'Jewish problem'.

Csáky's forecast of Hungarian policies was realised in part on 4 May 1939, with the passage through Parliament of the Second Jewish Law, which tightened the screw on Hungarian Jewry and significantly increased its civil disabilities. No Jew could now acquire Hungarian citizenship, stand for municipal office or (unless his or her family had lived in Hungary since 1867) vote in municipal or national elections. The Jewish 'quota' in the professions, established by the First Jewish Law, now shrank to 6 per cent; and in the financial and commercial sector, to 12 per cent. The new law potentially put the livelihood of as many as 250,000 Hungarian Jews at risk; however, since the economy, already under strain, could not sustain the loss of its most productive human resource, application of the law never became more than patchy. The hardest hit were those Jews whose activities made only an indirect contribution to the health of the economy—in the professions, offices and the media. According to one estimate,[20] by 1942 300,000 Hungarian Jews had been deprived of their livelihood and were dependent on the charity of the Jewish community. As events were to show, however, Hitler would not regard the creeping impoverishment of Hungarian Jewry as an adequate solution of the 'Jewish problem'.

Although still determined to secure Ruthenia and aware that this could not be achieved without German acquiescence, Horthy now underwent another of his recurrent bouts of nervousness that Hungary was edging too close to the Reich: Imrédy, whom he had appointed largely because of his good connexions in the West, had fallen increasingly under the spell of Hitler's success and Nazi showmanship. The Regent therefore used the coincidental discovery of apparent evidence that the anti–Semitic Imrédy had Jewish antecedents to shame him into resigning and to appoint the veteran Count Pál Teleki to the premiership in his place. Teleki, whose pro-Western sympathies had firmer roots than Imrédy's, nevertheless regarded the acquisition of Ruthenia as his government's first priority and used his expertise as an academic geographer to develop a public case for the reunion of Ruthenia with Hungary on environmental grounds—uncontrolled deforestation in Ruthenia was causing serious flooding of the Alföld by the River Tisza. When Hitler's widely anticipated dismemberment of Czechoslovakia began with an engineered pro-Nazi coup in Slovakia on 10 March 1939, Teleki decided that Hungarian troops should march into Ruthenia as soon as German troops crossed the Czechoslovak frontier. He informed the Italian and the Polish governments of this intention. Accepting that it would be more troublesome to rein in the Hungarians than to unleash them, Berlin signalled acquiescence in the operation, subject to stringent requirements for the protection of German interests in Ruthenia. When, therefore, the German army marched into Prague on 15 March, occupying Bohemia and Moravia, Hungarian forces simultaneously invaded Ruthenia, having provoked border incidents at Munkács and Ungvár on the previous day. Within three days, Hungarian troops were deployed along the Polish frontier, their objectives achieved and 12,000 sq. km of territory reclaimed for Hungary. Horthy had already despatched a fulsome message of gratitude to Hitler: 'I shall never forget this proof of friendship, and Your Excellency can at all times ever rely steadfastly on my gratitude'.[21] Eight weeks earlier, Horthy, giving an audience to the British and American Ministers in Budapest, had denounced the ambitions of 'the madman', Hitler: if Hitler provoked a war, Hungary would remain neutral and if German troops were to enter Hungary—'We would fight them to the last ditch and start a European war!'[22] The Hungarian press, oblivious to such inconsistencies, concentrated on hailing a rare success for Hungarian arms, heaping praise on the Regent who, to all outward appearances, had single-handedly made it possible.

Hungary's revisionist agenda was by no means exhausted: the issues of Transylvania and of former Hungarian territory within Yugoslavia remained to be addressed. In the meantime, however, Hitler's designs on Poland posed an awkward dilemma for Hungary, especially since Teleki's hope that success in Ruthenia would appease the extreme right had not been realised: the elections in May 1939 produced 750,000 votes for the Arrow Cross and National Socialists, giving the former party forty seats in Parliament and making it the second largest. Pressure on the government for an unambiguously pro-German policy was growing. Teleki and a majority of his ministers were nevertheless reluctant to incur the stigma of complicity in a German attack on Poland, Hungary's ancient friend and ally. Teleki was all too aware of the rapidity with which Hungary was painting herself into the Axis corner: Hungary's accession to the Anti–Comintern Pact had prompted the Soviet Union to sever diplomatic relations in February and her departure from the League of Nations in April had strained Hungary's relations with Britain and France. Support for German aggression against Poland, with whom both Britain and France had treaty ties, would extinguish such sympathy for Hungary as remained in the West. Urged by Mussolini in July to clarify Hungary's position in the event of a general conflagration, Teleki undertook, in identical letters to the Duce and the Führer, that Hungary would 'make her policy conform to the policy of the Axis'; but in a second letter, he stated that 'Hungary cannot, on moral grounds, be in a position to take armed action against Poland'. This assertion predictably provoked an explosion in the German Chancellery. Summoned to Berchtesgaden on 8 August, Csáky was subjected to a torrent of abuse from Hitler, who scorned the implication that Germany would need any assistance from Hungary in dealing with Poland and expressed incredulity that Teleki should write in such terms given that Hungary's territorial gains could not have been achieved without German help; there could be no question of German support for further revision. Browbeaten into a panic, Csáky disgracefully took it upon himself to say that his Prime Minister's letters should be considered withdrawn; on the following day Hungary's strongly pro-German Minister in Berlin, Döme Sztójay, delivered a formal *note verbale* revoking both letters. Learning of this, Teleki, who had not been consulted, immediately recalled Csáky to Budapest and reinstated the two letters; but the damage had been done and Hitler confirmed in his poor opinion of Hungarians. Csáky, moreover, survived. In an attempt to make an entry on the credit side of Hungary's ledger, Teleki addressed a personal message to the British Foreign Secretary, Lord Halifax, asserting that Hungary would not co-operate with Germany in hostilities against Poland and that she would remain neutral; but her geographical situation, he explained, precluded a formal declaration of neutrality.

The Hungarian government now pursued the hopelessly contradictory objectives of fending off insistent requests from Berlin for logistical support for the German invasion of Poland; securing German acquiescence in the recovery of Transylvania from Romania by force; and at the same time persuading the Western powers of Hungary's essential virtuousness. Having invaded Poland on 1 September, Hitler wished to supplement the eastward thrust of German forces with a supporting advance from the south, from Hungarian territory; for this he requested the use of the railway line that ran east from Kassa. On 9 September, following a meeting of the Hungarian cabinet, Csáky informed Ribbentrop that the transport of German troops across Hungarian territory for use against Poland would be incompatible with the honour of the Hungarian nation (Csáky had nevertheless told Count Ciano three days earlier that his government might accede to the German request if Berlin gave the green light for Hungarian action against Romania). Although Hungary eventually agreed to allow the unescorted transit by rail of German military supplies, her continuing refusal to countenance the passage of German troops allowed over 70,000 Polish soldiers and as many civilian refugees to cross the new common frontier into Hungary. The Hungarian government allowed those Polish troops who wished to continue the fight to make their way to western Europe: by 1941 nearly 50,000 had done so. Poles who elected to remain in Hungary were well cared for; special schools were opened for Polish children and the Polish Legation in Budapest continued to function, despite German protests, until November 1940.* Against this background, a perceptible cooling of Hungarian-German relations was unsurprising. Hitler suspended the shipment to Hungary of the arms on which the Győr programme of

---

* Much of the credit for this humane policy was due to József Antall, the government's Commissioner for Refugees; his son, József Antall Jnr, was to become Hungary's first democratically elected Prime Minister.

rearmament depended, a move that generated impatience among the Hungarian officer corps with Horthy's half-heartedness in supporting Nazi Germany; the Hungarian Chief of Staff, General Werth, threatened to resign.

Following the conclusion in August 1939 of the Nazi–Soviet Pact, which appalled Horthy, the Regent and his ministers had resolved that Hungary would cleave to a policy of armed neutrality in the looming European war. Horthy's faith in sea-power, moreover, sustained his inner conviction that when war came—it began on 3 September—Britain and her allies would ultimately prevail. But the growing strength of pro-German feeling both in the Hungarian army and outside it, combined with the impression made by the speed with which Germany had defeated Poland, caused Horthy to waver and to attempt to row back into German favour. In November, in a gesture of characteristic simplicity, Horthy despatched to the Führer a basket of Hungarian fruit (complete with instructions for its storage and consumption), accompanied by a rambling letter designed both to persuade Hitler of Hungary's unchanging goodwill towards Germany and to warn him of the dangers of supping with the Soviet devil. The letter concluded: 'We are a grateful and absolutely reliable people, and we realise what we owe to you and the German nation. We want the German people to feel that even though it wishes to fight its great battle alone, it need not face its cares alone. Whatever we can spare is at your disposal'.[23] Horthy, who signed himself 'Your Excellency's devoted friend', added that if the Führer should wish to avail himself of his services in any confidential negotiations, he was always available—'except for Easter'. Although the letter contained no reference to Romania, the importance of German approval for this next item on Hungary's revisionist agenda was clearly much in Horthy's mind when he sent it.

Hitler's reaction to Horthy's missive—and to the fruit which came with it—is unrecorded; he may have concluded that such naiveté could only betoken sincerity. German deliveries of arms to Hungary did, in fact, resume in December: but the resumption was accompanied by a renewed warning that Hungary should refrain from hostile action against Romania. Hitler regarded the maintenance of oil supplies from Romania, and consequently the preservation of peace in south-eastern Europe, as a vital German interest. Italy, too, urged the Hungarian government to put its territorial claims on hold until after the war. Teleki, however, with Horthy's full backing, had no intention of doing so. Matters came to a head in June 1940, when the Soviet Union demanded from Romania the cession of Bessarabia and northern Bukovina; the Hungarian cabinet immediately resolved to take this opportunity of pressing Hungary's claims in Transylvania, underlining the seriousness of its intentions by ordering the Hungarian army to deploy along the Romanian frontier. Alarmed, Hitler summoned Teleki and Csáky to Munich to discuss the situation. With Ribbentrop and Ciano in attendance, the Führer warned the Hungarians to desist from military action but undertook to find a negotiated solution to the problem; two weeks later, on 26 July, he urged the Romanian Prime Minister and Foreign Minister to work towards a peaceful revision of Romania's Trianon frontiers. There followed a virtual re-run of the scenario that had resulted in the First Vienna Award, with Romania replacing Czechoslovakia as Hungary's interlocutor: bilateral negotiations at Turnu-Severin on the Romanian-Yugoslav border duly collapsed after a week and Romania invited the Axis powers to arbitrate. Teleki, well aware that a resolution of the problem in Hungary's favour by Germany would have a hefty price tag attached, prevaricated; but ultimately had no choice but to accept a summons to travel to Vienna on 30 August to take delivery of whatever solution the Axis Foreign Ministers had decided to impose.

In the event, the Second Vienna Award disappointed both parties. Romania was required to transfer to Hungary 43,000 sq. km of territory in Transylvania, and with it 2.5 million inhabitants—including over a million ethnic Romanians. Hungary, for her part, had to accept that Romania would retain not only the economic heart of Transylvania but also more than 400,000 ethnic Magyars. The Romanians, indeed, accepted the outcome more philosophically than the Hungarians, using the occasion to embrace the Axis cause with gusto and agreeing to the transfer to Romania of a complete Panzer division tasked with training the Romanian army and putting it on to a war footing. The Hungarians took longer to digest the scale and implications of the price that Hitler, as Teleki had correctly predicted, exacted for his services. Hungary was required to accede to the Tripartite Pact, * thus committing herself unambiguously to the Axis cause; to increase supplies of food and raw materials to Germany, even if this impinged on domestic requirements; to allow German troops and armour to transit Hungarian territory by rail *en route* to Romania and to accept the stationing of German guards at Hungarian railway stations; to recognise the *Volksbund* as the exclusive political party of the Swabian minority in Hungary; to remove restrictions on extreme right-wing activity; and—not least in importance in German eyes—to take measures 'concerning the Jewish question'.

The Nazi bill was paid almost as quickly as it had been presented. On the day following Horthy's triumphal entry into Kolozsvár (Cluj), Transylvania's principal town, the government granted an amnesty to Ferenc Szálasi and released him from prison. Shortly afterwards the 1938 decree that forbade civil servants to join political parties, a measure aimed at the Arrow Cross, was rescinded. On 10 October, a new trade agreement with Germany effectively tied the Hungarian economy to the Nazi war machine. Finally, on 20 November, Hungary formally acceded to the Tripartite Pact—although Teleki refused to sign a secret protocol that would have obliged his government to ban all anti–Nazi publications in Hungary. Measures 'concerning the Jewish question' were on the drawing board but would not be implemented until the summer of 1941.

Horthy and Teleki had by no means forgotten about the remaining item on the revisionist shopping list—the areas of southern Hungary now incorporated in Yugoslavia—but for the time being gave priority to the cultivation of a closer relationship with Belgrade which, they hoped, would win good marks for Hungary in London and Washington. Hitler gave his blessing to a *rapprochement* that might bring Yugoslavia closer to the Axis and help to ensure her neutrality if, as seemed likely after the débâcle of Mussolini's invasion of Greece, Germany was

---

* The treaty concluded by Germany, Italy and Japan on 27 September 1940, under which the parties agreed to assist each other if attacked outside the contexts of the European or Sino-Japanese wars; the Tripartite Pact was in effect an insurance against an attack on the Axis or Japan by the United States.

obliged to march through south-eastern Europe to rescue her Italian ally. Negotiations in October and November led to the signature, on 12 December 1940, of a treaty between Hungary and Yugoslavia, of which the first article stated: 'Between the Kingdom of Hungary and the Kingdom of Yugoslavia there will be permanent peace and eternal friendship'. As Teleki had anticipated, the treaty received a warm welcome in London as a contribution to stability in the region; and the British Foreign Office also reacted favourably to the information that Teleki had made a contingency plan for the formation in London of a Hungarian government-in-exile, headed by István Bethlen, in the event of a German invasion of Hungary—a possibility the situation in Greece had made less remote. The British government nevertheless remained clear-eyed about Hungarian behaviour. On 6 February 1941, the British Foreign Secretary, Anthony Eden, warned Hungary's competent and effective Minister in London, György Barcza, that although His Majesty's Government had hitherto shown great forbearance in the face of a number of provocative Hungarian acts:

our forbearance had limits, and we therefore hoped that the Hungarian Government realised that our attitude after the war would inevitably be influenced by the degree and manner in which the Hungarian Government had endeavoured to withstand the Axis pressure and to maintain a genuinely neutral attitude. Recent events had suggested to many people in this country that the Hungarian Government were not merely submitting passively to Axis pressure, but even found it not unwelcome.[24]

Britain's attitude towards Hungary when the war was over would be determined by the extent to which Hungary stood up to pressure from the Axis; Eden hinted that Hungary appeared to be hiding behind this pressure as an excuse for revisionism.

Teleki hastened to reassure Eden, through Barcza, that for so long as he, Teleki, remained alive and at the head of Hungarian affairs, Hungary would not comply with German demands which were 'incompatible with the honour and sovereignty of the country'. It did not take long for demands of this nature to materialise. Although Yugoslavia had finally bowed to mounting German pressure by acceding, on 25 March, to the Tripartite Pact, the Yugoslav government had immediately been overthrown in a coup by pro-Western officers and politicians who ousted the Regent, Paul, in favour of the seventeen-year-old King Peter II. Enraged, Hitler at once activated existing plans for the invasion of Yugoslavia as well as Greece. The pro-German Hungarian Minister in Berlin, Sztójay, reported that Hungary's participation in the invasion, on which Hitler was counting, would be rewarded by the satisfaction of her territorial claims against Yugoslavia. A German military delegation arrived in Budapest to request the participation of five Hungarian army corps in the impending campaign.

Horthy, for whom revision usually took priority over other considerations, was from the first inclined to accede to the German request, despite the fact that the ink had scarcely dried on Hungary's 'Treaty of Eternal Friendship' with Yugoslavia; he argued, sophistically, that the change of regime in Belgrade had nullified the treaty. Teleki, mindful not only of Hungary's honour but also of the hostile reaction Hungarian complicity in the impending invasion would provoke in London, expressed strong reservations; but when the Supreme Defence Council met on 1 April he felt obliged to join the majority in voting for a military operation limited to the recovery of formerly Hungarian territory—a minority favoured total support for the German invasion, wherever it might lead. The council approved plans for a joint invasion by German and Hungarian forces. The Hungarian government's desperate efforts to find a pretext for Hungarian participation, such as evidence of Serbian maltreatment of the Magyar minority, yielded no facts to support mendacious reports in the pro-Nazi press. Demeaning attempts to salve the national conscience by tipping off Belgrade and Zagreb that invasion was imminent were too late to be useful. On 2 April, Barcza reported from London that if Hungary were to permit a German invasion of Yugoslavia from her territory, Britain would break off diplomatic relations; and that if Hungary were to take part in such an invasion, she would find herself at war with Britain and her allies. Barcza's telegram, confirming the Hungarian Premier's worst apprehensions, imposed on Pál Teleki a degree of strain and anguish he could not sustain: in the small hours of 3 April, he shot himself. He left a scrawled note, addressed to the Regent, by his bedside:

Your Serene Highness!

We have become breakers of our word—out of cowardice—in defiance of the Treaty of Eternal Friendship based on the Mohács speech.* The nation feels this, and we have thrown away its honour.

We have taken our stand on the side of scoundrels, for there is not a word of truth in the stories of atrocities! Neither against the Magyars nor against the Germans! We shall become grave robbers, the most rotten of nations! I did not hold you back. I am guilty. Teleki Pál.[25]

Pál Teleki had many qualities, not least of distinguished scholarship as an academic geographer; as a politician, he fell short of István Bethlen's calibre. His judgement and his moral sense, like that of so many Hungarian politicians of the inter-war period, had been deformed by the canker of Trianon; he none the less had a clearer perception than many of his contemporaries, including Miklós Horthy, of where Hungary's true interests lay, even though the magnet of revision had skewed his political compass. The epitaph accorded to him by Winston Churchill was perhaps over-generous: 'His suicide was a sacrifice to absolve himself and his people from guilt in the German attack on Yugoslavia. It clears his name before history'.[26] Teleki did not, on 2 April, vote against Hungary's participation in the attack on her ally; his resignation, in a separate note to Horthy, was posthumous. His suicide, moreover, did not 'absolve his people from guilt' since it made no impact on Hungarian policy: Horthy quickly appointed the Foreign Minister, László Bárdossy, to the Premiership and military preparations for the invasion of Yugoslavia continued without interruption. When, on 3 April, the British Minister in Budapest, Mr Owen O'Malley, called on the Regent to express his government's condolences on Teleki's death, Horthy informed him of Hungary's decision, explaining that Hitler had offered Hungary Croatia and Fiume in return for her support. In reacting, O'Malley pulled no punches: if the Regent:

entered into such a corrupt bargain with Germany or in any way acted as a Hungarian jackal to the German lion against a State with which he had just signed a Treaty of Eternal

* See page 368.

Friendship, his country could expect no indulgence, no sympathy and no mercy from a victorious Britain and United States of America and that he [Horthy] personally ... would be covered with well-deserved contempt and dishonour.[27]

Horthy, though moved, responded simply by saying that his mind was made up. On 4 April German military convoys began to rumble southwards through Hungary.

The German invasion of Yugoslavia began on 6 April; Hungarian troops only joined the operation five days later, when Yugoslav resistance had already been broken. Following Britain's severance of diplomatic relations with Hungary on 7 April, Minister Barcza paid his farewell call on Anthony Eden, who began by endorsing 'every word' that O'Malley had said to the Regent. It would always be a source of deep regret, Eden continued, 'that Hungary had chosen to dishonour her signature before even the ink was dry and to attack an ally, at a most critical hour in her history. The British people would not forget that act of treachery, which would be an enduring stigma upon Hungary's national honour'.[28] For the time being, Britain did not declare war; but Hungary had squandered her not inconsiderable credit in London. Teleki had been all too aware of the implications of this for the future of his country. Most Hungarians, however, including their Regent and his ministers, gave priority to celebrating another significant victory over Trianon: the recovery from Yugoslavia of 11,475 sq. km of what had been southern Hungary—the *Délvidék*—with over a million inhabitants, 36 per cent of them Magyars.

The two Vienna Awards, the occupation of Ruthenia and, now, the occupation of the Bácska, Muraköz and the 'Baranya triangle' restored to Hungarian rule a total of 78,567 sq. km of territory with 5.3 million inhabitants, of whom approximately 42 per cent were Magyars. From the revisionist perspective, the recovery of 53 per cent of the territory lost in 1920 represented a considerable achievement and ensured the continued popularity and authority of Regent Horthy. But this achievement, impressive though it appeared, remained provisional: it could become permanent only if Germany won the war—and even then would always be dependent on German goodwill, as would any further re-expansion of Hungary's frontiers. In the meantime, the price to be paid for this provisional gain was immense.

16

THE FAUSTIAN PACT II: THE PRICE

(1941–45)

The First Instalment

Although the fulfilment of Hungarian aspirations for the revision of Trianon was by no means complete, their realisation had in fact reached its high-water mark. Hungarians did not, of course, as yet know this—although the few realists among Hungary's politicians, including Count István Bethlen, suspected it. In the meantime, Hungary had to begin to pay the price; the bill was open-ended and the country eventually paid it in four instalments, each more dreadful than the last. Having forfeited the good opinion of the Western Allies, soon to include the Soviet Union and the United States,* Hungary had in effect sacrificed her independence in foreign policy; for good or ill, she was bound to the Axis. Hungary's independence in internal affairs, moreover, had also been placed in jeopardy.

The Third Jewish Law, promised as part of the price for revision in Transylvania and finally promulgated in August 1941, differed from its two predecessors in reflecting Nazi racism rather than imposing purely economic discrimination. Hungary's Jews were now stigmatised in law as an inferior race. The Third Jewish Law forbade mixed marriages and made sexual relations between a Jewish male and a non-Jewish female punishable by three years' imprisonment. The Minister of Justice, László Radocsay, explained to the Upper House: 'Mixed marriages had a definitely detrimental effect upon the evolution of our national soul; they brought into a position of influence that Jewish spirit whose harmful effect we have seen'.[1]

The passage of the law also gave the signal for the first deportations of Jews from Hungary. These were limited, for the time being, to non-Hungarian Jews who had sought refuge in Hungary from the German occupation of Czechoslovakia and Poland. The deportations, to camps in Galicia and the Ukraine, were none the less an ominous indication of the accuracy of István Bethlen's 1938

---

* Hitler invaded the Soviet Union on 22 June 1941; Britain and the Soviet Union concluded a treaty of mutual assistance on 12 July 1941; Winston Churchill and Franklin D. Roosevelt signed the Atlantic Charter on 14 August 1941.

prediction of the consequences of an alignment of Hungarian with German political values.* It should also be recorded, however, that between 1941 and mid-1943 the Hungarian Ministry of the Interior provided 14,000 Polish Jews with 'Christian papers' to exempt them from deportation;[2] and, when reports filtered back to Hungary of the wholesale massacre of deportees by the German SS in the Ukraine, the ministry ordered an end to all deportations, even recalling some trainloads already *en route*.

Early in 1942, the Hungarian occupation of northern Serbia—excluding the Bánát, which the Germans refused to hand over—brought new evidence of the contamination of Hungary, or at least of her armed forces, by the German alliance. Under the pretext of carrying out reprisals for alleged raids by Serb guerrillas, Hungarian officers presided over the massacre, by Hungarian troops, of over 3,000 civilians, including women and children, most of them Serbs and Jews, in the major town of Újvidék (Novi Sad): the victims were shot in cold blood and the corpses thrown into the Danube.** Following a belated government enquiry into the atrocities, in December 1943, a court martial sentenced five Hungarian officers to death and twenty more to long terms of imprisonment. The five principal culprits, all of Swabian origin—who, in accordance with military custom, had not been confined during the trial—escaped to Germany as soon as sentence had been passed, in German military vehicles escorted by SS personnel in plain clothes. In Germany, the five officers were rewarded with senior appointments in the SS; they were to return to Hungary, as officers in the German occupying force, in 1944.

In retrospect, the nine months that ended with the Újvidék massacre can be seen as the period during which Hungarians gradually awoke to the realities of their situation. The euphoria of revision gave way to a growing awareness of the threat to their way of life, and to the independence of their country, that their attachment to Hitler's Germany had created. As Nazi occupation, with all its attendant brutalities, engulfed so much of Europe, most Hungarians, apart from supporters of the extreme right, became even more conscious of, and began to value even more highly, the characteristics of their country that set it apart from all her neighbours. These included the existence of a small but active parliamentary opposition, both left-wing and conservative; the continued existence and activity of trade unions; the continuing publication, despite occasional interference, of daily newspapers—*Magyar Nemzet, Népszava, Szabad Szó*—that expressed liberal or social democratic views and criticised the government's pro-Nazi policies; and, despite their newly imposed economic and social disabilities, the relative security of a large Jewish population. Unlike many of their neighbours, moreover, Hungarians had enough to eat. During the next three years, Hungary's rulers would become increasingly concerned to protect these assets, to keep the human and material sacrifices demanded of them by Germany to a minimum, to restore

* See page 370.
** It should also be noted that the German/Hungarian invasion of Yugoslavia made possible Croatia's declaration of independence; and, in consequence, the massacre between 1941 and 1945 of 487,000 Orthodox Serbs, 30,000 Jews and 27,000 Gypsies by the fascist Ustashe regime under Ante Pavelič.

Hungary's good name in the West and, ultimately, to create circumstances that would enable Hungary to escape from the war with her territorial gains intact. Only the unique Hungarian capacity for self-delusion enabled these objectives to be seen as attainable.

When rumours of the impending launch of Hitler's 'Operation Barbarossa' against the Soviet Union reached the Hungarian General Staff in May 1941, General Werth, keen as ever to serve the German cause, urged Horthy and Prime Minister Bárdossy to offer the Führer the services of the Hungarian army in this anti–Bolshevik crusade. Werth's political masters demurred—Horthy out of pique that Hitler had not confided his invasion plans to him when the two men met in April, Bárdossy from instinctive caution. In order to demonstrate Hungary's enthusiasm for the anti–Bolshevik cause, however—during their April meeting, Horthy had actually urged Hitler to invade Russia—the Hungarian government severed diplomatic relations with the Soviet Union as soon as German troops had begun, on 22 June, to pour across the Polish frontier into the Ukraine. Hungary's relations with Moscow had in fact been developing well during the preceding months. In March, the Soviet government had taken the initiative in ceremoniously returning to Hungary fifty-six regimental standards which had been captured by Russian forces during the War of Independence in 1849; the gesture had been made in response to a decision by the Hungarian government—a decision many Hungarians would live to regret—to release the Communist Mátyás Rákosi from prison and allow him to travel to Moscow, where he spent the rest of the war. Now, on 23 June, Bárdossy's telegram to Moscow recalling the Hungarian Minister there, József Kristóffy, crossed with a telegram in the opposite direction reporting a conversation between Kristóffy and Molotov, the Soviet Foreign Minister, on the same day. Molotov had spoken in unusually cordial terms. The Soviet Union, he said, had no aggressive intentions towards or territorial claims against Hungary; Hungary's adherence to the Anti–Comintern Pact had been 'forgotten'; there was no need for Hungary to involve herself in a conflict between the Soviet Union and Germany; Moscow would have no problem with the satisfaction of Hungary's territorial claims against Romania. The Soviet government wished to know where Hungary stood. The implication, as Kristóffy, perhaps credulously, reported was that Hungarian neutrality in the new conflict would be rewarded with Soviet support for further revision in Transylvania—Romania was reported to have despatched ten divisions to fight alongside the invading Wehrmacht. For Bárdossy, who had already informed both the Russian and German Ministers of the decision to break off relations, this was an inconvenient development: he therefore suppressed Kristóffy's report, showing it neither to Horthy nor to the cabinet, a decision that the events of the next few days were to invest with some importance.

On 26 June, unidentified aircraft dropped a small number of bombs on the towns, now within Hungary, of Kassa and Munkács, causing civilian casualties. General Werth and the Minister of Defence, Károly Bartha, immediately informed Bárdossy that the raid had been carried out by Soviet aircraft. Horthy, unaware of Molotov's statements to Kristóffy three days before, approved Bárdossy's recommendation that Hungary should enter the war against the Soviet Union, a decision immediately confirmed by the cabinet. Bárdossy chose to ignore a report from a Hungarian air-force officer, Colonel Ádám Krúdy, who had taken off from Kassa airfield during the raid, that it had been perpetrated by German aircraft carrying Soviet markings. The true identity of the aircraft has never been satisfactorily established; a provocation devised by the German High Command in co-operation with the Hungarian General Staff seems the most likely explanation of the raid, which provided the pretext for Hungary's entry into the Second World War. On 27 June 1941, 40,000 Hungarian troops advanced through Galicia and crossed the Soviet frontier. Horthy despatched a message to the German Führer: 'I count myself happy that my army can take part, shoulder to shoulder, with the glorious and victorious German Army in the crusade for the elimination of the dangerous Communist horde and for the preservation of our culture'.[3]

Beneath the fine words, however, doubts were already beginning to fester. Horthy had been impressed by a memorandum—shown to him by his eldest son István, whose views Horthy invariably respected—by General Ferenc Szombathelyi, which forecast a long and bloody campaign in Russia that the Germans were by no means certain to win. Horthy, like Bárdossy, had also begun to lose patience with General Werth's unremitting Germanophilia and constant attempts to influence Hungarian policy in the German interest. When, on 19 August, Werth submitted yet another memorandum urging a greater Hungarian contribution to the German offensive, Horthy acceded to Bárdossy's insistence that the Chief of Staff should be dismissed; he appointed General Szombathelyi to replace him. Szombathelyi's influence soon made itself felt. When Horthy, accompanied by his new Chief of Staff, met Hitler at his new military headquarters, the 'Wolf's Lair' in east Prussia, he astounded the Führer by seeking his approval for the withdrawal from the Eastern Front of most of the Hungarian troops deployed there. Since the campaign had not yet begun to falter, Hitler—while doubtless mentally awarding the Hungarians another black mark—reluctantly agreed to a partial Hungarian withdrawal, with the proviso that four brigades should remain to occupy territory behind the front line. This marked the beginning of an increasingly bitter argument over the level of the Hungarian contribution to the German war effort, which would dominate the Hungarian-German relationship until it collapsed in 1944.

Prime Minister Bárdossy soon became increasingly pliable in the face of German pressure, which increased in proportion to the scale of the reverses which the Wehrmacht had begun to sustain on the Eastern Front. Bárdossy had by no means objected to General Werth's pro-German views, only to his interference in the political process; with Werth out of the way, he could now give free rein to his own sympathy with the German cause. In early November, Bárdossy readily acquiesced in a German demand for substantially increased deliveries of grain and oil; later in the month, during a visit to Germany, he agreed to a German request for the despatch of two more brigades to the Eastern Front; and when, in the wake of the Japanese attack on Pearl Harbor on 7 December, Germany and Italy declared war on the United States of America, Bárdossy, in response to German urging, took it upon himself to make Hungary's declaration of war on the USA without consulting either the Regent or the cabinet.* In January 1942, following

* Britain, Australia, New Zealand, Canada and South Africa had declared war on Hungary

the major Soviet counter-offensive in December, Ribbentrop arrived in Budapest to demand that the entire Hungarian army of twenty-eight divisions should be deployed on the Eastern Front; he made it clear that any further satisfaction of Hungary's revisionist claims would be dependent upon her compliance. In subsequent negotiations between Field Marshal Keitel, of the German High Command, and General Szombathelyi this requirement was whittled down to sixteen divisions; but the Hungarian government also agreed to order general mobilisation and to form a new force of 200,000 men, the Second Army, to fight in the east. Although Horthy approved these measures, the impact of the Russian winter on the German offensive and the growing strength of the Red Army's resistance deeply concerned him; his old belief that British—and now American—naval power would eventually prevail revived. Hungary needed greater flexibility and the capacity to manoeuvre. The time had come, Horthy decided, to part company with a Prime Minister whose strongly pro-German views and indirect association with the Újvidék massacre would rule him out in Western eyes as an acceptable interlocutor, should the need for one arise. Bárdossy, moreover, had failed to give his whole-hearted support to Horthy's pet project for installing his son István as Vice-Regent and heir to the Regency.* On 9 March 1942, Miklós Kállay replaced Bárdossy as Prime Minister.

When the British historian C. A. Macartney asked Miklós Horthy, in 1945, why he had dismissed Bárdossy, the ex-Regent replied: 'I came to the conclusion that he was not following a Hungarian policy'.[4] This accusation could never have been levelled against Miklós Kállay. The inconsistencies, ambiguities and zig-zags that characterised his policies—christened, after a Hungarian folk dance, the 'Kállay two-step' (kállai kettős) and 'see-saw policy' (hintapolitika) by contemporaries— arose precisely because, from the first, he endeavoured to pursue a course that gave absolute priority to the interests of Hungary and Hungary alone. Unlike his predecessors in the office of Prime Minister, Kállay survived both the war and its subsequent legal processes to write, from exile in the United States, a political memoir which, like all political memoirs, must be regarded as to some extent self-justificatory; but it is largely, in the present writer's belief, an honest work that does not attempt to gloss over those aspects of his policies that are the most obvious targets for criticism.[5] Kállay came from a land-owning family that had managed its estates in Szabolcs county since the twelfth century. He had been plucked from a post in the county administration to serve briefly as Minister of Agriculture in the Gömbös government, after which Horthy had appointed him to the Upper House of Parliament with the additional responsibilities—which he exercised from his Szabolcs estate—of national Commissioner for Floods and Irrigation. Those who knew him well, including Horthy, were aware that Kállay was not only passionately anti–Bolshevik but also deeply opposed to the Nazi and racist creeds; but, in retirement from public life, he had had no occasion to publi-

---

on 7 December 1941, in response to Hungary's participation in the German offensive against the Soviet Union. The USA did not get round to declaring war on Hungary until 5 June 1942.

* The Hungarian Parliament agreed to make István Horthy his father's deputy but not his constitutional heir.

cise his views and could present himself, to Germans and others, as a straightforward Hungarian patriot. Although its implementation tended to be ambiguous and contradictory, Kállay's policy was in fact straightforward: gradually to detach Hungary from her Axis alliance and to seek the protection of the Western Allies against the Soviet incursion into Europe which, he correctly perceived, would be the inevitable consequence of a German defeat.

Kállay's appointment on 9 March 1942 strengthened German suspicions concerning Hungary's reliability as an ally. Reports from the German Legation in Budapest would have made the Nazi leadership aware that the Hungarian Catholic Primate, Cardinal Serédi, regularly preached sermons critical of the Nazi regime and that the Bishop of Győr, Vilmos Apor, had publicly denounced Germany's persecution of the Jews. The German Legation may or may not have been aware that significant numbers of Allied prisoners of war who had escaped from camps in Germany and Austria found refuge in Hungary, unharassed by the authorities, and that the number of escaped Russian prisoners of war reaching Hungary had risen to a point at which the Hungarians found it necessary to install a Russian partisan captain in the Ministry of the Interior to minister to their needs. As Kállay is at pains to emphasise in his memoirs, exports of food to Germany actually fell between 1940 and 1943, by up to 25 per cent—although this decline probably had more to do with the Hungarian government's desire to keep its own population happy and well fed than with deliberate sabotage. From the German viewpoint, moreover, the volatility of Hungary's relations with Romania, which frequently threatened to explode in armed conflict, constituted a continuing and unwelcome threat to the security of deliveries to Germany of Romanian oil which, as the war went on, became indispensable to the German war effort. The Germans also became increasingly impatient with Hungarian foot-dragging on the Jewish question. When Kállay paid his first visit to the 'Wolf's Lair' in April 1942, he fuelled German dissatisfaction by deflecting Hitler's demand for more resolute measures, including deportation, against Hungary's Jews by describing the adverse impact of such action on the Hungarian economy and, consequently, on Hungarian deliveries to Germany. In December, moreover, Kállay formally rejected German demands for the deportation of Jews and for the harassment, including the requirement to wear a yellow star, of those who remained.

From 1942 onwards, as the irritants in the Hungarian-German relationship became more acute, the fear that Germany might, in the last resort, occupy Hungary took its place alongside the longer-term fear of Soviet occupation as a key determinant of Hungarian policy. László Veress, a young Hungarian diplomat then serving in the Press Office of the Foreign Ministry and destined shortly to play a key role in his country's affairs, well summarised the apprehension felt by many Hungarians:

From that time the fear of German occupation dominated the thinking and attitudes of Hungary. German occupation would have meant the destruction of an intellectual elite, anti–Nazi almost to a man, the destruction of left-wing political opposition, Social Democrats, Liberals, crypto-Communists, royalists, a wide spectrum indeed of anti–Nazis; and it would have meant annihilation for the Jews. It would also have meant something unacceptably humiliating for Hungarians: the Rumanians, the Slovaks, the Croats, and even the

Czechs becoming the favourites of Hitler's Germany and claiming their share in dominating or even occupying parts of Hungary.[6]

Hungarian concerns were particularly evident in Kállay's treatment of the Jewish issue: circumstances compelled him to make some concessions to Nazi pressure but not so many, as he put it, as to 'soil the national honour and reputation of Hungary'.[7] Kállay's inaugural speech to Parliament in March 1942 adumbrated the imposition of limits on Jewish land ownership; and in September Parliament approved a law restricting Jewish holdings to 100 *hold*, a measure that resulted in the confiscation by the state of 1.2 million *hold* of agricultural land and forest. The Law of Reception (*Recepció*), the 1895 high-water mark of Jewish assimilation, was annulled and conversion to Judaism forbidden. Since Jews were not deemed to be worthy of the honour of fighting for their country, they were conscripted into labour battalions and sent to dig trenches and clear mines on the Eastern Front, without winter clothing (a lack, it should be said in fairness, that they shared with most of the Hungarian army) or adequate rations. Out of the 50,000 Jews conscripted during the summer of 1942, only between six and seven thousand survived the winter of 1942–43. On the other hand, when in 1942 the Germans initiated mass deportations of Jews from occupied western Europe, the Hungarian government recalled to Hungary all Hungarian Jewish families whom they were able to contact in the countries concerned, thereby saving some 400 families from the camps. As late as April 1943, two Jewish members of the Hungarian Upper House were elected to serve on its Foreign Affairs Committee; and on the Finance Committee of the House, Jewish members were in the majority. Kállay's Defence Minister, Vilmos Nagy, did his utmost to mitigate the appalling plight of the Jewish labour battalions, to an extent that prompted the Germans to demand—and in July 1943, secure—his dismissal. Until 1944, Jewish schools and cultural institutions continued to operate normally; the performance of Jewish plays and musicals continued without interruption in Budapest's Goldmark Hall, the Jewish theatre.

The Second Instalment

On 20 August 1942—St Stephen's Day, Hungary's most important national holiday—the seventy-four year-old Regent sustained a personal blow of which the effect on his mental and physical wellbeing may have been greater than appeared at the time: it fell to Kállay to break the news to Horthy that his elder son István, the newly elected Vice-Regent, had been killed in a flying accident on the Eastern Front, where he was serving with the Hungarian Air Force.* Four months later, Horthy was given warning, by the General Staff, of a further, national, tragedy. The Hungarian 2nd Army, without armour, air support, heavy anti–tank guns or reserves and defending a sector of the front line along the River Don near Voronezh, 160 kilometres in extent, was exposed to the full force of the rapid

---

* In his memoirs, Horthy speculates on the possibility that his son had been the victim of sabotage by the Germans, who were aware of István's distaste for anti–Semitism and possibly of his conviction that the war was lost for Germany. There is no evidence, however, that his death was other than accidental.

advance of the Red Army following its devastating victory at Stalingrad in November. On Christmas Eve, Horthy besought Hitler, by telegram, urgently to supply the 2nd Army with the weapons and equipment that had been promised as a condition of its despatch to the front; Hitler issued appropriate orders, but they were too late. The anticipated Soviet assault on the Hungarian sector near Voronezh, in which the Russians outnumbered the 2nd Army by three to one in men and by ten to one in artillery, began on 12 January 1943. After forty-eight hours, one Hungarian division was in full retreat and three days later two divisions abandoned their positions without waiting for the Russians to attack; within a week, the 2nd Army had been virtually annihilated—130,000 men out of its total strength of 200,000 had been killed, wounded or captured. The Jewish labour battalions lost 36,000 men out of 40,000 but had nevertheless conducted themselves bravely. The commander of the 2nd Army, General Gusztáv Jány, in his Order of the Day for 24 January stated that to have lost a battle would have been a misfortune but not a disgrace: the disgrace, he continued:

consisted in the panic-stricken, cowardly flight of the troops, on account of which the German allies and our fatherland bear us contempt. They have good reasons for feeling so. No one will be allowed to return home, even if wounded or ill: everyone will recover here or perish. Order and iron discipline will be re-established, by summary executions if need be … Characteristic of the events of the last few days is that the Jewish labour service companies march in close order and in good discipline, whereas the so-called regulars give the impression of a horde sunk to the level of brutes.[8]

In a subsequent memorandum to the Regent, General Szombathelyi attributed the catastrophe in large part to the low morale of troops trained to defend the Carpathians but now required to fight two thousand kilometres from their homeland. Low levels of weaponry and equipment, together with the lack of suitable clothing and footwear to withstand temperatures that fell to minus 35 degrees Celsius, also, of course, played a significant role.

Until the last months of the war, there was an extraordinary contrast between the appalling hardships suffered by Hungarian armies in the field—stemming both from the poor quality of their equipment and from their treatment as expendable cannon-fodder by the German High Command—and the relative normality of life on the home front, at least in the capital. László Veress recalled:

Despite the desperate situation, the people of Budapest were enjoying themselves. Cafés and restaurants were full, and there was no real shortage of food and luxury consumer goods. In fashionable restaurants rationing was usually forgotten. In shops, rationing was used mostly as an excuse to prevent German visitors from buying up food or textiles. French escapees from German POW camps worked as waiters in classy restaurants such as the Ritz or the Gellért, serving the German guests with ill-disguised contempt. A delegation of Swedish journalists, entertained at the elegant Park Club, was surprised to hear the orchestra play 'Tipperary' at the request of Foreign Ministry officials.[9]

This was in early 1944. Less than a year later, the horrors and privations visited upon the citizens of Budapest would equal anything sustained by soldiers at the front.

The disaster at Voronezh, coming on top of the German defeats at El Alamein and Stalingrad, and the Allied landings in North Africa, strengthened Kállay's determination to find a route by which Hungary could leave the war with honour and territorial gains intact. Horthy gave this objective his approval but wished to remain in ignorance of the means by which it would be pursued. Kállay formed a small, informal group of ministers—Ferenc Keresztes-Fischer (Interior Minister) and Jenő Ghyczy (Foreign Minister-designate), Szombathelyi (Chief of Staff) and senior officials in the Foreign Ministry, all sharing the conviction that Germany could not win the war—to devise and co-ordinate means of making contact with the Western Allies. From early 1943 onwards, Hungarian envoys, both official and unofficial, fanned out through the neutral capitals of Europe (Stockholm, Lisbon, Berne) and Istanbul to make contact with Allied representatives. In Istanbul, the eminent physicist and Nobel laureate Albert Szentgyörgyi presented himself as the envoy of the democratic opposition in Hungary, which wished not only to deliver their country from the clutches of Nazi Germany but also to replace Horthy's authoritarian regime; his interlocutors unfortunately included a German agent posing as a British officer. In Stockholm, the Political Director of the Hungarian Foreign Ministry, Aladár Szegedy-Maszák, made contact with the British Embassy; and in Lisbon the young Foreign Ministry official László Veress met a British intelligence officer. The message that Kállay had authorised the 'official' envoys to convey was that Hungary would be ready to co-operate with British or American forces if and when they reached Hungary's frontiers. This offer, which Veress subsequently repeated to British agents in Istanbul, fell very far short of the unconditional surrender that Roosevelt and Churchill had agreed, at their January meeting in Casablanca, should be demanded of the Axis powers and their satellites. Although, therefore, these initial contacts evoked no substantive Allied response, they did prompt at least the British government to reconsider its hitherto undifferentiated refusal to enter into any kind of dialogue with enemy representatives; British arguments for a more flexible approach, however, cut no ice in Washington or Moscow.

In the meantime, relations between Hungary and Germany had cooled further. In February, the Germans had rejected a Hungarian request for the withdrawal from the Eastern Front of the tattered remnants of the 2nd Army; and the Hungarians had rejected a German alternative proposal for their reconstitution into three divisions to carry out occupation duties in Yugoslavia. The Hungarians eventually agreed to allow two divisions to remain in Russia. During a visit to Rome in early April, Kállay floated with Mussolini the idea of an alliance, within the Axis, between Italy and Hungary, which might pave the way for their gradual detachment from their German partner; Mussolini, in more need than ever of the German prop beneath his ailing regime and disintegrating army, was not enthused. Against this background, Hitler summoned Horthy to meet him at Schloss Klessheim, near Salzburg, on 16 April. Here, Horthy was subjected to a tirade from the Führer comparing the Hungarian military performance on the Eastern Front unfavourably with the Romanian, accusing the Hungarian government of preparing to defect from the Axis cause—Hitler specifically mentioned not only visits to Istanbul by Szentgyörgyi and András Frey, Foreign Editor of *Magyar Nemzet*, but also a mission to Switzerland by György Barcza—and demanding the dismissal of the 'political adventurer' Kállay. Above all, Hitler raged, the Hungarians had done nothing to tackle the Jewish question. Horthy stonewalled these complaints, entered a robust defence of Kállay and attempted, not surprisingly without success, to divert the Führer by describing his pet scheme for attaching manned kites to U-boats for observation purposes. Horthy refused to subscribe to a joint communiqué expressing his and the Führer's 'determined resolve to continue the war against Bolshevism and its British and American Allies till the final victory' but the Germans published it anyway; on Horthy's return to Budapest, Kállay published the text under the heading 'A German Declaration' and omitted from it the reference to the British and Americans, thereby further infuriating the Germans. On 7 May, Horthy addressed a letter to Hitler, once again refuting all the latter's complaints against Hungary, reaffirming his full confidence in Kállay and stating that such issues as treatment of the Jews were internal matters within the jurisdiction of Hungary alone. The Germans reacted by ordering their Minister in Budapest to have no further contact with the Hungarian Prime Minister and by suspending all official visits between the two countries.

The fall of Mussolini on 25 July 1943 and the prospect of Italy's defection from the German alliance revived Hungarian hopes that Anglo-American forces might, after all, reach Hungary's southern borders and enable her to change sides without risking German occupation. The British, however, had begun to lose patience with the continuing absence of a response to their suggestion, put to András Frey in February, that the Hungarians should send to Istanbul two army officers who could discuss with representatives of the British Special Operations Executive (SOE) the possible despatch of an SOE mission to Hungary. Kállay had hesitated to agree to this, partly because the British intermediary, György Pálóczy-Horváth, after allegedly acting as a spy for the Gömbös government, had embraced the extreme left and was suspected of having become a Soviet agent; and partly because talks between Hungarian officers and the SOE were more likely to be concerned with sabotage operations in Hungary than with the politics of Hungary's exit from the war. Torn between the risk of provoking German occupation and his desire to maintain contact with the Allies, Kállay was eventually impelled to act by a British message, relayed from the Hungarian Consulate in Istanbul, to the effect that if the Hungarians had taken no action by 20 July, contact would be broken off. The Prime Minister therefore entrusted László Veress with a second mission to Istanbul, with authority to inform British agents that if Allied forces— Soviet, Romanian and Czechoslovak troops excepted—reached Hungarian frontiers, they would not be opposed and would have free use of Hungary's airfields, roads and railways; this offer should be regarded as advance notification of Hungary's unconditional surrender, but in the meantime the Allies should refrain from bombing Hungarian targets. On 16 August, Veress and the Hungarian Consul-General, Dezső Újváry, met the Counsellor from the British Legation in Ankara, Sterndale-Bennett, to convey Kállay's message. The British response, conveyed to Veress during the night of 9 September by the British Ambassador to Turkey, Sir Hugh Knatchbull-Hugessen, aboard the ambassadorial yacht in the Sea of Marmora, had been approved by Churchill, agreed by Roosevelt and criticised by Molotov as too soft—the Russians would have preferred to demand Hungary's immediate unconditional surrender. The response required the Hungarian government to confirm their offer by furnishing the British with more authoritative credentials than Veress had been able to provide; to make 'at a suitable moment'[5] a public announcement of Hungary's unconditional surrender; pending such an announcement, to bring all co-operation with Germany to an end; and to obstruct the German war effort by any available means—modalities to be discussed in Istanbul by military representatives of the two governments. Veress returned to Budapest bearing not only this message but two radio transmitters and a code book so that contact with the British could be maintained.

The 'authoritative credentials' requested by London were in due course provided by the Hungarian Minister in Lisbon to his British counterpart. But in all other respects, the 'Istanbul agreement' remained a dead letter. Kállay simply could not bring himself to embark on concrete anti–German measures which, while they might have served to demonstrate Hungary's good faith to the Allies, would be virtually certain to trigger a German invasion and occupation of Hungary—a judgement that Hitler's swift occupation of defecting Italy was soon to vindicate. Along with other disastrous consequences, this would have amounted to a sentence of death for Hungary's 800,000 Jews. This consideration may not have been foremost in Kállay's mind; but it was certainly foremost in the minds of the Jews themselves, whose leading representatives repeatedly pleaded with Kállay to refrain from taking any steps which might put their people in jeopardy.* The conclusion of an armistice agreement with the Allies by General Badoglio's government in Italy on 3 September 1943, following the overthrow of Mussolini and the Allied invasion of the Italian mainland, arguably brought the Tripartite Pact, and Hungary's commitment to it, to an end; this might have been the logical moment for Hungary to announce her own defection. Indeed, Endre Bajcsy-Zsilinszky, speaking on behalf of the left-wing opposition parties, had already submitted a memorandum to Kállay urging that Hungary should withdraw all her forces from the Eastern Front, with or without German consent, publicly declare her neutrality, revoke the Jewish Laws and remove all pro-German elements from the cabinet and the General Staff, even if this were to provoke a German invasion. Occupation by force against Hungarian resistance, he argued, would be preferable to occupation borne 'with meekness and patience; because the forceful occupation will win the honour and the future of the country, maybe by suffering, possibly by very grave torments, blood and destruction to our unfortunate fatherland, but it will separate us from the fate of the German Reich'.[10] In principle, Bajcsy-Zsilinszky was right. The course he urged upon Kállay did offer Hungary's only road to rehabilitation and to any hope of sympathetic treatment at an eventual peace conference, not least with regard to her frontiers. But, quite apart from fear of the dangers and hardships to which occupation would expose most of the Hungarian population, Gentiles as well as Jews, there were other factors that rendered a clean break with the Axis impracticable.

Many among the older generation, remembering with distaste Italy's defection from the Triple Alliance during the First World War, were opposed on principle to Hungary's desertion of her allies. Horthy himself had always made it clear that personal honour would oblige him to give the Führer advance notice of Hungary's intention to seek an armistice: there could be no question, therefore, of presenting the Germans with a *fait accompli*. Moreover, pro-German sentiment

---

* Jewish representatives in London were taking the same line with the British government.

remained extremely strong in the military and civilian establishment, regardless of whether or not the Germans were winning the war; this attitude sprang, not from sympathy with Nazi ideology, which was confined to the extreme right, but from the deep-seated hatred of Communism the Béla Kun experience had instilled and which, together with gratitude to Hitler for the Vienna Awards, a majority of the population shared. With the exception of the Jews, most Hungarians, if given the choice, would have regarded occupation by Germany—so long as Slovaks and Romanians did not participate in it—as preferable to occupation by the Russians. This was the political reality of which Kállay and his colleagues had to take account. Kállay himself recorded the view that 'if we have to choose—until another factor has presented itself—between an essentially defensive [sic] Germany and an expansive Russia, we cannot but stand by Germany'.[11] This was what compelled him, despite Allied pressures and German threats, to continue to walk the tight-rope of seeking Allied favour without incurring the full force of German wrath. He could not know it, but Kállay's objective of surrendering to Western Allied troops when they reached the frontiers of Hungary and of winning recognition, in a peace settlement, for those frontiers as they stood in 1943, was already out of reach. Although Winston Churchill had argued long and hard for an Allied strategy that would involve, whether from Italy or Yugoslavia, a northward lunge against the 'soft underbelly' of the Axis that would deprive Hitler of his remaining allies and of his oil, Franklin Roosevelt supported Stalin's insistence, at the Tehran Conference in November 1943, that the Allies should give absolute and undiluted priority to the invasion of western Europe—long overdue, in the Soviet view. The Mediterranean strategy after which Churchill had hankered was therefore dead, and with it any realistic possibility of Western Allied forces beating the Red Army to the frontiers of Hungary. It followed—and would be confirmed when Churchill visited Moscow a year later—that central-eastern Europe and the Balkans would fall ineluctably into the Soviet sphere of influence, rendering Hungary's recent territorial gains, and much else, irrelevant. By the end of 1943, these unpalatable truths had begun to penetrate the clouds of wishful thinking in which most Hungarians, as ever, were living: the Allied advance through Italy had ground to a virtual halt, Britain had recognised the Communist Tito as leader of the Yugoslav struggle against Nazi occupation, and Hungary's inveterate foe Edvard Beneš had signed, in Moscow, a Czechoslovak-Soviet Friendship Treaty. On 12 January 1944, the British government sent Kállay a message to the effect that Hungary should not oppose the Red Army when it reached Hungarian territory; resistance would place Hungary in the dock alongside Nazi Germany. Hungarians could never quite believe that Britain and the United States, countries with whom they cherished so many affinities, were serious in their fidelity to and respect for their Bolshevik ally. Kállay himself admitted, with hindsight: 'One of the fundamental and catastrophic anomalies in the situation was that we were seeking the protection of the British and Americans, not only against our own 'allies', but against their allies also'.[12] The Western Allies, for their part—with the possible exception of Churchill and a handful of officials in the British Foreign Office—never fully understood that although the quest for the revision of Trianon had taken Hungary into alliance with Nazi Germany, it was the fear of Communist Russia which kept her there.

THE FAUSTIAN PACT II: THE PRICE (1941–45)

The Hungarian government's repeated requests for the release of Hungarian troops from the Eastern Front, so that they could man the Carpathian ramparts of their homeland against the Soviet advance, had met with flat rejection. Hitler had, in fact, given up on Hungary as an autonomous ally: as long ago as September 1943, when news of Italy's defection reached him, he had commissioned an operational plan, 'Operation Margarethe', for the occupation of Hungary. When, on 12 February 1944, Horthy made a further urgent plea for the return of Hungarian troops to defend the Carpathians against the Red Army's advance, Hitler concluded that Hungary was about to defect; preparations began for 'Operation Margarethe' to be implemented. Kállay had, in fact, authorised László Veress at this time to arrange a further meeting in Istanbul with British representatives; Veress informed them that the Hungarian government proposed to order all Hungarian troops serving on the Eastern Front to surrender to the Russians and requested British good offices in making the Soviet High Command aware of this intention. As belated evidence of good faith, Hungary had also agreed to receive an SOE mission, to send supplies to Tito's partisans in northern Yugoslavia and to allow Allied aircraft, *en route* to bomb German targets, the unimpeded use of Hungarian airspace. These moves, serious in intent, were to be overtaken by events. From 4 March, German troops and armour began to concentrate around Vienna; after conferring with Ribbentrop and Himmler, Hitler decided to obtain Horthy's agreement to the occupation of his country, without resistance, so that damage to its economic fabric would be minimised. Horthy was invited to meet the Führer at Schloss Klessheim—as the Romanian leader, Antonescu, had done a few days earlier—ostensibly to discuss the withdrawal of Hungarian troops from the Eastern Front. Aware of the German troop concentrations, indicating that invasion was imminent, Kállay attempted to persuade the Regent to decline Hitler's invitation; determined to do everything possible to bring his Hungarian soldiers home, Horthy nevertheless accepted it and, accompanied by Szombathelyi, Foreign Minister Ghyczy and Defence Minister Csatay, arrived at Klessheim on 18 March—unaware that 'Operation Margarethe' was to be launched in the small hours of the following morning.

Hitler did not beat about the bush. At their first meeting on 18 March, he informed Horthy that since Hungary was about to betray her allies he was obliged to take precautionary measures: in response to Horthy's question, he confirmed that these would involve occupation and the elimination of hostile elements. Hitler hinted that if the Hungarians created difficulties, Romanian, Slovak and Croatian troops were available to assist their German ally; he hoped that the occupation could proceed peacefully, with the Regent's agreement, but if necessary it would proceed without it. Horthy, speechless with anger, rose and left the room. At a second session of talks, following a tense and uneasy lunch, Horthy launched a vigorous counter-attack, warning the Führer not to make an enemy of his only true ally; Hungary would remain Germany's loyal friend if Hitler took no hostile action against her. Otherwise he, Horthy, would resign the regency. Unmoved, Hitler repeated his list of complaints against the Hungarian government, including its failure to act against the Jews. Horthy then announced his immediate departure for Budapest, only to be informed that this was impossible owing to an Allied air-raid that had also brought down telephone lines—a fiction designed both to prevent Horthy from reaching Budapest until the invasion had begun and to make communication with Kállay impossible. The exact nature of subsequent exchanges is unclear. Horthy, doubtless emotionally and physically exhausted, appears to have been swayed by an assurance from Hitler that German troops would be withdrawn from Hungary as soon as a government acceptable to the Reich had taken office in Budapest; his own entourage, which now included the pro-German Sztójay, urged him to avert bloodshed. At a final meeting, after 8 p.m., Horthy acquiesced in the German occupation of Hungary but refused to sign a communiqué asserting that the deployment of German forces to Hungary was taking place 'by mutual agreement'; this text was nevertheless published by the Germans. Horthy undertook that there would be no resistance to the occupation, that a new government would be appointed and that the Hungarian army would continue to fight the Bolshevik foe; according to some accounts[13] he also agreed, in a dangerous concession, that a substantial number of Hungarian Jews would be despatched for labour service in Germany. Horthy's train departed for Budapest at 9.30 p.m. During the journey, the Regent received Dr Edmund Veesenmeyer, Ribbentrop's principal adviser on east European affairs, whom Hitler had appointed earlier in the day to the new post of German Minister and Reich Plenipotentiary in Hungary. Veesenmeyer, an intelligent man, well informed on Hungarian affairs and an able servant of his Nazi masters, was to play a central role in Hungary's impending agony—as was another passenger on Horthy's train, the Gestapo chief Ernst Kaltenbrunner.

The Third Instalment

Eight German divisions—five from Yugoslavia, two from Austria and one from Poland—crossed Hungarian frontiers at 4 a.m. on 19 March 1944. A telegram to Kállay from Field Marshal Keitel, German Chief of Staff, warned that the response to any Hungarian resistance would be the involvement of Hungary's neighbours in the occupation. All discussion of resistance ended when a telegram from Szombathelyi on Horthy's train ordered that German troops should be given a friendly welcome. Only one shot was fired against the invaders; it came from the revolver of Endre Bajcsy-Zsilinszky when a Gestapo detachment arrived at his apartment building to arrest him. When Horthy's train drew into the Kelenföld station at 10 a.m., the Regent was greeted not only by his Prime Minister but also by a German guard of honour: the Germans already controlled all Hungary's communications and airfields. At a meeting of the Crown Council at noon, Kállay and his cabinet tendered their resignations. Horthy had already been informed by Veesenmeyer that Germany would like to see Imrédy appointed in Kállay's place, but Horthy advanced Imrédy's alleged Jewish ancestry as a reason for refusing to accept him. On 21 March, the Germans issued an ultimatum to the effect that if an acceptable government had not been constituted within thirty-six hours, military measures, including occupation of the Castle Hill, would be taken. Horthy eventually agreed to appoint Döme Sztójay, the former army officer who had served as Hungary's envoy to Germany—or, as some would and did argue, Germany's envoy to Hungary—for the past eight years; Sztójay presided over a cabinet of right-wingers, from both the Government Party and from the Party of Hungarian Revival whose leader, Imrédy, became Minister for the Economy. There were, however, no cabinet posts for the Arrow Cross Party, regarded in Berlin as insufficiently pro-German. Kállay, well aware of the ferocity of the storm about to burst over Hungary as the Germans set about forcing her into the mould of Nazi occupation, urged Horthy to dissociate himself from these events by abdication and retirement to his country estate. Horthy refused:

> I am still an admiral. The captain cannot leave his sinking ship; he must remain on the bridge to the last.... Who will defend the honourable men and women in this country who have trusted me blindly? Who will defend the Jews or our refugees if I leave my post? I may not be able to defend everything but I believe that I can still be of great, very great help to our people. I can do more than anyone else could.[14]

The Germans set about their political and racial cleansing from the first day of their occupation, with the active assistance of László Baky and other rightist collaborators. Ferenc Keresztes-Fischer and Endre Bajcsy-Zsilinszky, two of the few genuinely principled Hungarian politicians of the Horthy era, were arrested and imprisoned.* The same fate befell the senior Foreign Ministry officials who had been involved in Hungary's contacts with the Western Allies. István Bethlen escaped into hiding in the countryside, Kállay into the protection of the Turkish Legation. The Social Democratic, Smallholders' and Peasant Parties were dissolved. The escaped Allied prisoners of war who had enjoyed Hungarian hospitality, some of them for three years, were systematically rounded up—812 French, 5,450 Polish, 39 British, 11 American, 16 Belgian, 12 Dutch and 180 Russian, according to Veesenmeyer's report—and returned to captivity. Although the population at large reacted to these developments with apathetic resignation, one nodule of potential resistance came into existence in May, when, on the initiative of the underground Communist Party, a small group of representatives of the newly banned opposition parties came together to form the 'Hungarian Front', embracing, in addition to the Communists (temporarily rechristened the 'Peace Party'), the Independent Smallholders, Social Democrats, National Peasant Party and a monarchist group, the Blood Association of the Apostolic Cross. After establishing covert links with the trade unions and churches, the Front issued a manifesto in June, calling for an armed uprising against the German invaders and their Hungarian collaborators. Although the manifesto made no impression on the prevailing public apathy, the existence of the Front was to acquire greater significance in the months ahead.

Adolf Eichmann, who had arrived in Budapest with his special SS detachment (*Sondereinsatzkommando*) on 19 March, quickly settled down to work on 'the Jewish problem'. Sztójay personally approved a German request for the deportation to Germany—in fact, to Auschwitz—of 100,000 *Arbeitsjuden* and appointed Baky and another veteran of the extreme right, László Endre, to State Secretaryships in the Ministry of Interior with special responsibility for dealing with the Jews. An order from the Ministry to senior police officers opened by declaring: 'The Royal

---

* Keresztes-Fischer survived captivity but died in Austria shortly after liberation in 1945; Bajcsy-Zsilinsky was released in October 1944, and after attempting to organise armed resistance to the Germans, was captured and executed two months later.

Hungarian Government will cleanse the country of Jews within a short space of time'.[15] It was followed by a stream of discriminatory decrees, which ordered Jews to wear the yellow star; forbade them to purchase lard, sugar and other food items in short supply; confiscated their radios and telephones; froze their bank accounts; and closed down Jewish-owned businesses—18,000 shops in Budapest alone. Books by Jewish authors were publicly burned. By the end of April, 8,225 leading members of Hungary's Jewish community had been arrested. Endre and Baky then embarked on a systematic programme of deportation, including women and children. County by county, Jews were herded into ghettos in major towns, beginning with Kassa in the north east and then in Debrecen, Pécs and Székesfehérvár; Budapest was to be the last assembly point. There was no resistance; local Jewish Councils helped the authorities to conduct the operation in an orderly manner. From the ghettos, beginning on 15 May, entrainment and deportation to Auschwitz began. By mid-July, 458,000 Jews from the Hungarian provinces had been crammed into freight wagons by Hungarian gendarmes for the long, stop-start journey to Poland, a journey hundreds did not survive. With the Jewish population of Hungary outside the capital virtually eliminated, Eichmann now turned his attention to Budapest, where since May 170,000 Jews had been concentrated in 1,900 designated 'yellow star' apartment houses while over 120,000 lived illegally in Christian households. On 25 June, German-inspired government decrees imposed a curfew on all Jews between 5 p.m. and 11 a.m., forbade them to receive guests in their accommodation and barred them from all the parks and promenades of the capital. The deportation to Auschwitz-Birkenau of Budapest's 299,000 Jews was now scheduled to begin on 6 July. Hungary's three wealthiest Jewish families—the Chorins, Weisses and Kornfelds—and over forty of their relatives and friends were given a *laissez-passer* to Portugal by the SS in return for twenty-five-year leases on their factories, mines and banks. Several thousand more Jews were eventually saved by a series of deals, brokered by Rudolf Kasztner, between the Budapest Jewish Relief and Rescue Committee and the SS, who gave safe conduct to Switzerland to Jews named in lists submitted by the committee in return for large sums of cash, treasure and scarce commodities such as coffee.* A more ambitious and bizarre bargain proposed by Eichmann himself, under which the lives of one million Jews, including Hungarians, would have been spared in return for the delivery to Germany of 10,000 trucks and other *matériel* failed to clear the obstacles of disagreements among the Allies and Jewish organisations, together with suspicions, doubtless well founded, that the Germans would not deliver.[16]

The Western Allies and the neutral nations had at last begun to take notice of what was happening in Hungary. King George VI of the United Kingdom, King Gustav of Sweden, the Pope and the International Red Cross all addressed appeals to Horthy during the month of June for an end to the deportations. President

---

* Kasztner's activities, which inevitably involved frequent dealings with the Gestapo, had a tragic sequel in post-war Israel. Publicly accused of collaboration with the Nazis, Kasztner, in a resulting libel action that became entangled with Israeli party politics, failed to clear his name. In 1957 he was murdered, before the result of his appeal, which exonerated him, had been made known.

THE FAUSTIAN PACT II: THE PRICE (1941–45)

Roosevelt threatened the bombing of Budapest—and the first, British, air-raid on the capital had in fact taken place on 3 April. The Catholic Primate, Cardinal Serédi, told the Regent that he intended publicly to denounce the deportations unless the government intervened to stop them. Horthy himself, who had been reluctant to give credence to the increasing number of reports reaching him concerning atrocities against Jews and the true destination of the trainloads of deportees, finally decided to act. He was perhaps influenced in part by a letter from István Bethlen who, from his rural refuge, argued that the deportations had 'soiled the name of Hungary' and that the looting of Jewish property had 'become the source of the most atrocious corruption, robbery and theft in which, alas, very considerable portions of the Hungarian intelligentsia are also involved ... the whole Christian Hungarian society will soon be contaminated irreversibly'.[17]

On 26 June, Horthy presided over a meeting of the Crown Council that decided to halt the deportations; a Hungarian division, under General Bakay, took up positions in the capital to enforce compliance with this decision. Endre and Baky were dismissed from the Ministry of Interior. The deportations ceased. The Jews of Budapest were granted a breathing-space of which the legations of the neutral countries—in particular those of Sweden, under Raoul Wallenberg, and Switzerland—made good use in distributing certificates of protection (*Schutzpässe*). Emboldened by the discovery that he could still influence events and, doubtless, impressed both by the Allied invasion of France and by a series of heavy Allied air-raids on Budapest, Győr, Szolnok and Komárom, Horthy decided to replace Sztójay and his cabinet of pro-German rightists with a new government headed by senior army officers whom he believed he could trust. General Géza Lakatos took over the premiership on 29 August, with General Gusztáv Hennyey as his Foreign Minister. Eichmann and his special detachment left Hungary on the following day. Two pro-German ministers nevertheless survived the change of Prime Minister and, perhaps in part for their benefit, the first meeting of the new cabinet resolved that Hungary would continue the fight, shoulder to shoulder with her German ally.

Privately, however, Horthy was more than ever convinced that Hungary must withdraw from the conflict. Already Romania, unburdened by considerations of alliance loyalty, had adroitly changed sides, declaring war on Germany—and Hungary—on 25 August: Soviet troops were pouring into Transylvania. Even as the Red Army approached Hungary's eastern frontier, Horthy clung to the hope that the Western Allies could forestall it. The perverse refusal of Horthy and his ministers to accept that the Western powers could really be loyal to their Soviet ally was exemplified by their decision, on 31 August, both to send Hungarian troops, with promised German reinforcements, to attack the Russians in southern Transylvania and, in the same breath, to appeal to Britain and the United States to send airborne divisions to occupy Hungary. Horthy informed a meeting of the Crown Council on 7 September that he intended to negotiate an armistice with the Western Allies, after informing the Germans in advance; initial contact would be established through Baron György Bakách-Bessenyey, a retired Hungarian diplomat living in Switzerland to whom a line of communication already existed. The Council could not steel itself to endorse this proposal, deciding instead to present the Germans, through Veesenmeyer, with an ultimatum: unless five Panzer divisions were despatched within twenty-four hours to halt the Soviet advance, Hungary would be compelled to seek an armistice. On the following day, Veesenmeyer conveyed Ribbentrop's response, to the effect that reinforcements would be sent to Hungary and that Germany had no intention of abandoning Hungarian territory. When the promised reinforcements had not arrived by 10 September, Horthy convened an informal conference of trusted members both of the Council—including Bethlen, Gyula Károlyi and Kánya—and of the cabinet to discuss the modalities of an armistice; it should, Horthy proposed, follow the pattern devised by Finland, by which German troops would be allowed to leave the country unhindered while Hungarian troops ceased fighting without laying down their arms. Bessenyey had by now reported from Switzerland that there could be no question of a Western occupation of Hungary. It was agreed, therefore, that although an envoy, General Náday, should be sent to Italy in a last-ditch attempt to negotiate with the Western Allies, contact should also be established with the Soviet High Command. When this proposition was put to the cabinet, however, it met with unanimous opposition and the threat of collective resignation: the prospect of negotiating with the Russians was still anathema to both the military and the civilian establishment.

Horthy, with the help of a few close aides and his family, now took matters into his own hands, secretly despatching General Náday to Italy and Count Zichy to Slovakia—where an armed uprising, led by the Slovak National Council, was in progress against the puppet Slovak regime—to make contact with the Russian commander of pro-Soviet partisans there, Colonel Makarov. Zichy returned with a reassuring letter from Makarov, promising that if Hungary deserted Germany the Allies would guarantee her continued independence; territorial issues would be deferred to an eventual peace conference. A parallel mission to the Soviet High Command led by Baron Ede Aczél produced a similarly encouraging response. Horthy thereupon decided to send a delegation to Moscow, to be led by the Chief of Gendarmerie, General Gábor Faragho—a Russian speaker who had served as Military Attaché in Moscow; he would be accompanied by Professor Géza Teleki, son of the former Prime Minister, and by a senior diplomat, Domokos Szentiványi. Briefing the delegation on 27 September, Horthy gave Faragho a hand-written letter, in English, to convey to Marshal Stalin. After denying any Hungarian responsibility for the war and explaining that Kristóffy's report of his conversation with Molotov in June 1941 had never reached him,[*] Horthy's letter continued:

When sending with full authorisation my delegates to the negotiation of an armistice, I beg you to spare this unfortunate country which has its own historic merits and the people of which has so many affinities with the Russian people. Kindly exercise your great influence upon your allies, that you may make conditions compatible with our people's interests and honour, who would really deserve a peaceful life and a safe future.[18]

Faragho's delegation arrived in Moscow on 1 October. A week later, Molotov, after consulting the Western Allies, conveyed the preliminary terms of the Alliance for an armistice: within ten days, Hungary should withdraw all troops and civilian

---

[*] See page 385.

personnel from Czechoslovakia, Romania and Yugoslavia to behind her frontiers as they had been on 31 December 1937; should break off all relations with Germany and declare war immediately on her former ally; Makarov's letter should be considered null and void; Hungary's surrender must be unconditional. If these terms were accepted, a formal armistice agreement could be negotiated and signed in Moscow by a properly authorised Hungarian representative. Faragho reported this unpalatable news to the Royal Palace in Budapest by telegram, where it was laboriously decyphered by Horthy's son Nicky, his daughter-in-law, Ilona, and two of his personal aides. Soviet forces were by now sweeping into the Alföld, threatening Debrecen and Szeged. Horthy therefore summoned Lakatos, Hennyey and Chief of Staff Vörös (who, unbeknown to Horthy, maintained constant contact with the German military and with Veesenmeyer) to inform them, for the first time, of the presence of a Hungarian armistice delegation in Moscow and of the preliminary terms offered by the Allies; agreeing that Hungary had no choice but to accept them, Lakatos urged that the Regent should insist on a temporary halt to the Red Army's advance, which would give Hungarian units time to disengage and retreat. This condition accompanied Horthy's authorisation for the signature of a preliminary armistice and Molotov agreed to a short undeclared truce. Molotov and Faragho signed the preliminary armistice agreement at 7.57 p.m. on 11 October; Soviet forces were ordered to suspend hostilities against Hungarian units at midnight.

The pressure of these events had taken their toll on the elderly Regent. On 11 October, he was persuaded by his son Nicky to receive two representatives of the erstwhile opposition, the Smallholder Zoltán Tildy and a Social Democrat, Árpád Szakasits, to tell them in strict confidence that preparations for an end to Hungary's part in the war were well advanced and that a public announcement would be made shortly; he appeared to accept the suggestions of Tildy and Szakasits that when the time came arms should be distributed to the workers and all political prisoners released. At this point Horthy was thinking, and may have given his entourage and Lakatos an indication to this effect, in terms of announcing the armistice on 20 October; but on 13 October he suddenly decided, possibly in the light of well-founded rumours of an impending Arrow Cross coup, to bring this forward by five days, despite the fact that none of the preconditions for an armistice was in place. No orders had been issued for the withdrawal of Hungarian personnel to the Trianon frontiers; no preparations had been made for a declaration of war on Germany. Generals Miklós and Veress, commanders of the 1st and 2nd Armies respectively, had been given a codeword which, when received, would be their order to cease fire, make contact with the Soviet units nearest to them, and turn their guns on the Germans.* In the meantime, Vörös had merely ordered the armies to make a strategic withdrawal while continuing to resist the Russian advance. Horthy now planned to convene the Crown Council on the morning of 15 October, immediately prior to the public announcement of an armistice and

---

* According to Lieutenant General Antal Vattay, the Head of Horthy's Military Bureau, the staff officer whom Veress sent to collect the codeword, passed it and an explanation of its purpose to the Germans before conveying it to his commanding officer. See Nagy, K.: *Két Tábornok* ('Two Generals') (Budapest, 2000), p. 239.

to inform Veesenmeyer that it was about to be made; the coded order for a cease-fire would be issued immediately thereafter. But Horthy had not informed his Prime Minister, Ministers or Chief of Staff of the fact that a preliminary armistice had actually been signed in Moscow; neither had the Russians been warned that an announcement was imminent. Indeed, the Hungarian cabinet (minus its two pro-Nazi members), having been briefed by Lakatos and Vörös on 14 October on the hopelessness of Hungary's situation and having agreed that an armistice should be sought, was busily engaged in drawing up its own draft of an armistice agreement; it provided, among other hopelessly unrealistic conditions, for the occupation of Hungary by Western as well as Soviet forces. In order to make a good impression on the Allies, the cabinet also lifted the ban on the left-wing press and ordered the immediate release of all political prisoners.

The Russians, for their part, were fast losing patience with Hungary's continuing failure to implement the terms of the preliminary armistice—the 1st Army and most of the 2nd were still in place and, in the absence of final orders to the contrary, continuing to fight: on 14 October, the Soviet Chief of Staff delivered an ultimatum to Faragho demanding that within forty-eight hours Hungarian forces should turn their guns on the Germans, withdraw to the Trianon frontiers and provide the Soviet commander in Szeged with full details of the dispositions of both German and Hungarian units. Faragho transmitted this ultimatum to the amateur decoders in the Royal Palace; but Horthy was not informed of it until the morning of 15 October. The Germans, although still unaware of the Moscow armistice, had been informed of the orders issued to the 1st and 2nd Armies for a strategic withdrawal; General Guderian, Chief of the German General Staff, informed Vörös that unless the orders to withdraw were countermanded, Hungary would be declared 'a German strategic area' in which only German orders would have military validity. The receipt of ultimata from the Soviet Union and from Nazi Germany on the same day graphically demonstrated the acute difficulty of Hungary's situation. Hitler, moreover, had finally decided—not least in the light of the suspension of deportations of Hungarian Jews—that Horthy should be deposed and an Arrow Cross regime installed. As preparatory steps, General Bakay, commander of the Hungarian army corps defending Budapest, was abducted to Germany and SS-Hauptsturmführer Otto Skorzeny sent to Budapest to assist in the abduction of the Regent and his family.*

The Final Instalment

The date 15 October 1944 joined 29 August 1526, 13 August 1849 and 4 June 1920 as the most fateful days in the history of Hungary.** Accounts of the events of that day, several of them by direct participants, differ in a number of significant respects; the differences have given rise to bitter disagreements and acrimonious disputes ever since—over who knew what and when, who said what to whom

---

* Skorzeny had planned and led the dramatic rescue of Mussolini from captivity in the Abruzzi mountains in September 1943.
** The dates, respectively, of the Battle of Mohács, General Görgey's surrender to the Russians that ended the War of Independence and the signature of the Treaty of Trianon.

and why. The most reliable version is doubtless that in C. A. Macartney's epony-mous history; but his narrative occupies forty pages[19]—a luxury beyond the means of the present volume. The following account, necessarily condensed, reflects this writer's best judgement as to what actually happened. At 8.30 a.m. the Regent's son, Nicky, entered the office of the Director of Harbours in Pest. He had come, with an armed escort, to meet representatives of Tito's Yugoslav partisans, in the belief that they had important information to impart bearing on Hungary's efforts to leave the war. It is unclear whether the rendezvous was wholly spurious, a German invention designed to lure Nicky Horthy from the Royal Palace, or whether the Germans had simply become aware, through tele-phone tapping, of a genuine meeting. At all events Nicky, on entering the office building, was attacked by SS thugs, knocked unconscious, wrapped into a roll of carpet, whisked off to an airfield and flown to Vienna, whence he was taken to Mauthausen concentration camp. News of the abduction reached Horthy shortly before the meeting of the Crown Council which he had called for 10.30 a.m. and at which he intended to announce his decision to seek an armistice. The meeting consequently began a little late; but despite what must have been an appalling shock, Horthy retained his composure and opened the meeting with a prepared statement. The Regent said that he had 'called together the members of the Cabinets in this darkest hour of Hungary's history. Our situation is gravely critical. That Germany is on the verge of collapse is no longer in doubt; should that collapse occur now, the Allies would find that Hungary is Germany's only remaining ally. In that case, Hungary might cease to exist as a state. Hence I must sue for an armistice'.[20] Horthy went on to tell the Council, disingenuously, that he had ensured that Hungary would be offered 'acceptable conditions' by the Allies: he did not disclose, even now, that a preliminary armistice, on conditions the Council would certainly have rejected as unacceptable, had already been signed in Moscow. General Vörös informed the Council of Guderian's ultima-tum; the Council rejected it. After a legalistic discussion of constitutional law, the Prime Minister announced that since Parliament had not been consulted on the armistice issue, he and his cabinet must resign. Horthy accepted the resignations but maintained that as Supreme War Lord he could conclude an armistice on his own authority; he invited the cabinet to accept reappointment, which, to a man—including its two pro-Nazi members*—it did.

The next item on Horthy's predetermined timetable was a meeting with Veesenmeyer, at which he would fulfil his promise to give the Germans advance notice of Hungary's intention to leave the war; this had been arranged for twelve noon and Horthy left the Council meeting in order to keep the appointment. The Regent opened the audience with a bitter tirade against Germany's treatment of her Hungarian ally: Germany's record of economic plunder, broken promises and treachery had culminated in the abduction of his son, for which Horthy demanded an explanation. German behaviour had left Hungary with no option but to seek an armistice and withdraw from the war. After making a feeble

---

* Béla Jurcsek (Minister of Agriculture) and Lajos Reményi-Schneller (Minister of Finance).

defence of German conduct and passing responsibility for Nicky Horthy's abduction to the Gestapo, Veesenmeyer asked the Regent to receive a special envoy from the Führer, Ambassador Rahn, who had just arrived in Budapest. Horthy, respectful of protocol to the last, agreed to do so and Veesenmeyer departed. In accordance with a prearranged plan, Horthy's daughter-in-law, Ilona, had been listening to the conversation from an adjoining room; as soon as Horthy mentioned an armistice, she signalled to Horthy's Chef de Cabinet that he should hand to the waiting State Secretary for Press Affairs, Endre Hlatky, the text of the Regent's Proclamation to the Hungarian people, announcing his decision to conclude an armistice. Hlatky was then to arrange for the Proclamation to be broadcast immediately. After some confusion arising from the absence of a signature below the text, Hlatky did so: the one o'clock news bulletin on Hungarian Radio was interrupted for the first reading of the Proclamation—two further readings followed, separated by recorded martial music. After a rather disingenuous justification of past Hungarian policies—'Hungary was not led by any desire to acquire new territories'—and a recital of German misdeeds, including the treatment of the Jewish question 'in a manner incompatible with the dictates of humanity', the Proclamation concluded:

I informed a representative of the German Reich that we were about to conclude a military armistice with our former enemies and to cease all hostilities against them. Commanders of the Hungarian Army have received corresponding orders from me. Accordingly, the troops, loyal to their oath and following an Order of the Day now issued simultaneously, must obey the commanders appointed by me. I appeal to every honest Hungarian to follow me on this path, beset by sacrifices, that will lead to Hungary's salvation.[21]*

After the Proclamation, Hungarian Radio broadcast an Order of the Day, in the names of the Regent and Minister of Defence Csatay, requiring the unquestioning obedience of Hungary's armed forces to the orders that would reach them through their commanders; the order stated that the Regent 'had decided to request' an armistice. In the meantime, the coded message to the commanders of the 1st and 2nd Armies, triggering contingency orders for a ceasefire and co-operation with advancing Soviet units, had been despatched; and Horthy had received Rahn, who urged him to reconsider before handing his country to the Bolsheviks. Rahn's plea did, apparently, make a considerable impression on Horthy; but the Proclamation had already been broadcast. Amid the dramas of the morning, the very serious ultimatum issued by the Soviet Chief of Staff twenty-four hours earlier appears to have been completely overlooked.

Horthy never doubted the loyalty of the Hungarian army to himself nor that, when he eventually activated the order to disengage and withdraw on 15 Octo-

---

* According to some accounts, Prime Minister Lakatos and Foreign Minister Hennyey deleted from an earlier draft of the proclamation the words 'From today Hungary regards herself as being in a state of war against Germany', on the grounds that they were imprudently provocative. It is also claimed by some that the original version stated that the Regent 'had concluded', rather than 'was concluding' or 'was about to conclude' an armistice. Despite an indication to the contrary in C.A. Macartney's account (*October Fifteenth*, II, p. 405), it seems certain that the version actually broadcast put the request for an armistice in the uncompleted present tense—hence much of the confusion that followed.

ber, after announcing the armistice, it would be obeyed. When, at an earlier stage, General Hennyey had attempted to warn him that he should cherish no illusions about the loyalty of the officer corps, Horthy replied that he had 'a firm hold' over the army.[22] In this he was sadly deceived. Horthy had allowed himself to become detached from the army: he never attended military reviews, finding them too tiring, and had not visited a military unit for several years. He had alienated his senior commanders both by failing to consult them about military appointments and by his equivocal attitude towards the Germans and the war. This factor now became crucial. A significant number of Hungarian officers, both senior and junior, reacted with outrage to Horthy's broadcast Proclamation: the prospect of abandoning their German ally and of withdrawing from the battle against the advancing forces of Bolshevism was anathema to them. This reaction first manifested itself in the refusal of the Operations Section of the Defence Ministry, having guessed its significance, to transmit the Regent's coded message to the 1st and 2nd Armies. By his own account, General Vattay and his adjutant nevertheless succeeded in circumventing this obstruction by establishing direct contact with the two commanders concerned.[23] But worse was to come. During the afternoon, Veesenmeyer and a group of pro-German staff officers persuaded the pliant Vörös to issue a general order that in effect countermanded Horthy's Order of the Day: 'No one is to interpret the Regent's broadcast as meaning that the Hungarian Army is laying down its arms. So far it is only a question of negotiations for an armistice. The outcome of these is still uncertain, and thus every Hungarian soldier and unit must continue the fight, as before, and with all its strength, in the face of attack from any quarter'.[24]

This order was transmitted by telephone to all Hungarian units and broadcast on Hungarian radio in the early evening. It had an immediate and disastrous effect. A pro-German officer, Major General Hindy, arrested the commander of I Army Corps, charged with the defence of Budapest, assumed command and ordered all units to return to barracks. The 2nd Battalion of the Horthy Regiment, the Parachute Regiment, the Hussars, the police and the paramilitary gendarmes all declared against an armistice and for the Germans. Having issued his fatal order, Chief of Staff Vörös disappeared. Meanwhile, Horthy had rejoined the Crown Council, whose session had been interrupted by his meetings with Veesenmeyer and Rahn, to inform it of these conversations; but, even now, he did not reveal that the preliminary armistice, on Allied terms, was an accomplished fact. Meanwhile, the Germans methodically pursued their plans for the take-over of the capital and the installation, for which preparations had been in train for several days, of an Arrow Cross regime headed by Ferenc Szálasi, the growth in whose following had obliged the Germans to swallow their reservations concerning him and his party. By evening, all strategic points, railway terminals and the radio station were in German or Arrow Cross hands. A proclamation by Szálasi had been broadcast by Hungarian Radio. The Regent controlled only the Royal Palace and Castle Hill, which was surrounded by German troops. Although they thronged the streets, the people of Budapest watched these developments passively, without offering resistance or even protest. The prevailing mood was one of nervous apprehension.

The events of the night of 15–16 October are the most bitterly disputed, by those who participated in them,* of any in the whole sorry episode. The main point at issue is that of who, and on what authority, led the Germans to believe that the Regent was willing to resign, to place himself under German protection and to appoint a government acceptable to the Reich. This account cannot accommodate an examination of the evidence, nor adjudicate between the various conflicting testimonies. The salient facts were that German preparations for an assault, with armour, on the Castle Hill had been completed; and that the attack could be expected at any time after dawn on 16 October. At 10 p.m. on 15 October, Horthy had at last revealed to his Prime Minister and Foreign Minister that a preliminary armistice had already been concluded with the Allies, in Moscow, and that Hungary's failure to implement its terms had resulted in a Soviet ultimatum that would expire on the following morning. Appalled, Lakatos and Hennyey retired to the Prime Minister's office to consider the situation. Horthy's close aides, meanwhile, concerned above all for the personal safety of the Regent and his family, were endeavouring to persuade him to put himself under German protection; the government would simultaneously resign, leaving it to the Germans to appoint a new one without involving the Regent in the transfer of power. Horthy angrily rejected this proposal and retired to bed. In subsequent exchanges between General Vattay and the Prime Minister, the belief nevertheless arose and hardened that the Regent had, in fact, agreed to abdicate and to seek asylum with his family in Germany. This misrepresentation of Horthy's actual position seems to have arisen from the desire to protect him from violence, combined with wishful thinking inspired by the evident hopelessness of the situation and the wish to avoid bloodshed in a futile cause. At all events, Lakatos informed the German Legation in the small hours of 16 October that the government had decided to resign and that it was the Regent's wish to abdicate and to place himself under German protection. Hitler's assent to this proposal was sought and obtained. At 5.30 a.m., therefore, Veesenmeyer arrived at the Palace to escort Horthy, Lakatos and their aides to the Gestapo headquarters in the Hatvany Palace, a short distance away, while Otto Skorzeny and his SS troops carried out their assault on the Castle Hill; Horthy's family had already sought refuge with the Papal Nuncio. The confusion and misunderstanding resulting from the Germans' mistaken belief that Horthy had agreed to abdicate dominated the remainder of the day. Szálasi, confidently presenting himself at the Hatvany Palace to receive the Regent's benediction as head of the new government, was twice sent away by Horthy with a flea in his ear. Only when the Germans made it clear that Nicky Horthy's release from German custody would depend upon his father's compliance with their wishes did Horthy, depressed and exhausted, relent. He signed both a confirmation of Vörös's order to Hungarian armies to continue the fight and a short declaration to the Presidents of the two Houses of the Hungarian Parliament:

In a heavy hour of Hungarian history I make known this my decision: in the interest of the successful prosecution of the war and of the inner unity and coherence of the nation,

---

* In particular, by Generals Lakatos, Hennyey and Vattay in their respective diaries and memoirs.

to abdicate from my office of Regent and to renounce all legal rights accruing from my authority as Regent. I entrust Ferenc Szálasi with the formation of a Cabinet of national concentration. Given at Budapest on the 16th day of October 1944. Horthy.[25]

The Germans did not honour their undertaking to release Nicky Horthy; he was transferred from Mauthausen to Dachau, where he remained until the spring of 1945. On 17 October, Regent Miklós Horthy, with his family and under German escort, boarded a train for Bavaria. He never returned to Hungary.

Despite his distinctly selective moral sense, Miklós Horthy does not deserve too ill of posterity. Within the limitations imposed by his class, his early career and a shallow intelligence, he served his country unselfishly and acted at all times in what he perceived to be Hungary's best interests. Those interests demanded, in his view, the restoration of Hungary's territorial integrity and her protection from Communism. Both aims could best be furthered, so Horthy came to believe, through alliance with Germany. Although he found the style and conduct of Nazidom distasteful, he was impressed by raw power; *in extremis*, he nevertheless found the courage to withstand its pressure rather than to continue to assist it in an evil purpose. Horthy's reassuring predictability, his personal honesty and his stamina held Hungary together during two crisis-ridden decades. At the very end, although his natural dignity did not desert him, his age and naiveté left him at the mercy of events. After leaving Hungary for the last time, Horthy was detained, with his family, under house arrest in Bavaria until American forces reached the region in April 1945. As a possible war criminal, he was subsequently detained by the Allies in various west European locations until 1948, when he was permitted to enter exile in Portugal. He lived there, in very modest circumstances, until his death in 1957, in his ninetieth year. His remains were reburied in Hungary in 1993.

Although Hungary's attempt to leave the war did not have to fail precisely in the way that it did, it is difficult to see how it could have succeeded. Once the tide of war had turned against Germany, Hitler was bound to seek to retain control of Hungarian territory in order to protect southern Germany, with or without the consent and support of the Hungarian government; Hungary, moreover, had become Germany's second most important source of oil, after Romania.* Grateful loyalty to Germany on the one hand and fearful hatred of Soviet Communism on the other were both sufficiently strong in Hungary to make it doubtful that Horthy could have carried his government, army or people into a full armistice agreement with the Soviet Union—or even into the preliminary armistice, if knowledge of Faragho's mission had spread beyond Horthy's immediate entourage. As soon as Hungary had been lured away, by the prospect of regaining the lost territories, from her pre-war policy of armed neutrality, her fate was bound to that of Germany; she could have escaped from being dragged down with the Third Reich only by an open break with Hitler before March 1944, as Bajcsy-Zsilinszky and others had urged. This would have provoked the occupation and the holocaust which, although they could not be foreseen, were to be inflicted on Hungary in any case. But Hungary's honour would have been less damaged; and her claim to a more sympathetic post-war hearing from the Allies, stronger.

Forewarned by the Germans several months earlier that they should prepare to be given the reins of power, Szálasi and his Arrow Cross cronies came to office

---

* By 1944, Hungary's annual production of oil had risen to 840,000 tons.

with their priorities and their programme well prepared. After assuming, on 16 October, the office and title of National Leader (*Nemzetvezető*)—an act a thinly attended Parliament approved on 3 November—the new regime got down to work. Although Szálasi had in the past irritated the Germans by putting the interests of Hungary[7], as he saw them through the distorted prism of his ideology, ahead of all other considerations, his conduct in office pandered principally to the political and material requirements of the Nazis. The Arrow Cross plan for Hungary's surviving Jewish population of about 300,000, now concentrated almost entirely in Budapest, had been to use it for forced labour while the war lasted and then to deport it *en masse* 'to a place to be determined by international agreement'; but within hours of the Arrow Cross seizure of the radio building and transmitting station on 15 October, a stream of virulently anti–Semitic broadcasts was inciting the gangs of the extreme right to violence. Pogroms during the night of 15/16 October claimed the lives of several hundred Jews, many of them members of labour service battalions in Óbuda, who were herded on to the Danube bridges, shot and thrown into the river. Similar fates befell Jewish labour service battalions in the countryside. On 17 October, Eichmann returned to Budapest. Under his direction, Hungarian Arrow Cross detachments rounded up from the ghettos all able-bodied Jews between the ages of sixteen and sixty, male and female, to dig trenches and build earthworks in the southern suburbs of the capital. Many died of exhaustion, many were shot at the whim of their guards. From early November, with Szálasi's agreement, about 2,000 Jews a day were marched for 200 kilometres to the border checkpoint at Hegyeshalom to be handed over to the Reich, ostensibly for labour but in fact for extermination. Rationed to three or four bowls of thin gruel during the seven—or eight-day journey, large numbers perished on the way or were shot by guards for lagging. Back in the capital, intense pressure from the Vatican, the International Red Cross and neutral countries succeeded in extracting some minor concessions from Szálasi, including the creation of an 'international ghetto' for Jews holding *Schutzpässe* issued by the neutral legations; but the apartment buildings allocated for this purpose had been occupied largely by 'unprotected' Jews who were now evicted and joined the daily marches to Hegyeshalom. At the end of November, Hungarian police and gendarmerie, under the direction of Eichmann's *Sonderkommando*, herded all Jews who were neither 'protected' nor fit for forced labour into a new ghetto consisting of 162 apartment buildings in Budapest's 7th District, around the Dohány Street synagogue. By January 1945, the sealed ghetto housed nearly 70,000 Jews, mostly the very young, the sick and the aged. Both ghettos were subjected to frequent raids by Arrow Cross gangs, who looted and murdered at will. The terror intensified after the onset of the siege of Budapest: Arrow Cross gangs roamed the streets after dark, typically murdering fifty to sixty Jews in a night.* In late December and early January, three Jewish hospitals were ransacked, their patients and staff murdered. Between the onset of the pogroms in 1944 and the Red Army's 'liberation' of the capital in February 1945, 17,000 Jews died in Budapest.[26]

---

* The favoured method of execution was to tie three Jews together on the bank of the Danube and shoot the middle victim in the back of the head so that he fell into the river taking the other two victims with him, to drown.

The Szálasi regime's second priority was to put at the disposal of the belea-guered Reich such human and material resources as still remained in Hungary. All males aged between fourteen and seventy were conscripted for military or labour service. An absurd plan was announced for the transfer to Germany, for the win-ter, of the entire Hungarian population, with a promise of return to the homeland in the spring of 1945, by which time the Führer's secret weapons would have won the war for Germany. Tens of thousands of government officials, army personnel and able-bodied males did, in fact, leave for Germany as the Red Army advanced; but the great majority of Hungarians, including a rapidly increasing number of deserters from the army, ignored the government's orders and stayed put. After the encirclement of Budapest by Soviet forces on 27 December, most of them had no choice. Meanwhile, under German direction, the government systematically removed from the path of the advancing Red Army anything that might help sustain the German war effort. During the five months after 15 October 1944, over 2,000 trains and a large fleet of river barges transported to Germany 45,383 tons of wheat, 11,203 tons of lubricating oil, 7,905 tons of sugar, 3,040 tons of chemicals and pharmaceuticals, 189,753 tons of machinery and 100,000 head of livestock. In the process, Hungary permanently lost to the Germans 23,840 freight wagons and over 500 river craft.[27]

On 6 December, the Red Army's Second and Fourth Ukrainian Fronts, having swept across the Alföld in a week, broke the German line at Hatvan; three days later, they reached the Danube at Vác, north of Budapest, and drove southwards to link up with Marshal Tolbukhin's Third Ukrainian Front, which was advancing north-wards from the River Sava. Despite fierce and sometimes heroic resistance, in which Hungarian forces remained remarkably loyal to their German ally, Tolbukhin reached the outskirts of Buda on Christmas Eve and by 27 December the encircle-ment of the capital was complete. Szálasi, his cabinet and the rump Parliament had already left Budapest to set up shop in Sopron and Kőszeg, in western Hungary. The Minister of the Interior, Vajna, found time before departing to order the immediate renaming of all streets and squares named after eminent Jews. In Kőszeg, Ferenc Szálasi, impervious to the accelerating ruin of his country, settled down to compose his memoirs and political testament. Budapest, like Stalingrad before it, had acquired symbolic importance in the eyes of the two warring dictators. Stalin overrode the misgivings of the theatre commander, Marshal Malinovsky, and ordered the capture of the Hungarian capital before the general advance could be resumed; Hitler, for his part, rejected Hungarian pleas that Budapest should be declared an open city and ordered that *Festung Budapest* should be held to the last man.

The siege of Budapest began on 27 December, when Soviet forces cut the last two roads out of the capital, and lasted until 13 February; one of the great battles of the Second World War,* it was marked by appalling loss of life,** to the mili-

---

* Relatively unremarked by historians until the publication of Krisztián Ungváry's superb account in *Battle for Budapest: 100 days in World War II* (Budapest, 1998 and (trans.) London, 2005).
** The city was not evacuated; 38,000 civilians lost their lives, together with a similar number of Hungarian and German soldiers. The Red Army's casualties included some 80,000 dead.

tary on both sides and to the civilian population trapped in the capital, and by the physical destruction of most of the city. All the bridges linking Pest with Buda were destroyed. During the German commander's eleventh-hour attempt at a breakout, conducted on 11/12 February in defiance of his Führer's orders, over 19,000 German and Hungarian soldiers were killed and over 20,000 taken prisoner by the Russians.[28]

Meanwhile, developments were under way that would help to determine the political future of shattered Hungary. A pact, concluded in October 1944 between the revived Communist Party and the Social Democrats, designed to pave the way for a merger of the two parties after the war, was overtaken by events. On 20 November, on the joint initiative of Bajcsy-Zsilinszky (who had been released from internment by the Germans), the Communist László Rajk and anti–Nazi elements in the Hungarian army, a 'Committee of Liberation' had been formed to unite all anti–fascist parties and groups in an attempt to stimulate armed resistance to the Szálasi regime. Almost as soon as it had been constituted, the committee was betrayed by an *agent provocateur*. Bajcsy-Zsilinszky and his military collaborators—but not the Communists or other civilian participants—were hunted down and subsequently shot; but the surviving elements of the Committee—representatives of the Communist, Social Democratic, Independent Smallholders', National Peasants' and Citizens' Democratic Parties—assembled in Szeged under the aegis of two Hungarian 'Moscow' Communists, Ernő Gerő and Imre Nagy, to form the 'Hungarian Independence Front' (in succession to the earlier 'Hungarian Front'), whose National Committee would be regarded as the nucleus of a Soviet-sponsored Provisional Government of Hungary. The Front's programme called for land reform, extensive nationalisation and co-operation with the Western powers as well as with the Soviet Union. Horthy's armistice delegation—now led by the defecting Commander of the Hungarian First Army, General Béla Dálnoky Miklós—which since October had been watching events from Moscow with appalled apprehension, was now brought into play. Stalin proved to be surprisingly receptive to the concept of a broadly based, rather than wholly left-wing, provisional government in Hungary; indeed, at this stage he seemed concerned to ensure that the new government should not be regarded as Moscow's puppet.

The Hungarian armistice delegation accompanied Gerő and Nagy to Debrecen on 12 December 1944, in order to oversee the formation of a Provisional National Assembly, which would elect the new government. Orthodox elections were out of the question in the ravaged society the Red Army had left in its wake—and Hungary had not, in any case, experienced free elections for nearly two decades. The Provisional National Assembly consequently comprised representatives, chosen by repute and acclamation, from most of the municipalities and villages so far 'liberated' by Soviet forces. The Assembly's first meeting, held in Debrecen's Calvinist Collegium on 21 December, was attended by 230 delegates, of whom nearly one-third were Communists—reflecting the inevitable influence of the new occupying power; but all the erstwhile opposition parties were represented and the Provisional Government, which the Assembly elected on 22 December, covered most of the non-fascist political spectrum—three Communists, two each from the Independent Smallholders and Social Democrats and one member of the Peasants' Party. Two members of the armistice delegation, Faragho and Teleki, were included and its new leader, Béla Dálnoky Miklós, became Prime Minister. A Smallholder, János Gyöngyösi, received the Foreign Affairs portfolio and the former Chief of Staff, Vörös—the principal saboteur of Horthy's attempt to take Hungary out of the war but now, apparently, an enthusiast for the Soviet cause—became Defence Minister. In an inaugural Declaration, which clearly reflected Soviet drafting, the Provisional Government announced that it had broken once and for all with Hungary's German oppressors:

who have for centuries been subjugating the country and with the German alliance which has twice in the course of two generations plunged our fatherland into war, into national disaster. The Provisional National Government undertakes to compensate for the material damage which Hungary has caused by her war, waged against the Soviet Union and neighbouring peoples [and] makes every effort to establish good neighbourly relations and co-operation with all the surrounding democratic countries as well as with the United States and Great Britain; and sincere friendship with the Soviet Union, which is assisting our people in shaking off the German yoke.[29]

The Declaration went on to promise the repeal of all 'anti–democratic' laws; the dissolution of all fascist parties and organisations; rapid land reform, accompanied by the confiscation of the estates of traitors and members of the Volksbund; the restoration of the rights and liberties of the working class; and the inviolability of private property, which would remain 'the basis of the economic and social order of the country'. On 28 December, the Provisional Government formally declared war on Germany; its next duty was the conclusion of an armistice agreement with the Allies.

The armistice agreement, which had been agreed in negotiation between the Allies and which Gyöngyösi, on behalf of the Hungarian Provisional Government, signed in Moscow on 20 January 1945, contained no pleasant surprises. It obliged the Hungarian government to disarm and imprison all German forces remaining on Hungarian soil; to form and equip eight infantry divisions to serve under Soviet command; to release all prisoners of war and political prisoners; to guarantee freedom of movement to all Allied forces; and, inevitably, to withdraw all Hungarian military and administrative personnel from the recovered territories to the Hungarian side of the country's frontiers as they had been on 31 December 1937. The Vienna Awards were declared to be annulled. In addition, reparations in the form of goods to the value of $200 million were to be paid to the Soviet Union and $100 million-worth to Czechoslovakia and Yugoslavia. The armistice established an Allied Control Commission, chaired by Marshal Voroshilov, to direct the implementation of the agreement and oversee the work of the Provisional Government. This meant, in effect, that the new government could do nothing that did not have Moscow's prior approval. The Debrecen government was in any case virtually impotent, lacking as it did civil servants, money and transport. Only the Communists disposed of these administrative necessities; and it was no coincidence that the Provisional Government's first concrete achievement came from the Communist Minister of Agriculture, Imre Nagy, in the shape of a radical land reform which, at a stroke, transformed the countryside and Hungarian society.*

* See Chapter 17.

On 13 February 1945, Soviet forces completed their occupation of Budapest by seizing the Castle Hill: after nearly two months, the siege was over. Within a few weeks, the ravaged city began to come to life. The ghettos had been opened since mid-January, when the Russians occupied Pest. A pontoon bridge soon linked Pest with Buda; basic public services were in operation by the end of March; the dead were buried and the remains of the horses, whose meat had helped to keep many inhabitants of Buda alive during the siege, cleared from the streets. Although the Germans continued to fight stubbornly in western Hungary, the end was near. During the last week of March, Soviet forces took Székesfehérvár, Győr and Komárom. Szálasi and those of his colleagues who had not already fled or gone into hiding left Sopron for Austria, taking with them the Holy Crown and other coronation insignia. On 4 April, the last German military units left Hungary; nearly one million Hungarian soldiers and civilians went with them in order to escape the Red Army, whose advance across Hungary had been marked by virtually unrestrained rape and pillage. Hungary's ill-fated participation in the Second World War was over.

The war had cost Hungary 900,000 lives, of which 550,000 were Jewish. Six hundred thousand Hungarians, including 120,000 civilians, disappeared into captivity in the Soviet Union; half of them never returned.[30] Nearly half the country's national wealth had been destroyed or requisitioned, including 54 per cent of her industrial plant, 40 per cent of her railways and over half her livestock. All the prizes that had lured her into the Faustian pact with Hitler's Germany were lost. Worse, Hungary had forfeited the goodwill of the international community. At the Yalta Conference in February 1945, no voice was raised to mitigate her punishment, no concern expressed for her future. Churchill's informal understanding with Stalin that the West would retain a 50 per cent share of influence in Hungary (subsequently reduced to 25 per cent by Molotov with Eden's tacit agreement) was forgotten. The *fait accompli* of Soviet occupation was unchallenged. The year 1944–45 eclipsed the many previous tragedies and disasters in Hungary's history, perhaps excepting only the Mongol invasions of the thirteenth century. Hungary's will to survive had never faced a sterner test.

17

TWO FALSE DAWNS

(1945–56)

For the next decade, events in Hungary were largely determined by the priorities and policies of the Kremlin. By the autumn of 1944, when the conquest of eastern and central Europe by the Red Army was assured, Stalin had already decided on a differentiated policy towards the defeated or 'liberated' countries of the region. At the head of his list of priorities stood the immediate establishment of Soviet control over Poland, the crucial buffer zone between the Soviet Union and Germany, through the installation of a Soviet-sponsored government. Stalin had made progress towards achieving this objective at the Tehran Conference of the three Allies in 1943; he was to clinch it, overriding the feeble objections of his two Western partners, at the Yalta Conference early in 1945. Stalin was, nevertheless, concerned not to jeopardise his longer-term goal of securing Soviet hegemony over the whole of eastern Europe by pressing ahead too quickly in the other countries of the region. Stalin famously told Milovan Djilas: 'This war is not as in the past; whoever occupies a territory also imposes his own system as far as his army can reach: it cannot be otherwise'.[1] If the conversion of military occupation into overt political control were to be too brazen, however, the Western reaction might be hostile and the post-war co-operation an exhausted Soviet Union would need, put at risk.

In defeated Hungary, moreover, additional factors argued for caution: the extreme weakness of the indigenous Communist movement—the Hungarian Party could claim only around 2,500 members in 1944—and the pervasive hostility towards Communism that the Béla Kun experience had engendered. The Hungarian Communists who had spent years of exile in Moscow, and who were to be Stalin's instruments in 'liberated' Hungary, were therefore warned in 1944 that after returning to their homeland in the wake of the victorious Red Army they would have to co-operate with the bourgeois political parties, eschew any threat to private property and avoid any activity that might arouse Western concern. They would have to wait ten or even fifteen years for the creation of a 'dictatorship of the proletariat' in Hungary, which might come about only as the result of a major crisis in the capitalist system. In the meantime, Hungarian Communists should appear to be the soul of moderation and loyal members of a bourgeois-led coalition government. A secret instruction to Hungarian Party members in Moscow dated 12 November 1944 enjoined them: 'Leaders of the Party shall not thrust themselves into prominence; whenever possible, the party's objectives must be implemented through others, many times through another party'.[2]

This was the background to the formation of the Provisional Government and National Assembly in Debrecen, described at the end of the previous chapter. At grass-roots level, Hungarians were not fooled. As the writer Sándor Márai put it: 'A people that had already lived in servitude for so long seemed to know that their lot was not going to change: the old masters had left, and the new masters had arrived, and they would remain slaves as before'.[3]

An Illusion of Democracy

Initially, government by a coalition that embraced the entire Hungarian political spectrum (apart from outlawed fascists and their sympathizers)—Independent Smallholders (hereafter just Smallholders), Social Democrats (SDs), the National Peasants' Party (NPP) and Communists (HCP)—operated more smoothly than might have been expected. This was because all parties were agreed on the urgent necessity for radical change. The exigencies of war had frozen the social status quo in Hungary but comprehensive defeat shattered the mould. Although the land reform of 17 March 1945 was promulgated by a Communist Minister of Agriculture, Imre Nagy, it commanded the support of all parties in principle, even if there were differences over detail. Marshal Voroshilov in particular, at the head of the Allied Control Commission (ACC), demanded swift action on land reform in the belief that it would encourage mass desertion from Hungarian units, still engaged in bitter fighting alongside the Wehrmacht in western Hungary, by peasant soldiers anxious not to miss out on the redistribution. Under the reform decree, the government expropriated all estates of over 1,000 *hold* (slightly under 1,500 acres); the owners of estates of less than 1,000 *hold* were permitted to retain 100 *hold* if they were landowners in the traditional sense, 200 *hold* if they were peasants or 300 *hold* if they had been actively involved in anti–fascist resistance. Over 3,000 land-claimant committees, dominated by Communists and the NPP, implemented the redistribution, which was governed primarily by political considerations and paid scant regard to economic sense. Within three months, 5.6 million *hold* had been distributed, some of it to establish state farms and co-operatives; but the greater part (3.2 million *hold*) was parcelled out to over 642,000 dwarf-holders and landless peasants in small plots averaging 5 *hold* (7 acres)—much too small to be viable. The Communists defended the small size of the redistributed plots on the grounds that as many landless peasants as possible should become smallholders; critics of the reform, who included the American and British members of the ACC, suspected the Communists of deliberately ensuring that large numbers of smallholdings would fail, thus obliging their owners to join co-operatives.

The land reform transformed Hungarian society by destroying the erstwhile 'political class'—the gentry and the remnants of the aristocracy—and eliminating the elements of feudalism, which had persisted for longer in Hungary than anywhere else in Europe. The Catholic Church, which lost 90 per cent of its extensive estates, emerged with its economic and social influence greatly diminished. Hungarian society henceforth consisted of a relatively small bourgeois and professional class, significantly reduced by the disappearance of its large Jewish component; an impoverished rural class which included, even after the land reform, 300,000 landless peasants; and a growing urban proletariat. Against this social background the Communists, claiming credit for the land reform and enjoying the support of the occupying power, could look forward with confidence to the municipal and general elections that had been scheduled by the Provisional Government to take place in October and November respectively. The HCP had already concluded an electoral pact with the Social Democrats, under which the two parties would enter the elections on a joint ticket; and during the summer of 1945 the Communists conducted an energetic and indiscriminate campaign of recruitment, enrolling ex–Arrow Cross thugs as well as members of its more natural proletarian constituency, which increased its membership to 500,000 by October.

With the arrival of Mátyás Rákosi from Moscow in February 1945, the cast of the Communist leadership in Hungary was complete. Rákosi, then aged fifty-three, had been the acknowledged leader of the small group of Hungarian Communist exiles in Moscow during the war years and Stalin's personal backing made his installation as General Secretary of the HCP a foregone conclusion. The son of a Jewish village store-keeper, Rákosi showed great promise during his secondary education in Budapest and won a scholarship to study in Hamburg, after which he worked in London for a year as a clerk, adding knowledge of English to his German. Returning to Hungary on the outbreak of the First World War, Rákosi served in the Austro-Hungarian army on the Eastern Front until his capture in 1915 and emerged from a Russian prisoner-of-war camp in 1918 a convinced Communist and a fluent Russian speaker. After his repatriation, Rákosi threw himself into the revolutionary politics of Budapest and was rewarded with a junior post in Béla Kun's regime; fleeing the White Terror, with Kun, to Austria and then to Moscow, Rákosi found employment in the Comintern apparatus, played a significant role in helping to establish Communist Parties in western Europe and was arrested in 1925 while carrying out a Comintern mission in Hungary. Having served the resulting prison sentence, he was re-sentenced to life imprisonment by the Gömbös regime; but in 1940 Horthy consented to his extradition to the Soviet Union in partial exchange for the battle standards captured by the Russians in 1849.* A man of considerable intelligence, with a prodigious memory and an outstanding talent for languages, Rákosi was also a brutal, bullying sadist. Although he could deploy great charm when it suited him, his character was as unattractive as his squat, almost dwarfish appearance. His assumption of the leadership of the HCP in 1945 was an unmitigated misfortune for Hungary.

Three of Rákosi's principal lieutenants in the leadership of the HCP had shared the experience of exile in Moscow, and for longer periods. Ernő Gerő, a tall, ascetic and humourless economist, had joined the infant Hungarian Communist Party in 1918 and with the advent of the Horthy regime had been obliged to seek

* See page 385.

refuge in the Soviet Union. Like Rákosi, he had worked for the Comintern, mainly in Spain as a political instructor with the Spanish Communist Party during the Civil War; he had close connections with the NKVD* and was credited with grooming 'La Pasionaria' (Dolores Ibarruri), icon of the Spanish left, for political stardom. Mihály Farkas, a Slovak, had served his revolutionary apprenticeship in Prague with the Czechoslovak Communists, who sent him to Moscow for training; there, Farkas became an officer of the NKVD and, like Gerő, served in Spain, where his mission was to spy, and report, on Spanish Communists. A crude, boorish man, Farkas had no qualification for power save the love of it. József Révai, on the other hand, provided more intellectual ballast to the leadership; his role in the HCP was that of principal expositor and ideologue. A journalist by profession, Révai had served as Béla Kun's personal secretary and, in Moscow, as editor of Radio Moscow's broadcasts in Hungarian.

With Rákosi, these 'Muscovites' (as Communists returning to Hungary from exile in the Soviet Union were christened) comprised the 'quartet' that directed Hungary's affairs during the coming years of her greatest tribulation. Apart from considerable differences in personality, they had a great deal in common. Whether or not they were actually Soviet citizens, as some have claimed, their first loyalty was not to their Hungarian homeland but to the Soviet Union and Soviet Communism. They all had links with the NKVD, of which one of them had been a full member. Three of them had Soviet wives. All four were Jewish and had Magyarised their family names. It fell to them now to work with, and assert their authority over, the 'home Communists' whose different experience—that of underground work and frequent imprisonment in Horthy's Hungary—was reflected in a different mindset. The leading 'home communist', László Rajk, aged thirty-seven in 1945 and of Swabian (ethnic German) origin, had been active in the revolutionary movement since his student days and had then organised strikes in the construction industry; he served as political secretary to the Hungarian Battalion of the International Brigade in Spain and after the Republican defeat spent three years in internment in France. After escaping to Hungary in 1941, Rajk served several short prison terms but maintained his underground activities and campaigned against the war. Rajk's two brothers were prominent in the Arrow Cross movement—one of them, a member of Szálasi's government, is thought to have saved Rajk from execution after his last arrest in 1944. Rajk shared their anti–Semitism but nothing else: his Communist beliefs were fanatical, uncompromising and sympathetic to the promotion of the cause by violent means. His good looks, relative youth, courageous wife and, above all, his undeserved execution in 1949** have given him something akin to hero status in the eyes of many Hungarians; there is, however, no evidence that he would have been any less ruthless than Rákosi if his career had not been cut short. Of Rajk's fellow 'home Communists'—Géza Losonczy, Ferenc Donáth and, in particular, János Kádár—there will be more to say later in this narrative.

The 'home Communists', and Rajk in particular, found the restrictions imposed by Stalin on the HCP's political conduct hard to accept after the privations they

---

*The Soviet secret police, successor to the Cheka and predecessor to the KGB.
** See page 425.

had endured in the interests of the revolution. Révai tried to explain that 'England and America would not recognise a Communist government', adding pointedly:

'Those who want socialism and the dictatorship of the proletariat make the anti–German policy more difficult'.[4] Gerő, as soon as he arrived in Hungary, made the same point to the impatient 'home Communists': 'It is not a correct viewpoint to urge the construction of socialism on the rubble of defeat'.[5] As good Communists, Rajk, Kádár and their 'home' colleagues fell in behind the Party line conveyed from Moscow; but their patience was sorely tried by a situation in which collectivisation was taboo and in which, as a contemporary recalled:

The 'Short History' of the Bolshevik Party and many of the most militant and ruthless writings of Lenin and Stalin were not only not published in Hungarian, but were not sold in the bookshops in any other language either. The expression 'dictatorship of the proletariat' was severely forbidden. Those people who used it were denounced as reactionary trouble makers or stick-in-the-mud leftish deviationists.[6]

Despite the self-denying ordinance imposed upon them by Moscow, however, the Hungarian Communist Party, with the backing of Marshal Voroshilov, took prudent steps to ensure that it would be in a position rapidly to seize power as soon as Moscow allowed it to do so. In particular, the Communists took care to ensure that the Ministry of the Interior, and with it both the regular and the security police, were under their control. In the Provisional Government, the post of Minister of the Interior was held by Ferenc Erdei, nominally a member of the National Peasant Party but in fact an active Communist sympathiser. Erdei connived at the politicisation of the police force by the HCP and presided over the creation of a new body of secret security police, the ÁVO (*Államvédelmi Osztály* or State Defence Department). The ÁVO, a fateful addition to the Hungarian machinery of government, established itself in the former headquarters of the Arrow Cross Party at 60, Andrássy Avenue under a 'home' Communist, Gábor Péter, and at once set about its nominal task of bringing war criminals to justice but at the same time terrorising opponents of the HCP. Small but vicious pogroms took place near Budapest, in Gyömrő, where twenty-six people were killed, and also in Eger, Kaposvár and Kecskemét. The newly created People's Courts—instruments of the Communist Party as in other Soviet-occupied countries—engaged in an orgy of revenge and retribution, issuing a stream of sentences to internment, imprisonment and death: among those eventually executed were three former Prime Ministers (Bárdossy, Imrédy and Sztójay), Ferenc Szálasi and his entire cabinet.

Claiming credit for the land reform as well as for the restoration of food supplies to the capital (with the help of the Red Army), controlling the police and the enlarged state security apparatus, enjoying the active backing of the victorious army of occupation and disposing of greatly superior organisation and discipline, the Hungarian Communist Party approached the autumn elections with confidence. The HCP nevertheless laboured under several handicaps in addition to the deep-seated aversion of most Hungarians to Communism. The conduct of the Red Army had evoked widespread hatred and revulsion. Rákosi himself admitted in a letter to a former Comintern colleague, George Dimitrov: 'The excesses of the Red Army have become the Party's liability ... Cases of mass rape of women and robbery are repeated with the liberation of each region, as recently in Budapest too. Raids [in the streets] are being routinely conducted, in the course of which workers, some of them good party members, are taken to prisoner of war camps where they disappear'.[7] The activities of Gábor Péter's ÁVO, moreover, and the harsh sentences arbitrarily imposed by the newly established People's Courts—instruments of the Communist Party, as in other Soviet-occupied countries—aroused deep resentment, fear and hostility. The intervention, finally, of the formidable Catholic primate and Archbishop of Esztergom, József Mindszenty, made a significant impact. In a Pastoral Letter dated 1 November and read from the pulpits of every Catholic church in the land, Mindszenty declared:

that no Christian voter can support a party that rules by violence and oppression and that tramples underfoot all natural laws and human rights. Regretfully, we must agree with the British foreign minister who said that Hungary seems to have simply exchanged one totalitarian regime for another* ... Dear Catholic people, we call on you to vote only for those candidates who represent law, morality, order and justice ... There is only one way to vote in this election.[8]

In the event, these factors proved decisive. The autumn elections were the most free and democratic ever to be held in Hungary: the electoral law drawn up by the Provisional Government on the principles of universal, direct and secret suffrage enfranchised all Hungarians over the age of twenty; the vote was denied only to ethnic Germans and to anybody convicted or charged with pro-Nazi activities. In the municipal elections in Budapest, the natural constituency of the left, the Smallholders won 121 seats, eighteen more than the Communists and Social Democrats, who were running on a joint ticket. As a result, the Social Democrats insisted on fighting the forthcoming national elections independently, attributing their defeat in the capital to Communist unpopularity. When the national elections took place on 4 November 1945, however, the success of the Smallholders was even more emphatic: they secured 57 per cent of the vote, giving them 245 seats in the National Assembly, while the Social Democrats and Communists managed to win only just over 17 per cent each, giving them 69 and 70 seats respectively. The National Peasant Party secured 23 seats with 6.9 per cent of the vote and the Citizens' Democratic Party 2 with 1.6 per cent. The Smallholders could therefore command an overall majority of 81 seats in the Assembly and would have had no difficulty in forming a government by themselves, in accordance with normal democratic practice. In advance of the elections, however, the Smallholder leadership had buckled under pressure from Marshal Voroshilov, who—alerted by the municipal election results to the weakness of the Communist vote and having failed in his attempt to impose a single national list on the parties—had insisted that, whatever the outcome of the national elections, Hungary's government should continue to be an all-party coalition. Despite vigorous protests from the more courageous members of their rank and file, urging the formation of a purely Smallholder administration, Zoltán Tildy and Ferenc Nagy, respectively chairman and secretary of the Smallholders' Party, considered themselves bound by their earlier agreement.

* On 20 August 1945, Ernest Bevin had stated in the House of Commons, referring to Hungary: '... the impression we get from recent developments is that one kind of totalitarianism is being replaced by another'.

This was the first of many occasions on which the Smallholder leadership displayed reluctance or inability to stand up to Soviet pressure. Tildy, a Calvinist pastor, and Nagy, an intelligent and popular politician from a peasant family in southern Hungary, had together founded the Independent Smallholders' Party when they and their supporters had broken away from Count Bethlen's government party in 1930. They maintained active parliamentary opposition to Horthy's right-wing governments in the 1930s and early 1940s, were arrested by the Gestapo at the onset of the German occupation, worked underground after their release in October 1944, and then led the Smallholder group in the Provisional National Assembly in Debrecen. They were both honourable men, committed to the rebirth of a democratic Hungary and to promoting the interests of the rural population; but they considered it expedient to avoid confrontation with the Russian occupying power. They regarded any concessions to the Russians as temporary, and therefore unimportant, since they could be retrieved when the Soviet army withdrew from Hungary, as they assumed it would, following the signature of a Peace Treaty.

The protection of Hungarian interests during the deliberations of the Peace Conference in Paris and the negotiation of a final Peace Treaty had been a major preoccupation of both the Provisional Government and of the coalition under Tildy and Ferenc Nagy that succeeded it. The most pressing problem had arisen during the summer of 1945 in Czechoslovakia where President Beneš, having ingratiated himself with Stalin, exploited both Western guilt over Munich and Czechoslovakia's status as a victor power to extirpate the legacy of the Vienna Award in Slovakia. Beneš's obsessive hatred of the Habsburgs had survived their political demise and was now unleashed on the unfortunate Hungarians, whom Beneš regarded as representative of the Habsburg legacy. A succession of decrees by the government in Prague dismissed all ethnic Hungarians from public office without compensation or pension, confiscated all Hungarian-owned property of over 50 hectares, sequestered all Hungarian bank deposits and banned the use of the Hungarian language in any official or postal context. Hungarian appeals to the Allies fell on deaf ears, as did the Hungarian government's proposals for increased co-operation between the Danubian states and pleas for at least a modest revision of the Trianon frontiers to allow the repatriation of border regions with an overwhelmingly Hungarian population. The best that Gyöngyösi, the Smallholder Foreign Minister, could achieve, in an agreement concluded in February 1946, was an exchange of Hungary's small Slovak population for an equal number of Hungarians from Slovakia's much larger Hungarian community; the agreement left the balance of Hungarians marooned over the Czechoslovak border to fend for themselves in the face of Prague's continued persecution.* Visits to Moscow, Washington, London and Paris by Ferenc Nagy at the head of a government delegation that included Mátyás Rákosi, moreover, failed to make any impression on Allied insistence that the

---

* Hungary made her own contribution to the swelling tide of 'displaced persons' in Europe by expelling about 250,000 ethnic Germans, two-thirds of her Swabian population; Cardinal Mindszenty, himself of Swabian origin, campaigned vigorously against the expulsions and the United States protested—but to no avail.

Hungarian frontiers determined by Trianon should remain. The consequent perpetuation of the injustice of 1920 was the price Hungary had to pay for Horthy's failure to leave the war and thus escape the invidious status of 'Hitler's last ally'.

Adding insult to injury, the Peace Treaty Gyöngyösi signed in Paris on behalf of the Hungarian government on 10 February 1947 awarded three Hungarian villages opposite Bratislava to Czechoslovakia. Hungary's army was to be limited to 60,000 men and her air force to 5,000. The reduction of reparations payments from $300 million to $200 million in value represented the Allies' sole concession to Hungary. A clause that finally destroyed Ferenc Nagy's illusion that the Peace Treaty would bring the Soviet occupation of Hungary to an end stated that, following ratification, '... all Allied armed forces are to be withdrawn from Hungary within 90 days ... notwithstanding which the USSR shall maintain on Hungarian territory such armed forces as it may need for the Soviet army to maintain its lines of communication with the Soviet zone of occupation in Austria'.[9] The treaty also provided, of course, for the disbanding of the Allied Control Commission. In his final report the Head of the British Military Mission, Major General Edgcumbe, opined: 'Hungarians are on the whole very pleasant people, and in many respects highly cultured. They generally give the impression of being efficient and hard-working. Apart from outside influences, if they could think less about politics and their past, they should be capable of becoming a true democracy'.[10] Unfortunately, 'outside influences' had no intention of being 'apart' or of allowing Hungary to realise her democratic potential. The repeated concessions Tildy, Nagy and their Smallholder colleagues made in the face of pressure from the HCP, backed as it was by the occupying power and by the threat of violence in the streets, enabled the Communists to establish a stranglehold on the political process that would not be loosened for many years to come.

An important test of Smallholder resolve took place immediately after the party's victory in the elections of November 1945. After the completion of interparty negotiations on the distribution of portfolios in a coalition government, to be headed by Zoltán Tildy as Prime Minister, the Communists, backed by Marshal Voroshilov, threatened to withdraw from the coalition unless the Ministry of the Interior—already earmarked for the Smallholders—was reallocated to their party. Fearing that the Social Democrats and the NPP would follow the Communist lead, leaving the Smallholders to govern alone, Tildy, Nagy and even Béla Kovács, the usually robust secretary-general of the Smallholders' Party, gave way, thereby enabling the HCP to set about assembling the machinery of terror soon to dominate the Hungarian political landscape. The Western members of the Control Commission made no attempt to intervene in what they chose to regard as an internal Hungarian matter. The final composition of the government gave the Smallholders nine posts, including the Premiership, the Social Democrats and Communists four each and the NPP one. Once they had secured the Ministry of the Interior, now headed by Imre Nagy, the Communists were quite content with this. As József Révai later recalled: 'We were a minority in parliament and in the government, but at the same time we represented the leading force. We had decisive control over the police forces. Our force, the force of our Party and the working class, was multiplied by the fact that the Soviet Union and the Soviet army were always there to support us with their assistance'.[11]

On 1 February 1946, the National Assembly approved Law I (1946), which abolished the institutions of monarchy and established the Republic of Hungary. The new constitution created a Presidency, to which Zoltán Tildy was elected, and guaranteed individual rights and liberties. In the reshuffled government, Ferenc Nagy became Prime Minister and László Rajk replaced Imre Nagy at the Ministry of the Interior. The formal appearance of democratic freedoms in the new republic, however, were quickly exposed as a sham. The Communists embarked on a deliberate campaign to destroy the Smallholder majority. Voroshilov ordered the arrest of two Smallholder deputies who had opposed, in the Assembly, the immediate proclamation of a republic; and on 11 March the HCP announced the formation of a Left-Wing Bloc, embracing the Social Democrats, NPP and the Trade Unions in alliance with the Communists. The Bloc's first initiative, reinforced by street demonstrations, was to demand the expulsion from their party of twenty Smallholder deputies who were accused of holding reactionary views, evinced in their opposition to coalition with the Communists; Ferenc Nagy and his colleagues in the Smallholder leadership meekly acceded to this demand, in the interests, as Nagy subsequently claimed, of averting domestic disorder. One of those expelled, the prominent Smallholder Dezső Sulyok, formed with his fellow expellees a new opposition party, the Hungarian Freedom Party (*Magyar Szabadság Párt*). The Smallholders also acquiesced in the passage by the National Assembly of Law VII (1946), which established draconian penalties for any political activity or propaganda held to threaten the republic. Nagy did summon up the courage to challenge the predominance the Communists had established for themselves and their sympathisers in the bureaucracy, army and police; but his efforts foundered on the implacable opposition of László Rajk, who presided during 1946 over a creeping purge of so-called 'right-wing elements' from the public service, evicting some 60,000 officials from their posts. Planted evidence near the scene of the murder of a Russian officer in Budapest provided the pretext for Rajk's dissolution of the Catholic Youth Association; in succeeding months over two hundred social organisations, including the Boy Scouts and the National Association of Young Farmers' Clubs, suffered the same fate.

The Communists began their final assault on the Smallholders' Party early in 1947. Amid fanfares in the left-wing press, Rajk exposed an alleged conspiracy against the republic led by a group called the 'Hungarian Brotherhood Community' in which, Rajk claimed, leading Smallholders including two government ministers were involved. A number of arrests were made and subsequent interrogations duly implicated the Communists' real target: Béla Kovács. After submitting to interrogation—on the advice of Ferenc Nagy, anxious as ever to avoid a confrontation—Kovács was arrested by the Russians, in contemptuous defiance of protests by the Western members of the ACC, and whisked away to the Soviet Union, where the NKVD extorted a 'confession' and imprisoned him. This episode, which awakened the international community to the true state of affairs in Hungary, also precipitated the disintegration of the Smallholders' Party. In protest against the leadership's acquiescence in the abduction of Kovács, a junior minister, Zoltán Pfeiffer, led some fifty Smallholder deputies into opposition to form the

Hungarian Independence Party (*Magyar Függetlenségi Párt*). Ferenc Nagy, holidaying in Switzerland in May, was bullied into resigning the Premiership by Rákosi, over the telephone, with thinly veiled threats to his wife and young son; he never returned to Hungary.

Having virtually disposed of the Smallholders by what quickly came to be known as 'salami tactics',* the Communists turned to the ballot box to legitimise their de facto hegemony. As a necessary preliminary, the Leftist Bloc forced the passage through the National Assembly of Law XXII (1947), which disenfranchised every individual named in Rajk's 'B List' of suspected fascist collaborators, the entire ethnic German (Swabian) community and all Hungarian immigrants from Slovakia. These measures removed about 500,000 anti–Communist voters from the electoral roll. Naked threats to break up its meetings by mob violence compelled Dezső Sulyok to dissolve his Freedom Party; he fled abroad shortly afterwards. Elections had been called for 31 August, when many voters could be expected to be on holiday; in order to exploit this situation, László Rajk arranged for the printing of an excess quantity of 'blue slips'—the voting papers that enabled those holding them to vote in constituencies other than their own. 'Blue slips' were then issued to squads of Communist supporters who careered round the country on polling day in lorries and on motorbikes, casting votes for Communist candidates in selected constituencies. Despite this blatant fraud and other manipulations, which gained it as many as 300,000 votes,[12] the HCP increased its vote by only 5 per cent, to 22.3 per cent. The Social Democrats actually polled fewer votes than in 1945; but the Smallholders' vote shrank even more dramatically—from 57 per cent to 15.4 per cent—and although the new anti–Communist parties made a strong showing, the provision in the new electoral law for national as well as constituency mandates favoured the leftist coalition in terms of seats in the Assembly. The Leftist Bloc eventually commanded 271 (66 per cent) of the Assembly's 411 seats. The Communists nevertheless allowed the former Prime Minister, the pliant Smallholder Lajos Dinnyés, to form a new government in which the Leftist Bloc took the lion's share of cabinet posts. The Communists were now poised finally to dissolve the mirage of democracy in post-war Hungary.

Dictatorship and Terror

In September 1947, leading members of the European Communist Parties were summoned by the Soviet leadership to assemble in the small Polish health resort of Szklarska Poręba, in the hills of Silesia. Révai and Farkas represented the HCP. The Marshall Plan had been launched during the summer and Stalin, through his emissaries Malenkov and Zhdanov, had decided to lay down a new line for Communist Parties to follow in response to what he perceived to be a dangerous challenge from the West designed to undermine Soviet hegemony in eastern Europe. Proclaiming the division of the world into two camps, Zhdanov in effect took the assembled Communist leaders to task for obeying Stalin's earlier policy of restraint

---

* Both Rákosi and the Smallholder Zoltán Pfeiffer claimed to have originated this description of the process of destroying political opponents slice by slice.

and coalition. The Yugoslavs, who had flouted this policy by seizing power, were singled out for praise and held up as the example to be followed. The newly established Cominform was to have its headquarters in Belgrade. No effort should now be spared in transforming the societies and economies of the 'liberated' countries of Central and Eastern Europe in conformity with the Soviet model. In an attempt to deflect Zhdanov's strictures from Hungary, Révai boasted of the extent to which the HCP had penetrated both the machinery of government and the other non-bourgeois parties; Pfeiffer's Hungarian Independence Party, he promised, would pay for its success in the recent election—it would be destroyed 'by police action'.

Rákosi and Rajk lost no time in giving effect to Révai's promise. In October 1947, the ÁVO unleashed a vicious campaign of blackmail and coercion against both the Hungarian Independence Party and the Catholic Democratic People's Party; as a result of confessions extracted under torture or simply forged, 106 of the 109 deputies who had been elected to represent the two parties in the Assembly resigned their mandates and, in most cases, emigrated. Communists replaced them. Rákosi and his lieutenants next turned their attention to the Social Democratic Party; at the party's congress in March 1948, the Communist-influenced left wing turned on the centre, expelled the moderate leadership, including the popular Anna Kéthly, and obediently called for a full merger of the party with the HCP. The merger was formalised at a joint congress of the two parties on 12 June, which gave birth to the Hungarian Workers' Party (*Magyar Dolgozók Pártja*, HWP). Some 200,000 Social Democrats were either expelled from their former party or decided to leave it; many chose exile. The HCP, too, made the merger the occasion for a thoroughgoing purge of its own ranks, withholding new party cards from over 100,000 former comrades. Although the fellow-travelling remnants of the Smallholders and National Peasants' Parties were allowed to survive, subject to their good behaviour as loyal components of the Hungarian People's Independence Front—the umbrella organisation created in 1949—Hungary had in reality become a one-party state. Under a new constitution promulgated on 20 August* 1949, Hungary also became a 'People's Republic', defined by Rákosi as 'a dictatorship of the proletariat without the Soviet form'.

The new Hungarian constitution, closely modelled on that of the Soviet Union and virtually identical to those of the other 'people's democracies' of central and eastern Europe, assigned to the Hungarian Workers' Party (HWP), the 'advance guard of the working class', the leading role in the political, economic and social life of the nation. The government, headed by a Prime Minister as chairman of a Council of Ministers, became merely the executive instrument of the Party, the sole repository of power. The Party hierarchy consisted of a Party Congress at its base, to which the membership elected representatives on a local and institutional basis; a Central Committee of about seventy members, elected by the Congress; a Political Committee or Politburo, averaging a dozen members, elected by the Central Committee; and, in Hungary's case, a small group of three or four within

---

* 20 August, hitherto St. Stephen's Day, and Hungary's principal national holiday, now became 'Constitution Day'; the other major holiday, 4 April, marked the 'liberation' of Hungary by the Red Army.

the Politburo (Rákosi, Gerő, Farkas and occasionally Révai), which in effect held a monopoly of power so long as it commanded a majority in the Politburo.

The status of the National Assembly was reduced to that of a rubber stamp: meeting for very short sessions twice or three times a year, it converted into laws the decrees its own Presidium or the Council of Ministers had already issued and which already had the force of law. Composed, as it was, entirely of HWP members and fellow-travellers, the Assembly's votes were invariably unanimous. The Chairman of the Assembly's Presidium, a post occupied by the fellow-travelling Social Democrat Árpád Szakasits (who had succeeded Zoltán Tildy as President when the latter was forced out of office in July 1948) until 1950 and then by the alcoholic Smallholder István Dobi, carried out the functions of a head of state.

During the period from mid-1947 to late 1948—'the year of the turning point' (*'a fordulat éve'*) as HWP propagandists subsequently christened it—the exercise of Soviet power in Hungary became more open and proactive. Every government ministry, in which Hungarian Communists already monopolised the key posts, received its quota of Soviet 'advisers'. Around two thousand officers of the Soviet NKVD were attached to the ÁVO, renamed 'State Security Authority' (*Állam-védelmi Hatóság—ÁVH*) in September 1948. Under the direction of Farkas, as Minister of Defence, the Hungarian army and air force were remodelled according to the Soviet pattern; Soviet 'advisers' worked alongside HWP political officers in every army unit down to regimental level. On Soviet orders, and in defiance of the Peace Treaty, the Hungarian army grew between 1948 and 1951 from 70,000 to over 300,000 men, an expansion which necessitated the conscription of all eighteen-year-olds for three years' service. Officers who had served in Horthy's army, indispensable during the immediate post-war years, were progressively purged—many faced the firing squad—to be replaced by hastily trained youngsters from proletarian or peasant origins. No effort was spared to replace national loyalty by loyalty to the Soviet Union, liberator and ally. Nowhere was this imperative more implacably followed than within the Hungarian Workers' Party itself.

There was extraordinary irony in the fact that just a few months after the Yugoslav Communist Party had been held up to European comrades at Szklarska Poręba as a shining example to all builders of socialism, the Yugoslav leadership became the target for vitriolic condemnation by Moscow for alleged 'nationalist deviation', denigration of the Soviet Union and other offences against the Communist canon. Tito had succeeded too well for Stalin's liking: unlike the other 'people's democracies', Yugoslavia had liberated herself from Nazi Germany by her own efforts, without the help of the Red Army, and on this foundation Tito had established a Communist dictatorship that placed Belgrade's interests above Moscow's. Apprehensive that this example might prove attractive to other Communist regimes, Stalin, through the Cominform, pronounced an anathema on Tito and all his works in June 1948. The impact of the resulting crisis on Hungary, as on the other Soviet satellites, was immediate and devastating. Not only did the HWP have to demonstrate its loyalty to Moscow and be seen to cleanse itself of any Titoist or nationalist taint; but the crisis also provided Rákosi with a context within which he could act without restraint to consolidate his personal position and eliminate any potential threat to it from within the Party. After the Szklarska Poręba meeting, Rákosi had feared that László Rajk might use its outcome to claim that he, the radical activist, had been right to jib against Rákosi's Moscow-imposed policies of gradualism and coalition politics; after inspiring criticism of Rajk in the Politburo, therefore, Rákosi transferred him from the Ministry of the Interior to the much less powerful post of Minister of Foreign Affairs. The Yugoslav crisis now gave Rákosi a pretext for more drastic action, in which Farkas, who saw Rajk as a rival for the eventual succession to Rákosi, was his eager accomplice. On 30 May 1949, ÁVH officers arrested Rajk at his home; on 16 June he was expelled from the HWP. Some days earlier, a selection of party and government officials had been taken into custody, for the sole purpose of being tortured into making confessions which would implicate Rajk in the crimes of which he now stood accused: co-operating with Regent Horthy's secret police, espousing 'populism', spying for the imperialists and maintaining a secret liaison with Yugoslav Communists. When Rajk, despite days and nights of interrogation and torture, continued to maintain his innocence, Rákosi instructed János Kádár, now Minister of the Interior and Rajk's closest friend, to persuade him to confess to his misdeeds, for the good of the Party, with the promise of acquittal and safe conduct to exile in the Soviet Union. Rajk agreed to co-operate, partly to protect his wife who had been arrested with him. His trial, one of the first of a series of 'show trials' in Hungary and elsewhere in east-central Europe, opened on 16 September, under the stage-management of NKVD General Belkin; he was found guilty on all counts and executed a month later. Kádár, as the responsible Minister, was obliged to attend the execution: according to one account by a contemporary, Rajk spotted his former friend and shouted from the scaffold: 'This is not what you promised me …János, you have betrayed me'.[13] Whether this happened or not, there is no doubt that the whole episode made an indelible and corrosive impression on Kádár, which remained with him for the rest of his life.

Estimates of the number of victims of the reign of terror over which Rákosi presided between 1949 and 1953 vary, but it is certain that at least three-quarters of a million Hungarians were charged with offences against the state; of those found guilty—about half—over 200,000 underwent imprisonment, internment or forced labour. The death toll included not only some two thousand sentenced to execution but many more who failed to survive torture at the hands of the ÁVH or the privations of the camps. A process of continuous purge within the HWP itself targeted, first, virtually all the former Social Democrats in the Party's ranks—Szakasits was sentenced to life imprisonment—and then many of the 'home Communists', like Rajk veterans of underground work against Horthy and the Nazis, including János Kádár, who was arrested in 1951. His successor at the Ministry of the Interior, Sándor Zöld, fearing that criticism from Rákosi at a Politburo meeting presaged his own arrest, committed suicide after first killing his wife and children. His case was far from unique: under the pall of terror, suicides were common. In the summer of 1951, as part of a brutal drive to rid the capital of all whose class origins were suspect, some 15,000 people suffered expulsion from their homes and deportation to villages in the Alföld, where they were put to work as farm labourers; most of the deportees were surviving members of noble or gentry families and included former army generals, government ministers and industrialists. Party members moved into their vacant houses and apartments. A Social Democrat, himself a victim of the purge, recalled:

Every night was spent in horror and panic: at the sound of any fast motor-car or lorry after midnight the guessing started: 'Whose turn is it now?' The fast motor-cars took the victims to the ÁVO headquarters; the lorries took them to deportation camps ... In the deportation camps, as in the prisons and internment camps, the inmates were kept in appalling conditions, fed on swill and refuse. The former upper and middle classes ... were branded in an openly racist spirit: schoolchildren had their 'class background' marked in their documents and the child with the former 'exploiter's' blood in his veins was expelled from higher education and frequently pilloried in front of other children for the 'crimes' of his parents or grandparents.[14]

In a Hungary in which every vestige of democracy had been eliminated, every spark of free expression extinguished and nearly every link with the West severed, the Hungarian Workers' Party ruled unchallenged. In the elections of May 1949, its creature, the misleadingly named Hungarian Independence Front (*Magyar Függetlenségi Népfront* or *Népfront* for short) won 96.27 per cent of the votes cast by 96.04 per cent of the electorate; in 1953, the Front, throwing credibility to the winds, did even better, securing 98.2 per cent of the vote from 98 per cent of the electorate. Equipped with this monopoly of power, the HWP addressed the task of recasting the Hungarian economy and Hungarian society in the Soviet image.

A Land of Iron and Steel

The Second World War had left the Hungarian economy in ruins. In addition to the massive destruction of its infrastructure, compounded by ruthless Russian confiscations of raw materials and machinery, Hungary had been saddled with the burden of feeding and quartering 1.5 million Soviet troops until 1946 and 500,000 thereafter. The reparations imposed by the armistice agreement could be financed only by increasing the money supply, which soon resulted in the highest rate of inflation ever recorded. In October 1945, paper money with a face value of 106 billion *pengő* was in circulation, a figure that rose to 34 trillion in the spring of 1946 and to 47.4 quadrillion by July that year: this equated to an inflation rate of 10–12 per cent *per hour*. Only gold (and the US dollar) retained its value: many wedding rings were exchanged for a few days' food supply. Two measures rescued Hungary from a disastrous predicament that had imposed immense hardship on a population already oppressed by the human and physical losses inflicted by war and defeat. The first was the restoration to Hungary, by the United States, of the National Bank's gold reserves, which the Nazis had carried off to Germany in 1944; the second, the currency reform of August 1946, which created the forint. The new currency, issued at the rate of one gold forint for 4 trillion paper *pengő*, stabilised the financial situation remarkably quickly. The Provisional Government and the coalition that succeeded it in November 1945, could also claim credit for other positive developments. By mid-1946, over half the bridges blown up by the retreating Wehrmacht had been repaired, and Budapest's Liberty Bridge (*Szabadság Híd*) rebuilt; over 80 per cent of the country's rail track had been restored and rail traffic had achieved 50 per cent of its pre-war level; the coal mines, drained of flood water, were producing coal at 90 per cent of pre-war output. While government ministers and the civil service were entitled to their fair share of the credit for Hungary's recovery, much of it was due to the energy and resilience of the workforce: in the Ganz rolling stock works, for example, a workers' committee operated the plant for several months without pay and work continued on the shop floor on the same basis.

The Communists, however, seized control of the levers of the economy at a very early stage. Already in August 1945, Ernő Gerő, as Minister of Commerce in the Provisional Government, had concluded a trade and co-operation agreement with the Soviet Union that not only gave that country a virtual monopoly of Hungary's foreign trade (American and British protests were brushed aside) but also provided for the creation of Soviet-Hungarian joint companies, with tax–free status, which soon gave the Russians a dominant position in Hungary's bauxite and aluminium industry, in Danube shipping, in civil aviation and in the Hungarian oil industry. As 1945 ended, the HCP succeeded in persuading the Prime Minister, Ferenc Nagy, to sanction the creation of a Supreme Economic Council of which he would be the titular chairman but which would in fact be controlled by its Muscovite Communist secretary, Zoltán Vas. The Council, through a stream of decrees that had the force of law, regulated most areas of the economic life of the country and used its power progressively to reduce the size of the private sector. In parallel, the Bureau of Reparations—also under Communist control—established direct control of the industrial sector, purchasing two-thirds of its output for onward delivery to the Soviet Union. An artificially low exchange rate, imposed by the Russians, for the forint against the US dollar ensured that the volume of compulsory deliveries under the $200 million ceiling was cripplingly large: state purchases from the Manfred Weiss metallurgical plant accounted for 95 per cent of its output. As the Communist stranglehold on the coalition government tightened, so the assault on the private sector accelerated: the coal mines were taken into state ownership in July 1946; the Salgótarján Iron Works, the Manfred Weiss Steel and Metal Works, the Ganz locomotive and rolling stock plants and the Győr Wagon and Engineering Plant followed them in November; and in September 1947 it was the turn of the ten principal banks. By the latter date, 58 per cent of Hungary's industry and credit institutions had been nationalised. After the Szklarska Poręba meeting, the pace quickened further within the framework of a Three-Year Reconstruction Plan: in March 1948, all enterprises employing more than a hundred workers were taken into state ownership, without compensation, and at the end of 1949 the same fate befell all firms employing more than ten. By the end of 1950, the private sector of the Hungarian economy—apart from agriculture—had virtually ceased to exist.

Initially, during the period of the Three-Year Plan, these and other measures appeared to produce positive results and, apart from those dispossessed, probably enjoyed a broad measure of popular support. By 1948, industrial and infrastructural investment had increased from 3.7 per cent of national income (1945–46) to 22 per cent. In 1949, industrial production per capita had risen to 123 per cent of its pre-war level. The unveiling of the first Five-Year Plan, however, inaugurated a period of madness in economic policy—the mindless application of the Soviet model to Hungary—which inflicted lasting damage on the country and acute hardship on her population. It was driven in part, in Hungary as elsewhere in the Soviet bloc, by the conviction emanating from Moscow that a third world war could be expected before the end of the decade. Gerő, heading the newly established Council for the National Economy, proclaimed that Hungary had to become 'a land of iron and steel ... the fundamental issue of our Five-Year Plan is to develop our output of iron and steel at a tempo for which there is no precedent in the history of Hungarian industry'.[15] Determined to merit the title awarded him by the Party propaganda machine, that of 'Stalin's best pupil', Rákosi embarked on a programme of accelerated industrialisation that gave absolute priority to heavy industry. The level of investment laid down by the Plan, which came into effect on 1 January 1950, was already high at nearly 60 billion forints; but two upward revisions increased this to over 80 billion forints. During the period of the Plan, investment—of which heavy industry took the lion's share—increased twice as fast as national income, at the expense both of consumption and of agriculture. A crash programme to expand the production of iron and steel, in a country that (thanks to Trianon) lacked both iron ore and coking coal, grossly distorted Hungary's pattern of trade by necessitating disproportionate imports of those raw materials. The symbol of this policy, the new 'steel town' of Sztálinváros* on the Danube, became the showpiece of Communist Hungary for the next thirty-five years—despite being at least twenty-five years out of date at birth, modelled as it was on American plants of the 1920s. Other distortions imposed or encouraged by the planning regime were common to all socialist economies, including the Soviet Union itself. The emphasis on growth in volume, with attendant incentives to exceed centrally determined targets regardless of quality or marketability, encouraged factories to produce vast quantities of unsaleable—and in particular unexportable—goods. Between 1952 and 1954, the state-owned industries increased their production by 12.7 per cent; but stocks of unsaleable finished products rose by 72 per cent.[16] Unsaleable goods and uncompleted projects accounted for up to 20 per cent of national income during the Rákosi years. Gerő himself complained in 1951: 'As far as quality is concerned, the situation is absolutely intolerable. In 1945, 1946, 1947 and 1948, when we had far less means, when our economy was much weaker, there were not so many and such basic complaints against the quality of our export goods'.[17]

Attempts to remedy a situation in which, typically, 25 per cent of manufactured goods were rejected by inspectors or by the market resulted in a massive proliferation of regulations and controls, which in turn inflated the economic bureaucracy. In 1941, the ratio of blue-collar to white-collar workers had been 9:1; by 1953 it had become 4:1. The crude objective of growth for growth's sake was nevertheless achieved: by 1953, the industrial sector was growing at an annual rate of 20 per cent and during the Plan period the output of most metallurgical products doubled or even, in the case of aluminium, trebled. The industrial workforce grew by nearly half a million, an increase that eliminated urban unemployment and involved a significant transfer of population from the countryside into the towns.

In the industrial sector, therefore, there were a few short-term gains—at least on paper—to set against the adverse consequences of the Rákosi regime's policies, which in any case took longer to become apparent. In the countryside, however, the impact of Rákosi's treatment of agriculture was unrelievedly catastrophic. Although the ultimate Communist objective, in imitation of the Soviet

---

* Subsequently rechristened Dunaújváros.

example, was the total collectivisation of agriculture, this had to be soft-pedalled during the immediate post-war years. As in industry, however, Szklarska Poręba marked a watershed. Although a conference of the HWP in July 1948 had concluded—partly as a result of interventions by Imre Nagy—that Hungary's rural economy was not yet amenable to wholesale collectivisation and that the Party should continue to proceed cautiously, Rákosi announced a month later the inauguration of a programme of mass collectivisation, which would eliminate private farming within four years. Introducing the first Five-Year Plan, Gerő confirmed that 'one of the basic aims [of the Plan] is to lay down the foundation of socialism in the economy as a whole, not only in the towns but in the villages as well'.[18] But, ironically, land reform, for which the Party so eagerly claimed credit, had the effect of enhancing the proprietorial instincts of the peasantry and of increasing its natural resistance to collectivisation. Despite the regime's resort to forcible eviction and terror, co-operative farms replaced peasant holdings at only a very slow rate: 468 in 1948, 1,300 by the end of 1949, 5,224 by mid-1953. This last figure still represented only 26 per cent of Hungary's arable land. Vicious persecution of the 'kulaks', as peasants owning more than 25 *hold* were stigmatised in imitation of Stalinist terminology, alienated the entire peasant class. Many peasants abandoned the land altogether and migrated to the towns, leaving over 3 million *hold* of arable land uncultivated. Those who remained and resisted collectivisation were subjected to penal taxation and the burden of ever-rising compulsory deliveries of agricultural produce to the state at ever less favourable prices: in 1952, for example, agricultural prices fell by 10 per cent while the price of the manufactures peasant households needed rose by 37 per cent. In 1952, the combination of drought with draconian delivery requirements left two-thirds of peasant families with insufficient grain for sowing in the following spring and brought them to the brink of starvation. These policies had a disastrous effect on production, which in the case of wheat and wine fell substantially below pre-war levels, thereby necessitating imports Hungary could ill afford. The dismissal of agronomists who did not meet the regime's class criteria and the consequent neglect of research and modernisation, together with an acute shortage of tractors and other machinery, contributed to a critical situation in the countryside and to bitter discontent among a peasantry whose expectations of a better life had been raised by the land reform.

Rákosi's Hungary

Resentment of the Rákosi regime was by no means confined to the countryside. The period of the Three-Year Plan had seen a modest improvement in the standard of living of most of the urban population. The crash programme of industrialisation and soaring levels of capital investment, at the expense of consumption, threw this process into reverse from 1950 onwards. By 1952, real incomes had fallen on average to 66 per cent of their pre-war level. A 'reform' of wages and prices in 1951 increased wages by an average of 20 per cent but raised prices by between 50 and 100 per cent—the average price of consumer goods increased by 88 per cent over 1949 levels. The impoverishment of the urban workforce was made more acute by the compulsory purchase of state bonds—the so-called

'Peace Loan'—by enforced contributions to politically correct causes, such as aid to North Korea during the Korean War, and by compulsory subscriptions to Party newspapers and journals. These levies absorbed as much as 5 per cent of a weekly wage. Although rents were low, the shortage of urban housing, exacerbated by the influx of migrating peasants, became acute; fulfilment of the Five-Year Plan's target for the building of 217,000 new apartments fell short by 50 per cent, contributing to a shortfall of 340,000 apartments nation-wide. Inadequately maintained, the existing housing stock fell increasingly into disrepair. Many imported goods disappeared from the shops—citrus fruits, bananas and chocolate among them. Clothing was of poor quality and in short supply; endless queueing for bread, meat and other foodstuffs sapped energy and morale. Factory workers already in a state of permanent exhaustion were often obliged to leave their over-crowded apartments at 4.30 a.m. in order to reach their workplaces in time for the compulsory daily briefing on the contents of the Party newspaper, *Szabad Nép* ('Free People'). At the end of a working day made more gruelling by the progressive introduction of piece-work, they were frequently compelled to attend 'political education' classes until nine or ten o'clock in the evening. As in the other 'people's democracies' and in the Soviet Union itself, the trade unions ceased to represent the interests of the working class, becoming mere transmission belts for the Party's injunctions and propaganda.

The national environment in which the Hungarian people, urban workers and peasants alike, suffered these material privations had become arid and oppressive. In the field of education, as in others, the immediate post-war period had held out considerable promise. As early as April 1945, a National Council for Public Education, of which such leading cultural figures as Albert Szent-Györgyi, Gyula Szekfű and Zoltán Kodály were members, oversaw the completion of the reform of primary education that had been launched in 1940. Dezső Keresztury, the talented and energetic Minister of Education in both the post-war coalition governments, presided over the introduction of a single institution of primary education, the 'general school' (*általános iskola*) in which pupils spent four years on the 'three Rs' followed by a further four in which scientific and arts subjects were added to the curriculum. By the time implementation of the reform had been completed in 1949, however, politics had invaded the classroom, reducing the number of teachers by the rigid application of class criteria and distorting the curriculum to reflect Communist objectives. Primary education had also been the arena for a decisive showdown between the state and the Catholic Church, which until 1948 had maintained its control of a majority of primary and general schools. The Catholic Primate, Cardinal Mindszenty, defied the law passed in 1948, which established state control over 6,500 denominational schools by forbidding 18,000 Catholic teachers to become employees of the state. Mindszenty also organised a mass protest by Catholic parents against the secularisation of education, banned the use of new textbooks for even secular subjects, excommunicated Catholic civil servants involved in the reform and ordered priests and nuns to withdraw from the schools in which they gave religious instruction. From the summer of 1948, Mindszenty became the prime target for excoriation and slander by the government's propaganda machine; in December, he was arrested and, in February 1949, tried, in the first of Hungary's show trials, on charges of espionage and conspiracy against the state—offences to which he confessed after being drugged and beaten. Mindszenty, a brave but arrogant and rigid man, was sentenced to life imprisonment and thus acquired martyr status in and beyond the Catholic community worldwide.

Mindszenty's arrest inaugurated a concerted campaign by the HWP to eliminate the authority and influence of the Catholic and Protestant Churches of Hungary. In 1949, as soon as Mindszenty's trial had opened, the Catholic-supported Democratic People's Party dissolved itself and its leader, Barankovics, fled into exile; during the summer of 1950, following the arrests of large numbers of Catholic priests and the forcible closure of monasteries and convents, the Catholic episcopate undertook, in return for the government's promise of freedom of religion, publicly to endorse government policies. A year later, Archbishop József Grősz, Mindszenty's successor as head of the Catholic Church in Hungary, was arrested, tried and sentenced to fifteen years' imprisonment. The ÁVH thereupon took virtual control of all religious activity in Hungary: through the Office of Church Affairs, it used compliant clergy, the so-called 'peace priests', to monitor the activities of bishops and parish priests, open their mail and censor their sermons. The Protestant Churches, similarly, suffered a purge of their leadership and the imprisonment of many priests and pastors. Although Hungarians were still able to attend places of worship, their attendance was monitored and could adversely affect their secular lives.

Higher education suffered even more than primary and secondary education from the Party's determination to ensure proletarian purity in both the staff and student body of Hungary's universities. Large numbers of academics, including several scholars of international renown, lost their posts; would-be students who could not prove impeccably proletarian or peasant origins found that universities and colleges were closed to them. Lectures on Marxism-Leninism became compulsory for all students, translations of Soviet textbooks replaced their Hungarian equivalents and all Western books and journals were eliminated from university libraries; the magnificent library of the Academy of Sciences was purged of 4,000 volumes. The number of those admitted to higher education rocketed, reaching five times the level of attendance pre-war; but academic standards collapsed, both because a high proportion of the students admitted were ill-qualified to benefit from higher education and because many of their teachers were ill-qualified to dispense it. A bizarre casualty of the HWP's campaign to impose conformity on Hungary's educational system was the National Federation of People's Colleges (*Népi Kollégiumok Országos Szövetsége* or NÉKOSZ). The people's colleges, dedicated to the political and cultural education of young peasants and markedly radical in character, had sprung up after the war in response to peasant demand and had at first been favoured by the Communists as a useful training and recruiting ground for future Party members. Most graduates of the colleges, which by 1947 numbered a hundred with an enrolment of 6,000 students, did indeed join either the HCP or the NPP; but the colleges were jealous of their independence and resented attempts by the Party, in the 'year of the turning point', to force them into a common mould. The Party, for its part, became suspicious of an educational network that excluded the urban proletariat; and the arrest of László Rajk, an enthusiast for the people's college movement, tinged

NÉKOSZ with guilt by association. In September 1948, the Politburo pronounced an anathema on NÉKOSZ and decreed the absorption of its colleges—now numbering 160 with 10,000 students—into the mainstream higher educational system as student hostels, thereby adding a further grievance to those already harboured by the peasantry.

Not the least repugnant aspect of the transformation of their country into a Stalinist satellite, to Hungarians of all people, was the suppression of their national culture and its supplanting by that of Soviet Russia. As in other aspects of national life, the immediate post-war years were a time of hope: writers and poets such as Gyula Illyés, Sándor Márai and Sándor Weöres led a literary revival, centred on the journal *Magyarok*, which picked up the mantle of *Nyugat*. Another journal, *Újhold* ('New Moon') provided a focus for younger writers such as István Örkény, the Catholic János Pilinszky and Ágnes Nemes Nagy. After 1948, however, the dead hand of the censor silenced all but the sycophants and conformists, who took their cues from the journal of the Party-controlled Writers' Association, *Irodalmi Újság* ('Literary News'). Several Hungarian classics, including *The Tragedy of Man*, were banned. Translations of Soviet works took pride of place in the bookshops; Russian became a compulsory subject in general and high schools, and for the first two years of higher education. Even the veteran Marxist philosopher and Béla Kun's Commissar for Education, György Lukács, found himself under attack for heaping insufficient praise on Soviet literary achievements. In the visual arts, socialist realism held sway. The Party worked hard to establish a monopoly over the population's free time, such as it was. Red-kerchiefed Pioneers replaced the Boy Scouts; the Workers' Youth Association (*Dolgozó Ifjúság Szövetsége* or DISZ) mobilised Hungary's teenagers and students 'in the struggle for the victory of socialism'. Sport of all kinds was encouraged and generously financed, a policy that bore fruit in impressive crops of gold medals at the Olympic Games in London and Helsinki; to the extent that anything could give a temporary boost to national morale, Hungary's football squad, the 'Golden Team' of Puskás, Hidegkuti and Kocsis, achieved this, beating England 6–3 at Wembley and 7–1 in Budapest, as well as winning the Olympic title in 1952.* Every village had its 'People's House' where politically correct songs were sung and improving political lectures delivered. Soviet ensembles were the star turns in the theatres and concert halls of every city and town. A contemporary joke quoted an entry in the customs log at Záhony, on the Hungarian-Soviet border: 'Departed this day, destination USSR: 100 carloads of wheat, 200 carloads of corn, 5,000 barrels of wine, 250 new trucks, 70 optical instruments. Arrived this day, from USSR: 1 Moiseyev folk dance and song group'.[19]

By 1953 material privation, fear of the ÁVH and cultural starvation had combined to create a mood of bitter discontent and profound resentment in Hungary. In June of that year, 20,000 workers at the Csepel metallurgical plant (the former Manfred Weiss works, now the *Rákosi Mátyás Művek*) defied their union and the management by striking in protest against low wages, excessive production targets,

---

* But football was an unreliable political asset: when the Hungarian team lost to West Germany in the final of the World Cup in 1954, riots on the streets of Budapest continued for three days.

over-harsh discipline on the shop floor and food shortages. A substantial wage increase eventually muffled the protest; similar demonstrations in other industrial towns were bought off in the same way. No report of these episodes was permitted to appear in the media; but the Soviet Embassy and Soviet secret policemen working with the ÁVH watched developments closely and their reports aroused concern in Moscow.

The 'New Course'

When Stalin died in March 1953, Rákosi's position appeared to be impregnable. He had eliminated every possible challenge to his leadership from within the Party. Hungary's prisons were bulging with Party members who had been swept up in the permanent purge, along with tens of thousands of Hungarians from all walks of life—writers, academics, workers and peasants—who had been arrested simply *pour encourager les autres* or as a result of malicious accusations by the ÁVH's network of informers. Rákosi's latest victims were Gábor Péter, the sadistic and cynical head of the ÁVH, and the Minister of Justice, Gyula Décsi: both were Jewish and fell victim to Rákosi's dutiful imitation of Stalin's last purge, the anti–Semitic retribution for the alleged 'Doctors' Plot' in Moscow. Stalin's death saved them from execution but not from life imprisonment. Rákosi had decided to head the government as well as the Party, replacing Dobi as Prime Minister in August, 1952. This move provoked a warning from Moscow—for one man to hold both positions was contrary to Soviet practice—but Rákosi still believed that he could get away with it. The national elections of May 1953 had produced the predictable 98.2 per cent vote in support of the *Népfront*. Basking in the artificially generated adulation of a fearful and impoverished nation, he apparently felt no twinge of apprehension when the new leadership in the Kremlin—Malenkov and Khrushchev—signalled a softening of the Stalinist line and the initiation of a 'thaw'. He might, however, have been a little puzzled when, summoned to Moscow in June 1953 for consultations with the Soviet leaders, he was instructed to include in his delegation not only Gerő and Farkas but also one of his five Deputy Prime Ministers, Imre Nagy.

Like Rákosi, Imre Nagy, born into a poor peasant family in Somogy county in 1896, had discovered Communism as a prisoner of war in Russia during the First World War. After fighting for the Bolshevik cause in the Russian Civil War, he returned to Hungary in 1921 and embarked on political activity among the farm labourers of his native county, for which he was arrested in 1927. After a short spell in prison, Nagy emigrated to Vienna and then, in 1930, to the Soviet Union, where his wife and daughter joined him. During the 1930s, he held modest posts in the Agrarian Institute of the Comintern, the Soviet Bureau of Statistics and finally in the Hungarian service of the Soviet Broadcasting Commission. It has been alleged[20] that he acted as an informer for the Soviet secret police, a role forced upon many members of Moscow's émigré community. Although he consorted with his fellow émigré Hungarian Communists, he did not emerge as a leading member of the group; possibly because, unlike his colleagues, he refused to apply for Soviet citizenship, he was actually expelled from the émigré Hungarian Communist Party in 1936 and served a short prison sentence before being readmitted to the Party in 1940. Throughout his stay in the Soviet Union, Nagy maintained and deepened his agricultural expertise and was therefore a natural choice, when the Muscovite Communists returned to Hungary in the wake of the Red Army, for the post of Minister of Agriculture in the Provisional Government. He had the additional asset, in Soviet eyes, of not being Jewish; and in order to emphasise that they were not sponsoring a rerun of the Béla Kun experience, the Soviet leadership placed him fifth in the HCP pecking order, despite his relative obscurity. As Minister of Agriculture, as we have seen, he promulgated the land reform of 1945 and subsequently served the coalition as Minister of the Interior and then in the less influential post of President of the National Assembly. Agriculture and the defence of peasant interests nevertheless remained his prime interest and his opposition to Rákosi's policy of crash collectivisation cost him his seat on the Politburo and his government post. After only a year in the political wilderness, which he spent enjoyably as a visiting professor at the Gödöllő Agricultural College, his rehabilitation began with a severe test of his party loyalty—appointment to the post of Minister of Requisitions, in which he was responsible for extracting from peasant farmers the forced deliveries that were ruining them. His efficient discharge of this task was rewarded with re-election to the Politburo and the Central Committee Secretariat in 1951 and, a year later, with appointment to a Deputy Premiership with responsibility for rural issues. His career, and particularly its latest phase, had demonstrated his two dominant characteristics: obstinate defence of his convictions in his area of expertise, tempered when necessary by total loyalty to the Party and to Communism.

The Soviet leadership that confronted Rákosi and his colleagues in the Kremlin on 13 and 14 June 1953 was in an edgy mood. Not only were its members still feeling their way in the wake of Stalin's departure from the scene, not least in terms of their relationships with each other; but they had also found reports of strikes in Hungary, riots in Pilsen, Czechoslovakia and widespread unrest in East Germany, which threatened to develop into a full-scale uprising, deeply disquieting. The new Soviet leaders concluded that the screws of Stalinism had been tightened too recklessly; and that unless they were relaxed, the cohesion of the Soviet empire in eastern Europe might be put at risk—a circumstance that, at the height of the Cold War, they were not willing to countenance.

Malenkov, Khrushchev, Beria and their colleagues therefore accused Rákosi, in front of his delegation, of endangering socialism in Hungary by excesses in industrialisation, collectivisation, military expansion, the reduction of living standards, the staging of show trials and, not least, the encouragement of a cult of personality—Beria unpleasantly accused Rákosi of trying to make himself 'the Jewish king of Hungary'. On Malenkov's proposal, it was agreed that Rákosi should hand over the Premiership to Imre Nagy and co-operate with him in pursuing new policies that would retrieve the errors of the past.

Two weeks later, a stunned Central Committee of the HWP listened to speeches of self-criticism from Rákosi, Gerő, Farkas and Révai. On the proposal of Imre Nagy, whose appointment as Prime Minister was approved, the Committee passed a resolution that amounted to a comprehensive and damning indictment of Rákosi's policies: the Party leadership had:

- 'regarded industrialisation as an end in itself without considering the interests of the working class and working people …'
- '… neglected agricultural production and pushed collectivisation at much too rapid a tempo…'
- ignored 'the satisfaction of the needs of the people …with the result that the workers' living standard was reduced …'
- applied 'administrative measures against workers, such that people were victimised by the police and the courts […] the police imposed penalties in approximately 850,000 cases' between the beginning of 1951 and 1 May 1953.[21]

The resolution accused Rákosi personally of replacing collective leadership by 'direction by one individual' with its 'associated cult of personality'. Farkas and Révai lost their seats on the Politburo. Ominously, however, Rákosi retained his position as First Secretary of the Hungarian Workers' Party: this boded ill for the implementation of the Central Committee's other decisions, known collectively as the 'June Resolutions'. These called for a slow-down in industrialisation; greater emphasis on the development of light, rather than heavy, industry; measures to improve the people's living standards; a lower rate of capital investment, except in agriculture; a lightening of the burden of taxation and compulsory deliveries on the peasantry; more gradual collectivisation; and leave for peasants to withdraw from co-operatives if they wished.

On 4 July 1953, the National Assembly rubber-stamped a sanitised version of the June Resolutions, confirmed the appointment of Imre Nagy to the Premiership and approved additional government proposals for the abolition of internment camps, an amnesty for prisoners serving short sentences and a review of longer ones. Nagy's radio broadcast to the nation summarising these decisions, christened 'the New Course', made a profound impact, not least on the intelligentsia and the peasantry: the Rákosi nightmare, it seemed, had come to an end. During the next twelve months, the New Course did indeed produce some tangible results. Thirty-nine per cent of peasants enrolled in co-operative farms exercised their freedom to desert them and 18 per cent of all co-operatives dissolved themselves: the area of land farmed by cooperatives shrank from 2.5 million *hold* to 1.6 million. Compulsory deliveries were reduced, arrears cancelled, consumer prices lowered and wages increased; by 1956 the standard of living of the peasantry had risen by a third over 1949.[22] The improvement in living standards for the urban working class was less marked, at 15 per cent, but none the less significant. Investment in heavy industry fell by 41 per cent in 1954 and light industry began to revive. Nagy was able to report to the Central Committee early in 1955:

Retail trade has increased by 27 per cent and the sales volume for Christmas of 1953 exceeded that of 1951 by 36.6 per cent; trade has grown in rural areas by 38.2 per cent during 1954. Market prices in Budapest have fallen 13.3 per cent. There has been a 24.5 per cent increase in construction. Direct investments in agriculture in the second half of 1954 are 70.1 per cent greater than in the first half. We have granted eight thousand licences to artisans. The taxes on the peasantry have been reduced.[23]

The less important political prisoners began to trickle back from camps and prisons; many of those forcibly deported to the countryside returned to the capital to seek accommodation—their former homes were not restored to them. In other areas of policy, however, the New Course stalled in the face of persistent obstruction by the Party apparatus, at Rákosi's direction. Nagy could not command a majority in the Politburo, where he had no supporters; the Party Secretariat consisted entirely of Rákosi cronies. Rákosi chaired the Rehabilitation Committee, charged with reviewing the sentences of those whom he had himself imprisoned. Gerő headed the Ministry of the Interior as well as the Party's Economic Policy Committee. An opponent of Nagy, Béla Szalai, controlled the National Planning Office. A direct appeal by Nagy to the Soviet leadership against sabotage of the New Course evoked a rebuke to Rákosi and an injunction to co-operate; a counter-appeal by Rákosi against Nagy's alleged sidelining of the Party failed and in May 1954, Voroshilov, speaking at the Third Congress of the HWP, pointedly endorsed the principle of collective leadership and the policies of the New Course. Undismayed and unregenerate, Rákosi pinned his faith on an eventual change of wind in Moscow.

Despite his isolation in the Party, however, Nagy, with the wind from Moscow behind him for the time being, doggedly pursued the policies in which he believed. Majority support for the New Course in the Central Committee of the HWP held firm and its meeting in October 1954 quashed an attempt by the Politburo to impose draconian cuts on social and cultural expenditure, which would have undermined Nagy's popularity. Although he had never been, and never became, adept at political in-fighting, Nagy did have some success in countering Rákosi's spoiling tactics. In order to create a focus for popular support for his policies that would counter-balance the hostility of the Party leadership and its placemen, he converted the empty shell of the *Népfront* into a new umbrella organisation, the Patriotic People's Front (*Hazafias Népfront*), which would promote national rather than Soviet-socialist themes. Perhaps unwisely, he secured the election of his son-in-law, a Calvinist pastor, to the Front's secretary-generalship. The Front quickly helped to mobilise and articulate the considerable fund of goodwill Nagy's policies had generated, not least among the nations's writers and journalists, many of whom were beneficiaries of the 1953 amnesty. Despite Rákosi's opposition, and thanks to support from Khrushchev, Nagy succeeded in securing the release of a significant number of Party members from prison, including János Kádár. The editorial staff of the Party organ, *Szabad Nép*, became converts to the New Course; and Nagy succeeded in installing an ally at the head of the National Planning Office, in place of the hostile Szalai. Even Ernő Gerő began to waver in his support for Rákosi, whose star appeared to be on the wane.

Reaction

Clouds had nevertheless begun to gather over the New Course. Although agricultural production had increased with the reduction of taxation and compulsory deliveries, the relaxation of shop-floor discipline had led to a sharp decline in industrial productivity. Wage increases and lower consumer prices generated inflation. For reasons unrelated to Hungarian politics, the Soviet government announced that its deliveries of raw materials would be cut by half in 1955. Even if alternative sources of supply could be found to make up the shortfall, credits would be needed to use them, as they were already needed for the replacement of worn-out machinery in Hungary's industrial plants. Nagy's proposal that credits should be sought from the West foundered in the face of the Politburo's veto. Meanwhile, Hungary's trade balance, distorted by large imports of armaments at the behest of the Warsaw Pact, had slumped massively into the red. At the end of 1954, Rákosi spent several weeks in the Soviet Union, taking soundings of his many contacts there; what he heard encouraged him, on his return to Budapest, openly to attack Imre Nagy and the Patriotic People's Front. Rákosi's practised antennae had not deceived him: early in January 1955, the Hungarian leadership received a summons to Moscow for consultations with the Soviet Presidium. At a meeting that was a mirror image of that in June 1953, Malenkov led a furious denunciation of Nagy for bringing about a decline in industrial production, the destruction of co-operatives, social unrest, factionalism in the Party, tolerance of counter-revolutionary elements, opportunism, chauvinism and demagogy. In support of the charge of chauvinism, Malenkov adduced the fact that Nagy had publicly used a quotation from Petőfi: 'If the earth were God's hat, then our homeland is the bouquet upon it'. Despite this indictment, Nagy would be permitted to retain the Premiership if he admitted his mistakes and took corrective action. This, however, was not Nagy's way: unlike Rákosi eighteen months earlier when their situations had been reversed, he refused to admit his supposed errors or to engage in self-criticism.

There may have been some genuine concern in Moscow that the New Course risked carrying relaxation too far, to a point at which the authority of the HWP would be threatened. The more important factor behind the Soviet leadership's *volte-face*, however, was Khrushchev's temporary alliance with the Stalinists, with which he hoped to oust Malenkov (he succeeded on 8 February, when Bulganin replaced Malenkov as Soviet Prime Minister). Nagy and his policies became victims of the power struggle within the Kremlin. Although, back in Hungary, Nagy's obdurate refusal to recant, much less resign, further increased his popularity, it soon played into the hands of Rákosi, who took full advantage of Nagy's indisposition following a minor heart attack in February. Alarmed by Rákosi's reports, in Nagy's absence, of Soviet displeasure, the Central Committee deserted Nagy and attacked him, early in March 1955, for tolerating 'rightist deviationism'—Communist-speak for patriotism. When Nagy still refused to budge, Soviet Politburo member Mikhail Suslov, visiting Budapest for the 'Liberation Day' celebrations on 4 April, put his authority behind a further Central Committee resolution that accused Nagy, among other things, of attempting to form an opposition group within the Party. Ten days later, Nagy was expelled from the Politburo and Central Committee and stripped of all his Party offices; he nevertheless held on to the Premiership until, on 18 April, the National Assembly cravenly voted to dismiss him. He subsequently lost his university professorship and his membership of the Academy of Sciences; for the time being, however, Nagy remained a member of the HWP.

Rákosi, having secured the appointment of one of his trusties, András Hegedűs, to the Premiership, put the nation on notice of his return to absolute power by prompting the ÁVH to uncover an 'anti–Party conspiracy' in eastern Hungary: several hundred suspects were arrested of whom about a hundred were gaoled and six executed. Mihály Farkas paid for changing sides too quickly—he had incautiously expressed support for Imre Nagy in 1954—and lost his Politburo seat. Rákosi could not, however, restore the 1953 status quo as completely as he would have wished. Twenty-two months of the New Course had changed Hungary: having experienced some relief from the pressures and terrors of Stalinism, Hungarians would not readily submit to its reimposition. The international climate, too, had changed. The Austrian State Treaty signalled a tentative thaw in the Cold War;* and the visit of Khrushchev and Bulganin to Yugoslavia in May 1955 rehabilitated Rákosi's most bitter personal foe, Tito, who lost no time in publicly denouncing 'people who do not like the normalisation of relations ... There are such people, especially in Hungary.... These men have their hands soaked in blood, have staged trials, given false information, sentenced innocent men to death'.[24] Rákosi found it expedient, therefore, to resume his former policies with a certain degree of caution. The pace of industrialisation picked up again, but not to the pre-1953 level; the forced collectivisation of agriculture resumed, but peasant resistance to it increased despite a brutal campaign of intimidation in the countryside. At Moscow's prompting, and in order to improve Hungary's chances of admission to the United Nations, Rákosi was even obliged to moderate his persecution of the Church: Cardinal Mindszenty exchanged imprisonment for house arrest, while Archbishop Grősz and other priests were released from gaol.

A few presentational concessions, however, made no impact on the gradually emerging mood of discontent and protest that was both the legacy of the New Course and the reaction to its reversal. Nagy's policies had permitted a sufficient restoration of intellectual freedom to stimulate a resumption of activity by writers in the *Magyarok* and *Újhold* circles. Madách's *Tragedy of Man* had been restored to the Hungarian stage. The journal of the Writers' Association, *Irodalmi Újság*, had been transformed, under a new editor, from a sterile vehicle for socialist realism into a focus for intellectual support for the New Course. The rehabilitations of 1953 and 1954, moreover, had restored to the intellectual community dozens of men and women, many of them formerly loyal Party members, who had experienced terror at first hand and endured the squalor and humiliations of Rákosi's prison regime. They hated those responsible for the betrayal of their ideals; they hated themselves for following false prophets. The constituency of dissent now acquired both a forum and a martyr. In March 1955, DISZ—the Communist youth organisation—created a debating club, the Petőfi Circle, in order to snuff out its unofficial and unreliable predecessor, the Bessenyei Circle. HWP members, many of them products of the NÉKOSZ colleges, made up the leadership of the Petőfi Circle and most of its membership; in 1955, the Circle remained largely orthodox in character but it soon became a forum for relatively free expression. The martyr was, of course, Imre Nagy himself. In his enforced retirement, which he devoted to composing a reasoned defence of his views and policies, Nagy

---

* Signature of the Austrian State Treaty, and consequent withdrawal from Austria of occupation forces of the wartime Allies, removed the formal pretext for the stationing of Soviet troops in Hungary, namely protection of the lines of communication with Soviet units in Austria; but the virtually simultaneous creation of the Warsaw Treaty Organisation through the Warsaw Pact established a new rationale for the presence of Soviet forces in Hungary, as in the other satellite countries.

became a magnet both for like-minded Party members and for writers and journalists who saw in him the only hope for a socialist Hungary distinct from the
Soviet model and independent of Soviet control. When, in September 1955, an
issue of *Irodalmi Újság* was suppressed and its editor dismissed for making an implied
criticism of the Minister of Culture, fifty-nine leading Hungarian writers and artists, most of them Party members, sent a memorandum to the Central Committee
of the HWP protesting against cultural repression and 'anti–democratic methods'.
Most of the signatories of the 'Writers' Memorandum' were subsequently browbeaten by the Party leadership into disowning it; those who refused to do so faced
expulsion from the Party or severe fines. More importantly, Rákosi used the memorandum as an excuse to secure Imre Nagy's expulsion from the Party, on the
grounds that he had become 'a rallying point for the enemies of socialism'.

Rákosi's position was none the less under threat from two quarters. Imre Nagy
had indeed become a rallying point—not for enemies of socialism but for those
who, like him, believed that Rákosi had betrayed it; and, in Moscow, the convening of the Twentieth Party Congress set the stage for events that would shake the
Soviet empire to its foundations.

During the summer of 1955, Nagy wrote a number of essays, some twenty-five
in all, which together amounted to a vigorous defence of the New Course and a
withering indictment of Rákosi's perversion, as Nagy saw it, of the Communist
ideal. They also revealed a development of Nagy's own political beliefs into a
creed strongly resembling Tito's, a Hungarian version of 'national Communism'.
Far from averting the danger of a return to capitalism, Nagy argued, Rákosi's policies were actually increasing it:

No enemy propaganda … will destroy more completely the people's faith in socialism …
than a forced return to the old, mistaken, anti–popular pre-June [1953] policy. It is
undoubtedly this accursed blind policy that is strengthening the forces of reaction and
counter-revolution, and increasing the danger of capitalism. The Party membership and the
Hungarian people, those powerful supporters of the New Course and the June policy, do
not want a return to capitalism. They want a people's democratic system in which the ideals of socialism become reality …; they want a system that is actually ruled not by a degen-
erate Bonapartist authority and dictator but by the working people through legality and
self-created law and order.[25]

Similarly, Nagy maintained, the rejection of patriotism increased rather than
diminished the danger of 'chauvinism': 'socialism should not deprive the people
of their national character nor of their national sentiment and qualities; on the
contrary, it is with these that people enrich the universal moral-ethical values of
socialism. The unbreakable adherence of the Hungarian people to national ideals,
to the concept of loyalty, freedom and independence … is not a nationalism to be
condemned'.[26]

Because he had been denied an opportunity to defend himself against the charges laid against him in the Central Committee, Nagy submitted his essays to the
Party leadership as a defence *ex post facto;* he also sent copies to the Soviet leaders.
They were of course ignored. Loyal to a fault, Nagy had no intention of forming
an intra-Party faction or of appealing to a wider audience by publishing the essays;[*]

---

[*]The essays were published in the West, in French and English, in 1957.

but they circulated among Nagy's supporters within the Party and won new converts to his views. Nagy's defence of patriotism and his concept of 'national Communism' had immediate appeal to Hungarians. The essays acted as a solvent that accelerated the disintegration of the HWP during the early months of 1956, eventually isolating Rákosi and a shrinking group of cronies. When Nagy celebrated his sixtieth birthday on 7 June 1956, a stream of senior Party and public figures, including Kodály, Illyés and a government minister, called at his villa in Buda to pay their respects.

In the meantime, the latest turn of the wheel in Moscow had done Rákosi no favours. Khrushchev's denunciation of Stalin and Stalinism in his 'secret speech' to the Twentieth Party Congress created serious problems for 'Stalin's best pupil'. He did his best to bend with the wind. The Central Committee of the HWP dutifully reacted to Rákosi's report on the Twentieth Party Congress by passing a resolution that lauded the principles of collective leadership and socialist legality; economic planning should be sounder, cultural policies more liberal and victims of injustice rehabilitated. On 28 March 1956, Rákosi virtuously announced to a Party meeting in Eger that László Rajk, whom he described as the victim of a provocation by 'Gábor Péter and his gang', had been rehabilitated. But this, and subsequent half-hearted attempts at public self-criticism, were too little and too late to stem the erosion of Rákosi's authority. He began to be heckled and challenged at Party meetings. A young schoolmaster, György Litván,* told him to his face: 'Comrade Rákosi, the Hungarian people no longer trust you'.[27] In April, a young writer, Sándor Lukácsy, at a meeting of the Writers' Association, referred to Rákosi as 'a Judas whose hands are stained with blood'.[28] The Soviet-Yugoslav rapprochement—Tito, during a visit to Moscow in June, lobbied energetically for Rákosi's removal—and the dissolution of the Cominform underlined Rákosi's increasing isolation. Discipline within the Central Committee began to crumble. When János Kádár demanded the exposure of those responsible for Rajk's trial and execution, Rákosi played a tape recording of Kádár's treacherous promise to Rajk of exile in return for a full confession; when a replay was demanded, however, the Central Committee heard Kádár telling Rajk that he was acting on Rákosi's instructions. On the streets of Budapest, senior Party figures were openly insulted. Passers-by spat on official cars. Writers and journalists raised their heads, testing and frequently penetrating the boundaries of censorship. Dissident Party members, most of them supporters of Imre Nagy, began to dominate the Writers' Association; the Association's journal, Irodalmi Ujság, once again identified itself with the cause of reform. Opposition to Rákosi could be effective only within the Party: outside it, dissenters were vulnerable to summary trial and execution or imprisonment without any danger of adverse political repercussions.

Meanwhile, the Petőfi Circle, still dominated by Party members, had become a forum for political dissent and a microcosm of the fragmentation of the Party itself. Its debates attracted ever larger audiences and encouraged ever bolder interventions. A debate on education evoked demands for the resurrection of NÉKOSZ

---

* György Litván survived to teach sociology at Eötvös Loránd University, Budapest, and, as Director of the Institute for the History of the 1956 Hungarian Revolution, to edit *The Hungarian Revolution of 1956* (London, 1996). He died in November 2006.

and the People's Colleges; a historical debate on György Dózsa* became an exposé of the hardships inflicted on the peasantry by the Rákosi regime; in a debate on philosophy, the Marxist scholar György Lukács broke his self-imposed silence to attack Stalinist cultural policies, condemn the Marxist-Leninist monopoly of philosophical teaching and champion 'independent thinking'. In a debate on 18 June, on socialist legality, László Rajk's widow, Julia, dramatically raised the temperature to thunderous applause: 'I shall never rest until those who have ruined the country, corrupted the Party, destroyed thousands, and driven millions into despair receive their just punishment. Comrades, help me in this struggle'.[29]

A debate on the press, on 27 June 1956, attracted an audience of some five to six thousand, which necessitated its transfer to a larger venue, the former Officers' Casino (club). Loudspeakers were hastily installed to relay the proceedings to the crowds in the street outside. They heard the writer, Tibor Déry, call for freedom in literature and the press and for structural changes to the political system, rather than mere changes of personnel; and, in the small hours of the morning, Géza Losonczy—a 'home Communist' veteran and ally of Imre Nagy—demand Nagy's readmission to the Party. The name of Imre Nagy evoked a standing ovation of several minutes.

This was a turning point. Fortified by news of the riots in Poznań, Poland, as evidence of the dangers of relaxation, Rákosi persuaded the Central Committee to expel Tibor Déry from the Party and to suspend meetings of the Petőfi Circle *sine die*. The Committee's resolution accused 'a certain group which formed around the person of Imre Nagy' of responsibility for the Circle's 'onslaughts against the Party and the People's Democracy'. Not only was Nagy innocent of any involvement with the Circle; he would have disapproved strongly of much of what had been said there, by implication in his name. But Rákosi now had the bit between his teeth. On 16 July he confronted the Politburo with a blueprint for a massive counter-attack against the dissidents: Nagy and his group were to be arrested and tried, together with around 400 Communist sympathisers: the Writers' Association and the Petőfi Circle were to be dissolved; and *Irodalmi Újság* was to be closed down. This was more than even the Politburo could stomach: one of its members, unidentified, reported on the meeting by telephone to the Soviet Ambassador, Yuri Andropov.

The Soviet reaction was immediate: Mikoyan arrived in Budapest from Moscow within twenty-four hours, attended a reconvened Politburo meeting and informed Rákosi that he must resign. Rákosi's anguished telephone call to Khrushchev—'If I go, everything collapses'—fell on unsympathetic ears. On 18 July, Rákosi informed the Central Committee of his resignation on health grounds and immediately flew with his wife to the Soviet Union; he never returned to Hungary, dying in exile in Kyrghizia in 1971.

Mikoyan had brought with him the Soviet Presidium's 'recommendation' concerning Rákosi's successor as First Secretary of the HWP: it was to be Ernő Gerő. The choice of Gerő made continued unrest in Hungary inevitable: it could be argued, indeed, that the Hungarian Revolution began with the news of his appointment. The simultaneous election to the Politburo of two former victims

* See page 71.

of the Rákosi terror, János Kádár and the Social Democrat turncoat Marosán, did little to soften the elevation of a man whose unpopularity was second only to Rákosi's, particularly after the publication in May of a draft Second Five-Year Plan that promised a continued squeeze on consumption, triggering widespread strikes. To have appointed Imre Nagy, despite his refusal to recant, would have required more imagination, and knowledge of the true situation in Hungary, than the Soviet leadership possessed: but a revolution would almost certainly have been averted. Even the appointment of János Kádár could have had this effect, although there can be no certainties regarding this impenetrable man. As it was, the three months following Gerő's appointment were a period during which the gulf between the HWP leadership and the Hungarian people became unbridgeable. Strikes in protest against economic mismanagement and material deprivation proliferated throughout the country: the metallurgical plant on Csepel Island was paralysed by workers demanding improvements in their living standards. A local Party committee in Budapest later reported to the centre that 'the middle and lower functionaries were impotent, the ordinary members were confused, but everyone felt that there was something fateful in the air'.[30] The 'something fateful' was a decision by the Hungarian people, at first neither conscious nor well defined, to reassert their national identity.

18

REVOLUTION

(1956)

Gerő inaugurated his leadership of the Hungarian Workers' Party by proclaiming, confusingly, a war on two fronts: against 'leftist sectarianism' (Rákosi's legacy) and 'rightist deviationism' (Nagy). In a feeble attempt to retrieve the standing of the Party, he made a few concessions to the mounting tide of dissent and protest. The Politburo removed Mihály Farkas from all his Party offices and sanctioned a decree that banned the naming of any institution or street after a living Hungarian—the name of Rákosi consequently disappeared from countless inscriptions and street-signs. NÉKOSZ and its member People's Colleges were reinstated. Punitive proceedings, initiated by Rákosi against a number of writers and intellectuals, were halted. In order to strengthen Gerő's position, the Soviet government granted Hungary credits of 10 million and 60 million roubles. During the three months following Rákosi's departure—a period for much of which, as it happened, Gerő, Kádár and other members of the Politburo were away from Hungary on holiday or Party business—opposition to the leadership nevertheless continued to be voiced, and with increasing freedom. On 15 September, the Writers' Association held elections to its executive committee in which leading Party members, including the Minister of Culture, suffered defeat while seats were won by a significant number of non-Party candidates, among them the former Social Democrat Pál Ignotus,* who had been released from prison a year earlier. The association's journal, *Irodalmi Újság*, became the champion of artistic freedom and political reform: its circulation trebled in consequence—limited only by the rationing of newsprint—and copies changed hands at fifty times the cover price. The Petőfi Circle resumed its debates; Zoltán Tildy, the former Smallholder President, emerged from internal exile to take part in a debate on agriculture. The solemn reburial in Budapest's Kerepesi Cemetery, on 6 October, of László Rajk's remains, disinterred from the unmarked grave into which the ÁVH had flung his corpse in 1949, became a massive silent demonstration against the regime in which tens of thousands took part. Afterwards, a large group of university students marched from the cemetery to the Batthyány Memorial near Szabadság Square,

---

* Author *of Hungary* (London, 1972).

chanting anti–Stalinist slogans; the police did not interfere. In a gesture intended to mollify Tito, the Politburo decided, on the eve of the departure of Gerő and Kádár for a lengthy official visit to Belgrade, to readmit Imre Nagy to membership of the HWP.

From 20 October, when the students at Szeged University voted to break away from DISZ (the Party-sponsored youth organisation) and to establish the independent student association MEFESZ,* open opposition to the regime gathered momentum. *Irodalmi Újság* published a resolution passed by the Writers' Association calling for the early convening of a Party Congress which could, by secret ballot, elect a new Party leadership. Then, on 21 October, news reached Budapest of the outcome of Khrushchev's visit to Warsaw, which had taken place against a background of threatening troop movements designed to intimidate the Central Committee of the Polish Communist Party and deflect it from its determination to elect the 'national Communist' Władysław Gomulka to the First Secretaryship of the Party. The Poles had stood firm in the face of Soviet threats and Khrushchev had been obliged to accept the Central Committee's choice. This dramatic development further strengthened traditional pro-Polish sentiment in Hungary and offered an example from which Hungarians might learn. Students at universities throughout Hungary aligned themselves with their fellows at Szeged in joining MEFESZ and drawing up lists of demands, in conscious emulation of 'Young Hungary' in 1848. A meeting of students in the Philology Faculty of Eötvös Loránd University on the evening of 22 October decided to stage a demonstration, with slogans, on the following day. Simultaneously, a student meeting in the Technological University of Budapest, which was joined by young engineers and factory workers, produced a list of Sixteen Points on which satisfaction was demanded; the list was printed and, in the 1848 tradition, posted and circulated throughout the capital on 23 October.

The Budapest students' Sixteen Points deserve a brief summary, since—although this was far from the minds of those who drafted them—they were to become the agenda for a revolution.

The issues the list did not address are, moreover, as significant as those it included: recognition of the omissions is essential to a proper understanding of what the revolution was about. The students called for:

- the withdrawal of Soviet troops from Hungary in accordance with the 1947 Peace Treaty;
- new elections to the Central Committee by secret ballot;
- the appointment of Imre Nagy to the Premiership and the dismissal of Stalinists;
- the public trial of Farkas and his accomplices;
- multi–party national elections:
- a review of Hungary's relationship with the Soviet Union, guided by the principle of equality;
- a reorganisation of the national economy, on expert advice;

---

*The Association of Hungarian University and College Unions (*Magyar Egyetemi és Főiskolai Egyesületek Szövetsége*).

- the publication of foreign trade agreements [in order to expose the inequity of agreements with the Soviet Union];
- a revision of industrial norms;
- changes to the system of compulsory agricultural deliveries;
- the release of all political prisoners;
- freedom of expression, including the press;
- the removal of the statue of Stalin on György Dózsa Avenue and its replacement by a memorial to the freedom fighters of 1848–49;
- the restoration of the Kossuth coat of arms as the national emblem*;
- an expression of solidarity with Poland;
- the convening of a Youth Parliament on 27 October.

The Petőfi Circle, for its part, drew up its own list of Ten Demands, more moderate in tone than the Sixteen Points and omitting direct or implied criticism of the Soviet Union, other than a call for equality in Hungarian-Soviet relations. *Szabad Nép* published the Circle's demands on the morning of 23 October. Neither the Sixteen Points nor the Ten Demands called for the abandoning of any of the central planks of socialist policy: there was no call for the reversal of nationalisation, nor even for the abandonment of collectivisation. Nothing was further from the minds of the young reformers than a restoration of capitalism. They wished to see an alleviation of the burdens that extreme policies had placed upon workers and peasants alike. They called for an end to dictatorial, one-party rule. They demanded a reassertion of Hungary's national identity and the restoration of her national dignity.

The students' meeting that drew up the Sixteen Points also decided to call for a silent demonstration on the afternoon of 23 October to express solidarity with the Poles; the demonstration was to take place 'in a spirit of socialist democracy, order and discipline'. Radio Kossuth (the state radio) obligingly but inaccurately announced the arrangements for the demonstration in one of its morning bulletins. A later announcement, however, informed listeners that the Ministry of the Interior had banned all public meetings and demonstrations until further notice. In defiance of this, several thousand students gathered in Petőfi Square, on the Pest side, from noon onwards. Shortly before 3.00 p.m., when the march was scheduled to begin, Eötvös Loránd students brought news of a second announcement, withdrawing the ban. Gerő, who had just returned from Belgrade, may have hoped that the demonstration, if permitted, might become disorderly and give him and the ÁVH a pretext for a general clamp-down; more probably, the Minister of the Interior may have feared that the forcible dispersal of a crowd already numbering thousands would have unpredictable results. The students, therefore, sang the 'Kossuth Song' and the Marseillaise, and listened to the recitation by Imre Sinkovics of Petőfi's 'Hungarians Arise!' without interference, before setting off for the Margaret Bridge and Bem Square, where wreaths were to be laid. During the course of the march, the character of the demonstration underwent a significant

---

*The 'Kossuth arms' was the national symbol adopted during the revolution of 1848–49. It consisted of the traditional coat of arms of Hungary's medieval kings without the depiction of the Holy Crown which had surmounted it. The crown was restored in 1990.

change. The students and writers were joined by large numbers of workers whose shift had just ended; and pro-Polish slogans were drowned by chants of 'Russians go home', 'Nagy to the government' and 'Rákosi into the Danube'. The atmosphere nevertheless remained cheerful and orderly. The crowd, now numbering some 50,000, strained to hear a speech by the writer Péter Veres from the foot of General Bem's statue and then retraced its steps across the Margaret Bridge; along the route, Hungarian flags began to appear on the balconies of apartment buildings with their central communist symbol excised. The crowd continued to grow until, when it reached Parliament Square at about 6 p.m., it exceeded 200,000, among which students were now in a small minority. The cry went up for Imre Nagy to address the marchers. Nagy had returned to the capital that morning, from a celebration of the grape harvest near Lake Balaton, to find the demonstration in full swing; at a hasty meeting with a few of his supporters, he had urged caution and discipline, for fear of a provocation by the regime. With great reluctance, he allowed himself to be persuaded to speak in Parliament Square, only to be shouted down when he addressed the crowd as 'Comrades!'; his largely inaudible appeal for order and moderation came as a deep disappointment to the demonstrators, some of whom marched off to tear down the detested statue of Stalin on the edge of City Park while others made their way to the radio building in Sándor Bródy Street in order to demand that the Sixteen Points be broadcast.

At the radio building, a peaceful demonstration became an armed insurrection and then, with remarkable speed, a revolution. A strong detachment of ÁVH personnel was already installed in the building, as in other government and Party buildings, as a precaution against invasion by the crowd. While a delegation from the demonstrators argued with the radio authorities about relaying the Sixteen Points, Radio Kossuth broadcast, at 8 p.m., a characteristically ill-judged speech by Gerő, replete with references to 'the glorious Communist Party of the Soviet Union', 'the yoke of Horthy fascism and German imperialism', 'nationalistic well-poisoning' and 'provocation': the demonstrators heard themselves accused of spreading 'the poison of chauvinism' and of undermining the worker-peasant alliance. This angered a crowd already concerned about the fate of its delegation inside the building; in defiance of tear-gas grenades thrown from the radio building, it refused to disperse. A company of conscript soldiers despatched to Sándor Bródy Street to relieve a building apparently under siege quickly succumbed to the eloquence of the demonstrators, to whom they readily handed over their weapons. The first shot, probably loosed off by a panicky ÁVH guard, initiated sporadic exchanges of small-arms fire that continued until the arrival of an armoured regiment from outside the capital; according to one account,[1] one of its company commanders was shot by the ÁVH as he expressed his sympathy with the insurgents. His company thereupon joined the crowd, further reinforced at midnight by lorry-loads of workers armed with rifles looted from factory stores, in attempting to storm the building. After a pitched battle lasting most of the night, the radio building was stormed and seized by the rebels (as they must now be called) as dawn broke. Stalin's statue, meanwhile, had been cut off at the knees and was lying in fragments on the square it had dominated for five years. The capital was in turmoil, the streets seething with excited crowds. Communist symbols and red flags were torn down, the offices of *Szabad Nép* besieged. Stores of arms at police stations and military depots were broken into and stripped with little or no resistance from their guardians. A revolution had begun.

Ernő Gerő had not been slow to recognise, by the evening of 23 October, how serious the situation had become. As soon as reports from the radio building indicated that Hungarian troops could not be relied upon to suppress the insurgency, he requested—first through the Soviet Ambassador, Andropov, and then directly by telephone from Khrushchev—military assistance from the Soviet government. For form's sake, Khrushchev insisted that the request should be made in writing and this was done retrospectively in a letter signed by Hegedűs, as Prime Minister, a few days later; but the Soviet response was none the less immediate. During the night, two Soviet mechanised divisions crossed into Hungary from Romania to join the two already stationed there. Gerő had already convened the Central Committee of the HWP, which branded the uprising 'the work of counter-revolutionary, fascist forces' and agreed that it should be suppressed by force with Soviet help; it endorsed the imposition of martial law. The Central Committee also approved the appointment of Imre Nagy to replace Hegedűs as Prime Minister, together with the removal of six hardliners from the Politburo and their replacement by moderate reformers, including Nagy. Two of Nagy's closest allies, Géza Losonczy and Ferenc Donáth, were elected respectively to alternate membership of the Politburo and Secretaryship of the Central Committee; more prudent than their mentor, they declined to serve while Gerő remained in control of the Party. Gerő's co-option of Nagy to head the government did not represent a concession to the insurgents; it resulted, rather, from his astute calculation that Nagy's fundamental loyalty to the Party would impel him to advocate the restoration of order and that his voice would carry much greater weight with the rebels than Gerő's own. As an insurance, Nagy found himself confined, a virtual prisoner, in the headquarters of the HWP in Academy Street for the next three days. From here, on the morning of 24 October, Nagy broadcast to the nation, calling for an end to the fighting and 'the restoration of calm and order'. All those who laid down their arms by 2 p.m. would be exempted from the penalties of martial law:

Workers! Defend the factories and machines. This is your own treasure. He who destroys or loots harms the entire nation. Order, calm, discipline—these are now the slogans; they come before everything else … Stand behind the Party, stand behind the Government. Trust that we have learned from the mistakes of the past, and that we shall find the correct road for the prosperity of our country.[2]

When the Kremlin's chosen trouble-shooters, Anastas Mikoyan and Mikhail Suslov, arrived in Budapest on 24 October, Soviet troops and tanks had already been in action for several hours. They had sustained significant losses. Tanks are ill suited to urban conflict; unfamiliar with the city's layout, they frequently motored into narrowing streets and culs-de-sac, where they became easy targets for Molotov cocktails and, when their crews tried to escape, for small arms fire. Confronting them were between ten and fifteen thousand young Hungarians, mostly factory workers from the capital's poorest districts but including a small minority of hooligans and petty criminals who were unable to resist a fight against authority. Students, many of them appalled by what their peaceful demonstration had set in train, had by now largely faded from the scene. Most factories were now on strike and, in some, workers' councils had taken over the management of their plant—a phenomenon that became more general during the days ahead. Public transport ceased to operate; no newspapers appeared. The population depended on state-controlled Radio Kossuth for news and believed little of what they heard. They could, however, take at face value the announcement on 25 October that Gerő had been relieved of the post of First Secretary of the HWP and replaced by János Kádár—even though the positive impact of this news, the first fruit of Mikoyan's and Suslov's visitation, was reduced by the realisation that Gerő and his allies remained members of the Politburo and Central Committee. A second broadcast by Imre Nagy brought greater encouragement since, although he still referred to the insurgents as 'counter-revolutionaries and provocateurs', he announced the preparation of 'an all-embracing and well-founded programme of reforms', an impending government reshuffle and, not least, the initiation of negotiations on the withdrawal of Soviet forces stationed in Hungary. During the preceding twenty-four hours, the withdrawal of Soviet troops had replaced democratic reform as the revolution's primary and most urgent goal.

These announcements helped to produce a temporary reduction of tension in the capital. Instances of fraternisation between Hungarian citizens and Soviet troops had already begun and resulted, indirectly, in one of the most tragic episodes of the revolution, on the morning of 25 October. A large crowd, some of them riding on Soviet tanks, gathered in Parliament Square to demonstrate peacefully in support of the revolution's demands. A small detachment of ÁVH snipers, stationed by the Military Committee of the Politburo on the roofs of buildings surrounding the square, suddenly opened fire on the crowd—possibly in the belief that the Soviet troops were under attack but more probably as an act of deliberate provocation—causing severe casualties: well over 100 demonstrators, including many women, died and many more sustained serious wounds. Soviet tanks, stationed at the entrances to the Square, also opened fire. As news of the killings spread, bitter hostility to the regime and towards the security forces in particular welled up once more and tended to overlay Imre Nagy's promise of better times to come. The forces of revolution, moreover, acquired a de facto commander-in-chief. Colonel Pál Maléter, a tank commander who had fought with Soviet partisans against the Nazis during the Second World War, having been ordered to restore discipline in the Kilián Barracks where Hungarian troops had sided with the revolution, decided to join them instead; when the barracks were subsequently attacked by Soviet tanks, Maléter successfully led their defence. Meanwhile, the revolution had spread beyond the capital. Revolutionary committees sprang up in towns and villages throughout Hungary, replacing the local councils and brushing aside local Party institutions; the process was largely peaceful but in Mosonmagyaróvár, Miskolc, Kecskemét and a few other towns violence erupted, often provoked by the ÁVH, who became in turn targets for the vengeance of the local populace. In Budapest, Pécs and Miskolc, unofficial radio stations broke Radio Kossuth's monopoly of the airwaves; in the capital, 'Free Radio Kossuth' urged its listeners to place their radio sets on windowsills and balconies so that broadcasts could be heard in the streets. Substantial deliveries of foodstuffs, the peasants' contribution to the revolutionary cause, began to arrive in Budapest from the countryside.

Imre Nagy now began to feel his way cautiously towards an assertion of his authority as Prime Minister. On 26 October, he escaped from his enforced isolation in Party Headquarters and established himself in the Parliament building. His task, as he saw it, was to save socialism in Hungary and to justify the confidence the Soviet leadership had placed in him by securing his appointment to the Premiership. He remained totally loyal to the Communist cause and determined to protect it from anarchy and violence, which could be exploited by the 'imperialist' powers. A resolution Nagy guided through the Central Committee on 26 October promised elections for a new government, negotiations with the Soviet Union on a basis of complete equality, the return of Soviet troops to their bases as soon as order had been restored and an extension of the deadline for the laying down of arms. At a meeting with Nagy just before their return to Moscow, Mikoyan and Suslov agreed that non-Communists might be included in a future government but insisted that competence and unity should be restored to the leadership of the HWP; that the Party should have at its disposal an effective and resolute security apparatus; and that the Party should retain strict control of the media. Nagy found no difficulty with these propositions, while retaining his belief— which he had voiced in his first broadcast as Prime Minister—in 'a Hungarian way to socialism'. Accordingly, the new government which he announced on 27 October included a few 'safe' non-communists such as Zoltán Tildy, József Bognár and Ferenc Erdei as well as Béla Kovács, former Secretary-General of the Smallholders' Party and victim of the NKVD, who learned of his appointment to be Minister of Agriculture from the radio. To the disappointment of the more radical wing of the insurgency, which was strongest in the provinces, the majority of ministerial posts in the new cabinet were held by Communists.

As heavy fighting continued on the streets of Budapest on 27 and 28 October, resulting in the destruction of numerous buildings and the torching of a large number of Soviet tanks, Nagy recognised that the government could regain control of events only by making greater and more tangible concessions to the insurgents. The government had now replaced the Party as the focus of political authority. Gerő, Hegedűs and other 'yesterday's men' had fled to the Soviet Union. The HWP was already in an advanced state of disintegration; torn-up Party cards littered the streets of the capital. The time had come for Nagy to take the initiative. With Soviet approval (Mikoyan and Suslov had returned to Budapest on 27 October) and the support of the new Party leader, János Kádár, Nagy announced on 28 October the government's rejection of 'the view that sees the present formidable popular movement as a counter-revolution'; the government, he said, had ordered an immediate and general ceasefire. Soviet forces would withdraw from the capital and negotiation for their complete withdrawal from Hungary had been initiated. The new administration would abolish the ÁVH, restore the 'Kossuth arms' as the national emblem and make 15 March a national holiday. There would be no reprisals against those who had taken up arms. The provinces nevertheless remained sceptical. The 'Győr National Council', which had taken control of that large industrial town, threatened a general strike until Soviet troops had actually left Hungary and promised to come to the aid of the revolutionaries in Budapest unless there was an immediate end to the bloodshed there; the Council subsequently voiced the first demand for Hungary's neutrality and for free elections as soon as Soviet forces had departed. In Miskolc, the Workers' Council and Students' Parliament of Borsod County gave their provisional approval to Nagy's announcement but demanded the rapid translation of words into deeds. Overall, however, Imre Nagy appeared to have succeeded in regaining the initiative for the central government. By the morning of 29 October, fighting in the capital had virtually ceased and a measure of calm began to return to the city. Soviet armoured units began their withdrawal to bases outside Budapest. *Szabad Nép* marked its resumed publication with a striking editorial, attacking a *Pravda* article entitled 'The Collapse of the Anti–Popular Adventure in Hungary':

The events in Budapest were neither anti–popular, nor an adventure; nor was there a collapse. For five days bombs exploded and machine-guns were in action, spreading death. This city, torn by fate, shed blood and suffered for five days. But despite hundreds of deaths, the ideals of true patriotism and democracy were burning in every heart ... The revolutionary people of Buda and Pest want a people's freedom without arbitrariness, without terror and without fear. They want more bread and national independence. Is this what *Pravda* calls an adventure against the people?[3]

The *Szabad Nép* editorial reflected a mood of confidence and achievement which had begun to spread through the capital. The correspondent of the *New York Times* in Budapest began his despatch on 30 October with the words: 'The Hungarian people seem to have won their revolution'. There were, moreover, further reasons for optimism and even celebration. In the afternoon, Nagy announced that the government had abolished the one-party system and was placing 'the country's government on the basis of democratic co-operation between coalition parties as they existed in 1945'. A small 'inner cabinet' had been created, of which Nagy himself, Tildy, Béla Kovács, Erdei, Kádár, Losonczy and an unnamed Social Democrat were members. The Soviet government, Nagy said, would shortly be asked to withdraw its forces 'from the entire territory of the Hungarian Republic'. Zoltán Tildy followed Nagy at the microphone to announce the immediate abolition of compulsory agricultural deliveries and the resurrection of the Smallholders' Party, which should prepare itself for free elections. That evening, Moscow Radio broadcast a statement by the Soviet government concerning relations between the USSR and other socialist countries. The statement affirmed Soviet readiness to review with all members of the Warsaw Treaty the question of Soviet troops stationed on their territories; it went on to state:

The course of events has shown that the working people of Hungary, who achieved great progress on the basis of the people's democratic order, are rightfully raising the question of the need to eliminate serious defects in the field of economic construction, of improving further the material well-being of the population and of combating bureaucratic distortions in the state apparatus.

This movement, the statement averred, had been exploited by the forces of 'black reaction and counter-revolution', and for this reason the Soviet government had responded positively to the request of the Hungarian government for military assistance. However:

Since it considers that the further presence of Soviet Army units in Hungary can serve as a cause for even greater aggravation of the situation, the Soviet government has given orders to its military command to withdraw the Soviet army units from Budapest as soon

450

as this is considered necessary by the Hungarian government. At the same time, the Soviet government is ready to enter into corresponding negotiations with the government of the Hungarian People's Republic and other participants of the Warsaw Treaty on the question of the presence of Soviet troops on the territory of Hungary ...[4]

This was a highly significant statement, not only in its immediate implications for Hungary and longer-term import for the other satellite states, but also for the evidence it provided of the prevailing view within the Soviet Presidium at that time. It is noteworthy, too, that on 30 October Mikoyan and Suslov were making their third visit to Budapest in a week and appear to have approved, or at least accepted, the course Nagy had set towards a multi–party system and free elections.[5]

Members of the Soviet Presidium had in fact been arguing over the appropriate response to events in Hungary since 23 October. In one of the few accurate sentences in his otherwise suspect account of the episode in his 'memoirs', Khrushchev recalled: 'I don't know how many times we changed our minds back and forth'.[6] When the Presidium first addressed the issue, on 23 October after receiving reports of the siege of the radio building, Mikoyan had argued for restraint: 'Let the Hungarians themselves do the job of restoring order. If our troops intervene, we will only make things worse for ourselves'.[7] Mikoyan, shuttling between Moscow and Budapest with the hardliner Suslov as his 'minder', initially had the support within the Presidium of Malenkov, Saburov and the Defence Minister, Marshal Zhukov, for his view that Imre Nagy should be trusted to restore order (with Soviet help) and retrieve the situation for the HWP. The 'moderates' were opposed from the first by Marshal Voroshilov, Molotov, Bulganin and, when he was present, Suslov. Khrushchev, chairing the discussions, sat on the fence until a late stage. Nagy's announcement on 28 October, which in effect legitimised the uprising, rang loud alarm bells in the Kremlin and the Presidium met daily from then on. Even the hardliners, however, and Khrushchev in particular, harboured reservations over resorting to further military action; the Soviet Union should not be tarred with the same brush as the 'imperialists', who were at that moment living up to their name in Egypt. The 'moderates' took advantage of this hesitancy to secure the Presidium's approval, on the day of its publication, of the important government statement of 30 October. Nagy's announcement, on that same day, of Hungary's return to a multiparty system, however, aroused acute concern among other Party leaders in the Soviet bloc that the Hungarian example might be followed elsewhere. These concerns were made known to the Kremlin. The Chinese, in particular, through their senior Party delegation, which happened to be in Moscow at the time, expressed the firm view that Soviet troops should not be withdrawn from Hungary. Even Tito, at first sympathetic to the revolution, was beginning to have second thoughts. Khrushchev, moreover, had his own position within his Party to consider: an appearance of weakness would make him vulnerable to attack by those who had resented his denunciation of Stalin in his 'secret' speech a few months earlier. These factors combined to bring Khrushchev down on the side of the hardliners. Malin's note of the Presidium's meeting on 31 October records Khrushchev as saying:

...troops should not be withdrawn from Hungary and Budapest, let us take the initiative with regard to the re-establishing of order in Hungary. If we withdrew from Hungary, this would encourage the American, British and French imperialists. They would interpret it as a sign of our weakness, and would go on to attack. [By withdrawing] we would demonstrate the weakness of our position. In this case our Party would not understand us. Besides Egypt we would be giving away Hungary too. We have no other choice.[8]

In the wake of military intervention, the Presidium resolved, a new Hungarian government should be installed, probably under Ferenc Münnich (a veteran 'Muscovite', Hungarian Ambassador in Moscow under Rákosi and *persona grata* in the Kremlin) and János Kádár. Mikoyan returned from Budapest to find that the decision to crush the revolution had already been taken and that orders had been given to Marshal Konev to prepare for a further intervention. On 1 November, Mikoyan argued fervently for a postponement of military action and for Nagy to be given two weeks in which to stabilise the situation in Hungary. He won no support for his views. His travelling companion, Suslov, argued that 'only through occupation can we ensure a government which supports us'; Marshal Zhukov, a 'moderate' at an earlier stage, was even blunter: 'Determined measures must be taken. Get all the bastards. Disarm the counter-revolution'.[9] Khrushchev and his colleagues now set about ensuring that military action against Hungary would have the support of other Warsaw Treaty members and, crucially, of Marshal Tito. Meetings with the Polish leadership on the Soviet-Polish border and with the Romanians, Czechoslovaks and Bulgarians in Bucharest resulted in unanimous endorsement of Soviet intentions; a flying visit by Khrushchev and Malenkov to Tito on the Adriatic island of Brioni elicited the Yugoslav leader's full support for firm action.

There is some evidence that members of the Soviet Presidium were aware, when on 31 October they took the decision to crush the Hungarian Revolution by force, of developments in Budapest which may have further strengthened the arguments of the hardliners.* Accounts of the events that led to the massacre on Republic Square on 30 October differ, but it seems probable that early morning deliveries of food and other supplies to the Budapest headquarters of the HWP, on the Square, alerted nearby residents to the fact that the building was still occupied by a sizeable detachment of ÁVH personnel as well as by Party officials. In response to these reports, armed groups of insurgents who had not laid down their weapons after the ceasefire gathered in the square and, from about 10 a.m. laid siege to the building and attempted to enter it. The ÁVH thereupon opened fire, not only on the intruders but on anybody who broke cover outside. A fierce gun battle ensued, resulting in heavy casualties, which included women who had arrived to tend the wounded. Three armoured cars arrived to raise the siege and rescue the occupants of the Party building but their crews, on seeing the extent of the carnage, opened fire on the building instead. Imre Mező, First Secretary of the Budapest Party, a close friend and ally of Imre Nagy, ordered the ÁVH to cease fire and prepared to leave the building under cover of a white flag to negotiate a surrender. Insurgents burst into the building as Mező was about to leave it and shot him fatally; two army officers escorting Mező were also shot, as were

---

* See, for example, Victor Sebestyen's *Twelve Days: Revolution 1956* (London, 2006), pp. 215–16, and Charles Gati's *Failed Illusions: Moscow, Washington, Budapest and the 1956 Hungarian Revolt* (Washington, 2006), pp. 234–5.

ÁVH personnel leaving the building with their hands raised in surrender. Other ÁVH officers and men were rounded up and shot in cold blood; mutilated corpses were strung up from trees and lamp-posts in the square. In an uprising hitherto remarkably free from atrocities of any kind, and even from looting, this single shameful episode had great resonance; a photograph of young ÁVH men being gunned down with their arms raised flashed round the world.

Meanwhile, former politicians in the capital, many of them not long out of prison, were preparing to resume normal democratic activity in anticipation of the promised free elections. The Social Democrats elected Anna Kéthly to the party chairmanship; the Smallholders restored Béla Kovács to his former office of Secretary-General; the National Peasants' Party reinvented itself as the 'Petőfi Party'. All three parties acquired premises and prepared to relaunch their newspapers. Leading members who had collaborated with the Communist regime—Tildy, Dobi, Dinnyés and Bognár in the Smallholders, Szakasits in the Social Democrats and Erdei in the former NPP—found themselves excluded from office. Cardinal Mindszenty, released from house arrest, had already issued orders for the dismissal of all 'peace priests' from their parish and diocesan posts. The editors of *Irodalmi Újság* prepared the next issue of the journal, to be published on 2 November, which included Gyula Illyés's devastating evocation and indictment of the Rákosi period, written several years before, 'One Sentence on Tyranny'. Throughout the country, workers' councils had replaced the former HWP-dominated managements of factories, trading and transport enterprises and banks. A Parliament of Budapest Workers' Councils, established on 31 October, drew up a programme for the transfer of economic power from the HWP to the workforce; negotiation with government officials produced agreement for an end to strike action and a general return to work on 5 November. A Revolutionary Council took over the administration of the capital and elected a Smallholder mayor with a Social Democrat as his deputy. Revolutionary committees appeared in government ministries, courts of justice and the National Bank—and even in Hungarian diplomatic missions overseas. In his statement of 30 October, Nagy had confirmed that the government recognised 'the democratic organs of local autonomy, which have been brought into existence by the revolution', that it relied on them and sought their support. With remarkable resilience, Hungary thus prepared herself for a renewal of national life as a genuine democracy in which there would be a place for Communists and non-Communists alike. In a broadcast on 1 November, János Kádár announced the dissolution of the Hungarian Workers' Party and its reincarnation as the Hungarian Socialist Workers' Party (HSWP): 'In a glorious uprising, our people have shaken off the Rákosi regime. They have achieved freedom for the people and independence for the country, without which there can be no socialism'.[10] György Lukács, however, told a Polish journalist that Communism in Hungary had been 'totally disgraced': in free elections, Communists could expect only 5 per cent of the vote, or 10 per cent at the most. The Party would nevertheless continue to exist—'it will save the idea'.

As Hungarians celebrated the end of the darkest period of their national existence, moves were well under way further to prolong it. Early on 1 November, reports began to reach Imre Nagy in the Parliament Building of massive movements of Soviet troops across Hungary's eastern frontiers. Three thousand tanks had crossed into Hungary from the Ukraine and Romania; Soviet armoured units that had left Budapest two days before were now found to have dug in 10 kilometres from the capital; Soviet troops had occupied Ferihegy (Budapest) and other airports. When the Soviet Ambassador called on Nagy during the morning of 1 November, the Prime Minister (who had now taken over the additional portfolio of Foreign Minister), referring to these reports, warned him that if the Soviet government continued to flout its own statement of 30 October, Hungary would have no choice but to withdraw from the Warsaw Treaty. Andropov impassively took note, while maintaining that the troop movements were related to the impending Soviet withdrawal in accordance with the statement. When, during the course of the day, the reports were confirmed and further amplified, Nagy convened the cabinet and secured its unanimous agreement to Hungary's withdrawal from the Warsaw Treaty and to a declaration of Hungary's neutrality. Andropov was summoned at 5 p.m. to be informed of this in the presence of the entire cabinet, János Kádár and others. During this tense encounter Kádár, according to Deputy Foreign Minister György Heltai, who was present, told Andropov with great emotion that:

he knew full well that the declaration of neutrality meant the end of Communism for Hungary, and that meant the end of his life, because he had dedicated his whole life to the Communist Party ... But if the Soviets attempted to intervene in Hungary with the further use of arms, it would be the Soviets themselves who brought the counter-revolution to Hungary, and he would take to the streets with a pistol against Russian tanks and give his life for his country.[11]

When Andropov had departed to report to Moscow, Nagy telegraphed a note to the Secretary-General of the United Nations, Dag Hammarskjöld, informing him of the démarche to the Soviet Ambassador, who had been told that 'the Hungarian Government immediately repudiates the Warsaw Treaty and, at the same time, declares Hungary's neutrality and turns to the United Nations and requests the help of the four great powers in defending the country's neutrality'. Nagy requested that this matter should be added to the agenda of the forthcoming General Assembly.

The Western powers had other preoccupations. Although the Western media were giving massive coverage to the Hungarian Revolution, the Suez Crisis dominated both the front pages and, more importantly, the attentions of Western cabinets and chanceries. On 29 October, Israel—in collusion, as it subsequently transpired, with Britain and France who wished to reverse Egypt's nationalisation of the Suez Canal and topple the Egyptian leader, Colonel Nasser—had invaded Egypt. By prearrangement, Britain and France then delivered an ultimatum to Israel and Egypt threatening to intervene, ostensibly to separate the combatants but in fact to invade Egypt themselves. The strong opposition of the United States to these moves, of which she had been given no forewarning, magnified the crisis as the transatlantic alliance fell apart. On 30 October, therefore, as Soviet forces were beginning to pour into Hungary for the second time, the Security Council of the United Nations had convened in emergency session to debate the crisis in the Middle East. British and French vetoes of a United States resolution calling for an immediate ceasefire threw the crisis into the lap of the UN General Assembly, which accordingly met on 1 November, the day of Nagy's appeal to the

Secretary-General. This lamentable coincidence—and coincidence it was, *pace* the conspiracy theorists[12]—prevented the United Nations from taking cognisance of the Hungarian note until 3 November, by which time it had been overtaken by events.* Events in Hungary could not, in fact, have taken a different course even if the Suez Crisis had not arisen when it did. The West was concerned to avoid a confrontation with the Soviet Union, and not only because of the divisions in its own ranks over Suez. Washington and London—which Khrushchev and Bulganin had visited in April—did not wish to provoke a premature end to the new relaxation in East-West relations. Britain and the United States were at pains to reassure the Kremlin that they had no intention of exploiting the situation in Hungary to the Soviet Union's disadvantage. On 30 October, the US Ambassador in Moscow had delivered a note to the Soviet government, summarising a recent speech by the US Secretary of State John Foster Dulles and informing it that the United States did not regard the states of eastern Europe as potential military allies. A statement by the British government in the House of Commons on 1 November affirmed that 'it is not our intention to try and exploit the events taking place in Eastern Europe in order to undermine the security of the Soviet Union'. Pre-occupation with and disagreements over Suez certainly prevented the Western powers from making an early and united condemnation of Soviet actions in Hungary. This was helpful to Khrushchev, but not a decisive or even a major factor in his decision on 31 October to crush the revolution. There was never any question of military intervention by the West, Suez or no Suez. It is all the more regrettable that the American propaganda machine, through the medium of Radio Free Europe, had encouraged the youth of Poland and Hungary in particular to believe in the eventual liberation of 'the captive nations' by 'the forces of freedom'. This thoughtless rhetoric aroused expectations that could never have been fulfilled.

In Hungary, meanwhile, events had been moving towards their tragic climax. The four Soviet mechanised divisions already in the country had been joined by a further seven. By dawn on 2 November, Soviet troops had taken control of Hungary's railway system, occupying stations and placing guards on bridges and junctions. Budapest had been surrounded and major access routes cut. Imre Nagy, although now forced to recognise his betrayal by the Soviet leadership, nevertheless kept his nerve and maintained vigorous political and diplomatic activity. Notes to the Soviet government proposed immediate negotiations on Hungarian-Soviet relations with particular reference to the withdrawal of Soviet troops, nominating Hungarian political and military delegations for this purpose. A new appeal to the United Nations reported the latest phase of the Soviet invasion, called for recognition by the 'great powers' of Hungary's neutrality and asked the Security Council to instruct the Soviet and Hungarian governments to initiate negotiations without delay. On the following day, Nagy announced a government reshuffle which signified, as it was intended to do, the formal ending of Communist political hegemony in Hungary: three Social Democrats, a Smallholder and two repre-

---

* This is a considerable simplification, in the interests of brevity, of the series of exchanges that took place between the three Western powers about Hungary from 25 October onwards. These, and the situation in the United Nations, are very well summarised by Csaba Békés in Cox, T. (ed.): *Hungary 1956, Forty Years On* (London, 1997), pp. 51–66.

sentatives of the 'Petőfi Party' entered the government, leaving Communists in a minority of three—Nagy himself, his close ally Géza Losonczy and János Kádár. While these changes were being prepared for publication, Nagy sent for the Budapest Chief of Police, Sándor Kopácsi, and asked him if he knew the whereabouts of the former Minister of the Interior, Ferenc Münnich: 'You should know', Nagy continued (according to Kopácsi's recollection), 'that the First Secretary of the Party, János Kádár, also cannot be found. Yesterday he took part in all our deliberations. Today, he's disappeared without trace'.[13]

Although reliable first-hand evidence is lacking, it seems that in the late evening of 1 November Kádár, after hailing on the radio the Hungarian people's 'glorious uprising' and telling Andropov that he would fight Soviet tanks with a pistol or, according to other accounts, 'with his bare hands', had accompanied Münnich, at the latter's urging, to the Soviet Embassy. From there, the two men had been driven to the airport and flown to Moscow.*

On 2 and 3 November, Kádár and Münnich attended meetings of the Soviet Presidium. Kádár did most of the talking on the Hungarian side and gave a notably objective and dispassionate analysis of the situation in Hungary at the time of his departure. He made no attempt to conceal his support for the Nagy cabinet's decisions to leave the Warsaw Treaty and to declare Hungary's neutrality. He stressed the universality in Hungary of the demand for the withdrawal of Soviet troops. He pinpointed the appointment of Gerő to succeed Rákosi as the key Soviet error; and he showed sensitivity on the question of Communist affronts to Hungarian national pride. The next chapter of this narrative will look more closely at Kádár's motives in agreeing to fly to Moscow in secret: like most aspects of his personality, they were far from transparent. The immediate outcome of his testimony to the Presidium was a decision by the Soviet leadership to put him, rather than Münnich, at the head of a new Communist regime for Hungary and to fly the pair of them, together with other prominent Hungarian Communists who had been flown to join them in Moscow, back into Hungary in the wake of Marshal Konev's mechanised divisions.

In Budapest, negotiations between Hungarian and Soviet military delegations on the modalities of a Soviet troop withdrawal had begun on the morning of 3 November in the Parliament Building. Progress had been made, but not on the crucial question of timing. By mutual agreement, the talks resumed late that evening, at the Soviet military headquarters at Tököl, 25 kilometres south of Budapest. They were interrupted by General Serov, head of the Soviet KGB,**

---

* According to some sources—including Vali, F.: *Rift and Revolt in Hungary;* Kovrig, B.: *Communism in Hungary* and Khrushchev in *Khrushchev Remembers*—Kádár and Münnich were flown not to Moscow but to Uzhgorod, just over the Ukrainian border; and Kádár himself recalled in 1959 that he had come to Uzhgorod 'three years ago when the Hungarian people had been in great trouble'. But we now know from the Soviet archives that Kádár and Münnich attended sessions of the Soviet Presidium in Moscow on 2 and 3 November. References to Uzhgorod may have been designed to conceal this fact and to minimise direct Soviet involvement in the formation of Hungary's new government; or perhaps Uzhgorod had been a staging post *en route* to Moscow.

** Committee for State Security—the latest incarnation of the NKVD, which had changed its name three times since 1943.

who placed the entire Hungarian delegation under arrest. At dawn on the following day, Soviet forces launched an all-out assault on the capital and by 8 a.m. Soviet tanks had once more entered Parliament Square. Imre Nagy, his family and three dozen colleagues had accepted an offer of sanctuary in the Yugoslav Embassy. Just before leaving the Parliament Building for the last time, Nagy had broadcast, at 5.19 a.m., a final message to the world:

This is Imre Nagy speaking, the President of the Council of Ministers of the Hungarian People's Republic. Today at daybreak Soviet forces started an attack against our capital, obviously with the intention to overthrow the legal Hungarian democratic government. Our troops are fighting. The Government is in its place. I notify the people of our country and the entire world of this fact.[14]

In fact, very few Hungarian troops offered armed resistance to the invading Russians, having received no orders from their government to do so; units still ensconced in the battle-scarred Kilián Barracks, however, held out there for twenty-four hours before exhausting their stock of ammunition. Shellfire from Soviet artillery and tanks devastated the centre of the capital and caused widespread damage in the suburbs; machine-gun fire raked the boulevards. Several armed groups of workers nevertheless fought fiercely in the capital for several days; the most renowned of them, the Corvin Alley group commanded by the five Pongrácz brothers, kept up a brave and spirited resistance until 8 November. The Citadella on Gellért Hill fell on 9 November. On Csepel Island, metal workers fought on until 11 November, having brought down a Soviet reconnaissance aircraft with one of their own anti–aircraft guns.* During their westward march from the Ukrainian and Romanian borders, Soviet units had taken pre-emptive action against known insurgents in Debrecen, Miskolc and Veszprém, arresting hundreds; but around the southern town of Pécs, several thousand young workers and students dug themselves into positions in the Mecsek hills and resisted repeated Soviet assaults for three weeks. Long before that, however, Hungary had a new government.

In a broadcast at dawn on 4 November, Ferenc Münnich, speaking apparently from the town of Szolnok, east of Budapest but using Soviet radio frequencies, announced the formation of a Hungarian Revolutionary Worker-Peasant Government and explained that he, Kádár and other comrades had left the government of Imre Nagy, which had become incapable of dealing with 'the counter-revolutionary threat'; he cited the killing of Imre Mező and other leading Communists as evidence of the threat of anarchy. An hour later, the voice of János Kádár was heard on the same frequency, announcing his own appointment as Prime Minister in the new government, which would also include Münnich as his deputy, Marosán, Horváth, Apró and other anti–Nagy Communists. Kádár's statement mixed Stalinist claptrap with passages more sensitive to the realities of the situation:

Horthy's gendarmes and prison warders, the representatives of the hated and cursed oppressive system, have already set out to sit on the neck of the people … [and would have

---

* Simultaneously, at the Olympic Games in Melbourne, amidst rioting by a largely Hungarian-born crowd in protest against Soviet foul play, Hungary's water polo team beat the Soviet Union 4–0 and went on to win the gold medal.

brought] slavery, misery, unemployment and ruthless new oppression. Exploiting mistakes committed during the building of our people's democratic system, the reactionary elements have misled many honest workers, and in particular the major part of the youth, which joined the movement out of honest and patriotic intentions…[15]

Kádár went on to outline the new government's programme, largely moderate in content. There would be no reprisals against workers who had taken part in recent events; living standards would be raised as quickly as possible; compulsory agricultural deliveries would not be restored; and, although the new government had 'requested the Soviet Army Command to help our nation smash the sinister forces of reaction', it would negotiate the withdrawal of Soviet troops as soon as order had been restored. Escorted by Soviet tanks, János Kádár and the members of his government entered Budapest on 7 November. It was to be several weeks before they could claim to be in control of the country, even with Soviet military backing; in the meantime, Hungary was subjected to undeclared martial law administered by the Soviet army.

From 4 November, a swelling tide of Hungarian refugees filled the roads to the Austrian and Yugoslav frontiers, laden with as many personal possessions as they could carry or push in handcarts. By mid-December, over 200,500 Hungarians—2 per cent of the nation's population—had sought refuge outside their country. They left behind them at least 2,700 who had lost their lives in the revolution, including 196 children under fourteen, and 27,000 wounded. Soviet casualties numbered 669 dead and 1,450 wounded—an indication of the ferocity of the Hungarian resistance. Cardinal Mindszenty had sought refuge in the United States Embassy, where he was to remain, a virtual prisoner, for the next fifteen years.

The swearing-in of the 'Revolutionary Worker-Peasant Government' by the arch-survivor István Dobi, as Chairman of the Presidential Council, on 7 November marked the formal end of the Hungarian Revolution. It did not fail. It succeeded, to a degree that persuaded the Soviet leadership that it had to be crushed. The Hungarians did not revolt against socialism but against a political dictatorship sustained by terror; and against the occupation of their country by a foreign power. They showed no desire whatsoever to turn the clock back to Horthyite capitalism and quasi–feudalism; they would have settled, not just willingly but enthusiastically, for the reformed 'national Communism' represented by Imre Nagy. The revolution did not have nationalisation in its sights, only punitive production norms and artificially lowered living standards. True, Hungarian farmers had no taste for collectivised agriculture—but nor did the Poles, who successfully rejected it: the rural population of Hungary would nevertheless have readily reconciled itself to a socialist system without compulsory deliveries or penal taxation designed to extinguish individual farming. The original goals of the revolution did not—save for a small handful of extremists in the western provinces—include Hungary's withdrawal from the Warsaw Treaty or neutrality. Imre Nagy certainly regarded neutrality for Hungary as a long-term aspiration, writing in *On Communism*: 'The Hungarian people have become convinced by the terrible experiences of the two world wars that they cannot and must not become participants in the rivalries of free power groups'.[16] But the declaration of neutrality on 1 November was made in response to the second Soviet intervention—it did not provoke it; in making it, moreover, Nagy hoped to demonstrate to the Soviet leadership, and to the West, that Hungary had no intention of deserting one alliance for another. The Hungarian Revolution, therefore, was not the victim of its own ambitions. It was the victim of that fundamental paranoia that underlay most instances of bullying aggression by the Soviet Union. The underlying insecurity of a regime that had seized power by force and subsequently maintained itself in power by force rendered it incapable of tolerating diversity. It demonstrated this inability over Yugoslavia in 1948, in Hungary in 1956 and in Czechoslovakia in 1968.

In 1956, Hungarians had to relearn the harsh lesson of 1849: the West might applaud their aspirations for freedom and independence but would never actively support them. They nevertheless recovered their national self-respect, badly eroded by Trianon and the Nazi alliance; and they won the enduring respect of the non-Communist world. Unintentionally, they dealt a damaging blow to international Communism: formerly loyal comrades, who had with greater or lesser difficulty stomached the purges and other horrors of Stalinism, now deserted their Parties in droves. The year 1956 planted Hungary firmly in the world's consciousness: more has been written about the revolution, in all languages, than about any other aspect of Hungary's eventful history. 1956, moreover, prompted the peoples and governments of many countries to take a hard look at the values and priorities that informed their own policies: human rights moved up the international agenda.

19

THE SECOND COMPROMISE

(1956–88)

János Kádár

János Kádár, whose name is synonymous with the period of thirty-two years that followed the 1956 Revolution, was born János Csermanek in the Adriatic port of Fiume (Rijeka) in 1912. His father, a conscript in the imperial army, declined to marry his mother, a servant girl from Slovakia, who nevertheless followed him back to Hungary in the hope that he might change his mind. He did not. Young Csermanek's early years were therefore spent, with his mother, in acute poverty in a small village south of Lake Balaton. After the end of the First World War, the pair moved to Budapest in search of more regular employment for the mother—she found it, as a concierge—and better schooling for her son. János Csermanek completed the usual eight grades of elementary school and, at the age of fourteen, undertook an apprenticeship as a typewriter repairer. Losing his job in the Depression, Csermanek took part in the 1930 wave of strikes in the capital and, shortly afterwards, was recruited into the youth section of the illegal Hungarian Communist Party (HCP), where he acquired his first alias—Barna. Arrested in the round-up of suspected Communists following the Biatorbágy railway disaster of 1931,[*] János Barna spent two years in prison, where he encountered several leading members of the underground Party, including Mátyás Rákosi. Resuming illegal activities after his release, Barna paid for them with a further spell of imprisonment from 1937. Armed with these credentials and an evident talent for clandestine work, Barna worked his way up the Party's slender hierarchy, eventually securing election to its Central Committee, then under the leadership of László Rajk, in 1942. At this point he took the name Kádár ('Cooper'), by which he was known for the rest of his life. When the Hungarian 'Muscovite' Communists returned to their country in 1945 in the wake of the Red Army's advance, Kádár was a natural choice for co-option into the Politburo of the reconstituted HCP. His further career has been recorded in earlier chapters of this narrative.

[*] See page 344.

Kádár's complex personality is difficult to delineate with any confidence. An intensely private person, he revealed episodes from his past life, and their influence on him, only when he judged it politically useful to do so—usually to win sympathy as a victim of tragic events. His Communist belief sprang from instinct and emotion rather than from his intellect; he was not a student of the Marxist scriptures, of which he professed familiarity only with Engels's *Anti–Dühring*, a copy of which he claimed to have won in a chess competition in his youth. Sensitive, perhaps, to his lack of secondary or higher education, Kádár sometimes evinced hostility towards intellectuals. In 1956, he rounded on a group of journalists: 'You imagine that you are an important, influential force in society. You are not: the working class is the only such force and you are like flies sitting on the yoke. It's the oxen, not you, who are pulling the cart, whatever you may think'. And a year later, he lost his temper with a delegation from the Writers' Association: 'It's said that a people gets the government it deserves. Well, you writers deserve a far more repressive government than this'.[1]

Kádár nevertheless possessed intuitive intelligence of a high order. His tactical skill, sense of timing and judgement of the limits of the possible in any given situation were remarkable. These talents matured with experience of leadership. He had a natural aptitude for the manipulation of subordinates, for dividing and neutralising opposition. His aversion to personal publicity, the modesty of his private life, the simplicity of his preferred recreations—chess and the undemanding Hungarian card game, *ulti*—were undoubted political assets. The low-key, almost chatty style of his public speaking came as a relief to listeners sated with the formulaic Marxist rhetoric of his predecessors. He gave the impression, I thought when meeting him,* of being a little surprised to find himself where he was—he had none of the decisive confidence of movement or speech that power usually confers, although he had by then led his Party and country for over a quarter of a century.

I cannot claim that my personal encounters with János Kádár, which were inevitably formal in character, gave me any insights into the motives that had impelled him to betray the Hungarian Revolution, break all his public undertakings to the Hungarian people in its immediate aftermath and preside over a campaign of vicious retribution, which claimed the lives or liberty of thousands of his fellow Hungarians, including many of his former colleagues in Party and government. Nor is it easy to define the roots, in his life experience and political thinking, of policies that evolved into the second great compromise in Hungary's history, a compromise which, like the first in 1867, could be regarded either as a political tour de force or as an ignoble accommodation. My tentative conclusion was, and remains, that one aid to an understanding of Kádár is the central character, Rubashov, in Arthur Koestler's masterpiece, *Darkness at Noon*. Loyalty and service to Hungary's Communist Party were to Kádár the highest and all-embracing good. Unlike Rákosi, Gerő and Münnich, Kádár did not acknowledge an overriding loyalty to the Soviet Union; nor, unlike György Lukács and other Party intellectuals, did he see himself as the servant of Communism as an ideology, uni-

*The writer served as British Ambassador to Hungary from January 1980 until June 1983.

462

versally revelatory and universally applicable. Kádár's political motivation was more narrowly focused—on the HCP, and later the HWP and HSWP, as the only true protector, or so he believed, of the interests and wellbeing of the Hungarian people. All other considerations, including those of morality and personal honour, were for Kádár subordinate to the interests of the Party. He accepted his arrest and imprisonment in 1951 stoically, as an unpleasant but necessary sacrifice to the higher good. Whether or not he underwent torture in Gábor Péter's cells—there is no firm evidence either way—he, unlike Imre Nagy, obediently signed the fabricated confessions and self-criticism the Party demanded of him. After his release, he appears to have harboured no personal animus against Rákosi, meekly accepting from him a junior post in the Party's Budapest *apparat*. He kept his distance from the reformist group around Imre Nagy, allying himself to it only after the revolution had swept it to power.

The most likely explanation, in my view, for Kádár's agreement to join Münnich on their flight to Moscow, on 1 November 1956, is that he believed he had been summoned by the Kremlin to brief the Politburo on the true situation in Hungary; and that compliance with this summons would serve the interests of the Hungarian Party. The comprehensive, relatively objective and far from self-serving nature of the account he gave the Soviet leadership on 2 and 3 November* is more consistent, I believe, with this explanation than with the view that he deserted Imre Nagy and the revolution in order to advance his own political career. Once in Moscow, Kádár was left in no doubt of Soviet determination to crush the uprising. In acquiescing in Khrushchev's decision to place him at the head of a new client regime in Hungary, Kádár may have concluded that the Hungarian Party could be rebuilt only by a leader whom the Soviet leadership was prepared to trust and that fate had cast him in that role. The rest of his life was to be devoted to retaining that trust as the precondition for an unorthodox compact with the Hungarian people that would maintain the Hungarian Socialist Workers' Party in power. Although, at the very end of his career, the chemistry of power—together, perhaps, with the burden of personal guilt—corroded his judgement and mental balance, Kádár performed this task with remarkable pertinacity and skill.

Repression and Consolidation

Duly sworn in on 7 November 1956, and installed in the Parliament Building, the 'Revolutionary Worker-Peasant Government' was totally lacking in authority and in the means to tackle the chaotic situation that confronted it. Utterly discredited by Kádár's apostasy, the HSWP was universally reviled. In the factories, the Workers' Councils remained in control and, indeed, continued to grow in strength and cohesion: on 14 November the Central Workers' Council of Greater Budapest held its first meeting and adopted a programme drafted by István Bibó, whose 'Plan for a Compromise Settlement of the Hungarian Question' was already enjoying wide circulation among the capital's intelligentsia. The Council deman-

---

* See page 456.

ded the reinstatement of Imre Nagy as Prime Minister, free multi–party elections, the withdrawal of Soviet troops from Hungary and a general amnesty for all participants in the revolution. From their sanctuary in the Yugoslav Embassy, Imre Nagy and his closest supporters issued a similar programme in the name of the 'provisional executive committee' of the HSWP. Writers, journalists and youth organisations echoed these demands in the name of the newly formed Revolutionary Council of Hungarian Intellectuals, under the chairmanship of Zoltán Kodály. Although the revolution had been defeated, it had not died.

Initially, Kádár adopted conciliatory tactics in an attempt to gain control of the situation. In a broadcast following a meeting of the HSWP Central Committee on 11 November, he hinted at the desirability of involving other parties in the political process and testified, on the basis of his own experience as a member of the Nagy government, that neither Imre Nagy nor his 'political group' had willingly supported the 'counter-revolution'. Kádár expressed his readiness for negotiations with Nagy if the latter agreed to leave the Yugoslav Embassy. He repeated this offer to a delegation from the Central Workers' Council on 15 November, adding: 'We want a multi–party system and free, honest elections'.[2] On the same occasion, Kádár promised immunity from prosecution for those who had taken part 'in the great popular movement of the past few weeks'. There would be no deportations; the ÁVH had disintegrated, Kádár assured the workers' delegation, and was no longer needed—but its members should not be persecuted. It is not certain that Kádár gave these encouraging undertakings in deliberate bad faith; it is more likely that, in these early days following the defeat of the revolution, he was so concerned to establish a dialogue with the people, to break through the barrier of contemptuous ostracism that surrounded him and his Party, that he simply told his listeners what they wanted to hear. But at the same time Kádár was making preparations to establish the authority of the Party by deploying its traditional weapon, terror.

The first priority, however, not least in the view of the formidable trio of Soviet Politburo members—Malenkov, Suslov and Aristov—who had arrived in Budapest to oversee Kádár's activities, was to resolve the uncomfortable and embarrassing circumstance of Imre Nagy's asylum in the Yugoslav Embassy, which had already been the subject of frenetic triangular exchanges between Khrushchev, Tito and Kádár. On the strength of a written assurance from Kádár that, if asylum were to be withdrawn, the personal safety of Nagy and his companions would be guaranteed, Tito authorised his deputy Foreign Minister, Vidić, to negotiate Nagy's departure from the Embassy on this basis. What Tito did not know was that Kádár had already acquiesced in a plan concocted by his three Russian minders for the arrest and abduction of the Nagy group as soon as they left the Embassy building.[3] General Serov, head of the Soviet KGB, and Ferenc Münnich as Hungarian Interior Minister, made the necessary arrangements: on 22 November, shortly after boarding a bus that was to convey them, as they thought, from the Yugoslav Embassy to their homes and families, Imre Nagy and colleagues were seized by Soviet officers, detained in a military academy and, on 24 November, flown to Romania where they were later placed under house arrest. Budapest Radio had announced, prematurely on 23 November, that the group had departed for Romania voluntarily; following the announcement, at the instigation of the Central Workers' Council, the people of the capital staged a silent protest that emptied the streets and brought public transport to a halt.

Although, in the weeks immediately following the revolution, the Soviet military command assumed responsibility for security and most other aspects of central and provincial administration, Kádár lost no time in preparing to take these functions back into Hungarian hands. By 10 November he had initiated the formation of a 'Revolutionary Home Guard Militia',* loyal to the Party, which, by the end of the year, had sufficient strength to relieve Soviet units of internal security duties. Under Soviet military direction, the Hungarian army and frontier guard underwent a thorough purge; similarly, the KGB oversaw the reinstatement of the ÁVH. When, on 8 December, the Central Workers' Council called a general forty-eight hour strike in support of its political programme, Kádár felt strong enough to move against it. The Council was dissolved and its leading members arrested. A public declaration of support for the revolution by Kodály's Revolutionary Council of Hungarian Intellectuals, signed by 110 leading writers and journalists, attracted similar retribution: the arrest of several of the signatories was followed by the imposition of overall censorship. By the end of November, Soviet and Hungarian security personnel had made over 1,500 arrests resulting in imprisonment and nearly 6,000 detentions for investigation. The severity of reprisals increased after a long session of the Central Committee of the HSWP from 2 to 5 December had formally branded the uprising as a 'counter-revolution'. Government decrees proclaimed martial law and the restoration of internment. In Salgótarján, in northern Hungary, security forces opened fire on a workers' demonstration, killing over thirty and wounding dozens more; similar clashes occurred in Miskolc and Eger. The Soviet leadership could not, therefore, fairly accuse Kádár of lacking zeal in his efforts to restore order and extinguish the dying embers of revolution.

Khrushchev and his Politburo colleagues were, however, concerned that Kádár might be prepared to envisage, as his declarations of 4 and 11 November had hinted, legitimacy and some kind of political role for non-Communist parties. This was anathema both to the Kremlin and to the other Communist regimes in eastern Europe. The Soviet, Czechoslovak, Romanian and Bulgarian leaderships therefore assembled in Budapest on New Year's Day 1957 both to stiffen Kádár's resolve in restoring a Communist monopoly of power in Hungary and to make a demonstration of support for a regime regarded by the Hungarian people and by the non-Communist world as illegitimate. As soon as the Soviet and satellite delegations had left for home, on 5 January, Kádár issued a declaration that inaugurated two years of systematic repression and revenge: the dictatorship of the proletariat would be restored, by a HSWP which, together with other democratic forces which accepted the Party's leadership and policies, would alone enjoy the privilege of political activity. During the following weeks, government decrees stipulated minimum prison sentences of five years for a wide range of offences involving political dissent, to be tried by newly established 'people's courts' under an accelerated procedure; and empowered the police to intern or deport suspected

---

* Popularly known as the *pufajkások*, after the padded jackets with which they were issued.

offenders indefinitely. The Writers' Association was dissolved and several of its leading members, including Tibor Déry and Gyula Háy, arrested. In a measure more draconian than any introduced by Rákosi, participation in or incitement to strike action became punishable by death, a penalty to which even juveniles could now be liable, although the sentence was not carried out until the victim had reached the age of eighteen. The Party recaptured the factories from the workers, dissolving all workers' councils and replacing them with factory committees controlled by trade unions which were, in turn, under the thumb of the HSWP. During the period of reprisals, which slackened after the spring of 1959 but did not finally come to an end until 1961, 341 death sentences were carried out; two-thirds of the victims had been sentenced for revolutionary activity. Twenty-two thousand Hungarians were imprisoned, half of them for five years or more; among their number were the future President of free Hungary, Árpád Göncz, the future Director of the Institute for the History of the 1956 Hungarian Revolution, György Litván, and the political sage, István Bibó, who received a life sentence. About 13,000 people were sentenced to internment and many thousands more deported to internal exile or dismissed from their jobs.[4]

The most eminent victims of the reprisals were Imre Nagy and some of his leading associates: Pál Maléter, Géza Losonczy, Ferenc Donáth, the journalist Miklós Gimes and Nagy's secretary, József Szilágyi. Following a decision by Kádár and his inner circle in March 1957 that they must be 'called to account', a Hungarian police unit arrested the accused in Romania and brought them back to Budapest, where they were imprisoned. Mindful of the Romanian capacity for mischief-making, Kádár preferred to have this potential alternative to his own leadership under his direct control. The regime then took a long time to decide what to do with their prisoners. Nagy and Maléter refused to make any admission of guilt, although they volunteered explanations and a defence of their actions. This did not, however, offer a satisfactory basis for a public show trial. Losonczy died in custody, probably as a result of being force-fed during a hunger strike. The government eventually charged Nagy and Maléter with high treason and with plotting to overthrow the democratic order; the trial, *in camera*, opened in February 1958. Moscow then ordered a suspension of proceedings in order to avoid muddying the East-West waters on the eve of a projected summit meeting. The trial reopened in June and moved quickly to its preordained outcome of judicial murder. When the death sentence was passed, Nagy stated with dignity that he considered the sentence unjust. 'My sole solace in this situation', he said, 'is my conviction that sooner or later the Hungarian people and the international working class will exonerate me of the grave accusations, as a consequence of which I must sacrifice my life'.[5] According to another account, he added:[6]

Twice I have tried to save the honour of socialism in the Danube Basin—in 1953 and in 1956. It was Rákosi and the Russians who prevented it. If now my life is to be sacrificed to prove that not all communists are enemies of the people, I offer it willingly. After all that has happened, it has no value any longer. I realise that there will be another Imre Nagy trial at which I shall be rehabilitated and three times as many people will come to my reinterment as went to Rajk's. My only dread is that my eulogy will be given by those who betrayed me.

THE SECOND COMPROMISE (1956–88)

On 16 June 1958, Nagy, Maléter and Gimes were led to the scaffold. Szilágyi, who had refused even to offer an explanation of his actions, had already been executed, in April. Donáth received a prison sentence of twelve years.

It is difficult to identify the point at which what came to be known as Kádár's 'alliance policy' became a conscious strategy. It probably emerged from a succession of tactical decisions, dictated by the exigencies of the early post-revolution period, which gradually formed a pattern of political behaviour sufficiently coherent to be called a strategy. Kádár's overriding objective lay in the restoration, consolidation and maintenance of the HSWP's monopoly of power in Hungary. For this, there were two essential preconditions: continued endorsement of the regime by the Soviet leadership and, as a minimum, the absence of active opposition to the regime from the Hungarian people. For thirty years, all Kádár's policies were dictated by these two imperatives.

There was, therefore, no paradox in the fact that, as early as 1957, in parallel with a campaign of harsh reprisals designed both to reassure Moscow and to eliminate sources of potential hostility to the regime, Kádár took steps to win its acceptance, however grudging, by the Hungarian people. In this he was assisted by the reaction that followed the violent public mood-swings of 1956—from hope and exhilaration to disappointment and despair. The people of Hungary were simply exhausted: the majority lapsed, almost with relief, into passive fatalism. The habits ingrained by a decade of Communist rule, reinforced by official pressure, began to reassert themselves: several hundred thousand citizens were marshalled for the traditional march along Budapest's György Dózsa Avenue on May Day 1957, apparently prepared to give Kádár's regime the benefit of the doubt. Meanwhile, even as the wave of arrests and executions continued, Kádár took small steps towards reconciliation. Wage increases of up to 20 per cent were introduced, backdated to the advent of the new government; the abolition of compulsory agricultural deliveries was confirmed; and the tax burden on small traders outside the state sector was significantly reduced. These and other measures announced that the Rákosi era had not returned. Exemption from prosecution was promised to those who had left the country illegally and who confirmed before 31 March 1957 their intention to return: nearly 40,000 refugees did so. Although Catholic priests were among those sentenced to imprisonment for 'counter-revolutionary activities', the award of a state decoration to Archbishop Grősz and a statement of support for the regime from the Catholic episcopate symbolised reconciliation between Church and government. In July 1958, a Politburo resolution declared that 'the ideological battle against religious faith must not insult the religious sentiments of believers nor restrict their freedom of worship';[7] in the following year the Churches regained their state subsidies and permission to organise religious instruction in schools, outside school hours. This was already Communism with a difference.

By the time delegates assembled for its 7th Congress at the end of November 1959, Kádár had rebuilt the HSWP into a viable ruling party. Its membership, only 103,000 at the end of 1956, had grown to 402,000; once the Party's authority had been re-established by the repressive measures of 1957–58, careerists had flocked to join it. The Party's first national conference, held in June 1957, in closed session, had elected a leadership in which centrists were more strongly represented than hardliners: in the Politburo, Kádár could count on the support of, in particular, Béla Biszku, Jenő Fock, Lajos Fehér and Gyula Kállai in keeping dogmatists such as Károly Kiss and Antal Apró under control. The non-Communist youth organisation MEFESZ, which had sprung up on the eve of the revolution, had been replaced by the Federation of Communist Youth (*Kommunista Ifjúsági Szövet-ség* or KISZ); and the Party had acquired its own private army, the Workers' Guard (*Munkásőrség*), well armed and with an eventual strength of 60,000 loyal thugs. Most importantly, the revived Party had been given the Kremlin's seal of approval: when Krushchev visited Budapest in April 1958 to conclude agreements on long-term economic co-operation and trade, he made a point of lavishing praise on Kádár and expressing his confidence that the HSWP, under Kádár's leadership, would not repeat the mistakes of its predecessor. This confidence was reflected in Khrushchev's offer to withdraw several divisions of Soviet troops from Hungary; Kádár demurred, evidently calculating that their continued presence would allow him to pursue national policies without causing alarm in the Kremlin. The Patriotic People's Front was dusted down and, under Kállai's chairmanship, resumed service as the Party's electoral machine: in the parliamentary elections of November 1958, the Front duly delivered a vote of 99.1 per cent in favour of the single list of approved candidates, from a turnout of 98.5 per cent.

Following decisions taken by the Central Committee, which the 7th HSWP Congress rubber-stamped, the regime took urgent steps to make amends in the one area in which it was seriously vulnerable to criticism from Moscow: the standstill, even regression, in the collectivisation of agriculture. Half the agricultural co-operatives had been disbanded during the revolution, with the result that in 1958 only 15.6 per cent of Hungary's arable land remained under co-operative management. This compared with 55 per cent of the arable land in Romania, 75 per cent in Czechoslovakia and a virtuous 92 per cent in Bulgaria. In January, 1959, Kádár returned from the 21st Congress of the CPSU with a clear message from the comrades that something should be done to repair this disparity. The regime used both carrots and sticks to break down peasant reluctance to return to the co-operatives. Co-operative members were to be allowed to farm private plots of up to a *hold* and to hire machinery and equipment for this purpose from the co-operative at highly favourable rates. For the first time, farm workers in co-operatives became eligible for old-age pensions—the men at age seventy, the women at sixty-five. Tax concessions and improved social benefits became additional incentives to co-operative membership; but tax increases were threatened against those who stayed out and their children risked losing their places in secondary or higher education—a potent sanction. The combination of persuasion, by Party activists who descended on the countryside by the bus-load, and threats—but without the use of force—proved highly effective. By February 1961, the Party could announce with pride that 90 per cent of Hungary's arable land had been reclaimed for co-operative and state farms; and that only 6.5 per cent of the peasantry were farming privately. The countryside had been tamed.

A partial amnesty in 1960 for political prisoners, including Ferenc Donáth, Zoltán Tildy and leading writers, together with the dismantling of internment camps, helped to persuade the population that an end to the post-revolution spasm of terror and reprisals might be in sight. In the following year, an extensive reform of the criminal code, which banned the use of torture and abolished the practice of arbitrary internal deportation, convincingly drew a line under the Stalinist years—although imprisonment for political offences continued. The resurrection of the Writers' Association encouraged many writers to emerge from the silent exile they had imposed upon themselves and to resume creative activity; there was some relaxation of censorship. Khrushchev's denunciation of Malenkov, Molotov and Kaganovich at the Soviet Party's 22nd Congress, in October 1961, indicated to Kádár that he could safely move to eliminate the remnants of Stalinism in his own Party. During the run-up to the 8th Congress of the HSWP in November 1962, Kádár won the Central Committee's endorsement of a resolution condemning the crimes of the Rákosi years, rehabilitating their victims and expelling from the Party Rákosi (*in absentia*), Gerő, a number of their associates and fourteen former officers of the ÁVH. An ill-judged attempt by Marosán to mobilise the hardliners in revolt against Kádár's leadership resulted in his own expulsion. In order to underline the break with the past, Kádár took over the premiership from Ferenc Münnich, bringing the Muscovite's long political career to an abrupt conclusion. In a calculated bid for the co-operation of the intelligentsia, he publicly stressed the eligibility of non-Communists to occupy senior positions in state administration; and reversed the policy, reintroduced in the aftermath of the revolution, of discriminating against young people of middle-class origins in the competition for places in gymnasia and universities. When the 8th Congress opened on 20 November, all the scenery was in place for the unveiling by the regime of a new policy of reconciliation and alliance.

Reform

In January 1962, the Party daily, *Népszabaság*, had given prominence to a quotation from a Kádár speech: 'Whereas the Rákosi–ites used to say "He who is not with us is against us", we say "Those who are not against us, are with us"'. This aphorism became the slogan, not only of the 8th Congress of the HSWP, but of the entire Kádár period. Repeating it in his keynote speech to the Congress, Kádár announced the HSWP's rejection of 'the false thesis of the constant and absolute intensification of the class struggle' and bid for the co-operation of the 'many hundreds of thousands who are not Marxists but who respect our Party and our government for having created a legal order and a normal atmosphere in the country'. The Party would not capitulate to the enemies of Communism: but Hungary could achieve unity through 'political alliance and ideological debate'. Kádár's speech, and the proceedings of the Congress as a whole, revealed, as yet only in faint outline, the compact between the regime and the Hungarian people that became known (outside Hungary) as Hungary's second 'historic compromise'. If the people abstained from opposition to or criticism of the Party, and in particular from criticism of the Soviet Union and its military presence, the Party would in return gradually enlarge the area of personal freedom and improve the material quality of daily life. In the absence of any realistic alternative, an overwhelming majority of the population was prepared on these terms to accept the political status quo—provided that the regime delivered its side of the bargain. The reform and development of the Hungarian economy consequently became the key dimension of the regime's policies. The history of the Hungarian economy during the next thirty years became, in effect, the history of Hungary. The economic dislocation resulting from the 1956 Revolution and its immediate aftermath cost Hungary one-fifth of her gross national product (GNP). The imminent threat of economic crisis prompted a resurrection of the fundamental criticisms of the Stalinist economic model that had begun to emerge during Imre Nagy's first Premiership but which had been stifled by Rákosi's recovery of power in 1955. Many members of the HSWP's Central Committee. including Kádár himself, recognised that the rigidities of a command economy. in which central government laid down the levels of investment, wages, raw material purchase, energy use and labour intensity for every individual state enterprise, constituted an unsustainable handicap for a small, vulnerable economy. Professor István Varga, former economic adviser to the Smallholders' Party and appointed in December 1956 to chair a new government Economics Committee, reported six months later in favour of a radical overhaul of the command economy and the partial introduction of market prices. Although a few of Varga's recommendations, in particular those applying to agriculture, were accepted, most of them fell foul of political opposition from hardliners in the Politburo. Opposition to radical change was strengthened by the remarkable speed with which the economy appeared to have recovered from the disruptions of 1956: thanks in part to soft loans and credits from the Soviet Union, industrial production had regained its pre-revolution level by the autumn of 1957. The Varga report nevertheless fuelled a debate, which was to ebb and flow in Hungary during the next three decades, on the extent to which a socialist economy could be reformed without ceasing to be socialist.

The recovery of the Hungarian economy, in any case, proved to be short-lived. Hungary's burden of debt to countries both within and outside the CMEA* increased dramatically, from HF** 1,600 million in 1959 to HF 4,100 million in 1963, while a central planning regime that sacrificed quality to quantity resulted in an abysmal export performance. In the first quarter of 1961, between 15.6 and 54.5 per cent (depending on the manufacturer) of Hungary's production of shoes for export and between 16.3 and 60.3 per cent of textiles were rejected on quality grounds.[8] Recognition of the necessity for radical reform coincided with the defeat of the Stalinists at the 22nd Congress of the CPSU in Moscow and the subsequent ejection of conservatives from the leadership of the HSWP. In December 1964, the Central Committee charged the head of the Committee's Economic Department, Rezső Nyers, with the task of making a comprehensive critical analysis of the existing system of economic management. Nyers, a former printer and member of the Social Democratic Party until its merger with the Communists, had served as Minister of Finance during Münnich's Premiership; a highly intelligent man, his belief in the unique efficacy of market forces did not detract from his dedication to the socialist cause. By October 1965, the eleven expert committees working under Nyers's direction had produced a draft of what came

---

*The Council for Mutual Economic Assistance, otherwise known as Comecon: the mechanism through which the Soviet Union sought to integrate the economies of the Communist bloc to her own advantage.
** Hungarian forints.

to be known as the New Economic Mechanism (NEM). The Central Committee's approval of the draft was followed by two years of fierce public debate before the NEM, emasculated in several significant respects but still recognisable, finally came into effect on 1 January 1968.

The essence of the Nyers concept was the creation of a market economy within a socialist framework, in which the state would continue to own the means of production but would cease to control every aspect of their utilisation. Annual and Five-Year Plans would henceforth be indicative rather than comprehensively mandatory. Directives from the economic ministries would be replaced by economic regulators designed to discourage waste of materials or labour; to make production more sensitive to world prices; and to create material incentives to improved performance by each individual enterprise. The regulators included taxation of a company's wage bill, a tax on fixed assets, a tax on enterprise profits and rebates on production for export. Enterprise managers would be free to determine wage levels, within an overall ceiling, and thus to reward good work at the expense of poor performers—but not at the expense of the enterprise investment fund without incurring a tax penalty. The reform would introduce a three-tier price system: most raw materials would continue to carry fixed or maximum prices, while most finished manufactures would be freed from price control altogether and determined by the market. The prices of most food products would remain fixed and the production of basic essentials, for example staple foodstuffs and children's clothing, would continue to be subsidised; but price control in the construction industry would be abandoned. The prices of imported products would be adjusted better to reflect world prices. Co-operative farms would be encouraged to engage in ancillary activities, such as food processing; like manufacturing enterprises, they would be given a free hand in most aspects of their management. Constraints on private economic activity would be gradually removed.

Nyers did not shrink from the political implications of his proposed reforms: they would inevitably involve, with the devolution of economic decision-making, some 'democratisation' (he used the term) of public life. Some years later, he remarked that 'if you develop the mind of economic man, you develop the mind of man in general … we shall have to develop, in connection with the economy, our cultural and political institutions as well'.[9] It was therefore natural that the draft NEM should attract strong opposition within the HSWP and more widely. Nyers and his fellow reformers came under attack for promoting bourgeois materialism, for espousing petit bourgeois values and for betraying the socialist ideal. Orthodox Marxist economists claimed that the proposed reform would create runaway inflation and high unemployment. Senior members of the command economy's massive bureaucracy feared for their jobs and privileges in a system in which the freedom of enterprises to make their own decisions might make them redundant. It became clear that unless the draft NEM were diluted in a number of respects, it would be politically impossible to introduce it; the HSWP might split and Moscow would be likely to impose its veto. The reformers therefore had to settle for half a loaf: the tax on enterprise profits became absurdly high, a ceiling was clamped on wage increases in obedience to egalitarian dogma and the range of consumer goods within which prices would remain fixed became wider.

Moreover, a Politburo resolution imposed an institutional straitjacket: 'The structure of the state administration should remain basically unchanged until 1969. ... The present company structure should be retained essentially unchanged; changes on a large scale should be avoided'.[10]

Despite all these constraints and imperfections, however, the implementation of the NEM in 1968 constituted a minor earthquake in the Communist system. It did away with the command economy in Hungary and to a considerable extent liberated the natural talent of Hungarians for individual economic activity. An economist and historian who was directly involved in the reform process, Iván Berend, described the NEM as 'the first comprehensive, substantial and radical reform ever undertaken in a Comecon country'.[11]

The 'New Economic Mechanism', even in its emasculated form, produced immediate and positive results. Productivity rose by 6 per cent during the last two years of the Third Five-Year Plan (1966–70) and with it annual growth of Hungary's GNP, which reached 6.2 per cent by 1970. The supply of consumer goods improved significantly and living standards for most of the population took a marked turn for the better. The most dramatic change was in the agricultural sector, where the regime's permissive approach to private plots and co-operative autonomy produced an explosion of activity, which survived the suspension of economic reform in the 1970s. By 1978, private plots accounted for 18 per cent of Hungary's arable land and for an extraordinary 50 per cent of the country's horticultural and livestock production. Hungary became a grain exporter once more: agricultural exports in general accounted for one-fifth of all exports by the late 1970s and for over half Hungary's hard currency-earning exports to the West. Co-operative farms achieved useful economies of scale through amalgamation— their numbers fell from 4,600 in 1961 to 1,600 in 1978, their boundaries, and those of the state farms, often following those of the great estates of pre-war Hungary. Vertical integration with the food processing industries proved financially rewarding and the regime encouraged the trend. By 1979, Hungary held ninth place in the European league table of twenty-three agricultural producers and shared with Denmark second place in the world for meat production per capita.[12] In industry, where the constraints imposed on the NEM by the opponents of reform weighed most heavily, the improvement in performance was less spectacular; in particular, quality remained a serious problem and only one-fifth of manufactured products reached the standards demanded by the world market. Planning had already begun, however, for a second phase of reform, which would expose the economy even more directly to the influence of world prices: a committee chaired by Rezső Nyers reported during the summer of 1972 on the extent to which operation of the NEM had been held in check by 'circumstances' and on the need for further, more radical, advance.

Opposition to and criticism of the NEM from within the ranks of the HSWP had not, however, been silenced by the initial success of the reform. Events in Moscow, moreover, had created a climate within the bloc less favourable to change: the ouster of Khrushchev in 1964 and his replacement by Leonid Brezhnev inaugurated a period of dour conservatism in Soviet policies. This encouraged not only Kádár's domestic critics but also sniping from the leaderships of other ruling Communist parties, notably the East German and Czechoslovak,

73. Gyula Horn (1932–), former Communist official and subsequently leader of the Hungarian Socialist Party; Prime Minister 1994–8.

74. Viktor Orbán (1963–), founder member and leader of the Young Democrats' Alliance (FIDESZ); Prime Minister 1998–2002 and 2010–?

71. János Kádár (1912–89), as leader of the Hungarian Socialist Workers' Party, presided over both savage post-revolutionary repression and nearly three decades of relatively benign but authoritarian Communist rule.

72. József Antall (1932–93), leader of the Hungarian Democratic Forum and Prime Minister of Hungary's first democratically elected government.

69. Secret police (ÁVH) personnel forced out of the Budapest Party building on Republic Square; they were shot seconds after this photograph was taken.

70. Soviet tanks, after leading an all-out assault on Budapest to crush the Revolution, establish control of the capital.

67. Budapest celebrates the apparent victory of the Revolution which had begun on 23 October 1956. The *New York Times* reported on 30 October: 'The Hungarian people seem to have won their revolution.'

68. The giant statue of Stalin, toppled from its plinth by demonstrators during the night of 23/24 October 1956, lies in the street awaiting demolition.

65. Ferenc Nagy, founding member of the Independent Smallholders' Party and Prime Minister 1946–7, with the dwarfish Mátyás Rákosi, General Secretary of the Hungarian Communist Party and virtual dictator of Hungary from 1947 until the 1956 Revolution.

66. Imre Nagy, Prime Minister 1953–5, defending his 'New Course' in Parliament, flanked by the Party leaders Rákosi and Gerő who sabotaged his reforms.

63. Budapest, 19 March 1944: German troops take possession of Castle Hill after invading and occupying their last remaining ally—retribution for Hungary's unsuccessful attempts to negotiate a separate peace with the Western Allies.

64. Ferenc Szálasi, leader of the fascist Arrow Cross Party, arrives at the prime minister's office on 16 October 1944, to take over the government with Nazi backing, following Horthy's arrest by the Germans and enforced abdication.

61. Regent Horthy and his wife, Magda, at the opera during their state visit to Nazi Germany in August 1938, during which Hitler (standing between them in the imperial box) tried to bully Hungary into participation in the impending invasion of Czechoslovakia. The Hungarian party abstained from making the Nazi salute.

62. Hungarian troops march into Losonc (Slovakia) on 10 November 1938. Under the First Vienna Award, Czechoslovakia had been forced to return nearly 12,000 sq. km of the Slovakian territory of which the Treaty of Trianon had deprived Hungary. The slogan reads: 'Long Live Greater Hungary'.

57. Endre Ady (1877–1919), one of Hungary's greatest writers and poets, and certainly the most controversial.

58. Attila József (1905–37), the outstanding poet of the inter-war period, shortly before committing suicide.

59. Count István Bethlen (1874–1947), Prime Minister from 1921 to 1931. His programme of 'consolidation' restored political and economic stability after the turmoil of war and revolution.

60. Gyula Gömbös (1886–1936), extreme right-wing nationalist and racist, Prime Minister from 1932 until his premature death in 1936, which thwarted his ambition to transform Hungary into a fascist state.

who feared that the contagion of economic reform, and its presumed political consequences, would undermine their own authority. During the run-up to the Tenth Congress of the HSWP in November 1970, the NEM came under sustained attack from the dogmatic wing of the Party, on the grounds that the leadership had connived at the erosion of working-class unity by encouraging differentiation in incomes and by permitting 'creeping petit-bourgeois liberalism'. The sobriquets 'goulash Communism' and 'frigidaire socialism' were deployed by the dogmatists in scathing criticism of the reform measures. The NEM nevertheless survived the Tenth Congress, not least because Brezhnev, who attended it, had evidently decided to give Kádár the benefit of the doubt for the time being: his speech put the Kremlin's seal of approval on the HSWP's programme as a whole, including the economic reform. But the momentum the NEM had initially imparted to Hungary's economic performance had already begun to fade; the inequalities it produced, particularly between the countryside, where peasant incomes had risen significantly, and urban industry where improvements had been less marked, became more conspicuous than the overall rise in living standards. Divisions within the Party consequently deepened and these attracted unfavourable attention in Moscow. Ominously, an article in *Pravda* on the eve of a routine official visit by Kádár to the Soviet capital, in February 1972, referred to the appearance in Hungary of nationalistic tendencies, social problems, petit-bourgeois trends and, even, 'Zionist intrigues'. When Kádár faced Brezhnev and the Politburo across the table, he immediately came under attack for tolerating 'dangerous rightist deviationism, petty bourgeois tendencies in the cultural field, the restoration of petty capitalist conditions, neglect of social justice and the slackening of revolutionary vigilance'.[13] When, a few weeks later, the Hungarian Prime Minister, Jenő Fock, sought from his Soviet counterpart a substantial increase in deliveries of Soviet raw materials to Hungary, Alexei Kosygin curtly rejected the request.

Although Kádár rode out this storm, which produced no immediate change in Hungarian policy, he could not ignore the pointed prediction in *Pravda* six months later that the next meeting of the HSWP's Central Committee would 'increase the role of central planning and state control'.[14] The Central Committee, meeting in mid-November 1972, duly did so, inaugurating a dismal period of some six years during which most aspects of the reform programme were suspended or put into reverse. The oil crisis of 1973, which sharply increased the price, not only of oil but of all the imported raw materials on which the Hungarian economy depended, increased the pressures on the regime to abandon experiment, batten down the hatches and revert to more familiar practices. The creation of a State Planning Committee in 1973 helped the Hungarian government to reassert control over the largest industrial enterprises and to regain control of their investment policies. Financial incentives were reduced and the taxation of profits increased. Subsidy of unprofitable enterprises and price supports accounted for one-third of the state budget in 1977. As a result of trade union pressure, industrial workers pocketed a wage increase of 5 per cent regardless of the profitability of their factory or workshop. Enterprise and initiative on the co-operative farms were snuffed out and successful co-operative chairmen forced into retirement by waves of allegations of embezzlement and malpractice. Livestock production on private plots fell dramatically as it became less profitable: small farmers slaughtered their sows rather than face a loss on the rearing of their progeny. Kádár did not abandon the NEM but held aloof from it and acquiesced in the downfall of its leading champions. Rezső Nyers lost his place in the Central Committee's Secretariat in 1974 and was voted off the Politburo by the Eleventh Party Congress a year later; he was to spend the next decade in relative obscurity in the Institute of Economics of the Academy of Sciences. Jenő Fock, a reformer, lost the Premiership in 1975 to György Lázár, a colourless technocrat and former chairman of the State Planning Committee. Changes of personnel, however, were of little significance in the context of the crisis which, by 1978, had engulfed the Hungarian economy.

During the six years that followed the onset of the world oil crisis, the cost of Hungary's imports rose by an average of 70 per cent; the value of her exports increased by only 30–40 per cent, partly because of a fall in demand for them in Western markets. To make matters worse, the Soviet government, in 1975, replaced the system under which the prices of Soviet exports of energy and raw materials to CMEA partners were fixed for five years at a time with a crawling peg regime under which prices rose over three-year periods to levels that better reflected world market conditions. This had a devastating effect on Hungary, the CMEA member least well provided with natural resources: the average cost of her energy and raw material imports from the Soviet Union rose by 52 per cent, while prices of the machinery and agricultural produce which she exported to CMEA markets increased by only 15 per cent and 28 per cent respectively. The CMEA had ceased to be a benevolent society. Hungary's terms of trade, already marked by a rapidly widening deficit in Western markets, now suffered a drastic deterioration in the Soviet, Polish and Czechoslovak markets as well. It has been calculated that by 1980 Hungary needed to export to the Soviet Union eight times more buses to pay for a given quantity of oil than had been the case in the early 1970s.[15] Given the continuing political constraints that blocked any significant attempt to rationalise the Hungarian economy, the only remedial action open to the Kádár regime was to raise foreign loans to finance the trade deficit. Hungary's external debt in convertible currencies consequently increased from a relatively manageable $848 million in 1971 to $7,320 million in 1979; in addition, Hungary owed the equivalent of about $3,000 million to the Soviet Union and her other CMEA partners. Even hardliners in the HSWP's economic hierarchy were compelled to recognise, by 1978, that this situation was not sustainable.

During the period of retreat from economic reform, János Kádár had been careful to maintain support for the principles of the NEM while sanctioning a tactical pause in its application. He had, moreover, eased out of the Party leadership some of the NEM's principal opponents: Árpád Pullai, Imre Párdi and, most significantly, Kádár's deputy and presumed successor Béla Biszku had lost their Party posts by mid-1978. When, therefore, it became obvious that the emasculation and then virtual suspension of the NEM had been a costly error, its resurrection and the inauguration of a new wave of reform faced fewer internal political obstacles than they might have done. From 1978 onwards, the Kádár regime pursued a two-prong strategy. One prong was directed towards liberating the inbuilt talent of most Hungarians for generating wealth by individual economic activity,* by legitimising and actively encouraging the so-called 'second economy'. The second prong was manifested in a sustained effort to improve relations, in order to develop trade, with the West—an objective that also required measures assisting the credible presentation of Hungary as an attractive, civilised society deserving of Western sympathy and attention.

Already in late 1977, the Party daily, *Népszabadság*, had pronounced that 'it is in society's interest to develop, not to repress, the household plots'. New regulations permitted the enlargement of household plots by means of long-term leases on co-operative land. Two years later, a radical price reform freed from control the prices of most consumer goods, apart from basic necessities, and also adjusted the prices of energy and raw materials to reflect world, rather than CMEA, price levels. This resulted in price increases across the board averaging 57 per cent and obliged manufacturers to adopt stringent measures to eliminate waste. At the same time, the taxation of profits was reduced and the domestic price of manufactured goods was linked directly to their export price, i.e. to prices in the world market. In February 1980, the Politburo noted that half the Hungarian population was devoting up to 18 per cent of its working hours to the 'second economy' and that this activity was 'by and large useful: it relieves shortages and it is a major supplementary source for our development'.[16] This was the signal for an explosion of economic activity, in forms of which many were without precedent in Communist societies. A high proportion of state-owned shops, restaurants and canteens were leased out to private individuals who could retain all the profits, as well as bearing all the risks, of their small enterprise. Within factories the formation was permitted, indeed encouraged, of 'enterprise economic work partnerships' (VGMKs):** these were small teams of workers that contracted with their enterprise to carry out specified services, typically in the sphere of maintenance and repair, in their own time, when necessary renting enterprise tools or equipment for the purpose. Profits were distributed between members of the team. By 1986, there were 23,000 VGMKs in Hungarian plants and factories—125, involving 1,500 workers, operated in the Duna Steel Works alone—employing 260,000 workers outside normal working hours. The productivity of the VGMKs usually exceeded that of the enterprise as a whole by 25–40 per cent. The licensing of private taxis in Budapest in 1982 added a further, and welcome, dimension to the capital's 'second economy' (I recall the excitement of spotting, and hiring, a pioneering *magán taxi* in that year). By 1985, small-scale private activity accounted for nearly a third of Hungary's national income and involved members of seven out of ten Hungarian families. In 1984, the Central Committee of the HSWP gave its formal approval to an objective that had, in fact, already been largely achieved: the creation of a regulated market economy within a socialist society, combining state, co-operative and private ownership of the means of production. A few years earlier, this would have been anathema to Moscow; but Brezhnev had

---

* János Szentágothai, the distinguished neurologist and President of the Hungarian Academy of Sciences, told me soon after my arrival in Budapest in 1980 that 'the average Hungarian, working for himself, is a remarkably efficient money-making machine'.
** Standing for '*vállalaton belüli gazdasági munkaközösségek*'.

died in 1982 and his successor, Yuri Andropov, proved ready to trust the judgement of János Kádár, in whose rise to power he had been instrumental in 1956.

Pursuit of the first prong of Kádár's strategy, the revival and acceleration of the NEM, had carried obvious risks in terms of Hungary's relationship with the Soviet leadership. The second prong, the development of economic relations with the West, had, from the inception of the NEM onwards, been even more sensitive and potentially dangerous. The launch of the NEM had coincided with the Czechoslovak crisis of 1968, which confronted Kádár with an awkward dilemma. On the one hand, Alexander Dubček's programme of economic reform, and in particular his intention to authorise the opening of a West German trade office in Prague, could provide a useful stalking horse for Hungary's own reform programme; but, on the other, open support for Dubček against Antonín Novotný's hardline group would be likely to incur the wrath of Moscow, with unpredictable consequences. Although he was alarmed by what he considered imprudent haste on Dubček's part in pressing ahead with political as well as economic reform, Kádár nevertheless did his best, at two successive meetings of Soviet and East European leaders, to argue for moderation in dealing with him. At the second of these, in Moscow on 28 May 1968, at which Brezhnev warned that the Soviet Union would 'take any step to contain the Czechoslovak situation', Kádár was courageously outspoken: 'one cannot settle matters', he declared, 'by calling Mao Zedong and his associates crazy, Castro petit bourgeois, Ceauşescu nationalist and the Czechoslovaks lunatics. If we must criticise individuals, let us begin with comrade Novotný rather than with comrade Dubček'.[17] Even when, a few weeks later, a bad harvest in Hungary obliged Kádár to revisit Moscow with a begging bowl, he continued to argue against confrontation. But Dubček, with the publication of draft statutes that would have legitimised factionalism within the Party, was rushing into territory where Kádár could neither follow nor support him; he could only warn, and did so at a secret bilateral meeting with Dubček at Komárno on the Hungarian-Czechoslovak frontier. According to one Czechoslovak account, when the two men parted on the platform of Komárno railway station, Kádár asked Dubček 'almost desperately: "Do you *really* not know the kind of people you're dealing with?"'[18] By then, the Prague Spring was already doomed; Kádár, who had found himself isolated in the summer meetings of bloc leaders, could not in prudence withhold Hungary's participation in the invasion of Czechoslovakia, which began on 21 August. Hungary was, after all, herself an occupied country. Hungary's complicity in this tragic episode nevertheless constituted a major setback to the Kádár regime, which had only recently been rehabilitated in the international community; it was the worst possible backdrop to Kádár's incipient re-engagement with the West and also damaged his standing in Hungary itself—many Hungarians reacted with shame and anger, noting that Ceauşescu had withheld Romania's support for the invasion. Kádár himself cancelled all his engagements and disappeared from public view for two months, absorbing a significant increment to his existing burden of personal guilt.

The dropping of the 'Hungarian item' from the agenda of the United Nations in 1963, and Hungary's readmission to the organisation in return for an amnesty of political prisoners, had created a platform from which, subject to the permanent constraint of loyalty to the Soviet Union, the Kádár regime could develop political relationships with Western countries, which would assist the expansion of trade and the availability of loans. Relations with the Federal Republic of Germany (FRG) were the centrepiece of this policy, their improvement facilitated by the Chancellorship of Willi Brandt, the progenitor of *Ostpolitik*. The establishment of diplomatic relations with the FRG in 1973 opened the way to a dramatic increase in trade: by the 1980s, the FRG had become Hungary's second trading partner, after the Soviet Union. The events of 1968 faded from the collective Western memory even more quickly than had those of 1956; during the next fifteen years Kádár, now the elder statesman of the Soviet bloc, paid official visits to Austria, Italy, France and twice to the FRG, welcoming the leaders of those countries to Hungary in return. An improvement of relations with the United States followed the settlement of American claims resulting from the post-war confiscation of US property in Hungary and were given a major boost by the return of the Holy Crown to Hungary in 1978. This political background contributed to a major success for Hungary in 1982, when she was admitted to the IMF and the IBRD; although the Soviet Union had been informed that negotiations for admission were in train, Soviet sanction for their outcome was not sought—an indication of Kádár's growing confidence in Hungary's capacity to exploit East-West détente for national purposes.

The regime took an even greater risk of incurring Moscow's displeasure in making confidential approaches, also in 1982, to the British, French and FRG governments about a possible agreement between Hungary and the European Community. Soundings in Paris and Bonn elicited no encouraging response; but the dialogue with London, for which as British Ambassador I was the conduit, was active for several months. Initially, the Hungarians sought a free trade agreement covering industrial goods and improved access to EC markets for Hungary's agricultural produce. The urgency arose from the regime's fear of being locked into less favourable arrangements by the impending negotiations between the EC and the CMEA—with whom less than 50 per cent of Hungarian trade was by now conducted. As these negotiations approached, the Hungarians progressively lowered their sights. I reported to London that Hungary was trying to throw out an anchor to the West in order to resist a tug to the East; as time passed, she became willing to settle for the smallest anchor which was likely to hold—an agreement covering agriculture only. When even this raised apparently insuperable difficulties, the Hungarians lost heart and the dialogue withered on the vine.

Although it produced no result, the Hungarian initiative was interesting and significant. My interlocutor, the Deputy Head of the International Department of the HSWP, Gyula Horn (who was later to become Foreign Minister and, later still, Prime Minister of democratic Hungary), insisted that I should on no account disclose our exchanges to the Ministry of Foreign Affairs or to the Ministry of Foreign Trade; they were known only to a small circle within the Hungarian leadership—including, of course, János Kádár himself. The dialogue was to be conducted only with the Party's International Department and specifically with him personally. The reason for this extraordinary level of confidentiality was that the Hungarians had no intention of informing the Russians of their approach to the EC until it produced a concrete result. This carried the unspoken implication that Hungarian ministries were so effectively penetrated by

Soviet agents and 'advisers' that Moscow would become aware of any information passed to them. I reflected on the paradox that in Communist Hungary the only institution that could be relied upon not to leak secrets to the Russians was the Communist Party itself.

Although Kádár's cultivation of contacts with the West produced a steady flow of Western credits and, in 1982, an IMF rescue operation that saved Hungary from rescheduling her debts, the country's economic performance did not respond adequately to the stimulus of the revived and accelerated NEM. Foreign credits masked the basic weakness of the Hungarian economy, which the reform process alone could not remedy. Growth had slowed to less than 2 per cent in the early 1980s, while both Hungary's trade deficit and the burden of servicing mounting debts increased. In 1981, the Soviet Union added about $220 million to Hungary's hard currency import bill by suddenly imposing a 20 per cent reduction in the quantity of crude oil Hungary could purchase at favourable CMEA rates, thus forcing her either to buy Soviet crude with dollars or turn to Western suppliers. Hungarian reserves of convertible currencies fell from $2,000 million at the end of 1981 to only $500 million by March 1982. Hungary's fundamental problem lay in the inability, and unwillingness, of Kádár and his colleagues to carry economic reform to its logical conclusion. Hungary's major industrial enterprises, the dinosaurs of the economy, evaded much of the impact of the NEM by holding over the government the threat of bankruptcy and consequent unemployment: full employment remained an inviolate totem in a socialist society. The surge of activity in the 'second economy', moreover, was conducted at considerable cost to the 'first': factory workers belonging to VGMKs tended to be sparing with their energies during normal working hours in order to deploy them to maximum effect, and profit, after clocking off. Many workers, VGMK partners or not, had access to private plots in the countryside on which they produced fruit, vegetables and wine for sale. When my weekend riding and carriage-driving lessons took me through villages near Budapest, I was constantly struck by the contrast between the frenzy of weekend activity in the countryside and the sluggish pace of work in the factories I visited during the week; there, much of the workforce appeared to be recuperating from their weekend efforts in the 'second economy' and gathering strength for the next bout.

In mid-1983, I reported to London that the reform process had progressed as far as it could without coming up against ideological road-blocks: to push them aside would invite retribution from the Soviet occupying power, while to abandon reform would put in jeopardy its achievements to date. An atmosphere of inertia in government circles and faltering confidence caused me greater unease about Hungary's prospects than I had felt at any time during my three years in Budapest. My apprehension proved justified more quickly than I had expected, as the final chapter of this narrative will show. Hungary's net foreign indebtedness already amounted to $8.8 billion in 1984; it would rise to $10.7 billion in 1987. The national debt as a whole had risen to $20 billion by 1989, by a long way the highest per capita in the socialist bloc. Comparing their lot with that of their neighbours, Hungarians could nevertheless feel a measure of satisfaction. Romania had succeeded in substantially reducing her foreign debt, but only by inflicting massive hardship on her population; Poland's debt problem had not become quite as acute as Hungary's, but inflation reached 26 per cent by 1987 and real wages dropped by 17 per cent between 1980 and 1986; Czechoslovakia and East Germany, with their more developed industrial base, outperformed Hungary by most economic measurements but their peoples still lived in a political and social straitjacket. Nevertheless, if the Hungarian population was to remain largely reconciled to one-party rule and foreign occupation, the improvement in its living standards had to continue on an upward curve: when I left Hungary to take up a post in London, the improvement had already slowed to a halt. Soon afterwards, it was to go into reverse, with dramatic political consequences.

Kádár's Hungary

When I arrived in Hungary at the beginning of 1980, my first impression was of a society at ease with itself. Like most first impressions, this was only partly accurate, as I subsequently discovered; but it contained some truth. The Hungarian people had enjoyed well over a decade of unaccustomed and therefore welcome stability. They had more than enough to eat. Indeed, eating had become a national obsession, perhaps in reaction to past deprivations; Hungarians seemed to spend most of their time munching, not only in their homes, in restaurants and in cafés but on the streets, in the parks and by the swimming pools. One-third of the population had been officially classified as obese. Living standards had been rising steadily for a number of years and most families had acquired—albeit at a high price relative to wage levels—the basic symbols of material well-being: a refrigerator, a washing machine and a television set. Every third family owned a car, despite waiting lists of up to six years for East German Trabants, Soviet Ladas, Polish Fiats, Czechoslovak Škodas and Romanian Dacias (the CMEA's division of labour policy prevented Hungary from manufacturing her own automobiles, obliging her to concentrate on buses). Every second family owned or shared some form of country retreat, often a tiny prefabricated A-frame dwelling resting on a small but intensively cultivated plot of land. Although still subject to petty restrictions, foreign travel had become possible, to the West as well as to Hungary's socialist neighbours: Hungarians with invitations and a financial guarantee from an overseas host could apply for an exit visa, and a derisory $5 currency allowance, once a year; while tourist exit visas, with a $100 allowance, could usually be obtained every three years. By 1980, the number of journeys made by Hungarians travelling abroad to all destinations exceeded five million a year. Kádár confidently proclaimed: 'Let Hungarians see for themselves the so-called "Paradise of the West"—and be happy once they get back here'.[19] This confidence was not misplaced for so long as living conditions in Hungary continued to improve—very few Hungarians left the country illegally or failed to return from overseas trips; but when, as we shall see, living standards declined in the 1980s, the possibility of foreign travel ceased to be a political asset to the regime and became a serious liability. For the time being, however, foreign travel had become an important dimension of the enlargement of personal freedom that, in addition to greater material well-being, the regime offered in return for political good behaviour.

In political terms, the 'democratisation' of Hungarian society under Kádár was more cosmetic than real. A new constitution, introduced and rubber-stamped by

Parliament in 1972, contained wording designed to make it less of a Soviet clone and to give it a more national character: but in essentials it differed very little from the Stalinist version of 1949, which it replaced. The abolition, in 1966, of the single list of candidates in parliamentary elections and the restoration of the traditional system under which constituencies voted for one or more individual candidates appeared to be a step towards democratic practice; but since all candidacies remained subject to vetting and approval by the ruling Party it amounted to very little, especially since, in the great majority of constituencies, only a single candidate stood for election. Hungarians nevertheless benefited, during the Kádár years, from a number of measures designed to modernise and improve their social environment. By the 1970s, the provision of a state pension for men at the age of sixty and for women at fifty-five applied to the whole population and maternity benefits had been significantly improved. A dramatic increase in the recruitment and training of doctors brought about a significant improvement in routine health care, although it could not, as we shall see, make much impact on health problems stemming more from social ills than from disease. Similarly, a major increase in the number of schoolteachers, and improvements in their training, produced positive results in primary and secondary education. The Education Act of 1961 brought an end to the small village schools in which, of necessity, several grades had shared a teacher and a classroom, bringing the level of education in the countryside up to the level of that in the towns—although most rural schoolchildren now faced a lengthy bus journey to and from their nearest general school. Further reforms in the 1960s and 1970s produced a situation in which, on leaving general school at the age of fourteen, pupils could choose between continuing their academic education at high school (*gimnázium*), entering a vocational middle school (*szakközépiskola*) or embarking on an industrial apprenticeship combined with some general education in an apprentice school (*szakmunkásképző iskola*). By the late 1970s, nine out of ten children leaving general school were exercising one of these options and thereby continuing their education to the age of eighteen in the majority of cases. In the revitalised teaching profession, liberated from its Stalinist straitjacket, teachers were permitted to specialise, to select their own course materials and to choose, within the guidelines of a national curriculum, their own teaching methods. The average pupil-teacher ratio in general schools fell to an enviable fifteen. My own experience of Hungary confirms the judgement made by a Hungarian historian in 1999, that 'in terms of the body of knowledge that has been mastered, the average Hungarian completing high school during recent years has not just caught up with but, many would argue, overtaken the average 18 year-old in western Europe or America'.[20]

In higher education, of its nature more vulnerable to damage from the application of ideological and political constraints, progress during the Kádár era was less marked. Even in the 1970s and 1980s, the quality of scholarship and of the academic profession in Hungary still suffered from the imposition upon it of rigid political conformity during the two preceding decades. Academic standards at Hungary's universities suffered further from the deliberate concentration of research activity in research institutes under the direct control of the Academy of Sciences and under that of the Party, which could thus strangle at birth heretical or inconvenient findings. Quantitatively, however, the increase of the proportion of high school leavers going on to acquire a university degree or equivalent qualification from 2.3 per cent in 1960 to 7 per cent in 1984 was not insignificant. Although the university entry system had ceased to be distorted by positive discrimination in favour of students from working-class homes, the children of senior Party and government officials and other notables could still expect to be given privileged access.

The Kádár regime's tacit compromise with the Hungarian people inevitably imparted an element of cynicism to public and social life. Hungarians observed the rituals required of them in a Communist society—the rallies, the meetings, the slogan-mouthing—dutifully but without commitment or enthusiasm. Although it could not be voiced openly, anti–Russian feeling remained as strong as ever: Hungarian school pupils typically succeeded in undergoing eight years of compulsory classes in the Russian language without retaining more than half a dozen words of it. Apart from making money in the 'second economy', the one dimension of Hungarian life untouched by the prevailing apathy was that of nationhood and national identity. My last despatch to London from Budapest contained this passage:

My colleague in Warsaw* perceptively remarked, after only a few hours of a visit to Hungary, that the Hungarians are not a 'spiritual' people. He was quite right. The religion and culture of Hungarians is their nationhood. Their churches, their music, their poetry and their language are all, in one way or another, symbols of national survival and continuing national vitality. In a larger or more powerful country, this dominance of national sentiment might be distasteful, even disturbing. In a country two-thirds the size of England with a population only one-third larger than that of Greater London; a country which has been trampled on by, successively, Tartars, Turks, Austrians, Germans and Russians; a country which has lost every war it has fought in five hundred years—I have found the quality admirable and attractive.

It was a quality, too, with which the Kádár regime did its best to align itself, so far as this was possible without offending Soviet sensitivities.

In the aftermath of the 1956 Revolution, the HSWP had condemned all manifestations of national pride as symptoms of 'bourgeois nationalism'; Rákóczi's and Kossuth's fighters for independence were virtually written out of history textbooks for fear that their achievements and sacrifices might legitimise those of the freedom fighters of 1956. Kádár's 'alliance policy', however, soon obliged the regime to give cautious sanction to Hungary's irrepressible pride of nationhood. The still unhealed scars of Trianon were acknowledged, most publicly by Kádár himself in his speech to the final session of the Conference on Security and Cooperation in Europe (CSCE) in Helsinki in 1975. Less publicly, Kádár and government ministers made repeated representations to President Ceauşescu and the Romanian government about growing discrimination against the Hungarian minority in Transylvania. A committee of the Patriotic People's Front was authorised in 1968 to examine and report on conditions for Hungarian minorities in neighbouring states, a process that gained a much higher profile in 1985 when the regime established the Institute of Hungarian Studies to carry it forward. The constantly simmering but repressed tensions in the Hungarian-Romanian relationship were brought to the

* Sir Kenneth James, KCMG.

481

boil in 1986 with the publication of a massive three-volume *History of Transylvania* by a team of Hungarian academics led, as chief editor, by the Minister of Culture, Béla Köpeczi. A work of genuine scholarship, the *History* firmly but unpolemically promulgated the traditional Hungarian version of early Transylvanian history, namely that 'before the beginning of the thirteenth Century, there is no evidence—historical, archaeological or toponymic—for the existence of a Romanian population in Transylvania'.[21] In retaliation, leading Romanian historians publicly denounced the Hungarian work as 'a conscious forgery of history', even taking out a full page advertisement in *The Times* for the purpose. When Kádár sanctioned the 'Mother-tongue Movement', which brought together, in periodic conferences in Budapest, Hungarian speakers from across the world, including Czechoslovakia and Yugoslavia, Ceauşescu prohibited attendance by Hungarians from Transylvania. Although these activities gained for the regime some temporary credit from the Hungarian public, this was soon outweighed by their evident failure to produce concrete results: Ceauşescu remained impervious to Hungarian complaints and Kádár conspicuously failed to take up the cudgels on behalf of the heavily disadvantaged Hungarian minority in Slovakia. As was to become very apparent in the 1980s, the regime's unwillingness to risk incurring Moscow's displeasure by giving the plight of neighbouring Hungarian minorities the prominence that, in the view of many Hungarians, it deserved, became a further political liability.

Although he distrusted intellectuals, Kádár knew very well that his unwritten compact with the Hungarian people would not hold unless it commanded the support of, or at least acceptance by Hungary's writers and intelligentsia, traditionally the focus and the catalyst of dissent. The years of repression that followed the 1956 Revolution had borne heavily upon the literary and intellectual community, many of whose members suffered imprisonment or internment until the political amnesty of 1963 restored their freedom. Kádár entrusted the vital task of building a *modus vivendi* between the regime and the intelligentsia to György Aczél, like him a veteran of the illegal HCP in the 1930s and of Rákosi's prison cells in the early 1950s. Elected to the Central Committee of the HSWP in 1956, appointed deputy Minister of Culture in 1957, and subsequently a member of the Politburo and of the Party Secretariat, Aczél presided over the regime's cultural policies, and managed its relationship with the intellectual community for thirty years. He became Kádár's closest confidant and, given the importance of the creative arts in Hungarian life, virtually the public face of the regime. A subtle man, self-taught and widely read, Aczél could engage writers in debate on equal terms. A well-developed understanding of the complexities of human nature told him when persuasion was possible or the application of gentle—or less gentle—pressure necessary. Above all, Aczél possessed a fine sense of the point at which heterodoxy ceased to be helpful to the Kádár compromise and threatened to damage the Party's authority, of which he was an unswerving and sometimes implacable guardian. He defined three categories of writing and artistic work: the 'three Ts' (*támogatott, tűrt* and *tiltott*), which loosely translate into English as the 'three Ps'—promotable, permissible and prohibited. A Central Committee resolution in 1966, introduced by Aczél, sanctioned artistic works which were 'ideologically debatable and more or less in opposition to Marxism or socialist realism, as long as they [possessed] humanistic value and [were] not politically hostile'.[22]

Under this relatively benign formula, Hungarian writing, albeit sanitised in obvious respects, revived and flourished. Several leading poets, including Gyula Illyés, János Pilinszky and Ágnes Nemes Nagy, published some of their most important work during the 1960s. In prose, the tradition of social criticism in the Hungarian novel was carried forward by Déry, Ferenc Sánta and Ákos Kertész among others, while other writers including István Örkény and Géza Ottlik developed more experimental forms. The more serious sociological genre of the 'village explorers' in the inter-war years found new expression in the works of Gyula Csák and Sándor Csoóri. The retreat from economic reform in the early 1970s, however, was mirrored in a retreat from permissiveness in the cultural field. The young radical writer Miklós Haraszti was arrested in 1974 for his authorship of *Darabbér* ('Piecework'), about his experiences on the shop floor of a tractor factory,* which had begun to circulate in *samizdat* form; he received a suspended prison sentence. A sociological work by the novelist György Konrád provoked his arrest on charges of 'anti–socialist agitation'; but the authorities did not press the charges and the book, *The Intellectuals on the Road to Class Power*, was later published with excisions. In general, and thanks largely to Aczél's deft management, the cultural field suffered much less from the conservative counter-attack of the 1970s than the economic reform programme. When the spasm of reaction had passed, writers such as Péter Esterházy and Péter Nádas were able to carry the development of the Hungarian novel into a neo-modernist phase. Setbacks occurred only when new works took up overtly political themes. In general, the publication of a steady flow of new writing, together with the unrestricted reprinting of Hungarian and foreign classics, satisfied the Hungarian reading public. The same was true for theatre-and cinema-goers. The Kádár era, particularly the 1960s and 1970s, can be seen in retrospect as the golden age of Hungarian cinema: Hungarian film directors such as Miklós Jancsó, Károly Makk, Márta Mészáros and István Szabó were sometimes able to push back the bounds of the permissible more successfully than the writers and poets. Hungarians particularly appreciated, and gave the regime due credit for, increased access to Western plays and films; in a single week of October 1980, I noted that Budapest's theatres were performing plays by Arnold Wesker, Peter Shaffer, Alan Ayckbourn and Brian Clark in addition to five separate Shakespearean productions. In the world of music, all the previously banned works of Bartók were now being performed, including *Miraculous Mandarin*. György Kurtág was enlarging the repertoire of native Hungarian composition; and brilliant young pianists such as Zoltán Kocsis, Dezső Ránki and András Schiff were beginning to establish their international reputations. The richness and, despite political constraints, diversity of the nation's cultural life constituted a major factor in reconciling a majority of the Hungarian population to the loss of their political freedom.

And yet, in the last resort, János Kádár's provision of bread and circuses proved insufficient to sustain the compromise on which the HSWP's rule depended. After three years in Hungary, I recognised the deficiencies in my first impression, in 1980, of a society at ease with itself. Hungary's youth, in particular, with no

---

* Published in English as *A Worker in a Workers' State: Piece-Rates in Hungary* (London, 1977).

collective memory of 1956, let alone the horrors of the Rákosi era, found the acquisitive materialism their parents had embraced so enthusiastically unsatisfying and the society in which they lived uninspiring. The sector of social policy of greatest relevance to their daily lives, that of housing, was that in which the regime had most conspicuously failed to deliver. The housing shortage, especially in Budapest, remained acute throughout the Kádár years; state investment in municipal housing steadily diminished in real terms and failed to make up the shortfall in the replenishment of housing stock, which had grown ever since 1945. Most young couples were obliged to live with their parents or in-laws for anything up to ten years before their slow climb up the municipal housing list was rewarded with a cramped, ill-built two-room flat. Although the private building sector was considerably more buoyant in terms of units completed—typically double that of the state sector in any given year—its prices exceeded the means of most young home-seekers and the market was distorted by corruption. Corruption, indeed, was endemic in Kádár's Hungary, both petty—the 'brown envelope culture'*—and on a larger scale; but it was at its worst in the housing market. From this situation stemmed many of Hungary's social ills: a low birth rate, a high incidence of divorce and a suicide rate of 50–70 per 100,000 head of population, or 6.5 per cent of all deaths. Suicide had always been a significant social problem in Hungary; but the high incidence of suicides among young people now became a new and major source of concern. During the 1970s, suicide became the most common cause of death for fifteen—to nineteen-year-olds.[23] By the 1980s, alcoholism had also become a major problem in a country that had for a long time ranked high in the world league table for per capita alcohol consumption. At the beginning of that decade, there were about 500,000 registered alcoholics in Hungary;[24] during the next twenty years, this figure rose to 850–900,000, or 8–9 per cent of the population.[25] One-third of the population smoked, many of them heavily. By the 1990s, alcohol and tobacco accounted for 60 per cent of deaths among middle-aged men. Between 1960 and 1984, life expectancy for the Hungarian male fell from 66.4 to 65 years (although women were more fortunate, living on average to the age of seventy-three). The incidence of mental illness in Hungary doubled between 1970 and 1981 and doubled again during the 1980s. This is not a picture, clearly, of 'a society at ease with itself', as I acknowledged in my final despatch from Budapest. Social tensions arose not only from increasingly unfavourable comparisons, made possible by foreign travel and access to Western films, television and printed media, between living conditions in Hungary and those in Western Europe; but also from internal differentials in living standards, between Budapest and the provinces, and between relatively prospering Transdanubia and the much poorer eastern half of the country. For some of these tensions, animosity towards Hungary's growing Roma (Gypsy) minority served as an outlet: numbering around 400,000 by the 1980s, the Roma, with their large families and unorthodox lifestyle, came increasingly to be regarded as parasites and to a large extent replaced the now much less significant Jewish population as scape-

---

* The passing across desks of a brown envelope containing a small sum of money was a routine accompaniment to most interviews with doctors, teachers, retailers and bureaucrats at which a request was to be made or a favour asked.

goats for all the ills of Hungarian society. To this potentially volatile mix of problems and discontents was added, from the mid-1980s, an accelerating decline in the real incomes of most of the population: by 1988, these were on average 13 per cent below 1980 levels. Disposable incomes, which had grown at an average rate of 3.5 per cent annually during the 1970s, grew by only 0.3 per cent during the 1980s, a figure that concealed a dramatic fall from 1985 onwards. This resulted in part from the regime's introduction of financial measures which, though sensible and necessary in themselves, should have been implemented earlier and more gradually: price increases designed to close the gap between the domestic and world markets, a progressive income tax and a new value-added tax of 15–25 per cent all hit family budgets hard. The national consensus created by the Kádár compromise began to crumble. When the leaders and local delegates of the HSWP assembled in May 1988, for the third extraordinary conference in the Party's history, it was clear to all its participants that political change could no longer be postponed.

20

ROUND TABLE REVOLUTION
AND DEMOCRATIC HUNGARY

(1988–2000)

An Opposition Emerges

One of the features of Hungarian society that I found intriguing and attractive was, and is, the symbiosis between its writers and the people at large. In 1848, 1956 and now, in the early 1980s, Hungarian writers and poets demonstrated acute sensitivity to, and sympathy with, the mood and concerns of ordinary people and courage in articulating them. The funeral in 1979 of István Bibó, the political philosopher who had represented the Petőfi Party in Imre Nagy's 1956 government and who provided one of the last links with Hungary's pre-Communist political tradition, provided the genesis of a coherent reform movement in Hungary during the last decade of the Kádár regime. Attended by most members of Hungary's intellectual community, it resulted in the compilation of the *Bibó Memorial Book*, a massive collection of reminiscences, populist reflections (including one by Gyula Illyés), and dissident essays on the need for reform. Denied publication by the Party, it subsequently circulated piecemeal in samizdat, Hungary's first major excursion into a genre already well developed in the Soviet Union, Czechoslovakia and Poland. This, together with the inspiration provided by the rise of the Solidarity movement in Poland, led to the creation of the samizdat journal *Beszélő* ('Speaker'), which aimed to circulate uncensored news together with editorial comment and by the early 1980s had achieved a regular readership of 10,000. The collective editorship of *Beszélő*, led by János Kis, included Miklós Haraszti, and László Rajk, son of the victim of Rákosi's show trial, who played a major role in the distribution of the journal and other samizdat material. They suffered occasional harassment from the ÁVH—a body which, it should be noted, maintained a high level of malign activity throughout the Kádár years; but the regime took no formal action against the dissidents, partly because Kádár himself underestimated their influence and partly for fear of provoking more serious opposition. Further evidence of new currents flowing beneath the apparently tranquil political surface of Kádár's Hungary was provided by the parliamentary elections in 1985, the first to be held under a new law that obliged all constituencies to field more than one candidate. Although only seventy-one of the 154 non-official would-be candidates survived the nomination process, which the HSWP took care to control, thirty-five of them defeated their official opponents and entered Parliament to form the nucleus of the first independent—but not dissident or oppositionist—caucus.

The nascent reform movement had from the beginning exemplified the traditional Hungarian division between liberal urban intellectuals, represented by the editors of *Beszélő* among others, and the more nationalist Populists among whom writers and poets such as Illyés and László Németh were prominent. Although there was a great deal of common ground between them, the former group attached primary importance to democratic reform and human rights, while the latter put national independence and support for oppressed Hungarian minorities at the top of their agenda. A third group, potentially the most important, began to emerge after 1983: Marxist intellectuals and members of the HSWP, some of them in senior positions, who perceived the urgent need for reform if Hungary was to remain a socialist society. Immediately after the parliamentary elections in June 1985, the veteran reformist and ally of Imre Nagy, Ferenc Donáth, convened an unofficial conference near Monor, south east of Budapest, which brought together about fifty representatives of all strands of the reform movement to discuss the threat of a social crisis resulting from declining living standards. The proceedings of the conference were inconclusive and the three reformist groupings thereafter went their own ways.

In 1987, impelled by rising popular discontent and a mounting sense of crisis, each grouping significantly raised its profile. The editors of *Beszélő* produced a special edition entitled 'Social Contract', which opened with the words 'Kádár must go!' and went on to call for a public renegotiation of the 'Kádár compromise', a multi–party democracy and a national declaration of neutrality. A group of young HSWP economists produced a substantial report under the title 'Turnaround and Reform' (*Fordulat és Reform*), of which extensive leaks obliged the regime reluctantly to publish a sanitised version; this called for an accelerated programme of radical economic reform accompanied by political democratisation.

The Populists, for their part, organised a conference of intellectuals, on 17 September 1987, in the village of Lakitelek, on the River Tisza near Kecskemét, to which they invited Imre Pozsgay, whom they hoped might eventually lead the HSWP and whose presence might afford a measure of protection, and Mihály Bihari, author of a report entitled 'Reform and Democracy' (*Reform és Demokrácia*), which called for the separation of Party and state and for the legitimisation of factions within the HSWP. Pozsgay, an outstanding orator, electrified the conference with a ringing call for 'a new national coalition' which would prepare the way towards 'a democratic and socialist Hungary'; his speech subsequently earned him a reprimand from the Politburo. An intellectual with the appearance of a large, podgy schoolboy, Imre Pozsgay, after joining the Party in his teens, had begun his career as director of the Marxist-Leninist Evening University in Kecskemét; his doctoral thesis had amounted to a manifesto for socialist reform, arguing that economic and political reform were inseparable. He had been appointed Minister of Culture in 1976, a post in which he worked in uneasy partnership with the cultural overlord, György Aczél. In my own dealings with him in that capacity, I found him an engaging interlocutor, outside and above the common run of Communist ministers. Elected to the Central Committee of the HSWP in 1980, Pozsgay's reformist views barred him both from the Politburo and from succeeding Aczél when the latter lost his seat in the Secretariat in 1982. Instead, he reluctantly accepted the secretary-generalship of the Patriotic People's Front (PPF); he then used this position, with considerable skill, as a platform on which to establish a national reputation as the recognised leader of the socialist reform movement, the champion of social and religious minorities and the protector of the many reformist clubs and associations springing up in a more permissive environment. The Lakitelek conference marked the beginning of Imre Pozsgay's drive towards political leadership.

A second meeting was to take place at Lakitelek a year later, on 3 September 1988, held, like the first, in the back garden of a poet, Sándor Lezsák. Its closing declaration announced the creation of the 'Hungarian Democratic Forum' (HDF), soon to become the first opposition political party; its founding members, present on that occasion, included József Antall, soon to be the first Prime Minister of free Hungary, and Géza Jeszenszky, future Foreign Minister in the country's first democratically elected government.

Pozsgay's speech at Lakitelek had been delivered against a background of shifting political scenery in Budapest and the expectation of greater changes to come. The Central Committee, in a tacit admission of the Party's mismanagement of the economy, had transferred responsibility for economic policy to the government and, in June 1987, had approved Kádár's choice of Károly Grósz to take over the Premiership from György Lázár. Like Pozsgay, Grósz had joined the HWP in his teens, rising by 1962 to head the Party organisation in state radio and television, a post of considerable influence. He used his subsequent appointment to the propaganda department of the Central Committee to align himself with the Party's hardliners, a move that paid off when the reform process went into reverse in the 1970s. He established a reputation in Party circles as a straightforward, pragmatic and plain-speaking operator who got things done. Kádár trusted him sufficiently to put him, in 1979, at the head of the Borsod County Party Committee, which ruled Hungary's second industrial city, Miskolc; five years later, with Soviet approval, Grósz had risen to even greater heights as First Secretary of the Budapest Party organisation and a member of the Politburo. By 1987, he had sufficient confidence in the strength of his position to attach conditions to his acceptance of the Premiership: at his insistence, Kádár agreed that the Politburo would refrain from imposing policy decisions on the government and that Grósz would have a free hand in personnel matters—a major shift in the traditional balance of power between Party and government.

Kádár's personal authority was fast slipping away. Now aged seventy-five, his physical exhaustion had become obvious not only to his Party colleagues but also, from their television screens, to the general public. In his public speeches, he meandered and lost his thread. His holidays, often unscheduled, became longer and more frequent. Although Hungary was sliding into acute economic crisis, Kádár refused to contemplate the radical measures, such as the closure of Hungary's unprofitable industrial dinosaurs, which alone could avert it. But he continued to regard himself as indispensable to the HSWP and to Hungary; when, at the Central Committee meeting in June 1987 which approved the appointment of Grósz to the Premiership, Jenő Fock and Rezső Nyers bravely suggested that Kádár should exchange the general-secretaryship of the Party for the symbolic post of chairman, he adamantly refused. The question of his removal and, more contentiously, that of who should succeed him, nevertheless moved to the top of the political agenda. Pozsgay had clearly emerged as a potential leader, but he had many enemies within the Party who saw him as a threat to its authority. János Berecz, a Kádár protégé who had worked his way up the Party *apparat* to head the international department of the Central Committee and then to hold the ideology portfolio in the Party Secretariat, certainly regarded himself as a candidate for the succession. A political bruiser, he had more charisma than intellect; his unqualified condemnation of the 1956 Revolution and his pugnacious conservatism on cultural issues of which he had an imperfect understanding outraged the intelligentsia and alienated the younger generation. Károly Grósz, the intelligent pragmatist, positioned himself neatly between the more extreme positions of these two potential rivals; he greatly strengthened his position with a televised speech in Parliament in September 1987, in which he addressed with remarkable frankness the country's dire economic situation and the regime's responsibility for it. In a long televised interview on New Year's Day 1988, Grósz openly declared his qualifications for leadership of the HSWP and established himself as front runner in the succession stakes.

Endgame for the HSWP

The events of the next two years, 1988 and 1989, were as dramatic as any in Hungary's long and turbulent history. They took place against the background of, and were to a great extent determined by, the political earthquake in Moscow that had begun with the election of Mikhail Gorbachev as General Secretary of the CPSU in 1985. His policies of *perestroika* and *glasnost* were to transform—and ultimately destroy—the Soviet Union. Unlike his three predecessors, Gorbachev had the courage to face the stark facts of his country's economic weakness and vulnerability; and to draw the necessary conclusions from them. He recognised that the restructuring of the Soviet economy could be achieved safely, without endangering the socialist order, only in a stable international environment marked by *rapprochement* between East and West, particularly in Europe. In promoting the concept of the 'common European home', Gorbachev hoped to transform the cockpit of tensions between two mutually antagonistic political systems and alliances into a region of stability and constructive co-operation. He hoped, too, to create circumstances that would permit some reduction in Soviet military expenditure, which constituted a massive drain on the ailing Soviet economy.

These objectives at once placed the relationship between the Soviet Union and its east European neighbours high on the political agenda. The first hint of a radical change in that relationship had been given in November 1986 at the Moscow summit meeting of socialist leaders to discuss 'problems of economic co-operation'. The traditional pattern of trade, whereby the Soviet Union exported energy and raw materials to the countries of eastern Europe at prices well below world levels, receiving in return overpriced manufactured goods of poor quality, had become increasingly disadvantageous and costly to Moscow. The measures now proposed implied, in Gorbachev's words, 'an invitation to base economic relations within the Socialist community on market principles';[1] their implementation was to be obstructed by the more conservative East European regimes (although they were welcomed by János Kádár and by General Wojciech Jaruzelski of Poland) and finally overtaken by events in the countries concerned. Of even greater importance, however, was Gorbachev's public repudiation, at the 19th Conference of the CPSU in June 1988, of the 'Brezhnev doctrine', by which since 1968 the Soviet regime had claimed the right to intervene in the affairs of its socialist neighbours, if necessary by force, if socialism was deemed to be threatened. Gorbachev now proclaimed the freedom of every country to choose its socio-political system: 'In this situation, foreign imposition of a social system or a lifestyle through any method, and even more so through military measures, is a dangerous way of acting from the past'.[2] Finally, in his speech to the United Nations General Assembly six months later, Gorbachev announced that 10,000 Soviet troops and 5,000 tanks would be withdrawn from Hungary, the GDR and Czechoslovakia.

These historic declarations, together with the departure from the Politburo of foreign policy hardliners including Gromyko and Ligachev, told the peoples of eastern and central Europe that political and economic reform no longer incurred the risk of a punitive reaction from Moscow; and served notice on their Communist leaderships that the threat of Soviet intervention could no longer be used as a pretext for the obstruction of change.

The announcement that an extraordinary conference of the Soviet Communist Party (CPSU) would be convened in Moscow in June 1988 created irresistible pressure within the HSWP for a similar Party conference in Hungary: Kádár acceded to it and the conference was scheduled for May. The preparations for this event at which, as was generally accepted, the future leadership and direction of the Party would be determined, revealed the extent of the HSWP's disarray. The draft theses, or platform, for the conference, drawn up by Berecz and other hardliners, met with flat rejection not only by the most important local Party committees, including that of Budapest, but also by Pozsgay's PPF, the trade unions and the Party youth organisation, KISZ. In a last, fruitless attempt to defend orthodoxy, Kádár secured the expulsion from the Party of four of the young economists, including Mihály Bihari, who had contributed to the radical report 'Turnaround and Reform'; he also persuaded the Politburo to reprimand Pozsgay for his speech at Lakitelek and Rezső Nyers for agreeing to preside over a new reformist group, the 'New March Front'. These, however, were the last matters in which Kádár's wishes prevailed. When, at a meeting of the Central Committee on 10 May 1988, his proposals for relatively modest personnel changes in the Party leadership were voted down in favour of wholesale replacement, Kádár at last accepted that he would have to go. In a significant revelation of the burden his past imposed upon him, Kádár attached conditions to his resignation from the general-secretaryship: that he should not be called to account for László Rajk's confession in prison in 1949, nor for his role in the 1956 Revolution, nor for the punitive measures that followed it, nor for the reversal of the process of economic reform in the 1970s. On being given appropriate assurances, Kádár agreed to be 'promoted' to the new post of Party Chairman and to relinquish his seat on the Politburo. He would retain membership of the Central Committee.

When the Third Conference of the HSWP assembled on 20 May 1988, Kádár had already sought and obtained Moscow's approval for his own resignation and for the appointment of Károly Grósz to succeed him. His valedictory speech to the conference, which unexpectedly revived the hardline political vocabulary of the 1950s, lost him such support as he had retained and enabled Grósz to carry through a complete purge not only of the Politburo but of the Central Committee as well. Grósz himself, despite having promised the Premiership to Imre Pozsgay, became Prime Minister as well as General Secretary of the HSWP. This combination, together with the fact that the Politburo and Central Committee were now packed with his nominees, should have made his position impregnable. During the next few months he presided over a spate of economic reforms, introduced at a hectic pace, which he hoped would arrest the downward spiral of the Hungarian economy. Virtually all remaining controls on both prices and wages were removed. The Party abandoned its commitment to full employment. In an attempt to create a genuine market economy, state enterprises were permitted to transform themselves into private limited companies or public listed companies. The law which authorised this significant degree of privatisation was soon perceived, however, to be a licence for the managers of state enterprises, the 'red barons', to make their fortunes from the unregulated sale of state assets, which changed hands at absurdly low prices within a closed circle of Party members. The relaxation of censorship, leading to its complete abolition at the end of the year, enabled the media to give uninhibited coverage to this and other developments that further lowered the standing and authority of the HSWP. One issue that united several strands of the opposition movement was that of the joint Czechoslovak-Hungarian Gabčikovo-Nagymaros River diversion and hydroelectric dam project on the Danube Bend, a massively costly and environmentally damaging scheme which now threatened to come to fruition. Public demands for a change of leadership were superseded by demands for a change of regime. These were encouraged by events in the Soviet Union, where Gorbachev had clearly signalled his lack of interest in maintaining a Soviet hegemony in eastern Europe that was costly both politically and financially. Hungarians were not slow to appreciate that they were no longer obliged to accept one-party Communist rule as a condition of their national existence; and that they no longer needed the buffer between Budapest and Moscow that János Kádár had provided for over thirty years.

The MDF* was no longer the only organised opposition group. In March 1988, the foundation of the Young Democrats' Alliance (*Fiatal Demokraták Szövetsége* or FIDESZ) gave expression to the disillusionment and frustration that had been building up for years in Hungary's universities, where KISZ had long since

---

* Although I have retained the abbreviation—HSWP—for the anglicised name of the Hungarian Socialist Workers' Party, simply because, like CPSU for the Soviet Communist Party, it is more readily recognisable than the Magyar version, I have used Magyar-based abbreviations for the names of the new political parties that now came into being—anglicised abbreviations would be equally unfamiliar to non-Hungarian readers.

ceased to command respect or exert authority. In November 1988, the predominantly urban radicals, including the *Beszélő* circle, who had not been invited to the Lakitelek conference, formed their own party, the Alliance of Free Democrats (*Szabad Demokraták Szövetsége*, SzDSz). At the same time, a reform movement had begun to emerge within the ruling HSWP but outside Budapest, in the municipal and county Party organisations, the so-called 'reform circles' (*reformkörök*). These were composed largely of middle-aged intellectuals, committed to socialism, but concerned for the survival of the Party unless it embraced institutional reform and had the courage to take its chances in a multi–party system. From the meeting of the first reform circle in Szeged, late in 1988, the movement developed during the following months into a national network of discussion groups, which maintained direct contact with each other without reference to or sanction from the central Party organisation in Budapest. This challenge to the traditionally vertical structure of the Party was to pose a major threat to its leadership in 1989. Finally, the removal of censorship and the HSWP's apparent tolerance of political pluralism allowed Hungary's historic political parties to revive and to attempt to adjust to circumstances very different from those in which they had last been free to operate, over thirty years previously. The Independent Smallholders, the predominantly Catholic Christian Democratic People's Party, the Hungarian People's Party—successor to the Petőfi Party of 1956—and the Social Democratic Party re-established themselves and contributed to the avalanche of political pamphlets and journals beginning to flood the capital's kiosks by the end of the year. To varying extents, all were now able to benefit from financial support from outside Hungary. The Democratic Forum (MDF), however, having been first in the field and tapping the potent vein of Hungarian national sentiment, still constituted the most formidable opposition presence at the end of 1988.

Károly Grósz, meanwhile, had spent a busy summer during which, as it turned out, he sowed the seeds of his own political demise. During July, he paid official visits to both Moscow and Washington. Ostensibly, both visits went well; but both created hostages to fortune. In Moscow, Gorbachev received Grósz with great cordiality and undertook to give active consideration to Hungarian requests for guaranteed deliveries of oil and gas at current levels for the next six years, for Soviet approval of cuts in the Hungarian defence budget and for the urgent delivery of a new generation of machine tools for the modernisation of Hungarian industrial plant. In return, Gorbachev asked Grósz to mend Hungary's fences with Romania and to arrange an early meeting with Ceauşescu for this purpose. Hungarian-Romanian relations had indeed reached a nadir. The relaxation of censorship in Hungary had released a torrent of angry criticism of Ceauşescu's policy of 'systematisation'—the breaking up of rural communities and the herding of peasants into new satellite towns more amenable to political control, a policy that was being applied with particular ferocity to the villages of Transylvania with predominantly Hungarian populations. The Grósz government, having ordered the forcible dispersal of a popular demonstration in Budapest on 16 June to mark the anniversary of Imre Nagy's execution, had sanctioned an even larger demonstration two weeks later, under MDF auspices, to protest against Ceauşescu's abuses of human rights and persecution of the Hungarian minority in Romania. Against this unpromising background, Grósz rashly agreed to meet Ceauşescu at the end of August. As the venue for the meeting, Ceauşescu chose the formerly Hungarian, now Romanian, town of Arad where twelve Hungarian generals and a colonel had been hanged by the Austrians in 1849. Having set the stage, Ceauşescu used the occasion to effect a thorough-going humiliation of the inexperienced Grósz in a one-to-one session from which advisers were excluded,* and in which he vouchsafed not a single concession. Grósz, returning to Budapest empty-handed, incurred the contempt and enmity of the MDF and sustained serious damage to his authority in the country at large. In Washington, in July, Grósz had garnered prestige from a meeting with President Reagan in the White House; but he also agreed to meet representatives of the large Hungarian émigré community in the United States and, without prior consultation with his colleagues, acceded to their request that the remains of Imre Nagy should be disinterred and accorded a ceremonial reburial. This was to result, a year later, in the most powerful set-piece event in the collapse of Communism in Hungary.

These trials doubtless contributed to Grósz's decision, in November, to relinquish the Premiership and concentrate on strengthening his hold over the Party. Miklós Németh, a young economist who had been heading the economic department of the Central Committee Secretariat, became Prime Minister. Given subsequent events, it is easy to forget that in late 1988, and for some months afterwards, very few people indeed doubted that the HSWP would remain the dominant political party in Hungary for the foreseeable future, even in a multi-party system. None of the other parties that might contest the next parliamentary elections, due in the autumn of 1990, could even begin to match its 800,000 membership, its country-wide organisation or its physical and financial assets. Leadership of the HSWP, therefore, remained the supreme political prize and Károly Grósz was determined to retain it. For this he needed the continuing support of both the hardline majority, for which his rival was János Berecz, and that of the moderate reformers, for which Imre Pozsgay posed the main challenge. After jettisoning the Premiership, Grósz manoeuvred not unskilfully between the two. The extraordinary speech which he delivered to a Party rally in Budapest on 29 November, in which he warned against the activities of 'hostile counterrevolutionary forces' and against 'anarchy, chaos and … a white terror', strengthened his hold on the conservative constituency—a hardline speech by Berecz on the following day was mild by comparison—but also further alienated the reformers. On 28 January 1989, Pozsgay took advantage of this, and of Grósz's absence from the country, by revealing in a radio interview that the Party sub-committee charged with reviewing, under his own chairmanship, the history of the HSWP had determined that the 1956 Revolution had been 'a popular uprising against an oligarchical power', not the 'counter-revolution' the Party had condemned for so long. This revelation, and Pozsgay's simultaneously expressed support for a multi-party system, caused an immediate sensation and made him overnight the acknowledged champion of reform socialism.

If he had chosen to do so, Grósz could have mobilised a majority at the Central Committee's next meeting, in February, in favour of Pozsgay's expulsion from that

---

* This was a favourite tactic of Ceauşescu's: I saw him use it, fortunately to less effect, with the British Prime Minister, Harold Wilson, in Bucharest in 1975.

body and thus from the Politburo as well; he wisely decided not to hand Pozsgay the gift of martyrdom but to give him more rope instead. The Central Committee's communiqué in effect accepted the thrust of Pozsgay's radio interview and, more importantly, gave the Party's blessing to a plural political society in which non-Communist parties could operate legally, provided that they did so within the ideological framework of socialism and remained loyal to Hungary's military alliances. Grósz had not, however, finished with Pozsgay. A conference of reform circle members and other reformists, due to be held in Kecskemét on 15 April, became the focus of expectations that Pozsgay might split the HSWP by announcing the formation of a new party. Aware of the rumours, Alexander Yakovlev, Gorbachev's leading aide, took advantage of a chance meeting with Pozsgay in Rome to stress Moscow's support for Grósz; and Grósz himself, at a meeting of the Central Committee on 12 April, challenged Pozsgay to admit that he was planning to split the Party in Kecskemét. Pozsgay backed off. The speech he subsequently delivered to the reform conference was anodyne and uncontroversial, bitterly disappointing his supporters. Not for the last time, Pozsgay showed that for all his undoubted talents he lacked the killer instinct, which is an essential ingredient of effective political leadership. Grósz used the same Central Committee meeting to strengthen his hold on the Politburo by initiating the collective resignation of all its members, including himself, to pave the way for new elections to that body. Grósz's own re-election to the general-secretaryship of the Party was virtually unanimous; but among the Politburo members who failed to secure re-election was János Berecz—as Grósz had doubtless foreseen. Grósz's position, even within the Party elite, was nevertheless not so strong as it looked: he was going too fast for the comfort of some of his colleagues. When he asked the Politburo, on 19 April, to approve the declaration of an 'economic state of emergency', a concept with undertones of dictatorial power, the vote went against him; and the Prime Minister, Miklós Németh, showed his independence by publicly distancing himself from the proposal.

The Round Table Revolution

Beyond the walls of the 'White House' (the headquarters building of the HSWP), moreover, developments were in train that would transform Hungary's political landscape. The 'Independent Lawyers' Forum', which brought together 135 reform-minded members of the legal profession, may have been the smallest of the new opposition groups but it played a key role by inventing, in March 1989, the Opposition Round Table (*Ellenzéki Kerekasztal*). The declared purpose of the Round Table lay in bringing together all the leading opposition parties under one umbrella as the prelude to the initiation of negotiations with the regime on the pattern of the Polish National Round Table, at which representatives of the Solidarity movement were negotiating with the government of General Jaruzelski. The mounting strength of the opposition movement had just been demonstrated on 15 March, the anniversary of the 1848 Revolution: a commemorative demonstration organised by the opposition parties attracted over 100,000 participants, whereas only about 20,000 attended the official commemoration arranged by the HSWP. Following the 1848 tradition, the larger demonstration listened to a declaration of Twelve Demands to which all the opposition parties subscribed. These included a new constitution, free elections, multiparty democracy, national independence, neutrality in foreign policy, a new national coat of arms, an end to the political censorship of school textbooks, the disbanding of the Party's private army—the Workers' Guard—the withdrawal of Soviet troops from Hungary and an end of the division of Europe into two blocs. These echoes of 1848 and 1956 served a warning on the regime it could not ignore, not least because the cohesion of the HSWP was being steadily eroded by the activities of the reform circles in the provinces. The circles held their first national conference in Szeged in May, at which over 400 delegates represented 110 circles, and which heard speeches by both Imre Pozsgay and Rezső Nyers. According to one of his aides, Pozsgay had intended to use the occasion to launch a 'Movement for a Democratic Hungary' but, once again, his nerve apparently failed him.[3]

The combination of pressure from without—the opposition movement—and from within—the reform circles—had pushed the nominally ruling Party on to the defensive. It was seen to be losing control of events, an impression reinforced by a series of concessions on important issues. The Party youth organisation, KISZ, was dissolved in April and in May the ailing János Kádár was informed that he had been relieved of the Chairmanship of the HSWP and of his membership of the Central Committee. At the same time, the Party surrendered to the government its right to oversee non-party appointments and its control of the Workers' Guard, which became a militia under the Ministry of Defence. Németh, as Prime Minister, used his new independence to abolish the ÁVH-ridden State Office of Church Affairs, to suspend all work on the Gabčikovo-Nagymaros dam project and to set in train the arrangements for the reburial of Imre Nagy to which Grósz had agreed in Washington. On 26 June, the barbed wire fencing that marked Hungary's border with Austria was ceremonially removed in the presence of government ministers and the Western media; this first symbolic physical breach in the Iron Curtain was to have even more dramatic consequences three months later. Grósz, for his part, reluctantly acceded to the demand of the reform circles for a new Party Congress (although he preferred to call it a conference, with attendance controlled by the centre); and, crucially, agreed to negotiations with the Opposition Round Table on the terms and modalities of Hungary's transition to multi-party democracy. Grósz was all too aware that membership of the HSWP was haemorrhaging at a rate of thousands a week; 120,000 had left the Party by the end of March and the drift subsequently accelerated. He appears to have believed, however, that the Round Table would fall prey to internal disagreements and that if he could retain control of even a shrunken but disciplined HSWP until the 1990 elections, he could yet emerge as Hungary's first freely elected leader.

The ceremonial reburial of Imre Nagy, Géza Losonczy, Miklós Gimes, Pál Maléter and József Szilágyi in the Rákoskeresztúr Cemetery on 16 June 1989 should have given Grósz second thoughts. The reburial was preceded by a lying-in-state of the five coffins, with a sixth to represent all those other Hungarians who had given their lives in the 1956 Revolution, at which over a quarter of a million people paid homage; they listened to speeches of which several reduced the HSWP to the status of an ugly blemish on Hungary's past. One speech in particular, by a young leader of FIDESZ, Viktor Orbán, fired the imagination of the crowd and caught its mood. Recalling that on the day of another reburial, that of László Rajk in 1956, the party newspaper had promised 'Never again!', Orbán went on: 'In less than two years the HSWP ... sent to the gallows hundreds of innocents, among them its own comrades. We are not satisfied with the promises of Communist politicians that commit them to nothing; we must see to it that the ruling party can never again use force against us'.[4]

It was now clear to most of the leading members of the HSWP, if not to Grósz himself, that the Party would not survive without radical changes at the top. At the Central Committee's meeting in the last week of June, amid warnings from several speakers of the imminence of a split, it was decided that the Politburo would be replaced by a collective presidency of four—Rezső Nyers, Imre Pozsgay, Miklós Németh and Grósz, who would retain the post of Secretary-General but would relinquish to Nyers the leadership of the Party delegation in its negotiations with the Opposition Round Table. In elections to the Secretariat, János Berecz lost his place. Moscow's reaction to all these developments was benign: *Pravda* reported uncritically on 27 June that the HSWP's new objectives were 'democratic socialism, a law-based state, a multi–party parliamentary system and a market economy based on the decisive role of social property'.

Pozsgay, who had finally, on 7 June, summoned up the courage to launch his 'Movement for a Democratic Hungary' as a vehicle for his further advancement, became the Party's candidate for the Presidency of the Republic; but his vacillations in the preceding months had cost him the confidence of the reform movement, although his popularity in the country at large remained high. Parliamentary by-elections on 22 July threw the plight of the HSWP into stark relief: in all of the four seats at stake, the Hungarian Democratic Forum defeated its Communist opponents. At the beginning of September, the reform circles demonstrated their growing strength by fielding 357 delegates from 158 circles for their second national conference—now held, significantly, in the capital.

Meanwhile, from 13 June, trilateral negotiations had been taking place between the opposition parties, the HSWP and the HSWP's so-called 'auxiliary organisations'—the PPF, the National Council of Trade Unions, the National Council of Hungarian Women and others—which were obliged to subscribe to a common position but were recognised as carrying less weight in the negotiation than the two principals. The negotiating body as a whole became the National Round Table—although the table was in fact triangular. Although the Poles had already established a precedent for a negotiation of this kind (in Warsaw it had been bilateral rather than trilateral), it may nevertheless seem curious that Hungary's ruling Party was prepared to sit down on more or less equal terms with only recently legitimised opposition parties to discuss nothing less than the future of the nation. Rudolf Tőkés quotes a telling passage from an article by Mihály Babits, written just before the Second World War, which supplies part of the answer:

The Hungarian nation would have perished long ago if its political wisdom had not succeeded in preserving it ... In a strange way this squabbling and impetuous people had ensured the survival and the development of its country more by its sense of reality than by the military exploits imposed upon it by external necessities, or by its bravery ... It is very characteristic that it is by giving up the battle that it in fact consolidated its situation and possibilities in Europe ... And since then the whole existence of this people is only a series of lucid compromises, an uninterrupted meditation on actual possibilities.[5]

The Round Table thus followed a political tradition imposed upon Hungary, since the Battle of Mohács, by her vulnerability. But it also reflected an unvoiced determination by the whole political community, both Communist and non-Communist, that the crisis engulfing the regime must not be allowed to lead to violence on the streets. The reburial of Imre Nagy had just provided a powerful reminder of the tragedy of 1956 and its aftermath: it was common ground that this must never be repeated. The death of János Kádár on 6 July, only two months after his removal from the Central Committee of the Party which he had founded, reinforced the sense that an era had ended; and that Hungary had a precious opportunity to build for herself a better political future.

The twelve working groups of the National Round Table completed their work by mid-September 1989. Despite the shared commitment to an eventual agreement and mounting public pressure for an early outcome, the negotiations had been far from easy. The most intractable issue had been that of the Presidency of the future Republic. In Imre Pozsgay, the HSWP had a presidential candidate who regularly topped the popularity polls and could be expected easily to eclipse candidates from the opposition parties who were still virtually unknown to the voting public. The Communists consequently favoured an early presidential election, prior to the parliamentary elections in which their Party would be likely to sustain a heavy loss of seats. The opposition, for its part, at first insisted that the new president should be chosen by a newly elected parliament; but the opposition parties split on the issue. When the MDF, which since the Lakitelek conferences had maintained a co-operative relationship with Pozsgay, acceded to the HSWP's position, the matter appeared to be settled. It was not, as we shall see. Other questions giving rise to particular difficulty, and which were fudged in the agreement as it emerged on 18 September, included the future of the Workers' Guard, on which the HSWP resisted the demand of the opposition parties for its total abolition; the future of the HSWP's financial and physical assets, of which the ruling Party refused to divest itself to the benefit of the state; and the continued existence of HSWP cells in factories and other places of work, which the Party declined to withdraw. In the absence of satisfactory agreement on these issues, of which the timing of an election to the Presidency was the most important, both FIDESZ and the Alliance of Free Democrats, while refraining from sabotaging the negotiations by imposing a veto, declined to sign the final agreement. The agreement nevertheless represented a considerable achievement, providing as it did the basis for parliamentary legislation on a fundamental revision of the constitution; a new code for the financing of political parties; substantial changes to the Penal Code; and a new framework for parliamentary elections, which were to take place in March 1990.

During the next six weeks the Hungarian Parliament—still, of course, in its old, HSWP-dominated composition—worked with unaccustomed speed and energy to translate the Round Table Agreement into law; by the end of 1989, fifty-eight new acts had been passed. The most important, that setting out Hungary's new constitution, was published on the anniversary of the outbreak of the

1956 Revolution, 23 October—henceforth to be the national day of the Hungarian Republic (the designation that now replaced that of 'Hungarian People's Republic'). Its preamble declared that 'the Hungarian Republic is an independent, democratic state based on the rule of law, in which the values of bourgeois democracy and democratic socialism are equally recognised'. The constitution embodied a full range of guarantees for human rights; replaced the HSWP's 'leading role' with the guarantee of a multi–party system with safeguards against reversion to a single-party state; established the office of President, of which the incumbent would have limited rights to delay legislation or refer it to a Constitutional Court; and provided that the Parliament, composed of salaried deputies elected for a four-year term, would have the sole power to make appointments to senior government posts, to declare war and conclude peace and to authorise the deployment of the armed forces outside the country. A new electoral law put in place a system whose complexity reflected the difficulty of the Round Table's negotiations on the subject; essentially, it provided for a mixture of elections, in two rounds, by individual constituencies and by party, on the basis of national lists. A further law established the Constitutional Court, giving it powers to vet all legislation proposed for enactment by Parliament, to resolve constitutional disputes and to adjudicate in cases of claimed infringements of constitutional rights. On 23 October 1989, Mátyás Szűrös, Speaker of the Parliament and in that capacity interim president pending a presidential election, proclaimed the establishment of the Republic of Hungary to cheering crowds in Kossuth Square, outside the Parliament Building.

In the meantime, while the National Round Table was still in session, events had been taking place in and around Hungary that were of greater international interest and importance than the minutiae of constitutional and penal reform. The numerous camping sites around Lake Balaton, Hungary's 'inland sea', had long been the venue for summer holiday reunions of West and East German families and friends kept apart by the division of their country—Hungary was a country to which citizens of both Germanys could travel without difficulty. Hungary's frontier with Austria had begun to become porous since the removal in May of barbed wire fencing and frontier patrols. A 'pan-European picnic' organised on 19 August in Sopron, with the regime's approval, and accompanied by a temporary opening of the frontier, provided a strong stimulus to this process: several hundred East Germans were able to walk through the frontier gate and to make their way to Vienna, there to apply for passports and visas with which to enter the Federal Republic (FRG). The approaching end of the holiday season, moreover, obliged East German tourists to decide whether or not to return to Erich Honecker's barracks for the beginning of the school year. At least 3,000 of them sought to take advantage of the new political climate in Hungary by applying for passports at the West German Embassy in Budapest rather than in Vienna. When the FRG, unable to cope with the volume of applicants or with the wider implications for East-West relations, closed the Embassy, East Germans simply camped in the Embassy compound and in a neighbouring churchyard, making clear their refusal to return to the GDR. Miklós Németh and Gyula Horn, now Foreign Minister, attempted to broker an agreement acceptable to both German governments, which would resolve the impasse. When Chancellor Kohl agreed to authorise the issue of passports in Budapest, and the Honecker regime remained obdurate, demanding that Hungary fulfil her treaty obligations to the Warsaw Pact, the Hungarian government on 10 September gave permission to all East Germans in Hungary, who did not wish to return home, to travel to the FRG. By mid-September, some 23,000 had done so. Hungary's action, encouraged by the formation of a Solidarity-led coalition government in Poland and by clear signals of non-intervention from Moscow, led directly to the collapse of the Honecker regime in the GDR and then to that of Communism in the rest of eastern Europe.

The Fourteenth Congress of the HSWP, convened on 6 October largely at the insistence of the reform circles, became the occasion for the Party's disintegration. Although the reform circles, united for Congress purposes under the banner of the 'Reform Alliance', constituted the largest single voting bloc, they nevertheless accounted for less than 25 per cent of the 1,200 delegates, among whom the conservatives remained strong. Reformist morale had also been dented by a parliamentary by-election in September, in which a reform circle candidate with Pozsgay's personal backing had been soundly defeated by the MDF, whose candidate won 59 per cent of the vote. The Reform Alliance, which still looked to Pozsgay for leadership, was opposed by the 'People's Democratic Platform' under the leadership of Rezső Nyers, which gave top priority to the restoration of Party unity in preparation for the forthcoming elections. In an untidy compromise, Pozsgay and Nyers agreed to lead a rebranded and democratic 'Hungarian Socialist Party' (MSzP); in elections to the praesidium of the new Party, the Reform Alliance won nearly half the seats while the conservatives won none. Grósz and Berecz refused to join the MSzP and departed to lead a rump HSWP; but their political careers were effectively over. In the short term, the decision of the new leadership of the MSzP to adopt a membership policy of contracting in rather than contracting out—former members of the HSWP had to take the initiative in joining its successor—appeared to be a bad mistake: initially, only a small percentage of members of the old Party joined the new one. In the longer term, it gave credibility to the MSzP's claim to be a genuinely new party; and, as future events were to show, socialism still had a future in Hungary.

In the immediate aftermath of the National Round Table, the political initiative passed to the two parties that had declined to sign its final agreement, the Alliance of Free Democrats (SzDSz) and FIDESZ. Determined to block Pozsgay's path to the state presidency, which he still seemed certain to win if a presidential election preceded elections to a new Parliament, the two parties took advantage of the provisions of the new constitution to call for a national referendum, not only on that issue but also on the three other issues on which, as they saw it, the MDF had co-operated with the communists in producing a stitch-up in the Round Table—those of Communist cells in the workplace, the future of the Workers' Guard and the disposition of the HSWP's assets. To be successful, a petition for a referendum required at least 100,000 signatures: in a whirlwind campaign, the SzDSz and FIDESZ secured 114,470. By the time the referendum was held, on 26 November 1989, Parliament had already decided in favour of the SzDSz/ FIDESZ position on three of the four issues in dispute and had legislated accordingly; but Parliament had also resolved that a presidential election should be held on 7 January 1990, well in advance of the parliamentary elections in March. The referendum overturned this decision, by a narrow margin—a result that in effect brought an end to Imre Pozsgay's political career; he was not a fighter.

The break-up of the HSWP and the slow start made by the MSzP in winning popular support left Miklós Németh's government free to run the country for several months, prior to the 1990 elections, without party control or interference. Essentially a caretaker government, it nevertheless took several significant steps forward towards Hungary's post-Communist era. Since Gorbachev's speech to the United Nations General Assembly in December 1988, in which he promised a reduction of the Soviet military presence in eastern Europe, Hungarian-Soviet negotiations had been in train for the eventual withdrawal of Soviet troops from Hungary. These were brought to a successful conclusion by Németh and Horn in March 1990, with the signature in Moscow of an agreement providing for a complete Soviet withdrawal by 30 June 1991. Gyula Horn, in the same month, made the first public reference to the possibility of a Hungarian application to join NATO; and entered Hungary's application for membership of the Council of Europe. An agreement with the European Community on trade and economic co-operation had already been concluded in 1988—six years after Horn had first discussed the possibility with me. In a measure of importance for Hungary's transition to a market economy, Németh established a State Property Agency to manage the privatisation process and, it was hoped—over-optimistically—to put an end to the free-for-all which had enriched the 'red barons' and Party *apparatchiki* under the Grósz regime.

Democratic Hungary

Hungary's first fully free and democratic parliamentary elections, on 25 March and 8 April 1990, were contested by twenty-eight political parties, of which twelve met the criteria for running national lists; of these, six failed to achieve the 4 per cent of the national vote in the first round needed to proceed to the second. The six parties that succeeded in qualifying as parliamentary parties were the Hungarian Democratic Forum, essentially a mildly nationalist middle-class party that found support among both the urban and the rural population; the Alliance of Free Democrats, with a talented leadership, internationalist and technocratic, appealing mainly to the urban professional class and intelligentsia; the Hungarian Socialist Party, with a similar constituency and a new image as a social-democratic party; the Independent Smallholders' Party, supported principally by the older generation of farmers and peasants who wanted a return to the pattern of land ownership created by the 1945 reform; the Christian Democratic People's Party, strongest in predominantly Catholic regions; and the Federation of Young Democrats, left of centre, whose greatest appeal was naturally to the younger, university-educated generation and to first-time voters. Apart from the MSzP, very few of the party leaders were well known nationally, let alone household names. The MDF enjoyed some advantage in this respect, in that their new chairman, József Antall, had emerged during the National Round Table as a skilled negotiator and the natural leader of the opposition parties. Born in 1932, Antall was a latecomer to politics although his father had served as a Smallholder minister in two of the post-war coalition cabinets. After completing a doctoral thesis on József Eötvös,

501

Antall taught history in a *gimnázium* but lost his job in the post-1956 ideological crackdown; he then worked for twenty years in the Semmelweis Museum of Medicine, rising from a junior post as archivist to become the museum's director and a leading authority on medical history. He established a close relationship with Imre Pozsgay during the latter's tenure at the Ministry of Culture. Antall joined the MDF when it first became a political party in the autumn of 1988; his personality and natural talent for politics made an immediate impact. The rapport he enjoyed with Pozsgay undoubtedly contributed to the Round Table's achievement of an agreement, although it also gave rise to suspicions among the other opposition parties of too close a relationship between the MDF and the HSWP—suspicions that remained alive until Pozsgay's political demise.

In the first round of parliamentary elections, on 25 March 1990, in which over 65 per cent of eligible voters took part, József Antall led the MDF to a narrow lead over the SzDSz. The results were:

MDF:	24.7 per cent
SzDSz:	21.3 per cent
Smallholders:	11.7 per cent
MSzP:	10.8 per cent
FIDESZ:	8.9 per cent
Christian Democrats:	6.4 per cent

All other parties, including the rump HSWP led by Grósz and Berecz and the old Social Democratic Party, failed to cross the 4 per cent threshold and disappeared from the political landscape. In the second round on 8 April, in which the voter turnout fell to only just over 45 per cent, the MDF established a commanding lead:

MDF:	42.5 per cent (164 seats)
SzDSz:	23.8 per cent (92 seats)
Smallholders:	11.4 per cent (44 seats)
MSzP:	8.5 per cent (33 seats)
FIDESZ:	5.7 per cent (21 seats)
Christian Democrats:	5.4 per cent (21 seats)

In order to secure a parliamentary majority, Antall negotiated a coalition of the centre-right with the two parties closest to MDF's values, the Smallholders and the Christian Democrats; this gave him 59 per cent of the seats in Parliament—still short of the two-thirds majority which, under the new constitution, he would need to carry measures 'of constitutional standing'. In order to surmount this potential difficulty Antall negotiated, before the new Parliament assembled, an agreement with the Free Democrats—who would be the leading opposition party—which achieved a tighter definition of laws 'of constitutional standing', limiting this to measures directly related to the constitution; and paved the way for the introduction of the West German parliamentary device of a 'constructive vote of no confidence', under which the opposition could not remove the Prime Minister without securing a vote by at least 50 per cent of sitting deputies in favour of both a named replacement Prime Minister and a new government programme. The MDF–SzDSz agreement also settled in advance the thorny issue of the presidency: the new President of the Republic would be elected by Parliament, on a two-thirds majority vote, and the first President would be a Free Democrat, Árpád Göncz. Finally, the two parties agreed to vote for an amendment to the preamble to the constitution, which would delete its reference to 'bourgeois values and democratic socialism': the Republic of Hungary would now be defined simply as 'an independent, democratic state based on the rule of law'. These were wise arrangements, which gave Hungary a sound introduction to democratic parliamentary government. Hungary's new Parliament had a very different complexion from that of its predecessor. Ninety-five per cent of its members were entering parliament for the first time and 70 per cent of those were from professional backgrounds; 89 per cent had university degrees or equivalents and representatives of the working class accounted for only 4 per cent of the total. This was a new political society.

The opening of Hungary's first freely elected Parliament on 2 May 1990 is an appropriate point at which to put this narrative into softer focus. Thanks to a prolific and revitalised Hungarian press, there is no shortage of sources on the conduct of affairs by the three administrations which governed Hungary during the last decade of the twentieth century. Perspective, however, is lacking. I would not go so far as the former Chinese Prime Minister, Chou En-lai who, when asked for his views on the impact of the French Revolution on world history, famously replied that it was too early to tell. But Hungary's first fifteen years as 'an independent, democratic state' are not yet history. With the tragic exception of József Antall, most of the leading figures of that period are (in 2010) still living and some are playing an active part in Hungary's political life. Their memoirs and other writings, where they exist, are part of an ongoing political agenda. It is too soon to assess the wisdom or otherwise of many of their decisions or to be certain of their consequences. This closing passage can therefore be no more than a broad-brush sketch of events during the decade that followed the 1990 elections.

József Antall's coalition government faced the dual challenge of consolidating a plural political society; and carrying forward to completion Hungary's transformation into a market economy. In tackling these massive tasks, it was burdened with several handicaps: an ongoing economic crisis stemming largely from the Kádár regime's reckless borrowing, an inherited bureaucracy indifferent or hostile to its policies and, not least, its own inexperience of government. The dissolution of the CMEA in 1991 was welcome in political terms; but Hungary had already been obliged to suspend exports to the Soviet Union, who could no longer pay from them. Hungary was now dependent on Western markets in which her products were as yet uncompetitive; in the short term, this had a damaging impact on the country's trade balance, which fell into heavy deficit and remained there for several years. Against this unpromising background, the Antall government made creditable progress in steering Hungary through the choppy waters of transition. The privatisation of state enterprises and other assets proceeded, albeit at a modest pace: by the end of the coalition's four-year term the number of enterprises owned by the state had nevertheless declined by 60 per cent and the number of limited liability companies had risen from 450 to 79,000. A highly contentious issue bequeathed by the Communist era, that of compensation for the confiscation of private property by the state, found its resolution in a statesmanlike compromise involving partial compensation in the form of bonds redeemable for state assets including land; months of heated parliamentary debate on this question also demonstrated that the democratic process was putting down healthy roots. The government's hard work in laying down the legal foundations of a free market economy, together with Hungary's evident political stability, encouraged an accelerating inflow of foreign investment, which totalled over $8 billion by the end of the coalition's term. Antall also achieved considerable success in consolidating both the image and the reality of Hungarian independence. The last Soviet soldier left Hungarian soil on 19 June 1991, following a total of 100,380 of his fellow countrymen and women who had left Hungary for a more uncertain future in their own land; a long wrangle with the Soviet government over financial claims and counter-claims arising from over forty years of occupation ended in a settlement broadly favourable to Hungary. The conclusion of an agreement on associate membership of the European Community in 1991 and NATO's agreement in 1994 actively to consider the accession of Hungary, among others, to the North Atlantic Treaty further emphasised Hungary's escape from the Russian sphere of influence and gave her firm anchors to the West.

Despite these considerable achievements, however, the Antall government never achieved the popularity it might have been thought to deserve. There were several reasons for this. The most obvious was the impact of a deepening economic crisis on the living standards of most Hungarians. The Hungarian economy went into recession shortly after the coalition government took office and remained there for the rest of its term. By 1993, Hungary's GDP had fallen below its 1989 level by 18 per cent. Inflation spiralled, reaching an annual rate of 35 per cent in 1991 and not falling below 20 per cent thereafter. Real incomes had fallen, on average, by up to 15 per cent by 1994. At the same time, income differentials widened as pensioners and families with large numbers of children were driven into poverty. This situation threw into sharp relief the fact that Antall's MDF had no established popular following; the votes it harvested in 1990 had been cast more against the Communists than in favour of a party whose creed and policies had not been clearly articulated. The voting public nevertheless had high expectations of the MDF, simply because it was new and different. Economic circumstances made it inevitable that these expectations would be disappointed.

József Antall's personal style of government, moreover, did the coalition no favours. Although a model of clarity and persuasiveness across a negotiating table and in private discussion, Antall was a poor communicator to a larger audience. His public speeches, tortuous and prolix, tended to convey an impression of patronising remoteness, of 'talking down'—although they also revealed, to the patient listener, quite remarkable political prescience. His constant emphasis on national tradition, Christian values and the virtues of the middle class gave rise to suspicions, albeit unfounded, that his ideal for Hungary would be a re-creation of Hungarian society as it had been between the two world wars. The reburial, in Hungarian soil, of Admiral Horthy did nothing to allay such fears, although the decision to sanction this had been taken by President Göncz and Antall did not attend the ceremony. Antall's attitude towards Hungary's neighbours was also perceived to have inter-war overtones. His speech to the Third National Convention of the MDF contained a sentence he was not allowed to forget: 'I consider myself, in spirit, to be the prime minister for fifteen million Hungarians'. The wounds of Trianon were reopened. Although he had distanced himself from the populist element in the MDF, Antall was unremitting in his public support for the Hungarian minorities in Transylvania and Slovakia and did all he could, in international contexts, to keep open the concept of eventual frontier revision. He never developed that essential political quality, a thick skin. He was wounded by and bitterly resented criticism by the media of which, given the prevailing economic climate, there was no shortage. He became involved in acrimonious public disputes with the immensely popular President, Árpád Göncz, which seriously damaged his Premiership. He alienated the radical Populists in his own party and their leader, the nationalist István Csurka, led a group of them out of the MDF to found the extreme rightist 'Hungarian Justice and Life Party' (MIÉP). Above all, Antall's performance as party leader and Prime Minister was certainly affected by his ill-health and by the knowledge that his illness was terminal; his death in office on 12 December 1993 was a national misfortune. The extravagance of the monument to his memory in Budapest's Kerepesi Cemetery may signify belated recognition of this.

Following József Antall's death, the Premiership passed to Péter Boross, until then Minister of the Interior. He led the coalition competently until the parliamentary elections in May 1994, but made little impression on the problems that beset it. Remarkably, popular nostalgia for the Kádár era was already perceptible—memories of its antecedents had begun to fade. The Hungarian Socialist Party, moreover, now under the leadership of Gyula Horn, had been successfully remodelled into a credible social-democratic party while retaining control of many of the organisational and media assets of the HSWP—a tainted legacy. The MSzP leadership skilfully deployed their greater political experience in exploiting the failure of the MDF and its allies to arrest Hungary's slide into ever deeper recession. The scale of the MSzP's victory in the 1994 elections nevertheless came as a surprise—54 per cent of the vote as against less than 10 per cent for the MDF. The Free Democrats (SzDSz), in second place, achieved only 18 per cent, losing twenty-four seats. The Independent Smallholders, FIDESZ and the Christian Democrats could do no better than 5–6 per cent. Although Horn now enjoyed an absolute majority, he nevertheless invited the SzDSz to join him in a coalition, which then controlled an impregnable 72 per cent of parliamentary seats.

The new government's priorities were to tackle Hungary's continuing economic crisis and to thicken up her relations both with the West and with her neighbours; it achieved significant success in both. The centrepiece of the government's economic policy, the 'stabilisation package' of March 1995, was in fact devised and implemented by a Free Democrat, the Finance Minister Lajos Bokros. The package consisted of an immediate devaluation of the forint, to be followed by a continuing devaluation within a pre-designated band—the 'crawling peg'; a substantial reduction in the budgetary deficit, to be achieved by swingeing cuts in public expenditure, including welfare payments; and a curb on salary and wage increases in the public sector. This was harsh medicine but, accompanied by an acceleration of the privatisation process, which greatly enhanced government revenues and hard currency reserves, it worked. Gross national debt fell from $33 billion in 1995 to $27 billion by the end of 1996. Public expenditure fell from over 8 per cent of GDP to 4.6 per cent in 1997 and the current account deficit to a level below that of 1989. Hard currency reserves rose from $6.7 billion to $10 billion by the end of 1997. These improvements encouraged foreign investors dramatically to increase their exposure in Hungary, bringing the country to the top of the east-central European league table in attracting foreign investment. In foreign policy, the Horn government continued its predecessor's active cultivation of relations with the countries of the now renamed European Union and with North America; but it also mended fences with Hungary's neighbours, mindful that the formal resolution of outstanding differences would be a condition of eventual membership of both NATO and the European Union. Treaties with Romania and Slovakia—now an independent nation divorced from the Czech Republic—undertook to respect the Trianon frontiers in return for assurances of equal respect for the rights of Hungarian minorities.

None of these measures, essential though they were in terms of Hungary's national interests, increased the Horn government's credit with the Hungarian people. The 'stabilisation package' hit the pockets of the MSzP's natural supporters particularly hard; the privatisation process threw up spectacular and well-publicised cases of corruption; and the agreements with Romania and Slovakia were seen to bring scant improvement in the circumstances of the Hungarian minorities in those countries. Gyula Horn, whose considerable political talents had enabled him to hold together a notably fractious coalition for four years, nevertheless ran a poor campaign in the run-up to the next rounds of elections in May 1998. Before the first round, he conveyed an unattractive impression of arrogant over-confidence; then, when the results of that round showed that his government was in danger, he took refuge in old-style Communist rhetoric about threats from right-wing forces—the social-democratic mask (as many thought it to be) slipped, briefly but at a vital juncture. The second round gave FIDESZ a narrow victory with 38 per cent of the vote (147 seats) over the MSzP's 34.7 per cent (134 seats); the liberal SzDSz paid for its coalition alliance with the socialists with a collapse in its support, emerging with only 6.2 per cent (24 seats), well behind the Independent Smallholders who maintained their position with 12.4 per cent (48 seats). The MDF's vote declined further, to 4.6 per cent (18 seats); and in a development that alarmed many, Csurka's new extreme right MIÉP entered Parliament for the first time with 14 seats. FIDESZ, like the MSzP prior to 1994, had remodelled itself by moving from the centre-left to the centre-right, filling the gap in the political spectrum left by the eclipse of the MDF—with the rump of which it had concluded an alliance. FIDESZ also appropriated the MDF's nationalism, thereby winning the support of Hungarians who viewed with distaste Horn's accommodations with their neighbours. In Viktor Orbán, whose speech at the reburial of Imre Nagy was still remembered, the party had a young and charismatic leader whom eight years in parliamentary opposition had brought to political maturity. He was to prove an able Prime Minister and a confident champion of Hungarian interests.

These four-yearly turns of the political wheel have had the useful consequence of giving every major party some experience of government. They also showed that parliamentary democracy has taken firm root in Hungary and that its machinery has been well cast. It will take rather longer for the values of a true civil society—acceptance of individual responsibility, respect for the spirit as well as the letter of the law, aversion to corruption—to become embedded. It can nevertheless be conjectured that at the end of the twentieth century Hungary had achieved the internal situation and the external presence which would have been hers if the enforced detour of forty years of Communism had not taken place. That ugly interruption has, indeed, left scars, deep scars, which still from time to time disfigure Hungary's public life and the private lives of her citizens. The confrontational character of Hungarian politics tends to prolong the life of animosities and jealousies which it will take a generation finally to lay to rest. Hungary has nevertheless been able once again to pick up the threads of her long history. The continuity of national life has been resumed. The Round Table of 1989 revealed the same political talents as those which produced the historic Compromise of 1867. Hungary's formal accession to NATO in March 1999 symbolised her return to the western European community of nations to which King St Stephen had first joined her one thousand years before. Her full accession to the European Union in 2004 confirmed and made permanent an orientation which her culture has always expressed. Europe will be the richer for it.

On 4 June 2000, the anniversary of the Treaty of Trianon, Viktor Orbán made a speech, as Prime Minister, which concisely expressed the theme of this volume. He noted that each of the five empires that had invaded Hungary during the past thousand years—the Tartars, the Turks, the Habsburgs, the Nazis and Soviet Russia—had disappeared without trace: 'but we are still here, though—this must be said on the fourth of June—not in such large numbers and not in so large a country as that in which we once stood; but we still exist, we have survived them all and we are now planning our future'.

APPENDIX I

THE ÁRPÁD KINGS OF HUNGARY

[Dates are the years of reign. Italics indicate pretenders or usurpers]

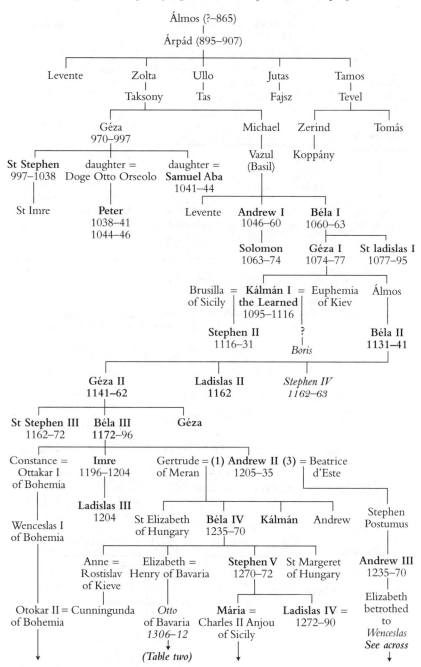

509

THE ANGEVIN & JAGIELLONIAN KINGS OF HUNGARY

[*Dates are the years of reign. Italics indicate pretenders or usurpers*]

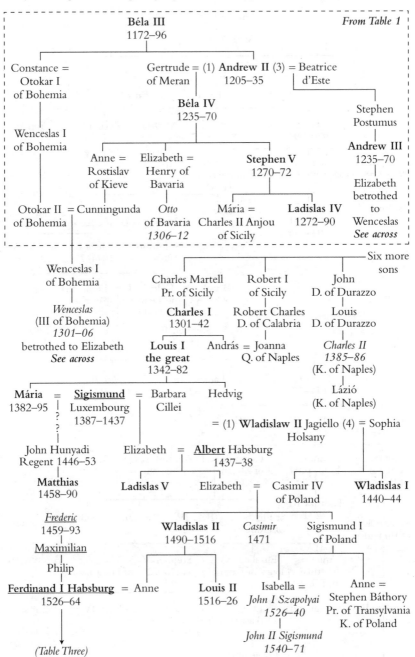

THE HABSBURG KINGS OF HUNGARY

*[Dates are the years of reign. **Emperors** underlined: (I) = Holy Roman, {I} = Austrian]*

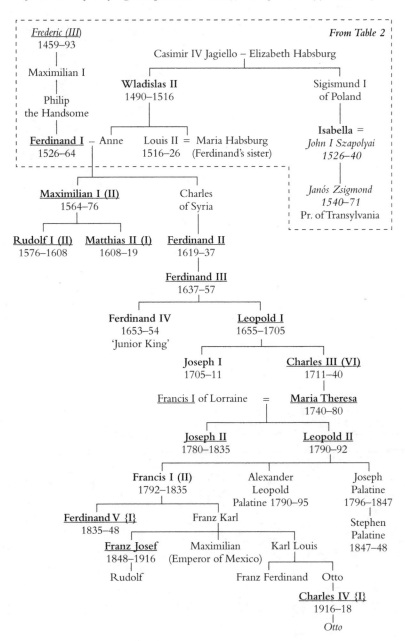

Frederic (III)
1459–93

Maximilian I

Philip
the Handsome

Casimir IV Jagiello – Elizabeth Habsburg

Wladislas II
1490–1516

Sigismund I
of Poland

From Table 2

Ferdinand I – Anne
1526–64

Louis II = Maria Habsburg
1516–26   (Ferdinand's sister)

Isabella =
John I Szapolyai
1526–40

Maximilian I (II)
1564–76

Charles
of Syria

Janós Zsigmond
1540–71
Pr. of Transylvania

Rudolf I (II)
1576–1608

Matthias II (I)
1608–19

Ferdinand II
1619–37

Ferdinand III
1637–57

Ferdinand IV
1653–54
'Junior King'

Leopold I
1655–1705

Joseph I
1705–11

Charles III (VI)
1711–40

Francis I of Lorraine   =   Maria Theresa
1740–80

Joseph II
1780–1835

Leopold II
1790–92

Francis I (II)
1792–1835

Alexander
Leopold
Palatine 1790–95

Joseph
Palatine
1796–1847

Ferdinand V {I}
1835–48

Franz Karl

Stephen
Palatine
1847–48

Franz Josef
1848–1916

Maximilian
(Emperor of Mexico)

Karl Louis

Rudolf

Franz Ferdinand   Otto

Charles IV {I}
1916–18

Otto

511

APPENDIX II

A Note on Hungarian Pronunciation

Readers who, like me, mentally 'pronounce' proper names as they read a book which contains unfamiliar ones may find this short and approximate guide to the pronunciation of Hungarian words helpful.

Vowels

a (short):   like the 'o' in cot
á (long):   like the 'a' in far
e (short):   like the 'e' in when
é (long):   like the 'a' in way
i (short):   like the 'i' in fit
í (long):   like the 'ee' in meet
o (short):   like the 'o' in ford
ó (long):   like the 'o' in open
ö: like the 'e' in herd
ő: like the 'u' in purr
u (short):   like the 'u' in put
ú (long):   like the 'u' in rule
ü: like the 'u' in cute
ű: like the 'oo' in coot

Consonants

c: like the 'ts' in fits
cs: like the 'ch' in choke
g: like the 'g' in gut
gy: like the soft 'd' in during
j: like the 'y' in yet
ly: again, like the 'y' in yet
ny: soft, as in the 'ne' in nearly
s: like the 'sh' in sheep
sz: like the 's' in soot
zs: like the 's' in treasure

In Hungarian, stress is almost invariably on the first syllable of a word.

B.C.

APPENDIX III

Hungarian Place Names

A number of historical Hungarian towns have changed their names during the course of their existence, sometimes more than once. Some have always been known by different names in different languages. This applies particularly to those towns which now find themselves outside the frontiers of modern Hungary, in Slovakia, Romania, Serbia and Croatia. This note lists the alternative names of the most important towns mentioned in the text.

H = Hungarian, Sl = Slovakian, R = Romanian, Se = Serbian, C = Croatian, G = German, Cz = Czech, P = Polish, U = Ukrainian.

Brassó (H):	Braşov (R); Kronstadt (G)
Eperjes (H):	Prešov (Sl)
Fiume (H):	Rijeka (C)
Győr (H):	Raab (G)
Gyulafehérvár (H):	Alba Julia (R); Weissenburg (G)
Karlóca (H):	Karlovci (Se); Karlowitz (G)
Károlyváros (H):	Karlovac (C); Karlstadt (G)
Kassa (H):	Košice (Sl); Kaschau (G)
Kismarton (H):	Eisenstadt (G)
Kolozsvár (H):	Cluj (R); Klausenburg (G)
Komárom (H):	Komarnó (Sl); Komorn (G)
Sadova (Cz):	Königgrätz (G)
Kremsier (G):	Kroměřiž (Cz)
Lwow (P):	Lemburg (G); Lviv (Ukrainian)
Nagyszeben (H):	Sibiu (R)
Nagyszombat (H):	Trnava (Sl)
Nagyvárad (H):	Oradea Mare (R); Grosswardein (G)
Olomouc (Cz):	Olmütz (G)
Pozsony (H):	Pressburg (G); Bratislava (Sl)
Sopron (H):	Oedenburg (G)
Szabadka (H):	Subotica (Se)
Szatmár (H):	Satu Mare (R)
Székesfehérvár (H):	Stuhlweissenburg (G)
Temesvár (H):	Timişoara (R)
Turócszentmárton (H):	Turčjanský; Sväty Marton (Sl)
Újvidék (H):	Novi–Sad (Se)
Várasd (H):	Varasdin (C)

ENDNOTES

PREFACE

1. Hanak, H.: *Great Britain and Austria-Hungary in the First World War* (London, 1962), pp. 2–3.
2. Townson, R.: *Travels in Hungary, with a short account of Vienna, in the year 1793* (London, 1797), p. 457.

1. THE MAGYARS: (400 BC–AD 1000)

1. The account which follows draws mainly on the following works: Bartha, A.: *A IX-X Századi Magyar Társadalom* (Hungarian Society in the Ninth & Tenth Centuries) (Budapest, 1975); Engel, P.: *The Realm of St. Stephen: A History of Medieval Hungary, 895–1526* (London, 2001); Fodor, I.: *The Pre-History of the Hungarian People and the Conquest* (Budapest, 1975); Kristó, Gy.: *Hungarian History in the Ninth Century* (Szeged, 1996); Róna-Tas, A.: *Hungarians and Europe in the Early Middle Ages* (Budapest, 1999).
2. László, Gy.: *A kettős honfoglalás* (The Double Conquest) (Budapest, 1978).
3. Philip Longworth in *The Making of Eastern Europe*, p. 278.
4. This speculation is pursued with perception and elegance in Sándor Márai's remarkable *Memoir of Hungary* (Budapest, 1996), pp. 72–4.

2. THE YOUNG HUNGARIAN STATE: (1000–1301)

1. For example: 'If a priest or *ispán* or any faithful person find anyone working on Sunday with oxen, the ox shall be confiscated and given to the men of the castle to eat'; and 'If someone eats meat on Friday, a day observed by all Christianity, he shall fast incarcerated during the day for a week' (Bak, J. M., Bónis, Gy. and Sweeney, J.: *The Laws of the Medieval Kingdom of Hungary* (Idyllwild, CA, 1989), pp. 3–4.
2. Zarek, O.: *The History of Hungary* (London, 1939), p. 74.
3. During the three centuries following the coronation of Stephen I, Hungary's ruling dynasty arranged at least sixty marriages with the royal houses of Europe (Rady, M,: *Mobility, Land and Service in Medieval Hungary* (London, 2000), p. 9.
4. Their friendship (they had first met as students in Paris) is still commemorated in a special annual celebration of vespers in Esztergom Basilica.
5. The 'inner' Royal Council was composed entirely of barons (*barones regni*) and bishops; there was also, on occasion, a 'greater' Royal Council, enlarged by the addition of invited magnates who wielded great influence in the kingdom without necessarily holding office under the Crown. This larger body eventually (in 1608) evolved into the Upper Chamber of the Diet.
6. Rady, M.: op. cit., p. 33.

7. Bak, J., Bónis, Gy. and Sweeny, J. (eds.): *The Laws of the Medieval Kingdom of Hungary*, Vol. I, p. 34.
8. A royal visit was calculated to cost the involuntary host twelve oxen, 1,000 loaves of bread and four barrels of wine.
9. Béla was the son of Álmos, who had expected to succeed Ladislas I. Ladislas gave the succession to Kálmán instead; Almos became a permanent thorn in Kálmán's side, leading three separate rebellions against him with foreign support. In 1112 Kálmán, his patience exhausted and his ecclesiastical background notwithstanding, incarcerated both Álmos and his son Béla and had their eyes put out; he also decreed that Béla should be castrated, in order to put an end to the line, but the court official entrusted with this task refused to carry it out.

3. HUNGARY ASCENDANT: (1301–1444)

1. Charles I also made effective use of exemplary punishment. When a noble, Felician Záh, apparently believing that his daughter had been violated by the Queen's brother, attacked the royal family with a sword as they dined in the palace at Visegrád and wounded the Queen, the ensuing retribution was formidable: not only was Záh himself cut down and quartered on the spot, but his children were tortured to death and all members of his kindred, up to and including the third degree of kinship, were slain. All Záh's more distant relatives were condemned to loss of property and perpetual serfdom. The kindred was wiped out.
2. The alliance, at least to the extent of a strong mutual sympathy, has endured to the present day; Hungarian politicians habitually refer to 'our Polish cousins' and *vice versa.*
3. Staple rights, granted to a town by the crown, entitled that town to oblige all merchants in transit to offer their goods for sale to the town's inhabitants, usually for a specified period; except during a trade fair, the transient merchants were forbidden to trade with each other. This was a crude way of building up the prosperity of strategically situated towns and of enriching royal treasuries with the dues and duties that resulted from the artificial concentration of trade. Charles I subsequently granted staple rights to Buda.
4. Over six and a half centuries later, in 1991, the Hungarians (whose first post-Communist Foreign Minister was a history professor) chose Visegrád as the venue for a meeting to discuss free trade and economic co-operation between the original Visegrád Three of 1335, although Bohemia had now become Czechoslovakia.
5. Before leaving Italy, Louis and Joanna had both agreed to the terms of an armistice proposed by Pope Clement VI, under which they would both leave Naples while the Pope launched an inquiry into the murder of Andrew. The inquiry never took place and Joanna soon felt able to flout the armistice with impunity. She was, however, eventually dethroned by Pope Urban VI, who in 1380 offered the Neapolitan crown to Louis the Great; Louis, by now an old man, declined it in favour of his cousin, Charles of Durazzo, to whom he promised military support. Joanna, dying as violently as she had lived, was strangled on Charles's orders in 1382.
6. The Battle of Nicopolis in 1396; see page 44.
7. Engel, P.: *The Realm of St. Stephen: a History of Medieval Hungary, 895–1526* (London, 2001), p. 177.
8. Kosáry, D.: *A History of Hungary* (Cleveland, 1941), p. 55.
9. Vardy, S. B.: 'The Image of Louis the Great in Modern Hungarian Historiography', in Vardy, S. B., Grosschmid, G. and Domonkos, L. S. (eds.): *Louis the Great, King of Hungary and Poland* (Boulder, CO, 1986), p. 352.
10. Zarek, O.: *The History of Hungary* (London, 1939), p. 166.

11. Murad himself did not live to see the consequences of his victory; he was murdered a few hours after the battle by a Serb who infiltrated the Ottoman camp.

12. On 15 June 1989, the 600th anniversary of the battle, a Serbian communist official named Slobodan Milosevic delivered to a cheering crowd of thousands on the former battlefield a speech designed to inflame Serbian nationalism and revive dreams of 'Greater Serbia'. This began the tragic chain of events that led to the disintegration of Yugoslavia, civil war and 'ethnic cleansing' in Bosnia Herzogovina and, later, in Kosovo.

13. The early history of Transylvania is a political minefield. Romanian historians have long maintained that the indigenous population of the Roman province of Dacia (roughly equivalent to the southern half of Transylvania) survived Roman occupation and that the Vlach (Romanian) people are directly descended from them. The fact that the Romanian language is Latinate, together with archaeological evidence, is commonly adduced as proof of this—and, consequently, of the theory that Vlachs were firmly settled in Transylvania long before the Magyars appeared on the scene. The Magyars, according to Romanians, were intruders and usurpers. The classic Hungarian account is of the Magyars arriving, late in the ninth century, in a pristine territory, rich in agrarian and mineral resources but populated only, and thinly, by Slavs; semi–nomadic Vlach shepherds wandered into the Transylvanian region later on. Because of the higher Vlach birth rate, the Romanian element in the Transylvanian population eventually out-numbered the Hungarian: but the Hungarians had got there first. The whole controversy blew up again as recently as 1986 (see Chapter 19).

14. Rady, M.: *Nobility, Land and Service in Medieval Hungary* (London, 2000), p. 115.

15. Bak, J., Engel, P. and Sweeney, J.: *The Laws of the Medieval Kingdom of Hungary*, Vol. II, p. 63.

16. The great Hungarian poet Sándor Petőfi (1823–49) parodied the medieval and early modern nobility:

I don't know how to read,
I don't know how to write,
I'm a proud privileged noble
And I am always right.

(Quoted in A. Komjáthy, 'Hungarian Jobbágyság in the 15th Century' (*East European Quarterly*, Vol. 10, 1976)).

17. Engel, P.: op. cit., p. 338.

18. During the early medieval period the designation '*jobbágy*' was applied to those freemen who worked in the households of barons and ispáns, to distinguish them from serfs; when these positions became the preserve of the nobility, and with the development of peasant farming, the *jobbágy* label moved downmarket to describe anyone who worked in subordination to a landlord, royal or otherwise. In the sixteenth century, the term was further debased, along with the peasantry, and implied serfdom.

4. FROM LIGHT INTO DARKNESS: (1444–1526)

1. Žižka's soldiers linked their wagons in a circle, enclosing the cavalry, and used them as platforms from which to repel their opponents with sword and pike; when the first force of an attack had been absorbed, the cavalry poured out through a gap in the circle and finished off the assailants.

2. At some point prior to this János Hunyadi's younger brother, also named János, had been killed in action against the Turks.

3. A curious aspect of the affair was Branković's gift to Hunyadi, precisely at this time, of a substantial part of the estates in Transylvania which had been given to Branković by

Sigismund as a reward for his loyal vassalage; the estates adjoined Hunyadi's own. This may have been a bribe to Hunyadi to encourage him to persuade the vacillating Wladislas I to authorise him, Hunyadi, to sign the 'Treaty of Szeged', from which, of course, Branković had much the most to gain.

4. Hunyadi took his revenge two years later when Vlad Dracul enlisted Turkish help in putting down a rebellion in Wallachia; Hunyadi intervened on the side of the rebels and defeated Dracul's Turkish supporters.

5. Recorded by János Vitéz and quoted in Held, J.: *Hunyadi: Legend and Reality* (New York, 1985).

6. The plague also carried off Erzsébet Cillei, whose arranged marriage to Matthias Hunyadi consequently never took place.

7. Addicts of the 'tingle factor' should try taking a stroll along Tóth Árpád Sétány (Promenade), a tree-lined avenue that runs along the west side of the Várhegy (Castle Hill) in Budapest, just before noon to hear the chorus of church bells ringing out all over the city below in commemoration of the relief of Belgrade five and a half centuries ago.

8. Quoted in Pamlényi, E. (ed.): *A History of Hungary* (Budapest, 1973), p. 108.

9. Matthias's first wife, George Podiebrad's daughter Katalin, had died in 1464.

10. The earliest comparative figures available are indicative, although they relate to the mid-sixteenth century: the annual income of a leading mining town in Hungary was then about 80,000 gold florins, compared with figures of between 300,000 and 600,000 gold florins for Milan or Naples.

11. The demand for copper in western Europe, for use in roofing, had grown rapidly. Towards the end of the fifteenth century Hungarian production began to fall as readily accessible deposits were exhausted and deeper mines abandoned because of flooding. After 1475 János Thurzó, a mining engineer from Slovakia, invented a method, involving water-wheels, of pumping out flooded mines and bought up a number of abandoned mines very cheaply. In partnership with the Fuggers bank, he developed a major enterprise that dominated the international copper market.

12. Engel, P.: *The Realm of St Stephen: A History of Medieval Hungary, 895–1526* (London, 2001), p. 321.

13. Knatchbull-Hugessen, C.: *The Political Evolution of the Hungarian Nation* (London, 1908), Vol. I, p. 62.

14. Komjáthy, A.: 'The Hungarian *jobbágyság* in the 15th Century' (*East European Quarterly*, Vol. 10, 1, 1976).

15. Quoted in Sinor, D.: *History of Hungary* (London, 1959), p. 144.

16. Hermann, Zs.: 'State Finances and the Value of Money in Pre-Mohács Hungary', (in *Századok*, no. 109), pp. 301–34.

17. Szalay, L.: *Magyarország története*, Vol. 3, quoted in Perjés, G.: *The Fall of the Medieval Kingdom of Hungary: Mohács 1526–Buda 1541* (Volume XXVI of *War and Society in East-Central Europe*, Boulder, CO, 1989), p. 108.

18. These issues are exhaustively examined in Perjés, G.: op. cit., pp. 176–88.

5. HUNGARY DIVIDED: (1526–1711)

1. Bishop Frangepán, quoted in Perjés, G.: *The Fall of the Medieval Kingdom of Hungary*. p. 123.

2. The siege of Eger was immortalised in a historical novel by Géza Gárdonyi, 'The Stars of Eger' (*Egri Csillagok*); it is available in an excellent English translation by the late George Cushing under the title *Eclipse of the Crescent Moon* (Budapest, 1994).

3. Benda, K.: *Hungary in Turmoil, 1580–1620*, (*European Studies Review*, Vol. 8, No. 3, 1978).

4. Those at Sárospatak and Debrecen are still flourishing and filling a wider role in higher education.

5. An extract from the poem 'How woeful it is for me' ('Siralmas énnéköm'), translated by Paul Tabori. Unless otherwise stated, all translations of Hungarian poetry in this book are reproduced, with permission, from *In Quest of the Miracle Stag: The Poetry of Hungary*, edited by Adam Makkai (Chicago, IL and Budapest, 1996).

6. Fekete, L.: 'Buda and Pest under Turkish Rule', *Studia Turco-Hungarica*, Vol. III (Budapest, 1976) p. 15. The figure of fourteen Christian families, based on Turkish taxation records, may have been an underestimate; Fekete cites, but does not endorse, another source which gives a total of eighty-eight Christian families in Buda and Pest combined at the same date.

7. In 1605, by which time the number of Christian worshippers in Buda had dwindled to a handful, the church of St Mary Magdalen was converted into a mosque, as the much larger Matthias Church (*Mátyás Templom*) had been at the beginning of the occupation.

8. Quoted in Gerő, A. and Poór, J.: *Budapest: A History from its Beginnings to 1998* (New York, 1997), p. 31.

9. A proportion, as R. Patai points out in *The Jews of Hungary* (Detroit, 1996), the Jewish community in the Hungarian capital maintained until the Nazi deportations of 1944.

10. The Hungarian adjective *puszta* means 'deserted' or 'empty'; the word is still used to describe the Great Hungarian Plain.

11. Sinor, D.: *History of Hungary*, p. 212.

12. Zimányi, V.: 'Economy and Society in 16th and 17th Century Hungary (1526–1650)', *Studia Historica Academiae Scientiarum Hungaricae* No. 188 (Budapest, 1987).

13. Quoted in Király, B. K.: *Hungary in the Late Eighteenth Century: The Decline of Enlightened Despotism* (New York, 1969), p. 115, footnote.

14. Makkai, L., in Evans, R. J. W. and Thomas, J. V. (eds.): *Crown, Church and Estates: Central European Politics in the 16th and 17th Centuries* (London, 1991).

15. From Milton's *Areopagitica*, quoted in Lukinich, I.: *A History of Hungary* (Budapest and London, 1937).

16. Quoted in Kosáry, D. G.: 'Gabriel Bethlen: Transylvania in the 17th Century' (*Slavonic and East European Review*, XVII, 1938).

17. These were the Perényis, the Losonczis and the Báthorys; see Pamlényi, E. (ed.): *A History of Hungary*, p. 133.

18. Schimert, P.: The Hungarian Nobility in the Seventeenth and Eighteenth Centuries', in Scott, H. M. (ed.), *The European Nobilities in the 17th and 18th Centuries*, Vol. II.

19. Benda, K.: 'Hungary in Turmoil, 1580–1620' *European Studies Review*, Vol. 8, No. 3 (1978).

20. Ibid.

21. Halsband, R. (ed.): *The Complete Letters of Lady Mary Wortley Montagu* (Oxford, 1965), Vol. I, pp. 297–301.

22. Berend, I. and Ránki, Gy.: *Economic Development in East-Central Europe in the 19th and 20th Centuries* (New York, 1974), p. 7.

6. THE STRUGGLE FOR INDEPENDENCE: (1547–1711)

1. One of them was Sir Richard Grenville, an Elizabethan soldier of fortune who fought in Hungary for two years against the Turks; he later became a distinguished naval captain. In 1591, commanding the *Revenge*, and cut off from the rest of his squadron, he engaged fifteen Spanish galleons unsupported. The battle, after which Grenville died of his wounds, was immortalised by Tennyson in his poem 'The Revenge'.

2. Sinan, the Grand Vizier, had been entrusted by the reclusive Sultan Murad III with oversight over all political and military matters.

3. Ignotus, P.: *Hungary*, p. 34.

4. Sinor, D.: *History of Hungary*, p. 179.

5. Quoted in Hengelmüller, L.: *Hungary's Fight for National Existence* (London, 1913), p. 18.

6. Bak, J. M. and Király, B. K. (eds.): *From Hunyadi to Rákóczi: War and Society in Late Medieval and Early Modern Hungary* (New York, 1982), p. 280.

7. Ibid, p. 283.

8. Daniel, D. P.: 'The Fifteen Years War and the Protestant Response to Habsburg Absolutism in Hungary' (*East-Central Europe*, Vol. 8, 1–2, 1981).

9. Both quotations are from Lukinich, I.: *A History of Hungary* (Budapest, 1937), p. 157.

10. Ibid., p. 158

11. Ibid., p. 160

12. Subtelny, O.: *Domination of Eastern Europe: Native Nobilities and Foreign Absolutism, 1500–1715* (Toronto, 1986), p. 78.

13. *Mátyás király életéről való elmélkedések* (1656) and *Az török áfium ellen való orvosság* (1660).

14. Quoted in Hanák, P.: *History of Hungary from Earliest Times to the Present Day* (Budapest, 1991), p. 63.

15. Quoted in Benczédi, L.: 'Hungarian National Consciousness as Reflected in the Anti–Habsburg and Anti–Ottoman Struggles of the late 17th Century' (*Harvard Ukrainian Studies*, Vol. X, 3–4, 1986), p. 426.

16. Ibid.

17. The Dutch Admiral de Ruyter subsequently seized one of the galleys on which the ministers were enslaved and set them free; his action is commemorated by an impressive memorial beside the Calvinist Great Church (*Nagytemplom*) in Debrecen.

18. Quoted in Zarek, O.: *The History of Hungary* (London, 1939), p. 255.

19. Quoted in Benczédi, L.: op. cit., p. 429.

20. '…pugnacious, reckless and rash…': Sinor, D.: *History of Hungary* (London, 1959), p. 204; '… young, ambitious, a good soldier…': Katalin Péter in Sugar, P. (ed.): *A History of Hungary* (London, 1990), p. 116; '… passionate make-up coupled with outstanding military and diplomatic talents…': Hanák, P.: *History of Hungary* (Budapest, 1991), p. 66.

21. There is no certainty about the derivation or meaning of the word *labanc;* one theory is that is was a corruption of the German *landsknecht* (knight), used ironically.

22. Vámbéry, A.: *Hungary in Ancient, Medieval and Modern Times* (London, 1886), p. 357.

23. Estimates of its size range from 120,000 to 250,000 men.

24. Some Viennese bakers celebrated their detection of one Turkish tunnelling party by baking small crescent-shaped pastries, the *croissants.*

25. Quoted in Wandycz, P.: *The Price of Freedom* (London and New York, 1992), p. 97.

26. There is a full and revelatory treatment of this episode in Malcolm, N.: *Kosovo: A Short History* (London, 1998), Chapter 8.

27. Knatchbull-Hugessen, C. M.: *The Political Evolution of the Hungarian Nation* (London, 1908), Vol. I, p. 166.

28. Rákóczi's inheritance included twenty estates, thirty-eight castles and 681 villages (Subtelny, O.: op. cit.).

29. His bride was Princess Charlotte of Hesse-Rheinfels, whose family could claim relationships to Louis XIV and other European monarchs; the marriage was not happy and when political events drove them apart after six years neither seems to have repined.

30. Quoted in Hanák, P.: op. cit., p. 71, and Bak, J. M. and Király, B. K., op. cit., p. 373.

31. Quoted in Bak, J. M. and Király, B. K.: op. cit., p. 373.
32. Hengelmuller, L.: op.cit., p.112
33. Bak, J. M. and Kiraly, B. K.: op.cit., p. 374.
34. Subtelny, O.: op. cit., p. 150.
35. Ibid., p. 152.
36. Quoted in Bak, J. M. and Király, B. K., op. cit., p. 450.
37. In 1906, Emperor Franz Josef sanctioned the return of Rákóczi's remains to Hungary. They are buried in the Cathedral of Kassa; ironically, Kassa has lain outside Hungary's borders since the Treaty of Trianon (1920).
38. In their poems and campfire songs, the *kuruc* made a significant and still treasured contribution to Hungarian literature.
39. Clause ix of the agreement, as quoted Knatchbull-Hugessen, C. M.: op. cit., Vol. I, p. 173.

7. HABSBURG RULE AND NATIONAL AWAKENING: (1711–1825)

1. The nobles demanded that the burden of the *contributio* (war tax) should be shared with the Austrian hereditary provinces; that Charles should recognise Hungary's right to a separate and independent government; that if a regency became necessary, the Regent should be the Palatine; and that a future Queen's consort should be crowned in Hungary.
2. Knatchbull-Hugessen, C.M.: *The Political Evolution of the Hungarian Nation* (London, 1908), I, p. 190.
3. From the beginning of the eighteenth century onwards, it is appropriate to refer to the upper stratum of the lesser nobility as 'the gentry'.
4. Barred by her gender from election to be Holy Roman Emperor, Maria Theresa initially bore the titles of Archduchess of Austria, 'King' of Hungary and Queen of Bohemia. Her efforts to secure the election of her husband, Francis of Lorraine, to the imperial crown were eventually rewarded in 1745; thereafter, she could be styled 'Empress'.
5. The last battle in which a King of England led his army in person.
6. Quoted in Balázs, É.H.: *Hungary and the Habsburgs, 1765–1800* (Budapest, 1997), p. 52.
7. Quoted in Knatchbull-Hugessen, C.M.: op. cit., p. 209.
8. Knatchbull-Hugessen, C. M.: op.cit., p. 196.
9. *Urbarium* was the term, in use since the early sixteenth century, to cover matters concerning landlord/peasant relations.
10. These figures are a reconciliation of those given in acres in Sugar, P. F.: *A History of Hungary* (London, 1990), p. 153 and those given in *hold* in Kann, R. A. and David, Z. V.: *The Peoples of the Eastern Habsburg Lands, 1526–1918* (Seattle, 1984).
11. Quoted in Király, B. K.: *Hungary in the Late Eighteenth Century: The Decline of Enlightened Despotism* (New York, 1969), p. 55.
12. Ibid.
13. Marczali, H.: *Hungary in the Eighteenth Century* (Cambridge, 1910), p. 123.
14. Quite apart from the disputes generated by the Turkish occupation, Hungarian laws on property were a lawyer's paradise. If a member of the nobility wished to sell land to a potential purchaser outside his family, he was obliged to offer it first to his immediate neighbours. If no neighbouring landlord was interested in buying, the outsider could purchase the land on, in effect, a thirty-year lease, at the expiry of which *any* branch of the original vendor's family could buy the land back for the original purchase price, plus an allowance for improvements.

15. Marczali, H.: op. cit., p. 146.
16. The exemption was not, in fact, complete: nobles owning property in Royal Free Towns were liable for the *contributio*, as were nobles who owned no land. See Dickson, P.: *Finance and Government under Maria Theresa, 1740–1780* (Oxford, 1987), Vol. II, pp. 257–8.
17. See Király, B. K.: op. cit., p. 100.
18. Marczali, H.: op. cit., p. 88.
19. Paget, J.: *Hungary and Transylvania: with remarks on their condition, social, political and eco-nomical* (London, 1839), Vol. II, p. 524.
20. Marczali, H.: op. cit., p. 45.
21. Townson, R.: *Travels in Hungary, with a short account of Vienna in the year 1793* (London, 1797), p. 194.
22. Marczali, H.: op. cit., p. 67.
23. A contemporary Hungarian account, cited by Marczali, H., op. cit., p. 69, noted that there were very few noblemen's houses in the country not built of wood and that glass windows were rarities even in towns. A noble family's wealth was displayed, not in its house or furnishings, which were usually primitive, but in jewellery, cloak fastenings, silver buttons and the like.
24. Király, B. K.: op. cit., p. 134.
25. Janos, A.C.: *The Politics of Backwardness in Hungary. 1825–1945* (Princeton, 1982), p. 30. Janos points out that this situation had important implications for the future: 'Having no legal title or claim to the lands they cultivated, these peasant families [the cottars] would acquire no proprietary rights under the Act of Emancipation of 1848 and … would form the bulk of the agrarian proletariat of the nineteenth and twentieth centuries'.
26. Király, B. K.: op. cit., p. 144. The building in Szarvas occupied by Tessedik's institute is still standing and can be visited, as can his farmhouse nearby; the local museum con-tains mementos of his activities.
27. Ibid., p. 143.
28. Bright, R.: *Travels from Vienna through Lower Hungary; with some remarks on the state of Vienna during the Congress in the year 1814* (Edinburgh, 1818).
29. Quoted in Janos, A.C.: op. cit., p. 49.
30. Ibid.
31. Quoted in Balázs, É.H.: op. cit., p. 47.
32. Marczali, H.: op.cit., p. 101.
33. Balázs, É.H.: op. cit., p. 201.
34. Knatchbull-Hugessen, C.M.: op. cit., I, p. 217.
35. Bright, R.: op. cit., p. 214.
36. Balázs, É.H.: op. cit., p. 211.
37. Ibid., p. 269.
38. Townson, R.: op. cit., p. 145.
39. Quoted in Wandruszka, A.: *The House of Habsburg* (London, 1964), p. 160.
40. Macartney, C.A.: *The House of Austria, 1790–1918* (Edinburgh, 1978), p. 21.
41. Király, B.K.: op. cit., p. 187.
42. Ibid., p. 230.
43. Macartney, C.A.: op.cit., p. 23.
44. This provision probably reflected the belief that exploitation of the royal salt monopoly by Leopold's predecessors had increased the vulnerability of the peasantry and poorer gentry to plague and epidemics by pricing salt beyond their reach.
45. Of the forty-nine counties that sent delegates to the 1790–91 Diet, twenty-two favoured Hungarian as the official language, nineteen wished to retain Latin and eight advocated the use of both (Kann, R. A. and David, Z.V.: op.cit.).

46. King Francis I of Hungary but Holy Roman Emperor Francis II until he resigned that title in 1806, having 'accepted' the title Francis I, Emperor of Austria in 1804.

47. Letter to Count Ferenc Széchényi, 1798, quoted in Cushing, G. F.: op. cit.

48. Sugar, P. F.: 'The Influence of the Enlightenment and the French Revolution in Eighteenth Century Hungary' (*Journal of Central European Affairs*, XVII, 4, pp. 331–55).

49. Visitors to Hungary noted this with surprise: Robert Townson attended a county assembly meeting in 1793 at which the proceedings were conducted entirely in Latin, while Richard Bright, visiting an estate in southern Hungary in 1814, witnessed a bailiff giving instructions in Latin to his subordinates.

50. Known as 'nobles in sandles' (*bocskoros nemesek*).

51. György Bessenyei (*c.* 1747–1811) came from a poor Protestant noble family in northeast Hungary; he studied the humanities at the Calvinist Collegium in Sárospatak but did not graduate. In Vienna, as a member of the Royal Hungarian Bodyguard, he found time to read the works of a wide range of west European authors including Locke, Pope, Rousseau, Voltaire (his favourite), Montesquieu and Holbach; he also founded a literary circle with the significant title 'Society of Hungarian Patriots'. His plays and novels were too overtly political to qualify for literary greatness but they were powerfully written and made an important contribution, in themselves, to the development of the Hungarian language.

52. Quoted from Bessenyei's pamphlet *Magyarság* by Bárány, Gy. in 'Hoping against Hope: the Enlightened Age in Hungary' (*American Historical Review*, 76, 2, April 1971).

53. Quoted in Evans, R. J. W.: in Scott, H. M., *Enlightened Absolutism: Reform and Reformers in Later Eighteenth-Century Europe* (London, 1990), p. 211.

54. Quoted in Cushing, G. F.: 'The Birth of National Literature in Hungary' (*Slavonic and East European Review*, Vol. XXXVIII, No. 91, 1960, pp. 459–75).

55. Mihály Csokonai Vitéz (1773–1805), the son of a Calvinist apothecary in Debrecen, was educated at the Calvinist Collegium in the same town and imbibed from his teachers there the ideas of the Enlightenment; he was expelled in 1795 for indiscipline. Having travelled to Pest to find a publisher for his early poems, he witnessed there the execution of the Hungarian Jacobins, which made a profound impression on him. He subsequently lived in Debrecen, in considerable poverty, where his writing evolved from the powerfully philosophical to the enchantingly lyrical; disappointed in love by the real-life heroine of his lyric poems, he gave way to despair. In 1805 he caught pneumonia while delivering a graveside panegyric at the funeral of one of his patrons and died shortly afterwards.

56. Bárány, Gy.: op. cit.

57. Ibid.

58. Deme, L.: 'Writers and Essayists and the Rise of Magyar Nationalism in the 1820s and 1830s' (*Slavic Review*, Vol. XLIII, No. 4, 1984).

59. Janos, A.C.: *The Politics of Backwardness in Hungary, 1825–1945* (Princeton, 1982), p. 10. (The definition of 'Hungarian' employed in this context was 'Magyar in language and custom', which would have embraced a wider proportion than ethnic Hungarians alone; the latter may therefore have accounted for even less than 44 per cent of the total).

60. From the beginning of the seventeenth century, when Michael the Brave briefly united Wallachia and Moldavia under his leadership, the inhabitants of those provinces can properly be designated 'Romanian' rather than 'Vlach' and 'Moldavian', reflecting their consciousness of a common ethnic identity.

61. Marczali, H.: op. cit., p. 207, footnote.

62. According to Macartney, the ethnic breakdown of Hungary's population in 1786 was as follows: Hungarians: 3.35m., Romanians: 1.5m., Slovaks: 1.25m., Germans: 1.0m.,

Serbs: 0.75m., Croats: 0.75m., Ruthenes, Jews, Gypsies and others: approx 0.5m. See Macartney, C. A.: *Hungary* (Edinburgh, 1962).

63. The figures for regional population growth between the two censuses of 1720 and 1787 are striking. The population of Transylvania increased by only 73 per cent during the period and that of north-west Hungary by 165 per cent; but in Transdanubia the growth was 220 per cent, in the region between the Danube and Tisza Rivers 352 per cent and in that between the Tisza and Maros Rivers a remarkable 944 per cent (Király, B.K.: op. cit., p. 7).

64. The best treatment in English of this subject is in Kann, R. A. and David, Z. V.: op. cit., Chapter 3.

65. The Ruthenians were Ukrainian by origin.

66. Köpeczi, B. et al. (eds.): *History of Transylvania* (Budapest, 1994), p. 427.

67. The part played by Hungarians in the Habsburg governance of Hungary is well described in R. J. W. Evans's chapter on 'Maria Theresa and Hungary' in Scott, H. M.: op. cit.

68. Bárány, G. in Sugar, P. F.: *A History of Hungary* (London, 1990).

69. Macartney, C. A., in Goodwin, A. (ed.): *The European Nobility in the Eighteenth Century* (London, 1953).

8. REFORM, LANGUAGE AND NATIONALITY: (1825–43)

1. Quoted in Iványi, B. G.: 'From Feudalism to Capitalism: the Economic Background to Széchenyi's Reform in Hungary' (*Journal of Central European Affairs*, XX/3, 1960, pp. 270–88).

2. Ibid.

3. Pardoe, J.: *The City of the Magyar; or Hungary and her Institutions in 1839–40* (London, 1840), Vol. II, p. 288.

4. Janos, A.C.: *The Politics of Backwardness in Hungary* (Princeton, NJ, 1982), pp. 77–8.

5. Hungary's official national anthem is the *Himnusz;* but sometimes the *Szózat* is also sung on ceremonial occasions. The distinction is similar to that, in England, between 'God Save the Queen' and 'Land of Hope and Glory'.

6. Translation by Kirkconnell, W., Makkai, A. and Herrick, E. M. in Makkai, A. (ed.): *In Quest of the 'Miracle Stag': The Poetry of Hungary* (Chicago, IL, 1996), p. 196.

7. Translation by Kirkconnell, W.: ibid., p. 227.

8. From the first of the two *Songs of Zrínyi*, translated by Kirkconnell, W.: ibid., p. 197.

9. From *Sóhajtás* ('Sighing'), ibid., p. 242.

10. István's father, Ferenc, and his forebears had spelt their family name with two accented 'é's—Széchényi; István Széchenyi chose to drop the accent on the second 'e'.

11. '[Ferenc Széchényi's] son, a beautiful boy about ten years old, spoke pretty correctly and fluently the Hungarian, German, Latin, French and Italian languages and, I believe, in some degree the Croatian'. Townson, R.: *Travels in Hungary* (London, 1797), p. 38.

12. Pardoe, J.: op. cit., Vol. I, pp. 263–4.

13. Crescence, widow of Count Károly Zichy.

14. Quoted in Bárány, G.: *Stephen Széchenyi and the Awakening of Hungarian Nationalism* (Princeton, NJ, 1968) p. 83.

15. Quoted in Janos, A.C.: *The Politics of Backwardness in Hungary, 1825–1945* (Princeton, NJ, 1982), pp. 51–2.

16. Quoted in Bárány: op. cit., p. 143.

17. Quoted from *Hitel* in ibid., p. 210.

18. Quoted in Wagner, F.S.: 'Széchenyi and the Nationality Problem in the Habsburg Empire' (*Journal of Central European Affairs*, Vol. XX, 1960, 3).

19. The formal union of the cities of Pest, Buda and Óbuda which created the city of Budapest did not take place until 1873, although the name 'Budapest' was current from 1849 onwards; until 1849, the capital was known as Pest-Buda.

20. Quoted in Pamlényi, E. (ed.): *A History of Hungary* (Budapest, 1973), p. 225.

21. Quoted in Kosáry, D.G.: *A History of Hungary* (Cleveland, OH, 1941), p. 190.

22. Quoted in Bárány: op. cit., pp. 212–13.

23. See Frank, T.: *Marketing Hungary: Kossuth and the Politics of Propaganda* in Péter, L., Rady, M. and Sherwood, P. (eds.): *Lajos Kossuth Sent Word ...* (London, 2003).

24. Hungary's first post-Communist President, Árpád Göncz, did the same when imprisoned after the 1956 revolution.

25. Deák, I.: *The Lawful Revolution: Louis Kossuth and the Hungarians, 1848–1849* (New York, 1979), p. 53.

26. Pardoe, J.: op. cit., Vol. I, p. 217.

27. Their name derived from the four 'circles' into which ancient Hungary had notionally been divided, one on either bank of the Danube and one on either bank of the Tisza.

28. His full title was *Personalis Praesentiae Regiae locum tenens*, 'Dignitary Representing the Presence of the King'.

29. Janos, A.C.: op. cit., p. 63.

30. The bridge at Marlow, in effect a scale model of Budapest's Chain Bridge, still links the two halves of the town and is in excellent condition.

31. Paget, J.: *Hungary and Transylvania: with remarks on their condition, social, political and economical* (London, 1839) Vol. I, p. 28.

32. Király, B.: *Ferenc Deák* (Boston, MA, 1975), p. 26.

33. Bárány, G.: op. cit., p. 349.

34. From Deák's report to the Zala county assembly, quoted in Király, B.: op. cit., p. 70.

35. Quoted in Bárány, G.: op. cit., p. 33. Any discussion of this issue is beset by a problem of translation. The Hungarian word *magyar* describes both the nationality of a Hungarian and the language which he or she speaks. But ethnic groups living under the Hungarian crown who did not speak Magyar were nevertheless Hungarian (*magyar*) by nationality and allegiance. It would be clear to a Magyar speaker, from the context, in which sense the word was being used; but this is less clear to an English speaker. When I reproduce, in this account, quotations from another source, I have left the wording unchanged, despite the risk of misunderstanding; when I have paraphrased, I have used the word 'Hungarian' to denote nationality and the word 'Magyar' to denote the language spoken by Hungary's largest single ethnic group.

36. Wagner, F.S.: op. cit.

37. Quoted in Bárány, G.: 'The Awakening of Magyar Nationalism before 1848' (*Austrian History Yearbook*, Vol. II).

38. Knatchbull-Hugessen, C. M.: *The Political Evolution of the Hungarian Nation* (London, 1908), Vol. I, p. 323. The translation problem is further complicated in this instance by the fact that the Archduke Joseph, who did not speak Magyar, would have delivered this speech, in the Upper House on 28 June 1843, in German, probably using the word *ungarisch* to mean both 'Hungarian' and 'Magyar'.

39. Wagner, F. S.: op. cit.

40. Literally 'Land of the Huns', an archaic and inaccurate designation; why Széchenyi chose it is a mystery.

41. Quoted in Bárány, G.: *Stephen Széchenyi*, p. 297.

42. Wagner, F. S.: op. cit.

43. Ibid.

44. Ibid.

45. During the reform period, the word 'nationality' (*nemzetiség*) was used to denote an ethnic group, *any* ethnic group, including the Magyars; later on, Magyars applied the term 'the nationalities' (*a nemzetiségek*) only to the non-Magyar ethnic groups, giving it a slightly disparaging overtone.

46. The Serbian language, like Magyar, had already been reformed and standardised, mainly through the efforts of the Serbian scholar Vuk Karadžić; but the Serb Orthodox Church insisted on retaining the Cyrillic alphabet, while Ljudevit Gaj refused to give up Catholic Croatia's Latin script. The outcome was a common spoken language, written in Cyrillic in Serbia and in Latin script in Croatia, a compromise that has endured to the present day.

47. Wagner, F. S.: op. cit.

48. Quoted in Sked, A.: *The Decline and Fall of the Habsburg Empire* (London, 1989), p. 95.

49. Deák's stand on taxation so infuriated the 'sandalled nobles' of Zala county that a serious attempt was made to burn down his house; a servant who tried to impede the arsonists was shot dead by one of them.

9. OPPOSITION, REVOLUTION AND WAR: (1844–49)

1. Quoted in Janos, A.C.: *The Politics of Backwardness in Hungary, 1825–1945* (Princeton, NJ, 1982), p. 58.

2. Knatchbull-Hugessen, C.M.: *The Political Evolution of the Hungarian Nation* (London, 1908), Vol. II, p. 49.

3. Quoted in Fejtő, F. (ed.): *The Opening of an Era—1848: An Historical Symposium* (London, 1948), p. 23.

4. Ibid., p. 45.

5. Macartney, C. A.: *The House of Austria: The Later Phase, 1790–1918* (Edinburgh, 1978), p. 78.

6. Quoted in Spira, Gy.: *A Hungarian Count in the Revolution of 1848* (Budapest, 1974), p. 18.

7. From George Cushing's translation of *Petőfi* by Gyula Illyés (Budapest, 1973), pp. 344–6. Illyés (1902–1983) was Hungary's greatest modern populist poet and writer.

8. From '*A puszta télen*' ('The Puszta in Winter'), ibid., p. 367

9. Quoted in Czigány, L.: *The Oxford History of Hungarian Literature* (Oxford, 1984), p. 191.

10. Illyés, Gy.: op. cit.

11. Translation by Makkai, A.: *In Quest of the Miracle Stag: the Poetry of Hungary* (Chicago, IL, 1996 p. 319.

12. Quoted in Spira, Gy.: op. cit., p. 32.

13. Macartney, C. A.: *The House of Austria* (Edinburgh, 1978), p. 89.

14. Patai, R.: *The Jews of Hungary* (Detroit, 1996), pp. 227–9.

15. Deák, I.: *The Lawful Revolution: Louis Kossuth and the Hungarians, 1848–1849* (New York, 1979), p. 96.

16. Quoted in Tóth, Z. L: 'The Nationality Problem in Hungary in 1843–1849' (*Acta Historica Academiae Scientiarum Hungaricae*, 1955, IV, 1–3).

17. E.g. by Knatchbull-Hugessen: op. cit., Vol. II, pp. 33–50.

18. Ibid., p. 60.

19. Wagner, F. S.: 'Széchenyi and the Nationality Problem in the Habsburg Empire' (*Journal of Central European Affairs*, Vol. XX, 1960, 3). The total population of the Empire at this time was about 36 million, of which 6 million were Magyars, 7 million were Germans and 15.5 million were Slavs.

20. Emancipation was not accompanied by title to land: over 900,000 cottar families—44 per cent of the peasant population—were emancipated but remained landless. 72 per cent of the Hungarian population lived off only 37 per cent of the land (Király, B.: *Ferenc Deák* (Boston, MA, 1975), p. 127.

21. Accounts of the course of events in May, June and July 1848 are frequently confused and contradictory in terms of chronology, if not in substance; I have tended to follow that given in Spira, Gy.: *A Hungarian Count in the Revolution of 1848* (Budapest, 1974) because it seems to be the best documented, although Spira's interpretation of the events he describes reflects a strong ideological bias.

22. Although the Hungarian word *országgyűlés* is used for both 'Diet' and 'National Assembly', I shall use the latter term from now onwards in order to distinguish the new parliament from its feudal predecessor; its two chambers will be referred to as the Upper House and the Lower House.

23. The Frankfurt Congress, convened in May 1848 by the leading liberals of the German states, was intended to promote and devise a constitution for a united Germany, including all or part of the Austrian Empire. The draft constitution provided that the rulers of German member-states could retain only personal links with, but not sovereignty over, their non-German territories. The Hungarians therefore saw in the Congress their best hope for achieving complete independence from the Habsburgs. The Congress foundered in 1849 on the rock of Prussian reaction.

24. Quoted in Spira, Gy.: op. cit., p. 261. By July 1848, Széchenyi's cherished Chain Bridge was nearing completion; eleven of its twelve suspension chains had been hoisted into place. When Széchenyi took his sons to witness the hoisting of the final chain on 18 July, a cable snapped and the chain crashed down on to the wooden pontoon between the piers on which the spectators were standing. Széchenyi and his sons were able to swim to the bank; but the incident flung Széchenyi back into one of his deepest depressions: the bridge would never be completed, Hungary would not survive, (ibid., p. 247).

25. Quoted in Knatchbull-Hugessen, C. M.: op. cit., Vol. II, p. 85.

26. With the cabinet's resolution of 27 August, quoted in Tóth, Z. I.: 'The Nationality Problem in Hungary in 1848–1849' (*Acta Historica Academiae Scientiarum Hungaricae*, 1955, IV, 1–3), p. 257.

27. Szabad, Gy.: *Hungary's Recognition of Croatia's Sef-Determination in 1848 and its Immediate Antecedents*, in Király, B. (ed.): *East Central European Society and War in the Era of Revolutions, 1775–1856* (Columbia, New York, 1984), p. 604.

28. Ibid, p. 244.

29. Quoted in Knatchbull-Hugessen, C. M.: op. cit., Vol. II, pp. 89–91.

30. Wagner, F. S.: op. cit.

31. E.g. by historians as far apart on the political spectrum as the Hon. C. M. Knatchbull-Hugessen and the Marxist György Spira.

32. Quoted in Knatchbull-Hugessen, C.M.: op. cit., Vol. II, p. 97.

33. Deák, I.: *Where Loyalty and Where Rebellion? The Dilemma of the Habsburg Army Officers in 1848–49*, in Király, B.: op. cit., p. 393.

34. Görgey, A.: *My Life and Acts in Hungary in the years 1848 and 1849* (London, 1852), Vol. II. p. 22.

35. During the Italian insurrection, Haynau had inflicted savage punishment on the insurgents in Brescia, ordering a number of them—including women—to be flogged. When, in retirement, he visited London, his reputation had preceded him: he was set upon by the workers in Barclay's Brewery and given a sound thrashing.

36. Once Radetzky had inflicted a final defeat on the King of Sardinia and the Piedmontese in Italy (at Novara in March 1849), it was only a matter of time before Austria

could considerably augment its forces on the ground in Hungary; the Empire could draw on immense reserves of manpower if it had to.

37. Quoted in Spira, Gy.: op. cit., pp. 105–6.
38. Quoted in Tóth, Z.I.: op. cit., p. 274.
39. Quoted in Spira, Gy.: pp. 171–2.
40. Görgey, A.: op. cit., Vol. I, p. 366.
41. Sproxton, C.: *Palmerston and the Hungarian Revolution* (Cambridge, 1919), p. 21.
42. Ibid, p. 37.
43. Görgey, A.: op. cit., Vol. II, p. 430. According to István Deák (in Deák, I, op. cit., p. 324) the surrender involved eleven generals, 1,426 officers and 32,569 other ranks of the Hungarian army; 144 guns; and sixty battle flags.
44. Those echoes persist to this day: a Hungarian friend, learning that I was engaged in writing this book, asked me to find out whether Görgey had been a traitor. I believe that he was not; so, apparently, does the Budapest City Council, since a handsome bronze equestrian statue of Görgey was erected on the Castle Hill in Buda in 1999. There is an elegant treatment of the subject by Professor László Péter: 'The Görgey Question', (*Slavonic and East European Review*, Vol. 76, No. 1, 1998).

10. THE POLITICS OF COMPROMISE AND DUALISM: (1849–1906)

1. The victims, subsequently remembered as the 'martyrs of Arad', were: Gen. Lajos Aulich, Gen. János Damjanich, Gen. Arisztid Dessewffy, Gen. Ernő Kiss, Gen. Károly Knézich, Gen. György Láhner, Col. Vilmos Lázár, Gen. Count Károly Leiningen-Westerburg, Gen. József Nagy-Sándor, Gen. Ernő Pöltenberg, Gen. József Schweidel, Gen. Ignác Török and Gen. Count Károly Vécsey.
2. On the eve of his execution, Batthyány had attempted to cut his throat with a knife smuggled into his cell by his sister-in-law, Caroline; his wound was suffciently severe to make hanging impracticable but did not save him from the firing squad. According to one Hungarian writer, the Archduchess Sophie (mother of the future Emperor Franz Josef), allegedly in love with Batthyány, had insisted on the death sentence in revenge for his liaison with Caroline (Ignotus, P.: *Hungary*, London, 1972, p. 63).
3. Kosáry, D. G.: *A History of Hungary* (Cleveland, OH, 1941), p. 251.
4. Király, B.: *Ferenc Deák* (Boston, MA, 1975), p. 139.
5. Ibid., p. 143.
6. See, for example, Szabad, Gy.: *Hungarian Political Trends between the Revolution and the Compromise, 1849–1867* (Budapest, 1977)—in other respects a valuable work.
7. Although, as A. J. P. Taylor has pointed out in *The Habsburg Monarchy, 1809–1918* (London, 1948), p. 105, the patent's provision that matters affecting only the non-Hungarian lands of the Empire would be debated in a 'narrower' parliament, in which Hungarian representatives would not be present, implied that the Empire was divided into two units—Hungarian and non-Hungarian—and that Pest-Buda equated to Vienna rather than to Prague: this was the first, coded, manifestation of the dualist concept.
8. Quoted in Knatchbull-Hugessen, C.M.: *The Political Evolution of the Hungarian Nation* (London, 1908), Vol. II, p. 183.
9. Quoted in Király, B.: op. cit., p. 164.
10. Quoted in Szabad, Gy.: op. cit., p. 119.
11. Ibid., p. 122.
12. Andrássy had been granted an amnesty in 1857 and returned from exile to become one of Deák's leading supporters.

13. In Hungarian, the name given to the relevant enactments of 1867 is *kiegyezés*, which is best translated as 'Compromise'. The German description of the equivalent legislation approved by the *Reichsrat* is *Ausgleich*, which is best translated as 'settlement'. Most Hungarian historians writing in English use 'Compromise' and I have followed suit.

14. See Péter, L.: The Dualist Character of the 1867 Hungarian Settlement' in Ránki, Gy.: *Hungarian History—World History* (Budapest, 1984); Hanák, P.: 'Hungary in the Austro-Hungarian Monarchy: Preponderancy or Dependency?' (*Austrian History Yearbook*, Vol. III, Pt 1, 1967); and Macartney, C. A.: *The House of Austria: The Later Phase, 1790–1918* (Edinburgh, 1978).

15. Quoted in Knatchbull-Hugessen, C.M.: op. cit., Vol. II, p. 220.

16. Quoted in Vermes, G.: 'Hungary and the Common Army in the Austro-Hungarian Monarchy', in Vardy, S. B. and Vardy, A.H. (eds.): *Society in Change: Studies in Honour of Béla K Király* (New York, 1983), p. 91.

17. Hanák, P.: in Chapter 6 of Pamlényi, E. (ed.): *A History of Hungary* (Budapest, 1973), p. 319.

18. Péter, L.: op. cit., p. 134.

19. Macartney, C. A.: op. cit., p. 205.

20. Décsy, J.: 'Gyula Andrássy' in Body, P. (ed.): *Hungarian Statesmen of Destiny* (Boulder, CO, 1989), p. 77.

21. Szabad, Gy.: op. cit., p. 163.

22. Quoted in Bárány, G.: 'Hungary: the Uncompromising Compromise' (*Austrian History Yearbook*, Vol. III, Pt 1, 1967).

23. Quoted in Gerő, A.: *Modern Hungarian Society in the Making: The Unfinished Experience* (Budapest, 1995), p. 132.

24. Seton-Watson, R. W.: *Corruption and Reform in Hungary* (London, 1911). Seton-Watson's Magyarphobia was later to play a fateful role in Hungary's dismemberment (see Chapter 12).

25. Janos, A.: *The Politics of Backwardness in Hungary, 1825–1945* (Princeton, NJ, 1982), p. 102.

26. Gerő, A.: op. cit., p. 134.

27. Vermes, G.: op. cit., p. 95.

28. Hanák, P.: op. cit., (1967), p. 298.

29. Macartney, C. A.: op. cit, p. 232.

30. Quoted (in Hungarian) in Gratz, G.: *A Dualizmus Kora: Magyarország Története, 1867–1918* (Budapest, l934, repr. 1992), Vol. II, p. 20.

31. Quoted in May, A. J.: *The Habsburg Monarchy, 1867–1914* (Cambridge, MA, 1951), p. 353.

32. A different version of the episode is advanced in Sugar, P.: 'An Underrated Event: The Hungarian Constitutional Crisis of 1905–6', in the (*East European Quarterly*, Vol. XV, No. 3 September 1981): according to Sugar, 'Speaker Perczel took out and waved his handkerchief and all of Tisza's followers did the same. Perczel ruled that this procedure was a vote, declared the motion … as adopted and recessed the House for three weeks'.

33. Quoted in Janos, A.: op. cit., p. 165.

11. ECONOMIC ADVANCE IN A TROUBLED SOCIETY: (1850–1913)

1. The statistics in this section, and in the paragraphs on Hungarian industry which follow. derive from the following authorities: Pamlényi, E. (ed.): *A History of Hungary* (Budapest, 1973), Chapters 6 and 7; Janos, A.C.: *The Politics of Backwardness in Hungary, 1825–1945*

(Princeton, NJ, 1982); Berend, I. T. and Ránki, Gy.: *Hungary: A Century of Economic Development* (Newton Abbot and New York, 1974); and 'Economic Factors in Nationalism: The Example of Hungary at the Beginning of the 20th century' (*Austrian History Yearbook*, Vol. III, Pt 3, 1967); *Economic Development in East-Central Europe in the 19th and 20th Centuries* (New York, 1974); 'The European Periphery and Industrialisation, 1780–1914' (*Journal of European Economic History*, Vol. 9 (1980); *Underdevelopment and Economic Growth: Studies in Hungarian Social & Economic History* (Budapest, 1979); *East-Central Europe in the 19th and 20th Centuries* (Budapest, 1977); *The Hungarian Economy in the Twentieth Century* (New York, 1985); Macartney, C. A.: *The House of Austria: the Later Phase, 1790–1918* (Edinburgh, 1978); Kornlos, J. (ed.): *Economic Development in the Habsburg Monarchy in the 19th Century* (Guildford, 1983); Hanák, P.: 'Hungary in the Austro-Hungarian Monarchy: Preponderancy or Dependency?' (*Austrian History Yearbook*, Vol. III, Pt 1, 1967); Ránki, Gy.: *Hungarian History—World History* (Budapest, 1984); Deák, G.: *The Economy and Polity in Early Twentieth Century Hungary: The Role of the National Association of Industrialists* (Boulder, CO, 1990). I have restricted statistics to the essentials and, to avoid cluttering the text, have not included individual references.

2. See, for example, Hanák, P.: op. cit.; Good, D. F.: *The Economic Rise of the Habsburg Empire, 1750–1914* (Berkeley, CA, 1984); and a good summary of the arguments in Sked, A.: *The Decline and Fall of the Habsburg Empire, 1815–1918* (London, 1989).

3. Szabad, Gy.: *Hungarian Political Trends between the Revolution and the Compromise (1849–1867)* (Budapest, 1977), p. 12.

4. Király, B.K.: *Ferenc Deák* (Boston, MA, 1975), p. 184.

5. Quoted in Janos, A.C.: op. cit., p. 115.

6. Patai, R.: *The Jews of Hungary* (Detroit, MI, 1996), p. 374.

7. Although fencing became a popular sport among Jewish students—Jews won Olympic gold medals for Hungary in 1908 and 1912—and Jews were often highly effective duellers when given the opportunity (Patai, R.: op. cit.).

8. Patai, R.: op.cit., p. 360.

9. Ibid., p. 356.

10. Janos, A C: op. cit., p. 178.

11. Patai, R.: op.cit., p. 358.

12. Quoted in Janos, A. C: op. cit., p. 162.

13. Romsics, I.: *Hungary in the Twentieth Century* (Budapest, 1999), p. 61.

14. It is worth recalling that although the Hungarian franchise, extending to only 6.3 per cent of the population in 1890, was very restricted, it was not exceptionally so by the standards of the time: the comparable figure at the same date for Belgium was 2.2 per cent, for Sweden 6 per cent, for the Netherlands 6.5 per cent and for Austria 7.2 per cent. France, Germany and Great Britain, however, had reached a more advanced stage with franchises of 29 per cent, 21 per cent and 16 per cent respectively.

15. Berend, I. T. and Ránki, Gy.: 'Economic Factors in Nationalism: the Example of Hungary at the Beginning of the 20th Century' (*Austrian History Yearbook*, Vol. III, Pt 3, 1967).

16. Quoted in May, A.J.: *The Habsburg Monarchy, 1867–1914* (Cambridge, MA, 1951), p. 82.

17. The full text of the Act is reproduced as Appendix III of Seton-Watson, R. W.: *Racial Problems in Hungary* (London, 1908).

18. The justification put forward for this legislation, in so far as it concerned denominational primary schools, was that it aimed to raise the level of teaching in those schools by enabling them, through state subsidies, to hire teachers of the same quality as those in state schools: these subsidies were conditional on the teaching of Magyar, so that if pupils moved from their native village they would not be disadvantaged by ignorance of the official language of their country.

19. Quoted in Janos, A.C.: op. cit., p. 111.
20. Seton-Watson, R.W.: op. cit., p. xix.
21. Seton-Watson, R.W.: op. cit., p. 204.
22. Knatchbull-Hugessen, C. M.: *The Political Evolution of the Hungarian Nation* (London, 1908), Vol. II, p. 333.
23. Between 1950 and the collapse of the Communist regime in 1989, Hungarian school-children received compulsory instruction in the Russian language during the last eight of their twelve school years. The great majority succeeded in emerging from the experience with virtually no knowledge of Russian whatsoever; exposure to the language certainly did not engender affection for the Soviet regime or for Communism.
24. Seton-Watson, H. and C.: *The Making of a New Europe* (London, 1981), p. 50.
25. Szekfű, Gy.: *Magyar Történet*, Vol. V, p. 569 and Lukacs, J. in *Budapest 1900: A Historical Portrait of a City and its Culture* (London, 1989), pp. 128–9.
26. Gratz, G.: *A Dualizmus Kora: Magyarország története, 1867–1918* (Budapest, 1934, reprinted Budapest 1992), Vol. I, p. 375.
27. The 'Buda' in Arany's poem is not the city but the brother of Attila the Hun, by whom, in legend, he was slain; Buda was believed to have settled on what became the site of the town, which took his name.
28. Translated by Zollman, P. in *In Quest of the Miracle Stag: The Poetry of Hungary*, ed. Makkai, A. (Budapest and Chicago, 1996), pp. 278–81.
29. Translated by Watson Kirkconnell, ibid., pp. 289–90.
30. From 'Song of a Hungarian Jacobin', translated by Sir Maurice Bowra, ibid., p. 414.
31. Translated by and quoted in Lukacs, J.: op. cit., p. 165.
32. From 'The Golden Age of Budapest', in Bátki, J. (ed. and trans.): *Krúdy's Chronicles* (Budapest, 2000), p. 198.
33. Quoted in Janos, A. C: op. cit., p. 172.
34. Lukacs, J.: op. cit., p. 14.
35. Gratz, G.: op. cit., Vol. I, p. 370.

12. WAR AND REVOLUTION: (1906–1919)

1. A more natural translation to English ears would be 'National Labour Party'; but this would convey a misleading impression of the new party's political complexion.
2. Quoted by Vermes, G.: *'István Tisza'*, in Bődy, P. (ed.), *Hungarian Statesmen of Destiny, 1860–1960* (Boulder, CO, 1989), p. 89.
3. Quoted by Vermes, G.: *István Tisza* (New York, 1985), p. 61.
4. The Slovak leader, Milan Hodza, told R. W. Seton-Watson that Franz Ferdinand had once remarked to him: 'It was very bad taste of those gentlemen [the Magyars] ever to come to Europe at all'. (Seton-Watson, H. and C: *The Making of a New Europe*, London, 1981) p. 96.
5. Count Kuno Klebelsberg, quoted in Vermes, G.: op. cit., p. 183.
6. According to Benda, K. (ed.): *Magyarország Történeti Kronológája, Vol. III* (Budapest, 1983) and to Diószegi, I.: *A Ferenc József-i Kor: Magyarország Története, 1849–1918*, those enti-tled to vote in the election of 1910 numbered 1,162,241 (6.4 per cent of the adult population); under the new law, this would have risen to 1,272,755 (6.8 per cent), based on the 1914 census. Romsics, I.: *Magyarország története a XX században*, postulates an increase from 1.1 million to 1.6–1.7 million, a rise of nearly 50 per cent. Vermes, G.: *István Tisza* (New York, 1985) believes that the reform would have produced 350,000 new voters, an increase of 28 per cent.
7. The works which I have found most useful and illuminating from the Austro-Hungarian perspective are: Bridge, F. R.: *From Sadowa to Sarajevo: The Foreign Policy of Austria-Hun-*

gary, 1866–1914 (London, 1972); Joll, J.: *The Origins of the First World War* (London, 1984); McCullough, E.: *How the First World War Began* (Montreal, 1999); and Williamson, S.: *Austria-Hungary and the Origins of the First World War* (London, 1991).

8. Quoted in Galántai, J.: *Hungary in the First World War* (Budapest, 1989), p. 23.
9. Quoted in Stone, N.: 'Hungary and the Crisis of 1914' (*Journal of Contemporary History*, Vol. I, 1966) p. 168.
10. Quoted in Williamson, S.: op. cit., p. 152.
11. Archduke Franz Ferdinand's hostility to Hungary was unwavering. On a personal level, he referred to them contemptuously as 'moustachioed gypsies'; on the political level, he regarded Dualism as the principal source of all the Monarchy's problems. In the late 1890s, he instigated the preparation by the General Staff of a contingency plan for the Austrian occupation of Budapest—anticipating by fifty years Adolf Hitler's 'Operation Margarethe'.
12. The full text of István Tisza's memorandum of 8 July is printed in Kaas, A. and de Lazarovics, F.: *Bolshevism in Hungary: the Béla Kun Period* (London, 1931), Appendix I.
13. Quoted in Vermes, G.: op. cit., p. 224.
14. Ibid., p. 225.
15. Excerpt from the German Ambassador's report, quoted in Vermes, G.: ibid., p. 229.
16. Ibid., p. 230.
17. Quoted in Galántai, J.: op. cit., p. 35.
18. Bridge, F.R.: op. cit., p. 369.
19. Károlyi, M.: *Faith without Illusion (Memoirs of Michael Karolyi)* (London, 1956), p. 56.
20. Quoted in Galántai, J.: op. cit., p. 43.
21. Ibid., p. 18.
22. Sked, A.: *The Decline and Fall of the Habsburg Empire, 1815–1918* (London, 1989), p. 258. The ultimatum was not, of course, 'designed' to start a European, let alone a world war; it was intended, unrealistically, to provoke a war with Serbia alone.
23. Stone, N.: op. cit., p. 155.
24. Quoted in Vermes, G.: op. cit., p. 328.
25. Ibid., p. 290.
26. Quoted from the newspaper *Falca*, ibid., p. 284.
27. Quoted in Galántai, J.: op. cit., p. 124.
28. Quoted in Stone, N.: *The Eastern Front, 1914–1917* (London, 1985), p. 124.
29. Quoted in Galántai, J.: op. cit., p. 120.
30. Ibid., p. 134.
31. Seton-Watson, H. and C.: *The Making of a New Europe* (London, 1981), p. 201 (note).
32. Quoted in Vermes, G.: op. cit., p. 338.
33. Vermes, G.: op. cit., p. 437.
34. Károlyi, M.: op. cit., p. 102.
35. Deák, I.: 'The Habsburg Army in the First and Last Days of World War I: A Comparative Analysis' (in Király, B. K. and Dreisziger, N. F. (eds.), *War and Society in Eastern Europe*, Vol. XIX (Boulder, CO, 1985), p. 310.
36. Károlyi, M.: op. cit., p. 144.
37. The Károlyi estates, including that at Kápolna, had been mortgaged to several banks to pay for Mihály Károlyi's personal debts. In 1917 the banks had appointed an estate manager, Elemér Studinka, to look after their interests and maximise revenue, which was paid to the banks. Although the estates were entailed, the Károlyi family could not apply for release from entail since this exemption could be granted only by the monarch; after Charles IV's abdication, this became impossible. Mihály Károlyi's redistribution was therefore technically illegal but arguably legitimate.
38. Nicolson, H.: *Peacemaking, 1919* (London, 1933 [1944 edition]), p. 237.

39. See, for example, Jászi, O.: *Revolution and Counter-Revolution in Hungary* (New York, 1924) and Károlyi, M.: op. cit.
40. Quoted in Jászi, O.: op. cit., p. 96.
41. Some accounts of this period in English use the word 'Soviet' instead of 'Council' as a translation of the Hungarian *tanács*. This has some advantages for the writer, since 'Soviet' can, in English, be used as an adjective as well as a noun, which is sometimes convenient; but terms such as 'the Hungarian Soviet Republic' or 'Hungarian Soviet Government' risk confusing the reader. The Hungarian Councils were certainly created in imitation of the Russian Soviets; but thirty years were to pass before Hungary became part of the Soviet empire.
42. Quoted in Janos, A.C.: *The Politics of Backwardness in Hungary, 1825–1945* (Princeton, NJ, 1982) p. 194.
43. Quoted in Kaas, A. and de Lazarovics, F.: op. cit., p. 91.
44. The text of the ordinance is in ibid., Appendix 14, p. 341 ff.
45. Ibid., p. 106.
46. Ibid., Appendix 6, p. 327.
47. Quoted in Jászi, O.: op. cit., p. 130.
48. Text reproduced in Deák, F.: *Hungary at the Paris Peace Conference* (New York, 1942), pp. 461–2.
49. Ibid.

13. THE ROAD TO TRIANON: (1914–20)

1. Substantial excerpts from the Foreign Office Memorandum are reproduced in Volume I of *The Truth About the Peace Treaties* by David Lloyd George (London, 1938), who presumably retained the copy he would have received as a member of the War Cabinet
2. Seton-Watson, H. and C.: *The Making of a New Europe* (London, 1981), p. 152.
3. Ibid., p. 154.
4. Quoted in Seton-Watson, H.: R. W. 'Seton-Watson and the Trianon Settlement', in Király, B. K., Pastor, P. and Sanders, I. (eds.): *Essays on World War I: Total War and Peace-making—A Case Study on Trianon* (New York, 1982), p. 46.
5. Quoted in Macartney, C.A. and Palmer, A.W.: *Independent Eastern Europe* (London, 1967), p. 84.
6. Ibid., p. 93.
7. The Romanian government proclaimed the annexation of Transylvania on 11 January 1919.
8. Nicolson, H.: *Peacemaking, 1919* (London, 1933).
9. Ibid., p. 34.
10. Ibid., p. 126.
11. Ibid., p. 127.
12. Ibid., p. 275.
13. Lloyd George, D.: *The Truth About the Peace Treaties*, Vol. II, p. 920.
14. Reproduced in Deák, F.: *Hungary at the Paris Peace Conference* (New York, 1942), p. 444.
15. In fairness to Austria, it should be noted that the Austrian delegation to the conference insisted repeatedly that there should be no transfer of territory without a plebiscite in the districts concerned: for no discernible reason, but probably from bureaucratic laziness, the conference chose to make the transfer without a plebiscite. A plebiscite in part of the region was, nevertheless, subsequently held, with interesting results: in Sopron, 72.8 per cent voted to remain in Hungary and in fourteen neighbouring villages, 54.6 per cent. The remainder of the Burgenland went to Austria without a plebiscite.

16. There are numerous different estimates of the ethno-demographic impact of the Treaty of Trianon and, in particular, of the number of Magyars consigned to alien rule—ranging from a conservative 2.5 million to Hungarian estimates of 3.75 million. The statistics with the best pedigree, on which I have relied in this account, are those appended to Harold Temperley's article 'How the Hungarian Frontiers Were Drawn' (*Foreign Affairs*, April 1928, pp. 432–47).

17. Lloyd George, D.: op. cit., Vol. I, p. 406.

18. *Documents on British Foreign Policy 1919–1939*, First Series, Vol. VII, p. 386.

19. Beveridge, W.: *Power and Influence* (London, 1953), pp. 155–6.

20. Nicolson: op. cit., p. 327. My italics.

21. Deák, F.: op. cit., p. 547.

22. Millerand's letter, in an over-literal translation from the French, is reproduced in Deák, F.: op. cit., pp. 551–4.

14. HORTHY'S HUNGARY: (1920–42)

1. Juhász, Gy.: *Hungarian Foreign Policy, 1919–1945* (Budapest, 1979), p. 34.

2. Deák, F.: *Hungary at the Paris Peace Conference: The Diplomatic History of the Treaty of Trianon* (New York, 1942), p. 550.

3. Sakmyster, T.: *Hungary's Admiral on Horseback: Miklós Horthy, 1918–1944* (Boulder, CO, 1994), p. 152.

4. Ibid., p. 12.

5. Jászi, O.: *Revolution and Counter-revolution in Hungary* (New York, 1924), p. 199.

6. Quoted in Janos, A.C.: *The Politics of Backwardness in Hungary, 1825–1945* (Princeton, NJ, 1982), p. 210.

7. From a speech delivered in the National Casino on 31 January 1932: quoted in Romsics, I.: *István Bethlen: A Great Conservative Statesman of Hungary, 1874–1946* (Boulder, CO, 1995), p. 303.

8. Rothschild, J.: *East Central Europe between the Two World Wars* (Seattle, WA, 1974), p. 160.

9. Romsics, I.: op. cit., p. 196 and Sakmyster, T.: op. cit., p. 133.

10. For a partial but entertaining account of the whole episode, see Windischgraetz, Prince L.: *My Adventures and Misadventures, 1899–1964* (London, 1966), Chapter 3.

11. Quoted in Juhász, Gy.: op. cit. p. 86.

12. Sakmyster, T.: op. cit., p. 166.

13. Juhász, Gy.: op. cit., p. 171.

14. Quoted in Sakmyster, T.: op. cit., p. 182.

15. Janos, A. C: op. cit., p. 220.

16. Ibid., p. 249, quoting Gaál, G.: *Napló* (Budapest, 1927).

17. Romsics, I.: op. cit., pp. 191–2.

18. There is an excellent account of the genesis of *Numerus Clausus* in Kovács, M. M.: *Liberal Professions and Illiberal Politics: Hungary from the Habsburgs to the Holocaust* (Washington, DC and Oxford, 1994).

19. Ibid., p. 58.

20. Patai, R.: *The Jews of Hungary: History, Culture, Psychology* (Detroit, MI, 1996), p. 483.

21. Ibid.

22. Ibid., p. 519.

23. Mócsy, I.: *Count István Bethlen*, in Bődy, P.: *Hungarian Statesmen of Destiny, 1860–1960* (Boulder, CO, 1989), p. 147.

24. Romsics, I.: op. cit., p. 195.

25. 'Three Million Beggars' (*Három millió koldús*) was the title of an exposé by the right-wing author György Oláh, published in 1928.

26. Illyés, Gy.: *People of the Puszta*, trans. G. F. Cushing (Budapest, 1967), p. 161.
27. This summary draws extensively on the very comprehensive account given by Romsics, I., in *Hungary in the Twentieth Century* (Budapest, 1999).
28. Translated by Vernon Watkins, in Makkai, A. (ed.): *In Quest of the Miracle Stag* (Chicago, IL and Budapest, 1996), p. 722.
29. Translated by John Bátki, quoted in Czigány, L.: *The Oxford History of Hungarian literature* (Oxford, 1984), p. 358.
30. Translated by Clive Wilmer and George Gömöri, in Makkai, A., op. cit., 722.

15. THE FAUSTIAN PACT I—THE PRIZE: (1936–41)

1. Quoted in Romsics, I.: *István Bethlen: A Great Conservative Statesman of Hungary, 1874–1946* (Boulder, CO, 1995), p. 306.
2. Bethlen, Count S.: *The Treaty of Trianon and European Peace: Four Lectures Delivered in London in 1933* (London, 1934), p. 65.
3. Ránki, Gy.: "'Unwilling Satellite" or "Last Satellite": Some Problems of Hungarian-German Relations', in Ránki, Gy. (ed.): *Hungarian History—World History* (Budapest, 1984), p. 267.
4. Ránki, Gy.: *Economy and Foreign Policy: The Struggle of the Great Powers for Hegemony in the Danube Valley, 1919–1939* (Boulder, CO, 1983), p. 137.
5. Ránki, Gy.: op. cit. (1984), p. 267.
6. Sakmyster, T.: *Hungary's Admiral on Horseback: Miklós Horthy, 1918–1944* (Boulder, CO, 1994), p. 191.
7. In a speech in Milan in October 1936, Mussolini enthused over the line between Berlin and Rome as 'an axis round which all those European States which are animated by a desire for collaboration and peace can revolve'. The Axis concept was not formalised into a treaty until 1938.
8. Juhász, Gy.: *Hungarian Foreign Policy, 1919–1945* (Budapest, 1979), p. 127
9. Ibid., p. 133
10. Sakmyster, T.: op.cit., p. 206.
11. Ránki, Gy.: op. cit. (1983), p. 192.
12. Juhász, Gy.: op. cit., p. 134.
13. Quoted in Macartney, G. A.: *October Fifteenth: A History of Modern Hungary, 1929–1945* (Edinburgh, 1957), Part I, pp. 160–1. This extraordinary work is the most authoritative and comprehensive history of the period in any language: spread over two lengthy volumes, it recounts Hungary's story during the inter-war and wartime years not just day by day but almost minute by minute. It contains insights, many of them deriving from the authors personal acquaintanceship with a wide range of Hungarian politicians, which are unique and indispensable to an understanding of this tawdry but tragic chapter in Hungarian history.
14. Ibid., Part I, p. 185.
15. Kertesz, S. D.: *Diplomacy in a Whirlpool: Hungary between Nazi Germany and Soviet Russia* (Notre Dame, 1953), p. 34.
16. Ibid., p. 35.
17. Sakmyster, T.: op. cit., p. 218.
18. Kertesz, S. D.: op. cit., p. 37
19. Ibid., p. 41.
20. Cited in Zweig, R.: *The Gold Train* (London, 2002), p. 30.
21. Sakmyster, T.: op. cit., p. 231.
22. Ibid., p. 230.
23. Szinai, M. and Szűcs, L. (eds.): *The Confidential Papers of Admiral Horthy* (Budapest, 1965), pp. 126–8.

24. Eden's despatch of 6 February to O'Malley (National Archives, FO371/26620).
25. A photocopy of the original is reproduced in Szinai, M. and Szűcs, L.: op. cit., between pp. 178 and 179.
26. Churchill, W. S.: *The Grand Alliance* (London, 1950), p. 168.
27. O'Malley's telegram No. 208 of 3 April 1941 to the Foreign Office (National Archives. FO371/26602).
28. Eden's despatch of 16 April 1941 to O'Malley (National Archives, FO371/26602).

16. THE FAUSTIAN PACT II: THE PRICE: (1941–45)

1. Patai, R.: *The Jews of Hungary* (Detroit, MI, 1996), p. 549.
2. Kertesz, S. D.: *Diplomacy in a Whirlpool: Hungary between Nazi Germany and Soviet Russia* (Notre Dame, 1953), p. 61.
3. Sakmyster, T.: *Hungary's Admiral on Horseback: Miklós Horthy, 1918–1944* (Boulder, CO, 1994), p. 267.
4. Macartney, C. A.: *October Fifteenth: Hungary 1929–1945* (Edinburgh, 1957), II, p. 82 (note).
5. Kállay, N.: *Hungarian Premier: A Personal Account of a Nation's Struggle in the Second World War* (New York, 1954).
6. Veress, L.-L.: *Clear the Line: Hungary's Struggle to Leave the Axis During the Second World War* (Cleveland, OH, 1995), p. 68.
7. Kállay, N.: op. cit., p. 123.
8. Quoted in Fenyo, M. D.: *Hitler, Horthy and Hungary: German-Hungarian Relations, 1941–44* (New Haven, CT, 1972), p. 105.
9. Veress, L.-L.: op. cit., p. 188.
10. Fenyo, M. D.: op. cit., p. 174.
11. Juhász, Gy.: *Hungarian Foreign Policy, 1919–1945* (Budapest, 1979), p. 280.
12. Kállay, M.: op. cit., pp. 378–9.
13. See Macartney, C. A.: op. cit., II, p. 239 and note.
14. Kállay, M.: op. cit., p. 433.
15. Fenyo, M. D.: op. cit., p. 183.
16. There is a full account of the Budapest Relief and Rescue Committee's attempts to save Hungarian Jews from the Holocaust in Braham, R. L.: *The Politics of Genocide: The Holocaust in Hungary* (New York, 1994), Volume 2, Chapter 29.
17. Quoted in Zweig, R.: *The Gold Train* (London, 2002), p. 62.
18. Juhász, Gy.: op. cit., p. 314.
19. Macartney, C. A.: op.cit., II, pp. 391–432.
20. Horthy, N.: *Memoirs* (New York, 1957), p. 230.
21. Ibid., pp. 259–60.
22. Sakmyster, T.: op. cit., p. 371.
23. Nagy, K.: *Két Tábornok* (Budapest, 2000), pp. 255–6.
24. Macartney, C. A.: op.cit., II, p. 416.
25. Ibid., II, p. 440.
26. For statistics relating to the Holocaust in Hungary, I have relied on Braham, R. L.: *The Politics of Genocide: The Holocaust in Hungary* (2 vols) (New York, 1994). There are vivid and harrowing accounts of the Holocaust in Budapest and the provinces by two of its surviving victims, Ernő Szép (trans. J. Bátki) in *The Smell of Humans* (Budapest, 1994) and Béla Zsolt (trans. Ladislaus Löb) in *Nine Suitcases* (London, 2004).
27. Figures quoted in Zweig, R.: op. cit., p. 65 and note.
28. Ungváry, K.: 'The "Second Stalingrad": The Destruction of Axis Forces at Budapest (February, 1945)' in Dreisziger, N.: *Hungary in the Age of Total War (1938–1948)* (New York, 1998), p. 168.

29. Juhász, Gy.: op. cit., p. 333.
30. Romsics, I.: *Hungary in the Twentieth Century* (Budapest, 1999), p. 216.

17. TWO FALSE DAWNS: (1945–56)

1. Djilas, M.: *Conversations with Stalin* (London, 1962), p. 105.
2. Quoted in Gati, C.: *Hungary and the Soviet Bloc* (Duke University Press, NC, 1986), p. 85.
3. Márai, S.: *Memoir of Hungary, 1944–48* (Budapest, 1996), p. 31.
4. Gati, C.: op. cit., p. 85.
5. Kovrig, B.: *Communism in Hungary: From Kun to Kádár* (Stanford, CT, 1979) p. 157.
6. Pálóczi–Horváth, G.: *The Undefeated* (London, 1993) p. 128.
7. Roman, E.: *Hungary and the Victor Powers, 1945–50* (London. 1996), p. 39.
8. Mindszenty, Card. J.: *Memoirs* (London, 1974), p. 267. [In this edition the document is incorrectly dated '1946'.]
9. Quoted in Romsics, I.: *Hungary in the Twentieth Century* (Budapest, 1999), p. 243.
10. Haraszti–Taylor, E.: *Britain and Hungary in the Post-War Years, 1945–51: A Parallel History in Narrative and Documents* (Nottingham, 2000), Vol. II, p. 104.
11. Kertesz, S.D.: *Diplomacy in a Whirlpool: Hungary between Nazi Germany and Soviet Russia* (Notre Dame, NC, 1953), p. 151.
12. See Kovrig, B.: op.cit., p. 217.
13. Méray, T.: *That Day in Budapest* (New York, 1969), p. 431.
14. Ignotus, P.: *Hungary* (London, 1972), pp. 212–13.
15. Quoted in Romsics, I.: op. cit., p. 275.
16. Berend, I.: *The Hungarian Economic Reforms, 1953–88* (New York, 1990), p. 9.
17. Berend, I. and Ránki, Gy.: *The Hungarian Economy in the Twentieth Century* (New York, 1985), p. 216.
18. Ibid.: p. 201.
19. Méray, T.: op. cit., p. 97.
20. Tőkés, R.: *Hungary's Negotiated Revolution* (Cambridge, 1996), p. 350.
21. Litván, Gy.: *The Hungarian Revolution of 1956: Reform, Revolt and Repression, 1953–63* (London, 1996). The text of the Central Committee's resolution was not published until 1986, when it appeared in a party journal intended for internal circulation.
22. These figures are taken from Romsics, I.: op. cit, p. 296.
23. Méray, T.: op. cit., p. 95.
24. Vali, F.: *Rift and Revolt in Hungary* (Cambridge, MA, 1961), p. 179.
25. Nagy, I.: *On Communism: In Defence of the New Course* (London, 1957), p. 49.
26. Ibid., p. 63.
27. Ignotus, P.: op. cit., p. 233.
28. Lomax, B.: *Hungary, 1956* (London, 1976), p. 39.
29. Ibid., p. 33.
30. Quoted in Kovrig, B.: op. cit., p. 295.

18. REVOLUTION: (1956)

1. Lomax, B.: *Hungary 1956* (London, 1976), p. 114.
2. Lasky, M. J. (ed.): *The Hungarian Revolution: A White Book* (New York, 1957), p. 61.
3. Ibid., p. 135.
4. Ibid., p. 146.
5. See, for example, the first-hand account in Kopacsi, S.: *In the Name of the Working Class* (London, 1989), p. 179.

6. Talbott, S. (ed.): *Khrushchev Remembers* (London, 1971), p. 418.
7. This account is drawn from two articles in *The Hungarian Quarterly*, Vol. 37, Nos. 142 and 143, by János Rainer; the articles are based on the manuscript notes taken at the Presidium's meetings by V. N. Malin, then Head of the General Department of the Central Committee of the CPSU, and unearthed by Russian researchers in the Presidential Archives of the Russian Federation. There is no reason to doubt their authenticity.
8. Ibid.
9. Ibid.
10. Lomax, B.: op. cit., p. 143.
11. Interview given by György Heltai to an American journalist on 12 December 1956 and reproduced in *The Hungarian Quarterly*, Vol. 37, No. 142 (Summer, 1996).
12. See, for example, Molnár, M.: *Budapest, 1956: A History of the Hungarian Revolution* (London, 1971), pp. 200–6.
13. Kopácsi, S.: op. cit., p. 208.
14. Lasky, M.J. (ed.): op. cit., p. 228.
15. Ibid., pp. 236–7.
16. Nagy, I.: *On Communism: In Defence of the New Course* (London, 1957), pp. 33–4.

19. THE SECOND COMPROMISE: (1956–88)

1. Both quotations are from Shawcross, W.: *Crime and Compromise: Janos Kadar and the Politics of Hungary since Revolution* (London, 1974), pp. 153–4.
2. Lasky, M. (ed.): *The Hungarian Revolution: A White Book* (New York, 1957), p. 262.
3. See Document No. 98 in Békés, Cs., Byrne, M. and Rainer, J.: *The 1956 Hungarian Revolution: A History in Documents* (Budapest, 2002), p. 435.
4. Ibid., p. 375. Estimates of the numbers of victim's of Kádár's repression vary widely, some sources giving higher and some lower figures than those I have quoted and which I have chosen because they come from the most recently published material.
5. Unwin, P.: *Voice in the Wilderness: Imre Nagy and the Hungarian Revolution* (London, 1991), p. 184–5.
6. Méray, T.: 'The Trial of Imre Nagy' in Király, B. and Jónás, P. (eds.): *The Hungarian Revolution of 1956 in Retrospect* (Boulder, 1978), p. 80.
7. Quoted in Romsics, L: *Hungary in the Twentieth Century* (Budapest, 1999), p. 327.
8. Berend, I. T.: *The Hungarian Economic Reforms, 1953–1988* (New York, 1990), p. 125.
9. I quoted this remark, made by Nyers in 1980, in a despatch from Budapest to the Foreign and Commonwealth Office in May 1983; I have not been able to trace the original source from which I gleaned it—I may have had it from Nyers himself—but I am confident of its authenticity.
10. Berend, I. T.: op. cit., p. 163.
11. Ibid., p. 166.
12. Romsics, I.: op. cit., p. 350.
13. Lendvai, P.: *Hungary: The Art of Survival* (London, 1988), p. 67.
14. Berend, I. T.: op. cit., p. 206.
15. Romsics, I.: op. cit., p. 354.
16. Berend, I. T.: op. cit., p. 281.
17. Tőkés, R.: *Hungary's Negotiated Revolution: Economic Reform, Social Change and Political Succession* (Cambridge, 1996), p. 50.
18. Mlynar, Z.: *Night Frost in Prague* (London, 1980), p. 157.
19. I noted this sentence from a speech I heard Kádár deliver in Parliament in 1980.
20. Romsics, I.: op. cit., p. 361.

21. Köpeczi, B., Makkai, L., Mócsy, A., and Szász, Z. (eds.): *Erdély Története* (Budapest, 1986),Vol. I, p. 301. See also footnote 13 to Chapter 3 of the present volume.
22. Kovrig, B.: *Communism in Hungary: From Kun to Kádár* (Stanford, CA, 1979), p. 402.
23. Shawcross,W.: op. cit., p. 215.
24. Lendvai, P.: op. cit., p. 101.
25. Hungarian Central Statistical Office: *Statistics of Centuries* (Budapest, 2002), p. 87.

20. ROUND TABLE REVOLUTION AND DEMOCRATIC HUNGARY: (1988–99)

1. Gorbachev, M.: *Memoirs* (London, 1996), p. 472.
2. Lévesque, J.: *The Enigma of 1989:The USSR and the Liberation of Eastern Europe* (Berkeley, CA, 1997), p. 80.
3. László Vass, quoted in O'Neill, P.: *Revolution from Within:The Hungarian Socialist Workers' Party and the Collapse of Communism* (Cheltenham, England, 1998), p. 130.
4. Tőkés, R.: *Hungary's Negotiated Revolution* (Cambridge, 1996), p. 330.
5. Ibid., p. 9.

BIBLIOGRAPHY

General Works

Benda, K. (ed.), *Magyarország Történeti Kronológiája* (4 vols, Budapest, 1981–83).
Bertényi, I. and Gyapay, G., *Magyarország Rövid Története* (Budapest, 1995).
Bideleux, R. and Jeffries, I., *A History of Eastern Europe: Crisis and Change* (London, 1998).
Bölöny, J., *Magyarország kormányai, 1848–1975* (Budapest, 1978).
Chirot, Daniel (ed.), *The Origins of Backwardness in Eastern Europe* (Berkeley, CA, 1989).
Eckhart, Ferenc, *A Short History of the Hungarian People* (London, 1931).
Gál, István, *Hungary and the Anglo-Saxon World* (Budapest, 1943).
Gerő, A. and Poór, J. (eds.), *Budapest: A History from its Beginnings to 1998* (New York, 1997).
Godkin, E. L., *The History of Hungary and the Magyars* (London, 1853).
Hanák, P. (ed.), *The Corvina History of Hungary* (Budapest, 1991).
Hóman. B. and Szekfű, Gy., *Magyar Történet* (5 vols, Budapest, 1935–8).
Ignotus, Pál, *Hungary* (London, 1972).
Jekelfalussy, J. (ed.), *The Millennium of Hungary and its People* (Budapest, 1897).
Johnson, L. R., *Central Europe, Enemies, Neighbours, Friends* (Oxford, 1996).
Klaniczay, T. (ed.), *A History of Hungarian Literature* (Budapest, 1983).
Knatchbull-Hugessen, G. M., *The Political Evolution of the Hungarian Nation* (2 vols) (London, 1908).
Kontler, L., *Millennium in Central Europe, A History of Hungary* (Budapest, 1999).
Köpeczi, B. et al. (eds.), *Erdély Története* (3 vols) (Budapest, 1986).
Kósa, L. (ed.), *A Cultural History of Hungary* (2 vols) (Budapest, 2000).
Kosáry, D.G., *A History of Hungary* (Cleveland, OH, 1941).
Lendvai, P., *The Hungarians, 1000 Years of Victory in Defeat* (London, 2002).
Longworth, Philip, *The Making of Eastern Europe* (London, 1992).
Lukinich, Imre, *A History of Hungary* (London and Budapest, 1937).
Macartney, C. A., *Hungary* (London, 1934).
———— *Hungary: A Short History* (Edinburgh, 1962).
Makkai, A. (ed.), *In Quest of the Miracle Stag: The Poetry of Hungary* (Chicago, IL and Budapest, 1996).
Molnár, E. (ed.), *Magyarország története* (2 vols, Budapest, 1964).
Molnár, M., *Histoire de la Hongrie* (Paris, 1996).
Pámlenyi, E. (ed.), *A History of Hungary* (Budapest, 1973).
Pascu, Stefan, *A History of Transylvania* (New York, 1990).
Patai, R., *The Jews of Hungary, History, Culture, Psychology* (Detroit, MI, 1996).
Péter, L. (ed.), *Historians and the History of Transylvania* (Boulder, CO, 1992).
Schulze, H., *States, Nations & Nationalism* (Oxford, 1998).
Sinor, Denis, *History of Hungary* (London, 1959).
Sugar, P., Hanák, P. and Frank, T. (eds.), *A History of Hungary* (London, 1990).
Sugar, P. and Lederer, I. J. (eds.), *Nationalism in Eastern Europe* (Seattle, WA, 1971).

BIBLIOGRAPHY

Vámbéry, Arminius, *Hungary, in Ancient, Medieval and Modern Times* (London, 1886).
Várdy, S. B. and Várdy, A. H. (eds.), *Triumph in Adversity* (Boulder, CO, 1988).
Vardy, S. B., *Modern Hungarian Historiography* (Boulder, CO, 1976).
Wandycz, P. S., *The Price of Freedom: A History of East Central Europe* (London, 1992).
Zárek, Otto, *The History of Hungary* (London, 1939).

Part One: The Medieval Kingdom

Bak, J. M. and Király, B. K. (eds.), *From Hunyadi to Rákóczi: War and Society in Late Medieval and Early Modern Hungary* (New York, 1982).
Bak, J. M., Bónis, Gy. and Sweeney, J. R. (eds.), *The Laws of the Medieval Kingdom of Hungary,. 1000–1301* (Idyllwild, CA, 1989).
Barraclough, Geoffrey (ed.), *Eastern and Western Europe in the Middle Ages* (London, 1970).
Bartha, Antál, *A IX-X Századi Magyar Társadalom* (Budapest, 1975).
Birnbaum, Marianna D., 'Buda between Tartars and Turks' in Krekic, B.: *Urban Society of Eastern Europe in Pre-modern Times* (Berkeley, CA, 1987).
Engel, P., *The Realm of St. Stephen* (London, 2001).
———— Kristó, Gy. and Kubinyi, A., *Magyarország Története, 1301–1526* (Budapest, 1998).
Fodor, I., *The Pre-History of the Hungarian People and the Conquest* (Budapest, 1975).
Fügedi, E., *Castle and Society in Medieval Hungary* (Studia Historica, Budapest. No. 187).
The Elefánthy: The Hungarian Nobleman and his Kindred (Budapest. 1992).
Györffy, Gy., *King Saint Stephen of Hungary* (New York. 1994).
Held, J., *Hunyadi, Legend and Reality* (New York, 1985).
———— *The Defence of Nándorfehérvár [Belgrade] in 1456* (in Ranki, Gy. [ed.]: *Hungarian History—World History* (Budapest, 1984)).
Hóman, Bálint, *Szent István* [Saint Stephen] (Budapest, 1938).
Kinross, Lord, *The Ottoman Centuries, The Rise and Fall of the Turkish Empire* (London, 1977).
Komjáthy, A., 'Hungarian Jobbágyság in the 15th Century' (*East European Quarterly*, Vol. 10, 1976).
Kosztolnyik, Z. J., 'Church and Court under Kálmán the Learned' (*East European Quarterly*, Vol. 18, 1984).
———— *Five 11th Century Hungarian Kings: Their Policies and Their Relations with Rome* (Boulder, CO, 1981).
———— *From Coloman the Learned to Béla III, 1095–1196* (Boulder, CO, 1987).
———— *Hungary in the Thirteenth Century* (Boulder, CO, 1996).
Kovács, Eva and Lovag, Zsuzsa, *The Hungarian Crown and other Regalia* (Budapest, 1980).
László, Gyula, *The Magyars, Their Life and Civilisation* (Budapest, 1996).
Maczak, A., Samsonowicz, H. and Burke, P., *East-Central Europe in Transition (from the 14th to the 17th Century)* (Cambridge, 1985).
Makkai, L., 'Agrarian Landscapes of Historical Hungary in Feudal Times' (*Studia Historica*, No. 140 [1980], pp. 5–18).
Malowist, M., 'The Problem of Economic Development in Europe in the Later Middle Ages' (*Economic History Review*, 2nd Series, Vol. 19, No. 1 [1966]).
Macartney, C. A., *The Magyars in the 9th Century* (Cambridge, 1968).
Pach, Zs. P., 'The Development of Feudal Rent' (*Economic History Review*, XIX, 1 [1966]).
Parry, V. J., *A History of the Ottoman Empire to 1730* (Cambridge, 1976).
Pelenski, J. (ed.), *State and Society in Europe from the 15th to the 18th Century* (Warsaw, 1985).
Perjés, Géza, *The Fall of the Medieval Kingdom of Hungary: Mohács 1526–Buda 1541* (Boulder, CO, 1989).

BIBLIOGRAPHY

Porter, R. and Teich, M. (eds.), *The Renaissance in National Context* (Cambridge, 1992).
Róna-Tas, A., *A Honfoglaló Magyar Nép* (Budapest, 1997).
Sedlar, J. W., *East Central Europe in the Middle Ages, 1000–1500* (Seattle, WA and London, 1994).
Sugar, P. F., *Southeastern Europe under Ottoman Rule, 1354–1804* (Seattle, WA, 1977).
Pach, Zs. P., 'The Shifting of International Trade Routes in the 15th-17th Centuries' (*Acta Historica Academiae Scientiarum Hungaricae*, XIX, 3–4, 1968).
Thuróczy, János, *Chronicle of the Hungarians* (ed. Engel, P.) (Bloomington, IN, 1991).
Vardy, S. B., Grosschmid G. and Domonkos, L. S. (eds.), *Louis the Great, King of Hungary and Poland* (Boulder, CO, 1986).

Part Two: The Habsburg Kingdom.

Ady, E. (ed. and trans. Cushing, G. and Vezér, E.), *The Explosive Country: A Selection of Articles and Studies, 1898–1916* (Budapest, 1977).
Balázs, É. H., *Hungary and the Habsburgs, 1765–1800: An Experiment in Enlightened Absolutism* (Budapest, 1997).
Banac, I. and Sysyn, F. E., 'Concepts of Nationhood in Early Modern Eastern Europe' (*Harvard Ukrainian Studies*, Vol. X, 3–4, Cambridge, 1986).
Bárány, G., 'Hungary, The Uncompromising Compromise' (*Austrian History Yearbook*, Vol. III, Pt 1 [1967]).
———— 'Hoping against Hope, The Enlightened Age in Hungary' (*American Historical Review*, Vol. LXXVI, 2 [April, 1971]).
———— *Stephen Széchenyi and the Awakening of Hungarian Nationalism* (Princeton, NJ, 1968).
———— 'The Awakening of Magyar Nationalism before 1848' (*Austrian History Yearbook*, Vol. II).
———— 'The Hungarian Diet of 1839–40 and the Fate of Széchenyi's Middle Course' (*Slavic Review*, Vol. XXII, No. 2, June 1963).
———— 'The Széchenyi Problem' (*Journal of Central European Affairs*, October 1960).
Bárdossy, L., *Magyar Politika a Mohácsi Vész Után* (Budapest, 1943).
Benczédi, L., 'Hungarian National Consciousness as Reflected in the Anti–Habsburg and Anti–Ottoman Struggles of the Late 17th Century' (*Harvard Ukrainian Studies*, Vol. X, 3–4, Cambridge, MA, 1986).
Benda, Kálmán, 'Hungary in Turmoil, 1580–1620' (*European Studies Review*, Vol. 8, No. 3, 1978, pp. 281–304).
Berend, I. T. and Ránki, Gy., *East Central Europe in the 19th and 20th Centuries* (Budapest, 1977).
———— *Economic Development in East-Central Europe in the 19th and 20th Centuries* (New York, 1974).
———— 'Economic Factors in Nationalism, the Example of Hungary at the Beginning of the 20th Century' (*Austrian History Yearbook*, Vol. III, Part 3 [1967]).
———— *Hungary, A Century of Economic Development* (Newton Abbot and New York, 1974).
———— 'The European Periphery and Industrialisation, 1780–1914' (*Journal of European Economic History*, Vol. 9 [1980], pp. 553–84).
———— *The Hungarian Economy in the Twentieth Century* (New York, 1985).
———— *Underdevelopment and Economic Growth, Studies in Hungarian Social and Economic History* (Budapest, 1979).
Bernard, P. B., *The Limits of Enlightenment, Joseph II and the Law* (Chicago, IL, 1979).
Bethlen, Count S., *The Treaty of Trianon and European Peace* (London, 1934).

BIBLIOGRAPHY

Blanning, T. C. W. and Cannadine, D., *History and Biography: Essays in Honour of Derek Beales* (Cambridge, 1996).

Blanning, T. C. W., *Joseph II* (London, 1994).

Body, P. (ed.), *Hungarian Statesmen of Destiny* (Boulder, CO, 1989).

Bridge, F. R., *From Sadowa to Sarajevo, The Foreign Policy of Austria-Hungary, 1866—1914* (London, 1972).

Bright, R., *Travels from Vienna through Lower Hungary; with some remarks on the state of Vienna during the Congress in the year 1814* (Edinburgh, 1818).

Buzinkay, G., *An Illustrated History of Budapest* (Budapest, 1998).

Crankshaw, E., *The Fall of the House of Habsburg* (London, 1963).

Cushing, G., 'The Birth of National Literature in Hungary' (*Slavonic and East European Review*, 38, 1960).

Czigány, L., *The Oxford History of Hungarian Literature* (Oxford, 1984).

Daniel, D. P., 'The Fifteen Years War and the Protestant Response to Habsburg Absolutism in Hungary' (*East-Central Europe*, Vol. 8, 1–2, 1981, pp. 38–51).

Deák, G., *The Economy and Polity in Early Twentieth Century Hungary: The Role of the National Association of Industrialists* (Boulder, CO, 1990).

Deák, I., 'The Habsburg Army in the First and Last Days of World War I: A Comparative Analysis' (in Király, B. K. and Dreisziger, N. F. (eds.), *War and Society in Eastern Europe, Vol. XIX (East Central European Society in World War I)* (Boulder, CO, 1985).

——— *The Lawful Revolution: Louis Kossuth and the Hungarians, 1848–49* (New York, 1979).

Deme, L., *The Radical Left and the Hungarian Revolution of 1848* (Boulder, CO, 1976).

——— 'Writers and Essayists and the Rise of Magyar Nationalism in the 1820s and 1830s' (*Slavic Review*, XLIII/4 [1984], pp. 624–40).

'E.O.S.': *Hungary and its Revolutions, with a memoir of Louis Kossuth* (London, 1854).

Evans, R. J. W. and Thomas, J. V., *Crown, Church and Estates: Central European Politics in the 16th and 17th Centuries* (London, 1991).

Evans, R. J. W., 'From Confederation to Compromise' (*Proceedings of the British Academy*, 87 [1995], pp. 135–67).

——— 'Széchenyi and Austria' (in *History and Biography—Essays in honour of Derek Beales*, Cambridge, 1996).

——— 'The Habsburgs and the Hungarian Problem, 1790–1848' (*Transactions of the Royal Historical Society*, 5th Series, XXXIX [1989]).

——— *The Making of the Habsburg Monarchy, 1550–1700* (Oxford, 1979).

Fejtő, F. (ed.), *The Opening of an Era—1848: An Historical Symposium* (New York, 1966).

Fekete, L., 'Buda and Pest under Turkish Rule' (*Studia Turco-Hungarica*, Vol. III, Budapest 1976).

Frank, T., *Picturing Austria-Hungary: The British Perception of the Habsburg Monarchy, 1865–1870* (New York, 2005).

Freifeld, A., *Nationalism and the Crowd in Liberal Hungary, 1848–1914* (Baltimore, MD, 2000).

Galántai, J., *Hungary in the First World War* (Budapest, 1989).

Gerő, A. (ed.), *Hungarian Liberals* (Budapest, 1999).

——— *Modern Hungarian Society in the Making: The Unfinished Experience* (Budapest, 1995).

Glatz, F., *Hungarians and their Neighbours in Modern Times, 1867–1950* (Boulder, CO, 1995).

Good, D. F., *The Economic Rise of the Habsburg Empire, 1750–1914* (Berkeley and Los Angeles, CA, 1984).

Goodwin, A (ed.), *The European Nobility in the 18th Century* (London, 1953).

BIBLIOGRAPHY

Görgey, A., *My Life and Acts in Hungary in the Years 1848–1849* (2 vols, London, 1852).

Gratz, G., *A Dualizmus Kora: Magyarország Története, 1867–1918* (2 vols, Budapest, 1934, reprinted 1992).

Hajdu, T., 'Army and Society in Hungary in the Era of World War I' (in Király, B.K. and Dreisziger, N. F. (eds.), *War and Society in Eastern Europe, Vol. XIX (East Central European Society in World War I)*, Boulder, CO, 1985).

——— 'Michael Károlyi and the Revolution of 1918–19' (*Acta Historica Academiae Scientiorum Hungaricae*, X, pp. 3–4 [1964]).

Halsband, R. (ed.), *The Complete Letters of Lady Mary Worthy Montagu* (Oxford, 1965), 3 vols.

Hanak, H., *Great Britain and Austria-Hungary during the First World War: A Study in the Formation of Public Opinion* (Oxford, 1962).

Hanák, P., 'Hungary in the Austro-Hungarian Monarchy: Preponderancy or Dependency?' (*Austrian History Yearbook*, Vol. III, Pt 1 [1967]).

——— *Magyarország a Monarchiában: Tanulmányok* (Budapest, 1975).

——— 'The Bourgeoisification of the Hungarian Nobility—Reality and Utopia in the 19th Century' (*Etudes historiques hongroises*, vol. 2 (1985), pp. 401–21).

Hatton, R. H. and Anderson, M. S. (eds.), *Studies in Diplomatic History: Essays in memory of David Bayne Horn* (London, 1970).

Hazard, P., *European Thought in the 18th Century* (New Haven, CT, 1954).

Hengelmüller, L., *Hungary's Fight for National Existence, 1703–11* (London, 1913).

Hobsbawm, E.J., *Nations & Nationalism since 1780* (Cambridge, 1990).

Hoensch, J., *A History of Modern Hungary, 1867–1986* (London, 1988).

Horváth, J., *Modern Hungary, 1660–1920* (Budapest, 1922).

Iványi, B. G., 'From Feudalism to Capitalism: The Economic Background to Széchenyi's Reform in Hungary' (*Journal of Central European Affairs*, XX/3 [1960], pp. 270–88).

Janos, A. C, *The Politics of Backwardness in Hungary* (Princeton, NJ, 1982).

Jászi, O., *Revolution and Counter-Revolution in Hungary* (New York, 1924).

Jeszensky, G., 'Peace and Security in Central Europe: its British programme during World War I (*Études historiques hongroises*, 1985).

Kaas, A. and de Lazarovics, F., *Bolshevism in Hungary: The Béla Kun Period* (London, 1931).

Kállay, I., *Management of Big Estates in Hungary between 1711 and 1848* (Budapest, 1980).

Kálmán, B. (ed.), *Magyarország Történeti Kronológiája*, Vol. II (Budapest, 1982).

Kann, R. A. and David, Z.V., *The Peoples of the Eastern Habsburg Lands, 1526–1918*. (Seattle, WA, 1984).

Kann, R. A., *A History of the Habsburg Empire, 1526–1918* (Berkeley, 1974).

——— *The Habsburg Empire: A Study of Integration and Disintegration* (New York, 1957).

Károlyi, C, *A Life Together: Memoirs* (London, 1966).

Károlyi, Count M., *Memoirs of Michael Károlyi: Faith without Illusion* (trans. Károlyi, C.) (London, 1956).

Keegan, J., *The First World War* (London, 1998).

Király, B. (ed.), 'The Crucial Decade: East Central European Society and National Defence, 1859–70' (*War and Society in East Central Europe*, Vol. XIV [New York, 1984]).

——— *War and Society in East Central Europe in the Era of Revolution, 1775—1856* (New York, 1984).

——— (ed.), *War and Society in East Central Europe, Vol. I* (New York. 1979).

——— *Ferenc Deák* (Boston, 1975).

——— 'The Emancipation of the Serfs of East Central Europe' (*Antemurale*, Vol. 15 [1971], pp. 63–85).

——— 'Total War and Peacemaking' (in Király, B. K., Pastor, P. and Sanders, I. (eds.) *Essays on World War I: Total War and Peacemaking—A Case Study on Trianon* (*War and Society in East Central Europe*, Vol. VI, New York, 1982).

BIBLIOGRAPHY

———— *Hungary in the Late Eighteenth Century: the Decline of Enlightened Despotism* (New York, 1969).

———— 'Neo-Serfdom in Hungary' (*Slavic Review*, Vol. 34, 1975).

Klapka, G., *Memoirs of the War of Independence in Hungary* (2 vols, London, 1850).

Komlos, J. (ed.), *Economic Development in the Habsburg Monarchy in the Nineteenth Century* (Guildford, 1983).

Köpeczi, B., 'Ferenc Rákóczi II' (*New Hungarian Quarterly*, Vol. 61, 1976).

Kosáry, D., *Culture and Society in Eighteenth Century Hungary* (Budapest, 1987).

———— *Gabriel Bethlen: Transylvania in the 17th Century* (*Slavonic and East European Review*, XVII, 1938, pp. 162–74).

Lukacs, J., *Budapest 1900, A Historical Portrait of a City and its Culture* (London, 1989).

Macartney, C. A., *Maria Theresa and the House of Austria* (London, 1969).

———— *The Habsburg Empire, 1790–1918* (London and New York, 1969).

———— *The House of Austria: The Later Phase, 1790–1918* (Edinburgh, 1978).

Makkai, L., 'Neo-Serfdom, its Origin and Nature in East Central Europe' (*Slavic Review*, Vol. 34, 1975).

Marczali, H., *Hungary in the Eighteenth Century* (Cambridge, 1910).

May, A. J., *The Habsburg Monarchy, 1867–1914* (Cambridge, MA, 1951).

McCagg, W. O. Jnr., *A History of Habsburg Jews, 1670–1918* (Bloomington, IN, 1992).

McCullough, E., *How the First World War Began* (Montreal, 1999).

McGowan, B., *Economic Life in Ottoman Europe, 1600—1800* (Cambridge, 1981).

Nagy, Zs., 'The 1918 October Revolution' (*New Hungarian Quarterly*, X, 33 [1969]).

Nicolson, H., *Peacemaking, 1919* (London, 1933, new edition 1944).

Niederhauser, E., *The Rise of Nationality in Eastern Europe* (Budapest, 1982).

Pardoe, J., *City of the Magyar, or Hungary and her Institutions in 1839–40* (London, 1840).

Parker, G., *The Thirty Years War* (London, 1984).

Pastor, P., The Home Front in Hungary, 1914–18' (in Király, B. K. and Dreisziger, N. F. (eds.), *War and Society in Eastern Europe, Vol. XIX (East Central European Society in World War I)*, Boulder, CO, 1985).

Péter, L., Rady, M. and Sherwood, P. (eds.), *Lajos Kossuth Sent Word* (London, 2003).

Polisensky, J. V., The Thirty Years War: Motive, Extent and Effect' (*Historica*, Vol. 14, 1967).

Rabb, T. K., *The Struggle for Stability in Early Modern Europe* (New York, 1975).

Ránki, Gy., *Hungarian History—World History* (Budapest, 1984).

———— *Hungary and European Civilisation* (Budapest, 1989).

Reményi, J. (ed. Molnár, A.), *Hungarian Writers and Literature* (New Brunswick, NJ, 1964).

Romsics, I., *István Bethlen* (Boulder, CO, 1993).

———— *Hungary in the Twentieth Century* (Budapest, 1999).

Rothenberg, G. E., 'The Habsburg Army in the First World War, 1914–18' (in Király, B. K. and Dreisziger, N. F. (eds.), *War and Society in Eastern Europe, Vol. XIX (East Central European Society in World War I*, Boulder, CO, 1985).

Schimert, P., 'The Hungarian Nobility, 1600–1800', in Scott, H. M. (ed.), *The European Nobilities in the 17th and 18th Centuries, Vol. II (Northern, Central and Eastern Europe)* (London, 1995).

Scott. H. M., *Enlightened Absolutism: Reform and Reformers in Late 18th Century Europe* (London, 1990).

'Scotus Viator' (Seton-Watson, R. W.), *Racial Problems in Hungary* (London, 1908).

Scribner, R., Porter, R. and Reich, M. (eds.), *The Reformation in National Context.* (Cambridge, 1994).

Seton-Watson, H. and Seton-Watson, C, *The Making of a New Europe* (London, 1981).

———— 'R. W. Seton-Watson and the Trianon Settlement' (in Király, B. K., Pastor, P. and Sanders, I. [eds.], op. cit.).

Seton-Watson, R. W., *Corruption and Reform in Hungary: A Study of Electoral Practice* (London, 1911).

―――― *Treaty Revision and the Hungarian Frontiers* (London, 1934).

Sked, A., *The Decline and Fall of the Habsburg Empire, 1815–1918* (London, 1989).

Slottman, W. B., *Ferenc II Rákóczi and the Great Powers* (New York, 1997).

Spira, Gy., *A Hungarian Count in the Revolution of 1848* (Budapest, 1974).

―――― 'Széchenyi's Tragic Course' (*Journal of Central European Affairs*, Vol. XX, [1960], 3).

―――― *The Nationality Issue in the Hungary of 1848–49* (Budapest, 1992).

Sproxton, C., *Palmerston and the Hungarian Revolution* (Cambridge, 1919).

Stone, N., 'Hungary and the Crisis of 1914' (*Journal of Contemporary History*, Vol. I [1966], pp. 153–70).

―――― *The Eastern Front, 1914–17* (London, 1985).

Stroup, E., *Hungary in Early 1848* (Buffalo, NY, 1977).

Subtelny, O., *Domination of Eastern Europe: Native Nobilities and Foreign Absolutism, 1500–1715* (Toronto, 1986).

Sugar, P. F., 'An Underrated Event: The Hungarian Constitutional Crisis of 1905–06' (*East European Quarterly*, Vol. XV, No. 3 [Sept. 1981]).

―――― 'The Influence of the Enlightenment and the French Revolution in Eighteenth.

Century Hungary' (*Journal of Central European Affairs*, XVII, 4, pp. 331–55, January 1958).

―――― 'The Nature of Non-Germanic Societies under Habsburg rule' (*Slavic Review, Vol. 22*).

―――― 'The Rise of Nationalism in the Habsburg Empire' (*Austrian History Yearbook*, Vol. III, Part I).

Szabad, Gy., 'Hungarian Political Trends Between the Revolution and the Compromise (1849–1867)', (*Studia Historica Academiae Scientiarum Hungaricae*, No. 128, Budapest, 1977).

Székely, Gy., 'La Hongrie et la Domination Ottomane (XV–XVII Siécles)' (*Studia Turco-Hungarica*, Vol. II).

Tanner, M., *Croatia, A Nation Forged in War* (New Haven and London, 1997).

Taylor, A. J. P., *The Habsburg Monarchy, 1809–1918* (London, 1948).

Teleki, Count P., *The Evolution of Hungary and its Place in European History* (New York, 1923).

Tóth, Z. L, 'The Nationality Problem in Hungary in 1843–1849' (*Acta Historica Academiae Scientiarum Hungaricae*, 1955, IV/1–3, pp. 235–77).

Townson, Robert, *Travels in Hungary, with a short account of Vienna in the year 1793* (London, 1795).

Vardy, S. B. and Vardy, A. H. (eds.), *Society in Change: Studies in Honour of Bela K. Király.* (New York, 1983).

Várkony, A. R., 'Historical Personality, Crisis and Progress in 17th Century Hungary'. (*Studia Historica Academiae Scientiarum Hungaricae*, Vol. 71, Budapest 1970).

―――― 'Habsburg Absolutism and Serfdom in Hungary at the turn of the 17th and 18th Centuries' (*Nouvelles Etudes Historiques publiées a l'occasion du XIIe Congrès International des Sciences Historiques par la Commission Nationale des Historiens Hongrois I-II*, Budapest, 1965).

―――― 'Repopulation and the System of Cultivation in Hungary after the Expulsion of the Turks' (*Acta Historica Academiae Scientiarum Hungaricae*, 1970, XVI, 1–2).

Verdery, K., 'Internal Colonialism in Austria-Hungary' (*Ethnic and Racial Studies*, Vol. 22).

Vermes, G., *István Tisza* (New York, 1985).

Wagner, F. S., 'Széchenyi and the Nationality Problem in the Habsburg Empire'. (*Journal of Central European Affairs*, Vol. XX [1960], 3).

Wandruszka, A., *The House of Habsburg* (Westport, CT, 1975).

Wangermann, E., *From Joseph II to the Jacobin Trials* (Oxford, 1969).

Williamson, S. R. Jnr, *Austria-Hungary and the Origins of the First World War* (London, 1991).

Zárek, O., *Kossuth, A Biography* (London, 1937).

Zimányi, V., 'Economy and Society in 16th and 17th Hungary, 1526–1650' (*Studia Historica Academiae Scientiarum Hungaricae*, No. 188, Budapest, 1987).

Part Three: Triple Tragedy and Rebirth.

Adám, M., 'France and Hungary at the Beginning of the 1920s' (in Király, B. K., Pastor, P. and Sanders, I. [eds.], op. cit.).

Barker, E., *British Policy in South-East Europe in the Second World War* (London, 1976).

Békés, Cs., Byrne, M. and Rainer, J. (eds.), *The 1956 Hungarian Revolution: A History in Documents* (Budapest, 2002).

Berend, I. T., *The Hungarian Economic Reforms, 1953–1988* (New York, 1990).

——— *Decades of Crisis, Central & Eastern Europe Before World War II* (Berkeley, CA, 1998).

Bone, E., *Seven Years Solitary* (Oxford, 1957).

Borsody, S. (ed.), *The Hungarians, A Divided Nation* (New Haven, CT, 1988).

——— 'Hungary's Road to Trianon: Peacemaking and Propaganda' (in Király, B. K., Pastor, P. and Sanders, I. [eds.], op. cit.).

Bozóki, A. et al. (eds.), *Post-Communist Transition: Emerging Pluralism in Hungary* (London, 1992).

Braham, R. L., *The Politics of Genocide: The Holocaust in Hungary* (2 vols, New York, 1994).

Cornwell, J., *Hitler's Pope: The Secret History of Pius XII* (London, 1999).

Cox, T. (ed.), *Hungary 1956—Forty Years On* (London, 1997).

Deák, F., *Hungary at the Paris Peace Conference: The Diplomatic History of the Treaty of Trianon.* (New York, 1942).

Deák, I., 'Hungary' (in Rogger, H. and Weber, E. (eds.), *The European Right: A Historical Profile* [Berkeley, CA, 1966]).

Dreisziger, N. (ed.), *Hungary in the Age of Total War, 1938–1948* (New York, 1998).

Eby, C., *Hungary at War, Civilians and Soldiers in World War II* (Pennsylvania State UP, PA, 1998).

Ehrlich, E. and Révész, G., *Hungary and its Prospects, 1985–2005* (Budapest, 1995).

Fehér, F. and Heller, A., *Hungary 1956 Revisited* (London, 1983).

Fél, E. and Hofer, T., *Proper Peasants: Traditional Life in a Hungarian Village* (Chicago, IL, 1969).

Felkay, A., *Hungary and the USSR, 1956–1988: Kádár's Political Leadership* (New York, 1989).

——— *Out of Russian Orbit, Hungary Gravitates to the West* (London, 1997).

Fenyő, M., *Hitler, Horthy and Hungary: German-Hungarian Relations, 1941–44* (New Haven, CT, 1972).

Frank, T. (ed.), *Discussing Hitler, Advisers of U.S. Diplomacy in Central Europe, 1934–1941.* (Budapest, 2003).

Gati, C, *Hungary and the Soviet Bloc* (Duke UP, NC, 1986).

Gorbachev, M., *Memoirs* (London, 1996).

Haraszti–Taylor, E., *The Hungarian Revolution of 1956: A Collection of Documents from the British Foreign Office* (Nottingham, 1995).

——— *Britain and Hungary in the Post-war Years, 1945—51: A Parallel History in Narrative and Documents* (2 vols, Nottingham, 2000).

BIBLIOGRAPHY

Held, J. (ed.), *The Columbia History of Eastern Europe in the 20th Century* (New York, 1992).

Horthy, M., *Memoirs* (New York, 1957).

Illyés, Gy., *The People of the Puszta* (Budapest, 1969).

Juhász, Gy., *Hungarian Foreign Policy, 1919–1945* (Budapest, 1979).

Kállay, N., *Hungarian Premier, A Personal Account of a Nation's Struggle in the Second World War* (New York, 1954).

Kecskeméti, P., *The Unexpected Revolution: Social Forces in the Hungarian Uprising* (Stanford, CA, 1961).

Kertész, S., 'The Consequences of World War I: The Effects on East Central Europe' (in Király, B. K., Pastor, P. and Sanders, I. (eds.), *Essays on World War I: Total War and Peace-making—A Case Study on Trianon* (*War and Society in East Central Europe*, Vol. VI), New York, 1982).

Kertesz, S. D., *Diplomacy in a Whirlpool: Hungary between Nazi Germany and Soviet Russia.* (Notre Dame, IN, 1953).

Király, B. and Bozóki, A. (eds.), *Lawful Revolution in Hungary, 1989–94* (Highland Lakes 1995).

Király, B. and Veszprémy, L., *Trianon and East-Central Europe* (Highland Lakes, 1995).

Király, B. et al., *The First War Between Socialist States: The Hungarian Revolution of 1956 and its Impact* (New York, 1984).

Komjáthy, A. T., *Give Peace One More Chance (Revision of the 1946 Peace Treaty of Paris).* (New York, 1993).

Kopácsi, S., *In the Name of the Working Class* (Toronto, 1986).

Kornai, J., *Evolution of the Hungarian Economy, 1848–1998, Vol. II* (Boulder, CO, 2000).

Kovrig, B., *Communism in Hungary: From Kun to Kádár* (Stanford, CA, 1979).

Lasky, M. (ed.), *The Hungarian Revolution: A White Book* (New York, 1957).

Lendvai, P., *Hungary, The Art of Survival* (London, 1988).

Lévesque, J., *The Enigma of 1989: The USSR and the Liberation of Eastern Europe* (Berkeley, CA, 1997).

Litván. Gy. (ed.), *The Hungarian Revolution of 1956: Reform, Revolt and Repression, 1953—63* (London, 1996).

Lloyd George, D., *The Truth About the Peace Treaties* (2 vols, London, 1938).

Lomax, B., *Hungary 1956* (London, 1976).

Low, A. D., 'The Soviet Hungarian Republic and the Paris Peace Conference'. (*Transactions of the American Philosophical Society*, Vol. 53, Part 10 [1963]).

Macartney, C. A., *Hungary and Her Successors: The Treaty of Trianon and its Consequences, 1919–1937* (London, 1937).

——— *October Fifteenth: Hungary 1929–1945* (2 vols, Edinburgh, 1957).

Macartney, C. A. and Palmer, A. W.: *Independent Eastern Europe* (London, 1967).

Mastny, V., *Russia's Road to the Cold War: Diplomacy, Warfare and the Politics of Communism 1941–45* (New York, 1979).

Max, S. M., *The United States, Great Britain and the Sovietisation of Hungary* (Boulder, CO, 1985).

Méray, T., *That Day in Budapest* (New York, 1969).

——— 'The Trial of Imre Nagy' (in Király, B. and Jónás, P. [eds.], *The Hungarian Revolution of 1956 in Retrospect* (Boulder, CO, 1978).

Mićunović, V., *Moscow Diary* (London, 1980).

Mindszenty, J., Cardinal, *Memoirs* (London, 1974).

Molnár, M., *Budapest, 1956: A History of the Hungarian Revolution* (London, 1971).

——— 'Imre Nagy (1896–1958)': in Bődy, P. (ed.): *Hungarian Statesmen of Destiny, 1860–1960* (Boulder, CO, 1989).

Montgomery, J. F., *Hungary, the Unwilling Satellite* (New York, 1947).

BIBLIOGRAPHY

Nagy, F., *The Struggle Behind the Iron Curtain* (New York, 1948).

Nagy, I., *On Communism, In Defence of the New Course* (London, 1957).

Nagy, K., *Két Tábornok: Vetter és Vattay élete, kora, hadművészete* (Budapest, 2000).

Nagy, Zs., '1919, The Hungarian Republic of Councils' (*New Hungarian Quarterly*, IX/31 [1969]).

O'Neil, P. H., *Revolution from Within: The Hungarian Socialist Workers' Party and the Collapse of Communism* (Northampton, MA, 1998).

Orde, A., France and Hungary in 1920: Revisionism and Railways' (in Király, B. K., Pastor, P. and Sanders, I. (eds.), op. cit.).

Pálóczi–Horváth, Gy.: *The Undefeated* (London, 1993).

Pastor, P., 'Hungarian Territorial Losses During the Liberal-Democratic Revolution of 1918–19' (in Király, B. K., Pastor, P. and Sanders, I. [eds.], op. cit.).

Prazmowska, A., *Eastern Europe and the Origins of the Second World War* (London, 2000).

Ránki, G., *Economy and Foreign Policy: The Struggle of the Great Powers for Hegemony in the Danube Valley, 1919–1939* (Boulder, CO, 1983).

———— 'Unwilling Satellite or Last Satellite: Some Problems of Hungarian-German Relations' (in Ránki, G. [ed.]: *Hungarian History—World History*, [Budapest, 1984]).

Révész, G., *Perestroika in Eastern Europe: Hungary's Economic Transformation* (London, 1990).

Roman, E., *Hungary and the Victor Powers, 1945–50* (London, 1996).

Romsics, I., 'The Great Powers and the Dissolution of Austria-Hungary' (*Hungarian Quarterly*, Vol. 41, Autumn 2000).

Rothermere, Viscount, *My Campaign for Hungary* (London, 1939).

Rothschild, J. and Wingfield, N., *Return to Diversity: A Political History of East Central Europe since World War II* (3rd edition, Oxford, 2000).

———— *East Central Europe between the Two World Wars* (Seattle, WA, 1974).

Rupnik, J., *The Other Europe* (London, 1988).

Rutter, O., *Regent of Hungary: The Authorised Life of Admiral Nicholas Horthy* (London, 1942).

Sakmyster, T., *Hungary's Admiral on Horseback: Miklós Horthy, 1918–1944* (Boulder, CO, 1994).

———— 'Great Britain and the Making of the Treaty of Trianon' (in Király, B. K., Pastor, P. and Sanders, I. (eds.), *Essays on World War I: Total War and Peacemaking A Case Study on Trianon (War and Society in East Central Europe, Vol. VI)*, New York, 1982).

Scarlett, D., *Window Onto Hungary* (Bradford, 1960).

Schmidt, M. and Tóth, L. (eds.), *From Totalitarian to Democratic Hungary: Evolution and Transformation, 1990–2000* (Boulder, CO, 2000).

Schöpflin, G., *Hungary Between Prosperity and Crisis* (London, 1981).

Shawcross, W., *Crime and Compromise: János Kádár and the Politics of Hungary since Revolution* (London, 1974).

Swain, N., *Hungary, The Rise and Fall of Feasible Socialism* (London, 1992).

Szász, B. (writing as Savorius, V.): *Volunteers for the Gallows: Anatomy of a Show Trial* (London, 1971).

Szinai, M. and Szücs, L. (eds.), *The Confidential Papers of Admiral Horthy* (Budapest, 1965).

Talbott, S. (ed.), *Khrushchev Remembers* (London, 1971).

Taubman, W., *Stalin's American Policy: From Entente to Cold War* (New York, 1982).

Temperley, H. (ed.), *A History of the Peace Conference of Paris* (6 vols, London, 1921).

———— 'How the Hungarian Frontiers Were Drawn' (*Foreign Affairs*, April 1928).

Tőkés, R., *Béla Kun and the Hungarian Soviet Republic* (London and New York, 1967).

Tőkés, R. L., *Hungary's Negotiated Revolution: Economic reform, Social Change and Political Succession, 1957–1990* (Cambridge, 1996).

BIBLIOGRAPHY

——— 'The Unwilling Satellite: Questions of Evidence and Interpretation' (in Ránki, G. (ed.): *Hungarian History—World History*, Budapest, 1984).

Ulam, A., *Expansion and Co-existence: The History of Soviet Foreign Policy, 1917–1967* (New York, 1968).

Ungváry, K., *Battle for Budapest: 100 Days in World War II* (London, 2003).

Unwin, P., *Voice in the Wilderness: Imre Nagy and the Hungarian Revolution* (London, 1991).

Vali, F., *Rift and Revolt in Hungary* (Cambridge, MA, 1961).

Vambery, R., *Hungary, To Be or Not To Be* (New York, 1946).

Veress, L-L., *Clear the Line: Hungary's Struggle to Leave the Axis During the Second World War.* (Cleveland, OH, 1995).

Vigh, K., 'Causes and Consequences of Trianon: A Re-examination' (in Király, B. K., Pastor, P. and Sanders, I. (eds.), *Essays on World War I: Total War and Peacemaking.*

——— *A Case Study on Trianon (War and Society in East Central Europe, Vol. VI)*, New York, 1982).

Windischgraetz, Prince L., *My Adventures and Misadventures, 1899–1964* (London, 1966).

Zweig, R., *The Gold Train* (London, 2002).

INDEX

INDEX

INDEX

INDEX

INDEX

INDEX

INDEX

INDEX